Judas Maccabaeus

TO BEENA SCHWEBEL BAR-KOCHVA
'Mine and yours are hers'
(*Babylonian Talmud, Nedarim* 50a)

Judas Maccabaeus

THE JEWISH STRUGGLE AGAINST
THE SELEUCIDS

BEZALEL BAR-KOCHVA

PROFESSOR OF ANCIENT JEWISH HISTORY,
TEL AVIV UNIVERSITY

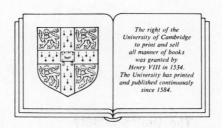

The right of the
University of Cambridge
to print and sell
all manner of books
was granted by
Henry VIII in 1534.
The University has printed
and published continuously
since 1584.

CAMBRIDGE UNIVERSITY PRESS

CAMBRIDGE

NEW YORK   NEW ROCHELLE

MELBOURNE   SYDNEY

Published by the Press Syndicate of the University of Cambridge
The Pitt Building, Trumpington Street, Cambridge CB2 1RP
32 East 57th Street, New York, NY 10022, USA
10 Stamford Road, Oakleigh, Melbourne 3166, Australia

First published 1989

Printed in Great Britain by the
University Press, Cambridge

British Library cataloguing in publication data
Bar-Kochva, Bezalel
Judas Maccabaeus: the Jewish struggle against the Seleucids.
1. Maccabaeus
2. Jewish soldiers. – Near East – Biography
I. Title
939   BS121.8.J8

Library of Congress cataloguing-in-publication data
Bar-Kochva, Bezalel.
Judas Maccabaeus.
Bibliography.
Includes indexes.
1. Judas, Maccabaeus, d. 160 B.C – Military leadership.
2. Jews – History – 168 B.C–135 A.D
3. Palestine – History, Military.
4. Seleucids.
5. Syria – History, Military.
6. Jews – Kings and rulers – Biography.
I. Title.
DS121.8.J8B37 1987   933'.04'0924–[B]   86–23212

ISBN 0 521 32352 5

CONTENTS

APPENDICES

EXCURSUS

ILLUSTRATIONS

MAPS

TABLES

DIAGRAMS

PLATES

NOTES

TRANSLITERATION OF HEBREW

In order to make it easier for the English reader, the following systems have been adopted in the book to render Hebrew in the Latin alphabet:

1. Biblical personal and place-names are given in the forms in which they appear in the standard English translations of the Bible.
2. The titles of mishnaic and Talmudic tractates are given as per H. Danby, *The Mishnah* (Oxford, 1938).
3. Hebrew names appearing only in the Books of the Maccabees (and not in the Old Testament) are given in the standard transliteration of Greek to English.
4. Modern place-names are given in the form employed in the English maps of Palestine published by the PEF and the Mandatory Government, and in the 1948 Index Gazetteer of Palestine.
5. Hebrew words are transliterated according to the following table:

א = ʾx	ז = z	נ = n	ר = r	X = xa	X = i
ב = b	ח = ḥ	ס = s	שׁ = š	X̣ = xā	ʾX = ī
ב = v	ט = ṭ	ע = ʿx	שׂ = ś	אX = xā	X = u
ג = g	י = y	פ = p	ת = t	הX = xā	וX = ū
ד = d	כ = k	פ = f		X = e	X = ō
ה = h	כ = k	צ = ṣ		הX = ē	וX = ō
ו = w	ל = l	ק = q		X = ē	(קטן)X = o
	מ = m			ʾX = ē	(ענ)X = e

KEY TO THE BRACKETS USED IN THE
TEXT OF I MACCABEES

[ ] Words improperly translated/transliterated into Greek or already garbled in the Hebrew original; letters or words garbled by copyists of the Greek text.

( ) Completion of phrases abbreviated in the Hebrew original or the Greek translation.

⟨ ⟩ Letters or words deleted or misplaced in the Hebrew or the Greek.

{ } Superfluous words added to the Greek by the translators or slipped in by mistake from other verses; glosses inserted by copyists.

ix

ACKNOWLEDGEMENTS

My Hebrew book, *The Battles of the Hasmonaeans*, *The Times of Judas Maccabaeus*, was published in 1980. The writing of that book was completed seven years ago. Since then I have rewritten the book, introduced numerous alterations and improvements, and expanded it by considerable additions in both the chapters and appendices, as well as some entirely new sub-chapters and appendices. The book has consequently been more than doubled in size, and the English version must therefore be regarded as superseding the former Hebrew book for all purposes.

I wish, first and foremost, to express my deep gratitude for the sincere help and constructive advice which the late Sir Moses Finley always readily placed at my disposal, and which has been of more value to me than I can say. My thanks extend also to a number of scholars whose criticism of basic issues or of minute points contributed to the improvement of various chapters: from England, Professor F. W. Walbank, and the late Mr G. T. Griffith and Professor H. W. Parke: from Germany, Professor Martin Hengel of Tübingen University; and, from Israel, Professor J. Efron and Professor M. Stern.

A more material debt is due to some bodies and individuals who by their generosity facilitated my work throughout the years. My research was carried out under the auspices of Yad Ben-Zvi in Jerusalem, the leading research institute for the history of the Land of Israel, which also published the Hebrew book. I am especially indebted to the Lucius N. Littauer Foundation of New York, and to its energetic president, Mr W. L. Frost, for covering the main expenses incurred in the preparation of the manuscript. Professor L. H. Feldman of Yeshiva University kindly supported my application, and Professor J. Ben-Shaul, the rector of Tel Aviv University, provided additional funds for that purpose. The hospitality of Professor Wolfgang Schuller, of Konstanz University in Germany, enabled me to bring the writing of the book to an end during my two years of most pleasant residence at Konstanz. To the Syndics of the Cambridge University Press, who undertook the publication of the book, I have the deepest sense of obligation.

Miss Naomi Handelman, of Tel Aviv University, skilfully improved the language and style of the manuscript, struggling with my handwriting and the recurring additions and amendments. The laborious work of editing was patiently and thoroughly handled by Miss Ann Johnston of the Cambridge University Press, who also made useful suggestions for improving the fluency of the book. I record their names here with much appreciation.

The book is dedicated to my wife, Beena. She closely followed my work with frequent discussion and fruitful advice, and provided practical and moral support, allowing me to devote myself to this study. The dedication to the book, quoting the celebrated Rabbi Akiva's maxim expressing gratitude to his wife Rachel, is just a token compensation for my wife's whole-hearted dedication.

B.B.

Even Yehuda, 1986

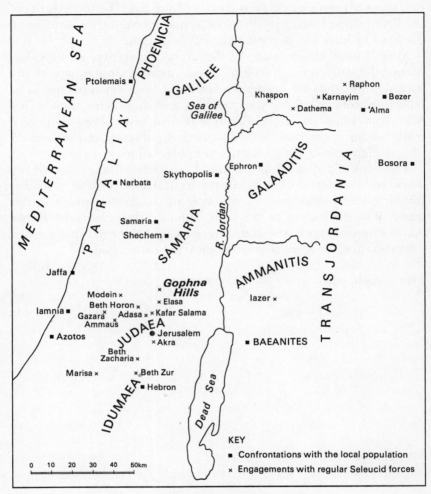

KEY

■ Confrontations with the local population

× Engagements with regular Seleucid forces

1 Sites of Judas Maccabaeus' battles

PROLOGUE

The biography of Judas Maccabaeus is in fact the story of the military and political struggle that he led against the Seleucid authorities from his father Mattathias' death (166 B.C.) up to his own heroic death (160 B.C.). Unfortunately, the sources do not elaborate on his earlier life and activity.

The period of Judas Maccabaeus' leadership can be divided into two stages: beginning a year or two after the inception of the religious persecutions, the first stage ended with the death of Antiochus Epiphanes and the purification of the Temple (Kislev-December 164 B.C.). During this period there were four major encounters with regular Seleucid forces: the battles against Apollonius and Seron, the campaign at Ammaus, and the clash at Beth Zur. After the purification of the Temple, when the child-king Antiochus V Eupator ascended the throne, there was a lull in the punitive measures of the Antioch authorities which was utilized by Judas Maccabaeus for conducting campaigns to rescue Jews in remote districts of Eretz Israel and for consolidating the defence of Judaea. During the second stage, which began in April 162 B.C. and ended two years later with the death of Judas Maccabaeus on the battlefield (160 B.C.), there were four additional important confrontations: the encounter with Lysias, the regent of Antiochus V, near Beth Zacharia and, after Demetrius I's accession (November 162 B.C.), the battles against Nicanor, the governor of Judaea, at Kafar Salama and Adasa, and the final battle near Elasa against Bacchides, the governor of the western regions of the empire. However, the resistance to the Seleucids did not die out after the disaster at Elasa. It was carried on by a skilful combination of diplomatic and military means by Judas Maccabaeus' brothers, first under the leadership of Jonathan (160–143 B.C.), and later under Simeon, up to the declaration of independence in 142 B.C.

Many evaluations have been made and numerous descriptions

given of the achievements of Judas Maccabaeus and the results of his
struggle, in general studies of the Second Temple period and particularly of the Books of the Maccabees, as well as in specialized
research and commentaries. Scholars have for the most part tended
to accept the picture presented in the sources, according to which the
Jewish force, poorly supplied with weapons, waged a war of the few
against the many, whereas the Seleucid foe, master of a great empire,
had unlimited manpower resources, and was provided with all the
advanced military equipment of the time. Such reservations as have
been expressed have been concerned mainly with the inflated numbers ascribed to the Seleucid forces and with the credibility of various
details in the accounts of the battles. There is, however, general
agreement that Judas Maccabaeus indeed achieved a glorious success
in most of the battles, the exceptions being the defeat at Beth Zacharia and at Elasa. All in all it may be said that dominant in scholarly
literature is the familiar romantic picture of fervent farmers going
forth to battle armed with primitive weapons and, despite their great
military inferiority, defeating the foe thanks to their religious and
patriotic zeal.

Other scholars seeking to explain the success of the Jews on the
basis of this information have tried to present a more balanced
picture. Thus they have pointed out that Judas Maccabaeus did not
gain a victory over a magnificent Macedonian army, such as that of
Alexander. According to this view, the Seleucid phalanx, the backbone of the enemy's army, had degenerated by that time, being
composed of Orientals and not of Greco-Macedonians as Alexander
the Great's renowned phalanx had been. Moreover, these scholars
have maintained, the standard of operation of the Seleucid phalanx,
its effectiveness, and its motivation were very poor. Furthermore,
these soldiers were for the most part mercenaries interested exclusively in money, not motivated citizens fighting for their home and
their country. Consequently, when confronted with difficult situations, they quickly took to their heels. Nor did the Seleucids have at
their disposal forces suitable for operating in the rugged mountainous
regions of Judaea, in which the battles took place. Accordingly the
Jews gained their victories not in a direct military confrontation, but
by utilizing ambushes and other guerrilla methods, by exploiting the
difficult condition of the terrain, by operating an efficient intelligence
service, and by taking the fullest advantage of their superior knowledge of the local topography.

These views, which were evolved in earlier generations, need to be
reconsidered and re-examined. More information about the Hel-

lenistic armies, their composition, armaments and operating methods is now available; the actual battlefields in the Judaean mountains are now accessible; the historiographical features of the literature of the Hellenistic period in general, and of the books of the Maccabees in particular, are clearer to us. Added to all this is the obligation imposed upon every generation to re-examine the past in the light of current attitudes, positions and lessons. Historians have always drawn abundant inspiration from the experiences and trials of their own time in interpreting the past, just as they have suggested that the lessons of the past can contribute to an understanding of the present.

Finally, a word on methodology: the subject requires an interdisciplinary approach. I believe, as many historians do, that politics and warfare can be better understood within the wider context of other aspects of human activity and culture.

The book is divided into two parts. The first part ('Historical Evaluation') discusses the essential historical problems arising from a study of the sources: the number of combatants on the two sides, the armaments of the Jewish force, the ethnic origin and effectiveness of the Seleucid phalanx, the fighting ability of the Seleucid armies in mountainous areas, the extent of Judas Maccabaeus' victories in the various encounters, and an analysis of the Jewish army's tactical methods and Judas Maccabaeus' leadership, policy and personality. The second part of the book ('Accounts of the Battles') provides the textual and factual basis for the discussion in the first part: it deals with the sources and seeks to reconstruct the course of the political and military events. The introduction analyses the Jewish writings: their date, provenance, sources of information, mutual connections, political and religious purposes, literary–historiographic school, and their general reliability. There follows a separate discussion of each battle including a detailed commentary on the battle descriptions as they occur in I Maccabees, the principal and most reliable source at our disposal. Each chapter is preceded by an introduction reviewing the historical and chronological background, the sources of the information available to the author of I Maccabees, and the value of the parallel sources. The commentary covers most of the linguistic and historical aspects, including some that do not directly refer to military operations and political developments, since these, too, have some bearing on the understanding of the course of the events, as well as on the evaluation of the credibility and character of the sources. Included in this second part are Judas Maccabaeus' en-

counters with the regular Seleucid armies, but not his struggles with
neighbouring nations which took place mainly in eastern Transjordania following the purification of the Temple. The latter have
been omitted both because for political reasons it is impossible to
carry out a full and thorough investigation of topographical and
archaeological questions which are decisive for an understanding of
the military events, and also because the Transjordanian campaigns
do not contribute a great deal to an elucidation of the basic and
significant historical problems. The book is supplemented by a series
of appendices on various subjects important to the main problems of
the book. Those subjects could not be discussed in detail in the
relevant places without interrupting the continuity of the main
argument.

PART I

HISTORICAL EVALUATION

1

Introduction: Deployment and tactics in field battles during the Hellenistic period

A brief survey of the combat methods of the Hellenistic period will make it easier for the reader to follow the discussion on the fundamental questions arising from the analysis of the courses of the battles. We shall deal here only with the two largest armies, the Seleucid and the Ptolemaic, omitting the Antigonid army of Macedon, and also the small armies of the 'splinter' states like Epirus, Pergamum, Pontus, Cappadocia, Armenia, etc. Although these armies included most of the components of the Seleucid and Ptolemaic armies, they differed from the latter in the number of the various types of units, in the ethnic origin of the soldiers and the way they were recruited, as well as in the total number of troops at their disposal, and consequently also in the way they operated on the battlefield. It must also be remembered that only the Seleucid and Ptolemaic armies utilized war elephants, which had more than a minor influence on the deployment of forces and the planning of a battle.[1]

[1] In the summary below of the armament and functions of the various tactical units only references relating to details and questions not sufficiently well known will be listed, and not those relating to matters familiar from the sources and that are generally accepted.

Notable among the many studies of the composition and operational methods of the Hellenistic armies are the comprehensive surveys in Rüstow and Köchly 1852: 336–435; Droysen 1888: 153–84; Kromayer and Veith 1926: 95–162. The last presents the conclusions deriving from Kromayer and Veith's five-volume comprehensive work analysing in detail the course of the chief battles fought in the Greek, Hellenistic and Roman worlds (1903–32). See also Couissin 1931: 65–93. A detailed treatment of the manpower sources of the Hellenistic armies, including recruitment methods, ethnic origin and tactical composition of the troops, appears in the monumental work of M. Launey, *Recherches sur les armées hellénistiques* (1949–50), which is also a mine of information on other questions, such as the armament of the Hellenistic armies, the service troops, the logistics and soldiers' pay, the social and civil status of soldiers of various categories, and the place of religious ritual in military life. Superior to it in analytical acumen and the critical view of the sources, though somewhat older, is Griffith, *The Mercenaries of the Hellenistic World* (1935), which deals also with the military settlements and the various units of allies and auxiliaries. The operational methods and tactics of the Hellenistic armies are the special subject of the excellent and fascinating work of W. W. Tarn, *Hellenistic Military and Naval Developments* (1930). On the basis of sundry papyrological material, there have been attempts to describe the structure of the Ptolemaic army, the most successful of which so far

3

The sources of information available to us are varied. They include primarily several dozen battle descriptions in the literary-historio-graphic works covering the Hellenistic period. As far as the Seleucid and Ptolemaic armies are concerned, the campaigns of Antiochus III, recorded by Polybius, are the most illuminating. In addition to battle descriptions, we have a number of treatises on the theory and art of warfare outlining mainly the composition of the various tactical units and sometimes also their deployment and operation on the battlefield. Noteworthy among them are the essays of the Tacticians – Aeneas Tacticus, Arrian, Onasander, Asclepiodotus – and Poly-aenus' collection of stratagems, the last being especially important as it gives succinct and reliable reports on many military episodes for which no other sources are available.

Besides the literary sources, there are papyrological and epigra-phical material and archaeological findings: the many papyrus docu-ments found in Egypt shed light on the structure of the units, the ethnic origin, and the table of organization of the Ptolemaic army, and consequently to an extent of the Seleucid army as well. The epigraphic documentation is scantier, and deals mainly with units of the Seleucid army and the military settlement system in Persia and Asia Minor. Especially valuable for an insight into the Hellenistic armies are the military regulations in regard to order and discipline, the practice in regard to sentry duty and patrols, maintenance of stores, handling of spoils, alertness, etc., in the tablets discovered in Amphipolis in Macedon and Chalcis on the island of Euboea, which reflect the practices of the Antigonid royal house during the reign of Philip V at the beginning of the second century B.C. The archae-ological finds relevant to our subject include statuettes, reliefs, draw-ings on tombstones, walls and mosaic floors, as well as coins show-ing Hellenistic warriors with their typical weapons, and also war elephants. Of great importance are the tombstones uncovered in military cemeteries in Alexandria, Sidon, and Demetrias in northern Greece, and especially the reliefs depicting arms and armour in the balustrade of the precinct of Athena Polias Nicephorus at Perga-mum. In recent years, at various Macedonian sites, discoveries have

---

is J. Lesquier's old book, *Les institutions militaires de l'Égypte sous les Lagides* (1911). On the composition and operational methods of the Seleucid army see Bar-Kochva 1979. A com-prehensive bibliography up to 1928 on armies and war in the Greek and Roman world appears in the two Kromayer and Veith works (1903–32, 1926). A bibliography covering the period 1917–38, along with summaries and assessments, appears in Lammert 1941: 1–114. Partial bibliographies for the post-1938 years are provided in the principal works published since, especially Launey (1949–50). See recent valuable summaries in Lévêque 1968: 261–90; Garlan 1972; Préaux 1978: 1.295–357; Garlan 1984: 353–62; Pritchett's excellent *The Greek State at War* (1974–85) is also relevant to the Hellenistic period.

been made of actual weapons in a satisfactory state of preservation, dating from just before and from the start of the Hellenistic period. Those published have come mainly from the royal tomb at Vergina-Aegae (Lower Macedonia) which is attributed to Philip II.

The Hellenistic armies presented a splendid sight on the battle-field: sometimes they numbered tens of thousands of soldiers, and the front line stretched for several kilometres, with the soldiers deployed in very close order. Some of the tactical units included in the array were equipped with long pikes which made them look like a bristling porcupine, while others had large shields covering most of the soldier's body. The many horsemen and the elephants also contributed to the variegated picture. The shields of white, silver, gold and bronze created an extraordinary visual effect together with the scarlet tunic or jackets of most of the soldiers, and the uniforms of a number of units in black, golden yellow and blue (see Plates V, IX, X). The difficulties of coordination resulting from the extended front line were overcome by a ramified signalling system using flags and bugles, which in themselves added to the somewhat theatrical atmosphere. All these, together with the war cry and the din of the advancing troops, were designed to instil confidence and enthusiasm in the soldiers, and fear and dread in the enemy. Among the many accounts reflecting the special effect that the Hellenistic armies created and the shock they gave the enemy, especially noteworthy is Plutarch's description of Mithridates' army in the clash in Greece with Sulla:

The rest of the commanders...deployed the army for battle and filled the plain with horses, chariots, shields and oblong shields (*thyreoi*). The air could not contain the shouting and noise of so many nations that came together for the battle. The conspicuousness and splendour of their equipment too had the power and might to spread dread; the shining brilliance of the arms, marvellously decorated with gold and silver and the hues of the tunics of the Scythians and Medes blended with the gleam of copper and iron and created a frightening play of fire when the army moved and separated, so that the Romans cleaved to the palisade (*kharakōma*) before the camp. And Sulla, who with no word (of reasoning) could remove their astonishment, and did not want to force on them (a battle) they might flee from, waited idly and found it hard to bear the sight of the barbarians who insulted him with boasting and condescending laughter. (*Sulla* 16[2–6])

The units and their deployment

The basic Hellenistic battle deployment consisted of heavy infantry
in the centre, cavalry that protected them on the wings, and light
infantry who served as 'skirmishers' and were deployed in the centre
in front of the heavy foot soldiers. Within the framework of the
general pattern of the formation it was sometimes necessary to introduce changes and variations such as the placement of cavalry units
between the heavy infantry in the centre, of light cavalry between
the foot skirmishers, and the like. All these were sometimes augmented by war elephants and, more rarely, by scythed chariots. The
position of the elephants varied from battle to battle depending on
the terrain and the tactical requirements.

The infantry forces positioned in the centre comprised mainly
phalangites, heavy units which were the backbone of the Hellenistic
armies. Their main offensive weapon was the *sarissa*, the long Macedonian pike to which was added a short sword, and for defence a
round shield, as well as a helmet and greaves or leg protectors
(*knēmides*). The *sarissa* both characterized and shaped the deployment
of the phalanx. In Alexander's time it was about 3.60 m long and
then grew gradually longer, reaching about 6.30 m in the Hellenistic
period. The *sarissa* was made of the flexible and strong cornel wood
with some metal components. It weighed 6.7 kg (Plate I).[2] Because
of its length, it was wielded with both hands. It is hard to know in
exactly what position the *sarissa* was held at the ready. Some believe
it rested on the shoulder or under the armpit, others that the soldier
held it with his arms stretched forward and down. It has also been
suggested that every row held it in a different position. Be that as it
may, it is clear that on the battlefield the soldier stood with his left
foot forward, holding the *sarissa* with both hands. Polybius reports
that one hand, certainly the right, grasped it two cubits (*ca* 90 cm)
from the back, and the distance between the two hands was also

[2] The various problems relating to the length, weight and manner of holding the *sarissa*
were the subject of a number of dissertations in Germany in the late nineteenth and early
twentieth centuries; a number of others deal with offensive and defensive weapons common
in the Hellenistic period. The most valuable of these is Lammert's comprehensive work on the
sarissa, a summary of which appears in *RE* (s.v. 'sarissa', cols. 2515–30). Objections have been
raised to some of Lammert's assertions, especially that the different rows of the phalanx had
sarissai of different lengths, which is contradictory to a definite statement of Polybius' (18.29.7).
On these see also Walbank 1957–79: 2.588; and on his estimates of *sarissa* dimensions and
weight (especially on the basis of metal parts found in Greece and Macedonia) see Markle
1977: 323ff.

90 cm. Thus the pike extended about 4.5 m from the soldier's left hand, that is, beyond the line. The phalanx soldiers were arrayed in the row in close order, being allotted only 90 cm each, including the distance to the next man, so that there was a space of about 45 cm between one soldier and the next.[3] This great compactness provided among other things maximum protection for the soldier in the formation: his shield covered the left half of his body as he inclined forward and the shield of the phalangite to his right provided some protection from that angle.

The shield of the Macedonian phalangite differed from that of the Greek hoplite, so well known from Classical art. As the phalangite held the long *sarissa* with both hands, his shield was necessarily smaller and flatter than the *hoplon*. It was held in place by a strap that fitted around the warrior's neck, and a second strap fixed to its inner surface through which the phalangite threaded his arm. Generally called *peltē*, the shield had a diameter of about 60 cm (see Plate II).[4] As to the material it was made of, in regular units the soldiers carried shields described as 'bronze shields' and in the elite units 'silver shields' and 'gold shields'. The latter were made of some metal simply plated with silver or brass respectively. It is also possible that these and the bronze shields, or some of them, were actually made of wood and covered with metal sheeting.[5]

---

[3] Many scholars think that the distance between the phalanx soldiers was even smaller; see the recent work by Pritchett (1974: 1.145–54).

[4] On the size ('eight palms') and form ('not too hollow') of the shield see Asclepiodotus 5.1; Aelian, *Tact.* 12. On the way that the *sarissa* was wielded and the shield held see Plut. *Cleom.* 11.2, *Aem.* 19.1–2. See also Couissin 1931: 76; Markle 1977: 326–31; contrary to Pritchett (1974: 1. 150–1) and others, who estimate the phalangite shield as 80 cm long or even more, that is, like the hoplite shield. For the term *peltē* for the phalangite shield, which itself indicates that it was smaller than the hoplon, see Plut. *Dem.* 49.2 (according to Polyaenus 4.9.3, Seleucus I was accompanied in that battle by the 'hypaspists', that is, the Royal Guard of the phalangites), *Aem.* 19.1–2; Livy 42.51.4–5, 44.41.2 (*peltē = caetra*; see Livy 28.5.11, 31.36.1); *I. Lindos* II. 2, c 127; and even Polyaenus 4.2.10 (on the period of Philip II, influenced by the shield of the Hellenistic phalangites). The name 'peltasts' too, that Polybius applied to the Royal Guard in the Hellenistic kingdoms (see p. 414 below) which was composed of genuine phalangites, testifies to the size of their shield. The codex of Amphipolis contains the term *aspis* (Feyel 1935: 31, line 4), as in Philopoemen's phalanx (Plut. *Philop.* 9.5; cf. Polybius 11.9.5). Pausanias' statement (8.50.1) that the shield of Philopoemen's men was an argive, i.e. of the traditional hoplon type (noted in Snodgrass 1964: 184), if actually based on reliable information, certainly does not attest the size of the phalangite shield of the Macedonians proper. For additional examples of phalangite shields see Head 1911: 233; id. 1932: 62 n. 5; Schober 1933: pls. 14–15; Hatzopoulos and Loukopoulos 1980: 39, 60–1.

[5] We have no explicit information indicating the use of a wooden base for the phalangite shields. There is, however, no reason to assume that the shields of the ordinary warriors, if not of the officers, differed in this respect from the Greek hoplite shields or the Galatian shields. Even the splendid ceremonial(?) shield attributed to Philip II that was found at Vergina was made of wood, and only the rim and a cruciform strut on the inner surface were of metal. On this

In some of the Hellenistic armies, the phalanx soldiers, or at least some of them, were equipped with metal coats of armour. That was the case with all of the phalangites of Philopoemen, the infantry commanders in the Antigonid army, and apparently also the picked units in the Seleucid phalanx. Other phalanx units may have used leather jackets. It may be that the provision of armour to certain units was decided for each battle according to the battleground and the enemy's armament.[6] Made of thick heavy metal, the coat of armour covered the upper part of the body, and interfered with the mobility of the phalangite, which was in any case limited. It was chiefly valuable against projectiles from a distance and, if the phalanx rows were broken up, in hand-to-hand combat. In a clash with heavy forces, the shield was enough to parry the blow of a pike, although the armour offered some possibilities of manoeuvring in such a confrontation (see Plate III).

The phalanx was generally arranged in rows sixteen deep. For special cases an even greater depth is recorded, such as in the battle of Magnesia for which thirty-two rows are reported. The space between rows was quite small, about 90 cm. Thus the *sarissai* of the second row protruded 3.60 m beyond the first row of soldiers, those of the third 2.70 m, of the fourth 1.80 m, and of the fifth 90 cm. The soldiers of the sixth and following rows held their *sarissai* at an angle upwards, ready at any moment to lower them and join in the fray in place of those who were hurt or exhausted, and meanwhile also producing a kind of 'hedge' protecting the forward rows against arrows, sling-stones and the like.

From the description above it is clear that every soldier in the front line was preceded by five pikes, the forwardmost extending 4.5 m ahead of him. The front line was thus a tangled porcupine of pikes, with great offensive and defensive power. The *sarissai* provided maximum protection, preventing enemy soldiers equipped with shorter offensive weapons from approaching for hand-to-hand combat. The close order protected the individual phalangite and reduced

---

shield see Hatzopoulos and Loukopoulos 1980: 220. On the wooden hoplite shields see Anderson 1970: 16. On the Galatian wooden shield see the hint in Diodorus 5.30.2. Galatian shields made of small pieces of wood covered in felt were found in the Fayum in Egypt and Hjortspring in Denmark, see Kimming 1940: 106–11; Rosenberg 1927: 103–14. On the plating of shields with hammered silver see Polyaenus 4.16 (the reign of Antiochus II). On bronze, gold and silver shields see also pp. 325–7 below.

[6] On the question of the phalanx soldier's body armour see Walbank 1940: 293; Griffith 1956–7: 3–10; id. 1979: 422–3; Bar-Kochva 1979: 54–6,65–6; cf. Plut. *Philop.* 9; Polyb. 11.9.5; Arrian, *Tact.* 3.2; Asclepiodotus 1.2 and the tablets from Amphipolis (Feyel 1935: 31, l. 7).

the chances of injury from the side. In an assault, if it succeeded in keeping its structure intact, the phalanx could cleave and crush any close formation in its way, either infantry or cavalry, unless the enemy was similarly equipped.[7]

The phalangites were organized as follows: the basic unit was the column (*lokhos*), generally made up of sixteen soldiers. The smallest tactical unit in the battlefield was the *syntagma* with sixteen columns totalling 256 soldiers, and the largest was the *stratēgia* or *phalangarkhia* made up of 256 columns totalling 4,096 soldiers. At times the formation comprised more than ten *stratēgiai*. It is hard to know whether there was some room between the subdivisions of a *stratēgia* or just between one *stratēgia* and the next. In any case, a phalanx formation of 40,000 fighters, for instance, occupied an area at least 2.5 km wide.

The massive structure described had a number of weak points deriving from the utilization of the *sarissai*: the long pikes which engaged both the soldier's hands prevented him from entering into hand-to-hand combat with any enemy soldiers who managed to penetrate the wall of *sarissai*. The short sword he was doubtless provided with (e.g. the *kopis*: Arrian, *Anab.* 1.15.8) was supposed to help in hand-to-hand combat, but to use it he had to let go of the *sarissa* and that was liable to produce a further break in the protective wall of the phalanx. In order to avoid penetration of that sort and provide the formation with the greatest power in the offensive, it was necessary to insist on the dense deployment of the rows and columns. However, that structure could be properly maintained only on more or less level terrain, and even there at the expense of speed. In rugged and difficult terrain, gaps appeared in the phalanx, especially when it was advancing. These enabled an enemy with high mobility to penetrate and engage in hand-to-hand combat in which the phalanx soldiers were almost helpless. The necessity of maintaining the set formation also limited the manoeuvrability of the phalanx and made it difficult for it to defend itself against a concerted frontal and flank (or rear) attack, especially if the force attacking the flanks was a fast, mobile unit like cavalry. In the case of such a simultaneous attack, the phalanx was vulnerable on its flanks, as it operated only in a forward direction. An attack from the flank alone would not disrupt the

---

[7] Data on the length of the *sarissa*, the distance between rows and soldiers, and on how far the *sarissai* extended beyond the front row are reported in detail in Polybius 18.29. The figures cited are based on the assumption that the Polybius cubit (*pēkhos*) was about 45 cm long. (Some reckon the Macedonian cubit was the equivalent of 46.2 cm, others 44 cm; for simplicity I have chosen to round off the figures to 45 cm.)

equilibrium of the phalanx because the whole formation could change direction and transform its flank into the front line.[8]

In order to counter a concerted assault on the phalanx, the Hellenistic armies deployed cavalry on both sides of the heavy infantry. Consequently the attacking cavalry had to strike at those flanking cavalry units before approaching the phalanx. That was the origin of the cavalry battles which played such a vital role in the wars of the period. When the phalanx formation was spread particularly wide, or when the surface abounded in obstacles which might produce dangerous gaps in the formation, cavalry units were deployed also at weak points within the phalanx formation in the centre of the battlefield. Cavalry was deployed among foot soldiers for the purposes of offence as well: in that way it was possible to locate easily gaps in the enemy's infantry line and reach them as rapidly as possible. If the wall of phalangites was pierced as a result of topographical conditions, uncoordinated advance, or heavy losses at certain points following protracted sniping by light skirmishers, the opposing cavalry could exploit the gap and penetrate the phalanx formation. Once inside, they could break up the phalanx from within in hand-to-hand combat where the cavalry also had the advantage of height and mobility. In addition to all the activities noted that were directly connected with the phalanx in the centre, the cavalry (if it was not too heavy), being mobile, was used to disrupt the enemy's mounted and unmounted skirmishers and snipers who endangered the integrity of the heavy foot formation by shooting from afar, and to break up semi-heavy foot formations, as well as for long-range pursuits.

The cavalry of the Hellenistic period can be classified in four categories: light, semi-heavy, heavy and 'super-heavy' or rather cataphracts (= 'covered with mail'). The lights included mounted archers and akontists who generally fought as skirmishers together with the light infantry in the front of the phalanx; we shall therefore deal with them later in the discussion on the skirmishers.

Units of 'semi-heavy' cavalry were made up of troops of various peoples who retained their traditional weapons. What was common to all was their relatively short offensive weapons and rather light defensive ones, facilitating rapid movement and action. Especially notable were the Thracians, who combined a thrusting spear about

---

[8] Some of the chief advantages and disadvantages of the phalanx formation are discussed in Polybius' famous excursus (in his report on the battle of Cynoscephalae) in which he compares the Roman legion with the Macedonian phalanx (18.28–32; cf. Plut. *Flam.* 8.4–8). Polybius notes especially the phalanx's dependence on the structure of the terrain, and the difficulty of forcing a broad, level battle site on its foe. On the same passage see also p. 126 below.

a metre long with a long sword and javelins, and protected themselves and their horse with an oval shield, but had no metal body armour at all (see Plate IV). These cavalry units were deployed on the battlefield on the flanks and among the infantry in the same way as the heavier mounted units, and proved especially valuable in situations requiring speedy action. At times, however, they operated like the light cavalry, as 'skirmishers' wielding their javelins.

There were two categories of heavy cavalry. In the mother country, Macedon, some were supplied with the *hoplon*, the heavy round shield of the Classical period, which together with the helmet constituted their defensive equipment. For offensive purposes they had a spear the length of a man of average height or less, and a short sword.[9] Yet the desire to lengthen the offensive weapon – expressed among the infantry by the use of the *sarissa* – was discernible in the cavalry as well. The second and more common type of heavy cavalry was armed with a *xyston* (a spear which judging by the illustrations of the period was as long as the *sarissa* of Alexander's heavy infantry: 3.6 m) and with the short sword.[10] The extension of the pike made it necessary to discard the shield, and the horsemen were protected by a heavy solid metal cuirass as well as a helmet. The rider was able to hold and control the long pike on the move thanks to a loop at the horse's neck that supported the shaft (Plate V). The length of the offensive weapon turned these heavy horsemen into a kind of mobile phalanx which, when able to maintain a tight formation, was superior to semi-heavy and heavy infantry (i.e. hoplites, not phalangites) as well as to semi-heavy and heavy cavalry armed with short spears. The form and weight of the armour, however, restricted the horseman's movements, and the elimination of the shield made the horse and to a degree the rider's face as well more vulnerable. As to the offensive weapon, it was still short compared with the *sarissai* of the Hellenistic phalangites, so that the heavy cavalry were not capable of making a frontal attack against phalanx units that maintained their close formation.

The defensive deficiency of the heavy cavalry and the desire to

[9] See, e.g., on the column erected by Lucius Aemilius Paullus at Delphi to commemorate the battle of Pydna, most recently published in Kähler 1965: 34, nos. 4, 9, 22, 26, and pl. 1. It is not clear from what has survived of the column whether the horsemen were also protected by suits of armour. One of the Macedonian horsemen (Kähler 1965: 34, no. 4, and p. 26) is wearing a tunic with leather strips, but that does not necessarily mean that he was equipped with a suit of armour, and in any case it is doubtful whether he had a shield.

[10] Markle (1977: 333ff.) argues for a Macedonian cavalry pike equal in length to the infantry *sarissa* already by the time of Alexander. His calculations are based on the assumption that the rider must always have grasped the pike in the middle. This was not necessary, however (see Plate V); the loop at the horse's neck permitted considerable flexibility in wielding the pike.

form a mobile force that would have the advantage over the earlier types of heavy cavalry and be able to face the phalanx was remedied to an extent in the 'super-heavy' cavalry, the cataphracts. This combat style which originated in central Asia was introduced to the Near East following Antiochus III's anabasis in 210–206 B.C. The brilliant success of the cataphract cavalry in the battle of Panium (200 B.C.), in which they quickly bested the Ptolemaic heavy horsemen facing them and then attacked the phalanx from the rear, led to the reorganization of most of the mounted contingents in the Seleucid standing army (apart from the national contingents) to suit that combat method and equipment.[11]

The precise equipment and combat method of the cataphracts in the Seleucid empire is not well known because of the paucity and brevity of the references to them. The only real information on their equipment appears in Livy's description of the deployment of the Seleucid army at the battle of Magnesia. After mentioning the cataphracts Livy states that next to them were the horsemen of the *regia ala*, one of the Royal Guard units, who were equipped with 'lighter armour for themselves and their horses' (37.40.12). Thus both the men and horses of the cataphracts were rather heavily armoured. And as the available illustrative material indicates a considerable increase in the length of the offensive weapon, it seems likely that that trend persisted in the new cavalry combat style as well. These conclusions make it possible to utilize the general information in the many pictorial and literary sources on cataphracts of the first to the third centuries A.D. who were similarly armoured, although in details (type and extent of armour, form of helmet, etc.) they differed as

---

[11] On the source and history of cataphract warfare see Rostovtzeff 1933: 217–21; Herzfeld 1920: 87ff.; Tarn 1930: 73ff.; Rubin 1955: 264–83; Eadie 1967: 162–8. On its introduction in the Mediterranean region by Antiochus III see Tarn 1930: 76. On the cataphracts in the battle of Panium see Bar-Kochva 1979: 156. In that battle the Seleucid right cavalry wing that tipped the scales was composed of cataphracts (and see Polybius 16.18.8). The retraining of all the cavalry in the Seleucid standing army for cataphract-style combat can be inferred from the deployment of the Seleucid cavalry (with the exception of the national contingents) at the battle of Raphia (217 B.C.) compared with their deployment at the battle of Magnesia (190 B.C.). At Raphia there were 6,000 regular Seleucid horsemen, of whom 2,000 were Royal Guard (on the permanent complement of the Royal Guard see Bar-Kochva 1979: 68ff.), all of them called simply 'cavalry' (Polybius 5.79.12; one Guard unit with no mention of its size appears in 5.84.1 and 5.85.12). At the battle of Magnesia, on the other hand, there were 6,000 cataphracts in addition to 2,000 Royal Guard (Livy 37.40.5–6,11). As to the Royal Guard units, their retraining for cataphract warfare of a certain variety is suggested by Livy 37.40.11. At the Daphne procession the mounted standing army numbered as usual 2,000 Royal Guard, plus 1,500 cataphracts and 1,000 'Nisaean horsemen' (Polybius 30.25.6–9). The latter rode Nisaean horses, an especially large, strong breed, intended from the outset for cataphract combat (see Tarn 1930: 77–81,156–7). On the identity and status of the other cavalry contingents that took part in the Daphne procession see p. 30 n. 3.

much from the Hellenistic cataphracts as they did among themselves.[12]

The unique aspect of the cataphracts, as their name indicates, was
their defensive equipment: instead of a solid suit of armour and a
shield, they were protected by scale armour which covered them
from neck to knees, and by a helmet which covered the face. The
horses too were amply protected by scale armour. As to their offensive weapons, they used a pike, the *kontos*, which was substantially
longer than the heavy cavalry's *xyston*, and almost equalled the
phalangite *sarissa* (Plate VI).

The extensive scale armour and long spear gave the cataphracts
a number of advantages over the heavy cavalry. Their armour
generally provided effective coverage against missiles, spears and
pikes of various kinds (although the chain mail was by nature more
penetrable than solid armour), and the pike enabled them to block
the enemy's advance and attack at a greater distance. These advantages gave the cataphracts great confidence which facilitated
bolder action. Their rapid advance made the thrust of the *kontos* more
effective than that of the infantry *sarissa*, so that it was said to be
possible to spear two enemy soldiers with one thrust. The infantry
phalangite did have a defensive advantage, however, for each soldier
in the front row had five *sarissai* before him, which terrified the horses
too, while the cataphract had only his own *kontos*.

The defensive and offensive reinforcement inevitably led to an
increase in weight. Compared with solid armour, the scale armour
allowed greater flexibility to the upper part of the body, but its
overall weight, the weight and length of the pike, and the horse's
scale protection made it necessary for the cataphracts to rely on their
close formation and to prefer level terrain. Furthermore, they were
vulnerable to attack from the flank and rear no less than the phalangites. According to the later sources these difficulties were exploited by infantry units which assaulted the cataphracts from the
flanks, attacking body parts of the riders and horses that were unprotected by armour (e.g. eyes, legs below the knees, and horses'
bellies), grabbing the pikes and turning them so as to unseat the
horseman who could no longer function, and the like. In order to
avert such disasters, the cataphracts needed the protection on their

---

[12] On the equipment and combat method of the cataphracts see especially Rattenbury
1942: 113–16; Eadie 1967: 170–3. The main literary sources are Heliodorus, *Ethiopica* 9.15ff.;
Plut. *Crass.* 18–19, 24–5, 27, *Luc.* 26–8; Cassius Dio 40.15.2; Ammianus Marcellinus 16.10.8ff.,
25.1.12; Julian, *Or. in Constanti laudem* 1.37c ff., 2.57c; Suidas s.v. θώραξ. The description
below of the cataphracts' equipment in the Hellenistic period is contrary to Rostovtzeff 1933:
218–21.

flanks of more mobile cavalry and infantry, mainly semi-heavy units skilled in hand-to-hand combat. Thus, in contrast to the heavy cavalry that preceded them, the cataphracts were not deployed at the extreme flanks of the formation unless some natural obstacle there provided sufficient defence.

The limitations of the cataphracts resulted in some variation in style. As noted above, in some picked units of the Seleucid army, the armour of horse and rider was less extensive, no doubt because greater mobility under special conditions was needed, and quite possibly the pike was shorter as well. At different times other variations were adopted, as for instance the use of the long *kontos* with scale armour for the horseman alone, not for the horse, or even a solid armour for the horseman (see Plate VII).

Hellensitic horsemen were deployed in eight rows of eight, composing the basic unit known as the *ilē*; the largest unit, the chiliarchy, was made up of sixteen *ilai*, a total of 1,024 cavalrymen. The cavalry in the Hellenistic armies was not particularly numerous, generally comprising between two and six chiliarchies. The light and heavy cavalry was allotted 1.80 m of space in the line per man abreast, while the cataphracts' deployment, being dependent on close formation, was certainly denser. Consequently the advance of the cataphracts was relatively slow. We have no definite and reliable information on the distance between the various cavalry units, or between one row and the next. According to one of the Tacticians, each horseman took up twice as much space from front to back as from side to side (Asclepiodotus 7.4). In cases where the plan was to exploit possible breaches in the phalanx wall so as to penetrate the formation and break it up from inside, the cavalry contingents were sometimes deployed in a triangle. The apex, made up of the picked horsemen or commanders, could penetrate the breach more quickly and efficiently, while the wider rows clashed with the soldiers on both sides of the breach whose situation was already precarious as the breach widened.[13]

---

[13] The various types of cavalry formation are discussed by three of the later Tacticians, Asclepiodotus (7.2–10), Arrian (*Tact.* 16) and Aelian (*Tact. theor.* 18). They note four main types: square, rectangular, rhomboid and finally the wedge or triangle (*emboloeidēs*). To the best of my knowledge, the only attempt to apply this information was by Marsden 1964: 68–73. On the basis of the statements that the Macedonians fought in the wedge formation (Asclepiodotus 7.3; Aelian, *Tact.* 8.4) and that Philip II trained them to fight that way (Arrian, *Tact.* 16.6), Marsden hypothesizes that Alexander's Macedonian horsemen all fought in that formation in the many battles in which they took part in the course of the anabasis, and he reconstructs the battle of Gaugamela accordingly. However, it is hard to accept that the Macedonian armies (and even less that the Diadochian or Hellenistic ones) gave up the impact of a solid row when facing infantry which was more flexible and mobile than the phalanx, or that the wedge formation could have bested a rectangular formation of cavalry with equivalent weaponry, especially on the defensive. The more common formation was the rectangular one,

Positioned in front of the phalanx were the skirmishers (*promakhoi*) – the majority archers and the rest slingers and akontists – some of them infantry and more rarely cavalry. The bow of the period was basically no different from that of the ancient East and the Aegean region in earlier periods. It was of composite construction, either single-arc or double-arc. The mechanical semi-automatic bow, the so-called scorpion, was used only in siege operations. According to the later Tacticians (e.g. Arrian, *Tact.* 3.3), the archers of the Hellenistic period forwent defensive arms to permit maximum mobility, but this was true of only some of those troops. We know that units of Cretans, evidently archers, employed round shields (e.g. Polybius 10.29.6), and infantry archers carrying shields and protected by helmets and greaves are known from Scythian art.[14]

The task of the skirmishers was to try and disrupt the phalanx formation and produce gaps in it by sniping from afar, in what would today be termed a 'softening up' operation by artillery, and make it possible for cavalry or semi-heavy infantry to penetrate and crumble the phalanx from within. The disruption of the phalanx was also designed to impede it in its forthcoming clash with the opposing phalanx. However, since the Hellenistic armies were all deployed similarly, the skirmishers did not generally succeed in accomplishing their task, for they had to face the skirmishers of the other side. Especially effective were the mounted archers which only the Seleucids had: as they were able to carry a much larger quantity of arrows than infantry archers, they could remain active in the battlefield for extended periods. Their high mobility and commanding position made them much more dangerous than infantry archers. (See Plate VIII.) In difficult terrain the mobile, flexible light forces acquired greater importance and could sometimes determine the tide of battle. In extremely rugged, broken terrain they bore the entire burden, while the heavy forces were occasionally left far to the rear.

An intermediate category was the semi-heavy infantry. These operated sometimes between the skirmishers and sometimes between phalanx units, and were equipped with characteristic national arm-

as the Tacticians report for most of the Greek armies (Asclepiodotus 7.4; Arrian, *Tact.* 16.9; Aelian, *Tact.* 18.5). The Macedonians trained and fought in a wedge when the circumstances required, especially when a chance to charge into a breach in the enemy phalanx line presented itself. The need to change the cavalry formation as required is noted also by Arrian, *Tact.* 16.2. The cataphracts, at any rate, did not use the wedge formation in any situation. The Tacticians' statements on the deployment of Macedonian cavalry in wedge formation is therefore inaccurate and arises from their predilection for rigid classifications and categories. For the view that Alexander's cavalry used the wedge formation only 'on occasion' see Griffith 1979: 413. See also Markle 1977: 339.

[14] See Sokolov 1974: nos. 26, 55–61, 157; Artamonov 1969: no. 270.

ament. Noteworthy among these was the Galatian style which featured a long elliptical shield providing the warrior with the greatest protection,[15] in contrast to the smaller, round shield of the phalanx, and a spear around 2 m long.[16] Among the semi-heavies were also Thracian soldiers, who in at least some of the battles of the period used the long, broad sword known as the *rhomphaia* and the elongated oval shield.[17] The relatively short offensive weapons allowed the individual soldier greater mobility and freer action in hand-to-hand combat, and manoeuvrability in uneven terrain. Consequently the deployment of the semi-heavies on the battlefield was less compact than that of the phalangites, with each soldier being allotted about 1.80 m of space. The main task of these units was to exploit any weak points and gaps in the enemy's heavy formation on the one hand, and on the other to defend their own phalanx against similar dangers. In order to accomplish this, the semi-heavies could be posted in the centre and front. In special cases, when because of numerical inferiority the front line of the phalanx was considerably shorter than that of the opposing phalanx, the semi-heavies (and even the lights, if necessary) were posted in the centre in order to expand the front line to the same length as that of the enemy. (See Plates IX–X.)

In quite a number of battles elephants were placed at various points of the formation.[18] The Seleucids' elephants came from India, and those of the Ptolemies from Africa. The African bush elephants

[15] On the Galatian shield see Couissin 1927: 307ff.; Launey 1949–50: 1, 529ff.; Anderson 1970: 14ff. However, contrary to these scholars and to what was generally thought in the past, it now appears that the oval shield, whatever its origin, was known to a certain extent in the Greek culture area before the advent of the Galatians in 279 B.C.: see esp. Maule and Smith 1959: 57 n. 207; Snodgrass 1964: pl. 18; and a recently discovered oval shield from Pylos, now in the Archaeological Museum at Thessalonike. Less decisive are the finds discussed by Fraser and Rönne 1957: 69–70 (pls. 1–2). At the same time, there is no doubt that the Galatian invasion of Greece and settlement in Asia Minor helped spread the use of that shield throughout the third century B.C. There is thus no reason not to continue to refer to the oval shield as the 'Galatian shield'. On the Galatian oval shield found in the Fayum, measuring 1.28 m × 0.635 m, see Kimming 1940: 106. Other Galatian shields, painted or incised on tombstones, seem to be somewhat shorter (see, e.g., Pls. IX, X, XIIIb, and esp. Burr 1934: 12).

[16] The tombstones from Sidon which provide a picture of semi-heavy Hellenistic military equipment show a pike about 2 m long. See, e.g., the Pisidian mercenary, Pl. X, and Mendel 1912: 263–4, 267–9.

[17] On the Thracian *rhomphaia*, whose nature has not yet been properly clarified, see esp. Livy 31.39.11–12; Plut. *Aem.* 18.3; and there also on the *thyreos*, the oval shield. On the latter source see Liedmeier 1935: 188; Snodgrass 1967: 119,123,142 n. 7.

[18] The exotic aspect of elephant combat has attracted numerous scholars, both historians and zoologists, who produced comprehensive monographs, the most recent and up-to-date of which is Scullard 1974. On elephants in Seleucid military service see Bar-Kochva 1979: 75–83. On the tactical exploitation of elephants, and on counter-measures, see Tarn 1930: 92ff.; Glover 1948: 1–11.

are larger and stronger than the Indian type, but the Ptolemies succeeded in taming and training only the forest elephant which was considerably inferior to the Indian breed. Both, however, proved to be quite effective in battle. The animal's thick hide was natural armour, its size and appearance frightened men and horses, and its speed and strength enabled it to crack dense formations and even break down walls. Elephants were also trained to hurl down enemy soldiers with their trunks and gore them with their tusks. The height and carrying capacity of the elephant were utilized by placing on its back a kind of tower that held three or four archers or *sarissa*-bearers, in addition to the mahout, the driver, who was seated on its neck (Plates XII–XIV). The elephant's weak points were the soft soles of its feet, and to a lesser extent its underbelly, ears, eyes and temples. Its main drawback as a fighting animal was its tendency to panic and lose control. A serious wound, incessant sniping from afar, or the death of the mahout could lead the elephant to stampede, about-face, and injure the soldiers behind.

In battles against peoples who had no experience with elephant warfare, herds of elephants were successfully used for assaults. They frightened the enemy and at times led to terror-stricken flight without a fight, and if they were required to attack, they shattered any dense formation of cavalry or infantry in their way.

In battles between Hellenistic armies, the value of the elephant in an attack was, however, quite limited. Just a few years after elephants were first employed in the Hellenistic battle array, the armies learned how to combat them by setting various types of traps such as pits, fires, and especially barbed chains that wounded the soles of their feet, and particularly by aiming for the mahout. In Alexander's time the armies had already learned how to amputate the elephants' feet with curved swords or hatchets wielded in daring assaults by units that were specially trained for the task. Another method was to pierce the elephant's temple by short-range sniping, or to isolate the animal and surround it with light infantry, etc. In order to protect the elephant and remove the traps in its way, a few dozen infantry lights, generally archers, were posted on its flanks, and they, together with the soldiers inside the 'tower', helped to repulse any approaching foe.[19] Sometimes the elephant was provided with armour for the more sensitive parts of its body. The need to attach an infantry guard and the weight of the 'tower' and its occupants reduced the

---

[19] See the sources in Bar-Kochva 1979: 82–3. Appian notes in his version of the battle of Thermopylae: τὸ στῖφος ὅ μετ' αὐτῶν ἀεὶ συνετάσσετο (*Syr.* 18 (83) = 'the unit which always accompanied them [the elephants]').

speed with which the elephant could attack infantry and cavalry formations, and sometimes enabled them to avoid it.

In a few cases when counter-measures could not be taken or were inadequate, it was possible to carry out a rapid advance by a frontal line of elephants. Their effectiveness was greatest against cavalry, as horses recoil at the sight of elephants. Furthermore, the lances of the Hellenistic cavalry (apart from the cataphracts) were not long enough, and the manner of holding them not steady enough, to stop the great power of a galloping war elephant. An elephant attack against phalangites was less usual: the wall of *sarissai* apparently discouraged the elephants to some extent, and they could be wounded in the eyes, etc., by the pikes (see Diodorus 18.34.2). On the other hand, a rush of advancing elephants produces panic or even shock in anybody in their path, and it takes extraordinary courage to stand firm against them. Furthermore, the *sarissai*, being mainly of wood, were by no means unbreakable. It was also possible to overcome the *sarissai* by equipping the soldiers in the 'tower' with long pikes (Polybius 5.84.2). In one case at least, at the battle of Panium, we know that a formation of phalangites was cracked by a group of elephants (Polybius 16.18.7, 19.11).[20]

As a result of the improved counter-measures and the limitation of their capacity in assault, elephants in the Hellenistic period served mainly in defensive and blocking operations, deployed together in a frontal line and protected on the flanks by infantry archers. In offensives they were used rarely, mostly between phalangites, where they advanced at the relatively slow pace suitable for heavy infantry. A deployment of this latter type is known from clashes of the Hellenistic armies with the Romans. As it was not possible to utilize the elephant's speed and strength, the animals served mainly to terrorize the enemy. The defensive roles of the elephants were confined mainly to blocking operations of various kinds. The most common was aimed against a cavalry assault. If the cavalry of one side was inferior, elephants could be placed in front to prevent its being defeated. In one case the elephants served as a 'mobile road block' to prevent cavalry that had been victorious in a clash between the flanks from returning to the battlefield and attacking the enemy phalanx from its rear. Sometimes elephants were placed behind the phalanx to protect it from an assault from the rear, or to serve as a last block in case the phalanx was broken by enemy infantry. Some were even posted in the front ahead of the light or semi-heavy

[20] Bar-Kochva 1979: 155–6; see also Polybius 5.84.9 (the 'peltasts' mentioned were to all intents and purposes phalangites – see Walbank 1957–79: 1.590–1, and p. 414 below).

infantry, in order to protect them from a phalangite attack. The number of elephants in the Hellenistic armies was relatively small, generally no more than a few dozen, so that they could not be used simultaneously in various operations or in several sectors of the same battlefield, aside from exceptional cases like the battles of Ipsus and Panium.

Descriptions of several battles of the Seleucid army mention the participation of chariots as well. Common in the East even earlier, the chariots were furnished with scythes attached to their wheels, which could cut to pieces soldiers or animals in their way (see the dramatic description of Appian, *Mithridates* 3.18). They were generally placed at the front of the formation, opposite the enemy sector which needed to be pierced. It was easy to combat them, however, and turn them into a danger to the forces behind them: the usual method was for the infantry archers to attack the horses and make them rear, turn tail and gallop through their own forces. Aware of the danger, the Seleucid commanders used chariots in very few instances. After the battle of Magnesia (190 B.C.) in which the chariots of Antiochus III caused the total collapse of the Seleucid formation, the military use of chariots was completely suspended, and they served primarily ceremonial purposes.

To complete the discussion on the various tactical units and their weapons, let us consider artillery pieces and siege machines. The development of these categories of equipment reached a pinnacle in the Hellenistic period, and for centuries thereafter only relatively few improvements were introduced. Most of the items were heavy and immobile apart from the mobile 'scorpion' (or *gastraphetēs*), a complicated device carried by a single warrior, which had a particularly large bow that could be described as 'semi-automatic'. The bow could be stretched long before it was used, more efficiently and easily than an ordinary bow, and the range set in advance. The warrior would set the bow with one end held against his stomach and the other against a wall or the ground; the arrow was shot by the release of a 'trigger'. While this bow had a longer range, accommodated heavier arrows, and could be aimed more accurately than the traditional bow, it was not widely used in battles in the open field, probably because of the need for time to set it and for a fixed counter when winding it.

The large artillery pieces were stationary models of the scorpion and various types of catapults, some propelling large arrows and some stones and iron balls (*petroboloi, lithoboloi*). The stationary scorpion continued to be based on the principle of the bow, but the

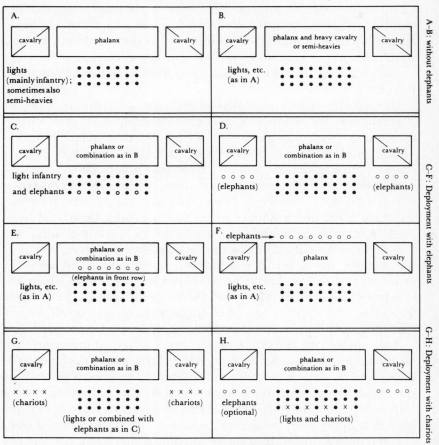

Diagram 1: *Main deployment plans of Hellenistic armies*

stretching was accomplished more easily and efficiently by turning a handle. The catapults, on the other hand, derived their energy not only from the bowstring but also from wound ropes which made possible a greater range and the ejection of heavier missiles. However, despite the intensive development of such devices, the Hellenistic armies made no use of artillery machines to break up close formations on the battlefield. The machines were not mobile, and assembling them on the battlefield was a lengthy process. Their range was limited to a few hundred metres, making it necessary to set the valuable machines up close to the enemy and thus risk having them fall into enemy hands. In addition, they operated rather slowly, and in the battle the opposing soldiers were soon intermingled while the accuracy of the machines left much to be desired (see especially

Polybius 11.12.4). For these reasons the stationary artillery machines and the mobile scorpions were not used on battlefields but only for siege campaigns or in blocking operations in passes, defiles and the like, where they were set up in advance in fortified, well-defended positions.

In siege operations the artillery pieces were aided by poliorcetic structures, that is, siege towers (*helepoleis*). The towers were designed to facilitate artillery fire into a city from a close, well-protected position, to provide archers with an elevated observation point over-looking the city and the defenders of its wall, to expedite direct access over the top of the wall, and to carry as near to the city as possible the battering ram used to demolish the city wall and towers. The engineers of the period built towers of different types, heights and sizes. The average was from 20 to 40 m high, divided into several storeys, and tapering toward the top from a base occupying any-where from 50 to 150 m². The towers were made of wood, pannelled with leather or tin plates to prevent them from catching fire from flaming torches, etc., tossed at them by the defenders. The whole construction was assembled near the site under siege, set on a large number of huge wheels and moved toward the wall by hundreds of well-protected men.[21]

The battle preparations, stages and turning-point

The tasks and armament of the various tactical units having been surveyed, we shall attempt to reconstruct the way battles were con-ducted in the Hellenistic period and clarify the various possibilities and developments, dealing only with two armies facing each other in an open field, and not with ambushes, blocking operations, siege campaigns, and the like.[22]

In battles on level ground against less sophisticated enemies the

[21] On various poliorcetic and artillery devices see esp. Droysen 1889: 187–268; Schramm 1918 and 1926: 209–43; the entries 'Helepolis', 'Katapulta', 'Lithobolos', 'Machinae', 'Skorpion' (by Lammert) and 'Gastraphetes' (by Droysen) in *RE*; Marsden 1969–71; Garlan 1974: 105–278. On the use of artillery in blocking operations see Hammond 1966: 49ff.; Bar-Kochva 1979: 161; and see Appian, *Syr.* 18(78); Livy 32.5.13. There was a considerable literature in antiquity on the construction of poliorcetic and artillery pieces, of which only Hero of Alexandria, Philo of Byzantium, Biton and Vitruvius have survived; see these sources in Marsden 1969–71: vol. 2; Garlan 1974: 279–404. See also additional bibliography in Lammert 1941: 54–61; Garlan 1974: xv–xxii.

[22] The summary below is based primarily on the study of the Seleucid army, see Bar-Kochva 1979: 105–206. For the battles of the other Hellenistic armies, the Diadochs, the Antigonid dynasty and King Pyrrhus of Epirus, see the analysis in Kromayer and Veith 1903–32: vols. 1, 2 and 4; Tarn 1930; Scullard 1974: 64–165; Lévêque 1957: 295ff.

Hellenistic armies would be deployed in the conventional manner, with the phalanx protected on the flanks by cavalry and in the front by skirmishers, among whom elephants were sometimes placed. The battle might begin with an elephant assault against the enemy infantry, but circumstances might favour starting with an assault by light infantry, phalanx or cavalry. When the Hellenistic armies had to fight against an army in broken terrain, they were generally content to use the light and semi-heavy infantry and cavalry units, depending on the possibilities presented by conditions in the area. At times they found ways to involve heavy forces in the formation, though in a rather limited and narrow deployment.

In battles between the Hellenistic armies themselves, generally on level ground, the armies were arrayed according to the regular system. Changes and improvisations depended on the particular topographical structure of the battlefield and its vicinity, and on the relative numbers and quality of the forces as estimated by the high command. Semi-heavy units were mingled with the phalanx if a sector of the terrain occupied by one of the sides was difficult to manoeuvre in, and in such circumstances cavalry too were sometimes placed among the phalangites. If the cavalry of one flank was inferior, elephants protected their front. But if the ground beyond the flanks of the front lines was level, there was a possibility of bypassing the elephants. Consequently the forces whose cavalry was inferior tried to post its flanks close to natural obstacles like bodies of water, stretches of sand, or mountains. A commander with large phalanx forces deployed them in as broad a line as possible, so as to force the enemy to post much lighter forces against them at various points. If the area was narrow and restricted on both sides by natural obstacles, he increased the number of phalanx rows, thus strengthening the heavies in the centre.

Obviously, then, the relative numbers, quality and tactical composition of the opposing forces affected the choice of battlefield. The commander whose cavalry was inferior hoped for an area restricted on both sides by natural obstacles. A similar arena, not very wide, was preferred also by a commander whose phalangites were considerably fewer than those of the enemy. A commander who had many semi-heavy and light infantry preferred rocky or steep ground, while a commander whose force was mainly heavy infantry or cavalry preferred a flat and level battlefield. The choice of battlefield took into account additional features which could make tactical surprise possible: a declivity beyond which reinforcements could be concealed and thrown into the fray thus upsetting the enemy's earlier calculations in deploying his forces; a hill overlooking a section of the formation and making possible a good view and rapid cavalry assault down the slope; a gully on the enemy flank or at his rear through which forces could be despatched to attack while the enemy was concentrating on its front; a nearby canyon behind the force to which some of the enemy cavalry could be drawn and then cut off and prevented from rejoining the main force; and so on and so forth.

After choosing a battlefield that suited him, the commander would set up his camp in the area. The enemy might avoid a confrontation and try to wait in a more congenial place, but that was not always possible: sometimes such avoidance would have been detrimental to morale, and sometimes time was vital because of a shortage of supplies, the approach of the rainy season, the soldiers' personal problems, etc. The side that could 'hold its breath' the longest was able to force its choice of battlefield on the foe. Sometimes during the waiting period one of the sides would move to another field, less suited to its requirements, in order to 'tempt' the other finally to join battle. The time and place of the battle could be forced in various ways: by cutting off lines of supply and retreat, by committing acts of sabotage and harassment, by arousing the local population to revolt, by systematically destroying sources of livelihood in the area, by taking punitive measures against the civilian population, etc. All these put heavy pressure on the enemy high command, reduced its ability to wait, and forced a quick decision, even to the extent of joining battle at a site convenient to the other side. Once it was decided to meet the challenge, the camp was set up on or near the battlefield. At times the rival camps were only one to three kilometres apart. The camps were normally protected by a palisade and sometimes by a more complicated system including a moat, a wall and watchtowers. There was also a tendency to rely on surface features which provided some natural protection. To these were added wide-awake sentries and patrols, primarily of horsemen who circled the camp day and night. The side that had chosen the battlefield generally refrained from interfering with the setting up of the rival camp or with the preparations so as not to discourage the enemy from making contact in that area.

In the days before the battle, the belligerents made preparations, mainly from the point of view of intelligence, taking note of each other's movements and endeavouring to get spies into the enemy camp or abduct some of the enemy soldiers in order to ascertain the exact composition of the opposing army. Sometimes attempts were made to tip the scales by making a nocturnal raid, bursting into the rival command tent, and the like. Long-distance exchanges of fire between the fortified camps and minor clashes near roads and sources of water and supplies were daily occurrences, and at times drew the opposing armies into a premature general confrontation.

In determining the exact day and hour of the engagement, careful consideration was given to local changeable conditions like the weather, direction of the sun, visibility and dust (cf. Vegetius 3.14). When one of the commanders had completed his preparations and concluded that the time was suitable, he left the camp and started to deploy his units across the field. Even at that stage, the rival army might refrain from emerging and remain within its camp. Because of the danger to morale, however, such a course was not customary at so late a stage unless the omens were unfavourable. It was also possible to besiege a camp if the enemy persisted in refusing to fight. Verbal harassment, threats and derision were likewise a consider-able factor in 'persuading' the enemy to take up the challenge.[23] The two armies then formed within sight of each other with no more than a few hundred metres between them. The commanders de-ployed their forces according to the units at their disposal, the terrain, and the advance information they had about the enemy, altering the placement of the units as further information became available on the enemy formation and composition. While deploying their forces, the contenders did not ordinarily interfere with each other, both of them fearing that a precipitous confrontation would upset their arrangements. The side that had dictated the choice of battlefield was the one that usually took up positions first and completed deployment, refraining from any harassment of the enemy which might lead to a last minute refusal to fight.

The battle itself was generally conducted in three principal stages: (a) *An exchange between skirmishers*: As noted above, the task of the skirmishers, posted in front of the centre, was to break up the for-mation of the enemy phalanx. However, as all the Hellenistic armies

---

[23] A discussion on the challenge to battle appears in Pritchett 1974: 2.147–56. Pritchett's view of the fairness in the preparations and placement of the two sides is somewhat rose-coloured. Thus for instance if a certain commander brands the avoidance of direct confron-tation and 'scorched earth' methods as unfair (ἀδίκως) and 'dishonourable' (ἀγεννῶς, Polybius 18.3.2; see Pritchett 1974: 2.148), it should not necessarily be concluded from his remarks that there existed a code requiring both sides to embark upon frontal battles. Closed-minded generals and political demagogues in their wake, as today, disparage indirect warfare deviating from the textbook models they were trained in. Pritchett's assessment perhaps applies to the Classical period, but there is no doubt that in the Hellenistic period the opposing forces did not deploy 'by mutual agreement' (ἐξ ὁμολόγου); the process was much more complicated and dynamic, as is indicated by the sources.

positioned infantry skirmishers in the front for the same purpose, these light units in fact neutralized each other. The battle began with the clash of skirmishers, sniping at each other and preventing the enemy from harassing the phalanx behind each of them. As the amount of ammunition a foot soldier could carry was quite limited, the engagement ended in a rather short time, and even if the skirmishers of one side had prevailed, they were not in a position to bother the opposing phalanx much longer. At this point the light forces generally withdrew to the rear of the phalanx. Although this opening stage was in fact a formality, neither side was prepared to forgo it for fear that the enemy would employ skirmishers, thus endangering the opposing heavy forces.

An effective variation was introduced if one of the contenders had mounted skirmishers, especially archers. These could carry large quantities of arrows, had the advantage of height and a good view of the field, and were able to move and act with great speed. These horsemen, however, were dependent on the structure of the terrain, and the horses were an easy target for enemy infantry archers. They could also be attacked by heavy cavalry. If while the enemy heavy cavalry was pinned down in protecting the flanks of its phalanx the mounted archers managed to overcome enemy light infantry, they might well go on to imperil the enemy phalanx formation.

(b) *A cavalry attack on the flanks*: At the time of the skirmisher clash or immediately after it, the battle was joined between the cavalry of the opposing sides. Normally a cavalry assault preceded the confrontation between phalanx units, as an early phalanx clash was wasteful. If one of the sides was having some success against the enemy phalanx while its own cavalry was being overcome, its efforts might be in vain. The cavalry moved and fought more quickly, and the battle would be decided before the phalangite clash ended. The phalanx whose cavalry was defeated would be in danger of being outflanked in the middle of the heavy infantry encounter, which would leave it no hope of success. That is why both sides preferred to wait for the outcome of the confrontation on the flanks before engaging their phalanx.[24]

Sometimes the cavalry engagement was delayed by the deployment of elephants in front of one or both sides. When the terrain permitted, the horsemen of one side bypassed the enemy elephants and attacked the opposing horsemen who sought cover behind the elephants. But if the elephants and cavalry had some natural obstacle

---

[24] That the phalanx refrained from attacking until the cavalry clash was over was rightly noted by Droysen 1889: 81, and Tarn 1930: 66–71.

on their flank, often a battle developed between the elephants of the two sides, unless the attacking cavalry found a way to divert the enemy horsemen or avert contact with the elephants through some clever manoeuvre. In confrontations between elephants, the Seleucids' Indian elephants always prevailed. As a rule, the defeat of an army's elephants led to the collapse of morale in its cavalry.

(c) *The clash of phalangites*: The cavalry engagement could end in several ways: one side could be victorious on both flanks, or win on one and be beaten on the other, and later come out on top in the confrontation between the two victorious flanks. If the victorious cavalry remained in the field it could decide the battle. A cavalry assault from the flanks of the phalanx together with a frontal attack of heavy infantry would leave the enemy centre with no real chance. It happened quite often, however, that the victorious flanks left the field to conduct a pursuit, or that the outcome of the cavalry clash was undecided, or because of successful blocking the opposing cavalry was never actually involved in the fighting. This left the decision to the phalangites. In a clash between phalanxes, the soldiers' physical condition and strength played a vital role, as did the coordination of the rows and columns and the number of rows in the formation. The number of rows affected the driving power of the entire force and its ability to 'freshen' the forward rows and so make it possible to continue fighting the exhausting battle for a long time.

In cases in which all the troops of one side fled the battlefield or surrendered, there was no doubt about who was victorious. But at times the outcome was unclear, when units of both sides remained on the battlefield or in its vicinity, but too exhausted to continue to fight. In such circumstances the side that managed to corral the bodies of the fallen was recognized at least formally as the victor (Diodorus 19.31.3–4). The side that then requested access to its dead thereby admitted defeat, and the victor promptly set up a trophy.

It is thus evident that it was the wise management and command of the cavalry that in most cases was the deciding factor in the battle. As a result the Hellenistic rulers and commanders always took their places in the forward flanks, among the cavalry. Combat on horses permitted them great mobility and a view of a large part of the arena, both of which were essential for orientation in what was happening and for directing the troops. The appearance of the kings and supreme commanders on the battlefield was a direct continuation of the Macedonian tradition documented in the period of Alexander the Great, and had a clearly political purpose. Since the

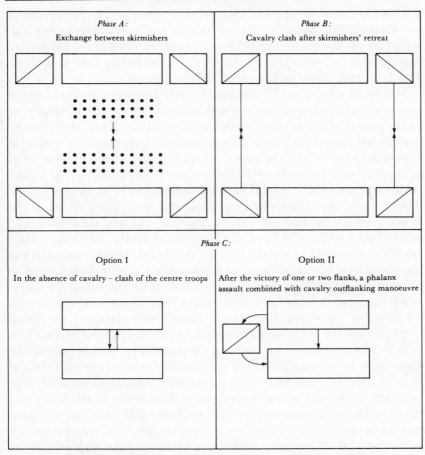

Diagram 2: *Principal battle phases (without elephants and chariots)*

Key

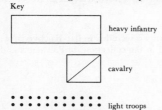

Hellenistic dynasties developed at the outset around the personalities of high-ranking officers, the king's military ability on the battlefield, his courage and the personal example he set served more than anything else to unite the Greco-Macedonian population of the empire behind him and to increase their reliance on him as a person worthy and capable of leading them and defending them throughout the hostile oriental expanse. However, the personal participation of the king or the supreme commander in the battle prevented him sometimes from seeing the overall picture, responding accordingly, and properly controlling the troops, and exposed him to danger which in itself could affect the course of the battle.

History does not record any two battles that were identical in the number and composition of participating troops or in the terrain, or in the phases of the battle. The description above should therefore be considered a schematic one, providing basic guidelines according to which the commanders planned the placement of the various units in the formation and the principal phases. During the actual battle, additional possibilities could develop: efforts could be focused on the flank where the commander-in-chief took his place; some of the cavalry could be directed even before the cavalry clash to a gap which had developed for some reason in the phalangite front; sham withdrawals could be effected on the flanks for the purpose of drawing the enemy's picked horsemen away from the battlefield and so preventing them from attacking the phalanx; reinforcements might suddenly appear from behind the front line, frightening the enemy soldiers and upsetting their commander's calculations; a surprise elephant assault from the flank could be made against the opposing cavalry; an ambush of mounted archers could be posted behind the front lines to the enemy's rear; the main effort might be directed toward breaking into the camp where the 'baggage' (*aposkeuē*) had been left, greatly affecting the morale of the soldiers in the field; and many other stratagems known from Hellenistic history. Rugged mountain terrain provided an even greater opportunity for an inventive and audacious commander because of the impossibility of deploying and moving the forces according to the standard tactical pattern.[25]

---

[25] A summary of the stratagems used by the Seleucid army is included in Bar-Kochva 1979: 203–5. A great many *stratēgēmata* of this type are featured in the collections of Polyaenus and Frontinus.

2

The number of combatants on each side

The difference in the number of combatants on each side is not necessarily a decisive factor in the course of military events. The quality of the personnel, the standard of weaponry, the capacity for tactical manoeuvring and the particular conditions of the battle site may cancel out or at least limit the importance of numerical superiority. Nevertheless, modern historians are wont to make the number of combatants the first piece of information given about rival armies and the course of a battle. In doing so they not only assume that quantity quite often becomes quality, but are following a prevailing historiographic tradition. Many a historian of antiquity stressed the numbers because often their significance was more comprehensible to him than was that of other components of military might. In accordance with that time-honoured procedure, we shall open our re-examination of the sources and of scholarly views with a study of the question of the relative size of the forces.

A simplistic view of the importance of the numerical factor in the course of a battle led, in most ancient literature, to a distortion of the data. This feature is not only characteristic of Oriental literature, but is familiar from Classical and Hellenistic historiography. The exaggerated figures cited by most Greek sources, beginning with Herodotus, for the Persian armies up to and including the era of Alexander the Great, are notorious. Needless to say, writers who had no real information at all on the actual numbers let their imaginations soar. But even senior officers and official chroniclers who had accurate information on the number of combatants in the forces and were eye-witnesses habitually magnified the size of the enemy army and minimized that of their own, even when they were absolutely accurate in their descriptions of the battles. The distortion of the relative strengths derived from a desire to enhance the glory of a victory, or diminish the gloom and frustration following a failure. In the case of a severe and decisive defeat, the figures relating to the side

favoured by the writer take a steep dive.[1] Only a few outstanding
historians such as Thucydides, Hieronymus of Cardia and Polybius
disregarded propaganda motives when reporting on events they took
part in, and when compelled to rely on information provided by
others, generally adopted various methods for separating the chaff
from the wheat so as to report reliable figures.

In order to arrive at a reasonable estimate of the number of
combatants, it is customary in the study of ancient history to attach
great importance to a consideration of the course of the battles
themselves so far as it can be reconstructed, to a comparison of the
statistical information in literary sources of unquestioned reliability
and in official documents that have survived, to an examination of
the battlefields in regard to the deployment and movement of the
numbers mentioned, to demographic data, to the synchronization of
events, to slips of the pen in sources which had access to authoritative
information on the events, and the like. These conclusions and
methods evolved and applied in a long series of investigations of
ancient military historiography oblige us to utilize the conventional means of testing the numerical data given in the sources regarding the armies of the opposing forces in Judas Maccabaeus'
battles.

The military force at the Daphne procession

The only direct data at our disposal from external sources on the size
of Antiochus Epiphanes' army relate to the various units that took
part in the parade that ruler arranged at Daphne near Antioch in
165 B.C.[2] The sum of the numbers given for those units comes to
41,000 foot soldiers and 4,500 'operative' cavalry.[3] No doubt need

[1] These rules are known to anyone familiar with historiographic literature. They can be
found in various discussions on writers of antiquity who cited army numbers. The distorted
troop figures in Xenophon and Arrian are treated at greater length on pp. 155–6 below.
Among the greatest military writers of antiquity, both were experienced army men themselves,
and the former was even an eye-witness of most of the events he reported. Notable among the
general surveys dealing with these questions is H. Delbrück's brilliant *Numbers in History* (1913:
esp. 12–25). The essay includes illuminating modern examples, in particular from the battles
of Napoleon and Frederick the Great, and from the revolt of the Swiss peasants.

[2] For the date of the procession see pp. 467ff. below.

[3] Among the cavalry listed, the 3,000 'civilians' (*politikoi*: Polybius 30.25.6), a representative unit of citizens (from Phoenician cities?) should be discounted. They did not figure in
the big battles and were at Daphne evidently for ceremonial reasons. The 1,000 horsemen
known as 'Friends' (*philoi*: Polybius 30.25.8) were nobles who did not constitute a military
body (see p. 240 below). It is true that both groups are listed in the first part of the procession
(30.25.1–11) together with definitely military units and not in the second part made up of
civilians, including women (30.25.12–19), but in the first part there are also mentioned
gladiators (30.25.6) who were certainly not part of the Seleucid army, and chariots hitched to

be cast on that information: the report of the parade which had been provided by Polybius (30.25.1–11), was preserved by Athenaeus (5.194–5), who is fairly reliable in his quotations from Greek and Hellenistic literature.[4] Polybius himself, the greatest historian of the period, was careful in choosing his sources, and meticulous in examining numbers of military forces (see esp. 12.17–22). Moreover, no overall figure on total military strength is given in this case, but rather a breakdown for each unit. The occasion itself was not a military campaign about which reports might be influenced by propaganda considerations, but simply a ceremonial procession, and the military units are listed together with civilian bodies such as 'the king's friends', gladiator groups, etc., in addition to boys, women and servants who appeared separately (ibid., 30.25.12–19). The parade was organized as a prelude to the great expedition to the eastern satrapies where there was considerable ferment at the time.[5] And indeed missing from the procession list are the various nationals from those regions who had served in rather large numbers as auxiliaries in earlier battles of the Seleucid army.[6] There is also an impressive correspondence between the listed size of the Royal Guard units, both foot and horse, and their size in earlier lists covering the Seleucid manpower situation,[7] such regular army units naturally having a fixed complement. All these points support the reliability of the list. The few textual garbles and the insertion of the civilian groups among the military do not detract from its credibility. The original text of the garbled lines can be reconstructed and the military groups can be distinguished from the civilian ones with a considerable degree of certainty, both through philological means and by comparison with other listings of Seleucid manpower.[8]

---

six or four horses or two elephants (30.25.11) which had no military value. The distinction between the two parts of the procession was not between army and civilians but between the armed and the unarmed, the latter carrying precious objects like crowns, perfumes and the like. In addition, the thousand 'selected' (*epilektoi*: Polybius 30.25.8) should not be counted, they being none other than the *agēma* mentioned later in the same sentence. The words χίλιοι οἷς ἐπηκολούθει (= after them a thousand...), preceding the reference to the *agēma*, should be deleted as they are mistakenly included under the influence of such phrases in other parts of the same excerpt (cf., e.g., para. 5). This is not the only garble in the excerpt (see p. 417 n. 21 below on the reconstruction of para. 5). In any case, no unit by that name figures in any battle, and the term 'selected' mentioned in I Macc. 4.1 (the battle of Ammaus) is only a general term. Cf. I Macc. 4.28, 6.28, 12.41, where the entire Seleucid army is described as 'selected'.   [4] See Brunt 1980: 482–4.

[5] On the purpose of the expedition and its chronology see pp. 466ff. below. On the situation in the Upper Satrapies see Mørkholm 1966: 166–80; Will 1967: 266–8.

[6] See Table 1. On these troops see Bar-Kochva 1979: 48–53.

[7] See further, pp. 416–17 below.

[8] Contrary to Markle 1978: 408–9. The textual garbles are a result of the vicissitudes of the texts of both Polybius and Athenaeus. On their reconstruction see n. 3 above and p. 417 n. 21 below. For the 'screening' of the civilians see n. 3 above.

Given the aims and circumstances of the procession and the absence of the auxiliaries from the eastern satrapies, it can be deduced that reserve forces of the military settlers stationed east of the Tigris[9] did not take part in the procession either: there was no point in summoning them to Daphne, hundreds and thousands of kilometres away, for purely ceremonial purposes, when the ensuing expedition was designed to subdue the upheaval in their own neck of the woods. The Daphne procession thus involves only units stationed or recruited west of the Tigris. Did these, however, represent the entire Seleucid mobilization potential in the western part of the empire, or was only part of that potential force called up for the procession? As the procession was organized within the framework of the military preparations and as their apogee, and extraordinary organizational and financial efforts were invested in making it a most impressive event, in all likelihood it involved the greater part (if not all) of the forces then in the western part of the empire available for such one-time tasks. Furthermore, the large centres of military settlement in the western empire, in Seleucis (the four large satrapies of northern Syria) and especially the central military headquarters and camps at Apamea,[10] were not far from Daphne, so that it was not particularly difficult to arrange for most of the available manpower to take part in the procession. It should be kept in mind that the ceremony was also meant to bolster the morale of the Greco-Macedonian military settler population. Obviously, 'available forces' does not refer to all the military forces in the empire. The authorities had to leave troops for border and regional defence. Those included mercenaries stationed in forts in sensitive zones,[11] and to a lesser extent military settlers who had to be left in their allotments or nearby fortresses[12] in order to prevent hostile elements from taking advantage of their assignment to other areas. Such troops did not take part at any time in expeditions or missions outside the limited territory they were assigned to, so that they are not to be taken into account in any estimate of the mobilization potential of the empire.

In order to verify the assumption that the military forces of the Daphne parade represent all the recruitment potential of the Seleucids to the west of the Tigris, it is worth comparing the figures for the Daphne procession with those for the Seleucid armies in the battle at Raphia (217 B.C.) and the battle of Magnesia (190 B.C.).

---

[9] On these units see Bar-Kochva 1979: 32–5.

[10] On the troops in these satrapies see ibid. 28–31.

[11] On them see ibid. 36–7.

[12] See, e.g., the settlers in Palai-Magnesia, ibid. 57–8. See further p. 101 below.

These two campaigns are the only Seleucid campaigns for which detailed numerical information is available, including a total figure and a breakdown by units. The two lists are reliable: the report on Raphia comes from Polybius (5.79), and that on Magnesia from Livy (37.40) and Appian (*Syr.* 32), both of whom took their information from Polybius.[13] In his description of the battle at Raphia Polybius used a Ptolemaic source[14] which noted a Ptolemaic numerical advantage, especially as regards the 'heavy' forces.[15] A source of that kind need certainly not be suspected of falsifying the true figures of the Seleucid opponent. Furthermore, the overall number of Seleucid forces at Raphia equals the sum of the figures for the units. The total in the description of the battle of Magnesia does not correspond to the sum of its parts, but some Seleucid units are not assigned any figure, and various evidence indicates that their numerical strength very exactly fills in what is missing for the total sum.[16] Finally, there is no discrepancy between the figures cited and the progress of the battles or the deployment and operational possibilities allowed by the battle sites at Raphia and Magnesia.

According to Polybius, in the battle of Raphia 68,000 soldiers took part on the Seleucid side, of whom 62,000 were infantry and 6,000 cavalry (5.79.13). At Magnesia the Seleucids had 72,000 in all, 60,000 infantry and 12,000 cavalry (Livy 37.37.9). The figures for the Daphne procession are thus less than those for the armies at Raphia and Magnesia. As noted above, troops from the eastern parts of the empire did not take part in the procession. In addition, it may appear that the reduction of the mobilization area was accompanied by a diminution in imperial forces in the western empire that had taken place since the reign of Antiochus III, or that the troops at Daphne did not truly reflect the mobilization potential of the western part of the empire. We shall see below that the last two alternatives do not apply, and that the numerical discrepancy must be attributed mainly to the territorial changes.

The forces at Raphia, Magnesia and Daphne were mobilized from three sources: the Greco-Macedonian military settlements that supplied reserve soldiers and Royal Guard, the peoples of the empire

---

[13] On Livy's and Appian's versions of the battles of Thermopylae and Magnesia as based on Livy see Nissen 1863: 114–18,181,195–7; Soltau 1897: 44; Witte 1910: 387–93; Klotz 1940: 13f.; Tränkle 1977: 27–30; Briscoe 1981: 2–3,241.

[14] See Bar-Kochva 1979: 128–9.

[15] Ibid. 253 nn. 11–12. The various proposals for correcting the numbers of the Greco-Macedonian Ptolemaic phalanx at Raphia made by Mahaffy (1899: 140–52) and Griffith (1935: 117,123,140) must be rejected. See Cavaignac 1951: 292–4; Peremans 1951: 214–22; Huss 1976: 58–60; Bar-Kochva 1979: 138–41; Galili 1976–7: 62ff.

[16] Bar-Kochva 1979: 8–9.

Table 1. Manpower sources for the Seleucid army

	Military settlers	Royal Guard (settlers' sons)	Mercenaries*	Vassals and allies*	Total
Battle of Raphia (217 B.C.)	20,000 Macedonians 4,000 cavalry 1,000 Thracians, (from Persis)	10,000 *argyraspides* 2,000 cavalry (*agēma* and *hetairoi*)	5,000 Greeks 1,500 Cretans 1,000 Neo-Cretans 5,000 Dahae and Cilicians	10,000 Arabs 5,000 Medes, Cissians, Cadusians and Carmanians 1,000 Cardaces (Kurds) 500 'Lydians' (western Media) 2,000 Persian and 'Agrianian' bowmen and slingers	
Total	25,000	12,000	12,500	18,500	68,000
Battle of Magnesia (190 B.C.)	16,000 Macedonians 3,000 Thracians (from Persis)* 6,000 cavalry (cataphracts)	10,000 *argyraspides* 2,000 cavalry (*agēma* and *hetairoi*)	1,200 Dahaen cavalry (Illyrians) 3,000 Tralli (Illyrians) 1,500 Cretans 1,000 Neo-Cretans 3,000 Galatian foot 2,500 Galatian horse 500 Tarentines	2,000 Cappadocians 2,500 Mysians 1,000 Light elephants guard 8,000 Cyrtians and Elymaeans 4,000 Pisidians, Pamphilians and Lycians 2,700 Orientals (Persians, Medes et al.) 1,500 Carians and Cilicians	
Total	25,000	12,000	12,700	21,700	71,400
The Daphne procession (165 B.C.)	15,000 Macedonians 1,500 cavalry (cataphracts) 1,000 Nisaean cavalry	5,000 *argyraspides* 5,000 'Roman style' 2,000 cavalry (*agēma* and *hetairoi*)	5,000 Mysians 3,000 Cilicians(?) 3,000 Thracians 5,000 Galatians	3,000 Cilicians(?)	
Total	17,500	12,000	13,000–16,000	3,000(?)	45,500

* For the provenance and status of these units see Bar-Kochva 1979: 8–9,42–53.

and the vassal peoples that supplied auxiliary troops, and mercenaries hired mainly from outside the empire. The large numerical discrepancy derives from the category of auxiliary troops. A total of 16,500 such took part in the battle of Raphia (10,000 Arabs and 6,500 from the eastern satrapies); auxiliary troops from Asia Minor were absent, they being controlled at the time by the rebel governor Achaeus. The battle of Magnesia involved 21,700 auxiliary troops, in almost equal numbers from the eastern satrapies and Asia Minor.[17] All these are entirely missing from the Daphne procession. The reason for the absence of the 'easterners' has already been mentioned. Asia Minor north of the Taurus was cut off from the Seleucid empire by the surrender to the Romans signed at Apamea in 189 B.C. As to the Arabs, their appearance en masse at Raphia is explicable both by the immediate interest of these caravan traders to ensure the amity of the ruler soon to control the ports of export, and by Antiochus III's desire to assure himself suitably experienced troops for desert warfare in territory where the decisive battle was expected to take place.

It should be noted in this context that the allies and vassals created difficulties in the Seleucid army. Their reliability, usefulness and military efficiency were doubtful, they caused considerable difficulty in coordination, and their participation has even been blamed for the defeat at Magnesia.[18] Thus their absence from Antiochus Epiphanes' army in 165 B.C. did not necessarily impair its ability, despite their numbers, and perhaps even contributed to the army's strength.

If the Seleucids wished to make up for the absence of auxiliary forces they could do so only by recruiting mercenaries from outside the empire, more precisely, from the regions north of the Taurus, who were certainly more experienced and better trained than the auxiliaries. The number of mercenaries at Daphne indeed shows some growth: 16,000 troops compared with 12,500 at Raphia and 12,700 at Magnesia.[19] A whole generation elapsed between the battles of Raphia and Magnesia, and if the similarity in the number of mercenaries taking part in the two is not accidental, it may well indicate the financial capacity of Antiochus III and the empire in general. His son, Antiochus IV, probably made an enormous effort when he increased the number of mercenaries, despite the reduced finances of the empire in his time and its tremendous debts arising

[17] Arab camel cavalry also took part in the battle, see Livy 37.40.12,41.11; Appian, *Syr.* 32 (167) and 33(173). The sources do not say how many. Judging by their location on the battlefield behind or beside the chariots, they seem to have been few.

[18] See especially Appian, *Syr.* 37(191). On the authenticity of the comment see Nissen 1863: 196; Ed. Meyer 1881: 123–4. Cf. Appian, *Syr.* 32(165–6).   [19] See Table 1.

from the payment of indemnities to Rome.[20] And to the financial difficulties were added the practical and political–legal problems that affected mobilization in the countries of the Aegean in the wake of the treaty of Apamea and the diminished sources of manpower in those regions.[21] All these difficulties limited the possibilities of bringing the overall numerical strength of the army up to the level it had attained in the reign of Antiochus III.

The most important component of the Seleucid army from the viewpoint of quality were the military settlers who provided the 'heavy' troops, both infantry and cavalry.[22] They were divided into two groups: the military settlers themselves serving as reserve soldiers, and their picked sons serving in the Royal Guard.[23] The Royal Guard was numerically constant; the infantry Guard numbered 10,000 at Raphia, Magnesia and Daphne,[24] while the two mounted Guard units numbered 2,000.[25] This consistency is of course not surprising in regular units naturally based on a fixed number of soldiers. More important for our discussion is the information on the strength of reserve troops in the various campaigns. The question of the overall number of the military settlers[26] is less relevant in this context, since, as has already been stated, it was not possible to mobilize all the military settlers for campaigns beyond their immediate vicinity.

The phalanx, composed of reserve soldiers from the military settlements, numbered 20,000 men at Raphia, 16,000 at Magnesia, and 15,000 at Daphne.[27] A cursory glance at these figures indicates relative consistency, the slight decline at Daphne deriving from the absence of the military settlers from the eastern parts of the empire and the unavailability of those from Asia Minor. However, as it is inconceivable that the military settlers from these two regions were so few, it is obvious that these figures are inadequate, and that the manpower potential of the military settlers from all parts of the

---

[20] On the financial straits see pp. 228–33 below in the comment on verses 29–31.

[21] On the mobilization restrictions see Griffith 1935: 146–7; and see p. 306 below re verse 30.

[22] On the military settlements as the main source of manpower for the phalanx see the evidence in Griffith 1935: 147–70; Bickerman 1938: 74–8; Jones 1940: 23–4; Bar-Kochva 1979: 20–2,56–8. For the heavy cavalry see ibid. 21,61–2,70–1,74.

[23] On the sources of manpower for the Royal Guard see pp. 98–9 below.

[24] See p. 416–17 below.

[25] See Bar-Kochva 1979: 68–73.   [26] On this see pp. 100–3 below.

[27] Raphia: Polybius 5.79.5; Magnesia: Livy 37.40.2 and Appian, *Syr.* 32(161); Daphne: Polybius 30.25.5. On the reconstruction of the text in the last excerpt see in detail below, p. 417 n. 21. Five thousand *argyraspides* (= bearers of silver shields) mentioned in the same paragraph were half the Royal Guard (see p. 417 below). The bearers of bronze and 'gold' shields were phalanx reserve soldiers from the military settlements.

empire that could normally be mobilized for one-time missions did not take part in the battles of Raphia and Magnesia in entirety.

The 20,000-man phalanx at Raphia in 217 B.C. did not include settlers from Cyrrhestica, a satrapy in northern Syria which had rebelled shortly before (Polybius 5.50.8, 57.4).[28] The number of rebels stood at 6,000, although it is impossible to know whether all the settlers rebelled, and how many of them could usually be mobilized for outside missions. In addition, the army at Raphia did not include military settlers from Asia Minor then controlled by the rebel governor Achaeus, whose numbers can be estimated likewise at about 6,000 on the basis of the number of soldiers who fought with Achaeus in Pamphylia.[29] Since the settlements in Asia Minor were concentrated in Phrygia and Lydia, a considerable distance from the battle site in Pamphylia, the estimate of 6,000 infantry accords with the number of troops that could be mobilized there for one-time distant missions. Thus the maximum number of reserve soldiers that could have been mobilized early in Antiochus III's reign, were it not for the revolts in northern Syria and Asia Minor, was about 32,000 with small margins for error in either direction.

The same total emerges from the information on the clashes with the Romans twenty-six years later at the end of Antiochus III's reign when there was a new generation of settlers at Cyrrhestica, and Asia Minor was again firmly under central control. A total of 16,000 phalangites, reserve soldiers, took part in the battle of Magnesia. A year earlier, in 191 in Greece, Antiochus III seems to have lost about 18,000 foot soldiers.[30] The description of the defensive deployment adopted by Antiochus at Thermopylae indicates that most of the soldiers were 'heavies',[31] and this is confirmed by the repeated stress in the sources on the fact that Antiochus was awaiting troops from the Upper Satrapies, probably mainly ethnic light troops who were delayed (Livy 36.15.5; Appian, *Syr.* 12(47), 17(74)). Of the phalangites who took part in the battle only a few belonged to the Royal

---

[28] On the settlers in Cyrrhestica and on this affair see Bar-Kochva 1979: 30–1.

[29] See ibid. 41.

[30] See ibid. 15–18. At the battle of Thermopylae most of the Seleucid soldiers (10,000 infantry and 500 cavalry), were killed and the rest who had been stationed in various places in Greece were taken prisoner.

[31] On the reconstruction of Polybius' text see Excursus V below. The reconstructed text indicates that the Seleucid centre was composed of the Royal Guard deployed before the rampart, while the phalanx stood on it and behind it. The left flank was manned by archers, slingers and dart throwers posted on the hills on the south outside the wall, who in view of their location could not have comprised more than a few hundred, and on the right near the sea were a few elephants followed by 500 cavalry commanded personally by Antiochus III. As to the light troops who blocked the Callidromus pass, they comprised solely Aetolians. See Livy 36.18.3,5 and 19.4; Appian, *Syr.* 18–19; Plut. *Cato Mai.* 14.1; cf. Bar-Kochva 1979: 160–1.

Guard. Otherwise it is impossible to understand the rapid retreat of the Guardsmen, who were elite soldiers and were deployed in the front of the battlefield, in contrast to the stubborn resistance of the phalanx of military settlers, who were reserve soldiers and older as well and were first positioned behind them.[32] The appearance of some 10,000 Guard soldiers at the battle of Magnesia, as emerges from an analysis of the figures and deployment in that battle,[33] similarly makes it unlikely that any large contingent of Royal Guard took part in the battle at Thermopylae: the 10,000 figure represented the full complement for that elite corps, and it could not have been reconstituted in less than a year if it suffered heavy losses at Thermopylae. Thus the number of reserve phalangite-settlers that could have been mobilized before the battle of Thermopylae was no more than 34,000.

The procession at Daphne was organized twenty years after the defeats at Thermopylae and Magnesia, when a new generation of military settlers had grown up.[34] Taking part in it were 15,000 reserve phalangites from the western part of the empire at the time, that is, from Syria and Mesopotamia alone. Absent were the 6,000 phalangite settlers from Asia Minor who were no longer under Seleucid control and had transferred their allegiance to the king of Pergamum;[35] absent too were the reserve soldiers from the eastern satrapies whose number is not given. Does the figure of 15,000 phalangites faithfully reflect the number of reservists from Syria and Mesopotamia who could under normal conditions be called up during the reign of Antiochus III as well? Direct data are unavailable but an estimate can be made. The 15,000 figure for reserve phalangites mentioned must be the minimum number of troops available in the west of the empire during Antiochus III's reign, for the number of military settlers could not have increased in the period after his death. The very small natural increase usual in Greco-Macedonian society must be offset by a certain percentage of natural decrease and losses which could not be made up. New recruits from Greece and Macedonia then controlled by the Antigonid dynasty could not reach the country, and Orientals were not accepted in the reserve units or phalanx.[36] Was, however, the number of warriors from the military settlements of Syria and Mesopotamia available

---

[32] For the sources and details see at the end of Excursus V, p. 570 below.

[33] See Bar-Kochva 1979: 9,168–9.

[34] In this connection it should be noted that the Seleucid casualties at the battle of Magnesia reported by Livy (37.44.1) are incorrect. The 1,400 captives are perhaps only the cavalry captives, while if the 50,000 figure can be treated seriously at all, it refers to the infantry captives (see Appian, *Syr.* 36(189)).

[35] On their new affiliation see Griffith 1935: 17ff.   [36] See in detail below pp. 92ff.

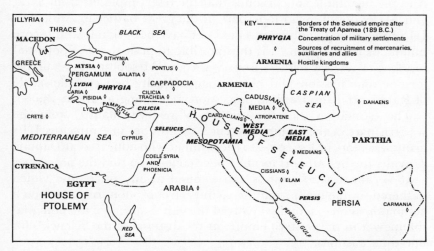

2 The Hellenistic world and manpower sources for the Seleucid army

for short-term missions during Antiochus III's reign considerably greater than 15,000? If we subtract that figure as well as the 6,000 settlers of Asia Minor from the round 32,000 to 34,000 total mobilization potential of reserve soldiers at the time, we find that the rest of the troops, which included reserve soldiers from the military settlements of the Upper Satrapies, numbered no more than 11,000 to 13,000. As there was a massive participation of national troops from the eastern regions at Raphia and Magnesia, the military settlers certainly were represented in numbers which reflected their recruitment capability. It is hard to imagine that the number of settlers from the Upper Satrapies available to the authorities for missions outside their area was less than that, or that in such a large area the number of military settlers was so small that 11,000–13,000 of them could not be called up for one-time missions so decisive for the future of the empire. The considerable activity of the large Diadochian armies in those areas and the hints of the early settlement of Greco-Macedonian soldiers there (esp. Diodorus 19.44.4, 46.1, 5),[37] the first successes of the military settlers from the Upper Satrapies in Molon's rebellion against Antiochus III's expeditionary force, and the confrontation of Molon's phalanx with the Royal phalanx not far from Babylon,[38] all indicate that the number of available troops could not have been less than the estimate mentioned above.

[37] See Tcherikover 1927: 159; Griffith 1935: 150.
[38] On this revolt see Walbank 1957–79: 1.571–85; H. Schmitt 1964: 116–49; Bar-Kochva 1979: 117ff. On the Seleucid military settlement east of the Tigris see ibid. 32–5.

And the inevitable conclusion is that the reserve soldiers from Syria and Mesopotamia who took part in the great battles in Antiochus III's time, though not fewer, could not have been significantly more numerous than 15,000. It is thus possible to posit that the potential number of reserve soldiers from Syria and Mesopotamia available for one-time missions did not change radically between the battle of Raphia and the Daphne procession, remaining at about 15,000.

The estimation that the number of reserve infantry from the western part of the empire (except Asia Minor) in Antiochus III's army was more or less equal to the number who appeared at Daphne provides further support for the above conclusion that the procession – whose aim was to impress and astound at any price, and which gathered, in the main from the vicinity, troops soon to embark on a combat mission – actually involved the vast majority of the potential manpower in the western empire at the disposal of the Seleucids for one-time missions.

The Seleucid armies in Judaea

The totals of 41,000 infantry and 4,500 cavalry are thus key figures for the assessment of the Seleucid mobilization potential in Judas Maccabaeus' generation. Since during Antiochus Epiphanes' reign there was constant tension and rebellion in the Upper Satrapies, the ruler had no possibility of moving the military settlers from those regions for a Judaean operation, and certainly not the auxiliary troops recruited from the local peoples.

However, the figures in the Books of the Maccabees for the Seleucid armies range from 100,000 infantry and 20,000 cavalry at the battle of Beth Zacharia (I Macc. 6.30) to the relatively modest 20,000 infantry and 2,000 cavalry at the battle of Elasa (I Macc. 9.4). Some of the figures surpass the mobilization potential not only of the western regions of the empire but of the empire as a whole, including all the eastern satrapies. Furthermore, when most of the Judaean battles were fought, the greater part of the Seleucid army (including soldiers from the western empire) was occupied in other arenas. According to I Maccabees itself, Antiochus IV left Syria for the East shortly before the battle of Ammaus in 165 B.C. (that is, shortly after the Daphne procession), taking with him 'half the army' (3.37). That expedition had far greater importance than the suppression of the rebellion in Judaea, and required the participation of particularly large forces. I Maccabees clearly exaggerates in the same passage in indicating that the main object of the expedition to Persia was to finance the campaign in Judaea (3.27–37). It may therefore be assumed that a considerably smaller number than 'half the army' was left to handle the Judaean operation. These figures enable us to evaluate the reliability of the numbers the Books of the Maccabees attribute to the Seleucid armies from the battle of Ammaus on.

According to I Maccabees the camp at Ammaus numbered 40,000 infantry and 7,000 cavalry, augmented by auxiliary troops from the coastal cities and Idumaea (3.39,41).[39] II Maccabees reports a total of 20,000 (8.9). Given the size of the Seleucid army at the time as noted above, there is clearly no foundation for the number given in I Maccabees. It thus seems reasonable to accept the hypothesis of the Dominican father, F. M. Abel, one of the great Holy Land scholars, that the figure was arrived at by association of the 'Aramite'–Seleucid force with the Aramite–Syrian one in a war of David's time related in I Chronicles (19.18).[40] The estimate in II Maccabees, citing less than half of Seleucid manpower then available, is surprising in view of the exaggerated numbers the book attributes to the Seleucid armies in Judas Maccabaeus' other campaigns, of the scanty information the author provides on the course of the battles, and especially of his tendency to exaggerate descriptive details. Presumably, the 'modest' number was the result of a palaeographical error, which is suggested also by an examination of the passage as a whole,[41] and the original estimate was much higher than 20,000. But in fact it is not impossible that together with the auxiliary troops from the coastal cities and Idumaea about 20,000

[39] On the substitution of אֲרָם (= arām) for the original אֱדֹם (= edōm) in I Macc. 3.41, and the use of the term 'Aram' in the original of I Macc. to designate the Seleucids, see pp. 209, 247 below.

[40] Abel 1949: 65. Chronicles does have rekev (= vehicles) and not pārāšīm (= cavalry), but in view of the tremendous number, the author of I Maccabees could very well have thought that cavalry was meant. Indeed in quite a few instances the Septuagint translation for rekev is ἱππεῖς or ἵππος (= cavalry), although not in the verse referred to in Chronicles. Be that as it may, the association and use of identical figures could have occurred to him only as a result of the reference to the Aramaean army in the Bible. A similar use of ἡνίαι (= chariots) referring to cavalry occurs in I Macc. 6.28 (see p. 305 below). The word rekev is quite commonly used to mean 'cavalry' in the Scroll of the War of the Sons of Light and the Sons of Darkness (see Yadin 1962: 179, especially no. 20).

[41] Contrary to the opinion of Niese (1900: 53), see Avi-Yonah 1972: 158. II Maccabees may have used the vague term myriōn (= myriads, tens of thousands in the genitive); cf. 11.4) and the number dis (= two) may have been attached to it under the influence of the expression diskhiliōn (= two thousand) in the following verse (8.10; the Lucian text has dismyriōn (= two myriads), which is certainly a mistake and clearly demonstrates the likelihood of an exchange between the two verses). The present text is affected also by the frequent repetition of the phrase 'two myriads' in the estimate of enemy losses in battles against the local elements in eastern Transjordania (II Macc. 10.17,23,31, 12.26; and cf. 12.19,23).

soldiers gathered at the Seleucid encampment at Ammaus.[42] At that stage, when two local commissioners or commanders had been beaten (I Macc. 3.10–26), it may be presumed that Ptolemy son of Dorymenes, the governor (*stratēgos*) of Coele Syria and Phoenicia, did not confine himself to the despatch of only a token force.[43] Furthermore, the chronological analysis shows that the negotiations between Lysias and Judas Maccabaeus began after the battle of Ammaus, and not after Lysias' first expedition.[44] Lysias would certainly not have opted for negotiations if Judas Maccabaeus had not first demonstrated his strength by defeating a large army.

The figures given in the two sources for Lysias' first and second expeditions must similarly be totally rejected. To the first expedition to Beth Zur, which began before the death of Antiochus IV during his expedition to Persia, I Maccabees ascribes 60,000 foot soldiers and 5,000 horse (4.28) while II Maccabees reports 80,000 foot and 'thousands of horsemen' (11.2,4). As to the second expedition which climaxed in the battle of Beth Zacharia, I Maccabees mentions an extensive mobilization of mercenaries which increased the expeditionary force to Judaea to 100,000 infantry and 20,000 cavalry (6.30), while II Maccabees states 110,000 on foot, but only 5,300 mounted (13.2). In *Bellum Judaicum*, containing information of great interest that does not appear in I Maccabees and is drawn from Nicolaus of Damascus, who also used some Seleucid source,[45] Josephus speaks only of 50,000 infantry and 5,000 cavalry (1.41).

The comparison of the overall recruitment potential of the kingdom with the numbers cited in the Books of the Maccabees makes any comment superfluous, but the estimate in *Bellum Judaicum*, though possibly influenced by the numbers attributed to the armies of Antiochus Epiphanes in the lost parts of Polybius' *Histories* and certainly rounded off, is not necessarily far from the truth: the numerical potential at the disposal of Lysias at the time of his second expedition, organized after the death of Antiochus Epiphanes, was greater than that available to the commanders of earlier expeditions to Judaea. Although I Maccabees reports that the troops that set out with the king returned from the East and headed for Antioch under the command of Philippus only after the battle of Beth Zacharia in

[42] No reliable data are available on the recruitment potential of the coastal cities, but if it is correctly concluded that the 'troops of the cities' who fought against Jonathan near Azotos (I Macc. 10.71) were composed exclusively of local militia (see Bar-Kochva 1975: 85–6), they did number close to ten thousand (ibid. 74). There is however no assurance that the figure cited for them in I Maccabees is correct.

[43] On the contradiction in the sources on the initiator and commanders of the expedition see p. 238 below re verse 38.

[44] Pp. 522–3 below.   [45] Pp. 189–90, 295–6 below.

the middle of Lysias' siege of the Temple (6.55–6), there are substantive and chronological grounds for assuming that a considerable proportion of the army that had left for Persia had returned to Syria earlier and even took part in Lysias' expedition to Judaea.[46] As his prestige as a regent and his aspirations to the crown were dependent on the success of this mission, Lysias had to bring with him to Judaea most of the troops he had at his disposal. The Seleucid army was apparently augmented by several thousand militia from the Hellenistic coastal cities and Idumaea, included in the grand total. As for the especially extensive recruitment of mercenaries referred to in I Maccabees, its dimensions must be doubted, for a comparison with earlier Seleucid armies and an examination of the sources of manpower available to them indicate that at most 16,000 men could have been recruited.[47] A mercenary army of that size took part in the Daphne procession, and was consequently included in the estimate of Seleucid recruitment potential noted above. The fact that the battle of Beth Zacharia involved the largest Seleucid force ever engaged in Judaea, and that the confrontation ended in a severe Jewish defeat, led the author of I Maccabees to indulge in particular exaggeration. Abel sought to explain the total of 120,000 Seleucid troops by association with the number of Midianites beaten by Gideon (Judges 8.10),[48] but in view of the opposite outcomes of the two battles it is doubtful whether in the present case the figure was indeed inspired by a biblical association.

Nicanor's two battles involved quite modest Seleucid forces. Both took place early in 161 B.C.,[49] whereas the Timarchus Revolt, which agitated the eastern satrapies, was suppressed only at the beginning of 160.[50] Like Demetrius I himself, presumably most of the Seleucid army was then mobilized exclusively for the solution of that serious problem, which was far more urgent than the events in Judaea. I Maccabees does not mention the number of Seleucid soldiers in these two battles. From its description of the first, which took place at Kafar Salama, it appears to have involved only the garrison that

[46] Pp. 546–7 below.
[47] P. 35 above and p. 306 below.
[48] Abel 1949: 116, followed by Goldstein 1976: 320.   [49] Pp. 373–5 below.
[50] A Babylonian astronomical tablet states that in 'the year 151, Tabitu 4' (i.e. 18 January 160 B.C.) Demetrius governed Babylonia (see Kugler 1922: 334; cf. Strassmaier 1893: 110). For the evidence of the literary sources see esp. Volkmann 1925: 393–5. Parker–Dubberstein 1956: 23 date Demetrius' rule in Babylonia as early as May 161 B.C. on the basis of a reference in a short list of cuneiform economic tablets in Kugler, ibid. However the tablet itself has never been published, its contents are unknown, and the reference to months which appear in Kugler's list does not necessarily indicate that Demetrius was in power already on the first date mentioned in the tablet. Olmstead 1937: 12 rightly disregarded this reference. Numismatic evidence does not offer any help since Timarchus' coins are undated.

Nicanor had in Jerusalem (7.27,31–2) and a relatively small number
of casualties (7.32). The second battle, at Adasa, was fought by the
garrison reinforced by some troops who arrived via the Beth Horon
ascent (I Macc. 7.39; *Ant.* 12.408). Certainly nothing can be learned
from the exaggerated figure of 35,000 Seleucid dead cited in II
Maccabees (15.27). The number of enemy dead in the various battles
described in that book comes to a total of about 230,000 and is
sufficient indication of the nature of the estimates there.[51]

Josephus, whose *Antiquitates* version is based exclusively on I Maccabees,[52] reports that 9,000 Seleucid soldiers took part in the battle
of Adasa (12.411), a number which does not figure at all in I
Maccabees. Josephus indeed sometimes invents numbers that do not
appear in the Books of the Maccabees, and does the same in his
version of Bible stories where none is actually given in the Bible.[53] As
regards the battle of Adasa, however, quite a high estimate could be
expected under the influence of the exaggerated figures I Maccabees
attributes to the Seleucid armies in the other battles, and in view of
the clear indication in the battle oration there of the great enemy
force (7.41), and especially because of the commemoration of the
victory by the proclamation of a regular holiday (7.49). Consequently it is hard to assume that in this case the relatively low figure
was invented by Josephus. It may be assumed that Josephus recalled
the 9,000 figure from Nicolaus' book which he used when writing the
abridgement in *Bellum Judaicum*, his earlier work. Quite possibly that
numerical estimate contains an element of truth, for the reinforcements were likely to include not only a royal army from Syria but
also local units from Coele Syria and Phoenicia.

Of all the numbers ascribed to the Seleucid army in the Books of
the Maccabees the only one that can be accepted with a substantial
degree of certainty is the estimate of Bacchides' forces at Elasa,
numbering 20,000 infantry and 2,000 cavalry (I Macc. 9.4). There
is no reason to question these: the battle took place in April of
160,[54] a short time after Demetrius' reconquest of Babylonia and the
suppression of the Timarchus rebellion, which subsided early in 160.
At that stage it was not yet possible to rely on the military settlers of
the Upper Satrapies (especially Media) who had taken part in the

---

[51] On this figure see Pfeifer 1949: 512. On the dubious value of the numbers cited as enemy
casualties in ancient literature see Brunt 1971: 694–6.   [52] See pp. 190–3 below.

[53] See the collection of examples in Drüner 1896: 36–41, and the detailed explanation of the
background to each and every figure. Drüner believes that Josephus invented the figure of
9,000 Seleucid warriors at the battle of Adasa (ibid. 8; see also Gafni 1980: 82 n. 8) but fails
to explain how Josephus contrived the figure, in contrast to his treatment of the other numbers.

[54] See p. 385 below.

Revolt.[55] It may therefore be accepted that the force at the disposal of Demetrius I was of similar size to the one that took part in the procession at Daphne. Thus 20,000 foot soldiers and 2,000 horse represent about half the Seleucid manpower at the time. The enthusiastic reception Demetrius I was accorded in Babylonia (Appian, *Syr.* 47(242-3)) should have made it possible for him to assign half the troops at his disposal to the suppression of the Revolt in Judaea, even if the satrapies east of the Euphrates had not been entirely subdued at the moment. In view of (1) the decisive defeat suffered by the previous meridarch, Nicanor; (2) the dismemberment of the corpse of Nicanor (I Macc. 7.47; II Macc. 15.32-3), who was a high-ranking officer in the Seleucid army before being appointed governor of Judaea (II Macc. 14.12); (3) the high rank of Bacchides, the commander of the expedition, who was in charge of the western satrapies of the empire (I Macc. 7.8);[56] and, above all (4) the danger of Roman intervention owing to the alliance between Judas Maccabaeus and Rome, concluded shortly before (I Macc. 8.17-32, especially 31-2),[57] and the diplomatic support Rome gave the Timarchus Revolt,[58] it cannot be assumed that the king would have risked sending a smaller force. In this case the author was forced to report the true figure for the Seleucid troops because of his overminimization of the Jewish force, designed to excuse Judas Maccabaeus' defeat.[59]

Finally, the possibility that the numbers the Books of the Maccabees give for the Seleucid armies include service troops such as armour-bearers, cooks, store-keepers, maintenance men, etc., must be rejected. In the Hellenistic armies such functions were carried out by people to whom the sources apply terms indicating their status

[55] See Diodorus 31.27a on the help the troops in Media gave Heraclides, the local satrap, who was Timarchus' brother. No information is available on whether the conquest of Babylonia had any immediate calming effect on Media, but in any case the loyalty of the troops there was rather questionable. On the settlers in Media see Griffith 1935: 150,160; Bar-Kochva 1979: 32-3,71-3,111,117-23, and there too on their tendency to separatism.

[56] For details of Bacchides' post and status, and the historical and administrative problems involved, see pp. 380-1 below.

[57] On the question of the overall authenticity of the document and its vicissitudes see Stern 1965: 74-82; Schürer... 1973-9: 1.171, and the detailed bibliography there. See also p. 374 below on the chronological question. On the background and Roman interests see Liebmann-Frankfort 1969a: 120ff.; and 1969b: 101-20; Briscoe 1969: 49ff.; Timpe 1974: 133-52. The proposal of Wirgin (1969: 15-20) that the treaty was signed four to five years earlier cannot be accepted. The same is true in regard to the recent attempts to question the authenticity of the document and the reality of the contacts between Judas Maccabaeus and the Romans, made by Gauger 1976: 155ff.

[58] Polybius 31.33, 32.2-3; Diodorus 31.27a,28-9; Appian, *Syr.* 47(243). On the background see Will 1967: 2.315-16.

[59] See pp. 62, 388-90 below for details.

outside the regular military organization, their disqualification for
military service, and their unarmed condition.[60] They were included
in the *aposkeuē* ('baggage') which covered, among others, soldiers'
wives, children, mistresses and slaves.[61] Apart from the special terms
applied to them, Diodorus explicitly states that the people of the
aposkeuē took no part in the military assemblies, were always left
behind being useless for pitched battle and were even incapable of
defending themselves (18.15.1, 19.42.3,80.4).[62] This information
proves that the Hellenistic armies – unlike modern ones – did not
have large 'service corps' as a standard, organic part of the military.[63] There are grounds for thinking that the supply system was
generally entrusted to private merchant contractors, who set up a
market (*agora*) in the camp. It was there that the soldier purchased
his food, with the special grant for that purpose added to his salary
(*sitōnion*).[64] Thus the service people were never included in the overall
total, and were always mentioned separately from the combat
units.[65] The wording of the Books of the Maccabees makes this quite
clear: like Hellenistic sources they specify and distinguish between
infantry and cavalry and there is thus no doubt that the authors wish
to report only on the fighting force. In any case, the number of service
people in the Seleucid and Ptolemaic armies did not constitute a

[60] ὄχλος and also ὅμιλλος (= mass); ὄχλος πρὸς μάχην ἄχρηστος (= a mass that is not
qualified for war); ἄοπλοι (= the unarmed); ἀπόμαχοι (= unsuited to military service).
Especially common was οἱ ἔξω τάξεων (= those outside the formation); see Holleaux 1938–57:
3.1–14,20–1. Cf. Welwei 1977: 2.101–3, who cites also the term ἀκόλουθοι (= escorts). On the
distinction between armour bearers plus the rest of the 'baggage' and τὸ δὲ καθωπλισμένον καὶ
πρὸς μάχην χρήσιμον (= armed and fit for battle) see Diodorus 19.80.4.

[61] For the exact meaning of *aposkeuē*, and the relevant sources, see especially Holleaux
1938–57: 3.15–26; Bickerman 1938: 91–2; Launey 1949–50: 2.780–90.

[62] This is indirectly indicated by the many sources reporting how easily the enemy forces
overcame the 'baggage' in the battles themselves; see, e.g., Diodorus 18.20.6 and 40.8;
19.42.2ff. and 84.7–8; 20.47.4; Plut. *Eum.* 5.5, 9.6ff., 16.9–11; Polyaenus 4.6.12–13. The few
defenders left behind were the only ones who tried to fill the breach (Diodorus 19.42.3).

[63] Contrary to Bickerman 1938: 90–2. Bickerman does not express his point clearly nor
support it with real evidence. The title ἡγεμὼν τῶν ἔξω τάξεων (= the commander of those
outside the formation) common in Ptolemaic papyri (see Launey 1949–50: 2.1–3) shows that
a military man was in charge of the service personnel, but this does not clarify the status of his
subordinates.

[64] On the ways the soldiers acquired their supplies and on the *agora* in Hellenistic armies
see Griffith 1935: 274ff. Cf. the abundant material from ancient Greece on merchants' activities
and 'markets' in army camps in Pritchett 1974: 1.30–52.

[65] The overall figure for the armies in various battles given in the principal sources accords
perfectly with the figure arrived at by adding up the combat personnel of the units the sources
list as taking part in those battles, leaving no surplus for service personnel in the total. See
especially the sources for the battles of Paraetacene, Gabiene, Ipsus, Sellasia, Raphia, Cynoscephalae and Pydna. On the figures in the battle of Magnesia see Bar-Kochva 1979: 8–9.
The number of service personnel is mentioned very rarely – Diodorus 20.41.1; Justin 38.10 (cf.
Diodorus 34.17). On the figures cited by Justin see Bar-Kochva 1979: 11.

very large percentage of the total manpower.[66] The numbers which the sources give for the Seleucid soldiers are therefore highly exaggerated in most cases.

Jewish manpower and combatants

The numbers ascribed to the Jewish forces are extremely modest in comparison with those cited for the Seleucid armies. The estimate ranges from 6,000 men near the start of the Revolt (II Macc. 8.1.16,21–2) to a maximum of 10,000 in the battle of Beth Zur (I Macc. 4.29), and diminishes in the last battle at Elasa to 3,000, of whom only 800 remained in the actual battle (I Macc. 9.5–6). The extreme overestimation in the Books of the Maccabees of enemy numerical strength, which indicates a clear intention to glorify and aggrandize Judas Maccabaeus' achievements, makes us suspect at the outset the figures given for the Jewish forces, and suggests the possibility of deliberate understatement. However, not all the numerical data for the Jewish army should be rejected out of hand. I Maccabees is absolutely accurate in describing the site and course of most of the battles and there are clear indications that the author personally witnessed some of them or at least utilized first-class written or oral sources.[67] Consequently there is no doubt that he had reliable information on the true size of the Jewish army. An examination of the direct information given for the Jewish forces in the battles must therefore be based, as is usual in the investigation of ancient historiography, on 'unsolicited' information of various kinds in I Maccabees itself, such as slips of the pen, numbers which can serve no propaganda purpose, and data preserved in official documents which are unquestionably genuine. In addition, an examination of the information given on the course of the battles themselves is likely to provide some help.

The numbers reported in the Books of the Maccabees for Judas Maccabaeus' army at the start of the Revolt cannot be checked or verified. No statistics are available besides those appearing in the battle descriptions. The campaigns were conducted with guerrilla methods where numerical strength is not a decisive factor. The most

[66] On the question of the number of armour bearers and service troops in general see also Bar-Kochva 1979: 100–1. It should be added that the Ptolemaic army could not have moved at a speed of 36 km a day through the Sinai desert in June 217 B.C. (ibid. 129) if it had included too many service troops.   [67] See below, pp. 153–5, 159–62ff.

that can be said is that the number was no less than the 6,000-man estimate II Maccabees states for the start of the Revolt. A numerical potential no smaller than that can be inferred from I Maccabees, which reports that after the careful screening and selection at Mizpah on the eve of the battle of Ammaus 3,000 men were left in camp (4.6). Both figures are certainly somewhat rounded off, and the latter is repeated in I Maccabees for the Jewish forces in other battles,[68] but according to the general spirit of these sources it may be assumed that if anything the figures are understated rather than overstated. At the same time there is no doubt that in the clashes themselves forces smaller than 6,000 men were utilized, as at Beth Horon and Ammaus, where the tactical requirements inherent in setting an ambush and conducting a long night march dictated the participation of only picked units (see I Macc. 3.16,23,56–4.6). It is illuminating that in the wake of the first successes, the camp gradually grew until even according to I Maccabees it reached 10,000 men at Beth Zur (4.29), a short time before the purification of the Temple.

The case is different with the numbers cited for the battles during the second phase, after the purification of the Temple. In analysing the battles, attention should be paid to the total lack of proportion between the minimal figures given for the Jewish force, and the large number of Seleucid soldiers reported in the battle of Elasa. The story goes (I Macc. 9.10–17) that there was a long and difficult struggle. The Seleucid army executed sophisticated manoeuvres and Judas Maccabaeus even pursued the enemy's strong right wing for a relatively long distance (and whether or not the retreat was a sham is irrelevant). There is no reason to doubt the details of the description for they accord very well with what we know of the Seleucid army, its units, deployment and operational methods. The course of the battle fits the topography, and it generally make sense.[69] However, 800 men were not capable of thus withstanding 20,000 infantry and 2,000 cavalry on a gently sloping plateau like the battlefield of Elasa,[70] and it is doubtful whether a Jewish force of that size would have dared to face Bacchides' army. The Seleucid army at the time included not only cumbersome phalangites but also thousands of picked troops that had been retrained in Roman combat methods

[68] I Macc. 5.20, 7.40, 9.5, 11.44. The figure of 3,000 given in I Macc. 4.15, 5.22 and 11.74 as the estimate of losses was selected to fit the number of Jewish soldiers in each battle; in other words, each soldier was supposed to have slain an enemy soldier with his own hands. Cf. also p. 271 below.

[69] For a detailed analysis of the battle see pp. 385ff. below and also pp. 70–3, 113–15.

[70] See pp. 385–8 below and Map 4, p. 73.

and were highly mobile, and the number of heavies was matched by a like number of semi-heavies and lights trained to fight in mountain areas.[71] The battle did not take place in a built-up area or in rugged terrain, where small contingents would have an advantage; it was a frontal clash in a limited area, in an open field on which it was relatively easy to move around.[72] Theoretically, then, there are three alternatives: either the report of the battle is basically false and merely the product of the author's imagination, or the numbers ascribed to the Seleucid army are grossly magnified, or else the size of the Jewish force is greatly minimized. On the basis of the probable reliability of the description and the evident size of the expedition led by Bacchides, the last possibility seems to be the correct one.

This conclusion gains support from a number of slips of the pen indicating that shortly after the purification of the Temple the true strength of the Jewish army reached at least 22,000, and the participation of additional thousands of soldiers must be taken into account in later phases. We are grateful to the German Jesuit scholar Josef Knabenbauer and to the late Michael Avi-Yonah, who seem to have been the first to pay attention to some of those *lapsus calami*. Avi-Yonah even estimates that Judas Maccabaeus had 22,000 soldiers at his disposal.[73] Both, however, seem to have been over-cautious, and do not apply their conclusion to the analysis of the main battles, and in any case the matter requires elaboration and support from other sources.

In telling of the Hasmonaean expedition despatched to evacuate the Jews scattered in remote districts of Eretz Israel, I Maccabees reports that Judas Maccabaeus took along 8,000 men to Gilead, while 3,000 followed Simeon to Galilee (5.20). There is no reason to doubt the general reliability of these numbers, as they serve no ulterior motive.[74] The rest of the force was left to defend the Judaean

---

[71] See pp. 120–9 below.

[72] Modern parallels customarily cited to prove that the Jewish army was capable of holding out against a superior force in open, traversable battlefield are not relevant. The distribution of the forces over a large area, the diversity of armament (including the aerial dimension), the technological qualifications required, the speed of movement and the ability to bring in reserves to block breaches in the various fronts, all these make for completely different conditions in modern warfare. In antiquity large groups of soldiers confronted each other face to face in a restricted space, utilized limited categories of short-range arms which did not require great technical skill, moved relatively slowly, and were unable to summon any substantial reinforcements. The final outcome was decided in a few hours at most on that specific battlefield, and was not the result of a complex of protracted clashes over an extensive area.

[73] Knabenbauer 1907: 17; Avi-Yonah 1972: 167, and 1964: 63–4.

[74] On the recurrence of the figure 3,000 in I Maccabees and its significance in the evaluation of the strength of the Jewish forces see p. 48 and n. 68 above.

Hills under Joseph and Azaria (I Macc. 5.18–19), probably because of the danger of attack by hostile neighbours, the Seleucid garrisons from the coastal plain, or even a surprise punitive expedition by the central authorities. Avi-Yonah estimated the total number of combatants at 22,000 on the assumption that Judas Maccabaeus certainly did not leave the defence of the Jewish heartland to a force smaller than the one he took along on his expeditions. Some support for this assumption is to be found in the Temple Scroll, composed probably just one generation after the Revolt, which stipulates that in a normal defensive war in Eretz Israel beyond the frontier, only a tenth, a fifth, or a third of the army should be sent out, or in great emergencies, half; but in any case half the military must under all circumstances stay within the country to avert the possibility of invasion (p. 58).[75] These stipulations, which are not based on any biblical verse, may very well reflect the practice in the Second Temple period. And indeed, during the Roman War in Galilee, each city sent half its men to the army, while half remained to serve the needs of the city (*Bell.* 2.584).

The above estimate of Jewish military potential at the time is confirmed by an investigation from another angle: in the course of the rescue expeditions to Gilead and Galilee, 2,000 men were killed during the battle conducted under the command of the sub-commanders Joseph and Azaria against Gorgias at the gates of Judaea (I Macc. 5.60). The number of casualties makes it possible to estimate the total number of soldiers. The proportion of dead varies from period to period in accordance with the methods of warfare and the effectiveness of the weapons, and it is possible to say with considerable certainty that in the battles of the Classical and Hellenistic periods, the percentage of casualties in the worst cases was 15%–20%, and ordinarily came to no more than 10%.[76] This estimate

[75] For the explanation of the passage see Yadin 1978: 2.183–4. On the dating of the scroll early in the reign of John Hyrcanus see ibid. 1.298.

[76] Cf. the data on Perdiccas' defeat of Ariarathes (Diodorus 18.16.2), on the battles of Paraetacene (Diodorus 19.27.1 and 31.5), Gabiene (Diodorus 19.40.1 and 43.1; Polyaenus 4.6.13; see Scullard 1974: 92, and Kromayer and Veith 1903–32: 4.426,432), Gaza (Diodorus 19.82,85), Asculum (Plut. *Pyrrh.* 21), Mantineia (Plut. *Philop.* 10; Polybius 11.10; cf. Polybius 2.65.7 on the recruitment potential of Sparta) and Raphia (Polybius 5.79.13 and 86.5). The estimates noted for these battles were drawn from the testimony of eye-witnesses like Hieronymus of Cardia, Phylarchus and Ptolemy of Megalopolis. The figures for the armies and casualties in the reliable report of Thucydides on the Peloponnesian Wars and the sources on the battle of Chaeronea indicate a very low percentage of dead. The sources on Alexander's wars can tell us nothing for they tend to exaggerate Persian military strength and do not generally cite the number of dead. On the other hand the Roman army inflicted a larger percentage of dead, up to 30%, on the Hellenistic armies. So it was for instance at Cynoscephalae (Livy 33.4.4–5 and 10.7; Plut. *Flam.* 7–8; Polybius 18.27.6). At the same time it should be noted that the number of dead attributed to the battle of Pydna (Plut. *Aem.* 21; Livy

does not apply, of course, to armies caught deep within enemy territory with no opportunity to retreat, nor to defeated foot soldiers whose way out was blocked by a particularly large number of cavalry, and the like.[77] According to II Maccabees, the battle against Gorgias took place near Marisa (12.35), on the edge of a hilly area inhabited by Jews. From there to Adullam, where the beaten Jewish troops gathered (12.38), there was a short and relatively convenient route for retreat.[78] Under such conditions, there is no reason to think that a large percentage of the force was killed in battle, especially since even according to II Maccabees Gorgias' force included no more than 3,000 infantry and 400 cavalry (12.33). The fact that Gorgias did not exploit his victory to invade the Judaean Hills, nor even to make a short pursuit, may also indicate that the bulk of the Jewish force was not destroyed. While the figure of 2,000 dead in I Maccabees may be rounded off slightly, the reasonable maximum of casualties was still 15%–20% and the average was less. Thus it does not seem to be an exaggeration to say that no less than 10,000 Jews took part in the battle of Marisa. The enemy was victorious, despite a considerable numerical inferiority, because the Jewish troops, being those left behind, had less battle experience and training, and were probably mostly new recruits. This conclusion confirms the estimate of at least 22,000 combatants available after the purification of the Temple. The number grew even larger with the transfer to Judaea of the many refugees from Gilead, Galilee and the coastal plain (I Macc. 5.23,45,53–4; and see 6.53). Many of those, who were grateful for their rescue and had no land or employment, certainly

44.42.7–9) is quite inflated, having been drawn from Poseidonius and Nasica who were prone to numerical exaggeration. On the exaggerated losses Livy attributed to the battle of Magnesia see p. 38 n. 34 above. In any case, the estimate above on the percentage of dead in Judas Maccabaeus' battles is based on data on Greek and Hellenistic armies and not Roman ones. The latter refrained from lingering around the 'baggage' in the course of a pursuit, and severe punishments ensured zeal in taking advantage of the weakness of the retreating foe.

[77] The most outstanding example of a case of this kind is the battle of Thermopylae in which Antiochus III lost almost his entire army of 10,000 foot and 500 horse (Livy 36.19.11; Appian, *Syr.* 20(90)). Note also the battle between Eumenes and Antigonus in Cappadocia (320 B.C.) in which Eumenes lost 8,000 of his 25,000 soldiers when the hills surrounding the level battle site were taken by Antigonus before the battle (Diodorus 18.40).

[78] On the identity of the episodes in I Macc. 5.55–62,66–7 and II Macc. 12.32–45 see Abel 1949: 441, as well as on the preference for the I Maccabees chronological order whereby the battle of Marisa took place at the same time as the expeditions to Galilee and Transjordania. Cf. Wellhausen 1905: 147–8; Dancy 1954: 108–9. The Jews had in mind to advance to the coastal plain against Iamnia (I Macc. 5.58), presumably in order to prevent some aggressive initiative planned by Gorgias. This purpose can be deduced from Gorgias' speedy reaction, and can explain the violation of the order given to the Jewish sub-commanders not to attack the enemy (I Macc. 5.19). Gorgias had indeed already advanced eastwards, and the battle took place near Marisa (I Macc. 5.66; II Macc. 12.35) in the hills of the Southern Shephela, which were not far from the borders of Judaea (I Macc. 5.60; II Macc. 12.38).

joined the Hasmonaean army. It stands to reason that in the great defensive wars at Beth Zacharia and Elasa, when all the earlier achievements were in jeopardy, men who had not taken part in the expeditions outside the Judaean Hills were mobilized. I Maccabees even reports explicitly, in a verse that may be termed a slip of the pen, on the considerable growth of the Jewish force following the purification of the Temple (6.6).[79]

It should be noted that there are insufficient grounds for the argument that I Maccabees deliberately inflated the number of casualties in the battle against Gorgias in order to show that only the Hasmonaeans were capable of saving the nation (which might be thought from I Macc. 5.61–2). The author of II Maccabees, who cannot be accused of such a bias since he mistakenly assigns the high command of the battle to Judas Maccabaeus himself (12.36),[80] makes it clear that it was a serious defeat. While he turns the great defeat at Beth Zacharia into a victory (though most laconically), with no mention of Jewish losses (13.22), in the case of the battle near Marisa he admits the death of Jewish soldiers (12.34) and the difficult situation that developed in the course of the fighting (12.36), and attempts to explain the losses by reporting that appurtenances of idolatry were found among the possessions of the dead (12.40). Furthermore, to claim that the number of casualties recorded in I Maccabees is designed to serve some dynastic-political purpose, it would be necessary to present clear evidence from another episode that the author is prepared to distort and falsify facts in order to

[79] The incautious and excited character of the verse is reflected by the word ἐν πρώτοις (= at first), referring to Lysias' first campaign which ended at Beth Zur. The 'herald' who supposedly reported Lysias' failure to Antiochus Epiphanes indicates knowledge of Lysias' second campaign to Judaea which took place a year and a half later. There are no grounds for interpreting ἐν πρώτοις as 'immediately', or the like, for Lysias did not leave the country in haste. There is no hint at any panic-stricken flight, and such a meaning is not acceptable linguistically either. The author of I Maccabees wished to stress the effect the events in Judaea had on the illness and death of Antiochus Epiphanes and, carried away by his enthusiasm, revealed some of the changes that had taken place in the numbers and armament of the Jewish troops after the purification of the Temple (see also p. 68 below).

[80] The possibility that the author of I Maccabees attributed a defeat of Judas Maccabaeus to the deputy commanders Joseph and Azaria must be rejected. He does not ever hide failures of the Hasmonaean brothers. The error in II Maccabees derives from the confused chronological order in that book, according to which the battle of Marisa took place as the expeditions to Transjordania ended (see p. 51 n. 78 above). On the other hand, it is hard to imagine jumbling in I Maccabees, given the definite stress on the fact that Judas Maccabaeus and Simeon were in Gilead and Galilee at the time (5.55), and because the responsibility for conducting the battle rested exclusively with the deputy commanders. Because of the author's excellent sources of information, it is inconceivable that he should have been mistaken or misled in such a vital matter connected with a serious defeat of the Jewish force. The crucial role of Azari(a) in that battle is mentioned in the II Maccabees version as well (12.36).

serve that same purpose; but such evidence is non-existent.[81] Moreover, in connection with one of the battles led by Jonathan, I Maccabees even tells of two sub-commanders saving the day when all Jonathan's men had fled, and keeps discreetly silent about what Jonathan himself did in the course of the flight (11.70). All in all, the mistake Joseph and Azaria made was not that they undertook to lead the people in battle (which seems to have been a preventive measure), but that by going forth to fight outside the Jewish centre in the Judaean Hills they in fact neglected the defence of that centre and imperilled it (see the explicit instruction in 5.19). The statement at the end of the battle description that Joseph and Azaria 'were not of the seed of those people to whom the salvation of Israel was entrusted' (I Macc. 5.62) is intended only to excuse the seriousness of the defeat. There is thus no justification for the opposite assumption that the number of dead was 'invented' in order to support the exclusive right of the Hasmonaeans to command and lead the nation.

Other data on the manpower potential of the early Hasmonaeans relate to the reign of Jonathan. In an authentic document of 152 B.C. (I Macc. 10.36) Demetrius I promises Jonathan[82] to absorb 30,000 Jewish soldiers into the royal army,[83] placing the recruits under the

---

[81] Geiger's well-known stand on this episode (1875: 207ff.) is derived from his general method which holds that I Maccabees diminishes the image of the Hasmonaean brothers in order to enhance that of Simeon and even glosses over some of the latter's failures and improper acts, such as the 'help' he extended supposedly to remove Jonathan and his sons (ibid. 206–19), in contrast to II Maccabees which embodies an 'anti-dynastic' approach. The evidence on which these assertions are based does not stand up to critical examination (see in detail in the discussion on the Kafar Dessau affair, p. 350; see also p. 197 on the Modein affair, and p. 302 on I Maccabees' omission of Onias' activities). On the absence of any 'anti-dynastic' tendency in Jason of Cyrene's book see also Niese 1900: 37–8; cf. Pfeifer 1949: 493.

[82] While the letter is not addressed to Jonathan but to the 'nation of the Jews' (10.25), this does not mean that the offer was not directed at him. See the arguments in M. Stern 1965: 97–8. It should be noted that the response to the document is given by 'Jonathan and the nation' (ibid. 46).

[83] On the credibility of the document see M. Stern 1965: 97–106. The fact that I Maccabees refrains from inserting Jonathan's name in the documents provides an added dimension of credibility. The reference to 30,000 Jewish troops who are said to have served in fortifications in Egypt in the Letter of Aristeas (para. 13) does not impugn the authenticity of the document in I Maccabees or the number given there, for I Maccabees was composed earlier than the Letter of Aristeas. The identity of the numbers is most likely accidental, and any connection between them means only that the author of the Letter of Aristeas took his figures from I Maccabees. So also M. Stern 1965: 104–5; Momigliano 1930: 163 and 1932: 161ff.; Murray 1967: 338–40; Schürer... 1973–9: 1.179. In any case, the fact that the numbers are identical does not outweigh the other considerations pointing to the reliability of the document as a whole. For the dating of I Maccabees to around 129 B.C. see pp. 162–3 below. With regard to the dating of the Letter of Aristeas, it behoves us to accept the view of a goodly proportion of scholars who place the 'Letter' in the last quarter of the second century B.C. see, e.g., Motzo 1915: 210–25; Février 1924: 1–22; Meecham 1935: 311ff.; Hadas 1951: 5ff.; Tarn 1951: 425ff.; Tcherikover 1958: 59–85; Jellicoe 1968: 48,378–9; O. Murray 1967: 337–71; Meisner

command of Jewish officers and allowing them to lead their lives in accordance with Jewish law (ibid. 37). Besides desiring additional manpower for the internal struggle for the throne, Demetrius was interested in getting Jonathan and the Jews on his side against Alexander Balas (esp. 10.22–3). Listed among numerous economic concessions, the offer which was meant to please the Jews must have been based on familiarity with the needs and requirements of the Jews (as is also indicated by the special service conditions mentioned above). All these concessions were obviously aimed at solving the deteriorating economic situation in Judaea which developed as a consequence of the frequent wars and the shortage of agricultural land resulting from a natural population explosion in the limited fertile area of the Judaean Hills.[84] The difficulties were aggravated by the reception of refugees from all parts of the Land of Israel. It can therefore be concluded from that document that many thousands of Jewish men who had reached military age had difficulty finding their living within the borders of Judaea. What is more important, the episode suggests that the Jewish manpower potential exceeded 30,000 men; it is not reasonable to suppose that Demetrius, who had caused the death of Judas Maccabaeus and once pursued Jonathan relentlessly, would jeopardize his reliability with a proposal that meant emptying Judaea of the entire available defence force. The emphasis on the restriction 'up to thirty thousand' (εἰς τριάκοντα χιλιάδας),[85] also implies that Jonathan had at his disposal an even

1972: 179–217; id. 1973: 37–44; and Bickerman's revised article in his 1976–80: 1.109–35. Attempts are made intermittently to date the book to the end of the first half of the second century B.C. or even the end of the third; see Schürer 1901: 3.611–12; Tramontano 1931: 48–91; Van't Dack 1968: 265–78; Rappaport 1968a: 37–50; Fraser 1972: 2.970–3. However, all the evidence presented can be refuted (see, e.g., Bickerman 1976–80: 1.127–8, and esp. n. 78 with regard to the title τῶν ἀρχισωματοφυλάκων (= of the chief bodyguards); cf. Mooren 1975: 22–3), while the opposing view has more solid support. A decisive argument which has not yet been raised appears from the description of the garrison in the Jerusalem citadel (ἄκραν τῆς πόλεως, paras. 100–4). The 'Letter' clearly points to the fact that the citadel was manned by Jews loyal to their country and religion and not by a foreign garrison; it was under the overall command of the high priest (προκαθηγουμένου, 103; cf. para. 122); and it was intended by its builder to safeguard and protect the Temple (paras. 102–4). Despite his celebrated tendency to idealize Jerusalem and the Temple, an Alexandrian writer of the Ptolemaic period would not have described the stronghold of Ptolemaic rule in Judaea in that way (cf. *Ant.* 12.133,138) unless he was writing in a period when that was the situation. The explicit assertion that the fort was 'in the highest place' from which the sacrifices could be seen (para. 103) may indicate it was north of the Temple. It is to be identified with the Hasmonaean stronghold constructed north of the Temple by John Hyrcanus (*Ant.* 15.403, 18.91). The Ptolemaic Akra was situated a few hundred metres south of the Temple and was considerably lower; see pp. 460–5 below.

[84] See in detail Bar-Kochva 1977a: 169ff. To the sources mentioned should be added the statement of Hecataeus of Abdera (quoted by Diodorus 40.3.8), written at the beginning of the Hellenistic period, on the increase in the Jewish population of the country.

[85] The word εἰς here can only be reconstructed as Hebrew עד (= up to), and it must be kept in mind that what we have here is a Greek document that was translated into Hebrew and then retranslated back into Greek.

greater number of soldiers who needed immediate employment. Indeed, a few years later Jonathan set out to confront Tryphon at Beth Shean with 40,000 men (I Macc. 12.41). That figure is cited incidentally in the course of the narrative, for a clash did not in fact take place: most of the Jewish army was sent back to Judaea and Jonathan was captured through a trick. Thus the report of the true number did not interfere with the author's bias, and is provided also in order to explain why Tryphon averted a confrontation and resorted to trickery.

It should be recalled, too, that 20,000 men were ascribed to the army of Simeon in the battle against Kendebaeus (138 B.C.), the governor of the coastal plain, whose forces were certainly quite limited (15.38, 16.4). I Maccabees does not give a modest number there, because the image of events and heroes changes from the start of the description of Simeon's reign, on the eve of the declaration of independence and the establishment of the Hasmonaean state in 142 B.C. (13.31ff.). The author no longer plays down Jewish might. He points out the royal (or to be more precise, the presidential) pomp of Simeon, the extension of borders, the diplomatic ties, the achievement of access to the sea, the prosperity and peacefulness. The text of the treaty between Simeon and the nation even stresses Simeon's public appointment as Chief of the Army with responsibility for manpower, arms and fortifications (14.42). That made it necessary to show that Simeon was worthy of his post and did a proper job.[86] The change of attitude is obvious also in the explicit reference to the participation of cavalry in the Jewish army (16.7),[87] although they took part in the Hasmonaean formation long before,[88] and to the utilization of the *helepolis*, an advanced Hellenistic siege device, during the siege of Gezer (13.44).[89] In any case, as I Maccabees was written and completed about 129 B.C.,[90] just a few years after the battle against Kendebaeus in the Aijalon Valley, the author could not allow himself too much contraction of the numerical strength of the Jewish force that took part in that battle,

---

[86] McNicoll (1978: 61–5) is of the opinion that the large number attributed to Simeon's army is not realistic and is intended to make it easy for the reader to understand how it was that Simeon succeeded where Judas Maccabaeus failed. However, the author of I Maccabees, who is frankly admiring the last of the Hasmonaean brothers, would have been belittling his achievements and success on the battlefield if he had inflated the number of soldiers at his disposal. It is likewise hard to believe that an author who wrote so shortly after Simeon's death would have magnified the size of the army, especially since it is doubtful whether by doing so he would have made any significant contribution to the elucidation of Judas Maccabaeus' failures.

[87] P. 71 below. [88] Pp. 69–71 below.
[89] P. 81 below.
[90] Pp. 162–3 below.

contrary to his practice in descriptions of the Judas Maccabaeus battles which were 30 or 40 years earlier.[91]

Although the number of people who followed Jonathan and certainly the number of soldiers Simeon had do not necessarily indicate the size of Judas Maccabaeus' army, it should be noted that (except for the two accidental pieces of information) the author of I Maccabees kept to his aim of minimizing the number of Jewish fighters, in regard to Jonathan's reign as well (see, e.g., 10.74, and the omission of figures on Jewish numerical strength in his other battles). The conclusion on the true size of Jonathan's army reinforces the evaluation that I Maccabees lacks credibility in connection with figures on Jewish military manpower. Since the demographic situation in Jonathan's time did not differ from that in Judas Maccabaeus', the above information too can confirm that after the purification of the Temple the inhabitants of the Judaean Hills were able to despatch to the battlefield tens of thousands of men of military age.

Does such a large recruitment potential seem probable in view of the population of the Judaean Hills during the Revolt period? Unfortunately the demography of Eretz Israel and its various districts in antiquity is a most controversial subject, and estimates on this question differ widely.[92] Consequently it is much safer to adopt the opposite approach and examine what a recruitment potential of 22,000–40,000 men implies regarding the size of the population as a whole, and whether the accepted figure is at all possible or is supported by other information and historical developments. In the absence of reliable data on the recruitment capacity of the Jewish population in either the First or the Second Temple period, we must turn to the Classical world. A recruitment of 15% of the free population is known from Classical Athens, and of 10% from Republican Rome.[93] The lower percentage at least can be considered for the time of the confrontation between Jonathan and Tryphon, when

[91] Some scholars who believe that the last chapters in I Maccabees are a later addition point out among various differences between the two parts of the book the attitude to the Jewish army and armament. However, the various theories in regard to the lack of unity in the book have been decisively refuted (pp. 165–6 below), and are consequently irrelevant to our subject.

[92] Estimates of the population and absorptive capacity of Eretz Israel in antiquity range from one million to five million. A survey of the problem, the various views, and interesting evidence for the minimalistic approach appear in Broshi 1979: 1–10 (see also Broshi and Gophna 1984: 147–57). Broshi estimates the number of people that could have lived in western Eretz Israel at a million, on the basis of the quantity of grain the country could provide for its inhabitants. However, in extreme situations that figure could be augmented by 200,000, even on the basis of Broshi's method.

[93] This emerges from the abundant data cited by Beloch 1886: 60ff., 99ff.; 1912–27: 2.386–418; Gomme 1933: 5–6,47; Brunt 1971: esp. 54 and 419. The recruitment potential of modern states fluctuates between 10% and 15%.

there was already a more than twenty-year-old tradition of recruitment under the Hasmonaeans, including compulsory enlistment. The number of Hellenizers need not be taken into account in any statistical estimate: it was insignificant, reaching just a few thousand (see II Macc. 4.40 and 5.5),[94] some of whom had already joined the ranks of the Jewish army by the time of Judas Maccabaeus,[95] and in any case the percentage of recruits from among the refugees was certainly very high and made up for the supporters of the Seleucids who failed to join the ranks. The overall population thus calculated would therefore be roughly 400,000.[96] Given the size of the region, its agricultural possibilities, and the absence at this stage in the history of Judaea of other means of livelihood, this evaluation indicates a considerable density of population.[97] And indeed, in addition to the above-mentioned letter from Demetrius I to Jonathan, a number of sources and considerations prove that the Judaean Hills during the Revolt period suffered from serious overcrowding and a shortage of land which later constituted the main factor motivating the conquests and territorial expansion of the Hasmonaeans.[98]

The logistic and economic problems involved in the organization

[94] There is no reason not to accept the estimate in II Maccabees, despite its being 'rounded'. Given the ideological and artistic framework of the book, there would be no reason either to exaggerate or minimize the number of Hellenizers. Jason's supporters mentioned in II Macc. 5.5 certainly did not collaborate with the authorities after their leader was deposed (see also 4.16). Presumably the thousand people attributed to Jason also included volunteers from the military settlements of the Toubians in Transjordania. Jason had earlier found refuge in Ammanitis (II Macc. 4.26) and apparently fled there to those settlers after the unsuccessful rebellion in 168 (II Macc. 5.7). The members of the settlements, at the time under the leadership of their compatriot Hyrcanus, aided Jason in accordance with the generally anti-Seleucid policy of their leader. Schürer (1901: 1.189ff.) and Bickerman (1937: 81,136) believe that the Hellenizers constituted the majority of the nation, but their evidence is not convincing: the statement in I Macc. 2.18 is made in a clearly rhetorical context; the word 'many' in I Macc. 1.11,43,52 does not provide a numerical indication. From the viewpoint of the conservative public of the Revolt period, a few thousand defiling the Sabbath and worshipping idols were 'many' compared to their numbers in the past. And in any case I Maccabees has the same word applied to the people faithful to the Torah (1.62, 2.29, etc.). Furthermore, in I Macc. 1.43 the reconstruction should be הסכימו (= they agreed [against their will]) and not רצו (= they wished; see Raban 1962: 383); I Macc. 1.13 and 10.14 are certainly not proof, for the Hellenizers are characterized there as τινες (= a few). As to Daniel 9.27 ('and he will strengthen a covenant for the many'), it has been pointed out more than once that the Hebrew text is quite odd. On the well-known hypothesis that the second part of the Book of Daniel was translated from Aramaic, it has been proposed that the source had קימא ויחל (= 'and he will violate a covenant') and the translator mistakenly read ויחיל (= 'and will he strengthen, enhance'), which accounts for the faulty translation; see Zimmerman 1938: 264. On the small number of Hellenizers see also Tcherikover 1961a: 477–8 n. 38, who believes among other things that the author of I Maccabees occasionally described them as 'many' simply to enhance the heroism of the Hasmonaeans.

[95] See pp. 82–4, 88 n. 54 below.

[96] This is also more or less the estimate of Avi-Yonah 1972: 163.

[97] This emerges also from Broshi's overall estimates of the population of the country, mentioned in n. 92.

[98] See in detail Bar-Kochva 1977a: 169ff.

and maintenance of so many soldiers before the battles were certainly not trifling. If most of them were reserve troops, one wonders how they were called up and summoned to the front. But these difficulties do not affect the hypothesis that quite a large army was at the disposal of Judas Maccabaeus. We sometimes magnify the logistic difficulties involved in the operation of the large armies of antiquity, having in mind modern models and not the conditions of people accustomed to be content with very little who are fighting on their own land. Fuel and equipment did not need to be transported, and each soldier brought along his personal weapon. As to supplies, various parallels with armies of the Classical and Hellenistic periods show that the amount of food allotted to soldiers even in peacetime, let alone emergency conditions, would today be termed 'starvation rations'.[99] According to Hellenistic law, farmers in the country dist-ricts (the *khōra*) were obliged to feed large armies;[100] when the Hasmonaean army set out, however, it most certainly had the willing help of the local farmers, for it was defending their national and religious, and sometimes even physical, existence and had many of them in its ranks as well.

The estimate of Judas Maccabaeus' recruitment capacity applies to the special circumstances of the big battles after the purification of the Temple, and there is no reason to suppose that that capacity was not used. The confrontation with Lysias at Beth Zacharia took place more than a year after the purification and the victories in the struggle with the surrounding peoples and Hellenistic cities. As the Seleucid expedition to Beth Zacharia was preceded by a protracted siege of Beth Zur, Judaea's southern gateway (I Macc. 6.31), Judas Maccabaeus was able to call up all his forces. According to II Maccabees, it even appears that Judas Maccabaeus' men stayed in the vicinity of Beth Zur for a long time in order to help the besieged and keep an eye on enemy movements (13.19–20), and I Maccabees indicates that, even before the expedition, Jewish troops took part in the siege of the Jerusalem citadel (6.32).

The clash with Nicanor at Kafar Salama occurred just a few months after the end of Bacchides' first expedition in 162–161 B.C. in which he put Nicanor and Alcimus in charge of Jerusalem. There are signs of differences of opinion in the Jewish camp during the first Bacchides expedition: the Scribes–Hassidim who called on Bacchides

---

[99] Cf., e.g., the 'starvation diet' in the Ptolemaic settlement of Kerkeosiris: Crawford 1971: 123, 132, and other examples there from Greek and Hellenistic history.

[100] Cf. Diodorus 18.32.3, 19.26.2, 20.73.3; Polybius 5.70.5. On the immunity of cities see, e.g., A. H. M. Jones 1940: 109–10; Préaux 1978: 1.309–10.

and Alcimus (I Macc. 7.12–15), undoubtedly did so despite Judas Maccabaeus' stand.[101] However, their attempts to parley with the authorities early in the reign of Demetrius ended in the murder of sixty Hassidim by Alcimus and the mass slaughter at Beth Zaith (ibid. 16,19) after which there was no room for illusions (ibid. 18).[102] The fact that Judas Maccabaeus refrained from confronting

[101] Many scholars have exaggerated the significance of the difference of opinion and gravity of the rift, describing the Scribes, the spiritual leaders, as aspiring only to religious freedom, and as ready to leave the rebel camp once that freedom was achieved. This interpretation is a milestone in the celebrated scholarly conception about the theocratical character of the aspirations of the Pharisee Sages and their alleged opposition to political independence and secular institutions expecting the appearance of the Saviour from the House of David. For a survey of the various nuances of this view in modern research, and an explanation of the disagreement between the Scribes and Judas Maccabaeus as being simply a matter of political tactics, see Efron 1980: 27–31. In addition to Efron's analysis of the verses in I Macc. 7.12–13, it should be stressed that the question of religious freedom could not have been the subject of the negotiations: the murder of the Hassidim and the 'Compliers' (I. Macc. 7.16,19; on the translation see the next footnote) initiated by Alcimus, the moderate high priest who certainly wanted the restoration of Jewish cult and practices, indicates that the Scribes submitted demands far beyond religious freedom. In any case, overall permission to practise Jewish precepts had already been granted by Lysias in the summer of 162 (II Macc. 11.24–5; I Macc. 6.59; see pp. 523ff. below). Moreover, the author of I Maccabees, who can be described as an extreme nationalist who advocated total independence and territorial expansion (see esp. 15.33), sincerely laments the death of the Hassidim, does not castigate them as traitors and deserters or condemn them in any way, and does not utter a word dissociating himself from their act. The attribution of a small number of soldiers to Judas Maccabaeus at the battle of Elasa (I Macc. 9.5–6), which has served as one of the chief pieces of evidence for the dimension of the dispute, is itself unacceptable (see below). In addition, there was no desertion from Judas Maccabaeus' camp following Lysias' offer in the spring of 164 of a conditional amnesty which included permission to observe the Torah precepts (II Macc. 11.27–33; see p. 539 below), and the number of Jewish warriors actually increased considerably subsequently.

The argument in the rebel camp was not therefore about the purpose and aims of the military struggle. Neither was it about the principle of conducting negotiations with the enemy. Judas Maccabaeus himself had contacts with the Seleucid authorities – with Lysias in 165 after the battle of Ammaus (II Macc. 11.17–21; see pp. 520–2 below) and after the battle of Beth Zacharia in early summer of 162 (I Macc. 6.60; II Macc. 11.23–6), and with Nicanor not long after the murder of the Hassidim (I Macc. 7.27–30; II Macc. 14.18–22). The dispute was of the sort that frequently occurs in liberation movements, about the timing of the contacts and their coordination with the military struggle. The question was one of tactics rather than of long-term strategy. In the wake of the lesson learned from the defeat at Beth Zacharia against a particularly large Seleucid force, Judas Maccabaeus avoided a clash with Bacchides' large force. He left the rural area to the mercies of Bacchides and dug in in his strongholds near Gophna. In that situation negotiations were the only way to save the rural area from the ire of the authorities. At first glance it also appeared that there was room for some parleying for Demetrius I, the new king, having usurped the legitimate successor, would not feel any obligation to carry on with his predecessor's policies, and indeed Bacchides sent envoys to Judas Maccabaeus 'with words of peace' (I Macc. 7.10). However, Judas Maccabaeus was reluctant to embark upon talks from a position of weakness while the superior force of Bacchides was in Judaea (ibid. 11: 'for they saw that they came with a great army'); the situation was different after Ammaus, and especially during Nicanor's incumbency, when the Jewish forces had a substantial numerical advantage. For further criticism of the 'theocratical' conception see below, pp. 475–6. And cf. p. 348 on Bacchides' first expedition.

[102] I Maccabees (7.24) does report the vengeance taken by Judas Maccabaeus after the massacre of the αὐτομολήσασι (במשלימים = compliers; for the translation cf. 9.24; Josh. 10.1,4 and II Sam. 10.19; there are no grounds for Cahana's rendering בנמלטים (= the

Bacchides even at this stage is no indication: according to I Maccabees, Bacchides came to the country with a large army (7.10) and
there is no reason not to accept that as true. It was just a short time
since the accession of Demetrius I, and it is reasonable to assume that
there were still contacts or negotiations with Timarchus and his
supporters in Babylonia, so that it was possible to send most of the
army to Judaea. Bacchides' lofty status in the Kingdom (I Macc.
7.8) points to the size of his army, which may very well have been
as large as the one Lysias took along on his second expedition. After
the experience of his severe defeat at Beth Zacharia a few months
earlier, Judas Maccabaeus refrained from embroiling himself again,
preferring to wait till the big army left the country. In fact shortly
thereafter Bacchides did return to Antioch, doubtless because of the
urgent need to direct most of the army to the suppression of the
Timarchus rebellion. It might appear that the anticipated negotiations between Judas Maccabaeus and Nicanor (I Macc. 7.27–30)
could also have led to a certain relaxation and lack of alertness in the
ranks of the rebels on the eve of the Kafar Salama clash (I Macc.
7.26–32),[103] but *ex post facto* there does not seem to be anything that
could have forced Judas Maccabaeus to join battle on the plain near
Gibeon[104] unless he had quite a substantial force at his disposal.
Even if it was smaller than the numerical potential estimated above,
it was certainly larger than Nicanor's modest force.

These considerations apply yet more closely to the battle of Adasa
(I Macc. 7.39–50), which likewise took place in the Gibeon
Valley.[105] After the earlier clash at Kafar Salama there was no doubt
of the hostile intentions of Nicanor, who went as far as to threaten
to destroy the Temple (I Macc. 7.35; II Macc. 14.33). Even scholars
who are of the opinion that some of Judas Maccabaeus' men were
content with religious freedom and did not aspire to national independence[106] must admit that they could not remain indifferent
to the danger that threatened the Temple. Despite his numerical advantage, Judas Maccabaeus steered clear of attacking the enemy in
Jerusalem for fear that Nicanor might react by menacing the Tem-

fleers) – the word never occurs in the Septuagint in the conventional literal meaning of
'deserters' or the like). But they are obviously not to be identified with the αὐτομολησάντων
of verse 19, for the latter were pursued and slaughtered by Bacchides, and they presumably
would not continue to favour a policy of complying after he left the country. They are to be
identified with the οἱ ταράσσοντες τὸν λαὸν αὐτῶν (עמם [?] מרניזי = harassers of their
people) in verse 22 (cf. 3.5). Perhaps the reading in verse 24 should be ἀνομήσασι (הפושעים
= the criminals) as in one of the minuscule manuscripts (no. 55) and the Syrian translation.
[103] On the imaginary nature of the description of the contacts and reconciliation between
the sides in II Macc. 14.19–30 see pp. 354–6 below.   [104] Pp. 356–8 below.
    [105] Pp. 363–5 below.   [106] N. 101 above.

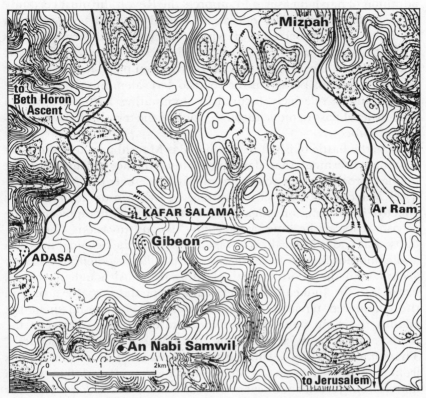

3 The mountain plateau and the Gibeon Valley

ple. Nicanor had left Jerusalem before the battle to welcome the reinforcement from Syria (I Macc. 7.39; *Ant.* 12.408). The two Seleucid forces met at Beth Horon and together climbed to the top of the mountain plateau. Judas Maccabaeus, who was encamped at Adasa, did not attack the enemy during the difficult ascent which would have facilitated the operations of a small army, but arranged the battle on the convenient level plateau close to the exit from the ascent.[107] It might be argued that Judas Maccabaeus' men, for some reason or other, arrived too late to take positions along the slope, but since the arrival of the Seleucid reinforcements did not change the situation in Jerusalem, it is hard to understand what sense there was in the deployment of the Jewish force on a broad plain unless it was numerically superior to Nicanor's army: if Judas Maccabaeus feared a change in the military situation in the Judaean Hills and the

[107] See pp. 365–6 below re verse 43.

adoption of harsh measures to suppress the Revolt, he must certainly
have known that enemy operations would have to be carried on
in areas under rebel control whose topographical structure was
advantageous to small bands of defenders. And if he feared drastic
action against the Temple, it would have been possible to attack the
enemy at various points on the road to Jerusalem in sections where
the ground is relatively fissured or dominating hills leave only a
narrow level pass to move through (such as the terrain slightly south-
east of Gibeon).

As to the battle of Elasa in which Judas Maccabaeus fell, the great
nationalist ferment that developed after Nicanor's death and the
holiday proclaimed in commemoration of the event (I Macc. 7.48–
9; II Macc. 15.36; Scroll of Fasting, 13 Adar) must have had the
effect of increasing, or at least not decreasing, the manpower of the
Jewish army at the time of Bacchides' second invasion. The possibility that Judas Maccabaeus was surprised by the Seleucid invasion
and could not therefore call on his entire military potential does not
accord with the information in I Maccabees. Although Bacchides
broke into the Judaean Hills very rapidly, he did tarry for a time in
the conquered territory north of Jerusalem, taking harsh action
against the rural population in order to ensure his control of the
roads, and probably also to draw Judas Maccabaeus into battle.[108]
That time should have sufficed for the mobilization of the soldiers
from a territory the size of Judaea, which was no larger than a day's
march from Jerusalem in every direction (see I Macc. 7.45; Ma'aser
Sheni 5.2). Even if we assume that Bacchides cleared the roads too
quickly for Judas Maccabaeus to organize his forces, the logic of
forming at Elasa with few soldiers is incomprehensible. If the purpose
was to prevent the conquest of Jerusalem (a step which was not
Bacchides' first priority but which the Jews necessarily feared), the
best way would have been to hole up in the besieged city and harass
the Seleucid troops from outside by means of Jewish forces who were
to arrive somewhat later. That would have been much more effective
than placing a small force on a rather level plateau facing a heavily
armed foe, a step which was doomed to failure at the outset. And if
the purpose was to rescue the Jews of the area north of Jerusalem
from the enemy, then too a delay of a few days was preferable to
suicide on the battlefield at Elasa.

It can therefore be concluded that the Jewish army grew considerably in the period between the battle of Beth Zur, before the
purification of the Temple, and the rescue expeditions to the remote

[108] See pp. 384–5 below, re I Macc. 9.2.

districts of the Land of Israel, and even received further reinforcement in later periods. In the four years after the start of the uprising
and the first victories, many volunteers gradually swelled the rebel
ranks, as often happens in national liberation movements which
begin with a small nucleus and in a few short years following successful operations turn into mass movements. The purification of the
Temple was a conspicuous turning-point, and the enthusiasm it
engendered contributed more than anything else to the numerical
growth of the Hasmonaean army.

Motives for distorting numbers

It is clear from the discussion at the beginning of this chapter on the
methods of ancient historiography that the magnification of the size
of the Seleucid armies and the minimization in regard to the Jewish
troops habitual in the Books of the Maccabees is inspired primarily
by the desire to glorify the victories of Judas Maccabaeus and his
soldiers. The numbers were affected also by the historiographical
nature of the books and the religious–didactic purposes of the authors. As has been stressed by many scholars, both authors desire to
show that the course of history is guided by the God of Israel.
Whereas II Maccabees points out direct divine intervention in
events, demonstrating a *deus ex machina* operating to extricate the
faithful from their plight, the author of I Maccabees constantly
implies the hidden hand of God concealed behind the scenes and
directing the progress of events.[109] He even says so explicitly in the
orations attributed to the Hasmonaean commanders (3.18,22,53,60,
4.8–10,24,30–2, 7.41–2, 9.46, etc.). As was usual in Greek and
Hellenistic literature, those orations are not authentic, and the most
they can indicate is the notions and aims of their author.[110] Had the
two authors reported the true strength of the Jewish and Seleucid
armies and thus revealed that the Jews had the numerical advantage
in some of the battles, they would have denied the didactic purpose
which was their main concern, for no divine help would be necessary
under such circumstances. As we shall see in considering the tactical

---

[109] On this see Niese 1900: 4–5; Abel 1949: xxii, xxxiv–xxxv; Dancy 1954: 1–2; Efron
1980: 24–5; Pfeifer 1949: 494–5,511–13; Arenhoevel 1967: 34–40,132–48. For the 'epiphanies' in II Maccabees see 3.25–8, 10.28–31, 11.8–10, 12.15–16,22, 15.12–16,27; cf. 8.24,36.
Although many scholars have pointed out the didactic tendentiousness of the authors, for some
reason they have not applied their conclusions in evaluating the nature and purpose of the
figures given for the soldiers in the Seleucid and Jewish armies. An exception is Arenhoevel
1967: 36–7.   [110] See details pp. 156–8 below.

composition and arms of the Jewish army, the same didactic purpose also led the authors to ignore the existence of cavalry and heavy or semi-heavy infantry in the Jewish army.

The size of the Jewish army in the battle of Elasa is thus minimized, even more than in other battles, to provide an excuse for the Jewish defeat and to enhance the hero's prestige in his last struggle. The small number of combatants is reported also in order to explain why in this case there was no divine help forthcoming: according to the religious conception of the author of I Maccabees, patent miracles do not occur, and God helps only those who are able and willing to counter-attack. His help is not forthcoming if the enemy has an unusual advantage, or when the Jewish side does not defend itself, or take steps to reduce its initial disadvantages (see, e.g., 2.29–37, 6.47, 7.12–19).[111] Such an approach differs considerably from that of II Maccabees where miracles occur even when the Jews are completely passive or are not particularly active in their own defence (e.g. 3.14–40; and see the battle descriptions in 11.8–10; cf. 10.29–31, 15.11–16, 26–7). Thus the oration ascribed to Judas Maccabaeus at Elasa contains no hint of any possible heavenly assistance (I Macc. 9.8–10). On the other hand, in this case the author of I Maccabees avoids his usual hyperbole in regard to numbers, since placing 60,000 Seleucid foot and 5,000 horse (the number reported for the Beth Zur confrontation), for instance, opposite 800 Jews would have led even the most gullible reader to distrust and reject the story. It is interesting that in regard to the battle of Beth Zacharia which likewise ended in defeat the number of Jewish combatants is not stated, there is no battle oration and the rout is accounted for by more than doubling the true strength of the Seleucid force in that campaign (to 100,000 infantry and 20,000 cavalry). The defeat at Elasa, which ended with the death of the commander and the resumption of Seleucid rule over Judaea and Jerusalem, was more critical, and the author therefore explains it by a drastic minimization of the Jewish numerical strength.

In addition to the national–panegyric and religious–didactic purposes of the authors, we must consider the literary background, the needs and requirements of the potential readers, and the information available to the authors. The author of II Maccabees belongs to the 'pathetic' school, and has a decided tendency to write in the 'tragic' vein.[112] The 'tragic' school of historiography believed that the

---

[111] For this see especially Oesterly 1913: 61, who cites the saying 'God helps those who help themselves'; see also Arenhoevel 1967: 89. For the ways by which God's help is granted to believers see in detail below pp. 214–15 re verses 19,22.   [112] See in detail pp. 172–8 below.

writing of history was in fact the writing of prose tragedy, with artistic means and purposes similar to those of the poetic variety. The purpose of tragedy, according to Aristotle's celebrated (and controversial) definition, is to produce catharsis in the spectator, cleansing and purifying him of negative emotions such as fear and compassion (*Poet.* 1449b27–8, and passim). The arousal of such feelings as intensively as possible in the play leads to relief and relaxation, and thus purifies and refines the spectator, freeing him from the negative effect of those emotions in daily life. In accordance with his literary objective, the author of II Maccabees established the relative strength of the opposing sides so as to arouse some of the emotions noted above. The contrast between the mighty Seleucid force, armed from head to toe, and the small ill-equipped Jewish army certainly filled the reader's heart with fear and dread. Being faithful to the dramatic devices of tragedy (and not merely for religious–didactic reasons), the author put in the *deus ex machina*, the deity who is revealed in the course of events in order to resolve the entanglements. Prodigies recur in II Maccabees also on other occasions (2.21; 5.2–3; 9.5ff.; 15.12–16), and are in fact characteristic of the pathetic school.[113] Another reason for the exaggeration of the numbers is inherent in the monographic and biographical character of the work, as these literary forms by their very nature led writers of the period to stress the importance of their subject by padding numbers and the like.[114] It turns out that they too habitually inflated numbers,[115] and the epitomist's prologue to II Maccabees indicates that Jason of Cyrene's original book abounded in numbers (2.24), probably to emphasize more strongly the superiority of the enemy and the inferiority of the Jewish force. Furthermore, the pathetic as well as the tragic school, as is indicated in the argument Polybius conducted with its followers, was by nature biased, having the stated purpose of praising the favoured side and denigrating the enemy.[116]

[113] On prodigies in pathetic literature see Diodorus 19.2.9,103.5,108.2, 20.29.3,30.2,70.1 (all based on Duris of Samos); Plut. *Them.* 10,32 (based on Phylarchus); Polybius 3.48.8. For other examples see Niese 1900: 34–7; see also Polybius 12.24.5–6 on Timaeus. For the religious bent of the prodigies see Polybius 16.12.3–11. See also E. Swartz in *RE* s.v. 'Duris' (3), col. 1855.

[114] On the distortion of the proportion in monographs see Polybius 3.32, 7.7.6, 10.21.8, 29.12.3–4; Lucian, *Hist. conscr.* 23. On the biographical form as a factor in the panegyric presentation of the hero see Leo 1901: 90ff.,207ff.,238ff.,316ff.; Petzold 1969: 12–14. The narrative framework of the epitome, if not of Jason's original work, is partially structured as a biography.   [115] See Reitzenstein 1906: 84ff.; cf., e.g., Lucian, *Hist. conscr.* 20.

[116] In many places Polybius points to inflated figures and distorted proportions being the rule among historians of his time (e.g. 3.33.17–18, 12.17–23). And see also Lucian, *Hist. conscr.* 7,20; Cic. *Fam.* 5.12.3. On the one-sided and panegyric character of pathetic historiography see Niese 1900: 34; Norden 1923: 1.82.

And in general, as Polybius notes in several places in his book, the 'pathetics' had no intention of reporting true facts, and historical accuracy was quite foreign to them (see also II Macc. 2.25,28–30).[117] Thus II Maccabees turned Judas Maccabaeus' defeat at Beth Zacharia into a victory (13.22),[118] and even refrained from reporting Judas Maccabaeus' death in the field at Elasa.

As to the sources of information available to the two authors, although the author of I Maccabees lived in Eretz Israel at the time of the Revolt and himself witnessed some of the military events,[119] it must be remembered that he is describing the war of liberation of his own people. Consequently he cannot be expected to give an accurate, objective report on the relative numerical strength of the two forces. Historians of antiquity more gifted and reliable than he, failed to do so in reconstructing contemporary events (probably because they had no such intention to begin with). Even the great Polybius admitted that it was the historian's privilege to show a bias in favour of his own people (16.14.6) and did just that in his biography of Philopoemen (10.21.8).[120] On the other hand, the author of II Maccabees, residing in distant Cyrene, had quite a vague and muddled notion of the battles. Judging from the information he provides, it is hard to believe that he had available any real data on the number of combatants involved.[121]

Unlike other historians of the Hellenistic period, neither of the authors had anything to fear from critics: I Maccabees was originally written in Hebrew, and there was no tradition of historiographic criticism in Jewish literature.[122] It was composed early in the reign of John Hyrcanus, some thirty years after the death of Judas Maccabaeus,[123] when few of those who had taken part in the battles were still alive and, in view of the limited distribution of books in general,[124] the chances that his book would reach them were small. Even if some readers had participated in the war or heard more accurate

---

[117] E.g. Polybius 2.58.12–13; also Lucian, *Hist. conscr.* 7,8. For detailed discussions of Polybius' criticism of his competitors see Koerner 1957; Walbank 1962: 1–12; Levi 1963: 195–202; Meister 1975. See also Bar-Kochva 1979: 146–7.

[118] See p. 294 below.   [119] Pp. 159–68.

[120] On the book and its panegyric purposes see Pédech 1951: 82–103; Errington 1969: 230,232ff.

[121] For a refutation of the view that Jason of Cyrene was an eye-witness of the events see pp. 180–2 below.

[122] On literary criticism in the Greek and Roman world see the general survey of Grube (1965). For the Hellenistic period see especially the various discussions on the historiographical methods by Polybius; see, however, n. 125 below.

[123] Pp. 162–3 below.

[124] On the difficulties which prevented books from being widely distributed in the Greek and Roman world see Hall 1913: 26ff.; Hadas 1954: 50–78; Tcherikover 1961b: 296–7; Reynolds and Wilson 1974: 1–37.

reports of it, there was no reason to fear that they would impugn the veracity of the legend of past heroism, for any criticism would detract from their own glory and that of the Hasmonaeans,[125] especially since at the beginning of John Hyrcanus' reign the ruling family had not yet aroused opposition in certain sectors of the Jewish population. II Maccabees, which was written in Greek, was aimed at the Jewish reader in the Diaspora who in any case was not in a position to have accurate information or confirm it. That was why the author allowed himself, among other things, to turn the Jewish defeat during Lysias' second expedition into a victory (13.22). The fact that Josephus was not familiar with II Maccabees[126] and the possibility that even Philo of Alexandria did not know of it[127] show that in the days of the Second Temple the distribution of the book was confined to the country where it was composed, or to limited areas and sectors of the Jewish Diaspora.

In general, in our day as well, the mass media allow themselves to distort, in accordance with their political inclinations, figures on the number of participants in military operations, demonstrations and mass meetings, disregarding the immediate testimony of thousands of eye-witnesses, not to mention numerical data that are not immediately visible such as numbers of refugees, casualties, etc. This fact is well known to contemporary historians of western countries, and even better to those dealing with eastern Europe and the Third World.

[125] On the absence of any criticism, even when it was clear to all that the information provided by the historian was far from the truth, see Lucian, *Hist. conscr.* 29.

[126] See p. 191 n. 124 below.

[127] An obscure passage in Philo's *Quod omnis probus liber sit* 13 (88–9), describing acts of cruelty perpetrated by despots who ruled Eretz Israel, led Schürer (1901: 3.486) to conclude that Philo was familiar with II Maccabees. As the purpose of the passage is to stress the Essenes' ability to tolerate suffering, however, it may very well refer to the persecutions under the Romans. It could in any case have been written under the influence of the descriptions of martyrs during the Hasmonaean Revolt which appeared in IV Maccabees, a philosophic sermon written before the destruction of the Second Temple and based exclusively on II Maccabees. There are various indications that Philo was acquainted with the former work. Thus, for example, the phrase ἀθλητὰς ἀρετῆς (= athletes of virtue) at the beginning of Philo's passage on the Essenes recalls the comparison of martyrs to athletes in IV Maccabees (17.16: τοὺς τῆς θείας νομοθεσίας ἀθλητάς = athletes of the divine law; and see also 6.10). On the resemblance between IV Maccabees and Philo in philosophical notions and biblical interpretations see Wolfson 1947: 1.22,95,398, 2.271–2. For the dating of IV Maccabees sometime between A.D. 18 and 54 see Bickerman 1945: 105–12 = id. 1976–80: 1.276–81; Hadas 1953: 95–6. Breitenstein (1976: 153–75) provides reasons for dating IV Maccabees after the destruction of the second Temple, but they are not convincing, and some even prove the contrary. The general chronological framework proposed by Bickerman accords with the widespread assumption that IV Maccabees was written under the impact of events in Caligula's time. The influence of the book on Philo noted above makes it necessary to date the book before the period of Philo's main literary activity, i.e. the late thirties or early forties of the first century A.D. At the time of the 'idol in the sanctuary', Philo was between 22 and 27 years of age.

3

The armament and tactical composition of the Jewish army

The Books of the Maccabees, the chief sources for the battles of Judas Maccabaeus, do not specify any Jewish tactical unit that took part in them nor any armament. I Maccabees usually confines himself to the general term ἄνδρες ('men', 'people': 4.6,29, 5.20, 7.40, 9.5) and II Maccabees is no less obscure (e.g. 8.1,22, 10.1,16,25, 11.6, 13.15), in contrast to the wealth of detail they provide for the enemy army. Such a presentation creates the impression that the arms at the disposal of the Jews were meagre and primitive. The author of I Maccabees even complains more than once of the shortage of basic fighting equipment at the start of the Revolt (3.12, 4.6,31). The complaints do not recur after the purification of the Temple, and the author incidentally notes the improvement that had taken place in the effectiveness and quantity of the armament at the disposal of the Jewish forces (6.6). But that was only a slip of the pen in the course of an explanation of the death of Antiochus Epiphanes in Persia as being the result of his disappointment at the failure of his Judaean plans.[1] Even here the author is not explicit, and is satisfied with a general and vague statement, and he continues to refrain from mentioning the types of weapons or units in the Jewish army even in descriptions of later battles.

There is no doubt that in the first four years of the Revolt, Jewish armament was pitiful. The description of Judas Maccabaeus' raid of the Seleucid camp at Ammaus states that 'shields and swords they had not as they wished' (I Macc. 4.6), an indication that in addition to archers and slingers, the traditional warriors of mountain peoples, in the first phase of the Revolt there were some Jewish units armed with shields and swords fighting very much like the classic Thracian and Scythian peltasts. With that equipment it was possible to carry out bold attacks against semi-heavy forces, including cavalry. Nevertheless, it was not enough to make possible a frontal battle on level

[1] See p. 52 n. 79 above.

68

terrain against heavy troops who with their long pikes could easily
prevent the Jews from engaging in hand-to-hand combat.

Cavalry and semi-heavy or heavy infantry

There are, however, clear indications that after the return to Jerusalem and the purification of the Temple there was a drastic change
in the tactical composition and armament of the Jewish force. A slip
of the pen in II Maccabees' description of the battle of Marisa,
Josephus' comments in *Bellum Judaicum* on the battle of Beth Zacharia, and an analysis of the course of the battle of Elasa and
Jonathan's confrontation with Apollonius, show clearly that in the
second phase of the Revolt, after the purification of the Temple, the
Jews had cavalry as well as infantry equipped with semi-heavy if not
heavy armament. The omission of any mention of the composition
of the Jewish army can be explained in the main by the panegyric
nature of the Jewish sources, their religious–didactic objectives, and
the literary character of II Maccabees. If the authors had written of
the utilization by the Jewish army of superior weaponry and tactical
units of the kind common in the armies of the time, as well as of the
true numbers for the opposing sides, that would have diminished the
wonder at the victories, and underlined the seriousness of the defeats.
At any rate, if the authors had set the outcome of each battle against
the actual equipment, the reader would not have felt the concealed
divine hand guiding the course of events, according to I Maccabees,
or the need for overt divine intervention, according to II Maccabees.
In order to uncover the truth it is therefore necessary to adopt
methods similar to those employed in Chapter 2 in the attempt to
reach a truer estimate for the number of soldiers at the disposal of
Judas Maccabaeus.

In describing the battle against Gorgias at Marisa, II Maccabees
casually mentions a Jewish horseman named Dositheus who distinguished himself in the battle against Gorgias' Thracian cavalry
(12.35). As that battle was an encounter of secondary importance
taking place on the border of Judaea while Judas Maccabaeus and
Simeon were occupied in the north (I Macc. 5.17–19,55–7),[2] it is
hard to believe that no Jewish horse soldiers took part in the great
decisive battles which took place after the purification of the Temple.
The II Maccabees mention of the type of unit the Jewish soldier
belonged to survived owing to the author's slip of the pen, as in the

[2] See pp. 50–3 above.

course of the description he was carried away by his admiration for the heroism of Dositheus, who tried to capture Gorgias, the enemy commander, alive with his own hands, and paid a heavy price (12.35). There is no reason to doubt the credibility of the information: it includes names, titles of units, and details on ethnic origin which do not appear to be fictional, and are well in line with Hellenistic military terminology. The possibility that Dositheus took part in the battle as a lone horseman must be rejected, as it would have been valueless, impractical and bizarre. In such a case we would also have to believe that the lone Jewish horseman in the camp managed to get close enough to the enemy commander for face-to-face combat without being hurt by other enemy horsemen. Furthermore, Dositheus is identified as τις τῶν Τουβιήνων (= one of the *Toubiēnoi*[3]), an expression which should be construed, on the basis of Hellenistic military terminology, especially in the Ptolemaic papyri,[4] as 'a fellow from (the unit of) the *Toubiēnoi*'. This description may suggest that the entire unit took part in the battle.

The conclusion on the participation of Jewish horse is confirmed through an examination of the course of the battle of Elasa: Judas Maccabaeus led a picked unit in pursuit of Bacchides' left wing which, as was the custom in the Seleucid army, included the elite horse,[5] from the battlefield between Beera (Al Bira) and Elasa, on

---

[3] The uncial MSS have τις τῶν τοῦ βακήνορος, but the phrase reads τῶν τουβιήνων in the Lucian MSS, one of the old Latin MSS (P) and in the Syrian version. See the various versions in the apparatus on this verse in Kappler and Hanhart 1967: 101–2. The version in the Lucian MSS and the Old Latin one has been preferred by most scholars. See especially Abel 1949: 422; Katz 1960: 60. In their view the word τουβιήνων (or rather τουβιάνων) was garbled to τοῦ βακήνων due to the separation of the τοῦ and the resemblance of the Ι to Κ. In the next stage βακήνων became βακήνορος because of the need to make the word genitive in form.

I see no justification for preferring the unknown name 'Bakenor' in this case, as believed by Hanhart (1961: 469–70, and in his edition of II Maccabees 1959: 101). It might be thought that the Lucian scribe was influenced by the mention of a certain Dositheus in the same chapter (12.19) in connection with the Toubians mentioned in a preceding verse (12.17), and that seems to be Hanhart's idea (though he does not express this explicitly). However, a simple reading should have shown the scribe that the Dositheus mentioned there was among the Judas Maccabaeus people who had come to rescue the Toubians, and not himself one (although that is presumably not so; see below). Moreover, the specification of the name in verse 35, after it occurred in several earlier verses, should have also shown the scribe that the reference was not to the same person. The form 'Bakenor' itself should not have given the Lucian scribe any trouble. In any case, we do not find that the Lucian version systematically altered Jewish names appearing in II Maccabees even if they were troublesome (such as 'Benjamin' in 3.4; 'Menelaus' in 11.29 and 32; the change of Αὐρανοῦ to Τυραννου noted by Hanhart in 4.40 is simply a slight palaeographic alteration not to be compared with a change of 'Bakenoros' to 'Toubiēnon').

[4] In the formula τις τῶν δεῖνων which refers to military settlers, the genitive plural indicates the ethnic, location, etc., of the members of the unit. Scores of examples of the use of these formulae are provided in Peremans and Van't Dack 1977.

[5] See p. 392 below re verse 12, and pp. 394–5 below re verse 14.

the southern approaches of Ramallah,[6] to *aśdōt hāhār* (= the mountain slopes).[7] The last phrase referred to the eastern slopes of the Judaean Hills (Josh. 10.40, 12.8). Given the deployment of the forces and the consequent escape routes, the place closest to the battlefield that could be so described is 1.5 km south of Beth El and 6 km north east of the battlefield, where the road to the Jordan valley begins its gradual descent. It should be noted that the place usually cited for the end of the pursuit is Baal Hazor, which is 12 km from the battlefield.[8] Judas Maccabaeus was perhaps capable (though that is doubtful) of striking Bacchides' flank with an infantry assault, but the pursuit of picked cavalry by infantry for such a distance (whether 12 or even 6 km) is simply not reasonable. Even though the flight of the Seleucid horse soldiers was a trick aimed at drawing Judas Maccabaeus into a trap,[9] the difference between the speed of the cavalry and that of the infantry is so great that a deliberate adaptation on Bacchides' part of the speed of retreat to that of infantry would immediately have revealed the secret of the plan of the Seleucid command. In any case, a sensible commander would never have left the bulk of his army on the battlefield and gone off with foot soldiers on such a long, hopeless pursuit after retreating picked cavalry. The desire to do away with the enemy commander-in-chief or capture the 'baggage' (*aposkeuē*) would not explain taking such action, unless we assume that the pursuing unit was composed of horse soldiers. The operation of the other Seleucid wing, which caught up with Judas Maccabaeus only near the mountain slopes (9.16), likewise indicates that the pursuit was carried on at cavalry rather than infantry pace.

A Jewish cavalry unit is explicitly mentioned in the description of Simeon's battle with Kendebaeus in the Aijalon Valley in 138 B.C. (I Macc. 16.7). But this is no grounds for claiming that I Maccabees would have reported the participation of cavalry in the Jewish forces earlier, if he had had information to that effect. We have already noted that beginning with Simeon's reign there is a substantial change in the author's purposes as shown by the stress on the military might of the independent state of Judaea.[10] The distribution of Jewish cavalry units among the infantry in this battle does not prove that the use of cavalry was an innovation in Simeon's time.[11] On the contrary, deployment of this kind is an indication that by then the

[6] On the location of the battlefield see pp. 385–8 below re verses 4 and 5.
[7] On the reading and reconstruction of the phrase ἕως 'Αζώτου ὄρος see pp. 395–7 below.
[8] On the identification proposals see pp. 396–8 below.
[9] See p. 395 below.   [10] P. 55.
[11] Contrary to Abel 1949: 279 and Dancy 1954: 194.

Jewish officers were already sufficiently experienced in cavalry warfare to depart when necessary from the current stereotypes (as did
Alexander's army in the battle of the Granicus and Antiochus III's
at Magnesia), which could not be expected of novices or amateurs.

It is true that there is no slip of the pen in the Books of the
Maccabees indicating clearly the types of Jewish foot soldier units.
Despite the silence of the principal sources on this point, however, an
analysis of some of the battles after the purification of the Temple
compels us to assume that at that time the Jewish camp included not
only light forces of archers and slingers but also units of semi-heavies
or perhaps even heavies. It is not possible to classify them more
precisely and stipulate the quality of their armament in Judas Maccabaeus' time, although there is no doubt that at least in Jonathan's
time the Jewish army already had a considerable number of men
who were fully fledged phalanx soldiers in equipment and combat
methods. These conclusions are based mainly on an examination of
I Maccabees' version of the battle of Elasa and of Jonathan's victory
near Azotos, and on Josephus' explicit statement in his description of
the Beth Zacharia battle in *Bellum Judaicum*.

The battle of Elasa took place on a gentle hilly site between Beera
and Elasa where the Seleucid phalanx, which was spread out to a
width of no more than 500 m, could move about quite comfortably.
The battle began with the confrontation of the light 'skirmishers'
(*promakhoi*) – the slingers and archers – following which two blocs of
Seleucid phalanx (apparently two *stratēgiai* of some 4,000 men each)
attacked the Jewish infantry in the centre (I Macc. 9.10–12).[12] The
battle between the two infantry forces lasted a long time, as I
Maccabees says, 'from morning to night' (9.13; cf. Exodus 18.13).
In the next phase Judas Maccabaeus assaulted the horse of the
enemy's right flank and pursued them beyond the battlefield (9.15).
The duration of the battle fought by the phalangites is described
with the biblical phrase quoted above, which, though perhaps an
exaggeration, certainly indicates a hard and protracted struggle.
Except in the description of the confrontation between Jonathan and
Apollonius, where its accuracy is undoubted (I Macc. 10.80),[13] that
phrase appears nowhere else in I Maccabees (nor do similar expressions), not even for the purpose of softening the effect of defeats.[14]

---

[12] For the site see pp. 387–8 below. For the analysis of the movements of the Seleucid force and
the identification of the various contingents see below pp. 390ff. See also the summary and
schematic presentation of the various stages on pp. 113–15.   [13] See p. 77 below.

[14] Cf. I Macc. 10.50 stating that the crucial battle between Alexander Balas and Demetrius
I lasted 'until the sun came'. There is no reason to suspect that the author was interested in
magnifying the story of that confrontation.

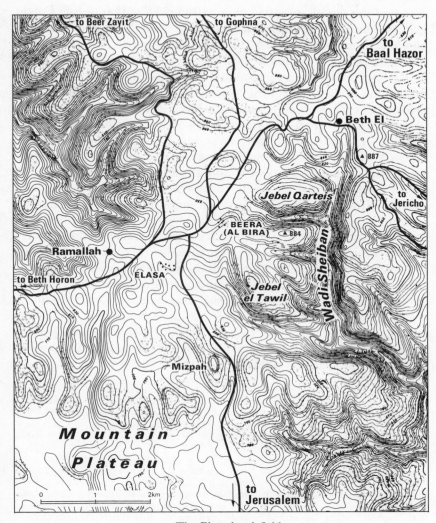

4 The Elasa battlefield

The activity of the wings also indicates that the decision between the
infantry came after a long fight, for if the foot soldiers who were the
bulk of Judas Maccabaeus' army had been defeated upon their first
contact with the enemy, there would have been no purpose in the
Jewish commander's assault on the cavalry in the enemy wing. The
duration of the battle in the centre, along with an analysis of the
various possibilities, tells something about the composition and arm-

ament of the Jewish infantry: on a battlefield like that of Elasa, light foot soldiers could not have stood up alone for so long against a large phalanx formation. In such circumstances neither religious fanaticism nor powerful national motivation would have been of much help. The dense massive phalanx blocs, taking up a substantial proportion of the width of the relatively easily manoeuvrable battlefield, would have crushed any light force in the area with the first blow. A concentrated barrage of arrows could not block an assault for long. The effective range of the bow was no more than 60 to 160 m,[15] and even less when the target was armoured phalangites. Furthermore, the quantity of ammunition that infantry slingers and archers were able to carry with them was extremely limited, and a substantial proportion at least of the ammunition of the Jewish lights had already been expended in the early struggle with the Seleucid lights who generally constituted no less than a quarter of the Seleucid army.[16] Only mounted archers were capable of protracted action on the battlefield.[17] However an examination of the description of Jonathan's battle against Apollonius[18] indicates that even in his day the Jews did not have mounted archers.[19] That kind of warfare required a great deal of tradition and sophistication. Be that as it may, if the Jews had had such archers, in the battle of Elasa the cavalry of the flanks would have been assigned to combat them, and not the foot soldiers of the Seleucid phalanx.

[15] On the effective range of the bow (as distinct from the distance it could reach) see McLeod 1965: 1–14; id. 1972: 78–82, and the detailed bibliography there. The differences in the sources as to the effective range can be explained by the varying abilities of the archers, and even more by the various materials composing the bows, their shape, size and workmanship, and also by weight, length and shape of the arrows, as well as by the protective equipment of the targets.

[16] See p. 117 below.

[17] Cf. the celebrated victory of the Parthian archers at Carrhae (53 B.C.). The Parthians were mounted, not foot soldiers. On horseback it was possible not only to carry a larger quantity of ammunition and easily replenish the supply, but also to reduce the distance from the enemy, and of course avoid the massive advance of the opposing infantry. Furthermore, in the battle of Carrhae the cavalry also used camels, one to every ten men. The camels carried loads of arrows, thus lengthening even further the duration of the shooting and ensuring its continuity. The Parthian side in that battle also included cavalry cataphracts whose task it was to block any advance against the archers. The bows themselves were capable of piercing armour (see especially Plut. *Crass.* 24).   [18] Pp. 76–7 below.

[19] Pseudo-Hecataeus' mention of the Jewish mounted archer, Mosollamos, in Alexander's army (Jos. *Ap.* 1.201) proves at the most that at the time of the composition of the book there were among the Jews of Egypt soldiers trained in that complicated military art. I have devoted a monograph to the treatise 'On the Jews' attributed to Hecataeus of Abdera (forthcoming). The monograph provides further evidence on the Jewish author of the work, dates it to the first years of Alexander Jannaeus, in the first decade of the first century B.C., and establishes the primary purpose of the Alexandrian Jewish author as justifying and legitimizing the existence of the Egyptian Diaspora during the period of political independence and prosperity in Judaea.

Since the overall object of the Seleucid campaign was to capture Judas Maccabaeus, who was then in the left flank, it could be argued that the Seleucid foot purposely refrained from crushing the Jewish foot in the first assault as it was Bacchides' plan to use his right wing to draw Judas Maccabaeus into a trap beyond the battlefield. It must however be remembered that hesitation on the part of an advancing phalanx against light troops could be fatal if it was not closely protected by its own adjacent lights or cavalry on the wings or in the centre: the opposing lighter infantry could cut into the wall of phalangites by sniping from afar, and then breaking through and crumbling the formation from within in hand-to-hand short-range fighting against which the phalangites were powerless. Even for the attainment of the goal of capturing Judas Maccabaeus it was not worth losing the military backbone of the empire. In any case, as noted above, light foot soldiers would quickly have exhausted their ammunition, so that the Jewish centre which carried on the battle for such a long time could not have been made up of light infantry.

The possibility that the battle dragged on because the Seleucid phalanx was enticed by the Jewish light units into the rough terrain adjacent to the battlefield must also be discounted. For that purpose, aside from lights and semi-heavies the Seleucids had by then soldiers who had been retrained in the Roman style of combat.[20] Be that as it may, it is doubtful whether even such Seleucid units would have engaged in a 'clean-up' operation of this type, for Jews who found safety in that rough terrain could not constitute any danger to the Seleucid army on a battlefield that was beyond the range of their stones and arrows. The fact that the struggle in the centre was of such long duration therefore obviates the possibility of assuming that the centre was composed exclusively of light infantry.[21]

As to the external sources, in the treatment of the battle of Beth

[20] Pp. 313–16, 416–18 below.

[21] It is far from correct to compare the battle of Elasa with mediaeval battles in which infantry archers overcame heavy horsemen. In the famous battle of Crécy (August 1346) between the English and the French, the English archers played a decisive role in the defeat of the French knightly cavalry, but the conditions were entirely different: the English longbow had a much greater effective range (200 to 350 m) than the bow used by the Genoese in the service of the French, and the former therefore prevailed in the clash of the archers; pouring rain made the hillside slippery and the French horsemen backing up the Genoese archers were unable to reach the English archers, who continued to snipe at them at long range with armour-piercing arrows; the range of the longbows and the condition of the terrain made for a considerable distance between the two sides so that it was easy for archers continually to replenish their 'ammunition'; and above all, the English archers did not fight on their own, but were covered from the rear by spear-throwing cavalry who prevented an assault by the French forces that did manage to get through despite everything; and finally, being generally undisciplined, the French army conducted an unbridled advance towards the enemy, and the officers lost control of the troops.

Zacharia in *Bellum Judaicum*, taken from Nicolaus of Damascus, Josephus reports that Judas Maccabaeus' brother Eleazar attacked one of the enemy elephants 'before the phalanxes of both sides clashed' (1.52: πρὶν δὲ συνάψαι τὰς φάλαγγας). Nicolaus himself based his version of Beth Zacharia on both I Maccabees and on an invaluable Seleucid source: the episode involving Eleazar was taken exclusively from I Maccabees and the rest from both sources, primarily from the Seleucid one.[22] While the sentence in question is included in the description of Eleazar's feat, it may be assumed that Nicolaus wrote it on the basis of information on the course of the battle emanating from the Seleucid source, for it refers to an event that occurred after Eleazar's death, and has no counterpart in I Maccabees. As to the term 'phalanx', it had a variety of meanings, occasionally denoting the overall battle formation, or the forces in the middle of the field, or even various tactical units.[23] In the Hellenistic period, however, the term was confined to *sarissa* -equipped units. Very rarely was it applied to heavy units made up of peoples outside the Hellenistic world who carried shorter offensive weapons, like the Roman legionaries and the Carthaginian foot soldiers.[24] Furthermore, it must be remembered that in the battle of Beth Zacharia the forward Seleucid units not only included phalangites, but also soldiers who had been retrained for combat in the Roman manner.[25] In any case, in the Hellenistic period the term did not designate light infantry.

If from the story of Judas Maccabaeus' battles it is hard to classify precisely the armament and combat tactics of the Jewish infantry, the description of Jonathan's battle against Apollonius near Azotos (I Macc. 10.74–83)[26] shows that in his day the Jewish army was

[22] See pp. 189–90 below.

[23] For the various meanings of the word 'phalanx' in Greek literature of various periods see the detailed survey by Lammert in *RE* s.v. 'Phalanx', cols. 1624–45. On the Hellenistic period, however, the treatment is inadequate, in that it concentrates on tactics, failing to deal with the question of terminology, and ignores papyrological material especially.

[24] The clearest evidence on the uses and forms of the word 'phalanx' in the Hellenistic period appears in Polybius, whose work abounds in military descriptions. Polybius is generally careful to restrict the word exclusively to *sarissa*-equipped foot soldiers, though in a few instances he applies it to the close formations of the Carthaginians (1.33.6 and 34. 6–7, 3.115.12) and in one place to Roman legionaries (3.73.7), whom in general he distinguishes from *sarissa*-bearers by other terms (*stratopēdon* for the legion itself, τὰ βαρέα τῶν ὅπλων (heavy arms) for its armament, etc.). In the post-Hellenistic literature, when *sarissa* combat almost disappeared, the term 'phalanx' was applied to legionaries' combat methods as well (e.g. Jos. *Bell.* 1.547; the legion itself is called *tagma*), or to the battle line as a whole (see Tarn 1948: 2.136). The strict official usage during the Hellenistic period is reflected in *OGIS* 229, line 103; *P.Bad.* IV, no. 47. On the flexible usage of the term by Zeno of Rhodes see Bar-Kochva 1979: 155–6.

[25] Pp. 126, 313–16 below.

[26] See the analysis of the background, rival forces and stages of the battle in Bar-Kochva 1975: 83–96.

made up chiefly of phalanx units augmented by cavalry on the flanks. Here, too, the author of I Maccabees refrained as was his wont from explicitly stating the composition of the Jewish force.[27] In that battle, which took place on a broad plain,[28] the enemy was arrayed in the usual way with the phalanx in the centre (ibid. 10.82)[29] and cavalry on its flanks (10.77, 79).[30] When the signal was given, Jonathan was surprised by mounted archers stationed in ambush who attacked him from the rear in unending volleys (10.79–80). In response the Jewish commander ordered his men to remain where they were (10.81). The hail of arrows continued for a long time (10.80), as the mounted archers were able to carry large quantities of ammunition. However, the enemy phalanx did not take advantage of the opportunity to then break the Jewish line, and eventually the archer-horsemen tired (ἐκοπίασαν = wa-yig‘ū, wa-yil’ū, 10.81) and the danger passed. As there is no hint of any assault against them, the implication is that their ammunition was exhausted and, as they could no longer contribute to the struggle, that they were compelled to withdraw from the battlefield. The fact that Jonathan ordered a passive 'absorption' formation which successfully withstood the hail of arrows, and also deterred the enemy phalanx from exploiting the continual 'softening up' for a frontal assault, makes it clear that the centre of the Jewish formation was not composed of a light infantry unit without shields, and not even of semi-heavies with spears much shorter than the *sarissai* of the phalangites. It may also be assumed that if Jonathan's soldiers had been lighter than the enemy's they would have taken advantage of their mobility to manoeuvre in the field. The passive tactics noted above required the use of the armament and formation of phalanx troops. The usual formation of phalangites facing such situations, especially confronting mounted archers, was the *synaspismos*, a 'contracting' manoeuvre of the shields in which they reduced the space between the columns to a minimum,

[27] The provocation in the letter Apollonius supposedly sent to Jonathan (I Macc. 10.70–3) does not prove that the Jewish force was lightly armed. The letter is not authentic, as is clear from its style, its formulae and terminology, the contents which contradict the situation which developed shortly thereafter with Jonathan's siege of Apollonius' garrison in Jaffa (10.75), and especially from the course of the battle. The letter is no different in value from the pre-battle orations attributed to the Jewish commanders, being a free invention of the author's reflecting the general purpose of the book to represent the Jewish force as inferior in numbers and equipment. Verse 73 itself is based on I Kings 20.23,25.

[28] The identification of the battlefield in Abel 1949: 199–200.

[29] In the original the word 'phalanx' appears in some Hebrew transliteration (פלנקס? פלנכס?) referring to the close formation of the *sarissa*-carrying unit stationed in the middle of a battle array; see the details in Appendix B, pp. 432ff.

[30] In addition to the ambush of mounted archers (verse 79), the participation of 3,000 cavalry is reported (verse 77); they were deployed in the flanks of the frontal formation in the usual Hellenistic manner.

no more than half the normal space, so that from the outside the rows presented a continuous structure of shields and pikes which protected the formation from sniping and possible assault.[31] If the phalanx happened to be unprotected on the flanks, the phalangites were accustomed to form a 'square' (*plinthion*) in which every side constituted a front. If, however, the infantry had the protection of cavalry on the flanks (like the Jewish infantry force; see below), the phalanx would present a frontal formation toward enemy forces only at its front and rear. This formation, by nature passive and static, could not make do with shields alone and needed *sarissai* to stop a possible assault by opposing phalangites. It is also hard to believe that an effective *synaspismos* could be formed without providing the front rows with coats of armour.[32] Regular phalanx troops habitually tended to refrain from skirmishing with the *synaspismos* formation because of the great compactness which gave it a substantial defensive advantage, and preferred to make use of 'lights' sniping from a distance and to wait for the formation to dissolve as the battle continued, morale difficulties developed, etc. In his paraphrase in *Antiquitates* Josephus properly understood Jonathan's action as *synaspismos* (13.95–6).

The analysis of the second phase of the battle also indicates the participation of the Jewish cavalry. When the mounted archers were 'neutralized', Jonathan's brother Simeon advanced toward the enemy phalanx (10.82).[33] The advance of infantry forces, which as noted were in this case composed of phalangites, against a phalanx formation protected by cavalry would have been suicidal unless the advancing phalanx had some protection on its flanks to prevent attack by the enemy cavalry (and this applies even more to light infantry). Moreover, it should be noted that it was not Jonathan who led the Jewish infantry advancing toward the enemy, but Simeon, although the order previously given to the infantry to switch to 'absorption' formation by Jonathan indicates that the latter com-

---

[31] On *synaspismos* see Kromayer and Veith 1926: 135; F. Lammert in *RE* s.v. συνασπίσμος, cols. 1328–30.

[32] The inside rows were on the other hand protected from arrows and 'steep trajectory' missiles by raised pikes and shields.

[33] The word συνῆψε in verse 82 should be reconstructed ויקרב (= and he approached) so that the sentence will read ויקרב אל הפלנכס (= and he approached the *fālanks*), as can be deduced from the Septuagint for Ezekiel 37.17. The Septuagint for Judges 20.30 has a similar construction to render ויערכו אל הגבעה (= and they arrayed themselves against Gibeah), but 'arrayed themselves' does not fit the context for our verse. Together with πρὸς πόλεμον, the verb συνάπτειν appears several times in I Maccabees and should be translated ויתגר עמם מלחמה (= and he contended with them in battle) as per the Septuagint for Deut. 2.5,24; see I Macc. 5.7, 21, 10.53. However, the word πόλεμον is missing from the present verse.

manded the entire formation. In Hellenistic tradition the commander-in-chief personally led one of the cavalry wings.[34] And most
important, the battle was decided when the enemy cavalry, that is,
the cavalry on the flanks, were exhausted (ἐξελύθη, 'tired': 10.82).
Only at this stage does the author refer to the advance of Simeon's
men and the retreat of the phalangites (ibid.).[35] It may thus be
inferred that units other than the infantry under Simeon's command
overcame Apollonius' cavalry on the flanks. It cannot be assumed
that these units were also heavy infantry, because the cavalry was
able to parry their blows easily and attack them from the flanks. It
is also hard to accept that this action was carried out by Jewish
archers; the enemy force, made up primarily of residents of
the Hellenistic coastal cities,[36] certainly also included infantry
specializing in that eastern art, whose function was to 'neutralize' the
'lights' of the Jewish side, in addition to its mounted archers. In any
case, if Jewish archers had beaten enemy cavalry, the author would
not have failed to provide the reader with some details on the factors
which led to the defeat of Apollonius' flanks. The accumulated data
cited above lead to the conclusion that Apollonius' cavalry flanks
were beaten by cavalry units led by Jonathan. The sequence of
events in I Maccabees and the wording of the description indicates
that Apollonius' phalanx was in fact not defeated by Simeon's heavy
infantry. Nothing is said about 'breaking' the phalangites, only
about 'breaking' the cavalry. Presumably Simeon advanced toward
the Seleucid phalanx when the turning point in the cavalry action
was apparent and close. The collapse of the cavalry laid Apollonius'
centre bare to the danger of a flanking manoeuvre, in addition to
that presented by Simeon's phalanx. Consequently, when the cavalry
'broke', the phalangites too fled for their lives, and that was why
there was no frontal clash between the heavy infantry of the two
sides. A similar though more complicated development is known
from the battle of Raphia between Antiochus III and Ptolemy IV in
217 B.C.[37]

[34] See pp. 26–8, 335 n. 70, 392 n. 38. Cf. Vegetius 3.18, where the second in command is
posted in the centre of the infantry.
[35] The plural verb καὶ συνετρίβησαν (וינגפו = were smitten) refers to cavalry (ἡ ἵππος)
and phalanx, both of which appear in the singular.
[36] On the identity of the 'troops of the cities' that set out with Apollonius for this battle (I
Macc. 10.71) see Bar-Kochva 1975: 85–6.
[37] See Bar-Kochva 1979: 136–7. A different picture from mine is drawn in a long detailed
article on the battle of Raphia by Galili (1976–7: 52–126). His reconstruction, however, derives
from an erroneous identification of the battlefield in the region of the Raphia crossroads
(pp. 74, 94–6), while according to Polybius (5.80.3,4,6–7 and 82.1–2) the battle took place 55
stadia from ancient Raphia (a-Sheikh Suleiman Rafaḥ), i.e. between the coastal dunes and
Kufr Shan.

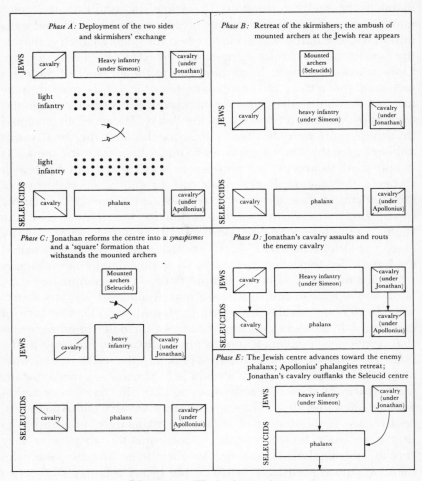

Diagram 3: *The battle near Azotos*

Despite the relatively detailed description of the battle in I Maccabees, the author does not specify 'cavalry' or 'phalanx' in the Jewish camp, although he does apply the terms to the enemy army (10.82), just as he does for the battles of Beth Zacharia and Elasa (6.45, 9.10–12). The battle near Azotos took place thirteen years after the death of Judas Maccabaeus, and it might be argued that the Jewish army had had enough time to organize and develop, so that its structure then would not reflect its composition at the time of Judas Maccabaeus. But the great importance of the episode for our subject is as evidence not merely that Jonathan had horsemen and phalangites, but especially that the author of I Maccabees maintained a consistent and deliberate silence regarding the composition of the Jewish field army.

To conclude the discussion of Jewish armament in the various battles, it is worth briefly considering siege warfare. As a rule, the *helepolis*, the large shooting tower and breaching device operated by Simeon the Hasmonaean in the siege of Gazara in 142 B.C. (I Macc. 13.43), is thought to be the first complicated war machine at the disposal of the Jews. This impression seems at first glance to be supported by the fact that the Jerusalem citadel was conquered only that same year (I Macc. 13.49–53). Possibly a superior poliorcetic device such as the *helepolis* was not available to the Jews before Simeon's time. I Maccabees casually mentions, however, artillery pieces (*mēkhanai*) employed by the Jews during the siege of the Jerusalem citadel on the eve of Lysias' second expedition (6.20) and during the defence of the Temple at the end of that campaign (6.52); probably most of the machines were part of the booty from the campaigns in eastern Transjordania (see, e.g., I Macc. 5.30). The expression 'and they made artillery devices' repeated in those verses indicates a considerable technical ability within the Jewish ranks which was demonstrated in the assembly of those complicated machines if not in their construction. It is not by chance that the author of I Maccabees speaks generally and vaguely of the artillery in the Jewish camp, and quite extensively and explicitly of the various siege machines at the disposal of the enemy (6.51). For Jonathan's time there is even mention of the concentration of 'many artillery devices' in preparation for the siege of the Jerusalem citadel (I Macc. 11.20). The specific mention of the *helepolis* in Simeon's time derives from the author's changed attitude and aim in the chapters describing Simeon's presidency. As to the conquest of the Jerusalem citadel, it should be noted that even in Simeon's time the citadel fell not because its walls were breached but because its residents were starved out. The siege machines of the Hellenistic period were not effective enough to break down the strong walls of fortifications that were particularly large and massive. The citadel was not overcome through starvation before Simeon's time because political-military considerations compelled the Hasmonaean brothers to allow its residents to bring supplies into the fort.[38]

[38] See pp. 458–9 below.

Source of recruitment and trainers

In the wake of the above considerations it is hard to avoid asking about the sources of the manpower and armament of the heavies, semi-heavies and above all the cavalry, in the Jewish army. Judaea was not a horse-breeding country, and its inhabitants had no tradition of cavalry warfare, or even semi-heavy, not to mention heavy, infantry combat. The horsemen themselves, and at least the instructors of the infantry, had to come from outside the boundaries of the Judaean Hills. As has been remarked above, Dositheus, the horseman who distinguished himself in the battle of Marisa, is described in II Maccabees (12.35) as 'one of the *Toubiēnoi*', which means that he belonged to the unit of the *Toubiēnoi*. The name *Toubiēnoi* indicates that the unit originated in the military settlements of 'the land of Toubias', the territory of the Toubias family in southern Gilead west of present-day Amman,[39] which had cavalry among their settlers.[40] Sosipatrus and another military man named Dositheus,[41] who figure in the list of Judas Maccabaeus' commanders during the expeditions to eastern Transjordania (II Macc. 12.19), were also military settlers from the land of Toubias (cf. ibid. 24, with I Macc. 5.13).[42] Most of Joseph son of Toubias' sons identified with

[39] A *kleroukhos* (= military settler) from the land of Toubias is mentioned in one of the Zeno papyri (*CPJ* 1, no. 1). On the boundaries of 'the land of Toubias' and the four settlements there whose names have survived in the sources see Tcherikover in *CPJ* 1.116. In the sale document, which was signed in 'Birta of Ammanitis', nothing is said about where the *kleroukhos* was from, although he may be presumed to be from Birta. In any case, there is no reason to think Birta was the only settlement.

An attempt to define the particulars of the arrangement by which the military settlers belonged to Toubias' unit was made by Bagnall (1976: 17). In his opinion, Toubias was recruited in the king's service, and advantage was taken of his status as head of a respected family in the region to make him responsible for the military settlers in the area. The matter needs further study.

[40] On the settlers who 'belonged to the horsemen of Toubias' see the papyrus noted above, and Tcherikover 1961b: 59–60; S. Applebaum has proposed (orally) locating the origin of the Toubiads mentioned in the battle of Marisa in a Babylonian place called Touia (Tovia?) which appears in *Notitia dignitatum orientis*, a fourth-century list of Roman stations, roads and installations (35.28: Touia contra Bi[r]ta). Despite the similarity of the names and data on the Babylonian Jews having engaged in military activities, the proposal seems somewhat far-fetched.

[41] The name refers to another person since the battle of Marisa coincided with the activity of Judas Maccabaeus in Transjordania (see pp. 50–1 and n. 78 above) and because II Maccabees specifies the hero of the battle of Marisa (12.35) several verses after reporting on the activities of Dositheus in eastern Transjordania.

[42] Various scholars (Abel, Avi-Yonah, Hengel et al.) believe that Dositheus and Sosipatrus came from the 'land of Tob' in northern Gilead east of Edrei (Judges 11.3; II Sam. 10.8; *PT Shebiith* 6.1 [36c]; for its identification see Z. Kallai, 'Land of Tob' in *Biblical Encyclopaedia*, vol. 3 (Jerusalem, 1955) cols. 366–7 (Hebrew); see Map 21 on p. 509). The proposal embodies a number of difficulties: the Septuagint gives the name Tob in exact transcription (Τωβ) while

Seleucid policy but the youngest, Hyrcanus, followed the Ptolemies, gathered a considerable force, and set up an independent principality in Ammanitis (*Ant.* 12.228–36). From there he tried to undermine Seleucid authority in Eretz Israel and provided funds for that purpose (as suggested in II Maccabees 3.11). He took his life sometime in the reign of Antiochus Epiphanes (*Ant.* 12.236), probably only in 168 B.C. after Antiochus Epiphanes' return from Egypt.[43] At any rate, there are signs indicating the direct involvement of the residents of the region in the happenings in Judaea, at least until that year: Jason, Onias' brother, who after being deposed from the high priesthood in 172 (II Macc. 4.26) fled to Ammanitis, probably to join Hyrcanus and his men, left his place of refuge at the time of Antiochus Epiphanes' second expedition to Egypt, and with a thousand men attacked Jerusalem, captured it, and pushed Menelaus and the Seleucid garrison back to the citadel (II Macc. 5.5–6). It is hard to understand how he could have overcome the Seleucid garrison and Menelaus' 3,000 men (II Macc. 4.39–40) without the help of Jews from Transjordania who had combat experience. Jason's connection with the military settlement in

the passages on these two commanders in the Books of the Maccabees have Τουβίου and Τουβιηνούς (I Macc. 5.13; II Macc. 12.17; cf. the form Τουβιήνων in II Macc. 12.35), all with the addition of the theophoric suffix; the form ἐν τοῖς Τουβίου (I Macc. 5.13) is not a translation of טוב ארץ (= land of Tob); the distance between Kaspin and the 'fort' of the 'Toubian Jews' was 750 *stadia* (about 140 km) according to II Maccabees (12.17; on the translation of the word *kharax* as 'fort' see below p. 510 n. 3). This estimate fits the rugged mountainous region of the settlement of Toubias, taking into account that merely as the crow flies the distance is about 100 km (the old Latin translation has '550 *stadia*' i.e. 105 km). Even though II Maccabees is no authority on topographical matters, it is hard to ignore totally this obvious correspondence in the distance to the land of Toubias in the south (cf. p. 276 below on the distance between Beth Zur and Jerusalem – 11.5); the military tradition of the settlements of the Toubias family in the Ammonite territory points in the same direction. Contradicting these considerations is the I Maccabees statement that the 'fort' was in Dathema (5.9,28–34), which is definitely near Kaspin. However, since Dathema was not within the boundaries of the 'land of Tob' either, it may be inferred that the Jews who managed to flee from the settlements of Toubias near Ammanitis, the power base of Timotheus (I Macc. 5.6), found a haven among their brothers in Dathema in northern Gilead, and that is indicated in II Macc. 12.17. The statement of the 'herald' that all the Jews in the settlements were slain and their wives taken prisoner (I Macc. 5.13) indicates that no Jews were left in the south. If the correspondence of the distance between Kaspin and the Toubias settlements is not coincidental, presumably the author of II Maccabees (or the epitomist) found some note in his sources on the distance between the Toubias settlements and the Kaspin region, and mistakenly interpreted it as relating to the distance between Kaspin and the place where the 'Toubian Jews' found a haven. Timotheus and his men were able to gain control of the Toubian settlements by exploiting the absence of a considerable proportion of the men of military age, who joined the army that was developing in the land of Judaea.

[43] Josephus' statement that Hyrcanus controlled his independent principality for seven years 'the whole time that Seleucus ruled in Syria' (*Ant.* 12.233) may actually refer to Hyrcanus' rule during the reign of Antiochus Epiphanes. If so, Hyrcanus' suicide occurred in 168 B.C. and was connected with Antiochus Epiphanes' return from Egypt in great disappointment. See Abel 1949: 320; Momigliano 1930: 185,193; Hengel 1973: 501.

Transjordania was demonstrated also in his flight to that region around the time of Antiochus Epiphanes' return from Egypt (II Macc. 5.7). A short time later Jason was forced to continue his wandering and seek refuge among the Arabs (II Macc. 5.8) in the wake of pressure in the Ammanitis area by the central authorities, which evidently led to Hyrcanus' suicide and the end of the independent existence of the principality. In any case, the weakness of Seleucid authority in Transjordania when Antiochus Epiphanes was absent from the area made it possible for Jews living in the territory of the former principality to continue to help anti-Seleucid elements in Judaea, as appears from the references to the horseman Dositheus and the commanders Dositheus and Sosipatrus. It is not surprising that members of settlements who cooperated with Jason should later have lent a hand to Judas Maccabaeus: first of all, we are not sure that all the settlers supported Jason and the moderate Hellenizers of his faction, rather than the conservative circles. Secondly, the clearly anti-Seleucid policy of some of the settlers, the persecution of Jason by the Seleucid authorities (4.16), and the strength and scope of the edicts that contrasted with the moderate approach of Jason's supporters, all these must necessarily have brought them closer to the rebel camp.[44]

II Maccabees' slip of the pen in regard to Dositheus therefore indicates in what direction the solution should be sought: evidently the horse soldiers and infantry instructors were Jews living outside Judaea, who were summoned to assist in the second phase of the Revolt, after the purification of the Temple. Inscriptions found at Arad show that Jewish infantry and cavalry served in the Negev in garrison duties during the Persian period.[45] As the time proposed for the relevant documents is the end of the Persian period, given the manpower policy of Alexander and his successors it is reasonable to suppose that these soldiers and their offspring carried out similar

[44] On this see also p. 88 n. 54 and p. 540 n. 40 below.

[45] See Naveh 1981: nos 7,12 (pp. 156,158), and see his conclusions, pp. 174–6, esp. p. 176. However, I would hesitate to accept the suggestion of Bickerman (1937: 55; id. 1938: 70) and Hengel (1973: 29–30), according to which the Jews from Judaea supplied auxiliary forces for the Seleucid army even before Jonathan's time. There is no evidence of this, and the entire assumption is based on Bickerman's healthy intuition that the operational capacity displayed by Judas Maccabaeus' warriors cannot be explained exclusively by religious devotion and nationalist motivation. Bickerman himself did not examine the battle descriptions and, despite the intuition noted above, in his various books repeats the conventional theme of the war of the few against the many, the ill-equipped against the well-armed, etc., in line with his general view, inspired by events of his time, that the Hellenizers constituted a majority of the Jewish people. That concept lends a dramatic, pathetic character to the struggle of monotheism against polytheism which he describes. On the modern relevance of *Der Gott der Makkabäer*, and

functions in the Hellenistic period. They may likewise have hastened to the aid of their brothers in the Judaean Hills. In addition, we should not reject the possibility proposed by a number of scholars that some help was extended by Diaspora Jewry as well.[46] It must be kept in mind that military occupations were widespread among Diaspora Jews in the days of the Second Temple. It is quite conceivable that the Jews of Egypt and Cyrenaica, who served in units of their own in the Ptolemaic army[47] and maintained close ties with the Temple in Jerusalem, were so shocked by the sacrilege committed[48] that they did not stand idly by. Indeed the Ptolemaic authorities may have encouraged such initiative for the purpose of stabbing the Seleucids in the back, especially since the Roman shield which had proved so efficient during 'the days of Eleusis' protected them from massive Seleucid retaliation. The same held true for the Jews of Phrygia and Lydia,[49] areas which were then under the control of the kingdom of Pergamum, the confirmed foe of the Seleucids. In addition there was the possibility of 'infiltration' by Jews from

its sources of inspiration in the struggle of European Jewry for survival when Hitler rose to power, see in detail my article in his memory (1982: 6–7).

[46] The possibility that Jewish reinforcements from outside participated was already noted in general by Hengel 1973: 32,180–1,501–2; and see also Applebaum 1979: 140. The principal evidence they proffer, however, based as it is on the common assumption that Jason of Cyrene was an eye-witness of the events, must be rejected. All signs indicate that Jason was not acquainted with Eretz Israel, and did not take part in the battles (see in detail pp. 380–1 below).

[47] On Jewish horsemen in Egypt see, e.g., *P. Tebt.* nos. 818,882; and see Tcherikover 1963: 30–43; Launey, 1949–50: 1.544. On the participation of Jews in the early Ptolemaic army, as individuals and in their own units, as early as the third century B.C. see Kasher 1978: 57–67; id. 1985: 38–48. On military settlers among the Jews of Cyrenaica see Applebaum 1955: 188–97; id. 1979: 118ff. The service of the Jews of Elephantine in the Persian army no doubt firmly established a military tradition among the Jews of Egypt. On their military organization see Porten 1968: 26–61.

[48] On the connection with Eretz Israel at the time of the Revolt see Beek 1943: 119–43; Tcherikover 1960: 1.45–6; A. Kasher 1980: 205–6.

[49] Jewish settlements in Phrygia and Lydia are discussed in Bickerman, 1976–80: 2.24ff.; Schalit 1960: 289–318; Bar-Kochva 1979: 45. The various *katoikiai* of Jews known in the area in the Roman period were former Seleucid military settlements, and the document in *Ant.* 12.148–53 noting the transfer of Jews from Babylonia to Phrygia and Lydia for the purpose of military settlement must be accepted as authentic. The recent attempt to impugn its authenticity by Gauger (1976: 23–154) is not convincing. The only serious argument proffered is the absence of any reference to Jews in the Seleucid manpower alignment at the battles of Raphia and Magnesia. It must be borne in mind, however, that Jews are not mentioned in the composition of the Ptolemaic army in the former battle either, although there is no doubt that at the time many Jews served in it in their own units. The reason is that, like their co-religionists from Elephantine in the Persian period, they functioned mainly in police and guard duties on the regional level, which accounts for their absence from the big battles. As to the various stylistic arguments, as has already been recognized, the document was redacted by Josephus (if not by some earlier writer) and this can be ascertained by comparing the documents of Jonathan's time appearing in I Maccabees with Josephus' version of the same documents in his *Antiquitates*.

military settlements within the Seleucid empire, in the regions of Babylonia and northern Syria.[50] In the Hellenistic world, borders were never hermetically sealed; the military forces of the Seleucid empire were engaged in mobile missions far from the border areas, and not in static defensive actions. Even mighty Republican Rome was unable to prevent the passage of troops and mercenaries from regions north of the Taurus and even beyond the Dardanelles into Seleucid territory, after the treaty of Apamea was signed. And finally, if Judas Maccabaeus and his brother Jonathan had such well-developed political instincts that in the middle of the battles they sent envoys to distant Rome (and Jonathan even to declining Sparta), is it likely that they failed to attempt the mobilization of their brothers outside Judaea who were well versed in warfare?

The identification of these Jews with the struggle in Eretz Israel did not develop overnight, and may not have been expressed in practice till four years after the outbreak of the Revolt, upon the purification of the Temple which led to a feeling of exaltation in the Diaspora of Alexandria (II Macc. 1.9). Successes can inspire volunteers from abroad, as we well know from events in the region in our own time. The same happened during the Great Revolt against the Romans whose early stage was marked by great successes; at that time volunteers came to Judaea, among them Monobazus and Cenedaeus from the royal family of Adiabene, Silas of Babylonia from Agrippa's army, Niger of the Peraea, and also some archers from the settlements of Zamaris in the Bashan. On these as well few sources have survived, despite the abundant material that has reached us through Josephus on the Great Revolt and its military progress, and despite the fact that Josephus had no need to conceal the participation of volunteers from outside.

It is true that aside from the mention of Dositheus and the unit he belonged to we have no hint of the participation in the battles of Jews from outside Judaea; however, in view of the patent didactic and panegyric purposes of the authors, it is not reasonable to expect them to provide more, especially since those soldiers fulfilled vital tasks in the tactical units whose very existence the authors deliberately ignore.

In this connection it should be noted that a document preserved in Josephus mentions military activity of Jewish officers and soldiers

[50] On settlements in Babylonia see Schalit 1960: 297; see also Appendix H, pp. 500–7 below. In Syria: Kraeling 1932: 137–9. On Jewish military settlements in the Diaspora in general see Hengel 1973: 27–31.

from Egypt in Coele Syria (*Ant.* 13.65), apparently during the reign of Alexander Balas.[51] As Jonathan was the third partner in the alliance involving Alexander Balas and Ptolemy VI Philometor, it is hard to believe that close cooperation did not develop between the Ptolemaic Jewish soldiers and officers who were stationed in the country and Jonathan's men in the latter's struggle against the forces siding with Demetrius I. Yet there is no information or intimation in I Maccabees on military help extended to Jonathan by those Jews, nor even on their presence in the country, despite the considerable detail given in the description of events. That fact supports the impression that such information did not suit the author's purposes. On the other hand it might be argued that as a Diaspora Jew, Jason of Cyrene would have had to point out ties with Jews abroad involving cooperation and assistance during the Revolt, if there were any. It should be remembered, however, that for him, religious–didactic and literary purposes were paramount, and his military descriptions are enveloped in an unreal atmosphere of fairy stories and miracles. As the letters in the beginning of the book (1–2.18) are not of his authorship, there is no evidence that he had any desire to indicate a special attitude on the part of Diaspora Jewry to what was happening in Eretz Israel in the midst of events.[52]

To sum up, if we put together the data cited above – the participation in the Jewish army of cavalry and reinforcements from the military settlements of Toubias in Transjordania, the existence of a military tradition including cavalry warfare among the Jews in the southern part of the country during the Persian period, the profusion of Jewish military settlements in the Diaspora and Transjordania, the inimical relationship between their Egyptian and Pergamene overlords and the Seleucid authorities, and the diplomatic efforts of Judas Maccabaeus and his brother – there are sufficient grounds for believing that the combatants in the Judaean Hills benefited from outside help. The fact is that the participation of military settlers from Coele Syria and Phoenicia alone is enough to account for the development and training of the infantry and cavalry that Judas Maccabaeus had at his disposal, and it is not necessary to assume that they were joined by many volunteers from afar. The number

---

[51] On the dating of the 'war' mentioned in the document see Kasher 1985: 133–4.

[52] This also applies to the legend of the mother and her seven sons (ch. 7) whose attribution (later) to Antioch is extremely dubious. Against the tradition on the martyrs' tombs in Antioch see Efron 1980: 56 n. 45, countering the view of Hadas 1953: 111; Gutman 1949: 35; see also Bickerman 1976–80: 2.192–209. In any case, the martyr stories seem to be an addition by the epitomist (6.17; and cf. p. 179 below).

of horse soldiers in the Seleucid kingdom was in any case not large, and it is possible to imagine a Jewish force including a few hundred cavalry, such as the 350 recruited and rapidly trained by Josephus during preparations for the Great War against the Romans in Galilee (*Bell.* 2.583). As to the infantry, the Judaeans could easily have been introduced to heavy or semi-heavy formations with the guidance and instruction of quite a small number of outside volunteers. The training and preparation of manpower in Hellenistic methods of warfare did not have to take more than a year or two, as can be inferred from the episode of the accelerated and efficient training of 20,000 Egyptian natives without experience or military tradition in phalanx warfare before the battle of Raphia, in 218–217 B.C.[53] The small number of volunteers, in proportion to the total strength of the Jewish army, made it easy to ignore their part in the war, and that is why there remain no slips of the pen besides the one in the description of the battle of Marisa and the references to the commanders Sosipatrus and Dositheus.[54]

We have some indications in regard to the source of armament of the Jewish troops. The volunteers who came from outside Judaea obviously brought their weapons with them, and I Maccabees notes explicitly that after the purification of the Temple Judas Maccabaeus' army was strengthened thanks to weapons taken as spoils (6.6). Those sources were not sufficient for so large a Jewish army, and a modest arms industry must have developed. Judas Maccabaeus' men, who assembled artillery pieces themselves, were certainly capable of making their personal weapons. And indeed I Maccabees reports on the manufacture of weapons on a large scale in Jonathan's time (10.6,21).[55] The raw materials needed were quite readily

[53] Polybius 5.65.9,85.9–10,107.1–3. On the performance of the Ptolemaic phalangites in the battle of Raphia see Bar-Kochva 1979: 138–41.

[54] Rhodocus, the Jew who defected at Beth Zur during Lysias' second expedition (II Macc. 13.21), may have come from the Hellenistic Diaspora, perhaps from the Toubian settlements in Transjordania. It is hard to believe that even before the establishment of the Hasmonaean state a Jew of Eretz Israel who did not belong to the Hellenizer community would have a Hellenized Iranian name of this kind. Greek names like Antigonus or Eupolemus given by pious Jews are no proof, for the first is connected with the name of a ruler who dealt fairly with the Jews while the second could have been adopted by a person who, like his father, travelled abroad frequently and had diplomatic contacts with foreigners. At the same time it is not impossible that the Rhodocus mentioned was among the followers of Jason, Onias' brother, who at one point probably began to collaborate with the rebels. On the names of Diaspora Jews, and especially the military settlers among them, see Hengel 1973: 114–19. One must however, take exception to his conclusions on the prevalence of Greek names among conservative elements before the declaration of independence. Some of the envoys with Greek names sent abroad by the Hasmonaean brothers (except Eupolemus) may very well have been formerly Jason's followers, or Diaspora Jews who settled in the country. On Eupolemus see p. 303 n. 7 below.

[55] The verb κατασκευάζειν should be reconstructed as להתקין (= to construct, repair, arrange); see Raban 1962: 383.

available and if necessary it was possible to use metal parts of household utensils and agricultural implements, and the like. The metal parts needed for the *sarissa* were relatively small and simple,[56] and the raw material for making the *sarissa* rod was readily available in the Judaean Hills. The common oak which abounded there and the Tabor oak of the coastal plain had properties similar to those of the Cornel wood from which the Hellenistic *sarissa* rods were made.[57] There was certainly no difficulty in producing the medium length pikes carried by semi-heavy troops. The Galatian shields, too, were made basically of wood, reinforced with felt and metal,[58] and the same may be true of the smaller shields of the rank-and-file phalangites. Village carpenters and blacksmiths able to make agricultural implements could fashion weapons of this kind. The technical skill required for making all these was considerably less than was necessary for fashioning effective bows, whose extensive utilization by the Jews is unquestioned.

Of all the personal gear in the Hellenistic armies, only the massive coats of armour presented any difficulty: the raw material and technical know-how for their manufacture were both relatively hard to come by.[59] However, only some of the Seleucid heavy and semi-heavy troops had armour of this kind.[60] In any case, the Jews could have been equipped with leather body armour of the kind that served the Roman army well at various times. As noted above, by the time of Jonathan's leadership, the Jewish forward lines at least may have been outfitted with some sort of body armour; otherwise it is hard to understand how they could maintain a closed passive formation for a long time in the face of mounted archers. Still, it is certain that in Judas Maccabaeus' time the Jews were inferior to the Seleucid troops in their ability to supply metal body armour, and that gave an advantage to the enemy units equipped with metal armour and pikes. And in any case the Jews were inferior in both number and equipment of cavalry. These defects were no doubt manifest in the battles where the Jews did not have overall numerical superiority, such as at Elasa and Beth Zacharia when the enemy were able to manoeuvre their 'armoured' forces, and tipped the scales against Judas Maccabaeus.

[56] See the components in Andronikos 1970: 91–107, and the discussion in Markle 1977: 323–6. Cf. Plate I below.

[57] The specific weight of dry Cornaceae wood is 0.7 to 0.8 g/cm^3, while that of oak is 0.66 to 0.79. The common oak reaches a height of more than 5 m, and the Tabor oak of up to 20 m. For the properties of the various woods mentioned see Panskin and de Zeeuw 1970: 1.569, 615–17.

[58] See p. 7 n. 5 above.

[59] On the expertise needed in the fabrication of armour see, e.g., Plut. *Dem.* 21.4–6.

[60] See p. 8 and n. 6 above.

4

The ethnic origin and fighting capability of the Seleucid phalanx

Like the other Hellenistic armies, the Seleucid army on the battle-field was composed of phalangites, heavy cavalry, semi-heavy and light infantry, and at times also light cavalry and elephants. The backbone of the army, however, was the phalanx force of military settlers[1] that was deployed in the centre of the battlefield and served as a sort of barbed and impenetrable porcupine which overran anything in its way as it advanced. It is rightly accepted that the eastern peoples had no proper answer to the massive power of the phalanx units, and that that deficiency enabled the Seleucids to control the complex variety of nations in the empire.

Polybius, the great historian of the period, consistently refers to the phalanx soldiers as 'Macedonians', and he does so even in his detailed description of the procession at Daphne in Judas Maccab-aeus' time (30.25.5).[2] Many scholars, however, hold that in the course of time the Seleucid phalanx deteriorated from the point of view of ethnic composition and operational ability. According to them, at the outset most of the military settlers making up the phalanx units were of Greco-Macedonian origin. But eventually they assimilated into the eastern environment through intermarriage with the local population, and when their offspring lost their military gifts, soldiers of indigenous Syrian origin joined the phalanx units (and perhaps also the settlements) and became a majority in them. The term 'Macedonians' applied to these units in the various sources thus denotes not national origin, but combat method, as it did in Ptolemaic Egypt. This was certainly the case at the time of Antiochus IV. The quality of the Seleucid phalanx thus degenerated considerably; the Syrian soldiers were much inferior in operational

---

[1] See the bibliography on p. 36 n. 22 above.
[2] On the reading of the sentence see p. 417 n. 21 below. 'Macedonians' refers to all the phalangites described in the sentence.

ability to the splendid Macedonian phalanx units that had earlier stormed the East.[3]

It is the practice today to express doubts and disbelief about assertions as to the presence or absence of military prowess in various races. Fighting ability is the result of variable elements and conditions in all areas of human activity (e.g. social structure, economic situation, climatic and topographical conditions, national and religious motivation, technological ability, strategic and tactical leadership, etc.) and may change drastically following alterations in one or more of these components. Care must therefore be taken to avoid passing a general judgement on the military ability of peoples and races. The Assyrians and Babylonians who at various times displayed excellent fighting qualities were eastern peoples, and it would not occur to anybody today to designate them as 'inferior' in fighting potential. However, despite reservations regarding 'racist' conclusions, it must be borne in mind that the fighting ability now under discussion is not general and timeless, but involves the specific qualifications for phalanx warfare in the Hellenistic period only. Among the variables that determine a nation's military capacity are its means and methods of fighting. For sundry reasons, some nations at certain times are more adept at a particular type of warfare than are others. In the same way, for the past twenty years athletes of the Far East have proved superior in table tennis while north Americans have excelled in basketball, but neither of them has shone in soccer. The phalanx was a Macedonian invention that was perfectly suited to the traits and gifts of the Macedonians, at least at the time of Philip and Alexander. Although it did not need very long training, it demanded certain qualities of the soldier: he had to be physically strong, quite tall, and imposing, and extremely disciplined. In these qualities the average Syrian (not elite troops) was inferior to the average Macedonian and even the average Greek.[4] And of course

---

[3] Bickerman 1938: 76; Launey 1949–50: 1.96,293,297,319, 2.109; Walbank 1957–79: 1.608; Ehrenberg 1960: 148; Tcherikover 1961a: 194 and 1961b: 172; Musti 1966: 121; Will et al. 1975: 461 (Will); G. A. Cohen 1976: 31–2. Against this view see Griffith 1935: 147–64; Tarn 1951: 35ff.; Tarn and Griffith 1952: 161–2.

[4] On the importance of physical strength and size (including height) for phalanx warriors see the information on Philip II's *pezetairoi* (Theopompus: *FGrH* 115, F348) and Antiochus of Commagene's Guard (Jos. *Bell.* 5.460), and the Tacticians' notations on stationing in the first rows of the Hellenistic phalanx especially large, strong warriors – Asclepiodotus 2.2, 3.5–6; Aelianus, *Tact.* 13.1–2; Arrian, *Tact.* 5.6, 12.1, and Arrian's statement that the 'phalanx must be frightening not just in its actions but also in appearance' (ibid. 12.4), and see also p. 392 below. Macedonian physical prowess and hardiness were fostered from infancy on. See, e.g., the well-known anecdote about Philip II in Polyaenus 4.2.1. The young Greek developed

the motivation and perseverance so important in every military
formation were certainly much weaker in Syrian soldiers fighting for
a foreign invader than in a Macedonian minority fighting for its
existence in the hostile East. The alleged 'mixed' and Syrian origin
of the Seleucid phalanx soldiers is therefore relevant to the assessment
of their operational ability and consequently deserves a careful
investigation.

Native Syrians and the Seleucid phalanx

We now turn to the suggestion that native Syrians were enlisted in
the phalanx units. There is no doubt that the term 'Macedonians'
was not construed as a purely national term: it covered not only
natives of Macedon, but also Greeks from the entire Aegean
region.[5] However, the evidence cited for the more extreme view that
the term 'Macedonian' as used for the Seleucid army was a synonym
for 'phalanx' which was made up mostly of Asiatics does not hold
water. Some of this evidence refers to elite units of the Seleucid army
and some to the army in general.

In regard to the elite units, it is mainly the statement of Polybius
that the *argyraspides*, the infantry Royal Guard, the elite contingent
of phalangites, were armed in the Macedonian style (5.79.4) that is
cited as proof that the soldiers themselves were not Macedonians.
However, a close examination of the functions and development of
this contingent as well as some direct information shows clearly that
it was composed of Macedonians,[6] and that Polybius had obvious
substantive and stylistic reasons for describing the *argyraspides* as he
did and not simply as 'phalangites'.[7] It was also pointed out that
Livy noted that the *regia ala*, one of the two elite cavalry units of the
Royal Guard,[8] was composed of 'Syri plerique...Phrygibus et Lydis
immixti' (= mostly Syrians...mixed with Phrygians and Lydians,

his capacities through gymnasium education. On the connection between gymnasium
education and military training in the Hellenistic period see Launey 1949–50: 2.813ff.
    [5] This conclusion seems to be acceptable to all, and is often valid not only for mentions of
Macedonians in the context of military operations. It was expressed most aptly by Griffith
1935: 42 (less clearly on p. 41). The analysis of the numerical data on the heavy infantry forces
after Alexander's death indicates that out of 50,000 soldiers called 'Macedonians', only 30,000
were actually Macedonian. As the sources clearly distinguish between a 'Macedonian phalanx' and a 'mixed phalanx', that is, a unit composed mainly of Asiatic soldiers (see Diodorus
18.30.5, 19.14.5 and 27.6) the remaining 20,000 who are also called 'Macedonians' could only
have been Greek mercenaries.
    [6] See in detail pp. 418–26 below.   [7] See the discussion on pp. 420–1 below.
    [8] On this unit see also Polybius 5.53.4,84.1,85.12, 16.18.7, 30.25.7; Polyaenus 4.9.6; and cf.
Bar-Kochva 1979: 68–75.

37.40.11). There is no doubt, however, that his source, Polybius, did not mean native Syrians but rather military settlers of Greco-Macedonian descent who lived in Syria. The Royal Guard was of different composition from the regular units, and as usual in the armies of antiquity included only picked soldiers (a custom preserved in some royal armies to this day), enough of whom could be found only in a great reservoir of experienced soldiers. Thus for example the *agēma*, the other cavalry Guard unit, was composed mainly of Medes (Livy 37.40.6),[9] people who had always excelled in cavalry warfare. We have no intimation, however, that there was such a reservoir of native Syrians, Phrygians and Lydians. Quite the contrary: as cavalry warfare demands a long tradition deriving from the nature of the country and the topographical features, it is hard to believe that native Phrygians and Lydians fought on horseback, and even less reasonable to suppose that they served in the elite cavalry unit. In the Classical and Hellenistic periods, nationals of those peoples figured as fighting forces very rarely and in rather small numbers, and at any rate never as cavalry.[10] On the other hand, a survey of the Seleucid military settlements indicates that the military settlers of Asia Minor, the Greco-Macedonian *katoikoi*, were concentrated exclusively in Phrygia and Lydia.[11] It may therefore be assumed that these 'Phrygians' and 'Lydians' were simply military settlers of Greco-Macedonian origin, and this conclusion should be applied as well to the 'Syrians' mentioned in the same sentence. And in fact, a military settlement in Syria of horsemen of Greco-Macedonian origin is recorded in the sources: the residents of Larissa in the satrapy of Apamea, who came from Thessaly, are explicitly described

[9] Appian's version – Μακεδόνων (Macedonians: 32(163)) – is the result of a palaeographic garbling, for the rest of the clause in Livy (*eiusdem regionis multarum gentium equites* = cavalry of many races from the same region), which certainly comes from Polybius who was the source for Appian as well (see p. 33 n. 13 above), shows clearly that the reference is to indigenous Medes (contrary to Bickerman 1938: 59). On this unit see further Bar-Kochva 1979: 68–75.

[10] The sources appear in Launey 1949–50: 1.449–51,481–3. See also the small number of Phrygians and Lydians among the infantry soldiers in the famous list of Persian vassals in Herodotus 7.73–4 (and their complete absence from the cavalry – ibid. 86). Three hundred Lydian horsemen are mentioned by Curtius (6.6.35), but his wording suggests that they were not native Lydians: '...from Lydia 2,600 foreign troops and 300 horsemen of the same nation'. The term *peregrinus* (foreign) was not applied to other nations, not in this list of reinforcements nor in others. They may have been Hyrcanian horsemen from the Caspian Sea region who were settled as a garrison by the Persians. On the Hyrcanian plain and Hyrcanian settlement in the region see Strabo 13.4.13 (629). It should be noted also that, given the composition of the unit they belong to, the Lydian infantry mentioned in the account of the battle at Raphia were evidently a Median tribe (on 'Lydians' in western Media see Grintz 1969: 56f.). In any case these Lydians are javelin-throwing infantry (akontists) and not cavalry. See also Bar-Kochva 1979: 69.

[11] See ibid. 22–7, especially p. 26.

as serving in the Royal Guard (Diodorus 33.4a).[12] Diodorus also cites an entertaining episode involving the son of a Macedonian settler in eastern Syria, who served in a cavalry unit assigned to Alexander Balas (32.10.2–9), probably the *regia ala*.[13]

As to the sources relating to the Seleucid army in general, Livy (36.17.5) and Plutarch (*Flam.* 17.5; *Moralia* 197d) call the Seleucid troops that fought the Romans at Thermopylae (191 B.C.) 'Syrians'. Elsewhere Livy states that the Macedonian settlers in the Seleucid kingdom degenerated into Syrians (38.17.11: 'in Syros...degenerarunt'). Plutarch cannot be considered an independent source, as he evidently based his report on Livy.[14] As to Livy himself, the above description should not be taken as grounds for any conclusions, for its purpose is clearly to belittle the ability of the Seleucid army. Livy even specifically stresses that the Syrians are 'the lowest of peoples, with the character of slaves' (36.17.5).[15] These pejorative remarks all appear in orations attributed to Roman commanders,[16] and it has long been recognized that the editing and expansion in the commanders' exhortations in Livy (as in other orations in his books), far exceeded the amount he allowed himself in the strictly narrative material.[17] Furthermore, the disparaging expressions noted appear in orations that were not in the main taken from Polybius, Livy's principal source for the Roman–Seleucid confrontation, but were invented by Livy himself.[18] Livy ascribed to the Roman commanders offensive comments on the ethnic origin of the Seleucid troops on the

[12] While Diodorus actually speaks of the 'first *agēma* of the cavalry' and not of 'the royal ala', it appears that the name of the latter was changed to the more respected name of *agēma*, when the satrapies beyond the Tigris were detached from the Seleucid empire in 147 B.C., cutting off the *agēma*'s reservoir of Median manpower. The new unit was composed not of military settlers' sons, but of the settlers themselves, and was a regular reserve unit. See Bar-Kochva 1979: 70.

[13] On this episode see further p. 426 below.

[14] On Livy as one of the sources for Flamininus' biography and the chapter under discussion see Nissen 1860: 291.

[15] For the sources of this view of the Syrian peoples see Hengel 1976: 77ff.; and of the Mesopotamian peoples, Eddy 1961: 104–6.

[16] Sharing this bias is also the oration in Livy 35.49.8, in which the orator calls all soldiers from the Upper Satrapies 'Syrians', although he specifies their countries of origin ('the many names of unheard-of nations, Dahae and Cadusians and Elymaeans – they were all Syrians'). On these units see also Livy 35.48.5; 37.40.

[17] See Nissen 1860: 25–7; Ullmann 1927: 133ff.; Lambert 1946: 58ff.; Walsh 1963: 219–44; Paschokowski 1966; Tränkle 1977: 120–31; Burck 1977: 430–63.

[18] See Ullmann 1927: 20,147–8; Tränkle 1977: 128–31; Briscoe 1981: 245–6. There is no justification for Hengel's contention (1976: 85) that Livy's information is taken from Poseidonius. The Roman campaign against the Galatians of Asia Minor in 189 B.C. was evidently not reported in Poseidonius' historiographical work which started at the point where Polybius' work ends.

assumption that such remarks would encourage their own soldiers before battle.[19] Thus he also had the consul M. Manlius Vulso comment, before the battle against the Galatians in 189, on the 'ethnic degeneration' of the Galatians of Asia Minor, and on the difference between them and the brave Gauls that the Romans had encountered in the past (38.17).[20]

In addition to the sources noted above, the hypothesis that the Seleucid 'heavies' included a large number of indigenous Syrians is probably based on information from the end of Alexander the Great's period and the start of the wars of the Diadochs that reports the arming of Asiatic soldiers as phalanx fighters and also on inferences from the history of the Ptolemaic army. The sources relate that on the initiative of governors of cities and satraps, 30,000 young Persians or other Asiatics gathered in Susiana wearing Macedonian uniform and trained in the Macedonian fighting system (Arrian, *Anab.* 7.6.1ff.; Diodorus 17.108.1ff.; Plut. *Alex.* 71). Later Eumenes of Cardia put into the battlefield eastern phalangites who, in one case in 321 B.C., numbered 15,000 or even 20,000 men (Diodorus 18.29.3,30.5).[21] However, those were sporadic attempts which did not last long.[22] On Alexander's part, this was an endeavour of the type that embodied a combination of the demonstrative and the ostentatious, or else it reflected an acute shortage of manpower,[23] while in Eumenes' case, he had no choice but to enlist easterners in the phalanx in the face of Craterus' enormous numerical superiority

---

[19] On this manner of exhorting soldiers to fight by means of literary orations in Livy see Tränkle 1977: 130, and pp. 128–31 on the oration attributed to Manlius Vulso. On the main themes serving in Livy's orations to arouse the soldiers' enthusiasm see Bornecque 1977: 410–12.

[20] See also Tarn 1951: 35 and n. 1 on disparaging expressions regarding the Seleucid army. A critical view of them appears also in Briscoe 1981: 214, and G. M. Cohen 1978: 2 n. 7. Hengel (1976: 85–6) is of the opinion that in 38.17.11 Livy is referring not to the ethnic 'contamination' of the Macedonians but to the influence on them of the local nature and climate (according to para. 10). However, since in 36.17.5 Livy seems to be deliberately giving the reader a feeling that the Seleucid army was composed of autochthonous Syrians, I am not sure he did not mean the same also in the oration before the clash with the Galatians noted above.

[21] See also Diodorus 19.14.5,27.6. On the estimate of the number of Asiatics in Eumenes' phalanx see Griffith 1935: 41. A. B. Bosworth (1980: 17 n. 138) believes on the contrary that in the battle against Craterus, Eumenes' phalanx was entirely Asiatic.

[22] Griffith (1935: 42) and Milns (1975: 92,127–8) believe that the contingent was demobilized already in Alexander's time, or immediately after his death. That is possible, but it may be that the Asiatic soldiers in Eumenes' phalanx had received their training in that unit. In any case, they disappear from the arena after Eumenes' downfall in 316, and their numbers diminish even earlier to between 3,000 and 5,000 as a result of the reinforcement of the Macedonian base in Eumenes' army.

[23] For the second explanation see Bosworth 1980: 19 and passim.

in Macedonian phalangites (see Diodorus 18.30.1,4). An identical policy on manpower cannot be extrapolated from these episodes for the Seleucid rulers. In any event, in neither were these soldiers called 'Macedonians' or assigned to mixed units with Macedonian soldiers, but kept within their own special framework.[24] Diodorus even states explicitly that the 30,000 young men who gathered at Susiana were supposed to be an *antitagma*, a counter-army to the Macedonian phalanx (17.108.3),[25] while describing Eumenes' Oriental phalanx as being 'of every race'. In contrast, as noted above, the soldiers of the Seleucid phalanx were called 'Macedonians' as late as the reign of Antiochus Epiphanes.

For our question the comparison with the Ptolemaic army is more relevant and deserving of a more extended treatment. In a general way, it is possible to say that the southern superpower at first built its army according to a system somewhat resembling that of the northern kingdom.[26] The Ptolemaic army, too, was based on military settlers, mercenaries and auxiliary troops, and its heavy units were recruited from among the military settlers. The composition of the units and their development, however, were completely different. When the Ptolemaic army first started operating in the third century, its light infantry forces already included native Egyptians (Diodorus 19.80.4),[27] while the phalanx comprised only a minority of Macedonians supplemented by settlers from other countries outside Egypt, at first Greeks from the Aegean islands and Asia Minor, and later also others from Asia Minor and even Jews and members of Iranian peoples who had no tradition of phalanx warfare.[28] Only in

[24] See Milns 1975: 128; and Bosworth 1980: 17ff.

[25] For the meaning of the expression see Briant 1972: 51–60.

[26] On the structure of the Ptolemaic army see Lesquier's still outstanding work, *Les institutions militaires de l'Égypte sous les Lagides* (1911: esp. pp. 1–30). Various chapters in the two volumes of Launey 1949–50 are a valuable guide to the Ptolemaic army. Other works of value on the subject are Schubart 1900; F. Oertel in *RE* s.v. 'Katoikoi', cols. 1–26; Meyer: 1900; Bouché-Leclercq 1907: 4.1–69; Griffith 1935: 108–41; Crawford 1971; Uebel 1968; Heinen 1973: 91–114; E. Van't Dack 1977: 77–105; Tcherikover 1960: 1.11–15; Kasher 1985: 38–55, 186–91.

[27] The native Egyptians should be counted separately from the 22,000 Macedonians and mercenaries according to Kromayer and Veith 1903–32: 4.436; Griffith 1935: 109,112. The counter-argument of Seibert (1969: 166), which denies the credibility of the statement in Diodorus 19.81.1 on Ptolemaic numerical superiority, is not convincing. The same chapter contains a comparison between the training for top command of young Demetrius (not of the sub-commanders in his camp) with that of Ptolemy and Seleucus. Demetrius' greater number of elephants also suggests that Ptolemy had a considerable numerical advantage. For a refutation of Seibert's linguistic argument see Huss 1976: 59 n. 244. See also Lesquier 1911: 6–7,19–21; Launey 1949–50: 1.589.

[28] This description of the composition of the Ptolemaic phalanx is based on three main points: (a) the relatively small number of Macedonians compared with mercenaries in the Ptolemaic phalanx at the end of the fourth century (see Griffith, 1935: 109–11); (b) the use

the case of one unit of the Royal Guard at Alexandria (the *therapeia*) was the Macedonian character preserved at least up to the end of the third century B.C.[29]

The system of military settlements worked well in the first generation. The settlers received the land in exchange for their undertaking to be ready for duty at any moment. Being experienced soldiers, they retained their military fitness even though engaged exclusively in agriculture, and when called upon in emergencies carried out their duties satisfactorily. The second and third generations of settlers, however, were no longer an effective fighting force. The ethnic heterogeneity in the settlements which diluted the national motivation, the settlers' lack of military experience and the long intervals between the great Ptolemaic campaigns all made the system unworkable. At the outbreak of the fourth Syrian War in 219 B.C., when Antiochus III invaded Coele Syria, Ptolemy IV did not have the proper forces to stop him. The *epigonoi*, the offspring of the military settlers, were useless, and Ptolemy had to give them a year or two of intensive training before he could meet the Seleucid ruler in the battle of Raphia (Polybius 5.62.7–65).[30] Because of the deterioration and degeneration (militarily speaking) of the residents of the military settlements, Ptolemy was compelled also to recruit and train for phalanx warfare indigenous Egyptians who had formerly been employed only as light infantry. Those Egyptians thereafter

in documents of the term 'Macedonian' as a pseudo-ethnicon for settlers of various nations who fought as phalangites; and (c) Polybius' designation of the Ptolemaic phalanx at the battle of Raphia as simply 'phalanx' (5.65.4), with no national definition, although close by stress is placed on the national origin of the phalanx of Greek mercenaries and of the Libyan and Egyptian natives (5.65.5) who took part in that battle alongside Ptolemy.

So far as we know, the term 'Macedonian' in pseudo-ethnic application appears only from 215 B.C. onwards (cf. *P. Hamb.* 189 to *BGU* 1958). It might then be argued that only from the battle of Raphia onwards were peoples other than Macedonians accepted in the phalanx, just as in that battle Egyptians were equipped with Macedonian weaponry in separate units. But the small number of Macedonians in Egypt at the end of the fourth century and the impossibility (for political reasons) of recruitment in Macedonia make it difficult to assume that in the third century the phalanx, which had to be the major force in the army, could have differed in composition from the phalanx at the battle of Raphia (except for the unit of indigenous Egyptians which was an innovation introduced on the eve of the battle). The absence of clear papyrological evidence on 'pseudo-Macedonians' before Raphia is apparently purely fortuitous. On 'Macedonians' as a pseudo-ethnicon see Lesquier 1911: 2,11–12,109,283; Heichelheim 1925: 38–43; Launey 1949–50: 1.321,325,335; Tcherikover 1960:1.14; id. 1963: 42–3; Uebel 1968: 30,59,120,133,281,313 and passim, and esp. p. 382; Préaux 1978: 1.315.

[29] On this unit see Fraser 1972: 1.80 and 2.152 n. 224.

[30] This explanation for the appearance of the phalanx of indigenous Egyptians at Raphia first emerges in Griffith 1935: 117,123,140. However, the low figure of 5,000 he attributes to the Macedonian–Ptolemaic phalanx at Raphia must be rejected. See p. 33 n. 15 above. Other explanations for the introduction of the indigenous Egyptians do not hold water. See a summary of the various suggestions in Huss 1976: 58 n. 243.

constituted almost half the phalanx force, and were later even given land, though much less than had been allotted to other settlers. The military settlements and consequently the phalanx were thus no longer composed of purely foreign elements.[31] The change was not salutary: native Egyptians, who were aware of their power and importance in the imperial military configuration, demanded privileges and embarked upon a mutiny which lasted more than thirty years.[32] The provision of arms and the fostering of the military potential of the local population has often led to the collapse of empires (cf., e.g., the rejection of the British Raj in India after the Second World War during which a large number of Indians were called to the colours), and constituted a special danger in the Hellenistic empires where the dominating peoples were only a small minority even in their own power bases, Egypt and northern Syria.

We have no information available on a similar process in the Seleucid army, and all signs indicate that such a deterioration did not occur there, at least not till the second half of the second century B.C. The key to understanding the method that helped maintain the Macedonian character of the Seleucid phalanx force lies in the organization and history of the *argyraspides* (= silver shield bearers), the infantry Royal Guard of the Seleucid army. A separate appendix provides a detailed review and discussion of the sources on this unit.[33] The following paragraphs include a summary of the findings and the conclusions relevant to the present subject.

Generally comprising 10,000 soldiers, the contingent was equipped and operated as a regular phalanx, and was composed of the picked young sons of the military settlers, every settler being obliged to despatch one of his sons. They apparently assembled at the military school at Apamea in northern Syria (see Strabo 16.2.10 (752)) where they received their basic training. Those who proved apt served later on as a permanent unit at the disposal of the court at Antioch. The high quality of the unit was maintained by the demobilization of soldiers whose prowess had diminished or who presented disciplinary problems, and the enlistment of new, strong young men who proved themselves suitable. In that way throughout the years the new generation of military settlers served in the Royal Guard for longer or shorter periods, in numbers roughly equal to the number of their elders who had served in it. The contingent's tasks

[31] On the 'mixed' composition of the Ptolemaic army after the battle of Raphia see Griffith 1935: 122–3,139–41; Peremans 1951: 214ff.; Fraser 1972: 1.68ff.

[32] The revolt of the Egyptian soldiers is mentioned in Polybius 5.107.1–3 and 14.12.4; and see Milne 1928: 226–34; Préaux 1936: 528–52; Will 1967: 2. 35–6.

[33] See pp. 413–31.

included carrying out police and guard duties in government centres in the Seleucis region, the four Macedonian satrapies in northern Syria, and especially in the capital, Antioch, manning forts and key positions, and being prepared at a moment's notice to proceed to distant corners of the empire to subdue uprisings. When a soldier left his unit to return to the military settlement he came from, he took his place in the ranks of the reserve force, and may well have released his father from that obligation.

A similar system probably applied to the military settlers who served in the cavalry. Exclusively Greco-Macedonians and Iranians (mainly Medes who excelled in cavalry warfare), they sent their sons to serve in the royal '*ala* of the companions' and in the *agēma*, the two cavalry units of the Royal Guard.[34]

An organization of this type was designed to preserve the military fitness of the settlers. Their sons, having served in the Royal Guard, did not forget the art of war even when they became ordinary farmers, and because of the mechanical nature of phalanx warfare, not much time was required to refresh experience previously acquired. It could be said that 'once a phalangite, always a phalangite'. The system also operated to establish a connection between the settler and the central authorities. The vast distances between the military settlements scattered throughout the empire and the centre in Antioch could undermine the settler's loyalty to the regime and incline him to support local satraps and commanders who from time to time sought to rid themselves of the yoke of the dynasty. This danger was especially likely to afflict the offspring of the military settlers who were not acquainted at all with the Seleucid royal house and with the Macedonian population's particular commitment to it. The service in Apamea and Antioch led the soldiers of the Guard, the future settlers, to a direct recognition of an identification with the royal house, and inculcated the duty of loyalty to it. This was demonstrated in the behaviour of these soldiers in the Achaeus rebellion and the revolt of Molon, the satraps of Asia Minor and Media, when they refused to fight against Antiochus III (Polybius 5.54.1–2 and 57.6–7).

The organizational system of the Royal Guard must have prevented the deterioration of the military settlements as a stable, permanent manpower potential for the phalanx. As a result there was no need to recruit native Syrians to those units, and the Seleucid phalanx could have continued to be composed mainly of Macedonians and Greeks.

[34] Bar-Kochva 1979: 60–1,70–1.

The above conclusion is based mainly on probability: since the Seleucid army had a system for preserving the military aptitudes of the Macedonian settlers, it had no need to enlist Asiatics, unlike the Ptolemaic army in Egypt. Is there any direct evidence to support that conclusion and prove that there were no native Syrians in the Seleucid phalanxes?

Even the scholars who claim that the Seleucid phalanx at the time of Antiochus Epiphanes included a large number of Syrian soldiers do not believe that there was no separation between the Macedonian and Oriental contingents (even the Ptolemies kept them separated) but that the phalanx included also many units of eastern soldiers. The decisive fact, however, is that Polybius, the most reliable historian of that age, applied the term 'Macedonians' to the phalanx of Antiochus III which took part in the battles of Thermopylae and Magnesia,[35] as well as to the heavy troops of Antiochus IV who marched in the Daphne procession (30.25.5). In describing the campaign against Molon, the battles of Raphia and Panium, and the expedition through the Elburz mountains, he used only the term 'phalanx' or 'phalangites' (5.53.3,79.5; 10.29.5,30.5; 16.18.4). If that phalanx included also Oriental soldiers, Polybius would have considered it necessary to distinguish somehow between them and the Greco-Macedonians, just as he listed the phalanx of the immigrant military settlers separately from the phalanx of the Egyptian and Libyan natives, aside from the phalanx of the Greek mercenaries, in describing the Ptolemaic deployment in the battle of Raphia, although all of them were positioned next to each other (5.65.3–4,5,8–9). Furthermore, as a historian who tried to explain the rise of Rome and the decline of the Macedonian world (including the Seleucid kingdom) by political, social and military factors,[36] Polybius would certainly have avoided disguising the true composition of the Seleucid phalanx and calling its soldiers 'Macedonians' if in fact it had degenerated and comprised mainly native Oriental personnel.

In addition to this, the data on the numerical strength of the Seleucid phalanx in relation to that of the Greco-Macedonian military settlers indicate that at most it included an insignificant number of native Syrians. The Seleucid phalanx (excluding the Royal Guard) at the Daphne procession numbered 15,000 (Polybius 30.25.5).[37] As shown above,[38] the army that appeared at Daphne

---

[35] See below pp. 418–19, esp. nn. 25–7, and pp. 569–70.

[36] On this matter see Walbank 1980: 41–58. In that article Walbank does not dwell on the military reasons for the dominance of the Roman world (esp. Polybius 18.28–32).

[37] See pp. 416–17 below and esp. n. 21.   [38] See pp. 30–40 above.

represented the entire potential of the forces in the western part of
the empire that could be mobilized at the time for a one-time mission,
and it is universally agreed that the military settlements supplied
soldiers for the phalanx units. And indeed the number of military
settlers in that part of the realm already considerably exceeded the
figure of 15,000 cited for phalanx warriors. Two of the four large
military settlements in northern Syria whose population is explicitly
described in the sources as Greco-Macedonian – Antioch and
Cyrrhus – numbered 5,300 and 6,000 citizens respectively, and the
last number held true for the *eleutheroi*, the free population of Seleucia, at least some of whom were soldiers.[39] It is not likely that
Apamea, where according to Strabo most of the Macedonians were
concentrated (16.2.10 (752)),[40] had fewer citizen–settlers. Aside
from the large settlements in northern Syria, the military settlement
in Syria and Mesopotamia can be described as rather modest: the
number of known settlements is small,[41] and judging from Dura
Europus, the only one for which we have relatively abundant information, the number of settlers in each was no more than a hundred
or at most two hundred, as was the case in the Ptolemaic Kerkeosiris
and the Seleucid *katoikiai* in Asia Minor.[42] The overall strength of the
military settlers in the western part of the empire seems therefore to
have stood at about 25,000–30,000, which is almost double the
number appearing in the Daphne procession. Leaving half the
settlers at home for local defence was reasonable and was also the rule
for Jewish armies during the Second Temple period.[43] In any case,
these numerical data make it unnecessary to conclude that the
phalanx force at Daphne included soldiers of Oriental ethnicity or
any at all from any besides the old Greco-Macedonian settlements.

It is true that the information cited above as to the size of the
citizen population in the great north Syrian military settlements applies to the last quarter of the third century B.C., and it might be
argued that in the time elapsed up to Antiochus IV the number of
Greco-Macedonian settlers had diminished, or the number among
them capable of fighting had, and their places were filled by recruits
from the local Oriental population. Such a policy reversal involving

[39] On the citizens, inhabitants and soldiers of these three cities see Bar-Kochva 1979: 28–
31. For the numbers see esp. Polybius 5.50.7–8,57.4,61.1; Malalas 201.12–16. Cf. Downey
1961: 81–2.
[40] See further Bar-Kochva 1979: 28–9.
[41] See ibid. 31–2.
[42] On the small number of military settlers in Dura Europus see Rostovtzeff 1940: 1.498,
and in the *katoikiai* of Asia Minor, Bar-Kochva 1979: 43. On Ptolemaic Kerkeosiris see
Crawford 1971: 122–3.   [43] See p. 50 above.

the participation of Oriental soldiers in the phalanx forces would presumably have led to a considerable increase in the number of phalangites in comparison with the earlier period when they were drawn exclusively from the Macedonian settlements. The need to reinforce the heavy troops must have arisen in the wake of the lessons learned in the earlier battles: at Raphia the Seleucid army was defeated to a large extent because of the numerical inferiority of the phalanx force at its disposal compared with the Ptolemaic phalanx which was reinforced with native Egyptians.[44] At Thermopylae the Seleucid army as a whole was smaller than the enemy and was therefore compelled to deploy for defence in the narrow pass.[45] At Magnesia the heavy forces of the opposing sides were equal in number but the Seleucids failed in their attempt to decide the issue through an abundance of light and semi-heavy troops of mercenaries and auxiliaries, partly because of their inefficiency and the difficulties of coordinating those varied troops.[46] Moreover, the ejection of the Seleucids from Asia Minor after the battle of Magnesia meant that at least 6,000 phalangites from Phrygia and Lydia were lost to the Seleucid manpower pool.[47] And yet there was little discernible difference between the number of phalangites from Syrian and Mesopotamia during Antiochus Epiphanes' reign and during the long reign of his father, Antiochus III.[48] This numerical stability itself suggests that the phalangites continued to be drawn from that same human reservoir, the Greco-Macedonian military settlements.[49] It should be noted also that the information on the infantry Royal Guard, the elite permanent contingent of the phalanx, indicates that

[44] In all 35,000 Seleucid phalangites of all provenances (military settlers, Royal Guard, mercenaries) *versus* 61,000 Ptolemaic phalangites. On the numbers see Bar-Kochva 1979: 132,136–41, and there on the influence the numerical inferiority of the Seleucid phalanx had on the calculations of the two sides, the choice of battle site, and the course and outcome of the battle.

[45] Although there were 18,000 Seleucid soldiers in Greece, only 10,000 infantry and 500 cavalry took part in the battle along with 4,000 Aetolians, facing the Roman 20,000 infantry and 2,000 cavalry; see Bar-Kochva 1979: 15–18,158. On the influence the relative strength had on Antiochus III's choice of battle site and conduct of the battle see ibid. 160.

[46] In that battle the Seleucids had 60,000 infantry and 12,000 cavalry against 30,000 Romans, but only 26,000 of their infantry were 'heavies' facing 22,000 Roman legionaries. See ibid. 165–9. On the 'contribution' of the auxiliary troops to the defeat at Magnesia and the insufficient utilization of the phalanx see ibid. 171–3.

[47] See p. 37 above.　　　　　　　　　　　　[48] See pp. 37–8 above.

[49] G. M. Cohen (1978: 31–2) argues that there is an increase in the size of the phalanx from 20,000 at Raphia to 25,000 at Daphne despite the restrictions on recruitment stipulated by the Treaty of Apamea, and that in his view indicates that the phalanx was no longer purely Macedonian. These figures are incorrect: the phalanx at Raphia numbered 35,000, of whom 20,000 were reserves from military settlements, 10,000 Royal Guard, and 5,000 Greek mercenaries, while at Daphne there were 15,000 reserve soldiers and 10,000 Royal Guard. On the figures cf. also pp. 36ff. above.

its members were recruited from the Macedonian military settlements even early in the second half of the second century when the restrictions against enlisting local Syrian forces in the Seleucid army were lifted.[50]

The conclusion regarding the refusal to recruit native Syrians as phalangites is indirectly supported by an examination of the composition of the Seleucid light troops. The Seleucid kings included in their armies light units from all over the empire as well as the immediate neighbourhood. It was relatively cheap and easy to call up units from among the peoples of the empire who had inexpensive traditional weapons and not very complicated combat methods, whose base was often quite near the battle area, and could supply manpower in almost unlimited quantity. Accordingly, soldiers were recruited from most of the nations of the empire. The Seleucid army included of the Iranian peoples Elymaeans, Cyrtians, Cissians, Cadusians, Carmanians and Cardacians; from the Near East, Arabs and Jews; from Asia Minor – Cilicians, Cappadocians, Galatians, Pamphylians, Carians, Pisidians and Mysians.[51] However, the Syrians and the various Mesopotamian peoples are entirely missing from the three available lists of Seleucid manpower, including even the Daphne procession during the reign of Antiochus Epiphanes when the Seleucid army was in dire need of light forces owing to the absence of the contingents from the eastern satrapies then seething with rebellion.[52] Furthermore, the procession was conducted in Syria, and if way had been found to include in it light and semi-heavy forces from the regions north of the Taurus from which the Treaty of Apamea forbade recruiting (such as Mysia, Galatia, as well as Thrace), Syrian units of that type would certainly have participated in the procession if it was in fact customary for native Syrians to fight in the Seleucid army.

The Seleucid rulers were guided by a sound instinct in their consistent refusal to recruit Syrians in light units (not to speak of heavy ones). They were cautious about enhancing the military potential of Syrians and Babylonians or giving them weapons, because they realized that arming the natives inhabiting the nerve centre of the empire might endanger its very existence in the case of insurrection, as happened in Egypt after the battle of Raphia, while rebellion by Persians or Medes, for example, would not jeopardize the power base of the dynasty, and heavy forces could quickly be

[50] See pp. 422–4 below.
[51] See Table 1, p. 34, and on the status and identification of the various nations Bar-Kochva 1979: 43–8.   [52] See Table 2, p. 117 below.

deployed from northern Syria to suppress it. The Diaspora Jews (as distinct from Palestinian Jews)[53] were the only 'Syrian' people admitted to the ranks of the Seleucid army since, being a foreign element where they resided, they could presumably be trusted to identify with the central authorities and not cooperate with the local population when put to the test. And indeed that assumption generally proved to be valid. Two occasions are known in which Jewish soldiers acted effectively when the main imperial forces were occupied in other sectors: at the start of the 'Brothers War', in the 230s B.C., Jewish soldiers from Babylonia blocked a Galatian attempt to invade Babylonia from the north-west; and around 210 B.C. some two thousand Jewish soldiers helped to restore order in Phrygia and Lydia (*Ant.* 12.147–53).[54] Even so, those Jews do not seem to have served in the great battles as phalangites, but operated in one or another tactical deployment in the region they were responsible for.

The few references to 'Syrian' soldiers in other sources cannot shake the conclusion regarding the extreme caution displayed by the Seleucid authorities in connection with providing Syrian natives with arms of any kind. The 'Syrian' expeditionary force which according to Pausanias took part in the defence of Thermopylae against the Galatians in 279 B.C (10.20.5) should be identified as Macedonian military settlers from Syria. It was altogether natural that the Greek Pausanias, in reporting on various elements in the Hellenistic world coming to the rescue of the mother country, should refer to their place of residence rather than to their ethnic origin.

Syrian mercenaries, as distinct from regular soldiers, are mentioned in two cases: 400 'Syrian' mercenaries figured at Corinth in the service of Antigonus Gonatas (Plut. *Arat.* 18.2–4 and 24.1; Polyaenus 6.5.1). However, it has been suggested that the word 'Mysians' was confused with 'Syrians' in the primary source for the story.[55] In any case, the story provides no evidence that native Syrians were employed by the Seleucids themselves. The same is true for Josephus' statement that Alexander Jannaeus had Pisidians and Cilicians in his army but not Syrians, because the latter were hostile (*Ant.* 13.374). Substantively speaking, probably in both cases the reference is to the offspring of military settlers in northern Syria who

---

[53] See p. 84 and n. 45 above.   [54] See pp. 500–7 below, and pp. 85–6 above.
[55] Griffith 1935: 68 n. 3.

sought a livelihood outside their native land[56] and hired out for army work. At any rate, in the second half of the second century B.C. the employment of native Syrians in the Seleucid armies was initiated,[57] so that the situation in the time of Jannaeus cannot be projected to apply to the composition of Antiochus Epiphanes' army.

The question of mixed marriages in the military settlements

In addition to the assumption that Syrians were enlisted in the Seleucid Phalanx, the second suggestion noted at the beginning of the chapter has been that the soldiers from the military settlements themselves were no longer 'racially pure', and were the offspring of several generations of mixed marriages. In order to clarify whether the Seleucid army degenerated, what actually interests us is not the question of absolute racial purity, but whether the ethnic composition of the Seleucid phalanx deteriorated to the point where it would necessarily diminish its military capacity below that of the Macedonian armies of Alexander the Great and the Diadochs. To confirm this it is not enough to cite isolated instances of mixed marriages or even the impression that they were not uncommon. It is necessary to be convinced that the miscegenation was so widespread that the nature of the military settlements changed, their way of life having become more Oriental than Greco-Macedonian, and especially that the descendants of the first settlers in the course of the generations acquired the traits of the Orientals and lost the capabilites essential for the phalanx which had characterized the Macedonians at the end of the fourth century B.C.

The claim concerning widespread intermarriage is based first and foremost on the precedent established in Alexander the Great's time when he recognized the marriages of 10,000 Macedonian soldiers to Asiatic women (Arrian, *Anab.* 7.4.8 and parallels). Some of the men were among the ten thousand veterans who later left those wives and their children in the East to return to Macedonia with Craterus (ibid. 7.12.2). As the Greco-Macedonian phalanx at the disposition of the Diadochs upon which the Seleucid military settlements were later based numbered about 50,000 men,[58] this means that up to

---

[56] Cf. the son of a settler from Magnesia in Asia Minor who was a physician at Amphissa in Greece, in Schwyzer 1922: no. 369; and see Bar-Kochva 1979: 225 n. 97.

[57] See p. 437 below.   [58] See Griffith 1935: 41.

20% of the first settlers had Asiatic wives. However, that says nothing about the other settlers, and in fact following a possibly stricter policy on the part of the authorities, the offspring of those first mixed marriages may well have made every effort to marry Greco-Macedonian wives. It would be going too far to cite as evidence the policy and deeds of Alexander the Great, who himself married Asiatic women, whether because he wished to set an example of Asiatic–Macedonian integration, or for other political reasons of the time.[59] The Hellenistic courts, though they did not eschew marriage with commoners, insisted that spouses should be Greco-Macedonian (with the single exception of Seleucus I whose marriage to the Persian princess Apamea, formalized in the mass ceremony at Susiana, endured).[60] Their policy on the possibility of the ethnic integration of the military settlers therefore deserves consideration without reference to Alexander's demonstrative actions.

Along with the precedent mentioned, a number of assumptions have been made that seem to prove that mixed marriages continued to increase among the military settlers. Thus it is said that the first settlers, the demobilized soldiers, were an exclusively male community, that the import of women from Greece and Macedon was impossible, and that therefore the continuity of life could not be maintained in the settlements without Asiatic women, and abstention from marriage with the Oriental women was not feasible in view of the way the settlements were scattered all over the empire. The first assumption (which is the crucial one) is not correct. The Diadoch armies, the chief nuclei for the Seleucid military settlements, were regularly accompanied by the soldiers' wives and children who were counted as part of the army 'baggage' (*aposkeuē*; see, e.g., Diodorus 19.43.7; Justin 14.3.6). There is no reason to reject the notion that a considerable proportion of these wives were not Asiatics but had gone along when their husbands were recruited in Greece and Macedon at various times, or arrived later from the Aegean lands. These women certainly settled down in the new military settlements as did in later times the families of the Cretan mercenaries in Myus (*Milet* 3, nn. 33ff.) and the Jewish soldiers in Phrygia and Lydia (Jos. *Ant.* 12.149).[61] As to the other assumptions, they do not necessarily hold, for enough immigrant ethnic groups are known in

---

[59] On the rejection of the traditional explanation about a deliberate 'fusion' policy and the explanation of the intermarriages for other reasons, mainly the desire to legitimize the rule of Alexander and the satraps by marriage with local princesses, see Bosworth 1980: 10–12.

[60] See Seibert 1967: 1,122.

[61] See the discussion on the last two inferences in G. M. Cohen 1978: 33–5. On the 'baggage' cf. also pp. 45–6 and n. 61 above.

history (ancient included) who successfully maintained their ethnic particularity despite dispersion and isolation. A debatable question is whether the Macedonian settlers had a good enough reason and high enough motivation for avoiding intermarriage, and if their segregation had a salutary or nefarious effect on their ability to maintain their strength, power and existence. The effects are in fact mixed, and rather than rely upon speculations that are often quite academic, it is preferable to examine the sources.

For purposes of this discussion, a distinction must be made between rural military settlements and the urban ones which were granted the status of *polis*. It might seem at first glance that the former, which were smaller and more widely scattered, would be more fertile ground for the spread of mixed marriages than the large urban ones of northern Syria. Yet it is doubtful whether such marriages were particularly numerous even in Ptolemaic Egypt where native Egyptians were accepted in the army. Of the large amount of surviving material, there is little evidence clearly indicating mixed marriages.[62] At any rate, there is no justification for speaking of a general trend, nor of an attenuation of the Greco-Macedonian national character of the settlers in those villages. The relatively meagre Seleucid material includes the story of Diophantes, evidently a military settler at Abae on the edge of the Syrian–Arabian desert (Diodorus 32.10.2–9). He married a local woman, but his children had Greco-Macedonian names, and his hermaphrodite daughter Heraïs married a Macedonian. When she turned into a man, he enlisted in the Macedonian cavalry unit, so that as the story shows, despite the Syrian-Arab mother, the family obviously remained Greco-Macedonian in spirit and way of life.[63] Be this as it may, such marriages in remote settlements certainly prevented the degeneration that inbreeding could produce[64] and did not lead to a decrease in the fighting capacity of the settlers' sons.

The dimensions of the intermarriage phenomenon in the rural settlements, however, are of little relevance to our main interest, for the phalangites who fought against Judas Maccabaeus (and the Seleucid phalanx in general) came chiefly from the urban settlements. They included reserves from among military settlers in the western part of the realm, and the Royal Guard. The former came

---

[62] See, e.g., *OGIS* 130; *W. Chr.* no. 51; *SB* 1567. *P. Rainer* (*SB* 8008, l. 49) refers to concubines of the soldiers stationed in Syria and Phoenicia and not to legitimate wives. On this question cf. Vatin 1970: 134–5; Fraser 1972: 1.71ff.; Hengel 1976: 87.

[63] See also G. M. Cohen 1978: 34–5, and Vatin, 1970: 139.

[64] On the marriage of relatives at Dura Europus see p. 109 n. 75 below.

mainly from the large settlements with *polis* status in northern Syria[65] and the latter, which comprised settlers' sons from both the west and east of the empire, also consisted primarily of men from urban settlements, for the majority of settlers in the Upper Satrapies were concentrated too in the cities of eastern Media.[66] Thus for the present problem the important question is to what extent the original descent and tradition of the Greco-Macedonian population was preserved in the cities.

The direct relevant information available on the Seleucid empire is not very plentiful and is limited mostly to written material found in the Dura Europus excavations. Unfortunately most of the surviving material is from the Parthian period, after 116 B.C., when the Parthians conquered the city, rebuilt it and resettled it. And yet quite a lot can be learned even from that material. The fortified place that was called Europus during the Seleucid period was a military settlement with the status of a *polis*,[67] founded by Macedonians (Isidorus of Charax, *GGM* 1.248, l. 9). The settlers who were citizens of the town, the *Europaioi* (unlike the others), all had typically Macedonian names throughout the Seleucid period (*P. Dura* 15, 34).[68] During the period of Parthian rule a few Oriental names possibly started to appear among them, though the evidence is only from the Roman period (*P. Dura* 17c).[69] Tarn has pointed out that from 33–32 B.C. onwards there was in the place a *genearkhēs* (= head of the clan) – a position that did not exist in the Seleucid period. Tarn correctly concluded that this official's function was to ensure the Greco-Macedonian character of the *genos* in the place to which new ethnic elements had been added.[70] No women's names have survived from the Seleucid period, but the names of women of the ruling class found in two temples of a later date at Dura are definitely Macedonian.[71] It might be argued that they could have been Asiatics who changed their names, but in cases of that kind, as we

---

[65] See p. 101 above.

[66] See Bar-Kochva 1979: 32 on these settlements and their status, and p. 39 above on their numerical potential.

[67] See esp. the parchments in *P. Dura* nos. 12,15, and Welles' notes ad loc. See further Griffith 1935: 156–7. On the status of Dura Europus as a military settlement see Bar-Kochva 1979: 39, and ibid. 22 for the criteria for distinguishing a military settlement.

[68] Welles 1951: 262–3; id. in *P. Dura* pp. 7,58. The numbers designating the parchment rolls and papyri noted in the Welles article do not correspond to those in the final edition.

[69] Welles 1951: 255,262; id. *P. Dura* p. 7.

[70] See Tarn 1951: 37–8.

[71] Welles 1951: 263, and see: *P. Dura* 48; *The Excavations at Dura Europos Conducted by Yale University and the French Academy of Inscriptions and Letters, Preliminary Report of the Third Season, 1929–1930* (New Haven 1932): 18–35,51–3; *Preliminary Report of the Fifth Season, 1931–1932* (New Haven, 1934): 131ff.

know from other places, usually the Oriental name is retained as well, and only one such instance was found at Dura (*P. Dura* 19), and it does not predate Trajan.[72] It should be noted as well that of the graffiti scratched in Greek on the city gates during the Parthian period only 20 % are Semitic names, and even those are attributable to wayfarers (on the basis of their content and form) and not to the citizens, or even to the other residents of Dura.[73] It was only in the Roman period, after A.D. 240 that the local citizens were no longer called Europaioi but by the Oriental name Dourenoi (or *Dourani*, in Latin) and at that time the number of Orientals there increased significantly.[74] It may therefore be concluded that, despite the paucity of material from the Seleucid period itself, it is very unlikely that the Macedonian settlers intermarried to any significant extent with the local women while serving in the Seleucid army.[75]

Tarn, who in his books frequently opposes the prevalent notion about the military settlers' loss of Greco-Macedonian identity and ethnic particularity, presents further evidence from literary sources.[76] Not all of it stands up to criticism,[77] and the rest needs to be further clarified. As to the situation in the city settlements, information on the definitely Macedonian character of a former military settlement, Seleucia on the Tigris, in the first century B.C is provided by Tacitus (*Ann.* 6.42) and Pliny (*Nat. Hist.* 6.122). Tacitus, based here on a Greek source,[78] is more detailed and can be construed as applying to the cultural rather than the ethnic plane,[79] which Pliny likewise may suggest ('Macedonumque moris'). Yet the two planes are connected, and it is difficult to believe that the *polis* of Seleucia could have retained its Macedonian character in the first century B.C., some four centuries after its establishment by Seleucus Nicator, if marriage with natives had already been a common practice in the reign of Antiochus Epiphanes. Tarn also mentions the appellation

[72] Welles 1951: 265.
[73] Ibid. 266, and see *The Excavations at Dura Europos, Preliminary Report on the Second Season 1928–1929* (New Haven, 1931): 153ff.
[74] Welles 1951: 262,270ff.; id. *P. Dura* pp. 6–7.
[75] Vatin (1970: 137) claims that mixed marriages were common in Dura Europus from the start of Macedonian settlement there, but does not provide any real evidence. The example he cites of the marriage of related Macedonians is isolated and late (of the first century A.D.) and at most suggests that there was an avoidance of mixed marriages. See also G. M. Cohen 1978: 34.
[76] Tarn 1951: 34–8.
[77] The evidence in Livy 37.54.18 (Tarn 1951: 37) is irrelevant because the Rhodes delegates are referring to the ancient cities of Asia Minor (as suggested by Polybius 21.22.14).
[78] See Hengel 1976: 83.
[79] 'civitas potens...neque in barbarum corrupta sed conditoris Seleuci retinens' (= a powerful city and never degenerated into barbarism but retained [its faithfulness] to [the memory of] Seleucus [its] founder).

μιξέλληνες (= mixed Greeks)[80] which in Plutarch (*Crassus* 31.1) is applied by a Greek to two people in the camp of the Parthian general, Surenas, around 50 B.C.[81] If it is not a pejorative because they bowed to Crassus, the term suggests that even under the Parthians a distinction was made between Greeks and half-Greeks.

To end this discussion it is worth considering the data regarding the practice elsewhere in the eastern cities, particularly in the Ptolemaic empire. As the Ptolemies were not especially concerned to safeguard the Macedonian character of their army, and later even its 'foreign' character was diluted, Ptolemaic material can be cited as evidence only if there was a strict policy in regard to the maintenance of the Greco-Macedonian ethnic exclusivity in urban population concentrations. The fact is that in the few Ptolemaic settlements that had the status of *polis*, mixed marriages were expressly forbidden even in the second century A.D., and the offspring of such were not granted all the privileges of citizenship in the Greek polis (*P. Gnomon* §38–51; *W. Chr.* no. 27).[82] If that was the Ptolemaic practice, how much more so that of the Seleucids. It is therefore possible to conclude quite confidently that most of the Greco-Macedonian soldier-settlers retained their ethnic exclusivity.[83]

In addition to the reasons given above regarding the exclusion of full Orientals from the Seleucid phalanx (most of whose warriors were settler-citizens in the towns), it should be emphasized that people who rejected intermarriage with native inhabitants of the *polis* certainly did not admit full Orientals into the citizen body. Against the integration of such people there also operated the principle that was common in the Greek and Hellenistic world, whereby citizenship was granted only to individuals who, in addition to having an ephebic education, could prove that at least one of their parents was a citizen of that town.[84] It is not reasonable to suppose that one group of phalangite-settlers was so discriminated against in respect to civil rights in comparison with their fellow-soldiers who

---

[80] See Tarn 1951: 38,51.

[81] Cf. *Syll.*³ 495, ll.110ff.; Livy 38.17.9; Latyschev 1916: no. 32 (Olbia).

[82] See esp. Fraser 1972: 1.71–3,76–8, 2.787; cf. Rostovtzeff 1940: 1.324–5, 2.1058, 3.1394 n. 121; A. H. M. Jones 1971: 302–3,473; Vatin 1970: 132–6; Hengel 1976: 82. On the complex and controversial question of civilian rank and the relationship between membership in a *politeuma* and the *polis* see the comprehensive treatment in Fraser 1972: 1.46ff., and Kasher 1985: 168ff., as well as Kasher 1977: 148–61.

[83] For a correct view of the reluctance of the Greek and Macedonian settlers in the East to contract mixed marriages (although the author does not restrict his conclusion to the military settlements) see Hengel 1976: 82–93. At the same time Hengel believes that a change took place after the battle of Magnesia which was even more drastic among the Seleucids than among the Ptolemies.

[84] See Fraser 1972: 1.71–2 and A. H. M. Jones 1940: 160; Taubenschlag 1955: 582.

were also phalangite-settlers in the very same city. This conclusion is also supported by the numerical stability of the military settlers owning land in the capital, Antioch, for which some demographic data are available. At the start the city had 5,300 citizens, some of them Athenians, undoubtedly settled in nearby Antigonea earlier by Antigonus Monophthalmus, and Macedonians settled by Seleucus I Nicator (Malalas 201.12–16).[85] This figure is only slightly smaller than the number of citizens Plato considered ideal for a city (*Leges* 737.5,740.4–5) and approximately the number in nearby Seleucia and Cyrrhus. It was doubled only in Julian's time, despite the great expansion of the urban population (Strabo 16.2.5; John Chrysostom, *PG* 50.591; Libanius, *Epist.* 1137). The number of land parcels in the town then, in the fourth century A.D., came to only 10,000 (Julian, *Misopogon* 362.3).[86] It thus appears that although the city, originally founded as a military settlement, acquired a civilian tinge, the land was kept for the descendants of the first settlers.

The Seleucid phalanx in action

With regard to the phalanx standard of performance, the data and descriptions from the time of Antiochus III, in the third or fourth generation of military settlements, indicated no deterioration. Appian and to an extent even Livy (following Polybius) describe it as a very experienced and well-trained force whose members were outstandingly brave (Appian, *Syr.* 32(161),35(181–2),37(190); Livy 37.43.7). It suffered serious setbacks at Raphia, Thermopylae and Magnesia, but in all three cases there were reasons related to developments on the flanks and the rear rather than to the performance of the phalanx itself.[87] On the other hand, in the battle of Panium where the flanks of the Seleucid phalanx were not exposed to the onslaught of enemy cavalry, it demonstrated its ability by 'breaking' the heavy Ptolemaic formations (Polybius 16.18–19).[88]

[85] See also Downey 1961: 81.
[86] That Julian is referring to public land parcels (suggested by Liebeschuetz 1972: 149–50, and Downey 1951: 318) is not likely; the passage is clearly phrased and the word ἰδίᾳ (= privately) is stressed, while the antonym κοινῇ (= in common) does not appear at all. For other grounds against this suggestion see Liebeschuetz himself.
[87] On the exposure of the phalanx to cavalry assault from the flanks at Magnesia and Raphia see Livy 37.42; Appian, *Syr.* 35; Polybius 5.85.6. Despite the last source, apparently only the Seleucid phalanx was exposed on both flanks at Raphia, while the Ptolemaic right wing remained in the field and outflanked the Seleucid centre; see Bar-Kochva 1979: 135–7. On the danger of an attack from the rear at Thermopylae and the threat to the Seleucid camp and 'baggage' (*aposkeuē*) in that battle see Appian, *Syr.* 19(86–7).
[88] See Bar-Kochva 1979: 155–6.

As to Antiochus Epiphanes' time, the verdict of a good number of modern historians is that after the Treaty of Apamea the Seleucid army was a broken reed. That verdict is based not on that army's performance in the battlefield, but on the assumption that the heavy casualties in the phalanx (as well as in other units) at Magnesia, the removal of Asia Minor from Seleucid hegemony, and the recruitment restrictions north of the Taurus all irremediably destroyed the Seleucid army's manpower base. An analysis of the specific data, however, shows that assumption to be oversimplified. The phalangites from the military settlements west of the Taurus who fell at Magnesia were replaced by the younger generation, as shown by the numbers in the Seleucid phalanx who took part in the Daphne procession.[89] As for Asia Minor north of the Taurus, which the terms of the treaty amputated from the Seleucid body, it provided no more than 6,000 phalangites and some 500 horse that could be assigned outside their immediate neighbourhood, all together less than 20 % of the Seleucid phalanx force and an insignificant percentage of its cavalry.[90] With regard to other troops, while the Treaty of Apamea did forbid both the recruitment of mercenaries from the countries north of the Taurus and the utilization of war elephants, the Seleucids ignored these provisions, as is shown by various reports on the appearance of mercenaries from Asia Minor, Thrace and Crete, and on the use of elephants in the army of Antiochus Epiphanes. Despite the financial burden entailed by reparations payments to Rome, there is a certain increase in the number of mercenaries at Daphne, compared with Magnesia and Raphia.

Unfortunately, the chapters in Polybius and Diodorus describing the military accomplishments of Antiochus Epiphanes have not survived. Consequently we do not have sufficient information on the operational capacity of the army as a whole and the phalanx in particular in Judas Maccabaeus' time. Still, the rapid conquest of Egypt and the breakthrough westward from Pelusium in 169 and 168 B.C., which had not been accomplished by any Hellenistic army since the days of Perdiccas, indicate that the army was by no means ineffectual. While it is hard to imagine that Egypt would have fallen to Antiochus Epiphanes so easily if authority had not then been wielded by the pleasure-seeking Lenaeus and Eulaeus (see especially Diodorus 30.15), it must also be borne in mind that the Egyptians were the aggressors and therefore were not taken by surprise.[91]

---

[89] See p. 38 below.   [90] See Bar-Kochva 1979: 41–2.

[91] The events are reconstructed on the basis of the scanty and fragmentary sources in Mørkholm 1966: 64–101; Will 1967: 2.265–6; Bunge 1974: 57–85, and detailed bibliography

Moreover, internal crises of the same kind had occurred earlier in the history of Hellenistic Egypt (especially after 204 B.C.), but the Seleucid kings had not dared take advantage of them to invade the land of the Nile. The success of Antiochus IV must then have been a result of the superiority of his heavy troops.

The battle of Elasa, in which the Seleucid phalanx faced Judas Maccabaeus' heavy or semi-heavy forces, shows the former's admirable capacity for tactical planning, coordination of forces, restraint and perseverance (I Macc. 9.1–22).[92] The campaign was conducted at a late stage of the Revolt when the Antioch authorities had had time to become familiar with the extraordinary personality of Judas Maccabaeus, and hoped that his capture or death would enable them to put an end to the uprising. The expedition itself made its way swiftly through the eastern slopes of the Judaean Hills – an unexpected route which prevented Judas Maccabaeus from setting an ambush or clashing with the enemy during its ascent.[93] On reaching the Beth El mountain, by systematically destroying the population and property in the area north of Jerusalem, Bacchides compelled Judas Maccabaeus to join battle in the gentle hilly region south of Ramallah without further delay. At the time Judas Maccabaeus could not apply the 'scorched earth' method, both because he had become the unofficial leader of the Jewish population and because he was at odds with the supporters of the high priest, Alcimus, regarding the political objectives.[94] The battlefield Bacchides chose facilitated a controlled operation and a properly planned feigned retreat, the two elements that were the teeth of the tactical trap. The Seleucid army deployed for battle according to the classic pattern: in the centre were two large phalanx contingents (*phalangarkhiai* or *stratēgiai*), in the wings cavalry, and ahead of the phalanx light forces (*promakhoi*) of slingers and archers. Bacchides himself led the right wing where the picked cavalry was. Following the preliminary clashes between the light skirmishers, Bacchides gave the phalanx units the unusual order to attack the centre units of the Jewish army, and left the cavalry in the wings where it was. The Seleucid phalanx actually conducted a delaying action against the Jewish centre in order to seduce (or force) Judas Maccabaeus, who was in the Jewish left wing with his horsemen, into intervening in the battle. Bacchides hoped thus to draw him into a trap and prevent his

there. Notably the author of the Book of Daniel, a contemporary of the events, also evaluates the conquest of Egypt as a great achievement; 'And he shall do that which his fathers have not done, nor his fathers' fathers' (11.24).

[92] See in detail pp. 390ff. below.
[93] See also pp. 382–3, 552–9 below.   [94] Pp. 384–5 below.

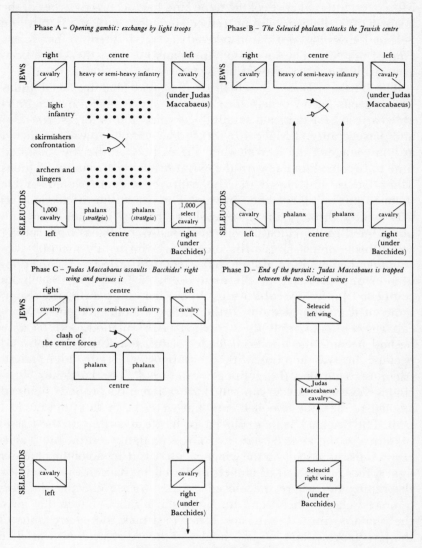

Diagram 4: *The battle of Elasa*

leaving the battlefield as he had done at the time of the defeat at Beth
Zacharia. A direct assault by the Seleucid cavalry would have
'broken' the Jewish cavalry and led to their retreat. As Bacchides did
not take the offensive and the Jewish infantry was in trouble, Judas
Maccabaeus could not allow himself to stand aside and not intervene.
The only remaining possibility as the forces were then deployed was

for him to attack Bacchides himself on his right wing and by killing the enemy commander to turn the tide. Aware of the methods Judas Maccabaeus had used in previous battles (cf. I Macc. 7.43), Bacchides expected such a reaction and planned accordingly. When Judas Maccabaeus attacked from the wing, Bacchides' cavalry deliberately retreated and drew Judas Maccabaeus into pursuing them far from the battlefield. At the same time some of the cavalry on the Seleucid left wing closed off Judas Maccabaeus from behind. The right wing turned to face the pursuers, and the 'victorious' Jewish wing was caught between hammer and anvil, unable to escape.

The battle of Elasa took place in a gentle, hilly plateau while the military encounters of the expedition to Egypt were certainly on level ground. But, even on uneven mountainous terrain where it was difficult to move about such as that of the Beth Zacharia area, the Seleucid heavy troops demonstrated quite satisfactory operational ability and relative flexibility.[95] A general decline in the composition, number and fighting ability of the Seleucid phalanx began in 152 B.C.: the war of succession in Antioch split the army among the various aspirants to the throne and interfered with the traditional system of recruitment and training for the Royal Guard and the reserve troops. The situation was aggravated by 147 B.C. with the loss of Media, which in addition to a concentration of cavalry also had a large number of military settlers who served as phalanx soldiers.[96] The rivals for the crown were obliged to recruit the Syrian population as an essential supplementary force against their opponents.[97] Native local manpower became a regular component of the imperial armies and lowered their powers of resistance both against mutinous domestic elements such as the new Hasmonaean state, and against external enemies such as the Ptolemies and the Armenian kingdom, not to mention the rising Roman and Parthian superpowers.

[95] See pp. 126–9 below.
[96] See Bar-Kochva 1979: 32–5,42,69–70. On the detachment of Media see Will 1967: 2. 339.
[97] See, e.g., I Macc. 10.30,71–8, 11.44–50. Cf. p. 437 below.

5

The Seleucid army and mountain warfare

Just as the mistaken notions about the national origin and military ability of the phalangites were employed to explain the failures of the Seleucid troops, so the victories of Judas Maccabaeus were explained on the premise that the phalanx combat method was antiquated and rigid, and prevented satisfactory performance in terrain that was hard to traverse. In this chapter we shall examine the available information on the number and weight of the light infantry contingents in the Seleucid army, the tactical composition of the units that operated in Judaea, as well as the ability to operate in mountainous areas of the light warriors separately and the army as a whole, including the phalanx troops.

The Seleucid army had no lack of units fit and well trained to fight in mountainous terrain. The various surveys of Seleucid manpower list soldiers from mountainous countries in the Aegean area, Asia Minor and the eastern satrapies making up the light and semi-heavy forces. These contingents comprised about half the total infantry,[1] and sometimes even more. They were assuredly not inferior to Judas Maccabaeus' men in fitness for mountain combat. Among the units mentioned as operating in Judaea at the time of the crisis the only nationals specifically noted in the Books of the Maccabees are the Cypriots, Mysians and Thracians.[2]

The Cypriots are referred to as serving in the garrison of the Jerusalem citadel in 172 B.C. (II Macc. 4.29), and perhaps elsewhere in the country in 164 B.C. (II Macc. 12.2). As a matter of fact, native

---

[1] Polybius 5.53,79, 7.15.4, 10.29.6, 30.25; Livy 35.48.5,49.6, 37.40; Appian, *Syr.* 32; Lucian, *Zeuxis* 8; Polyaenus 4.15, 8.39; Justin 27.2.10, 36.1.4; Plut. *Flam* 17.5; Phlegon, *FGrH* IIB, no. 257, F 36; *OGIS* 229, line 105, and many other sources.

[2] No informative value should be attributed to Josephus' statement on the settlement of Macedonians in the Akra (*Ant.* 12.252) as it is merely an interpretive paraphrase of I Macc. 1.33–4. See p. 443 below and n. 26 for details. Porphyry, *FGrH* IIB, no. 260, F50, is certainly based on Josephus; Porphyry used Josephus extensively throughout his work (cf. F57, l. 7).

Table 2. *The Seleucid army and its tactical units* *

	Phalanx	Semi-heavy infantry	Light infantry	Heavy cavalry	Light cavalry	Total
Battle of Raphia (217 B.C.)	20,000 Macedonians 10,000 *argyraspides* 5,000 Greeks	1,000 Thracians	1,500 Cretan archers 1,000 Neo-Cretan archers 500 Lydian akontists 10,000 Arabs 1,000 Cardacians 5,000 Dahae and Cilicians 2,000 Persian and 'Agrianian' bowmen and slingers 5,000 Medes, Cissians, Cadusians and Carmanians	4,000 military settlers 2,000 Royal Guard		
Total	35,000	1,000	26,000	6,000		68,000
Battle of Magnesia (190 B.C.)	16,000 Macedonians 10,000 *argyraspides*	3,000 Tralli(?) 3,000 Thracians 2,000 Cappadocians 3,000 Galatians 4,000 Pisidians, Pamphylians and Lycians(?)	3,000 Tralli(?) 1,500 Cretan archers 1,000 Neo-Cretan archers 2,500 Mysian archers 8,000 Elymaean archers and Cyrtian slingers 2,700 'Orientals' 1,500 Carians and Cilicians 4,000 Pisidians, Pamphylians and Lycians 1,000 elephant guard	6,000 cataphracts 2,000 Royal Guard	1,200 Dahaeans (Scythians) 2,500 Galatians 500 'Tarentines' (mounted archers)	
Total	26,000	8,000–15,000	18,200–25,200	8,000	4,200	71,400
The Daphne procession (165 B.C.)	15,000 Macedonians 5,000 *argyraspides*	5,000 'Roman style' 3,000 Thracians 5,000 Mysians(?) 5,000 Galatians	3,000 Cilicians 5,000 Mysian (archers?)	1,500 cataphracts 1,000 Nisaeans 2,000 Royal Guard		
Total	20,000	13,000–18,000	3,000–8,000	4,500		45,500

* For a clarification of the weapons of the various units see Bar-Kochva 1979: 48-75.

Cypriots, who were probably armed with light weapons, did not leave any impression on Hellenistic military history.[3] It would therefore be more likely that these 'Cypriots' were some garrison troops who had formerly served the Ptolemies in Cyprus and defected to the Seleucid side, as was done by Ptolemy Macron, their governor, a few years later, in 168 B.C.[4] The Cyprus garrison comprised a variety of troops from Greece (Achaeans), Crete, Thrace and Asia Minor (Ionians, Lycians and Cilicians), who were organized in their own communities.[5] In light of the comparative material about these nationals, the Achaeans were heavies, the Cretans lights and perhaps also some heavies, the Thracians semi-heavies, and the troops from Asia Minor semi-heavies (Ionians and Lycians) and lights (Cilicians). As heavy infantry certainly was not stationed to guard a built-up area, the 'Cypriots' in the Jerusalem garrison should be seen as one of these groups of nationals, armed with light or semi-heavy equipment.

The Mysians gained control of Jerusalem by force on the eve of the religious persecutions (II Macc. 5.24; I Macc. 1.29–40). Mysia being at the time outside the boundaries of the Seleucid kingdom, these soldiers doubtless served as mercenaries, like the 5,000 of their compatriots who took part in the Daphne procession (Polybius 30.25.3). Their weapons are not mentioned in I Maccabees nor in the description of the procession. At the battle of Magnesia, some 2,500 Mysian archers took part (Livy 37.40.8),[6] but the fact that they were despatched to fight a civilian population in a built-up urban area may indicate that by the reign of Antiochus Epiphanes they were already semi-heavies equipped in the Galatian style which had spread throughout Asia Minor and been adopted by other peoples such as the Cappadocians, the Pisidians, the Pamphylians, and the Bithynians.[7] That style of combat had partisans in the region both because of the great impression the Galatians had made on the local inhabitants during their invasion of the Ionian cities in 279 B.C., and because the method itself was 'all-purpose' and well suited to the conditions and needs of those countries. Quite possibly the Seleucids, who controlled Asia Minor till 190 B.C., encouraged the local people to equip themselves thus in order to have a reserve

[3] See Launey 1949–50: 1.487–9.
[4] See in detail pp. 536–7 below.
[5] On the *koina* of the mercenaries in Cyprus see Launey 1949–50: 2.1032–6.
[6] On the Mysians in other Hellenistic armies and their armament see Launey 1949–50: 1. 438–44; Griffith 1935: 143,145 and passim.
[7] For the equipment of these peoples see Launey 1949–50: 1.433ff.; and especially Livy 37.40.10,14; and see the gravestones from the Sidon necropolis (Plates IX, X).

of semi-heavy soldiers available. And indeed the Menas inscription provides testimony illustrating the equipment of a Mysian soldier in that style in about 150 B.C.[8] It is less likely that they were phalangites recruited from the military settlements on the border between Mysia, Phrygia and Lydia, who were known as 'Myso-Macedonians'.[9] After the battle of Magnesia, the Greco-Macedonian military settlers in Asia Minor began to serve the Attalids, their new lords, in accordance with the usual conditions and obligations of Hellenistic military settlement.[10]

Thracian cavalry figures in Gorgias' army at the battle of Marisa (II Macc. 12.35), and apparently the army of Seron which made the Beth Horon ascent consisted of Thracian infantry.[11] An inscription recently discovered in Jerusalem which may be attributed to the garrison in the city citadel at the time of the Revolt seems to contain some indication of the Thracian descent of at least some of the soldiers.[12] These Thracians were indigenous, probably equipped as semi-heavies in the Thracian style which was somewhat lighter than the other semi-heavies of the period.[13] Thracian soldiers occupied a respectable place in the armies of the Hellenistic period,[14] and 3,000 of them even took part in the Daphne procession (Polybius 30.25.5).

[8] Bar-Kochva 1974: 14–23, esp. 15.

[9] On them see Griffith 1935: 145,167,178–9; Magie 1950: 2.974; Bar-Kochva 1979: 41.

[10] Griffith 1935: 171ff.; and see Welles 1934: no. 51.   [11] See p. 133 below.

[12] See the inscription *SEG* 30, no. 1695, and the photograph in Applebaum 1980: 49. If the Ares referred to in the opening line is not a person's name (which is still a possibility), the oath-takers seem to have belonged to the Seleucid garrison in Jerusalem during the period of the Revolt: the oath by Ares, the God of war, along with words connected with war and casualties (l. 7), suggest that the oath-takers were Hellenistic soldiers. Since the inscription was incised on a small, simple piece of chalkstone of the kind common in Jerusalem in the neighbourhood of the High Commissioner's Residence and of the Mount of Olives, there is little chance that it was brought to the city from a distance, and it most likely originated in Jerusalem. The palaeography points in general to the second century B.C. The poor quality stone on which the inscription is incised and the use of a vow of revenge in the name of Ares ('flogging the priests' in l. 4), which was usually accompanied by a rather cruel ceremony (Aeschylus, *Sept.* 42), indicate that the oath-takers were in dire straits and rather frustrated. That was the case for the garrison at various times in the course of the Hasmonaean Revolt, especially after the death of Nicanor in 161 B.C. However, a definite dating requires thorough epigraphical examination. The word *akra* itself is not mentioned in the remaining part of the inscription (against Applebaum 1980: 50–1).

As to the origin of oath-takers, the description of Ares as a flute player (Αὐλητής) may suggest that they were Thracian, for that epithet is not found among the many attached to Ares in the Greek and Hellenistic culture (Tymnes, *Anth. Pal.* 6.151, refers to a trumpet announcing the start of the battle), all of which stress his warlike attributes, cruelty, lack of restraint, etc. The epithet can be explained however, by the connection between Ares and Dionysus in the Thracian culture. Described as 'the flute player' in inscriptions and literary texts (Αὐλωνεύς: see, e.g., Farnell 1909: 5.306, no. 93), Dionysus was known in Thrace as a god of war (see ibid. no. 60), and Ares, who like Dionysus originated in Thrace, is a nickname for the latter (ibid. no. 60b) or his stand-in, or even his twin (Gruppe 1906: 2.1380–1).

[13] See p. 16 above.

[14] The sources are in Launey 1949–50: 1.366ff.; Griffith 1935: 253–4.

Because of the constant ferment in the eastern satrapies, they probably could not come from the Thracian military settlements in the satrapy of Persis.[15] The Thracian units stationed in Eretz Israel were therefore composed of ordinary mercenaries who fought with their traditional weapons. And indeed, the Thracian equipment – the shield and *rhomphaia*, the broad, long sword — was most suitable for countering the dangerous congregation of masses of people in urban areas, being 'demonstration dispersal' or 'crowd control' equipment of a sort. At various stages of the Revolt, especially at the beginning, these mobs constituted the greatest danger to the security of the representatives of the central authorities and their henchmen in Jerusalem and other places (cf. II Macc. 3.18, 4.41–2).

The participation of other than heavy forces is stated or hinted at on other occasions too: II Maccabees stresses the great ethnic variety of the Seleucid army in the battle of Ammaus (8.9). As the phalanx comprised mainly Greco-Macedonians, this points to the involvement of a considerable number of lights and semi-heavies in the campaign. The picked troops who accompanied Gorgias on the difficult night march to surprise Judas Maccabaeus at Mizpah (I Macc. 4.1,5) must have been composed of soldiers of this type. Slingers and archers are mentioned explicitly in the description of the battle of Elasa (I Macc. 9.10). The analysis of the battle of Beth Zacharia, too, indicates that the Seleucid army brought along a large number of lights,[16] and it was in that spirit that Josephus understood the description in I Maccabees (*Ant.* 12.372–3).

It was not only the ethnic contingents who demonstrated ability to manage in mountain areas. Some of the heavy units were even specially adapted for mountain warfare. The list of contingents at Daphne indicates that 5,000 men, half the Royal Guard, the spearhead and elite force of the phalanx formation, were retrained during Antiochus Epiphanes' reign in Roman weapons and tactics (Polybius 30.25.3).[17] The typically Roman armour is noted in the description of the battle of Beth Zacharia (I Macc. 6.35),[18] so that there is no doubt that soldiers of that contingent appeared in Eretz Israel at least after the death of Antiochus Epiphanes. The retraining was undertaken not only because of Antiochus IV's great predilection for Roman institutions and customs, he having lived in Rome

[15] On the military settlements of Thracians in Persis see Bar-Kochva 1979: 33–4,42, 50–2.

[16] See pp. 126–7, 329–30, 333–4 below.

[17] On the units the 5,000 'Roman' soldiers belonged to, and on the Royal Guard in general, see pp. 413ff., esp. 416–17, 431 above. Cf. pp. 98–100.

[18] See pp. 313–16 below.

as a hostage, but also in order to facilitate the operation of the army in the difficult mountain terrain that it would have to fight in on its expeditions to satrapies beyond the Tigris. Replacing the long cumbersome Macedonian *sarissa* with the *pilum* (or *hasta*), the shorter Roman lance, and increasing the distance between the individual soldiers as well as between the various *manipulae* added to the efficiency and versatility of the re-trained forces, enabled the individual soldier to fight on his own, and made the army as a whole more manoeuvrable.

An examination of the performance and achievements of the Seleucid army in mountainous areas shows that the light and semi-heavy troops knew how to manoeuvre and operate in battle arenas of that nature. The rupture of the Ptolemaic blocking formation at the Porphyrion pass on the Lebanese coast (south of the town of Damour) and on the cliff commanding it (Polybius 5.69; 218 B.C.) is a good example, as was the siege of Sardis against the rebellious satrap Achaeus in 214 B.C. (Polybius 7.15–18).[19] In these engagements the various Seleucid units operated in fine coordination according to a precise schedule in difficult topographical conditions. The battle at Porphyrion (Ras Nabi Yunas) merits brief attention.[20] The Ptolemies deployed a triple line of defence at the pass: some of the force, assisted by various traps, blocked the narrow passage between the mountain and the sea which at some points was no more than 50 m wide. A second contingent took up positions on the cliff that soared above the pass (Hill 59). The steep northern part of it commanded the bottleneck of the pass, and from the eastern more gently sloping part it was possible to come down into the pass in case of blockage. The third contingent was placed on the slopes of the Lebanon range, apparently on Hills 275 and 348 which blocked the mountain paths from the east to the pass. Antiochus left behind the heavy contingents, and his light troops reached the place from the north along the coast. The attack began simultaneously in all sectors: two arms of the Seleucid force carried out a diversionary action, one trying to climb to Hill 59 from the east, while the other fought at the pass itself to break through southwards. At the same time another arm commanded by Theodotus the Aetolian made a surprise attack on the blocking units on Hills 275 and 348 after

---

[19] On the background, topography and planning of the latter operation see Walbank 1957–79: 2.63–6; Hanfmann and Waldbaum 1975: 36.
[20] For a detailed reconstruction of the battle see Bar-Kochva 1979: 124–7. Cf. Galili 1954: 60–1 and 1968: 53–6. For various reasons it seems that the pass was not at Ras el Sadiyatt which Galili proposes (following Abel 1951: 77) but at Ras Nabi Yunas, north of Porphyrion (Bar-Kochva 1979: 125).

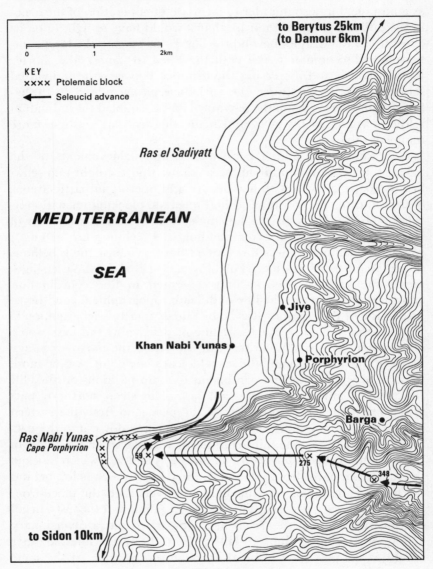

KEY

xxxx Ptolemaic block

◀━━━ Seleucid advance

to Berytus 25km
(to Damour 6km)

Ras el Sadiyatt

MEDITERRANEAN

SEA

● Jiye

Khan Nabi Yunas ●

● Porphyrion

Barga ●

Ras Nabi Yunas
Cape Porphyrion

59

275

348

to Sidon 10km

5 The Porphyrion pass

bypassing it from the east. With the removal of the Ptolemaic
blocking forces Theodotus continued on his way and, with the advantage of height, assaulted the Ptolemaic troops dominating the
pass. Theodotus' capture of Hill 59 tipped the scales and enabled the
arm fighting at the pass on the coastal strip to break through the pass
and rout the enemy.

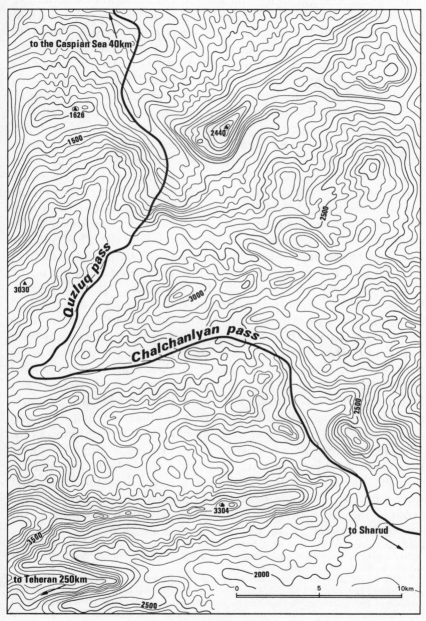

6 The Elburz pass

It was not only the lights and semi-heavies that were well trained for combined mobility in difficult terrain, but the army as a whole as is demonstrated especially in the description of Antiochus III's expedition through the dangerous pass in the Elburz range in the course of the 'anabasis' to Parthia and Bactria in 210 B.C. (Polybius 10.29–31).[21] Of great interest is the Seleucid plan for advancing which included the modern element of a 'soft patrol' to seek out an ambush, a method which does not seem to have many parallels in the Greek or Roman armies: the Seleucid expedition, which included forces of all sorts (among them phalangites, artillery, engineer units and pack animals), had to cross the Elburz range. On this route, which was 300 stadia long (57 km, ibid. 30.2), he had to cope with two passes, the Chalchanlyan and the Quzluq.[22] The road itself ran mainly through a canyon flanked on both sides by terrifying high cliffs. In addition, the canyon was obstructed at various points by rocks and fallen trees (ibid.). About 6 km before the Chalchanlyan pass, the canyon becomes very narrow, and the battle may well have been fought in that sector. Antiochus feared that Arsaces' troops (ibid. 29.1–2) or the Tapurians, the 'barbarian' allies of the Parthians, would gain control of those heights. In fact the latter did set an ambush from the dominating cliffs (ibid. 30.2–3), and the main problem was to find those hiding places and prevent the enemy from attacking the heavy troops. Antiochus despatched light forces to the cliffs, who with the help of local guides gained control of the heights on each side of the pass (ibid. 29.4, 30.7,9); into the pass itself he sent first a unit of Cretan archers equipped with shields which slowly made its way forward, in the hope that its vulnerable nature would draw enemy fire and so lead to the disclosure of the ambush points. The 'soft' archers were followed by semi-heavies equipped with the long Galatian shields covering almost the whole body who were to stop the Tapurians if they managed to break into the pass. After them came another semi-heavy unit equipped only with some body armour (ibid. 29.5–6), and probably armed only with swords in the

[21] Galili's reconstruction (1968: 52–3) is unacceptable. His mistake seems to arise from insufficient attention to the verb ἐφεδρευόντων (Polybius 10.30.9) which is the key to the understanding of the *stratēgēma* Antiochus used in that battle. See the linguistic and substantive analysis in Bar-Kochva 1979: 144–5.

[22] For the location of the expedition route and the problem involved see Walbank 1957–79: 2.236–9; Pédech 1958: 74–7. It should be added that Polybius mentions only one ascent (ἀνάβασις). But in fact the road that crosses the Elburz has two: from the plain near Shahrud the road ascends northwards to the Chalchanlyan pass and descends westward to the prominent bend where it turns northward and ascends to the Quzluq pass, from which it winds down through the plain of the Caspian Sea. Polybius apparently had only a general idea of the structure of the road, and for that reason does not locate the area of the battle very precisely either.

7 The battle arena near Beth Zacharia

Aerial view from above Kh. Beit Zakariya (Beth Zacharia) southwards (see also Map 15 on p. 310)

Key:
1 Ḥalḥul–Beth Zur ridge, the starting point of the Seleucid march
2 Beit Ummar ridge
3 Valley of Blessing
4 Kefar 'Etsyon Hill–Jewish ambush (?)
5 Russian Hill–Jewish ambush (?)
6 *Wadi Shukheit defile–the proposed battle site*
7 Yellow Hill
8 Tree Hill (Baluṭat el-Yerza)
9 Saddle north of the defile (the way to Beth Zacharia) – main Jewish force
10 Houses of Allon Shvut
11 'Ein 'Arrub

Thracian style of combat who were supposed to climb up and engage in hand-to-hand combat with the forces hidden in the cliffs in case the light snipers seizing the peaks were unsuccessful in breaking up the ambush. The phalanx and the 'baggage' brought up the rear. The plan worked out well: the 'barbarians' opened fire on the 'bait', thus revealing their positions to the snipers who had previously occupied the crest. The well-aimed arrows of the Seleucid lights neutralized the Tapurians and so endangered them that they left the ambush and fled (ibid. 30.7–9).

The ability to operate in this manner had not changed a generation later in the reign of Antiochus Epiphanes. On the contrary, in his day even the phalanx gave evidence of the capacity for acting, manoeuvring and winning in mountainous terrain, although it undoubtedly preferred to fight on level ground. Polybius' conclusion that phalanx warfare is useless in mountainous terrain (18.31.5–12) is based on the assumption that the phalanx operated only in a broad front line (ibid. 7). Although it refers to phalanx combat in general, that judgement is in fact based mainly on the conventional deployment adopted by the Antigonids with whom Polybius, a prominent cavalry officer of the Achaean League, was well acquainted. And indeed, Polybius' statement is included in the excursus to the battle of Cynoscephalae (197 B.C.) in which the Macedonian army of Philip V was beaten by a Roman task force commanded by Titus Quinctius Flamininus. In contrast, the Seleucid kings, at least in the second century B.C., had learned how to array the phalanx on a narrow front as well, and thus derive the greatest advantage from it in mountainous terrain too.

The adaptability of the Seleucid phalanx is exemplified in the illuminating description of Lysias' march from Beth Zur to Beth Zacharia, and of the battle that was fought near Beth Zacharia (I Macc. 6.28–47).[23] The route that the Seleucid forces followed goes through broad valleys, mountain ridges and passes. Judas Maccabaeus himself deployed around the Wadi Shukheit defile south of Beth Zacharia. The wadi, where the main confrontation took place, is overlooked on both sides by two hills and on the north by a saddle (I Macc. 6.31–3,40; *Ant.* 12.370; *Bell.* 1.41). It is hard to know whether Judas Maccabaeus set an ambush for the enemy or openly took up positions on the commanding peaks; perhaps he was bold enough to deploy openly on the saddle while concealing forces in the hills on either side of the defile. Which course he chose depends on the forestation of the area and the coverage available, matters which cannot at present be clarified. In any case, the advance and formation of the Seleucid troops was aimed at anticipating all possibilities.

The basic unit of the Seleucid army in that expedition (*ma'arākā* = 'formation', in the original Hebrew of I Maccabees) was composed of an elephant surrounded by 1,000 phalangites (500 on each side), themselves covered on the flanks by 500 horsemen (250 on each flank). Some of the 'formations' replaced the phalangites with foot soldiers equipped in Roman style (I Macc. 6.35,39). The result

[23] For a discussion of the sources, the location of the battlefield, the Seleucid formation and strength, the considerations taken into account by both sides and the reconstruction of the course of the battle see pp. 291ff. below.

was a 'mini-formation' of the conventional Seleucid deployment
involving phalangites in the centre and cavalry in the wings, with
elephants sometimes placed at centre, front or between the phalanx
units. All together, eight 'formations' of this type took part in the
action, augmented by light and semi-heavy infantry and cavalry.
The deployment of the Seleucid army changed in the course of the
expedition to adapt to changes in the terrain: in the broad valleys
such as the Valley of Blessing at the entrance to the 'Etsyon region
the 'formations' spread out the full width of the valley, with the
entire line provided with cavalry cover on the wings (I Macc. 6.38).
Each formation occupied between 120 and 150 metres, so that the
eight of them abreast stretched across the valley for about 1,700
metres. The light forces moved in front of the 'formations'. Upon
entering the defile the deployment was in file, with one 'formation'
following another, the first being preceded by a mounted, advance
scout company (*prodromoi*), while the rest of the light and semi-heavy
infantry and cavalry spread out on the hills on both sides of the defile
(I Macc. 6.40; *Ant.* 12.371). The transformation of the line, if Judas
Maccabaeus did set an ambush for the enemy, fits in with the rules
for movement and advance which Xenophon had recommended
and Alexander utilized on his way to the battle of Issus: varying the
marching order from a broad frontal line to a long column deployment according to the terrain when the enemy's position is unknown and a surprise attack is likely (Xen. *Hipp.* 4.1–3; Arrian, *Anab.*
2.8.2–4). Thus the advancing army is always on the alert ready to
return fire at any moment. If Judas Maccabaeus openly awaited the
enemy, the advance of the Seleucid army in a broad deployment
might be construed as a challenge to the Jewish combatants. It
could, however, be predicted that the challenge would not be taken
up and Judas Maccabaeus would not be induced to leave the positions he held dominating the pass. Thus spreading the army out, a
procedure which certainly slowed the advance, must have been
intended purely as a demonstration of power calculated to inspire
dread, as Antiochus III did on his way to besiege Larissa in Greece
in 191 B.C. (Livy 36.10.4). The impression a column was likely to
make was less than that of a full simultaneous display providing a
clear view of the elephants with their towers and handlers, their gold
and silver ornaments and opulent carpets, the horses with their
purple saddles, the soldiers' colourful garments, and in particular
the polished shields, armour and other equipment shining in the sun
(I Macc. 4.23, 6.35,37,39,43).

The desire to arouse dread by visual and vocal means and thus lower the Jews' morale and will to fight is very obvious in the overall Seleucid plan and especially in the utilization of the elephants. From the purely military point of view there was not much value to the elephants in this battle, for placing single elephants within heavy units prevented the exploitation of their speed and physical power in an assault. The aim was chiefly psychological: most of the Jewish soldiers were not familiar with the combat methods of the elephants and probably had never even seen an elephant in their lives.[24] Indeed the description in I Maccabees contains a clear echo of the shock the appearance of the Seleucid army gave the Jewish troops (6.38: 'frightening'; 6.41: 'and all trembled'). Resplendence in the battlefield, one of the characteristics of the Hellenistic armies, quite often paralysed the rival army's will to fight.[25]

The arrangement of the 'formations' one behind the other while traversing the defile explains the reason for this particular tactical structure. The object was to create a flexible, complete, self-sufficient and independent unit capable of changing its dimensions according to the width of the various defiles along the route; thus it could operate on its own in any possible sector in a reduced formation which exemplified in miniature the conventional tactical units and deployment of the Hellenistic combat system. Each of the 'formations' could be compressed into the narrowest part of the defile which was only about a hundred metres wide by reforming the phalanx into 32 rows. Some of the forward 'formations' also included soldiers equipped and trained for Roman-type warfare (instead of the phalangites of the rear 'formations') which increased the flexibility and operational capacity of the spearhead in the defile. We can only admire the originality of this solution in seeking a suitable way of exploiting the qualities and advantages of the conventional Hellenistic battle array even in an inconvenient topographical structure. The Jewish chances of success against the troops advancing in the defile were no greater than anticipated in a broad, level terrain: on the over-looking hills a battle was joined between well-trained Seleucid light and semi-heavy units and the Jewish defenders, who were thus prevented from attacking from above the 'formations' advancing through the defile. On the level though narrow ground of Wadi Shukheit and on the saddle, the Jewish

[24] Cf. the effectiveness of Antiochus I's Indian elephants against the Galatians the first time they appeared in Asia Minor (Lucian, *Zeuxis* 10–11; on the overall authenticity of the descriptions see Bar-Kochva 1973a: 1–3; and the activity of the elephants of King Pyrrhus of Epirus on his expedition to Italy (Plut. *Pyrrh.* 21.7; Justin 18.2)).

[25] See, e.g. Polybius 11.9; Appian, *Syr.* 33(169); Plut. *Eum.* 14, *Sulla* 16, *Luc.* 27; Onasander 28,29.

troops could do little against the crushing power of the Seleucid heavies who achieved their target as efficiently as they were accustomed to on the broad level field more convenient for heavy combat.

The great innovation in the battle of Beth Zacharia was the paramount function assigned the heavy forces despite the inconvenient terrain thanks to their flexible deployment, in contrast to their concentration in the rear in the Elburz expedition so as to prevent any contact with the enemy (Polybius 10.29.4 and 30.5). The danger of assault from the flanks threatening the Seleucid phalangites was less on the relatively low hills surrounding Wadi Shukheit than in the great Elburz range. On the other hand, the fear of an organized, massive frontal assault which was less likely at Elburz necessitated at Beth Zacharia the forward placement of the heavies right behind the mounted skirmishers. If the Jews had managed to scatter the light horsemen, they would have had to face the 'Roman' infantry or the impenetrable phalanx protected on the flanks in each 'formation' by cavalry which could embark upon an assault against the Jewish flanks or undertake a pursuit. It must also be taken into account that Antiochus III could not afford to lose phalanx soldiers in a confrontation of secondary importance in the Elburz pass *en route* to prime targets in Parthia and Bactria, while the high point of Lysias' expedition was the battle of Beth Zacharia.

6

The military achievements of the Jewish forces

As we have seen, the Jewish army more than once outnumbered the enemy and its equipment was by no means primitive. On the other hand, the Seleucid army was fit, experienced and rather familiar with mountain warfare, so that the standard of manpower and the battle site would not necessarily have constituted an advantage for the Jews. We should consequently re-examine the conventional admiration for the dimensions of the Jewish military achievement. Is that admiration justified? In order to reply to that question we must clarify whether and when the Jews fought against forces that properly represent, at least formally, the royal Seleucid army in number and quality and what the balance sheet of achievement against them was. It appears that of the various clashes of Judas Maccabaeus with the regular Seleucid forces, it was at Ammaus, Beth Zacharia and Elasa alone that his force was required to face royal armies. In two of these battles he failed, and only at Ammaus did he gain a glorious victory.

The scope of the first two battles, against Apollonius and Seron, was quite modest in scale and importance. Apollonius was apparently then the governor (*meridarkhēs*) of Samaria[1] and fought the rebels either because their main base was in the toparchy of Aphairema-Gophna, then part of his meridarchy (I Macc. 11.32) or because the troops that were stationed in Judaea and Jerusalem were incapable of taking effective action. The force that set out with him was composed of 'gentiles and those from Samaria' (I Macc. 3.10). The reference is to garrisons that were stationed in the region of Samaria, probably Mysian mercenaries, as well as members of the military settlement called Samaria, and perhaps also Samaritans.[2] Whatever the exact meaning, the Samaritans did not take part in the major battles of the period, and are not known from the various

[1] As per the document in *Ant.* 12.261; see pp. 202–3 below.
[2] See the various reconstructions and interpretations, pp. 203–4 below.

Hellenistic armies,[3] so that no real qualitative weight can be attributed to them. The size of the military settlement of Samaria is not known;[4] but, as already noted above, the total number of military settlers in Syria and Coele Syria, aside from the large military settlements in Seleucis in northern Syria, was quite small, so that each locality could have had no more than a few dozen

[3] The Josephus story of 8,000 soldiers brought to Alexander by Sanbalat during the siege of Tyre (*Ant.* 11.321) is basically suspect, as is that on the settlement in Egypt of Sanbalat's soldiers. A negative view of these stories is quite widespread among scholars (e.g. Tcherikover, 1961a: 43ff. For further bibliography see Seibert 1981: 271–4). All attempts to confirm them fail to provide an answer to the fundamental questions: why is there no mention in the detailed sources on Alexander's military activities in the area of the considerable Samaritan reinforcements which were supposed to amount to a quarter of the total force camped near Tyre? Why is the role of Samaritans in the big battles of the Ptolemies and Seleucids unrecorded? And why has no real evidence been found of the extensive Samaritan military settlement in Egypt that such a number of soldiers as attributed to Sanbalat would have produced? The evidence provided for Samaritan military settlement (the sources in Launey 1949–50: 1.. 548–50,554; cf. Kasher 1978: 63–5) is quite weak. The only mention of a Samaritan soldier in Ptolemaic papyrology ('Adamas son of Libanus, *Samarites*' *P.Ent.* 62.1.1–2) lists him in a mercenary unit, not in one of military settlers. The military settlement of Samaria in the Arsinoite nome was basically a Jewish settlement. Of the twenty names of inhabitants that have been preserved (see the list in Launey 1949–50: 2.1232–5), seven are defined as Jews (*CPJ* I, nos. 22,128) and one (Hagai: ibid. no. 28) cannot be Samaritan, being typical of the Restoration period. The place may have been founded at the time of the dispersal of the Israelites from the northern kingdom as early as the period of the First Temple (implied in Isaiah 11.11), although the possibility should not be rejected that its origin was in the combined deportation of Jews and Samaritans to Egypt at the time of Ptolemy I (*Ant.*12.7). Even if the Samaria mentioned was a Samaritan settlement, it should be kept in mind that the military settlements in Egypt were quite small, including an average of only 100 soldiers (Crawford 1971: 122–3). In any case, these meagre data out of the plentiful papyrological material on military settlement in Egypt do not add much credibility to the story of Sanbalat's soldiers, nor indicate the existence of a military tradition among the Samaritans of Eretz Israel. In contrast to the Samaritans, the names of hundreds of Idumaean military settlers are known (Launey 1949–50: 2.1235–41), although they were not a conspicuous element in the settlements. See also the arguments of Tcherikover (1961a: 331 n. 13), who notes that Alexander the Great did not use auxiliary troops from the local populations until he reached central Asia. It has already been acknowledged that the information about the Samaritan revolt at the time of Alexander's stay in Egypt (Curtius Rufus 4.8.9–11) and the persecution of the Samaritans shortly after the Macedonian occupation (as appears from the papyri of Wadi Daliah) discredit both the story about the establishment of the Samaritan temple by Alexander, as well as that about Sanbalat's soldiers.

[4] The archaeological excavations carried out in Samaria provide no answers to the question of the number of military settlers: the Hellenistic acropolis was limited in size (230 × 120 m), but at least some of the settlers would be living outside the upper city, near their lands, as was reported regarding a group of the settlers from the Seleucid military settlement in Magnesia in Asia Minor (*OGIS* 229, lines 100–4). The same is reported about Samaria itself in Herod's time (*Ant.* 15.296). The data on Magnesia indicate that it included some civilians (ibid. line 35 and passim), which makes it even harder to draw any conclusions about Samaria from the archaeological finds. On the composition of the population in Magnesia and its fortress, Palai-Magnesia, and on the scattering of the settlers there see Bar-Kochva 1979: 22–3,57–8. On the dimensions of the Hellenistic acropolis in Samaria see N. Avigad in Avi-Yonah 1978, s.v. 'Samaria', p. 1047. On doubts about the size of the Hellenistic city see in brief Crowfoot et al. 1942: 31. In *Ant.* 15.297, Josephus reports the circumference of the Herodian city as 20 *stadia*, but according to him the area was larger than that of the previous city .

settlers.[5] As to the garrisons of mercenaries in the district as a whole, in order to assume that a large army was stationed in Samaria, it would be necessary to find evidence of many forts in that meridarchy, but none is available. All in all, the military supervision of the various districts in the Seleucid kingdom was limited to a modest number of fortresses and military settlements, with the exception of certain districts where there was a concentration of military settlements, mainly for reasons of global strategy.[6]

Much the same can be said about the clash with Seron, the second of Judas Maccabaeus' battles. I Maccabees calls Seron ἄρχων τῆς δυνάμεως Συρίας (= head of the Syrian army), which is a translation of the Hebrew שׂר צבא ארם (śar ṣevā arām = [chief] commander of the army of Aram – see II Kings 5.1 and the Septuagint ad loc.). However there is no possibility that Seron was the commander-in-chief of the Seleucid army, if only because the king himself was the overall commander of the armed forces and even led them in the battlefield.[7] Nor can it be assumed that Seron was a high officer appointed for purposes of the mission in Judaea, as the author himself admits in an illuminating slip of the pen he acted on his own and exceeded his authority (3.14).[8] I Maccabees, although he was aware that Seron was not chief of staff, presumably did not know Seron's exact position and therefore allowed himself to exaggerate his rank, which served to magnify the military achievement. Josephus in *Antiquitates* writes that Seron was the *stratēgos* of Coele Syria and Phoenicia (12.288), that is, the civil and military governor of the satrapy which included Judaea. But that is only an attempt to explain the title given in I Maccabees which is not based on any information or other source.[9] Josephus' suggestion must be rejected because the *stratēgos* of Coele Syria and Phoenicia at the time was Ptolemy son of Dorymenes (I Macc. 3.38; II Macc. 4.45, 8.8); and if Seron had served in that central post, the author of I Maccabees, who is knowledgeable about less important matters, would have had to know it, and would certainly have used the specific title rather than a vague term, and would, as was his wont, have noted the rank

[5] See p. 101 above.

[6] On the planning of the empire's defence, the placing of the military settlements and the strategic considerations see Bar-Kochva 1979: 26,36,43–4.

[7] On the hierarchy of the Seleucid command see ibid. 85–93.

[8] That is the meaning of the expression 'I will make a name for myself' according to its biblical origin (in Gen. 11.4 and II Sam. 8.13) and its meaning in I Maccabees itself (5.57).

[9] Contrary to Michaelis 1778: 68–9; Abel 1949: 57; Avi-Yonah 1966: 46, and others. See also p. 209 below. On Josephus' reports on the battles as paraphrases based exclusively on I Maccabees see pp. 207–8 below.

of nobility awarded to an official of such a rank (cf. 3.32,38, 7. 8,26, 10.65, 11.30).[10]

The name Seron itself appears only once in the Greco-Macedonian onomasticon.[11] If we take into account certain possibilities of error arising from the Hebrew pronunciation and the transliteration from the Hebrew original to Greek, the name is reminiscent of a number of Thracian names.[12] The information we have on Seleucid satraps and *stratēgoi* shows that, except for semi-independent Armenia where local princes were appointed governors, they were always of Greco-Macedonian origin,[13] while the national units of mercenaries, vassals and allies often remained under the command of their own compatriots.[14] All the considerations and data noted above tend to show that Seron was no more than one of the commanders of the mercenary garrisons in the region. The propinquity to Beth Horon suggests Gezer (I Macc. 4.15, 7.45, 9.52; cf. 13.43–8) or the garrison at Iamnia which included Thracians (I Macc. 5.58–9; II Macc. 12.35). Although the proposed conclusion indicates that the enemy army was rather small, this should not be construed as detracting too much from the military–tactical achievement. The participation of Thracian soldiers in the expedition demonstrates the great effectiveness of the ambush set by Judas Maccabaeus and the fighting ability of the Jewish army. The Thracians, who were semi-heavies, were well trained in warfare in areas similar to that of the Beth Horon ascent, while the phalanx – despite everything said above on its operational methods – found it difficult to defend itself effectively on such a steep winding slope, just as the more flexible and mobile Roman legionaries failed there in the Cestius Gallus expedition (*Bell.* 2.546–50).

The third Seleucid expedition against Judas Maccabaeus, which culminated in the battle of Ammaus, was initiated and planned by Ptolemy son of Dorymenes, the *stratēgos* of Coele Syria and Phoenicia

---

[10] On the Seleucid titles of nobility see especially Corradi 1929: 318–43.

[11] Plut. *Apopth. Lac.* s.v. Λοχαγος (actually: Σειρων). On his identity and dating in the first half of the fourth century B.C. see Poralla 1913: 113. The similar form, Σέρας, appears twice in the inscription of late Sparta: Bradford 1977: 371. This form also appears twice in Lycia: Zgusta 1964: 167,467.

[12] See, e.g., the names Σιρούων, Σοῦρις, Σοῦρα, Τήρης and similar forms among the Thracian inscriptions in Mikhailov 1956: nos. 203,507,844,1690,2149,2274,2291,2314,2330,2337,2338; and also the names Σερεῖον, Σῖρες, Σῖρος, Σῖρρος, Σεῖρος, Σύρα, Ζῆρα, in Tomaschek 1893: §§1.43,46; II.19; III.76,77,81,102.

[13] Bengtson 1964: 2.29,37,61–2,157–8 and passim. Cf. Heuss 1949: 309, and see Bengtson 1964: 188–93 on the status of the *stratēgos* as civil governor after the battle of Magnesia and the detachment of Asia Minor in 190 B.C.

[14] See Polybius 5.79,7,9,10–11. Cf. also I Macc. 10.37. The loyalty of the soldiers in the various units was given to their national leaders, and not necessarily to the central authorities. Cf. pp. 423, 537 below.

(II Macc. 8.8–9).[15] Among the participants was Gorgias, the meridarch of Idumaea adjacent to Judaea (II Macc. 10.14, 12.32), and Nicanor, who was perhaps meridarch of the coastal region (*paralia*). Although as noted above the estimate of Seleucid numerical strength reported by I Maccabees is greatly inflated and based on a biblical association, and the statement that half the Seleucid recruitment potential was sent to Judaea also seems an exaggeration, presumably a military force despatched by the *stratēgos* of a satrapy could not be very small. Together with the auxiliary troops from Idumaea and the coastal plain adjoining (3.41),[16] it was several times larger than Judas Maccabaeus' select task force of 3,000 combatants (I Macc. 4.6) which broke into the Ammaus camp at dawn.

In view of Lysias' status, the force he brought along on his first expedition to Judaea which was called off at Beth Zur (I Macc. 4.26–35) must have had a numerical strength that was certainly not inferior to the ten thousand attributed to Judas Maccabaeus, but it is doubtful whether in this case it is possible to speak of a real Jewish victory in battle. Contrary to the practice of I Maccabees, especially in regard to encounters with similar large armies, the battle account is condensed and the sentences extremely laconic ('and they charged and there fell some five thousand men of Lysias' camp', 4.34). The abridgement and 'compression' are evident also in the description of the actions and achievements of the Seleucid army before the battle.[17] Furthermore, the defeat of an army as large as Lysias' should certainly have led to panic-stricken flight and a pursuit (cf. 3.24, 4.15, 7.44–6), but the Seleucid army's retreat was slow, deliberate and planned, and there is no allusion to any pursuit (4.35). It thus appears that the scope and dimensions of the Beth Zur clash were rather modest, and in view of the circumstances and nature of the area, could be no more than a nuisance raid of the 'hit and run' variety on the Seleucid army camped at Beth Zur in preparation for a breakthrough to Jerusalem. If the phrase 'and they charged' (4.34)[18] refers only to the Jewish force perhaps the author did not ignore (though he did somewhat blur) the real nature of the confrontation, and his words may be construed as referring to a foray into the enemy camp. In any case, the raid itself did not have any decisive results: the pace of the Seleucid retreat suggests that Lysias

---

[15] According to I Maccabees the initiative for the expedition came from the regent, Lysias, and Ptolemy son of Dorymenes took part in the expedition itself (3.38). But on this point the II Maccabees version is preferable. See p. 238 below.

[16] See pp. 41–2 above and pp. 247–8 below.   [17] See pp. 286–7 below.

[18] On the reconstruction of the original Hebrew text (and the proper translation) see p. 288 below.

was obliged to leave Judaea not because he suffered a serious blow but for external reasons. An examination of the chronology shows that the news of Antiochus Epiphanes' death in Persia must have reached the Seleucid commander while he was encamped at Beth Zur.[19] Accordingly, Lysias, who was serving as regent, hastened back to Antioch to settle the matter of the succession.[20] The author of I Maccabees was misled by his source with regard to the sequence of events and the reason for Lysias' withdrawal, as he was with regard to the course and dimensions of the military operations in that expedition.[21] Even if the end of the expedition preceded Antiochus Epiphanes' death (a possibility which is very remote indeed), the unusual form of the description nevertheless suggests that Lysias left the country for some reason unrelated to the campaign. Quite a number of factors could have obliged the regent to return to the capital even if Antiochus Epiphanes was still alive at the time in the Upper Satrapies.

Early in the reign of Demetrius I, Judas Maccabaeus struck at Nicanor twice in a row. Before that, Nicanor had held the eminent position of supervisor of all the war elephants in the kingdom (II Macc. 14.12). His appointment as military governor of the little meridarchy in the hills of Judaea (ibid.) indicates how much importance the central authorities attached to the suppression of the Revolt. At the same time, as noted above, most of the manpower of the Seleucid army was then occupied in the eastern satrapies. Nicanor's forces in the first confrontation comprised only men from the Jerusalem garrison (I Macc. 7.27,32), and in the second also some reinforcements from Syria (7.39). In view of the circumstances, those reinforcements cannot have been very numerous.

The Seleucid troops who clashed with Judas Maccabaeus at Beth Zacharia and Elasa properly represented the military power of the kingdom, for at least half if not more of the Seleucid manpower potential could have taken part in those battles. And indeed both of them ended in a clear Jewish defeat. The fact that it was only at such a late stage that large Seleucid armies were engaged, and even then only intermittently, should not be surprising in view of what is known about the Seleucid suppression of other revolts in the same period, and about the Seleucid order of priorities. The Upper Satrapies, with their vast territories and inexhaustible resources that

---

[19] See pp. 279–80 below.

[20] Zeitlin 1950: 27,105, already figures that, but he does not analyse the description and in fact bases it on a mistaken chronological system for calculating the dates mentioned in I Maccabees. Cf. Bunge 1971: 418, who proffers reasons which in the main do not pass the test of critical appraisal.   [21] See in detail pp. 281–2 below.

were in a constant state of unrest, were more important to the Seleucids economically and as a source of manpower than tiny, poor Judaea. Because of its isolation, the propinquity of the Judaean Hills to the strategically vital coastal plain could not give the suppression of the Revolt in Judaea priority over the restoration of calm in the Upper Satrapies. Although any rebellion could be infectious and was likely to spread to adjacent regions, the Seleucids could well rely on the neighbours' hatred of the Jews to divert them from their true needs and desires and impel them to direct their energies to the persecution of the Jews. It was only after the purification of the Temple that the Jews began to constitute a danger to security in the coastal plain (I Macc. 5.22,23,58,68; II Macc. 12.1–9, 32–7). It should also be taken into account that the obvious weakness of the Ptolemies during the reign of Antiochus Epiphanes no doubt relegated the suppression of the Jewish Revolt to a low place in the order of priorities. Moreover, as long as the Hasmonaeans made no attempt to occupy the Jerusalem citadel, the symbol of Seleucid control of the country, and as long as they made no alliances with hostile powers, the authorities were not impelled to abandon their urgent tasks in other places and hasten to Judaea. It is illuminating that of the Seleucids' two large expeditions, the one to Beth Zacharia was undertaken in response to an attempt to gain control of the citadel (I Macc. 6.18–28), and the other, to Elasa, to obviate direct Roman intervention in the happenings in Judaea (I Macc. 8.23–9.22).

The general slowness of action on the part of the authorities seems to parallel the methods adopted a generation earlier by Antiochus III in suppressing the rebellions of Molon and Achaeus which were much more dangerous and detrimental to the vital interests of the Seleucid empire than the uprising in Judaea. The forces initially sent to put down the rebellions were rather small, and from time to time the king even turned his attention to urgent missions in other parts of the realm. It was only after three years that Antiochus III led a large army to settle matters in the eastern satrapies under Molon's control, while Achaeus' rebellion in Asia Minor was not crushed till six additional years had passed.[22] The suppression of Molon's rebellion had priority because a large proportion of the Seleucid cavalry was recruited from Media and its environs. It is interesting to note that Achaeus had a relatively small force at his disposal, no more

[22] For the Achaeus–Molon rebellion see Polybius 5.40–54,107.4, 7.15–18, 8.15–35; and see Schmitt 1964: 116–49,158–74.

than 6,000 infantry and 500 cavalry.[23] And yet Antiochus III was not in a hurry to confront the rebel and recover his hegemony in the districts north of the Taurus.

The success and achievement of Judas Maccabaeus in his struggle with the Seleucids were chiefly on the strategic–political plane and not the tactical–military one. The Hasmonaeans were defeated in the big battles, but in the end emerged victorious from the conflict. The fact that the Seleucids were slow to react led to the escalation of the Revolt and eventually to Jewish independence. The time factor operated to the advantage of the Hasmonaeans: the substructure of the resistance movement and of the Jewish army became so solid that military defeats could not lead to their collapse. On the other hand, the Seleucids were not able to leave large enough armies in Judaea to protect their gains because of the limited number of soldiers at their disposal and the frequent rebellions in other regions. The increasing power and solidity of the Jewish forces already made clear to the enemy in Judas Maccabaeus' day that it was necessary to repeal the restrictions on religion, and compromise in political and administrative areas as well. In Jonathan's time, as the Seleucid empire gradually sank into court intrigues and struggles for succession, the military power that had accumulated in the country made it possible to manoeuvre among the contenders in Antioch, and to derive the greatest political advantages from the dependence of the various aspirants to the crown on the help of the Jewish military force.

[23] On the size of Achaeus' army see Bar-Kochva 1979: 42. On the settlers and horsemen in Media and on the composition of Molon's army, ibid. 18,32–3,69–72.

7

The battlefields, tactics and leadership of Judas Maccabaeus

Military historians tend to laud Judas Maccabaeus' talents for guerrilla and indirect warfare, and his ability to exploit to the fullest the advantages provided by rugged mountainous terrain. This is a fair evaluation of the first phase of the military struggle, before the purification of the Temple. But care should be taken not to extend it to cover all the stages of Judas Maccabaeus' military operations.

After entrenching themselves in their mountain refuge in the Gophna region, Mattathias and his sons began with measures against internal opponents (I Macc. 2.43–7, 3.8; II Macc. 8.6) and perhaps also against elements that were compliant, undecided or fence-sitters. Since the religious question was the central one at this stage of the Revolt, some religious coercion was applied by the Jews as well: on the one hand the destruction of altars for idol worship (I Macc. 2.45) and on the other forced circumcision (ibid. 2.46: ἐν ἰσχύι = by force). II Maccabees even gives some details of the tactical methods adopted by Judas Maccabaeus in accomplishing his ends: making surprise raids against towns and villages, probably against homes and estates of opponents, burning them down, setting nocturnal ambushes, and the like (8.6–7). It appears from I Maccabees that at this stage no actions were taken against the civil authorities or the Seleucid forces. However, one may presume that raids on small Seleucid supply convoys had already been carried out by then.[1]

The first clashes with the authorities were initiated by the local Seleucid officials and commanders as they tried to restore order in Judaea; Judas Maccabaeus employed guerrilla warfare methods against them as well. That the campaigns were of this nature is

---

[1] The allusions to clashes with the authorities in the song of praise to Judas Maccabaeus in I Maccabees (3.1ff.) are not contradictory evidence, for the song compresses together various of his activities pertaining to later periods. As to the II Maccabees 8.6–7 summary, it may very well refer to the operations against Apollonius and Seron (see below). In any case, it is a fact that in the course of its sequential account I Maccabees makes no mention at all of any confrontation with Seleucid troops until the clash with Apollonius.

specified in I Maccabees in regard to the Beth Horon attack where
the enemy was surprised from ambush (3.23), and despite some
vagueness (4.12–14) can be understood from the description of the
various stages in the campaign at Ammaus.[2] The author of I Maccabees knew nothing about the clash with Apollonius, and therefore
confined himself to a medley of verses from the David and Goliath
episode (3.11–12).[3] Possibly that battle should be counted among
the surprise attacks and ambushes II Maccabees reports in the
summary of Judas Maccabaeus' military activity prior to the battle
of Ammaus (8.6–7).[4] I have attempted to show that in the operation
at Beth Zur as well, whatever its dimensions, the methods employed
were in fact those of guerrilla warfare.[5]

   Of the four battles that took place before the purification of the
Temple, only for the one at Ammaus does the text provide the full
details which enable us to appreciate the traits and virtues of Judas
Maccabaeus' army (I Macc. 3.38–4.25; see Map 10, pp. 222–3).[6]
The Seleucid army was encamped near Ammaus at the eastern edge
of the Aijalon Valley, and it intended to stay in the area for a while in
order to gain control of the various routes leading to the mountain
region, and so prepare the ground for an extensive mopping-up
operation of the rebel strongholds. Judas Maccabaeus assembled his
people at Mizpah, on the plateau north of Jerusalem, and apparently
found a way to leak information on the assembly to the enemy in
order to tempt the Seleucid troops into an immediate action against
him and thus draw them into a trap. The same day Judas Maccabaeus conducted a series of religious ceremonies at Mizpah and also
a careful screening of his soldiers. And in fact, Gorgias, one of the
enemy commanders, was tempted into thinking that he would succeed in surprising the rebels, and at sundown set out from Ammaus
with a picked force for the purpose of making a nocturnal assault on

---

[2] The special conditions of the battle of Ammaus make it impossible to imagine a regular
frontal clash between the two armies that confronted each other. The 'screening' conducted
in the Jewish army (I Macc. 3.55–6), the night march (3.57, 4.1–5), the short stay of Judas
Maccabaeus' force in the area south of Ammaus (3.57) which was a hilly area most certainly
unobservable from the Seleucid camp on the plain near Ammaus (3.40), the observation of the
enemy camp (4.7), and above all the undertaking of the march at a time when most of the
Seleucid force at Ammaus expected Gorgias and his task force to be surprising the Jews at
Mizpah (4.1–4), all these indicate that Judas Maccabaeus planned on a relaxed and un-
prepared atmosphere in the Seleucid camp, and broke into it from a commanding position. This
is even stated explicitly in 4.4. In any case, if Judas Maccabaeus had not judged conditions
suitable for a surprise attack on the camp, he would certainly have taken on Gorgias, who led
a small force on a hard night march through hilly terrain. The vague description in I
Maccabees (4.13–14) may be misleading and seems to refer only to the forward patrols of the
enemy camp.   [3] See pp. 204–6 below.
[4] See pp. 200–1 below.   [5] Pp. 134–5 above.
[6] See the detailed commentary, pp. 241ff..

the camp at Mizpah. Judas Maccabaeus was informed in time of Gorgias' departure, left Mizpah, and with 3,000 picked men quickly traversed 27 km descending to the hilly region south of Ammaus. That night Gorgias looked in vain for Judas Maccabaeus in Mizpah and the mountainous plateau in its vicinity. At dawn, Judas Maccabaeus burst into the enemy camp at Ammaus where most of the Seleucid force was, by taking advantage of the complacency of the command, which was sure that Gorgias' expedition would be successful. The picked Jewish soldiers put the enemy to flight, but did not allow themselves to be drawn into a long-distance pursuit, and also refrained from taking spoils, being aware that Gorgias would be returning to the camp. When the latter came down from the mountain region and saw his camp in flames in the distance, he fled with his soldiers, avoiding battle with the Jews who were waiting for him in the valley.

The reconstruction above shows that the Jewish army had first and foremost a fast and efficient intelligence system, without which Judas Maccabaeus would not have learned in time of Gorgias' departure from his camp *en route* to Mizpah, and would certainly not have managed to reach the Ammaus area that same night. Effective military intelligence was also vital in ascertaining the exact site of the enemy camp and the weak points of its defence. The long night march that Judas Maccabaeus led through a long mountain route from Mizpah to Ammaus with 3,000 combatants exemplifies several additional characteristics: absolute control of the central command and a high standard of discipline, an excellent sense of direction displayed by officers of all ranks in quite tortuous terrain, a high degree of physical fitness in the rank and file, great mobility and speed. These qualities were demonstrated even more clearly in the sunrise attack on the enemy camp, which was conducted just a few hours after the conclusion of an exhausting march, with careful attention to the element of surprise. Control over the army and adherence to the goal is put to the greatest test in a pursuit. Here too the high level of discipline was maintained, and at least some of the units left off in time to meet the force returning with Gorgias. Even the plentiful spoils, a bait that was a stumbling block for more than one Hellenistic army, did not affect the alertness and discipline of Judas Maccabaeus' army. The physical ability alone to conduct a pursuit following a night march and sunrise assault, and to return in time to the Ammaus area cannot but arouse wonderment. These military qualifications were augmented by a fighting spirit and religious and national zeal which were fostered in various ways, among them the assembling of the camp deliberately at Mizpah so as to recall the victories at the time of the judges and early kings, the carrying out there of various precepts connected with the Temple, fasting on the eve of a battle and the selection of soldiers and their classification according to the regulations in Deuteronomy. Judas Maccabaeus' tactical planning was thus based on his army's outstanding qualities: effective intelligence, centralized command, strict discipline, a sense of direction, superior physical fitness, mobility and speed, adherence to the goal, high motivation and a fighting spirit. These qualities, which are vital to the success of the indirect approach, enabled Judas Maccabaeus to carry out his basic tactics in the battle of Ammaus, involving a split of the enemy force, a diversionary action, and surprise.

It is hard to know to what extent those qualities were evinced in the other battles that preceded the purification of the Temple, and whether in those too Judas Maccabaeus' tactics were as complicated. There is no doubt that the perfect performance at Ammaus derived in large measure from the individual excellence of the soldiers, chosen in a highly selective process. Such a selection may also have been conducted before the ambush on the Beth Horon ascent was set. The defeat of Seron's Thracian mercenaries[7] required a carefully planned ambush and assault using only picked troops. In any case, the absence of detailed information on the phases of the other battles does not mean that the Jewish tactics in them were any less sophisticated. The author of I Maccabees enlarged upon the battle of Ammaus because he himself actually took part in it, while for the others that preceded the purification of the Temple he had only hearsay evidence or second-hand descriptions.[8] In any case, some of the qualities manifested in the battle of Ammaus are evident in the expeditions to Transjordania (e.g. I Macc. 5.24–34, esp. 28,29,33).

The purification of the Temple marked the beginning of a new phase in Judas Maccabaeus' military activity, characterized by readiness to meet the foe in frontal combat and sometimes even on level ground quite convenient for waging 'heavy' warfare.[9] For the

---

[7] See p. 133 above.   [8] See pp. 159–62 below.

[9] In an article published shortly after the Hebrew edition of this book, Y. Harkavi (1981) 63–71 reaches a similar conclusion without analysing the battlefield or course of the battles. He calls attention to several salient facts: the number of confrontations between the two sides during the years of the revolt was very small, which suggests frontal clashes rather than guerrilla sorties; the Seleucids did not spread their army throughout the country but kept it together, an arrangement which discouraged a war of attrition and assaults on small groups; and finally, the Seleucids proceeded to Judaea with 'heavy units', in the Beth Zacharia campaign even with elephants, which indicates that they expected frontal confrontation with Judas Maccabaeus' army.

battle of Beth Zacharia, where the enemy had a decided qualitative and quantitative superiority, it is difficult to decide whether Judas Maccabaeus set an ambush or advanced for a conventional frontal clash.[10] In any case, the Jewish commander set the confrontation in a place likely to be of considerable advantage to a local force that had settled in earlier. In the battles against Nicanor at Adasa and Kafar Salama the Jews unhesitatingly met the enemy in frontal battles on an absolutely level plateau,[11] confident presumably because of their great numerical superiority and because they had no lack of proper weapons for fighting in such terrain. At Elasa the enemy had a clear advantage in heavies and cavalry. The convenient plateau site was forced upon Judas Maccabaeus, and the clash itself was conducted with the conventional methods of the Hellenistic period. Domestic political considerations compelled Judas Maccabaeus to join the battle against his will. Bacchides had sowed terror and dread among the rural population in the Beth El region north of Jerusalem, and as the leader of the Revolt Judas Maccabaeus could not allow himself to stand idly by.[12] Still, if he had not been successful in similar encounters on similar terrain against Nicanor, he would probably have avoided a clash this time too as he had during Bacchides' first expedition to Judaea, a short time after the defeat at Beth Zacharia (I Macc. 7.8–25).

The change in Judas Maccabaeus' combat methods after the purification of the Temple came in the wake of a drastic increase in the manpower potential at his disposal, and of an improvement in weaponry including the introduction of cavalry and artillery which led to a significant change in the tactical composition of his army, and made it 'heavier'. Hasmonaean control of all areas of the Judaean Hills opened the way for the organization of reinforcements and adaptation of the forces in preparation for the military undertakings. This was not possible earlier, when the rebels operated in semi-underground conditions, assembling on mountain cliffs in the Gophna region and in desert areas. The changes in the size, equipment and combat method came about not only as a result of possibilities that became available to the Jews, but in particular owing to the realization that they were essential in view of the altered political and territorial situation: Judas Maccabaeus now became the recognized leader of the people, in control of all Jewish territory in the Judaean Hills. He had to protect existing territorial gains, especially Jerusalem and the Temple, as well as safeguard the rural

[10] See pp. 332–3.   [11] See pp. 58–62.
[12] See pp. 384–5.

population in the periphery which was his main support in logistics and manpower. A 'scorched earth' policy or the abandonment of the population and the holy city to the mercy of the foe while seeking refuge in rugged terrain and waiting for an opportunity to strike indirectly no longer suited the circumstances. On one occasion when Judas Maccabaeus avoided battle, the first time Bacchides appeared in the country, the result was the resumption of control by the Seleucid army and the imposition of Alcimus as high priest (I Macc. 7.20), and a little later also the exposure of the Temple once again to the danger of defilement and even destruction (I Macc. 7.35–6; II Macc. 14.33).

The need to defend territory led to a willingness to enter upon a siege. This is evident even before the purification of the Temple during Lysias' first campaign that was stopped at Beth Zur.[13] After the Temple was purified, intensive fortifications were undertaken for the Temple Mount and for Beth Zur (I Macc. 4.59–60, 6.7). Judas Maccabaeus' people who were confined to Beth Zur withstood a protracted siege at the start of Lysias' second expedition (I Macc. 6.31,49–50; II Macc. 13.19–22). After his victory in the battle of Beth Zacharia, Lysias began a long siege of the Temple (I Macc. 6.50–62). The confinement in the siege managed to provide a breathing space before and after the battle of Beth Zacharia: the siege of Beth Zur enabled Judas Maccabaeus to concentrate his forces in the area south of Jerusalem in an attempt to block Lysias, and after the defeat at Beth Zacharia the confinement in the Temple made it possible to prevent the enemy's seizure of the sanctified area with all the consequences to Judas Maccabaeus' status as well as to the preservation of ceremonial sanctity. The siege also made it possible to detach a large section of the enemy's troops and prevent them from continuing to pursue the defeated rebel contingents. Confinement in the Temple ultimately also helped the rebels to obtain political concessions in the wake of developments in Antioch (I Macc. 6.58–9; II Macc. 11.23–6).

The heavy equipment acquired by the Jewish forces after the purification of the Temple also included artillery, which made them more inclined to conduct static warfare, such as laying siege. In the rescue operations that Judas Maccabaeus conducted in Transjordania, Idumaea and the coastal plain, no siege machines are mentioned, whether because of the rapid nature of the campaigns, the low combat level of the local militia,[14] or because none was yet

---

[13] See also pp. 286–7 below.
[14] See p. 515 below on the identification of Timotheus' army.

at the disposal of the Jewish forces. At the time Judas Maccabaeus
was carrying out fast sorties against fortified settlements and areas (I
Macc. 5.5,36,44,65,68; II Macc. 12.13,21) based on rapid moves,
deception and surprise, depriving the enemy of time to organize a
defence. A year later, Judas Maccabaeus besieged the Akra, using
artillery (I Macc. 6.20).[15] Weapons of that kind were collected in the
Temple, and when Lysias after the decisive battle of Beth Zacharia
laid siege to the Temple, the Jews may have used them against the
enemy (II Macc. 6.52).

As to the operational ability of the forces in open field battle after
the purification of the Temple, we have no real descriptions of the
combat methods and tactics of the Hasmonaean army at this stage,
and Jewish activity is depicted in quite sketchy terms. It is consequently impossible to know how well the Jews adapted to Hellenistic arms and combat methods, how they applied them in the
battlefield, and whether they manifested any initiative or originality
within the limitations of those tactics. The paucity of details on some
of the battles of the post-purification phase cannot be explained by
the absence of information or the utilization of secondary sources.
The descriptions of Seleucid deployment and tactics in the battles of
Beth Zacharia and Elasa in I Maccabees show that if the author
himself was not an eye-witness he certainly made use of excellent
first-hand testimony,[16] and there is no doubt that he was even more
familiar with the deployment and tactics of the Jewish forces in those
battles. The real reason lies in the author's desire to refrain from
revealing the change and improvement in the Jewish arms and
combat methods, so as not to prejudice his national–panegyric and
religious–didactic purposes. Any detailed explanation would have
forced the author to disclose the true composition of the Jewish
army, as the author of II Maccabees accidentally did (12.35).

The only thing that can be said about the Jewish tactics at this
stage is that the greatest effort was made to strike down the enemy
commander (I Macc. 7.43,9.14–15; cf. 6.43–6). There is even an
explicit statement that special forces were concentrated opposite the
wing led by the enemy commander (I Macc. 9.14). The death of the
commander could have a tremendous impact if the army was small
and the soldiers in the vicinity noted his fall. This is what happened
at the battle of Adasa where Nicanor's death resulted in a hasty
retreat (I Macc. 7.44). When the Seleucids had a large force in the

---

[15] I Macc. 4.41 does not speak of a siege but of the confinement to the Akra of the troops
in order to avert trouble during the purification of the Temple. See also pp. 458–9 below.
[16] See pp. 159–61 below.

field, as in the battle of Elasa, the death of the commander would necessarily have had a much smaller immediate impact on the rank and file (who may even have been unaware of it). The purpose of attacking the commander in this case was mainly to disrupt as soon as possible the enemy's ability to manipulate and control its forces.

Finally, a few words on the personality of Judas Maccabaeus as a military leader. Any attempt to evaluate it objectively and cool-headedly is difficult because of the great admiration the sources display for their hero, and especially because of the extremely pan-egyric nature of II Maccabees.[17] Despite these limitations it is possible to point to a number of qualities that certainly characterized the Jewish commander: the elegy dedicated to Judas Maccabaeus in I Maccabees (3.1–9) indicates his great physical strength and courage (ibid. 4).[18] In the same context (verse 3) there is also mention of his superior personal arms, referring doubtless to the second phase of the rebellion when the Jewish arsenal contained heavier equip-ment and Judas Maccabaeus led his army in conventional frontal battles.[19] In one case he served as an example to the men by endangering himself and taking the lead in an assault (I Macc. 5.43; cf. John Hyrcanus in I Macc. 16.6). His gift for tactical planning, directing and controlling forces in expeditions and battles is shown by what was said above about the qualities of the Jewish army as manifested in the battle of Ammaus. To that must be added Judas Maccabaeus' ability to direct, operate and command cavalry, as the analysis of the battle of Elasa shows.

As to military discipline in the Jewish camp, the only information we have concerns the execution of a number of officers who during

[17] Among the many attempts to evaluate the personality and accomplishments of Judas Maccabaeus, the most noteworthy are Bevan 1904: 77–9; Dancy 1954: 132–3. Like their predecessors, however, those summaries are of a compilatory nature, putting together material without discriminating between sources, and without examining each case and episode on its own merits. For a military evaluation see Avi-Yonah 1972: 178–82.

[18] C. F. Burney (1920: 319–25) attempted to show that the poem is an acrosticon based on the name 'Yehuda Makaba' (sic), which itself stresses the enthusiastic panegyric character of the poem and excludes it as a source of information. Burney's attempt was, however, properly refuted by G. O. Neuhaus (1971: 12–15). All in all, Burney's method of reconstruction is contrived and arbitrary.

[19] I would venture to attribute informative value to the sentence 'and he wore armour like a hero'. The verse cannot be described as merely biblical rhetoric for, despite linguistic and stylistic similarity, its content contrasts strikingly with the story of David's preparations for the duel with Goliath (I Sam. 17.38–40), and the author seems to be proud that Judas Maccabaeus was outfitted like the enemy commanders. Yet the location of the sentence in the laudatory poem at the beginning of the Revolt story does not mean that Judas Maccabaeus was thus equipped in the early stages of the Revolt. The poem definitely refers to later operations (see also n. 1 above).

a siege allowed some Idumaeans to escape for a price (II Macc.
10.21–2).[20] All signs point to the unusual efforts made by Judas
Maccabaeus to foster the morale and religious–national ardour of his
men. Although the wording and content of the speeches are mainly
the creation of the authors of the Books of the Maccabees,[21] it is likely
that the pre-combat exhortations in fact spoke of past successes and
trust in God in the present. The choice of Mizpah as an assembly
point before the battle of Ammaus, the ceremony conducted there,
and especially the fasting and screening of the soldiers in the spirit of
the war laws in Deuteronomy (I Macc. 3.46–60) indicate an understanding of the importance of motivation and historical–religious
consciousness for the troops. On the political–strategic plane, Judas
Maccabaeus demonstrated great sensitivity to public opinion, and
was prepared to join battle in inconvenient conditions at Elasa to
avert a diminution of his status as commander and leader. The same
concern affected the choice of tactics in that battle.[22] On the other
hand, like other nationalist leaders, Judas Maccabaeus took drastic
measures against his opponents within the community (I Macc. 3.8,
6.24). Still, he should not be represented as an unrestrained religious
zealot and nationalist. He was generally able to evaluate the relative
strength of the belligerents and consequently refrained from purifying the Temple before the death of Antiochus Epiphanes, and later
from interfering with the 'supply corridor' to the Jerusalem citadel,
and so avoided activating the entire military strength of the
empire.[23] In this matter he erred after the death of Antiochus Epiphanes, before the battle of Beth Zacharia, owing to an under-
estimation of the degree to which Lysias was then in control of what
was happening in the kingdom.

Judas Maccabaeus' political acumen is illustrated by his establishment of diplomatic contacts with the enemy when he believed he
could derive some benefit from them. Three times he negotiated with
the authorities from a position of strength: after the battle of
Ammaus,[24] when Lysias was forced to abandon the siege of the
Temple in the course of his second campaign (I Macc. 6.60–1), and
during Nicanor's incumbency (I Macc. 7.26–30).[25] However, he
refused to do so from a position of weakness, preferring to abandon

---

[20] On I Macc. 7.24 see p. 59 n. 102 above.
[21] Pp. 156–8 below.   [22] Pp. 384–5, 393–4 below.
[23] See pp. 458–9 below.   [24] See p. 533 below.
[25] The II Maccabees version of the negotiations with Nicanor (14.18–30) must be rejected
out of hand, implying as it does that at a certain point Judas Maccabaeus was prepared to
desist from all rebellious action and accept a post in the Seleucid administration in the country.
See pp. 354–5 below.

the rural districts when Bacchides invaded the country with his large army.[26] On the other hand, it is doubtful whether there is any reason to share the admiration of many scholars who extol the broad geo-political insight that Judas Maccabaeus exhibited in establishing relations and concluding a pact with the Romans. While the text of the pact mentions that Demetrius was warned not to oppress the Jews (I Macc. 8.31–2), the Roman warning evidently merely im-pelled the Seleucid ruler to take carefully planned drastic measures to capture Judas Maccabaeus and put an end to the Revolt once and for all. From the Roman angle the pact remained devoid of practical significance, like the mutual defence treaties concluded with various elements in the Hellenistic world, including small islands like Asty-palaea in the Aegean Sea. Commitments of that kind were im-plemented by Rome only when the time appeared ripe and it suited her interests. Judas Maccabaeus and his advisers may not have known that; the Seleucid king, who had spent years in Rome as a hostage, was well aware both of the unlikelihood of any immediate Roman action, but also of the potential danger represented in the long run by such a pact.

The sources say very little about the private life of the rebel leader, and it would appear that he was totally devoted to the cause. Consequently he apparently never married. (II Maccabees does mention his marriage, but the episode there is not credible and appears to be a literary invention.[27]) Although the wives of the other Hasmonaean brothers are not mentioned either in I Maccabees, their children are, in various contexts, but no reference is made to any offspring of Judas Maccabaeus. While a number of well-known generals and leaders of antiquity were endowed with unusual stature or beauty that contributed to their glory and were important elem-ents in their charismatic authoritativeness, Judas Maccabaeus evi-dently had no such advantages. Otherwise I Maccabees, which abounds in scriptural associations especially from I and II Samuel, would not have overlooked the opportunity to laud him in terms borrowed from verses describing Saul, David and Absalom.[28] I Mac-cabees does not even use such terms in the song of praise introducing the history of the man (3.1–9). In this connection it is worth con-sidering the possibility proposed by some scholars that the epithet 'Maccabaeus' is derived from the word *maqvān*, a man with a head like a *maqevet* (= mallet; cf. Bekhorot 7.1), presumably a hammer with one end pointed and the other broad, i.e. that his forehead and

---

[26] See also p. 59 n. 101 above and p. 348 below.   [27] See p. 355 below.
[28] See I. Sam. 9.2, 10.23–4, 16.12, 17.42; II Sam. 14.25–6, and cf. I Sam. 16.7.

back of his skull protrude. A slight deformation even contributed to the charisma of some historical figures.[29] The other known suggestion which explains the epithet 'Maccabaeus' as an indication of his physical strength, is, however, no less possible.[30]

[29] See especially Schiffer 1973: 32,60–1, and the psychoanalytic explanation there.

[30] See the summary of the various etymologies in Schürer... 1973–9: 1. 158 n. 49. Vermes notes: 'a nickname originally indicating a bodily peculiarity could easily have acquired, in changed circumstances, the meaning "hammer (of God)"'. A change of meaning is certainly possible, but 'hammer of God' would have been in Hebrew *maqavyā* or *maqevetyā*, like other theophoric names. The explanations 'strong as a hammer', 'striking his enemies like a hammer', 'having a hammer-like blow', and the like, are linguistically more appropriate.

PART II

ACCOUNTS OF THE BATTLES: INTRODUCTION, TEXT AND COMMENTARY

8

The sources: their date, provenance and characteristics

The main sources for reconstructing the course of the battles are I
and II Maccabees. The complex questions connected with the identity of the authors, the language and date, the provenance, aims
and characteristic features of these two books have often been discussed and reviewed in scholarly literature, so that there remains
only to refer the reader to the numerous introductions to and studies
of the Books of the Maccabees.[1] In the present survey we shall deal
only with those questions that are of decisive importance in reconstructing the course of the battles, or where an analysis of battle
accounts contributes to a solution.

The First Book of the Maccabees

I Maccabees, originally written in Hebrew, reached us in Greek
translation. It covers the period from the plunder of the Temple by
Antiochus Epiphanes in 169 B.C. (1.16ff.) until the murder of
Simeon the Hasmonaean by Ptolemy son of Abubus in 135 B.C.
(16.11–22). After a short introduction reporting briefly the successes
of Alexander the Great, the dissolution of his empire, the accession
of Antiochus Epiphanes and the Hellenistic reform in Jerusalem
(1.1–15), the book surveys at length the coercive edicts (1.16–64),
the start of the Revolt under the leadership of Mattathias the Hasmonaean (2.1–69), the period of Judas Maccabaeus' leadership until
his death in the battle of Elasa (3.1–9.22), the leadership of Judas'
brother Jonathan and the political and military struggle in his
time – 160 to 143 B.C. (9.23–12.52). It ends with the period of

[1] Of the concise summaries those especially worth pursuing are: Bickerman in *RE* s.v.
'Makkabäerbücher', cols. 779–97; Abel 1949: i–lix; Pfeifer 1949: 461–524; Dancy 1954: 1–
22; M. Stern, 'The Books of the Maccabees', in *Biblical Encyclopaedia*, vol. 5 (Jerusalem, 1958)
cols. 286–303 (Hebrew); Habicht 1956: 167–94. Studies and commentaries dealing with
specific problems are cited below.

Simeon after the achievement of independence and the start of the
Hasmonaean state – 143 to 135 B.C. (13.1–16.16). The book contains
no information on the identity and sources of its author, except
for the final verses (16.23–4), where the obscurities outweigh the
specifics.

The date of the composition of I Maccabees, the identification of
its sources, and the degree of its accuracy have been subjects of
dispute ever since an exhaustive study was first made of the book in
the middle of the eighteenth century. Thus a few scholars assign the
date of its composition to early in the administration of John Hyrcanus (which commenced in 135 B.C.), that is, about a generation
after the death of Judas Maccabaeus, while others date it later, after
the death of Hyrcanus, that is, in the time of Alexander Jannaeus
(from 103 B.C. on). Of those who assign it to an earlier date, some
maintain that the author belonged to the generation of the Revolt
and based his work mainly on his personal impressions and on the
descriptions of eye-witnesses, and was also assisted by official archives
and a Seleucid chronicle. Those who assign the composition of the
book to a later date assume that the author relied on a written source,
such as a detailed chronicle of the Hasmonaean dynasty, as well as
on archival material, a Seleucid chronicle, and perhaps also some
reminiscences and second-hand oral reports. In general the tendency
is to consider the sources of the author's information as fairly reliable.
Some have certain reservations, however, about the stylistic and
substantive presentation of the material, claiming that the author's
partiality for biblical phraseology and associations has a misleading
effect, occasionally obscuring and even distorting the historical
picture.

In addition to these views, which are accepted in one form or
another by most scholars, extreme opinions have also been expressed
on the above problems. While in the past there were some who
sought the sources of I Maccabees even in Jason of Cyrene,[2] the
author of the book that II Maccabees is based on, in the last generation the German scholar K. D. Schunck and others who followed
in his footsteps sought to apply to I Maccabees the methods of the
'Documentary Hypothesis', familiar from the classical criticism of
the Bible. Thus they assumed that the book constitutes a mosaic of
several written sources, such as 'the Mattathias source', 'the Judah
source', 'the Jonathan source', 'the Simeon source', and so on, each
with its own objectives and attitude.[3] Here and there voices may

[2] Schlatter 1891: 2ff.; Kolbe 1926: 134ff.
[3] Schunck 1954; id. 1980: 291; Arenhoevel 1967: 70,98ff.; Schaumberger 1955: 524–6;
Bunge 1971: 368–85 and passim; id. 1976: 64. Schunck's book earned enthusiastic reviews,

even be distinguished which, denying the historicity of most of the events described, declare them to be imaginary and tendentious accounts formed by merging general information which the author had about the Seleucid kingdom and army and about the early days of the Hasmonaeans into pertinent, stylistic and ideal 'models' and 'patterns' known from the Bible.[4]

From the analysis of Judas Maccabaeus' battles which is given later, there emerges quite a favourable picture of the reliability of the book. Some accounts of the battles, mainly those at Ammaus and Beth Zacharia, may be counted among the better military historiography of the period. Replete with detailed information, these accounts provide a living and colourful picture of the course of events, in which there is complete accord between the military movements and the terrain, and they include information whose reliability can be confirmed by the knowledge at our disposal from external sources about the tactical composition, the command, the armaments and the operational methods of the Seleucid forces. It is not suggested, however, that these accounts are the acme of perfection and satisfy all the demands of the modern reader. As usual in ancient military literature, the reporting is elliptical and selective, and at no time covers all parts of a battlefield. Often it deals exclusively with the movements and actions of the commander or his relatives, and omits other details of interest to the historian (e.g. 6.43–6, 9.13–17). Nor, despite its great brevity, is there reason to doubt the accuracy of the information relating to the other cam-

and traces of it can be discerned in quite a number of articles. A method similar to Schunck's was proposed a year before Schunck's book appeared by W. Mölleken (1953: 205–26; see p. 345 n. 91 below for further details).

Schunck's theory exhibits some of the negative features of classic biblical research: arbitrary shifting of verses and parts of verses from place to place; predetermination of features and trends, bisection of passages and even verses on the basis of advance assumptions, total disregard of the fact that differences in emphasis frequently arise from the nature of the events, and 'discovery' of non-existent stylistic differences. Specific objections to Schunck are voiced by G. O. Neuhaus (1974b: 162–75); the article is basically 'technical' in nature. A recent critical article in Hebrew (Kochabi 1983) attacks Schunck's view on the basis of an examination of general historiographic and theological aspects. Without going into detail, it must be stressed that such a theory of sources could be entertained only if it could be proved that a long interval elapsed between the events and the composition of the relevant book. As we shall see below, the author in this case belonged to the generation of the Revolt, and was even an eye-witness of some of the events.

[4] The view that the influence of the Bible on I Maccabees goes beyond linguistic and stylistic features to affect the way events and episodes are described has recently been espoused by Goldstein (1976: 6–8,73,264,322,342, and passim). In many cases these 'influences' are imaginary. Thus nobody could possibly agree that the description of Judas Maccabaeus' resourceful deed at Ammaus (I Macc. 4.3ff.) was composed under the inspiration of I Chron. 14.14–16 and II Sam. 5.23–5; or that the impressive appearance of the enemy in the battle of Beth Zacharia (I Macc. 6.35–41) follows Ezek. 21.8–23 and Hab. 1.6–9; or that the victory at Adasa (I Macc. 7.43–6) reflects I Sam. 14.20–2 and Jud. 7.21–4.

paigns and battles, such as the encounter with Seron at the Beth
Horon Ascent, the expeditions into Transjordania and the battles
against Nicanor. If we study the language of the passage carefully,
we shall find that the account of the clash at Beth Zur, though at first
sight likely to raise doubts, may yet likewise agree with historical
events, despite the misleading laconic style. The favourable evaluation of the accounts of the battles and their developments in I
Maccabees is reinforced when compared with the fictitious record of
II Maccabees on the one hand and the informative summary of the
battle of Beth Zacharia in *Bellum Judaicum* on the other. It is only in
respect to the struggle against Apollonius, at the beginning of Judas
Maccabaeus' career, that we regard the author as unreliable. For
having no actual information on the battle, he contented himself
with a collection of biblical phrases drawn from the contest between
David and Goliath, thereby also conveying to the reader an appropriate echo of and a close association with that heroic episode.[5]

The numerous biblical associations in the other accounts of the
battles do not detract in any way from the credibility of the information, since they have in every instance considerable factual support. So, for example, where part of the Seleucid force in the battle
of Beth Zacharia is described as 'armoured with chain and bronze
helmets on their heads' (6.35), this is not just a matter of using
phraseology influenced by the description of Goliath's weapons (I
Sam. 17.5). Although the author made use of a biblical vocabulary
and syntax, and emphasized items of armaments similar to those
mentioned in the case of Goliath, there are slight deviations from the
biblical text which bring the narrative up to date. In the light of the
information we have there is no doubt that his statements faithfully
reflect the armaments of part of the Royal Guard, the elite unit of the
Seleucid army, which was retrained in the Roman combat method
and armament (Polybius 30.25.3).[6] In that connection it is worth
noting the author's great precision in specifying names and topographical data. The first and second battles against Nicanor, he
states, took place at Kafar Salama and Adasa (I Macc. 7.31,40), two
small undistinguished hamlets situated about a bowshot from Gibeon, which was well known and populated also in the days of the
author.[7] Had he specified Gibeon as the place of the encounter, he

---

[5] See pp. 200, 204–6 below.   [6] See pp. 313–16 below.
[7] Gibeon is mentioned in the Restoration list (Neh. 7.25 and apparently also Ezra 2.20)
and at the time of the Great Revolt (*Bell.* 2.516,545). There is no doubt that it was populated
during the Hellenistic period, though relatively sparsely: see Pritchard 1962: 76.

would have added an important element to the image of the Hasmonaeans as reviving the commandment to conquer and settle the
country (see I Macc. 15.33), and would have aroused pleasant associations with Joshua's and David's great victories at Gibeon (Josh.
10.10–14; I Chron. 14.16), all the more so in the battle of Adasa
where the enemy doubtless fled down the Beth Horon Descent to the
Aijalon Valley on its way to the Seleucid stronghold at Gezer (I
Macc. 7.45; cf. Joshua 10.11–12, 33; I Chron. 14.16).

The favourable evaluation referred to above applies only to the
battlefields, to the tactical deployment, and to the military movements. As has previously been mentioned in the analysis of the size
of the armies, most of the numbers given do not stand up to criticism
and are only meant to serve national as well as didactic, religious
and even literary purposes. This does not, however, justify rejecting
the accounts of the battles themselves. Thus for instance Xenophon,
the greatest military writer of Classical Greece, who took part in the
battle of Cunaxa beside the rebel Cyrus as commander of the Greek
mercenaries, and made a detailed and reliable report on the course
of the battle, asserts that nine hundred thousand soldiers fought with
King Darius (*Anab.* 1.7.12).[8] The credible traditions on Alexander's
great battles reported in Arrian's *Anabasis* likewise attribute exaggerated numbers to the Persian armies,[9] although the information is
mainly based on the memoirs of Ptolemy son of Lagus who took an
active part in them and, as a senior commander in Alexander's
army, was well informed on details. To give just one example, in
regard to the battle of Issus, Arrian states that 600,000 Persian
soldiers took part in it against 40,000 of Alexander's (2.8.8).[10] But
the battlefield was only about six kilometres long, and confined on
one side by the sea and on the other by the almost vertical slopes of
the Amanus range.[11] That arena could contain only a small percentage of the number cited by Arrian, the more so in this case when
the army was composed mainly of cavalry.[12] Evidently these data

[8] For an analysis of Xenophon's description and the figures attributed to the armies see
Kromayer and Veith 1903–32: 4.221–42.

[9] This matter is familiar to many, and detailed bibliographical notes would be superfluous.
It is worth remembering Tarn 1948: 2.137, who notes the exaggeration in the number of
enemy troops, and the minimization of the number of Alexander's troops and casualties in the
battle of Hydaspes (pp. 190ff.). See also the explanations of Griffith 1935: 19.

[10] Thus also in Plutarch (*Alex.* 18). In Justin (11.9.1) and Diodorus (17.31.2), 500,000; in
Orosius (3.16.6), 400,000; in Curtius (3.2.4–9), 312,000.

[11] Regarding the battlefield see Janke 1904: 5ff.; Judeich 1931: 4.355ff.; Hammond 1981:
94ff.; Bosworth 1980a: 203–4.

[12] See the assessment of the deployment possibilities for the cavalry in Alexander's time in
Polybius 12.18.4.

were taken from Ptolemy's book,[13] but even if they were not, it
should be borne in mind that Arrian was a native of Asia Minor and
served under Hadrian as the governor of Cappadocia which is not
very far from the battle area. Arrian must have been aware of the
features of the terrain around the Bay of Alexandretta which were
well known because of its importance as a major route. As an
experienced military man he was capable of discerning the absurdity
of the figure he reported, especially since he was presumably familiar
with the harsh criticism Polybius levelled at Callisthenes (12.17–18),
himself an eye-witness to the battle of Issus, though the latter attributed a considerably lower figure in that battle to the Persians –
only 30,000 cavalry and 30,000 infantry.[14] Such disproportions in
reporting military numbers are of course common in the writings of
authors who lacked military experience and were not present on the
battlefield.[15]

The negative evaluation of the authenticity of the speeches included in the book, like the negative evaluation of the reliability of the
military numbers cited, does not detract from I Maccabees' overall
credibility. Although he was an eye-witness of some of the battles,
the author of I Maccabees was not part of Judas Maccabaeus' inner
circle;[16] he did not serve as a staff reporter and thus did not record
the battle orations as they were given. Even a precise and meticulous
eye-witness was at a later stage incapable of reconstructing the
wording of a speech delivered in the emotional atmosphere preceding

[13] See Brunt (1976: 1.151 n. 5, 462–3) on the meaning of the word ἐλέγετο (= it is told)
in this context. Bosworth (1980a: 209), on the other hand, speculates on the basis of the
expression ἐλέγετο γάρ that Arrian or the source he used had reservations about the number
attributed to the Persian army. However, both had the opportunity to know other numbers,
Ptolemy directly and Arrian from the sources he used. Thus even if the expression noted does
suggest certain reservations, this is not enough to clear Arrian or Ptolemy of the charge of
incorporating an unreasonable number (and none other) in the military report.
[14] It does not matter that Polybius erred in considerably reducing the size of the battlefield
at Issus (to 14 *stadia* = 2.7 km); see Walbank 1957–79: 2.367. The difference in the estimate
of the area far from justifies the vast difference in numbers between Callisthenes and
Ptolemy–Arrian. On Polybius' criticism see also Meister 1975: 81–90, and earlier bibliography
there.
[15] If we are restricted to just one example from Greek history, it is worth recalling Timoleon's expedition to Sicily (Diod. 16.77.4 and 78.2; Plut. *Tim.* 25.3; etc.). Timoleon was
much admired by the Sicilian sources underlying Diodorus' and Plutarch's accounts (especially
Timaeus: see Westlake 1938: 68–72; Brown 1958: 83–7; Talbert 1974: 22–38). Those sources
glorified their hero by attributing a tremendous numerical advantage to his enemies, which
does not fit the various phases of the battles or the options open to the two sides. On Timaeus'
lack of familiarity with military matters see Polybius 12.23–4, 25f 7,25h 2. On Timaeus' gift
for invention see Polybius 12.12,25i 5,25k 1. Talbert's analysis of the battle figures (ibid. p. 64),
despite his description of them as 'unreasonable', seems too credulous, and ignores the
tendentiousness of the sources.
[16] See pp. 238, 281, 335 below.

a battle, however impressive the speech may have been, and however experienced he might be in the use of the mnemonic devices favoured by the rhetoricians of the period.[17] At most he could hope to retain the spirit of the oration or an isolated sentence of particularly forceful rhetoric. The author's reports of the commanders' orations are unreliable, just like those contained in the writings of his contemporaries and of distinguished historians, including eye-witnesses, who preceded him. Every student of Ancient History is acquainted with Thucydides' much discussed admission that the orations embedded in his writings contain what 'in my opinion was demanded of them [i.e. the speakers] by the various occasions (περὶ τῶν αἰεὶ παρόντων τὰ δέοντα μάλιστα εἰπεῖν), of course adhering as closely as possible to the general sense (τῆς ξυμπάσης γνώμης) of what was really said' (1.22.1). This legacy of the father of critical historiography in one way or another guided the best of Greek and Hellenistic historians.[18] Less qualified historians incorporated in the speeches their own views, using them as a means of emphasizing lessons of a religious, moral or nationalistic nature. Some of them did not even take the trouble to adapt the contents and wording of the speech to the circumstances.[19]

The battle orations in I Maccabees are in the main the product of the author's imagination, as they are for the most part patterned on the declaration of '(the priest) anointed for battle' (משוח מלחמה) in the war code in Deuteronomy (20.3–4). Occasionally the timing of their delivery does not accord with the circumstances. Thus for instance during the ambush at Beth Horon, when the maintenance of absolute silence was vital, Judas Maccabaeus is described as delivering an oration proper just before the assault (3.17–23). At the battle of Ammaus when Judas Maccabaeus intended to raid the complacent Seleucid camp, the Jewish force was discovered by a forward sentry of the enemy, and it was therefore necessary to take immediate action. Nevertheless in that case too the author has Judas Maccabaeus making a detailed speech when encountering the enemy camp, before breaking into it (4.8–11).[20] More than once the length of the oration is out of all proportion to

[17] On these methods see Blum 1969.

[18] See Walbank 1965; on Polybius: id. 1957–79: 1.13–14. On Xenophon see Kelley 1977; on Arrian see Tarn 1948: 2.286–95.

[19] See Walbank 1965: 4ff. On the orations inserted in Hellenistic historiography see Scheller 1911: 50–6; Norden 1923: 1.89–99. See, for example, on the speeches in Livy, p. 94 n. 17 below. See also the criticism of Polybius 2.56.10; Plut. *Praecept. ger. reip.* 6 (803b); and the comment of Lucian, *Hist. conscr.* 58.

[20] On the oration before the ambush at Beth Horon see pp. 214–16 below re verses 19–23; on that at Ammaus see pp. 266–7 below re verse 8.

that of the information given on the battle itself (3.17–22, 4.30–3).
As for the contents, the emphasis is always on the enemy's numerical
advantage, the object of the speeches being to inculcate in the reader
the religious and educational lesson of Heaven's covert assistance to
the combatants. This is done even in cases where Judas Maccabaeus'
forces could be numerically superior, but for tactical reasons he
deployed only a small part of his combatants (Beth Horon: 3.18–22),
and where the historical circumstances do not permit attributing any
numerical advantage to the enemy (Adasa: 7.41–2).[21] It is interesting
to note that the battle orations in I Maccabees are completely
different from those ascribed in II Maccabees to the same battles.
Although in *Bellum Judaicum* Josephus consistently provided a word-
for-word paraphrase of I Maccabees, he nevertheless freely adapted
the orations in the spirit of Hellenistic rhetoric and presented a text
entirely different from that in the source he had used. For Josephus
himself understood that too much importance was not to be assigned
to the existing text, and preferred to follow the recognized and well-
known Hellenistic literary tradition, the terms and style of which
were likely to be accepted with considerably more interest and
understanding by the potential Greco-Roman reader.[22]

As to the different views on the date of the composition and on the
sources of I Maccabees, stress should be laid on the impression,
which is gained from an analysis of the battles of Ammaus and Beth
Zacharia, that the author was an eye-witness to the events and even
took an active part in them. Conspicuous in the account of the battle
of Ammaus is the congruity between the complex, detailed timetable
(3.47,57, 4.1,3–6), the numerous topographical details (3.40,46,57,
4.1,3,6,7,12,14,15,18,22), and the varied and sophisticated military
movements. In view of the inadequacy of battle accounts preserved
in ancient times in second-hand sources, it is difficult to believe that
the author would have been capable, on the basis of an oral or written
source, of providing such a detailed and accurate report of so complicated a battle, unless he had himself been present during the
action. Thus in *Antiquitates*, although Josephus sought, by following
I Maccabees verse by verse, to give a continuous and faithful

[21] See p. 213 re verse 16 below on the tactical compulsions at Beth Horon, and p. 365 re verse 41 on the purpose of the battle oration at Adasa.
[22] Despite the general agreement among scholars on the non-credibility of most of the war orations in Greek and Hellenistic literature, this evaluation has for some reasons not been applied to the speeches in I Maccabees. The reservations thus far expressed related to the poetic parts of the speeches (e.g. 3.50–3, 4.8–11), and even then for reasons of form, not substance. See Abel 1949: xxiv; Dancy 1954: 4. See, however, the total rejection by Pfeifer 1949: 486–7; also Zunz 1832: 123; Bartlett 1973: 17.

paraphrase of the battle of Ammaus, he nevertheless omitted any mention of either Mizpah, where Judas Maccabaeus concentrated his force, or of the temporary encampment south of Ammaus, two topographical details without which it would be impossible to reconstruct either the course of events or Judas Maccabaeus' tactical plan.

From a study of the report on the battle of Beth Zacharia, some scholars, basing their view on the description of the shields glittering in the sun (6.39) and Eleazar's struggle with the leading elephant (6.46), have arrived at a similar conclusion regarding the author's personal participation in the battle.[23] But, as a matter of fact, details like those relating to the first point have been preserved even in a secondary or tertiary source, such as Plutarch (*Eumenes* 14, *Sulla* 16), and several objections must be raised in connection with various details in the episode of Eleazar's struggle with the elephant,[24] although these are not enough, if account is taken of the 'fog of battle', to reject the possibility that the author took part in the encounter. On the other hand, the description of the Seleucid army's special 'formations' (*ma'arākōt*) in the battle (6.35–9)[25] is unique: neither their composition nor their deployment could have been drawn from contemporary military literature (as, e.g., in II Macc. 15.20), for both deviated from the standard procedure because of the special conditions of the terrain; had the author taken all this from a written source, it would not have been preserved in such great detail and with such accuracy. In any event, the deployment and advance of the 'formations' side by side in an extended line in the first stage of the Seleucid force's movement in the broad valley before entering the defile (6.35) and before contact was made between the opposing forces would certainly not have found a place in a compressed, concise account of the kind we have here, if the author had not personally witnessed and been stirred by it. It is no wonder that Josephus in *Antiquitates* omitted this stage entirely, and did not describe the special deployment in the broad valley. Furthermore the author reports that the Jewish force heard the din of the soldiers, their marching and the clanging of their weapons only after he says that the Seleucid army entered the defile in the second stage of its advance (6.41), and not earlier in the account of the first stage (6.33–9) when describing in detail the Seleucids' impressive and menacing extended line in the broad valley. This sequence fits in admirably with the particularly contrasting acoustical properties of

---

[23] Abel 1949: xxiv; Zeitlin 1950: 27; Dancy 1954: 3; Torrey 1963: 73.
[24] Pp. 336–7 below.   [25] See pp. 126–7 above, and below, pp. 312–17.

the broad valley and the defile.[26] As for the shields glistening in the sun, which are mentioned only at the end of the first stage shortly before the report of the entry into the defile (6.39), this could not have happened earlier in view of the season, the timing and the direction of the Seleucid advance. The author also displays the utmost accuracy in referring to the gradual rising of the sun, which produced the stated effect.[27] Despite Josephus' striving after accuracy, he made a mistake in *Antiquitates* as regards this 'superfluous' detail and even introduced it into the wrong context, when explaining that after entering the defile, on giving the command to sound the battle cry and charging the Jews, the king instructed the soldiers to uncover their shields, which produced a brilliant light (12.372). It is noteworthy that the hearing of the shouts of the soldiers was mentioned by Josephus only in connection with the commencement of the battle itself, even before the gleam of the shields. Josephus' version, in which there is great military logic (for one unacquainted with the features of the battlefield and the uniqueness of the situation), demonstrates what can be expected to happen to details of this kind in an author who was not an eye-witness. It should be added that *Bellum Judaicum*, which is based on a secondary source, mentions neither the visual effect created by the shields nor the noise made by the troops in their advance.

Despite all that has been stated, it can be said with a great deal of certainty that the author was not a member of Judas Maccabaeus' general staff. He makes no reference to Judas Maccabaeus' intelligence activity and tactical considerations in the battle of Ammaus, without which it is difficult to understand its diverse movements. Moreover he errs in his explanation of the status and function of the leading elephant at Beth Zacharia, as well as Eleazar's motives in attacking it (6.43–4).

As for the other battles, the description of the battle of Elasa may be based on an eye-witness report. This cannot be definitely proved, however, since in the detailed account of the actions and movements of the Seleucid army there are almost no details which deviate from the deployment and standard method of operation customary in Hellenistic armies. The reference to the advance of the phalanx with its two parts, which contrary to the usual practice in this instance preceded the cavalry attack and did not even directly affect the outcome of the battle (9.12), does not necessarily prove that we have here the direct report of an eye-witness: this piece of information is neither superfluous nor irrelevant, since it is of considerable impor-

[26] See pp. 331–2 below.   [27] See pp. 327–9 above.

tance for an understanding of Judas Maccabaeus' reaction on his wing,[28] and the author was likely to comprehend this on his own. Nor do the many lacunae in the I Maccabees description of the battle of Elasa, such as the absence of any reference to the results of the clash at the centre and to the developments on the right wing of the Jewish force (cf. Lucian, *Hist. conscr.* 49), rule out the possibility that the author was an eye-witness. The report centres round the actions and reactions of the commander, since this was his final hour. The author may also have been stationed on the left wing of the Jewish battle line which, in the course of the pursuit, moved far from the battlefield, so that he had difficulty in following developments in the other sectors when the left wing made contact with the enemy. But if the author did not take part in the battle and based his statements on the testimony of others, he is certainly to be classed as a first-rate military historian. A comparison with Josephus' paraphrase in *Antiquitates* is enough to establish him as such. If we had only Josephus' account it would have been impossible to reconstruct the operations of the Seleucid army in the battle of Elasa.

That the author was an eye-witness to the battle of Beth Horon is less likely, since the description is not particularly detailed nor does it contain 'superfluous' details. The accounts of the confrontation with Apollonius and of the battles of Beth Zur, Kafar Salama and Adasa certainly do not reflect the testimony of eye-witnesses: the absence of any substantial details on the battle against Apollonius, the great brevity, the general nature of the reports, and the lack of detailed accounts of the movements in the field at the battles of Beth Zur and Kafar Salama, all indicate that the sources at the author's disposal were not of the best quality. The author of I Maccabees or his sources may have deliberately curtailed the description of the operation at Beth Zur in order to obscure the nature and actual results of the encounter, so glorifying the deeds and achievements of Judas Maccabaeus.[29] As for the battle of Adasa, if we take into account that it was fought at a late stage in the Revolt when a regular record of events was undoubtedly kept, and especially the powerful impression of the victory that was celebrated for generations, it is difficult to believe that the author of I Maccabees, who is generally held to have had free access to the Hasmonaean court, did not have extensive information on the encounter. The shallow, obscure description of the battle can be taken as indicative of the way in which the author adapted information about events at which he himself was not present, and reinforces the supposition that

[28] See pp. 393–4 below.   [29] Pp. 134–5 above, and 275–6 below.

the author was an eye-witness of the battles of Ammaus and Beth Zacharia, and perhaps also of Elasa.

It may thus be assumed that the accounts of the battles of Ammaus, Beth Zacharia and Elasa are based on notes made by the author or also by others shortly after the events. Decades later, when he came to incorporate them into his book, he had no difficulty in reliving the battles, and thus succeeded in preserving the details which enabled him to depict a consistent and coordinated picture of the developments. In the descriptions of the other battles, the author may have drawn for some of them on oral reports, for others on current chronicles or similar written material. The former case appears to be a reasonable assumption for several battles in the first stage of the campaign before the purification of the Temple, while the latter appears to be applicable to the encounters with Nicanor.

The various hints that may help to determine the date of the composition of the book do not contradict these conclusions. Differences of opinion have centred around its closing verses: 'and the rest of the story (τῶν λόγων = דברי) and his wars and the deeds of valour he [John Hyrcanus] performed and the building of the walls he built and his deeds, lo they are written in the book of his high priesthood from the time when he was the high priest after his father' (16.23–4). Some scholars point to these verses as proof that the book was written after the death of John Hyrcanus, that is, not before 104 B.C., whereas those who date its composition earlier maintain that these verses are a later interpolation or an adaptation, devoid of any significance, of the well-known biblical phrase.[30] But there is no need of these assumptions. The reference in these verses to 'the book of his high priesthood' does not necessarily indicate that the writing of the chronicle had already been completed. Moreover the only significant act with which the verse credits Hyrcanus, as distinct from the general statement about 'his wars and the deeds of valour', is 'the building of the walls'. What is meant here is the rebuilding and enlargement of the walls of Jerusalem after they had been demolished by Antiochus VII Sidetes on the raising of the siege at the outset of Hyrcanus' rule (*Ant.* 13.247; Diodorus 34–35.1.5).[31]

[30] I Kings 15.23, 16.5,27; II Kings 10.34, 13.8,12, 14.28, 20.20. See Momigliano 1930: 36ff.; id. 1980: 565–6; Dancy 1954: 8; and others.

[31] According to Diodorus (34–35.5) and Porphyry (in Eusebius, Schoene edition, vol. 1, p. 255), Antiochus Sidetes destroyed the city wall of Jerusalem. Josephus in *Antiquitates* writes: καθεῖλε δὲ καὶ τὴν στεφάνην τῆς πόλεως (= and destroyed the crown of the city), and some scholars deduced from that phrase that only the battlements of the wall were demolished. However, it would have been little use destroying the battlements and not the wall, and in any case such a limitation is contradicted by Diodorus, Porphyry and even by what is implied in I Macc. 16.23. We must conclude that Nicolaus, the peripatetic author who was Josephus'

This was undoubtedly done by Hyrcanus shortly after the death of Antiochus Sidetes in his great expedition to the eastern satrapies in 129 B.C. What is decisive is that, of the considerable achievements of John Hyrcanus – which included conquering Samaria and Idumaea, the plain of Esdraelon, Galilee,[32] and some Transjordanian cities, as well as proselytizing the Idumaeans and settling Galilee and the Coastal Plain – the author contrived to mention specifically only the rebuilding of the walls, an undertaking which was carried out at the beginning of Hyrcanus' rule and which, with the change in the political conditions and the enormous territorial expansion in the course of the years, actually lost its importance. How is it that the author, who stresses the Jewish right to reconquer the country (15.33–4) and admires Hyrcanus, failed to mention the latter's conquests in his summary? It follows therefore that the author was unacquainted with John Hyrcanus' other activities, and that the book was completed when the restoration of the walls was still regarded as his most important achievement, that is, between 129 and 126 B.C.[33] The words 'his wars and the deeds of valour he performed' accordingly refer to John's first military operations at the end of his father Simeon's reign and during the initial six years of his rule, which included the war against Kendebaeus in the Aijalon Valley and his struggle with Ptolemy son of Abubus, the governor of Jericho, Antiochus Sidetes' siege, and the expedition against the Parthians in which he took part as the latter's vassal. The phrase 'and the deeds of valour' does not necessarily signify particularly large military successes, but was included in order to stress John Hyrcanus' personal bravery (see esp. I Macc. 16.6).

Accordingly it may be assumed that 'the book of his high priesthood' relates to a current chronicle which was being written in the Hasmonaean court from Hyrcanus' accession to the presidency in 135 B.C. The unusual reference to a chronicle which had not yet been completed was necessary because the conclusion of the book cut short the story of John's activities. Although the author devoted the literary framework of the book exclusively to the first five Hasmo-

source for this point, used 'crown' as a figure of speech to stress the importance of the wall for the security and prestige of the city, whereas Diodorus' restricted vocabulary and dry style retained the wording of the source he used, probably Poseidonius of Apamea. On the sources for this incident see Bar-Kochva 1977: 181–4. The building enterprise may have included the so-called 'first wall', but this is still not to be compared with Hyrcanus' great conquests.

[32] On the problem of the conquest of Galilee and its dating see p. 554 n. 5 below.

[33] On the dating of John Hyrcanus' first round of conquests see pp. 560–2 below. Momigliano (1980: 564–6) dates the book no later than 129 B.C. because of the absence in chapter 8 of any reference to the elimination of Pergamum and the establishment of the Roman province Asia.

naeans, he did not end it with the death of Simeon (16.16), but told
of his son John's vigilance and swift action in seizing power, since he
felt the need to set the reader's mind at rest with the information that
the machinations of Ptolemy son of Abubus had failed, and that the
rule had remained in the hands of the Hasmonaean family. Having
already mentioned Hyrcanus at the beginning of his career, the
author had to refer his readers of future generations to some source
for the continuation of the high priest's activities. When the work
was written, not long after 129 B.C., he could point only to the official
chronicle that was being written in the Hasmonaean court. Actually
the wording of the verse in the spirit and style of the concluding
remarks to the historic accounts of the kings of Israel and Judah
served an additional purpose. It awoke in the reader an association
between the leaders of the Hasmonaean dynasty and the rulers of the
nation in its glorious past during the First Temple period (cf.
9.22).

The fundamental mistakes in the book about the Roman regime
and history, and especially the favourable, enthusiastic view of
Roman imperialism (ch. 8), fit in more with the level of information
about and attitude towards Rome early in John Hyrcanus' reign.
Under Alexander Jannaeus, Greek–Oriental literature (especially
the writings of Poseidonius of Apamea) showed increasing interest in
the regime and society of that rising Western power. While Roman
involvement in the affairs of the region grew more serious, the
Hasmonaean state no longer had need of any patronage and diplomatic help. There are also indications of Jannaeus' anti-Roman
policy; at any rate, in contrast to his predecessors, he did not renew
the pact with Rome, nor did the interests of the great power now
coincide with his aims.[34] The anachronistic allusion to the conquest
and destruction of Corinth in 146 B.C., mentioned in the account of
the alliance with Rome in the days of Judas Maccabaeus (I Macc.
8.10), does not compel us to postpone the date of the book's composition much beyond 146 B.C.: in that chapter the author summed
up the knowledge he had about Roman imperialism, and was not
precise about the chronological order. It may also be that he was
unaware that the final conquest of Greece occurred only after the
death of Judas Maccabaeus. Under the conditions of communications that prevailed in the ancient world, there is nothing surprising
in this. Nor can it be expected of an author, who states that Media
and India were transferred to the rule of Eumenes (sic) after the

[34] On the relations between Jannaeus and Rome see Rappaport 1968b: 329–45; M. Stern
1981: 28–9.

battle of Magnesia (I Macc. 8.8), that he should take a lengthy
journey abroad, for instance, and search in libraries and archives to
find out when exactly Corinth fell. Having heard a report of the
conquest of Greece and the destruction of cities, he introduced it into
his account to stress the achievements of the rising power. Nor does
the statement that the tombs of Mattathias and the four brothers
were in Modein 'unto this day' (13.30) prove the lateness of the
book. The unusual syntactical construction of the verse and its
artificial and forced introduction in the passage suggest that it is a
later interpolation. Be that as it may, it could have been written close
to 129 B.C. The verse refers to the monumental structure set up by
Simeon immediately after the death of his brother John sixteen years
earlier, and the biblical phrase may have been selected to emphasize
that Simeon intended to perpetuate the memory of the members of
his family (see 13.29: 'for a perpetual memory').

Dispensing at this stage with a complicated chronological discussion, it should be noted that even the acknowledged disruption in
the continuity of events in I Maccabees – with the purification of the
Temple (4.36–60) and Judas Maccabaeus' rescue expeditions (ch. 5)
preceding Antiochus Epiphanes' death (6.1–17) – does not refute
the conclusion that the author was a contemporary of the events.
The analysis of the special circumstances of that year, the author's
status and locus at the time, the sources of information available to
him, and the chronological systems he used, all these explain the
error.[35]

In connection with the conclusion drawn from the closing verses
of the book regarding the date of its composition, note should be
taken of the view held by several scholars who, following von Destinon, maintain that the final chapters in I Maccabees (13.31ff.) are
a later addition and do not belong to the main body of the book.
They note in particular that Josephus, who consistently paraphrases
I Maccabees in *Antiquitates*, bases himself, from the account of
Tryphon's accession to the throne (*Ant.* 13.213–29), on another
source.[36] This proof, like other arguments, has been rejected by
various scholars who have advanced positive and weighty reasons in
favour of the integrity of I Maccabees.[37] However, further objections
and doubts on this score are nevertheless still heard from time to
time.[38] Among other objections, mention is made of the many docu-

---

[35] See in detail pp. 281–2 below.

[36] Von Destinon (1882: 80–91) and many who followed in his footsteps. See the detailed
bibliography in Schunck 1954: 7–8.

[37] Especially Ettelson 1925: 249–384; Schunck 1954: 10–15; Arenhoevel 1967: 94–6.

[38] E.g. Baer (1968: 105–6) considers chh. 1–7 a separate unit.

ments inserted in the account of the period of Jonathan and Simeon
(or already close to the death of Judas Maccabaeus; chh. 8ff.); the
omission of the events that took place during Jonathan's rule in the
seven years between 159 and 152 B.C. (I Macc. 9.54,73, 10.1); and,
mainly, the glaring disproportion between the length of the account
devoted to the first of the brothers (about six and a half chapters
for a period of six years) as against the comparative brevity of the
account of Jonathan and Simeon (seven and a half chapters that
describe a period of some twenty-five years).

All these cannot, however, disprove the integrity of the book. The
documents in the report on Jonathan's leadership are numerous
due to contemporary conditions: through diplomatic contacts he
exploited the violent internal struggle for power in Antioch to obtain
concessions, which found their official expression in these documents,
whereas by contrast Judas Maccabaeus conducted negotiations with
the central authorities only once,[39] and during Nicanor's governorship maintained some brief contact with the local administration.[40]
The silence about 159 to 152 B.C. arose from the absence of any
important events during those years. Demetrius I's rule had attained
stability and full control, and as a result the scope and possibilities
of Jonathan's activities had narrowed greatly. After the considerable
achievements and actions of Judas Maccabaeus, the period of Jonathan's stay at Michmash seemed a 'day of small things', unworthy
of being recorded. And finally, the author dealt in great detail with
the military events in the days of Judas Maccabaeus, mainly because
he was personally involved in some of them, whereas under Jonathan
and Simeon he was already of advanced age and did not participate
in the principal events. Moreover, the length of time that had elapsed
since the events of Judas Maccabaeus' time imparted a greater glory
and splendour to them than to more recent developments. In fact,
the military struggle that occurred in the days of Judas Maccabaeus
was certainly more heroic and exciting, since in general it involved a
united regime waging war against the Jewish people and not various
contenders for power seeking the help of the Jews against internal
rivals.

In contrast to what is known of II Maccabees, there is no room for
accepting the suggestion made by some that I Maccabees is an
abridgement of an earlier more comprehensive work. I Maccabees
is marked by consistency and continuity. It does not contain references to events or people never before mentioned (in contrast, e.g.,
to II Macc. 5.27, 8.30, 10.14), or gross geographic mistakes caused

[39] See Appendix I, pp. 517–23, 533, 538.   [40] Pp. 349–51, 354–6 below.

by abbreviation (as in II Macc. 12.10), or allusions to later events
not noted in the book itself (as in II Macc. 4.11). Despite I Maccabees' terse style in comparison with the flowery loquacity of II
Maccabees, the former contains no verses compressing a number of
occurrences into a few words (in contrast to, e.g., II Macc. 5.27 and
14.25). The precision in the battle descriptions is the best indication
that the book is not an abridgement, for it is in the nature of an
epitomist to mutilate and garble.

In considering the sources of I Maccabees many scholars have
noted the use the author made of official archives from which
documents cited in the book were taken, and of written chronicles.
The clear evidence of the use of a chronicle or chronicles is the many
dates cited, all of them based on the calendar employed in the
Seleucid empire. Contrary to the general practice in antiquity, the
Seleucids did not begin a separate count for each king, but commenced their dating from 312 or 311 B.C., commemorating the conquest of Babylonia by Seleucus Nicator. There were, however, two
systems: as the Macedonians in Syria started their year in the
traditional opening month of Dios, corresponding more or less to
October, their count began in the autumn of 312 B.C. In Babylonia
the year started in *Nisanu* (about April), and the Babylonian sources
accordingly count from the spring of 311 B.C.[41] It has been assumed
that as the ancient Hebrew calendar also began the year in the
spring, the Babylonian version of the Seleucid calendar was adopted
by the Jews in Eretz Israel. However, Bickerman has succeeded in
proving that both systems are used in I Maccabees. The Babylonian
system is utilized for domestic affairs such as the death of Mattathias
and the purification of the Temple, while for external affairs (like the
dates of Seleucid expeditions, events in Antioch, and so on) the
Macedonian–Syrian system is applied.[42] In II Maccabees, on the
other hand, in which all dates except two appear in the official
documents in ch. 11, it is natural that only the Macedonian–Syrian
system is used.[43] As the adaptation of the two sets of dates to the two

[41] On the start of the Babylonian reckoning see especially Kugler 1907: 1.211; Parker and
Dubberstein 1956: 10–26; Bickerman 1968: 22–6,71; Samuel 1972: 142–3.

[42] First in the entry on 'Makkabäerbücher' in *RE*, cols. 781–4, where he thought that the
'internal' count began in April 312, but he later set April 311 as the start of the 'internal'
count; see Bickerman 1933: 241; id. 1937: 155–8. For evidence based on the Babylonian
chronicle of the Seleucid kings published in 1954, see Schaumberger 1955: 423–7; Hanhart
1964: 55–96. For refutation of the arguments against Bickerman's system see pp. 562–5
below.

[43] Thus Bickerman in *RE* s.v. 'Makkabäerbücher', cols. 789–90; id. 1937: 157. This does
not necessarily relate to the dates in the first document at the beginning of the book (1.7,9),
which like the second document is not, all agree, from Jason of Cyrene's book, and in any case
is a document written by the Jerusalemites. On the date that appears in II Macc. 13.1 in the

categories of events could not have been done by the author himself or with his knowledge, it was concluded that he at least utilized a Seleucid source from Syria. Since the book does not abound in information on events in the empire, at court or in the army, it stands to reason that that source was quite a short one. The brevity and the many dates suggest that it was a chronicle. The 'domestic' dates could have been reported by the author himself from his own knowledge, but the possibility should not be eliminated that he made parallel use of some Jewish chronicle on the times of Judas Maccabaeus, perhaps a family chronicle of the Hasmonaean dynasty.

In summing up it may be said that an analysis of the battles reveals the satisfactory level of accuracy of I Maccabees as a whole and of the accounts of the battles in particular. This favourable evaluation does not, however, apply to the numbers of the forces and to the orations of the commanders. Written in the days of John Hyrcanus shortly after 129 B.C. and about thirty years after the death of Judas Maccabaeus, the book has, as its source of information, the author's personal experiences, reports and accounts of other eye-witnesses, notes which he himself or others had kept, as well as official documents found in the Hasmonaean archives, and also at least one Seleucid chronicle.[44]

A proper understanding of I Maccabees is impossible without an accurate reconstruction of the original Hebrew text. For the present, the only attempt at a comprehensive one is the Hebrew translation by Abraham Cahana,[45] which also included sporadic suggestions made by Michaelis and Grimm in their commentaries on I Maccabees. Following his predecessors, Cahana assumed that the author of I Maccabees used only biblical expressions, and that the Greek translator of I Maccabees kept to the Greek vocabulary and the method of translation used by the Septuagint.[46] Accordingly,

course of the story see p. 549 below; the author determined the date and inserted it in the wake of a series of dates in the documents in ch. 11, and consequently it too is based on the Macedonian–Syrian system, as is the date of the high priest Alcimus' call on Demetrius I upon the latter's accession to the throne (14.4; see in detail the reasons given by Goldstein 1976: 544). There are no grounds for the contention of Bunge (1971: 341ff.) that the two dates given in the narrative are based on the Macedonian–Babylonian system, and none for the view of Zeitlin (1950: 253) that the count in II Maccabees starts in the autumn of 311.

[44] This does not mean a systematic inclusion of passages from a Seleucid chronicle as suggested by Schunck (1954: 36–51), but rather a haphazard gleaning of information. Neuhaus (1974: 165–8) correctly argues that the verses which Schunck attributes to the Seleucid chronicle do not embody the components typical of Seleucid chronicles, and that the verses indicate a critical stance, at times even a clearly anti-Seleucid approach. On the question of I Maccabees' use of written sources see also pp. 401–2 below re verse 22.

[45] Cahana 1957: 2.95–175.

[46] See especially the evidence of Grimm in the introduction to his exegesis on I Maccabees (1853: xv–xvii) and in the body of the book, passim; Ettelson 1925: 303ff.

Cahana sought to reconstruct the language of the original through a rigorous examination of every word that occurs in the Greek text of I Maccabees and its usages in the Septuagint.[47] Cahana did his work with commendable assiduousness, but while the method is fundamentally correct, the assumptions on which it is based are too categorical: there are definite indications that the author of I Maccabees, when unable to find the suitable biblical expressions, used Greek words in some Hebrew transcription for current Hellenistic terms, such as 'gymnasium', 'phalanx', 'helepolis', and perhaps others.[48] For reasons which are not clear, he at times even used the language of the Sages.[49] For his part, the Greek translator of I Maccabees more than once deviated from the usual vocabulary of the Septuagint, and translated a biblical word with a Greek one used in the Septuagint for another purpose.[50] At times he preferred Greek words that do not occur in the Septuagint at all.[51] In a number of these instances Cahana translated the Greek text by biblical expressions that are wide of the mark. On the other hand, for no apparent reason Cahana sometimes diverged from the principle he had laid down for himself by deviating from the method of the Septuagint. Another shortcoming in Cahana's translation arises from different biblical words having been frequently translated in the Septuagint by the same Greek expressions, for which only the context and a philological and historical analysis can determine the appropriate Hebrew word to be reconstructed for I Maccabees. More than once Cahana's choice is wrong because of an inaccurate interpretation of a verse.[52] In the commentary on the accounts of the battles in I Maccabees I have, on the basis of these criticisms, tried to correct and improve the reconstruction of the text suggested by Cahana and his predecessors, in cases where this is important in

[47] A similar attempt at reconstruction of the poetic passages only was recently made by G. O. Neuhaus (1974). Some of his secondary assumptions are erroneous, e.g. the notion that if the Greek translation contains words or phrases which in the Septuagint render a variety of Hebrew terms, the term to choose is the one that appears in the biblical books written near the author's time (1974: 50-1). The book is deliberately archaizing in the choice of vocabulary and expressions.

[48] I Macc. 1.14, 13.43, and see pp. 432ff. below on φάλαγξ (9.12, 10.82). Cf. on this also Baer (1968: 105), although his approach is rather extreme. Thus it is hard to agree with him that the Hebrew original of βωμούς (I Macc. 1.54) was bōmōsiōt and not bāmōt: see ibid. p. 108 n. 12a. The latter fits in with the author's intentions and evokes known biblical associations.

[49] So too Alon 1958: 2.153-9; and p. 214 below re verse 18; pp. 312 and 332 below.

[50] See, e.g., pp. 267-8 re verse 12; p. 283 re verse 26; p. 340 re verse 50; p. n. 2.

[51] See below p. 284 re verse 28; pp. 332 re verse 41; and also pp. 391-2. Cf. Ettelson 1925: 322-5; Pfeifer 1949: 497-8.

[52] For additional critical comments on Cahana's translation see Melamed 1932; Schwabe 1933-5: 274-7; Raban 1962; Baer 1968: 105 n. 9; Neuhaus 1971-2.

understanding the verse or the linguistic practice of the author of I Maccabees.

The Second Book of the Maccabees

II Maccabees is, as is well known, an abridgement of a five-book work by Jason of Cyrene. There is no doubt that the abridgement, like the original work, was written in Greek. The original work has not survived, and no explicit information is available on Jason's time, on his connection with the events, or on his sources. Nor is anything reported about the identity, time and location of the epitomist. What is known about the identity of the original author, the content and purpose of his book, the literary character and aims of the abridgement, is contained in the epitomist's short flowery introduction (2.19–32).[53] The epitome itself covers the entire period from the exacerbation of the internal crisis in Jerusalem in Seleucus IV's last regnal year (176 B.C.) which led to Heliodorus' attempt to plunder the Temple (3.1ff.) up to Judas Maccabaeus' defeat of Nicanor in the battle of Adasa and the subsequent proclamation of

[53] An interesting curiosity is the theory that II Maccabees is not an abridgement at all, and that Jason of Cyrene and his five books never existed but were invented by the author of II Maccabees. According to that theory the details about the abridgement in the introduction actually refer to the screening, arrangement and styling of the material in the sources at the disposal of the author, including mainly oral sources. See Kosters 1878: 491–558; Kamphausen 1900: 81,84; Richnow 1968: 7–12,36–42 and passim. The main effort of this last doctoral dissertation is aimed at proving this thesis, but the arguments proffered are unconvincing. According to Richnow the epitomist nowhere in the book states where and how he made the abridgement (but see 10.10); it is not possible that an historian of the Hasmonaean Revolt who wrote five books on the subject would end his book with Nicanor Day (see n. 95 below on this); a work of five books could not be so large that it would need to be abridged (but if they were like, e.g., the first five books of Polybius, they definitely merited abridgement); and finally, various authors in the Hellenistic period frequently cited sources in part fictitious (on this see especially Quintilian, *Inst.* 1.8.21 – but the reference is to reliance on sources for a book the author represented as his original work, not an epitome of a non-existent source). On the other hand all these ignore the clear evidence of the abridged nature of II Maccabees: the discrepancy between the definition of the historical framework (2.19–22) and the contents of the book; the abundance of participles which are a definite sign of abridgement (see p. 178 n. 85 below); a brief mention of events and persons, sometimes with no specification, in a form that definitely indicates a detailed description in the source the epitomist used or a reference to them in another context (4.11, 5.27, 10.37, 12.36, 14.19; and see pp. 181, 198 below); insertion of matters out of context and at incorrect times (e.g. 5.27, 8.30–3; pp. 196–9, 511–12); extreme brevity or truncation in a few episodes (e.g. 5.7, 8.1–7, 10.10–13,19, 13.21–3; 14.19) and exaggerated prolongation in others (mainly chh. 3, 6–7, 14–15), etc. Above all, why should any author describe his book as an abridgement of a non-existent work, attributing it to a man of no reputation and placing him in Cyrene, so far from the site of events? Would that make his book appear to provide good, authoritative and reliable testimony on events in Judaea? For other objections to Richnow see Doran 1981: 81–3.

Nicanor Day (15.36). In contrast to I Maccabees, II Maccabees enlarges upon the conflict of factions and personalities in Jerusalem and upon the Hellenistic reform (3.1–5.10) and the torture of the martyrs (6.1–7.42). The historical story is preceded by two epistles to the Jews of Egypt regarding Hanukkah (1.1–2.18), which are generally believed to have been written neither by Jason nor by the epitomist. All in all, along with corresponding stories in both books, there are some in II Maccabees lacking in I Maccabees and some in I Maccabees lacking in II Maccabees.[54]

A re-examination of II Maccabees serves only to confirm the presence of all those well-known features discerned by scholars in the past. The style of the narrative is diffuse and florid, permeated with pathos, and stands in complete contrast to the concise and to-the-point text of I Maccabees; the didactic–religious purpose to show that God will not allow his people to fall even if He is angry at them and punishes them, affects the presentation of the historical and military material in particular through stressing divine intervention in the course of events; the author's unfamiliarity with the geography of Eretz Israel obscures the course of the military developments. All this detracts from the quality and reliability of the accounts of the battles.

Despite the customary denigration of the accounts of the battles in II Maccabees, attempts have been made to glean various items of information from them to supplement the accounts in I Maccabees, sometimes even giving preference to the parallel information in the former source. In general it may be said that the author of II Maccabees had at times a better knowledge of the status of the Seleucid commanders and the hierarchy of the command than I Maccabees (e.g. II Macc. 8.8–9, 14.12 *versus* I Macc. 3.38, 7.26), just as in regard to external, political and administrative matters he occasionally had richer and more varied information. In some places the book contains valuable complementary information lacking in I Maccabees, such as the heroism of Dositheus in the battle of Marisa (12.35) and the treachery of Rhodocus at the siege of Beth Zur during Lysias' second campaign (13.19–21). There is no justification, however, for the attempts of certain scholars to rely on other fragments of information, such as, for example, the number of 20,000 combatants which II Maccabees ascribes to the Seleucid army in the battle of Ammaus (8.9). As a rule the figures in II Maccabees for the enemy forces are much more exaggerated than those in I Maccabees

[54] See a list of the passages and a comparative table in Pfeifer 1949: 472–4.

and in the case of Ammaus there was evidently a textual error in II Maccabees.[55] Nor is a preference for II Maccabees' version of the structure of the Jewish command, the tactical deployment of the force, and the form of attack in that battle (8.21–4) supported by any critical, methodical reasoning: if the author of II Maccabees was quite ignorant of the terrain, not much value can be attached to his statements about the form in which the attack was organized and the way in which it was carried out, and in any event these statements are not to be preferred to the detailed account of I Maccabees, firmly based as it is on the conditions of the terrain.[56] Neither are there any grounds for reconstructing the route of Lysias' second expedition to Judaea and the route Judas Maccabaeus followed in reconnoitring the Seleucid army on the basis of II Maccabees, which mentions a fictional earlier encounter at Modein (13.14–16),[57] or accepting the description of the deployment of the Seleucid force in the battle of Adasa given in II Maccabees, which mentions among other things elephants 'in an advantageous wing' (15.20), although at the time the Seleucid army no longer had any elephants.[58]

Within the context of the general evaluation a vital question is the identity of the literary school to which the book belongs. The author of II Maccabees is usually regarded as a distinguished representative of the pathetic–rhetorical school which was dominant in the Hellenistic period[59] – hence the atrocity stories and the human suffering, the epiphanies, the exaggerations, and the verbosity. However, although Jason of Cyrene undoubtedly belonged to this school, there are indications that he was at least influenced by the 'tragic' school, while the epitomist seems to have had a decided preference for writing in the style and structure characteristic of the latter school.[60] The determination of the literary school and its features

---

[55] See also p. 41 n. 41 above.

[56] See also pp. 256, 268 below. Cf. pp. 486–7.

[57] See pp. 197–8, 293–4 below.   [58] See p. 366 above re verse 43.

[59] Niese 1900: 32–9; Ed. Meyer 1921: 2.459; Bickerman in *RE* s.v. 'Makkabäerbücher', cols. 792ff.; id. 1937: 147; Abel 1949: xxxvi–xxxvii; Pfeifer 1949: 518; Hadas 1959: 126–7.

[60] F. Jacoby (in *RE* s.v. 'Jason' (10), col. 779) called Jason's writing 'tragic' but he does not explain his view. The 'tragic' tendency of II Maccabees has recently been briefly noted also by Christian Habicht in the introduction to his commentary on II Maccabees (1976a: 189–90). Against this opinion see Doran 1979: 110–14; id. 1981: 89ff. The latter proposes viewing II Maccabees as the annals of a city, concentrating on its defence by the local deity through epiphanies, on the pattern of literary works of this kind written in the Hellenistic period. However, despite the abundance of epiphanies in II Maccabees, the Temple and city of Jerusalem are not saved through an epiphany and they suffer conquest and profanation by Antiochus IV. The very existence of such a literary pattern is not proved: the references in the Lindos inscription to the authors who mention certain epiphanies which saved cities or holy places are no proof that they were written on the pattern suggested by Doran.

affects the assessment of the credibility of many informational details,[61] and for that reason it is worth noting the characteristics of the 'tragic' school and the form they assume in II Maccabees.

The existence of a 'tragic school' was first pointed out by Eduard Schwartz at the end of the last century.[62] Since then many scholars have added evidence and made various and contradictory proposals concerning suitable terminology, the sources of influence, the inception of the school, and the works that can be attributed to it.[63] A few voices (though venerable ones) doubted the existence of a school that deliberately and consciously applied the principles of tragedy, arguing that tragic features were permanent ingredients of Greek historiography since its very beginning.[64] However, the evidence presented by the majority seems convincing and in any case the difference of opinion does not basically affect our subject, for nobody denies that certain writers of the Hellenistic period were more influenced than their predecessors by the artistic rules that guided the tragic poets, even if the former did not at the outset consciously attempt to imitate tragic works with all their components and characteristic features.

The 'tragic' school is believed to have preached that the aim and some of the artistic means of an historiographic work should be similar to those of the poetic tragedy. The difference between them was deemed to be mainly in the form, for whereas the latter is constructed in metre and dialogue, the former is in literary prose. Since no complete prose work belonging definitely to the 'tragic' school is extant, it is difficult to ascertain the precise principles which guided the author. The general assumption is that Aristotle's distinctions in the *Poetics*, or at least rules he had internalized and the accepted practice, served as a guide for the 'tragic' historians as well. There is, however, no doubt that 'tragic' history writing could not

[61] See, e.g., the figures for the opposing forces, the course of the battles, the attitude to combat on the Sabbath, the figures of Antiochus Epiphanes and Nicanor, the marriage attributed to Judas Maccabaeus, Timotheus' blasphemy and his being 'killed off' twice, etc. See pp. 64–5, 198, 220, 277, 355–6, 361, 487–91, 512–13 below.

[62] Schwartz 1896: 123–5; id. 1897: 56ff.; id. in *RE* s.v. 'Diodoros', col. 687, and s.v. 'Duris', cols. 1853ff. The term 'historico-tragic' itself first appears in E. Will 1913: 76ff.

[63] Leo 1901: 110; Reitzenstein 1906: 84ff.; Scheller 1911: 38–72; Laqueur 1911: 347ff.; Norden 1923: 91–5; Ullman 1942: 25–53; Venini 1951: 54ff.; von Fritz 1958: 85–128; Zegers 1959; Brink 1960: 14–16; Syme 1964: 50–1; Strassburger 1966; Wardman 1974: 168–79; Momigliano 1978: 8. The main extant sources are: Polybius 2.16.14 and 56.6–13, 7.1–2, 15.36.7; Duris of Samos, *FGrH* IIA, no. 76, F 1; Diodorus 20.43.7; Plutarch, *Per.* 28, *Them.* 32, and *Alex.* 75; Lucian, *Hist. consc.*; Cicero, *Fam.* 5.12.3–5; Aristides, *Or.* 49 (vol. II, p. 513, ed. Dindorff); Horace, *Carm.* 2.1; *AP* 333–4.

[64] Walbank 1938: 55–9; id. 1945: 8–15; id. 1955: 4–14; id. 1960: 216–34; Meister 1975: 109–26; Kebric 1977: 11–18; Doran 1979: 107–10; id. 1981: 84–9. Cf. Giovannini 1943: 308–14; Wehrli 1946: 9–34; id. 1947: 54–71; Laistner 1947: 14ff.

be completely faithful to the *ars poetica* of the tragedy, especially as regards the external structure, because of its different formal character, the factual, historical basis on which it was structured, and the historian's personal or emotional involvement in events. Allowing for these, it may be said that most of the fundamental principles of the tragedy are indeed present in II Maccabees.

Just as a tragedy does not depict what has actually taken place but rather what would probably happen (*Poet.* 1451a.35–1451b.5), so the 'tragic' historian has to be faithful not to the facts but to artistic 'truth'. Accordingly II Maccabees strove for a complication of the plot (cf. *Poet.* 1452a.15,b.30), even if it meant departing from the historical truth.[65] The aim of an historiographic work, like that of a tragedy, is to bring the reader to catharsis, a 'cleansing' and 'purification' from emotions such as fear and pity (*Poet.* 1449b.25–30, 1452b.30). Hence II Maccabees plays on these emotions, often by misrepresenting the relative strength of the forces on the two sides,[66] by increasing tension, and by multiplying miraculous acts and horror, misery and human suffering.[67] Aristotle was against presenting such scenes on the stage and excluded them from serving as 'tragic' elements (*Poet.* 1453b.1–10), but they were undoubtedly common in his day, as can be seen, too, from the tragedies of Euripides. In any event, Aristotle himself recommended that these be described through the dialogue (loc. cit. 5).

The principle of unity of action, which is in Aristotle's view also characteristic of Greek tragedy (*Poet.* 1450b.25, 1451a.15–35), to some extent directed the epitomist, if not Jason himself. II Maccabees is in fact composed of two 'tragedies' similar in structure and content (3.1–10.9, 10.10–15.36), each with a 'beginning', 'middle' and 'end' (*Poet.* 1450b.25–35), and with a 'complication' (δέσις) and a 'dénouement' (λύσις) of the conflict (*Poet.* 1455b.24–35). In the two 'tragedies' the Temple is at the centre of events, and both have an identical and symmetrical dimension: an unsuccessful attempt by the enemy to gain control of the Temple (the episode of Heliodorus; the expeditions of Lysias); the enemy's conquest of the city (Antiochus Epiphanes; Nicanor); the salvation of Judas Maccabaeus (purification of the Temple; the battle of Adasa). At the conclusion of each 'tragedy' a festive day is instituted (the festival of Hanukkah; Nicanor Day).[68] The book is far from displaying the perfect unity of

[65] See, e.g., the description of the contacts between Judas Maccabaeus and Nicanor in II Macc. 14.18–30 (see pp. 354–6 re verse 27), the Heliodorus affair (3.8–39) and the description of Antiochus Epiphanes' death (9.1–18).   [66] See pp. 64–5 above.

[67] 3.24–7,33, 5.1–4, 6.18, 7.42, 9.5–12, 10.10,29–30, 11.8, 14.45–6.

[68] Cf. Pfeifer 1949: 510–11.

action demanded by Aristotle, as can be seen from the duplication
of the structure and the inclusion (especially in the second part) of
some superfluous episodes, unrelated even to one another. Some
ancient poetic tragedies likewise did not attain this perfection (*Poet.*
1451b.34–6, 1456a.10–20), which is obviously difficult to achieve in
an historiographic work. The absence of the other two well-known
unities, the unity of place and the unity of time, cannot invalidate
this view, since the principle of the unity of place was accepted only
from the period of the Renaissance on, while the unity of time is to
be found only in some of the Classical tragedies (*Poet.* 1449b.12–13)
and is by its nature opposed to comprehensive historiographic writing. The positive and optimistic conclusion of the two 'tragedies' in
II Maccabees, the purification of the Temple and the victory over
Nicanor, does not conflict with the principles of tragedy: Aristotle
states that in a tragedy the hero goes 'from bad fortune to good or
from good fortune to bad' (*Poet.* 1451a.14), although he himself
regards the passage from good to bad fortune as the more sublime
and appropriate form for a tragedy. Of these two forms, the first
finds expression even in four tragedies of Euripides (*Iphigenia*, *Alcestis*,
Ion and *Helen*), although, contrary to others, he concludes most of his
tragedies with bad fortune (*Poet.* 1453a.25). So, too, the tragedy of
the exodus from Egypt by Ezekiel, the Hellenistic Jewish poet, the
only 'Jewish' tragedy of which fragments are extant, was structured
from bad fortune to good.[69] The double *dénouement* of the plot, one
for the good and the other for the bad, which occurs in the two parts
of the book was accounted inferior by Aristotle, from whose remarks
it is, however, apparent that such instances were not uncommon in
ancient tragedies (1453a.12–35).

In addition to the basic principles of the tragedy, other dramatic
elements characteristic of Greek tragedy are to be found in II Maccabees. Frequent use is made of the sudden reversal (*peripeteia*; *metabolē*) in the fate of the heroes which stands counter to the direction
in which the plot is developing (cf. *Poet.* 1452a.22; Polyb. 3.4.5,
15.36.2), especially in describing the fate of Jason, Antiochus Epiphanes, Menelaus, and Judas Maccabaeus himself;[70] as usual in
tragedy, the author adds laudatory or pejorative epithets to the
names of several of the heroes in the book,[71] and curses, opprobrious
appellations, and furious remarks are legion;[72] the villains in the

[69] Preserved by Eusebius, *Praep. Evang.* 9.28–9. See the edition of J. Wieneke (1931).
[70] 4.26, 5.5–10,27, 9, 13.3–9. On the *metabolē* see in detail pp. 201, 277, 487 below.
[71] 3.11, 4.19,25,38,47, 5.16,23, 6.18,23,28, 7.27,34, 8.14,32,34, 9.9,13,28, 10.35, 11.11,
12.15,27,35,43,45, 13.4,7, 14.27,30,31,38,43, 15.12, 32,33. See also Richnow 1968: 118–25.
[72] E.g. 4.13,19, 8.34, 14.27, 15.3.

book transgress with overweening pride (*hybris*), often utter abuse against God (*blasphēmia*), and even lift a hand against Him (*theomakhia*).[73] While these motifs are not alien to the Bible, they are even more common in Greek tragedy. The frequent use made of epiphanies is reminiscent of the *deus ex machina* who unravels the entanglement in the later tragedy (*Poet.* 1454b.1–5), while the 'tragic' principle of retaliation and poetic justice (*ius talionis*) is employed more than once.[74] The abridgement of the considerable information provided by Jason of Cyrene (II Macc. 2.24,31) and the monographic form of the book are among the characteristics of 'tragic' historiography.[75] Since tragedy deals not with entirely evil people but with average characters (*Poet.* 1452b.30–53a.10), the author tries to maintain some balance in presenting them (see, e.g., the favourable sides of Antiochus Epiphanes and Nicanor),[76] although in many instances his personal attitude to the characters (principally Jason and Menelaus) prevails over his artistic judgement. Another balance is to be seen in the prevention of excessive tension. In order not to agitate or depress the spectator too much, the chorus in the tragedy has from time to time the task of proclaiming what is about to happen.[77] Thus in critical situations, with no solution in sight, the narrator interrupts the continuity of the account to explain in an optimistic tone what is happening, or to hint at a coming change.[78] The limited number of heroes and the disregard for the personalities and activities of the father and brothers of Judas Maccabaeus, the principal hero, can also be explained by the need, usual in a dramatic experience, to take into consideration the spectator's ability to absorb things. Some of these components and artistic devices are traceable also in the rhetorical–pathetic school, but the occurrence of all of them together points to the deliberate presentation of the historical material in the spirit of the historiographic 'tragic' school, or at least of 'tragic' theory.

If the above evaluation is correct, the epitomist may be hinting at the way the book was designed in his programmatic introduction.

[73] E.g. 5.21, 7.19,34, 9.7–8,10, 10.34,36, 12.14,16, 15.3–6. On *theomakhia* and its harsh punishment in II Maccabees and in Greek tragedy see also J. Gutman 1949: 29–32 (= Bar-Kochva 1980a: 195–8).

[74] 4.26,38,42, 5.8–10, 8.34–6, 9.6,8,10,28, 10.36, 12.6, 13.8, 15.32–3. See also Niese 1900: 34; Zeitlin 1952: 54; Marcus 1966: 26–8.

[75] See Duris of Samos, *FGrH* no. IIA, 76,F 1; Cicero, *Fam.* 5.12.5–6; Lucian, *Hist. conscr.* 7, 23, 32; cf. Aristotle, *Poet.* 1451a15–20, 34–5; 1456a13–16.

[76] 3.35–9, 4.19,37–8, 9.11–27 (esp. v. 17), 11.13–14, 13.23,26, 14.23–9. See also pp. 355–6 below.

[77] On this aspect of the function of the chorus see G. Murray 1965: 106,109,119.

[78] 4.16–17, 5.17,20,27, 6.12–17, 8.11, 9.4, 15.5.

He defines his chief aim as the provision of 'pleasure' (ψυχαγωγία) to the reader, together with 'usefulness' (ὠφέλεια). The second aim is served by the religious–didactic approach. The two terms 'pleasure' and 'usefulness' are common both separately and together in Hellenistic literature in defining the purpose of historiographic writings (see esp. Luc. *Hist. conscr.* 9–13; Dion. Hal. *Pomp.* 6), and they appear together even in a realistic writer like Polybius (1.4.11, 6.1.3,8, 15.36.3), who by 'pleasure' refers to the enjoyment that can be derived from understanding historical processes (see 6.1.8ff. and cf. 39.8.7). However, when the word is used by a 'tragic' writer, it is reminiscent of Aristotle's well-known statement that effective representation (μίμησις) which, as previously mentioned, does not represent reality as it is, can bring enjoyment (ἡδονή) to the spectator (1448b.5–20). Similarly Duris of Samos, of the tragic school, in his criticism of Ephorus and Theopompus, demanded 'imitation' and 'pleasure' of historiographic works (*FGrH* 76 n. 1).[79] Elsewhere the epitomist compares Jason, the author, to the architect of a new building who attends to all the details, and himself to a painter who is responsible only for its 'adornment' (διακόσμησις, 2.29). The comparison of the historian with the artist, too, was common in the Hellenistic period and likewise appears in Polybius.[80] But in the case of a 'tragic' writer, it may perhaps be explained in the light of Aristotle's remark that, like the work of painting, the shaping of the characters and contents in a tragedy differs from and is superior to reality (*Poet.* 1448a.5–20, 1454b.8–12; cf. 1447a.13–16).

Is the 'tragic' presentation of the events the product of the epitomist alone, or were there at least some 'tragic' features in Jason of Cyrene's original work? The example of the architect and artist suggests that the architect – that is, Jason of Cyrene – concerned himself with all details of the house, including its adornment.[81] Thus the adornment was already present in the original work, although it

---

[79] On the conventional interpretations of the terms μίμησις and ἡδονή in Duris see the survey in Meister 1975: 109–14. Meister's attempt (pp. 115–17 – and in his wake, Doran 1979: 110) to explain μίμησις in Duris as intending a realistic description of the situation must be rejected. The use of the term in the sense proposed by the disciple of the peripatetics who himself wrote essays on tragedy and tragedians is not reasonable, especially since it appears adjacent to 'pleasure'. Meister's explanation of the last term, as enjoyment from an exact description of reality, seems strange when the author in question is Duris. The Duris fragments certainly do not fit the conception proposed. Meister's main arguments revolving chiefly around the evaluation of the nature of the works of Ephorus and Theopompus are not decisive and can be refuted.

[80] For the metaphor of the painter and painting cf. Arist. *Poet.* 1447a15–20, 1448a5–10, 1454b8–12; Polybius 12.25h.2–3,28a.1; Plut. *Alex.* 1.3; Lucian, *Hist. conscr.* 13.50–1.

[81] See also Vitruvius' description of the qualifications and training of architects in *De architectura* 1.1.3,4,13,16.

was less conspicuous because it was mingled with other elements which did not contribute to the 'adornment'. The epitomist's work focused exclusively on that enhancement of the adornment. It was confined on the one hand to the abridgement of superfluous or tiresome details (2.24,28,31) such as the external background of the events and their exact and detailed development (2.30, 10.10) as well as the many numbers (probably of armies, dates, etc. – 2.24) and similar material.[82] As a multiplicity of details prevents arousing in the reader emotions which is the main objective of 'tragic' writing, the abridgement itself operates to emphasize the 'adornment'. On the other hand, the epitomist of II Maccabees saw to the preservation in entirety of the accounts which are more in keeping with the artistic details ('whoever undertakes to paint and copy should seek the suitable [useful] for adornment', 2.29). At the same time it must be stressed that the epitomist deleted not only details he considered 'superfluous' or 'obstructive' but also complete episodes. He did so mainly to maintain the unity of the plot (see also below on the termination with Nicanor Day).

It can therefore be concluded that in redacting and abridging Jason of Cyrene's books, the author of II Maccabees' role was primarily to provide the book with a 'tragic' framework, or to give prominence to the 'tragic' features already there. Consequently some stories were retained intact, some were abridged a little or a lot, and some were omitted altogether.[83] The epitomist is responsible for ending the book with the victory over Nicanor. He added transitional sentences in certain places (4.17, 5.17–20, 6.12–17, 10.10) and may have changed the location of some parts.[84] There is no way of knowing to what extent the epitomist's individual style affected the language of the book. The 'compression' of a number of stories resulted in the proliferation of participial forms, as is usual in epitomes.[85]

The above conclusion on the function of the epitomist also has implications regarding the estimate of the time, sources and credi-

[82] Despite the epitomist's warning, II Maccabees contains more than fifty numbers, of troops, of losses and captives, of sums of money, etc. From this it may be concluded that Jason's book really abounded in numerical data. For another interpretation of II Macc. 2.24 – that it refers not to the omission of numbers but to the reduction in the number of lines – see Bickerman 1976–8: 1.256 n. 36; Doran 1981: 77–8.

[83] See also the summary of Pfeifer 1949: 320–1, in whose opinion the criterion for the epitomist's choice of material was the lessons that could be learned. Others have proposed considerations of another kind.

[84] See p. 181 and n. 95 below on the victory over Nicanor; on transitional sentences see Habicht 1976a: 171.

[85] On the large number of participles in certain parts of II Maccabees see in general Mugler 1931: 419–23; and in the episode of Onias' murder at Daphne see M. Stern 1960: 7–8.

bility of Jason of Cyrene's original work. The consideration of these questions was complicated by the difference of opinion on the extent of the epitomist's involvement in the shaping of the book. Many scholars believe that entire episodes are his creation, but they differ in their identification of those episodes.[86] We have to rely on the epitomist himself, who in only one case, in the introduction to the martyr stories, reports (if we understand him correctly) that the episodes were inserted on his own initiative (6.17). And indeed there are other reasons, too, for believing that the martyr stories were not taken from Jason of Cyrene. As to the source of the other parts of the book, there is no reason to disbelieve what the epitomist says in his introduction, and claims to the contrary are groundless. As Jason of Cyrene was not so famous an author that it was worth adhering exclusively to him, and his remoteness from the site of the action did not enhance his credibility for the readers, the epitomist could be expected to give some hint of his own additions (as he did in regard to the martyr stories), or his use of other sources, if his interventions had reached the point of including descriptions that did not appear in Jason's original work. And if some readers happened to be familiar with Jason's books, they could have easily discerned that the epitomist was not faithful to the original if he had incorporated many stories of his own. The abridgement was an accepted literary genre in the Hellenistic period, and the few examples extant show that the epitomists were quite faithful to the contents of the originals, and if they deviated from it, they specified the fact.[87] In any case the II Maccabees epitomist notes the 'epiphanies' which are definitely 'tragic' and 'pathetic' features, as one of the chief characteristics of Jason of Cyrene's book (2.21–3: 'And the visions from the heavens shown to the warriors... by Jason of Cyrene narrated in five books'). This remark itself can serve as the basis for identifying episodes certainly taken from Jason's book.

In order to assess properly the descriptive level of Jason of Cyrene's original book and its sources, it is therefore necessary to examine those accounts in which the epitomist's abridgement is relatively restricted, and the description is detailed, fluent, consistent and includes epiphanies (e.g. chh. 3, 6, 7, 9, 11.1–15, 14.26–15.36). The examination of those chapters does not produce conclusions very

---

[86] See especially Grimm 1853: 12–15; Willrich 1900: 132–4; Büchler 1906: 297ff.; Churgin 1949: 230–55; Zeitlin 1952: 18–30; and, in more restricted form, Bunge 1971: 336ff.; Habicht 1976a: 170–3.

[87] See esp. the explicit declaration of Marcian of Heraclea (*GGM* vol. 1, p. 567, lines 16–33), noted by Doran 1981: 83–4. On later epitomists see Begbie 1967: 333–8; Brunt 1980: 475–94. Cf. the preface of Justin, para. 4, which recalls that of II Maccabees.

different from the general negative assessment of other parts of the book. Consequently, the suggestion of a number of scholars that Jason of Cyrene was an eye-witness of the events must be rejected.[88] Even an author with the greatest inclination for didactic–pathetic writing would not have managed to distort the military events to such an extent if he himself had witnessed them. Furthermore, all indications show that Jason of Cyrene was not acquainted with Eretz Israel: the statement that the flame lit on the beach at Iamnia was visible in Jerusalem (12.9) and a number of distinctly mystifying estimates of distances between various places and Jerusalem (10.27, 12.9,29) which originated with Jason and not the epitomist,[89] totally eliminate the possibility that the author was familiar with Eretz Israel. The claim that Jason's religious views accord only with those of the Eretz Israel Hassidism[90] and therefore he must have spent considerable time in the country,[91] must likewise be rejected. His views actually embody nothing that could not have been acceptable to at least some Diaspora Jews during the second half of the second century B.C. or even in the middle of that century.[92] On the other

[88] In contrast to Tcherikover 1961a: 382–7; Abel 1949: xli; Hengel 1973: 180–1; Applebaum 1979: 139–40; and in fact also Niese 1900: 37; Habicht 1976a: 175, 177.

[89] See further p. 514 and n. 14 below.

[90] Pfeifer 1949: 515; Abel and Starcky 1961: 18–25; Hengel 1973: 182.

[91] So Hengel 1973: 182.

[92] Hengel points out the views of the author of II Maccabees regarding a defensive war on the Sabbath, forbidden foods, and belief in angels and in resurrection. However, II Maccabees does not negate defensive war on the Sabbath (see below pp. 484ff.), and in any case the understandable desire of Jewish settlers in the Diaspora to free themselves of military obligations on the Sabbath may have led Jason of Cyrene to describe rather strictly the attitude of warriors in Judaea to Sabbath observance. The matter of forbidden foods was respected and kept by Diaspora Jewry. It is especially stressed in the Letter of Aristeas (paras. 142ff.), which was written in Alexandria early in John Hyrcanus' reign (p. 53 above n. 83), and in III Maccabees (3.4,7), which is of a later date. The heavenly figures that appear in the epiphanies in II Maccabees do not indicate a real angelology. They are impersonal, lacking human traits, and anonymous (see 3.26, 10.29–30, 11.8; cf. 12.22, 15.27). The epiphanies contain nothing that deviates from the Hellenistic epiphanies of the time. See, e.g., the description of the rescue of Delphi from the Galatians in 279 B.C. in Justin 24.8.3; Pausanias 10.23.2. For other parallels from Greek literature see Doran 1981: 98–103. Cf. also another work of Diaspora Jewry, III Macc. 6.18–20. All this is in complete contrast to variegated, ramified angelology, including the names and traits of angels, which was already common in Judaea at the time of the Book of Daniel, and developed in the writings of the Judaean Desert Sect. As to belief in resurrection of the flesh, who can say that this belief was not widespread among the Jews of the Egyptian–Cyrenaic Diaspora? They were probably most willing to accept it because of its similarity to the age-old Egyptian belief. The fact that IV Maccabees (14.6, 16.13), which used the material of II Maccabees, speaks of the eternity of the soul and not the resurrection of the flesh is not proof to the contrary (as against Pfeifer 1949: 514–15; Hengel 1973: 182 n. 321). The author of IV Maccabees 15 is much more refined and sophisticated than Jason of Cyrene. His book is a philosophical treatise in the spirit of the Stoic school, and the general belief in the resurrection of the flesh acquires a restrained note that better suits his intellectual level. The views of the author of IV Maccabees cannot therefore reflect the popular faith of Diaspora Jews, and this is even more valid in regard to Philo's works (see Cavallin 1979: 282–5, 288–93, and p. 323 on the Platonic influence on IV Maccabees' and Philo's conception

hand, it is hard to imagine that a Jew who spent a long time in Eretz
Israel could be so confused regarding the 'four kinds' of the Feast of
the Tabernacle, or the basic regulations on the purity of Jerusalem
and the Temple.[93]

Similarly the attempt of scholars to identify Jason of Cyrene, the
source of II Maccabees, with Jason son of Eleazar, one of the two
emissaries sent by Judas Maccabaeus to Rome (I Macc. 8.17),[94] must
be utterly rejected. In the main, this identification is based on the
unusual manner in which Eupolemus, the second emissary, is
mentioned in II Maccabees. In praising the favourable attitude of
the Seleucid authorities towards the Jews in the reign of Antiochus
III, the book states that the contacts with the Antioch authorities
were made 'by John the father of Eupolemus who has gone as envoy
to the Romans' (4.11). Neither Eupolemus nor even the embassy to
Rome is mentioned again in II Maccabees. The unusual use, too, of
the son's name in order to identify the father calls for an explanation.
Hence some have assumed that Jason of Cyrene was none other than
Jason son of Eleazar and that he was acquainted with Eupolemus
from their joint mission, which accounts for the strange manner in
which the latter is introduced into the verse. In view of what has
been said above, however, there are no grounds for assuming that
Jason of Cyrene was an associate of the rebel leadership. It must
accordingly be accepted that the verse refers to Eupolemus because
the embassy to Rome was mentioned in detail in Jason's original
work, but omitted by the epitomist in II Maccabees, since for literary
and didactic reasons he preferred to conclude the work with an
account of the institution of a festive day, namely, Nicanor Day.[95]

---

of resurrection). Furthermore, in Judaea itself at the end of the Second Temple period, the
Pharisees believed only in the eternity of the soul (*Bell.* 2.163–4; *Ant.* 18.14), although in the
Book of Daniel the belief in the resurrection of the flesh is already explicitly expressed, and the
mishnaic sages, the Pharisees, accepted it only later (see, e.g. Sanhedrin 10.1; Sotah 9.15). On
the various approaches in the Palestinian Apocrypha and Pseudepigrapha see Nickelsburg
1972: 174–5. In the Middle Ages, too, a number of Jewish philosophers favoured the idea of
the eternity of the soul, contrary to the views of the rabbis and the ordinary people. See also
pp. 571–2 below on the sect affiliation of the author of I Maccabees and of Jason of
Cyrene.

[93] See p. 370 below in the commentary on verse 47 ('opposite Jerusalem'). It must be added
that the spiritual world of the author of II Maccabees could by no means be counted among
the evidence of Hellenization of the Jews of Eretz Israel, as suggested by Hengel (1973:
176–82, esp. p. 176).

[94] All in the wake of Herzfeld 1863: 2.445; Keil 1875: 275. See esp. Hengel 1973: 180–1;
Applebaum 1979: 140.

[95] On the hypothesis that Jason did not end his book with Nicanor's death see Geiger 1875:
228; Schlatter 1891: 50–1; Willrich 1900: 134; André 1903: 50; Meyer 1921: 456ff.; Pfeifer
1949: 509–10; Churgin 1949: 230–1; Zeitlin 1950: 24; Tcherikover 1961a: 384; Bunge 1971:
173ff.; Hengel 1973: 176–7; There is a wide variation among scholars as to the exact
chronological framework for Jason's book. Against this view see Wacholder 1974: 31 n. 14,

The first references to Judas Maccabaeus in the book (5.27, 8.1) are a good example of the lack of method and consistency on the part of the epitomist, who at times failed to identify names and events which were certainly described in detail in an earlier context in Jason's original work, but are not mentioned in II Maccabees.[96]

The determination of the exact dates of Jason of Cyrene or his epitomist is in this case of marginal importance, because even if Jason did belong to the generation of the Revolt, the didactic and artistic presentation of his historical material and the author's remoteness from the scene of the events are more relevant to the evaluation of the book's credibility than is the time it was written.

The question of the sources of II Maccabees and the connection between it and I Maccabees is more important for our study and can provide guidance as to the possibility of relying on the parallel or complementary information in II Maccabees. The question has long preoccupied German scholars in particular, who have devoted long, detailed discussions to it, their proposals covering almost all the theoretical alternatives. There is no denying that along with considerable additions and divergences, there are definite points of contact between I Maccabees and II Maccabees. For that reason several scholars assumed that both were based entirely on Jason of Cyrene's book, or part of I Maccabees (chh. 1–7) is taken from Jason. Others speculated that the author of I Maccabees and Jason both based themselves on the same written source, or stories told to them by eye-witnesses of the events. Still others contend that Jason of Cyrene made direct or indirect use of I Maccabees. One scholar rejects all these possibilities and believes that Jason of Cyrene used only a non-Jewish source on Seleucid history which he then reworked as was his wont in a Jewish spirit. In addition, more complicated theories were developed, such as, for example, that II Maccabees is based mostly on an anonymous source older and more reliable than I Maccabees, and partly on Jason of Cyrene. Or that Jason's work is constructed according to a series of sources such as 'The Annals of Onias', 'The Annals of Jason', 'The Annals of Menelaus', a Seleucid

though his argument is not convincing: the final verse of II Maccabees (15.37) does not attest to the contents of Jason's original book but derives from the purposes and literary character of the epitomist's work. Wacholder's assumption (pp. 38–9) that Jason of Cyrene was familiar with Eupolemus' book on Jewish history and made use of it does not in itself explain the mention of the latter's diplomatic mission to Rome (II Macc. 4.11) as Wacholder believes, and thus does not negate one of the main arguments for the hypothesis on the broad chronological range of Jason's original book: if Eupolemus' mission had not been described by Jason, the epitomist and Jason himself would have presented him as 'Eupolemus the historian' and the like, and not as the man who set forth on a mission to Rome. See also pp. 185, 374 below.   [96] See pp. 196–9 below; cf. 8.30,32,33, 10.19,37, 12.36, 14.19.

chronicle and documents from the Jerusalem archives. There have also been speculations regarding a Samaritan source, a book written by Onias IV, the history of Eupolemus son of John son of ha-Kotz, and so on and so forth.[97]

Most of these hypotheses must be rejected out of hand. The amazing exactitude of the geographic descriptions and of the reports on the course of the battles in I Maccabees could not have been drawn from the book of a person living in distant Cyrene, and the unrealistic character of the battle descriptions in Jason of Cyrene's original book has already been pointed out. In view of Jason's place of residence it is hard to imagine that he got his information from oral stories of an eye-witness. The nature of some of the many points of contact between the two books also excludes this suggestion. To cite just one example: both books report that slave traders took part in the Seleucid expedition that ended with the Ammaus defeat (I Macc. 3.41; II Macc. 8.11). Slave traders undoubtedly took part in the other expeditions as well, and oral sources would have noted this in regard to the other battles. How is it then that Jason, who wished to stress the Jews' desperate condition before the battles, expanded and developed the slave-trader story in connection with the Ammaus expedition in his own imaginative fashion, but failed to mention their participation in other battles? And see pp. 202 n. 18, 485–92.

The question remains whether the two books relied on a common written source, or whether Jason of Cyrene used mainly I Maccabees (directly or indirectly) for the parallel episodes. The evidence presented so far in favour of the first possibility fails to convince that this is the only solution. The basic argument is that II Maccabees contains some episodes connected with the activity of Judas Maccabaeus that are absent from I Maccabees, along with some exclusive pieces of information in the parallel episodes which do not seem to be the invention of Jason of Cyrene. Hence it has been suggested that a common source was selectively used by the two books. However, the author of I Maccabees states that 'the rest of Judah's story and the wars and braveries...were not written' (9.22), which means that neither he nor other written sources at his disposal described those additional events (see further pp. 401–2 below). The additional episodes in II Maccabees were not therefore taken from a common

[97] Grimm 1857: 14–19; Geiger 1875: 219ff.; Hitzig 1869: 2.412–16; Keil 1875: 272–3; Schlatter 1891: 2ff.; Willrich 1895: 68,76; Niese 1900: 94; Schürer 1901: 3.483; Laqueur 1904: 72–87; Wellhausen 1905: 130,145,158; Büchler 1906: 277ff.; Kolbe 1926: 134ff.; Bévenot 1931: 10–12; Pfeifer 1949: 472–5,481,516; Zeitlin 1952: 20–4,69–70; Schunck 1954: 116–28; Bunge 1971: 527ff.; Goldstein 1976: 56–61,92 and passim; Habicht 1976a: 172ff.; Toki 1977: 69–83; Bickerman 1976–80: 2.159ff.

source. As for the additional information in the parallel episodes, they could be drawn from the same source (or sources) that supplied the additional episodes themselves. It should be stressed that the author of I Maccabees, as a contemporary of the events, and even an eye-witness to some of them, could well have composed his account without having to rely on a previous comprehensive and detailed book. As a matter of principle, an unknown primary source must not be introduced when it is not needed. I tend to believe, therefore, that I Maccabees was known to Jason of Cyrene in one way or another.

Be that as it may, Jason of Cyrene must also have used another or even several written sources, from which he drew the stories that do not appear in I Maccabees, such as the Heliodorus affair, events that preceded the Revolt, the documents in ch. 11, as well as other details incorporated into the parallel descriptions. It is such a source (or sources) that provided him with the vast knowledge that he demonstrates of the internal affairs of the Seleucid empire, as well as the correct information that Antiochus Epiphanes' death preceded the purification of the Temple. Whether Jason relied on I Maccabees directly or indirectly,[98] whether he used one additional source or more than one, and the identity, nationality, time and place of the author or authors of those sources – all these are anyone's guess, and any attempt at this stage to achieve greater precision is doomed to failure.[99]

---

[98] Because of the paucity of dates in II Maccabees and the discrepancy in dates between I Maccabees (6.20) and II Maccabees (13.1) regarding Lysias' second expedition, it might be thought that Jason of Cyrene was acquainted with I Maccabees only through an intermediate source which had omitted all dates, and that the erroneous date – the year 149 which appears in II Maccabees (see p. 549 below) – was taken from some other source he made use of. This is not necessarily so, however: the above date begins the episode on Lysias' second expedition to Judaea. The first part of the expedition episode (13.3–9) deals with the execution of Menelaus, and was certainly drawn from a source other than I Maccabees. It is possible that as a result Jason paid no attention to the chronological information in I Maccabees, and subsequently added the date – the year 149 – under the influence of the dating of three of the documents in ch. 11 (taken from another source), which he believed to be connected with Lysias' first expedition in 148 (see pp. 516ff.). It should be noted that the date under discussion, and the date of Alcimus' mission to Demetrius I (14.4), are the only ones appearing in the narrative in II Maccabees (other dates occur in the opening documents and those of ch. 11), and it seems that the epitomist omitted the other dates in line with his tendency to reduce the amount of tiresome details and numbers in the book (2.24). He left in the date of Lysias' second expedition so as to differentiate it clearly from the first, which is by implication dated by the documents in ch. 11. It is hard to know why he retained the date of Alcimus' mission; perhaps he felt that his previous statement – that Demetrius landed in Tripolis 'after three years' (14.1), meaning three years after Antiochus Epiphanes' death and not three years after the last event reported in the book (Lysias' second expedition) – might mislead the readers. It is less reasonable to assume that Jason's original book was completely lacking in chronological data, and that it was the epitomist who added 'the year 149' in the wake of the documents in ch. 11. For another explanation of the omission of dates by the epitomist see Bunge 1971: 337.

[99] Against several of the theories proposed in regard to Jason of Cyrene's sources see the stringent comments of Doran 1981: 11–23.

Of the various theories, it is worth considering Gutman's interesting proposal that Eupolemus, the diplomat and author, found refuge in Cyrene after Bacchides seized control of Judaea in 160 B.C., and even wrote a book on Judas Maccabaeus which was used as a source by Jason.[100] The suggestion is based mainly on an analysis of a passage ascribed to Eupolemus' book on the kings of Judah. This fragment, surviving in Clemens of Alexandria (*Strom.* 1.141.4), establishes the number of years elapsed from Adam (and Eve) to Demetrius' fifth regnal year, and the twelfth year of a certain Ptolemy's rule of Egypt. It has been established that the only date that fits both those timings is 157 B.C. It was in fact the fifth year of King Demetrius I of Syria's rule, and the twelfth of Ptolemy VIII Physcon's. As the latter in that year ruled only in Cyrene, and yet Eupolemus ended the period since the creation of the world with his reign, Gutman supposed there was a particular connection between the writer and Cyrene, and proffered the interesting speculation on Eupolemus' peregrination. The text itself, however, does not define Ptolemy as king of Cyrene at that time, but as king of Egypt, a mistake it is hard to imagine in a contemporary author like Eupolemus. It has already been shown that the passage as a whole was revised and underwent a later adaptation,[101] perhaps by Ptolemy of Mendes.[102]

As for the epitomist's place of residence and of origin, the transmission of the information in Jason's book without any topographical elucidation does not support the view that he was ever a resident of Eretz Israel. For other reasons, too, this view has been rejected.[103] Conspicuous in the accounts of the battles in Transjordania are grave geographical inaccuracies and mistakes, especially as regards the distance between Transjordania and Iamnia, which evidently have their origin in the adaptation and abridgement of these accounts.[104] They testify that the map of Eretz Israel was entirely foreign to the epitomist.

[100] Gutman 1958: 2.76–8. The hypothesis that Eupolemus was Jason's source appears also in Habicht 1976a: 177–8.

[101] Von Gutschmid 1893: 191; F. Jacoby in *RE* s.v. 'Eupolemos' (11), col. 1228; Wacholder 1974: 40–3.

[102] Wacholder 1974: 43–4.

[103] See Willrich 1900: 134; Pfeifer 1949: 519; Abel 1949: xxxiv; M. Stern in *Biblical Encyclopaedia*, vol. 5 (Jerusalem, 1958) col. 294 (Hebrew); as opposed to Geiger 1875: 226–7; Dancy 1954: 15; Bunge 1971: 202; Doran 1981: 112.

[104] See pp. 513–14 below, esp. n. 14.

Josephus – *Bellum Judaicum* and *Antiquitates*

In his first book, *Bellum Judaicum*, Josephus reports on Judas Maccabaeus' activities (1.38–46) in the summary of the period of persecution and Revolt that introduces the work (1.31–49).[105] The summary exhibits the influence of I Maccabees and even of the Book of
Daniel (1.32 as against Dan. 12.7), and also contains information
that does not appear in the Books of the Maccabees or contradicts it.
It is generally accepted that the summary has no great value: it is too
'compressed', fragmented, inexact, and full of errors on essential
points.[106] But that judgement certainly does not fit the illuminating
description of the battle of Beth Zacharia within that summary
(41–6), which is detailed and consistent and includes a number of
supplementary facts that accord very well with the circumstances
and military and topographical possibilities.[107] For that reason it is
worth clarifying the sources of the summary in general and of the
description of the battle of Beth Zacharia in particular.

Bellum Judaicum begins with the affair of the internal crisis, the
persecutions and Revolt, after which comes the history of the Hasmonaean state and the Herodian dynasty. Following Hölscher,
there has been general agreement that Nicolaus of Damascus was
Josephus' sole source for his account in *Bellum* of the last two
periods.[108] Josephus based himself exclusively on Nicolaus for reasons
of technical convenience: like other epitomists of antiquity, he found
it awkward to handle several scrolls at one time. Nor did he believe
it necessary to make any special effort, for Jewish history up to
Herod was not his main concern, and was included merely as an
introduction to the Great Revolt against the Romans. Hölscher
drew a similar conclusion regarding Josephus' summary of the persecutions and Revolt,[109] which has not been generally accepted.[110]
Hölscher pointed out various features in the description of the persecutions and Revolt which he believes indicate that the summary is
an epitome of a written source, and that the description has a non-

[105] At this point we are considering the summary of events only up to the death of Judas
Maccabaeus. For the summary on the period of Simeon (50–4) see p. 452 below.
[106] See the list of errors in Hölscher 1904: 4–5; and esp. Goldstein 1976: 60. See also below
n. 115.
[107] See pp. 295–6 below.
[108] Hölscher 1904: 8–19; id. in *RE* s.v. 'Josephus' (2), cols. 1944–9.
[109] Hölscher 1904: 4–8,17; id. in *RE* s.v. 'Josephus' (2), cols. 1944ff.
[110] The scholars who agree with Hölscher in regard to the source of the story of the edicts
and Revolt are the following: Schlatter 1891: 1; Meyer 1921: 164–5; Thackeray 1929: 40;
Bickerman 1937: 150,163,165; id. in *RE* s.v. 'Makkabäerbücher', col. 796; Dancy 1954: 30;
Michel and Bauernfeind 1962: 1.xxv–xxvi.

Jewish tone. While his evidence failed to prove the point,[111] the Josephus summary has an admittedly conspicuously 'foreign' tinge and clearly Hellenistic features which could not possibly have been composed by Josephus; all of them, however, are confined to the description of the battle of Beth Zacharia.[112] Niese, on the other hand, properly pointed out the characteristically Jewish features.[113] It has been suggested that Josephus did not directly utilize any written source at all for the period in question, but relied on his memory of various sources he had read in the past.[114] None of these proposals solves all the difficulties. In view of Josephus' practice of using just one source in relation to the Hasmonaean state and the Herodian dynasty, and of the compression and confusion in the

[111] Hölscher's main evidence for the abridgement of a written source is as follows: (a) abridgement in most of the description in contrast to elaboration in regard to Beth Zacharia (on this see further below). (b) The mentions of the sons of Toubias (para. 31) and supporters of Ptolemy in Jerusalem (32) with no explanation of their identity. But there is no need for additional explanation in the framework of a brief description: the reader understands that the sons of Toubias were among the 'Jerusalem notables' mentioned in the preceding sentence and among the supporters of the Seleucids, while the supporters of Ptolemy are the notables backing Onias, the rival of the sons of Toubias. (c) Antiochus decides on the coercive edicts, among other reasons because of 'the memory of the suffering he underwent during the siege' (34), while before that (32) the text says simply that 'Antiochus conquered the city by force'. This is, however, only an invention of Josephus' in an attempt to explain the coercive edicts and was not taken from any source. There is no trace of any real siege of Jerusalem at the time, not in I Maccabees nor in II Maccabees, and a siege is wholly improbable, given the circumstances and the balance of power. (d) Josephus forgets to report the death of Antiochus V Eupator, so the reader mistakenly believes that Antiochus VI (48) is Antiochus V and not Alexander Balas' son. But the Antiochus mentioned is described as 'the son of Antiochus', i.e. of Antiochus V. Josephus, when writing *Bellum*, was not greatly interested in the history of the Revolt and the Syrian kings, and thought that the young king, Tryphon's protégé, was Eupator's son. If he had had a written source to refer to, it is doubtful whether he would have erred in this way.

As to Hölscher's evidence that Josephus' source was pagan, the anti-Seleucid attitude he himself points out and the sharp disparagement of the Seleucids and their generals are certainly no proof of a non-Jewish source. Hölscher argues that the description of events is secular in character, and the quarrel among the Jews does not revolve around a difference in religious–cultural approach, but rather around authority and political orientation. II Maccabees, too, describes the clash in Jerusalem as a struggle for power (3.4ff.) and hints at a difference in political orientation (3.11; see also *Ant.* 12.221ff.). The Hellenizing movement is not mentioned in *Bellum*, but as it is given minimal space even in I Maccabees, it is not surprising that Josephus omitted it in a description designed to be short. On the other hand, the coercive decrees (34) and the purification of the Temple (39–40), the other events with religious significance, are reported in relatively great detail.

[112] See in detail on p. 296 below.

[113] Niese 1900: 103–5. Among Niese's evidence, worth noting are the expression ἀλλοφύλων ('Gentiles' 37); the period of three and a half years for the profanation of the Temple (32), which is influenced by the Book of Daniel (12.7; cf. *Ant.* 12.322); the sharp condemnation of Antiochus and the commanders (34–5); the praise of the Hasmonaean dynasty and the presentation of the Jewish people as united under its leadership (37); the application of the terms 'profanation' and 'holiness' for the altar and the Temple (40).

[114] Churgin 1949: 197–8; Tcherikover 1961a: 392–5; id. 1961b: 135–45, esp. 144–5; Goldstein 1976: 60–1.

description of the internal crises, persecutions and Revolt as a whole, it is not likely that for the superficial description of the Revolt he used more than one written source; the description of the battle of Beth Zacharia is too detailed to be based on Josephus' memory; and we did not find that Josephus added 'Jewish features' in such quantity to Nicolaus' description in his summary of the history of the Hasmonaean state and the Herodian dynasty in *Bellum Judaicum*.

It therefore appears that the sources for the description of the battle of Beth Zacharia should be discussed separately from the summary of the period of persecution and Revolt as a whole. The report on Beth Zacharia is consistent, contains logical supplementary information, and shows definitely Hellenistic features. In addition it is hard to discern characteristically Jewish features in it, or any identification on the author's part (despite the influence of I Maccabees in the Eleazar episode – see below). This is in striking contrast to Josephus' report on other events, marked by extreme brevity, errors, fragmentation, and Jewish features.

It appears likely, then, that in regard to the rest of the description, apart from the battle of Beth Zacharia, Josephus did not carry out an orderly abridgement of Nicolaus' book, but rather briefly noted what he recalled from material he had read earlier in Nicolaus, in I Maccabees and in the Book of Daniel, and that accounts for the mistakes and inaccuracies (especially in the names of people and in the chronology – a common occurrence when relying on memory alone[115]), the much greater brevity than in regard to the Hasmonaean State and the Herodian dynasty (despite the obvious parallels with the time of the Great Revolt, the subject of his book[116]), the Jewish features inserted by Josephus and the absence of Hellenistic ones. Probably Josephus decided in this case to refrain from total adherence to Nicolaus' text because he properly felt that it would not be appropriate to describe the crucial Jewish national–religious uprising from the viewpoint of a non-Jewish writer whose description

---

[115] (a) Substitution of names: Onias for Jason (para. 31; and see Tcherikover 1961a: 393–5); Bacchides as the Seleucid commander killed by Mattathias (36); Akdasa instead of Elasa (47); Antiochus instead of Demetrius (47); Antiochus (VI) instead of Alexander Balas (48: and see Goldstein 1976: 60 n. 37); (b) errors connected with names: the foundation of the temple of Onias is attributed to Onias the Jerusalem high priest (Onias III) rather than his son, Onias IV (33); Judas Maccabaeus is described as Mattathias' first-born and not Simeon (37); (c) errors in chronology and sequence: Mattathias ejects the enemy from Judaea and becomes the leader (37); the treaty with Rome is set at the start of Judas Maccabaeus' activities (38); Judas Maccabaeus repulses a second invasion by Antiochus IV (38; the reference is evidently to the battle of Ammaus); the Seleucids station their troops in the citadel only during the period of Judas Maccabaeus' leadership, a short time before the purification of the Temple (39).

[116] See p. 193 below and n. 134 there.

was too detached and did not correctly present the Jewish angle (although Nicolaus did criticize what Antiochus Epiphanes did in the Temple; see *Ap.* 2.84). Josephus took the liberty of adopting this method in the present case because the events of the persecutions and Revolt which led to the rise of the Hasmonaeans were better known to the people of the Second Temple period than others because of their importance, and certainly to a person like Josephus who considered himself a descendant of the Hasmonaeans. In regard to the battle of Beth Zacharia, on the other hand, he decided to enlarge the picture, presumably because of the participation of the elephants, which added interest and variety to the description,[117] and therefore reverted to adherence to Nicolaus.

As to Nicolaus' sources for Lysias' second expedition and the battle of Beth Zacharia, the many reliable pieces of information on the expedition and the battle, some of which were deliberately omitted in the Books of the Maccabees, and are less flattering to the Jews (esp. the flight to Gophna – 45), point to a Seleucid source. On the other hand, the episode on Eleazar (42–4) included in the story of Beth Zacharia seems to have been taken directly from I Maccabees. The contents in the two books are completely identical, and Nicolaus obviously tried to select wording synonymous with that of I Maccabees.[118] Nor did he add a single thing that does not appear in I Maccabees.[119] Josephus cannot have taken the Eleazar episode directly from I Maccabees: it is extremely unlikely that for the Beth Zacharia story he would have used two written sources, since in the rest of the description of the persecution and Revolt he exhibited considerable sloth and relied on his memory alone, while for the Hasmonaean state and the Herodian dynasty he based his version entirely on Nicolaus of Damascus. Furthermore, the episode in ques-

---

[117] Cf. the Byzantine extracts from Diodorus' version of the battle of Ipsus, in which actually only the function of the elephants in the battle is mentioned – De Boor 1906: 344, no. 236 (= Diodorus 21.2). And see also the considerable elaboration on the confrontation of the elephants and their combat methods in the description of the battle of Raphia in Polybius (5.84) which is out of all proportion to the contribution and importance of the elephants in the course of that battle and its outcome.

[118] Eleazar saw (*Bell.*, πρυϊδών; I Macc., εἶδεν) the tallest elephants (*Bell.*, ὑψηλότατον; I Macc., ὑπέραγον), and then he thought (*Bell.*, ὑπολάβων; I Macc., ᾠήθη) that the king was seated on it. He ran (*Bell.*, ἐκτρέχει; I Macc., ἐπέδραμεν) into the close formation (*Bell.*, τὸ στῖφος; I Macc., φάλαγγος) of the enemy, went under the elephant, hit him and was crushed to death. Both books treat Eleazar's exploit as one designed to bring him glory and fame (*Bell.*, εὐκλείας; I Macc., ὄνομα αἰώνιον).

[119] On the gilt wall crenellations of the tower in *Bell.* 1.42 as the explanation for the difficult expression 'the king's armament' in I Macc. 6.43 see below pp. 334–5, and p. 76 above on the source of the information that Eleazar advanced toward the elephant before 'the clash of phalanxes' (ibid.).

tion contains one of the clearly Hellenistic features,[120] no sense of identification, and the description as a whole is cool and even fraught with reservations (in paras. 43–4 especially). Nicolaus himself relied in this case solely on I Maccabees because the Eleazar episode, which was insignificant from the Seleucid point of view, certainly was not reported in the external sources.

Regarding II Maccabees, there is no evidence that Josephus or Nicolaus was acquainted with it or with the original work of Jason of Cyrene. It is true that the review of internal events in Jerusalem contained in the summary, which probably ultimately derives from Nicolaus (via Josephus' recollections from an earlier reading), is somewhat reminiscent of the story in II Maccabees. However, the mention of the Toubians, which does not appear in II Maccabees, shows that a different source was used. This is even more clearly shown in the expanded version of the same story that appears in Josephus' *Antiquitates* (12.237–40). The rest of the summary in *Bellum Judaicum* has no connection with II Maccabees.

To sum up: Josephus relied on his memory for most of his short survey in *Bellum Judaicum* of the period of the persecutions and Revolt, influenced by I Maccabees, Nicolaus of Damascus, and the Book of Daniel, while in regard to Lysias' second expedition and the battle of Beth Zacharia, he made direct use of the written version of Nicolaus. Nicolaus himself drew his information from a Seleucid source as well as from I Maccabees, and for the episode on Eleazar's bravery, from I Maccabees alone. Be that as it may, the brief references to Judas Maccabaeus' military campaigns in *Bellum Judaicum* do not contribute anything to an understanding of them. On the other hand, Josephus' version of Lysias' second expedition and the battle of Beth Zacharia is invaluable for the reconstruction of the campaign and the battle.

A detailed description of Judas Maccabaeus' accomplishments appears in Book 12 of *Antiquitates*, Josephus' later work (287–434). It is included in the paraphrase of I Maccabees (12.246–13.212) that covers events up to Simeon's time.[121] The paraphrase was made directly from I Maccabees and not from any intermediate source.[122]

---

[120] Eleazar's death is a portent (κληδών) of the outcome of the battle (45); and see p. 296 below.

[121] See the detailed textual comparisons in Bloch 1879: 80–90; Drüner 1896: 35–50; Ettelson 1925: 255–80,335–41. These points were accepted by all. See also the following note.

[122] Drüner 1896: 35–50; Schürer 1901: 3.195–6; Ettelson 1925: 253ff.; Thackeray 1929: 62–4,83; as opposed to the well-known view of von Destinon (1882: 60–79); Hölscher 1904: 52.

Here and there Josephus inserted details or incidents that do not appear in I Maccabees.[123] As already shown, this information was not taken from II Maccabees or Jason of Cyrene's original works,[124] but from other sources, some Jewish and some non-Jewish. Among the latter it is possible to identify with considerable certainty Polybius and Nicolaus of Damascus.[125] An examination of the descriptions of Judas Maccabaeus' battles confirms the assumptions noted. Josephus' version is generally a faithful paraphrase of the battle descriptions in I Maccabees. Still at times he tried to explain extraneous episodes in I Maccabees on the basis of information he remembered from the writings of non-Jewish historians (e.g. 386, 389,402). Some influence of another source which was acquainted with the campaigns themselves is discernible. This may well be Nicolaus of Damascus who, as stated above, inspired Josephus' version on the persecution and Revolt in *Bellum Judaicum*. This does not mean that Josephus used this source simultaneously when writing his paraphrase on the battles in *Antiquitates*. He may well have recalled various pieces of information from the sources he had used earlier, especially since he made assiduous use of Nicolaus' work in the subsequent books of *Antiquitates*. In any case, he did not forget his own former version in *Bellum Judaicum* (see the indication in *Ant.* 12.244–5).[126] This is the origin of the location of the Akra in the

---

[123] Extensive use of other sources is obvious in the description of the background to the coercive edicts (12.237–45), the document of the 'Sidonians in Shechem' (257–64), Antiochus Epiphanes' activities in Jerusalem (253–6), Menelaus' death (383–5), the founding of the temple of Onias (387–8), and the ascension of Demetrius I (389–90). In addition there are marginal supplements to the information in I Maccabees which must be ascribed to his utilization of other sources.

[124] See esp. Grimm 1857: 20,27; Nussbaum 1875: 8–9; Niese 1900: 105–7; Willrich 1900: 146ff.; id. 1924: 14–29; Schürer 1901: 3.486; Bickerman 1937: 167ff.; M. Stern 1960: 8–11.

[125] On Polybius see *Ant.* 12.358–9 (in connection with Antiochus Epiphanes' death), 12.136, *Ap.* 2.84 (profanation of the Temple). On Nicolaus of Damascus see below. All the other proposals regarding Josephus' sources of information are speculative. On this see also the balanced comments of S. J. D. Cohen (1979: 44 n. 77). The only thing that can be said is that the Samaritan document, the story of Menelaus' execution, and the erection of the temple of Onias were taken from one or more Jewish sources. On Josephus' sources in his Book 12 see Grimm 1853: xxvii–xxviii; Nussbaum 1875: 5–22; Bloch 1879: 96–100; Büchler 1896: 186; Niese 1900: 103; Momigliano 1930: 20ff.; Bickerman 1937: 163; Zeitlin 1950: 56–7; Dancy 1954: 30–1; Golstein 1976: 55–61,558–74; S. J. D. Cohen 1979: 44–5; see also pp. 346, 452 below.

[126] On the relationship between Josephus' version of the persecution and Revolt in *Antiquitates* and *Bellum Judaicum* see Drüner 1896: 51–6; Niese 1900: 101–3; Hölscher 1904: 8; Dancy 1954: 31; M. Stern 1960: 12–13. Drüner even tries to prove that Josephus revised the material from I Maccabees when he wrote *Antiquitates* by means of a detailed comparison with what he wrote earlier in *Bellum*. However, the comparison of the two versions (Drüner 1896: 53) does not necessarily prove this, and the verbal resemblance derives from the fact that Nicolaus, the source for *Bellum*, made use of I Maccabees (see p. 189 above). Drüner's evidence from the comparison of *Bell.* 1.81ff. with *Ant.* 13.314ff. (p. 55) is not relevant to the summary of the edicts and the Revolt because both those passages in entirety were taken from Nicolaus.

Lower City (*Ant.* 12.252; cf. *Bell.* 1.39), and may also be the explanation for the information about Nicanor's 9,000 soldiers in the
battle of Adasa (12.411), of which there is no mention in I Maccabees,[127] as well as for the description of the change from an extended line to a single file in which the 'formations' lined up behind
each other on entering the defile in the battle of Beth Zacharia
(12.371). Since some details relating to the movement of the Seleucid
force in that battle can in fact be deduced from I Maccabees, as well
as from the force's manner of deployment in the broad valley at the
entrance to the defile, Josephus would have had no difficulty in
recalling the clearer reconstruction of the deployment mentioned in
the source he had drawn on some fourteen years earlier. It is,
however, an undeniable possibility that the account of the Seleucid
deployment on entering the defile is an original interpretation by
Josephus (even though it undoubtedly accords with historical
fact).

In his accounts of other battles, Josephus from time to time took
the liberty of adding details based on information at his disposal
about the operational methods of the Hellenistic armies.[128] Other
additions were intended to explain difficult passages in I Maccabees,[129] or to bring the material more within the range of the
comprehension and outlook of his book's potential Gentile reader,
unacquainted with Eretz Israel and with the Jewish way of life,
religion, and conceptual world.[130] As usual, Josephus omitted details
that were liable to hurt the feelings of the Greco-Roman reader or
might depict the Jews in too unfavourable a light.[131] At times he
deviated from the original intention of a verse because of a too literal
reading of the Greek text of I Maccabees, without taking into
account that the Greek translator had used the special dialect of the
Septuagint, and occasionally employed words in a sense different
from that usual in the literary Greek of the Hellenistic period.[132] The

---

[127] See p. 44 above.
[128] E.g. 12.306 ('leaving lights burning in an abandoned camp'); 432 (removal of the dead
'by agreement'), and see pp. 263, 399–400 below.
[129] E.g. 12.288 ('*stratēgos* of Coele Syria') *versus* I Macc. 3.13 ('[chief] minister of the army
of Aram'); 12.296 ('half of the army and of the elephants') *versus* I Macc. 3.34 ('half the army
and the elephants').
[130] E.g. 12.271 (the religion of our Lord') as the explanation of I Macc. 2.27 ('who complies
with the covenant'); 12.278 ('altars') *versus* I Macc. 2.24 ('platforms'); 12.300–1 (Judas
Maccabaeus' oration stressing mourning practices) instead of I Macc. 3.46–56 (fulfilling ritual
obligations during the ceremony at Mizpah). See also the distances specified in *Ant.* 12.370,408.
[131] Compare 12.410–11 (the omission of the maltreatment of Nicanor's body) with I
Macc. 7.47.
[132] E.g. 12.287 ('he killed...and wounded') compared with I Macc. 3.12 (τραυματίαι =
the wounded; in the Septuagint – the dead; see p. 205); 12.299 ('from Syria and from the
adjacent region') compared with I Macc. 3.41 ('the army of Aram and of the land of the
Gentiles [Philistines]'); see below p. 247.

greatest deviations from the text and from the intention of I Maccabees are to be found in the orations attributed to the Jewish commander before the battles. Contrary to his usual custom when describing the battles themselves, Josephus wrote the oratory with the scantiest regard for their contents as given in I Maccabees. This is particularly conspicuous in the Ammaus speech, which is steeped in Hellenistic ideas and concepts that have nothing whatsoever in common with the world of ideas of the author of I Maccabees.[133] On the other hand, in the battle orations at Beth Horon (12.291) and Elasa (12.424–5) at least the principal ideas expressed in I Maccabees have been preserved. In some of the orations Josephus added reasons for presenting the Hasmonaean war as a 'just war', hinting covertly at the difference (in his view) between it and the Great Revolt against the Romans.[134]

Josephus' too literal reading of the Greek text of I Maccabees referred to above refutes the view repeatedly expressed in different variations during the last two centuries that, when writing *Antiquitates*, he made use of both the Hebrew original and the Greek translation of I Maccabees at the same time.[135] A careful study of the accounts of the battles shows that all the differences between Josephus and the Greek text of I Maccabees, which are quoted as proof of his having used the Hebrew original, can be explained by his tendency to simplify the description and interpret it on the basis of, or adapt it to, the concepts and point of view of the Greco-Roman reader. Besides the evidence derived from Josephus' too literal reading of the Greek text, there are other clear indications that he did not use the Hebrew original of I Maccabees.[136]

---

[133] Compare 12.303–4 with I Macc. 3.57–60, 4.8–12; see also Mattathias' testament *Ant.* 12.279–85 compared with I Macc. 2.48–67; and see Zeitlin 1950: 55.

[134] See in detail Gafni 1980: 81–95. See also Farmer 1956: 11–23.

[135] Michaelis 1778: 28, 138 and passim; von Destinon 1882: 69; C. C. Torrey, 'Maccabees Books', in *Encyclopaedia Biblica*, vol. 3 (London, 1902) 187–95; Joüon 1922: 204–6; Zeitlin 1950: 33,57–8; Melamed 1951: 122–30; Goldstein 1976: 14. Against them see Grimm 1853: xxviii–xxix; Bloch 1879: 80–90; Drüner 1896: 50; and esp. Ettelson 1925: 331–42. Most of the evidence cited by these latter is not decisive, however.

[136] P. 347 below: 12.299 ('allies from Syria and from the adjacent region') compared with I Macc. 3.41 ('the army of Syria [Edom] and of the land of the Gentiles [Philistines]'); p. 323: 12.371 *versus* I Macc. 6.37 ('on each one men of valour thirty-two [four]') – omission of the number of warriors on the elephants; p. 356: 12.404 *versus* I Macc. 7.29 ('[and the ambushers] were prepared to seize Judah') – no mention of ambush; p. 398 below: 12.429 ('up to Mount Aza that is so called') *versus* I Macc. 9.15 ('to the [slopes of] the mountain'). See also *Ant.* 12.251 compared to I Macc. 1.29: Josephus had trouble with the Greek translation of I Macc. here – ἄρχοντα φορολογίας (= the officer in charge of taxation; Hebrew: *śar ha-misim*), and therefore deleted his part in the events. The well-known reconstruction *śar ha-missim* (= 'minister [commander] of the Mysians', according to II Macc. 5.24), which is spelt identically in Hebrew, has been generally accepted, and there are no grounds for questioning that reconstruction.

9

The beginning of the Revolt and the battle against Apollonius

The episode at Modein and the escape to the Gophna Hills

Organized popular opposition to the religious persecutions began with Mattathias' charismatic action at Modein, described in great detail in I Maccabees (2.15–18). Sporadic outbreaks of resistance no doubt occurred in various places at the same time. Mattathias' public defiance was the signal for the rural population to raise its head and rally around the leadership of the Hasmonaean family. The audacity and initiative to assault the representative of the government doubtless derived from the special personality of Mattathias and his family. However, since Mattathias himself resided in Jerusalem at the start of the persecutions (I Macc. 2.1) and refrained from responding to Seleucid provocations in the city, most certainly geographic and accessibility factors contributed to making Modein the site of the most serious spontaneous uprising against the authorities, and the cradle of the general revolt.

Modein, today Tel al-Ras near the village of El-Midya, is located close to the meeting point of three geographical regions, and is itself on relatively gentle and easily accessible terrain. East and north of it, however, stretches rugged, mountainous terrain that is not easily traversable. Modein is situated at the north-eastern extremity of the Low Shephela. South of Modein is the Shephela, the hilly transitional region between the steep rugged slopes of the Judaean Hills and the coastal plain. The Shephela consists of two parts, a higher one that is more difficult to traverse and a lower one which is relatively easy. The boundary between them passes by Ni'lin, slightly east of Modein. The High Shephela extends from Ni'lin to Kharbata, east of which are the mountain slopes. As to the area north of Modein, Wadi e Natuf, whose main bed is a kilometre

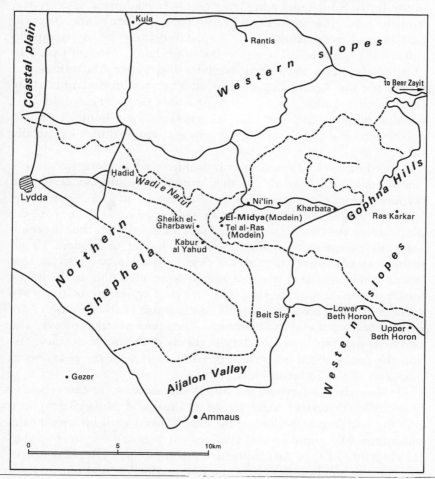

8 Modein and the western Gophna Hills

north of El-Midya, marks the northern boundary of the Shephela. North of the wadi there is no transitional area, and the long extensions of the mountain plateau go all the way down to the coastal plain.

It may be assumed that the authorities refrained from applying the coercive decrees in the mountain communities on the slopes, and concentrated their efforts in more easily approachable regions such as the mountain plateau north and south of Jerusalem and in the hills of the Low Shephela which were also close to the Seleucid forts in the Jerusalem citadel and Gezer on the coastal plain respectively. Modein was situated in a relatively accessible area, and Seleucid officials and troops consequently appeared there in an attempt to enforce the coercive decrees. On the other hand, Modein's propinquity to the steep and rugged western slopes gave Mattathias and his people the feeling that they would be able to find immediate refuge and organize in the adjacent hills before there could be a massive military response. The nearness to their homes certainly encouraged the people of the villages and made things logistically easier.

According to I Maccabees, Mattathias and his sons fled to the 'mountains' (2.28) while another group of 'justice seekers' who favoured passive resistance (see p. 481 below) found a haven in the 'desert' (2.29). The sources give no more precise indication of the place where the rebels assembled. Avi-Yonah believed that the main assembly points were in the Gophna Hills east of Modein.[1] That seems reasonable since that area is close to Modein, and also because it was mentioned as a place of refuge later, after the defeat in the battle of Beth Zacharia (Jos. *Bell.* 1.45). The nature of the place made it an ideal base for guerrilla forces: most of the mountains are extremely rugged and hard to reach. The slopes abound in caves and crevices providing cover in case the enemy did manage to penetrate, and the peaks afford a safe and convenient view of the roads north and west of the Judaean Hills.

II Maccabees describes the initial organization of the rebels in quite different terms: 'And the Maccabaeus (ὁ Μακκαβαῖος) who was the tenth, after he fled to the desert, lived with his men in the mountains like animals, and they fed on grass all the time so that they should not take part in the defilement' (5.27). The closeness of the verse to the description of the devastation carried out in Jerusalem by Apollonius, commander of the Mysian troops (5.24–6), gives the impression that Judas Maccabaeus fled from Jerusalem to the desert before the promulgation of the anti-Jewish decrees, and there began to organize and shape a core of rebels. This does not fit in with the tradition noted above whereby Mattathias raised the flag of Revolt in his native village of Modein only after the decrees had been issued, and then found refuge in the 'mountains' together with his sons and supporters. Various scholars are of the opinion that the 'realistic' tone of the verse makes it preferable to the 'artistic–legendary' story in I Maccabees on Mattathias' charismatic action

[1] Avi-Yonah 1964: 57; id. 1972: 148.

and the start of the Revolt in Modein.[2] Niese even claimed that the
Modein story originated in the days of the Hasmonaean State and
was designed to serve later dynastic purposes: it was meant to present
the Revolt as beginning on the initiative of Mattathias, Simeon's
father and founder of the dynasty, and not of the brother, Judas
Maccabaeus, who left no offspring. According to this conception,
Simeon was wrongly presented as the 'brain' who planned the
battles after Mattathias' death (I Macc. 2.64).[3] Tcherikover proffered another argument in support of the later origin of the story: it
is hard to imagine that Jason of Cyrene would have overlooked as
exciting a story as the Modein tradition if he was acquainted with it,
and the same applies to the epitomist.[4]

Far-reaching conclusions should not, however, be drawn from
that verse. Judas Maccabaeus' sudden appearance without any introduction or prior information, the reference to the men who
accompanied him to the desert, and the many participial forms
(cf. p. 178 n. 85 above), all show that the verse is an abridgement (or
summary) of a detailed story in Jason's original book, which contained information on additional people in the leadership of the
Revolt at its inception. This story may well have begun with the
Modein episode, and it is not impossible that among the ten people
were Judas Maccabaeus' brothers and Mattathias who fled from
Modein (cf. I Macc. 2.17,20,28). In any case there are signs that
Jason of Cyrene was familiar with the tradition on Modein: the book
relates that during Lysias' second expedition, before the siege of Beth
Zur, the Seleucid army camped at Modein and Judas Maccabaeus
burst into the camp at night (13.14–15). This statement is completely
unrelated to the geographical background, and is not at all con-
gruous. It can only be that Jason, who did not know where the
Seleucid camp was, inserted the name of Modein which was famous

[2] Niese 1900: 45–7; Kolbe 1926: 139; Tcherikover 1961a: 205,384; Nickelsburg 1971:
519,523; and others. Objections to Niese (without providing counter-arguments) were already
voiced by Wellhausen 1905: 132–5; id. 1901: 257 n. 1. A variation on Niese's method appears
in Schunck 1954: 64–6, who argues that the story of Modein was originally connected with
Judas Maccabaeus and that the name of Mattathias was substituted in order to give prominence to the founder of the Hasmonaean dynasty. Against him see Neuhaus 1974b: 168; and
the persuasive remarks of Kochabi 1983: 286–9.
[3] Niese 1900: 45. Against the theory on the presence in I Maccabees of pro-Simeonic or pro-
dynastic distortions, see pp. 52–3 esp. n. 81 above, and pp. 350–1 below. According to II
Maccabees as well, who is not suspected of any partiality to Simeon, the latter filled positions
of command and was the second most important figure. Jonathan seems not to have had any
important function at the start of the Revolt because he was too young, while later, when
Judas Maccabaeus was gone, he was recognized as the leader because of his natural
qualifications.   [4] Tcherikover 1961a: 384.

from the onset of the Revolt in order to whet the reader's interest.[5] The description of the Hasmonaean brothers as commanders of various units of the Jewish forces in the battle against Nicanor and Gorgias (8.21–3), having no factual basis either (see p. 256 below), shows that the author was well aware of the tradition on the division of labour in the Hasmonaean family (cf. 2.19). All in all, it is quite certain that Jason of Cyrene was acquainted with I Maccabees and used it as one of his main sources (pp. 182–4 above).

As to the sequence of events, there is no doubt that the verse on Judas Maccabaeus' flight to the 'desert' is not in the proper place in II Maccabees. According to II Maccabees, Judas Maccabaeus and his men were careful 'not to take part in the defilement', but according to the sequence of the description Jerusalem was defiled by idolatry only later (6.1–11).[6] Displacement of verses and passages from their original context by the author or the epitomist is not a rare occurrence in II Maccabees (see, e.g., 8.30–6, 10.24–38, 11.1–13). Artistic considerations from the realm of the poetics of tragedy may explain the location of the verse under discussion: it may have been displaced not accidentally but in order to hint at the saviour to come, and thus somewhat dispel the feeling of depression and helplessness that developed in the wake of the events described in the chapter and reached its peak in the subsequent chapters on the suffering of the martyrs (cf. p. 176 above). The extremely abridged nature of the verse suggests that the transfer was made by the epitomist. As for the statement that Judas Maccabaeus found refuge 'in the desert', it is not adequately grounded in the tradition of manuscripts,[7] and must in any case be seen in the light of Jason of Cyrene's vague notions of the geography of Eretz Israel (see p. 180 above), the information he had on the flight to the desert of some of the believers (6.11; and also I Macc. 2.29), and his acquaintance with biblical references to the Judaean desert as a hiding place for rebels and insurgents. Jason could also have been influenced by conditions in the neighbourhood of his native Cyrene. Even Josephus, who was not acquainted with II Maccabees and based his

---

[5] The absence of Mattathias from the opening verses in the prologue to II Maccabees (2.19–22) which define the contents of Jason's book is not counter-evidence, because also missing from those verses are Onias, Menelaus and Demetrius I who play important roles in the events in the II Maccabees narrative.

[6] See also Bévenot 1931: 197; Habicht, 1976a: 228 n. 27c.

[7] The words εἰς τὴν ἔρημον are in the Venetian manuscript, the Lucian version, and the ancient Latin and Syrian translations. This may be an addition meant to complement the participle ἀναχωρήσας that precedes the phrase. See Hanhart 1959: 29,70. Against him see Habicht 1976a: 228 n. 27b.

version solely on I Maccabees, makes the conventional statement that Mattathias found refuge in the desert (*Ant.* 12.271). Thus it is impossible to glean from the verse either the time or the place of Judas Maccabaeus' first uprising against the authorities.[8]

The deletion of the Modein tradition by the epitomist or Jason himself was motivated by literary–artistic considerations. Bickerman believed that this was done in order to achieve dramatic unity by limiting the framework of the plot to the heroic image of the principal protagonist, Judas Maccabaeus.[9] The conclusions about the 'tragic' form of the book support this evaluation: too many heroes overburden the absorptive capacity of the spectator or reader. Likewise noteworthy is the opinion of Momigliano, who believes that the omission of Mattathias' exploits derives from the tendency of II Maccabees to shape events according to the historiographical framework and conception of the Book of Judges. Like the charismatic characters in Judges, Judas Maccabaeus becomes a commander of the army and leader of the Revolt thanks to his initiative and qualifications, and not because of descent.[10]

First military confrontations

The rebels' first operations are described in I Maccabees in a prose text and in a rather general poetic passage. These indicate that the major effort was directed against the Hellenizers and their periphery, and not against the Seleucid officials and troops in Judaea (2.43–7, 3.8; the verses opening the poetic passage are a summary of Judas Maccabaeus' later accomplishments – cf. p. 138 n. 1 above). Thus we can infer that the garrison in the Jerusalem citadel, apart from Beth Zur the only Seleucid fortress in the Judaean Hills region, was forced to be content with supervising the population in the city, lacking as it did the power to restore order in the northern part of the region.

The Apollonius expedition was the first response by Seleucid forces summoned from outside Judaea to confront Judas Maccabaeus

[8] The assertion of I Maccabees that Mattathias left Jerusalem and moved to Modein (2.2.) lends no support to the view that Judas Maccabaeus' activity began in Jerusalem and not in Modein. The tradition about the Revolt starting in Modein and the family's close ties with the place is frequently reiterated in I Maccabees (2.17,70, 9.19, 13.25–30). The family's connection with Jerusalem can be explained by their ritual functions within the Yehoiarib clan; see also Alon 1958: 2.156; Mazar, 1941: 105–7.

[9] Bickerman 1937: 149. See also Efron 1980: 54. Cf., e.g., Lucian, *Hist. conscr.* 49; Klein 1939a: 248.

[10] Momigliano 1975: 86; cf. Pfeifer 1949: 487.

and his men. The author does not date the episode directly, but it is included in the narrative framework of the year 146 by the Seleucid count (2.69–3.37),[11] which is mentioned in connection with Mattathias' death (2.69). Since the date refers to a domestic event, it is based on the Seleucid–Babylonian system, thus applying to the year between April 166 and April 165 B.C. The engagement with Apollonius was preceded by various preliminary operations of Judas Maccabaeus on the internal front, and the ambush of Seron which followed likewise took place the same year. The first battle should therefore be dated somewhere between the summer of 166 and the spring of 165 B.C.[12]

The I Maccabees description of the clash with Apollonius (3.10–12) is vastly inferior to those given of later battles. The author seems to have had very little information about this event. He does not mention the rank and function of the enemy commander, the number of soldiers he had, the composition of his army, the route the expedition took, the site and course of the battle, the number of casualties, or the direction of retreat, details which for the most part are provided for the other battles. In the absence of real substance, he fills in with a mosaic of biblical phrases mostly taken from the story of the contest between David and Goliath. There is no doubt that the sources he utilized were not eye-witnesses, and the author himself certainly did not take part in that episode.

II Maccabees does not mention the battle against Apollonius nor the second battle against Seron. However, it contains an illuminating summary of Judas Maccabaeus' feats against the Seleucid foe in the early phases of the Revolt up to the battle of Ammaus: 'And the Maccabaeus being in the battle, the Gentiles could not withstand him (ἀνυπόστατος ἤδη τοῖς ἔθνεσιν) since the wrath of God turned into grace; and coming unexpectedly to cities and villages he would burn them, after selecting suitable places, and made quite a number of the enemy flee; and he generally took advantage of the nights for

---

[11] For the annal-like arrangement of the book see 1.54 (the year 145), 2.70 (146), 3.37 (147), 4.52 (148), 6.16 (149), 6.20 (150), 7.1 (151), 9.3 (152), 9.54 (153). This framework is maintained consistently only up to the start of Jonathan's leadership.

[12] The next date appearing in I Maccabees – the year 147, referring to Antiochus Epiphanes' expedition to the East (3.37) – is an external date that must be calculated according to the Macedonian–Syrian system, and thus extended from the autumn of 166 to the autumn of 165 B.C. This does not mean, however, that the battles against Apollonius and Seron preceded the autumn of 166 and were fought between April and the autumn of 166. The author was not aware that he was using two different chronological systems and assumed that the year stated for Antiochus' expedition to the East likewise began in Nisan. It is against this background that the celebrated I Maccabees error – setting the purification of the Temple before Antiochus Epiphanes' death – should be understood (4.52 *versus* 6.15; and see p. 281 below).

assaults of this sort, and the fame of his courage spread everywhere'
(8.5–7). These verses probably apply to the clashes with Apollonius
and Seron,[13] as well as to occasional raids on supply convoys, in
addition to punitive measures against Hellenizers and collaborators.
Attacks against the enemy from dominating positions while exploiting the surprise element, sometimes even at night, as noted in that
passage, are identical with the methods Judas Maccabaeus employed
in the battle against Seron and in the campaign at Ammaus, and
presumably the clash with Apollonius was of the same character. It
is hard to determine definitely why these episodes were not described
in detail in II Maccabees, and whether they were included in Jason
of Cyrene's book. At first glance it may appear that Jason, who in
other cases gives evidence of a better knowledge than the author of
I Maccabees of the hierarchy and status of commanders of the
Seleucid army, was aware of the low ranks of Apollonius and Seron
and therefore did not report the confrontations with them, except in
a few summarizing verses. On the other hand, II Maccabees describes various battles with low-ranking Seleucid officers and local
commanders in Transjordania. It may well be that these initial
small-scale victories were deleted in order to clear the way for the
account of the great victory at Ammaus, thus highlighting the immediate extreme change in the situation after the sacrifice of the
martyrs and the appearance of Judas Maccabaeus, in line with the
didactic and literary purpose of the book (see in detail pp. 277, 487
below). In any case, the multiplicity of participial forms in these
verses indicates a certain 'compression' made by the epitomist.[14]

The description of the battle against Apollonius in *Antiquitates*
(12.287) is a prose version of the flowery one in I Maccabees. It
adds nothing of value except the statement that Apollonius was the
stratēgos of Samaria, which Josephus apparently deduced from the
'Sidonites in Shechem' document that he included in his book
following the report on the religious persecutions (ibid. 257–64).

I Maccabees 3.10–12

3.10 And Apollonius mustered Gentiles and those from Samaria a
      large army to fight Israel.

11   And Judah knew and he went forth toward him and smote

---

[13] See also Niese 1900: 53; Bevan 1902: 2.176; Büchler 1906: 282 n. 4; Churgin 1949: 242;
Bunge 1971: 232.

[14] Against Büchler, ibid.

him and slew him and many fell dead and the remainder
fled.

12 And they took their spoils and Judah took Apollonius' sword
and fought with it all the days.

COMMENTARY

3.10 *Apollonius mustered*: His rank and function are not mentioned. He
certainly cannot be identified with Apollonius son of Menestheus,
who was satrap of Coele Syria and Phoenicia early in the reign of
Antiochus IV (II Macc. 4.4; cf. 4.21).[15] It has been proposed to
identify him with the Apollonius mentioned in the 'Sidonites in
Shechem' document (*Ant.* 12.261) as the governor (*meridarkhēs*) of
Samaria.[16] Josephus already believed the two were not to be
separated, for in his version of the battle he specifies: 'Apollonius,
stratēgos of the land of Samaria' (ibid. 287). The proposal is
reasonable as the verse clearly indicates a connection between the
man and Samaria. Others have sought to identify him with
Apollonius, commander of the Mysians, who, according to II
Maccabees, led the troops who broke into Jerusalem on the eve of
the religious persecutions (5.24).[17] The name of the Mysian
commander is missing in the I Maccabees parallel (1.29). As it is
quite certain that the name did figure in the original version of I
Maccabees,[18] the author himself may well have known that the
Apollonius who fought Judas Maccabaeus was identical with the
Mysian commander mentioned earlier in his book in the proper
historical sequence, and therefore did not feel it necessary to define
him here.

Indeed there is no reason to deny the possibility that Apollonius,
commander of the Mysian troops, was appointed governor of
Samaria: he might have been a Macedonian, for in the Seleucid
army the mercenary contingents were sometimes commanded by

[15] Contrary to Bengtson 1964: 2.163 n. 3.
[16] So, e.g., Grimm 1853: 52; Abel 1949: 55–6; Dancy 1954: 88; M. Stern 1965: 63, and
many others. On the authenticity of the document of 'the Sidonites in Shechem' see Bickerman
1976–80: 2.105–35; M. Stern 1965: 52–3; Schalit 1970–1: 131–83.
[17] Ewald 1864–8: 4.403 n. 3; Schlatter 1891: 11; Bévenot 1931: 66; Schunck 1980: 308.
[18] The account of Apollonius' capture of Jerusalem in II Maccabees (5.24–6) seems to be
a paraphrase of the story in I Maccabees (1.29–39). The timing of the episode on the Sabbath
is only an imaginary interpretation of Jason based on the phrase 'words of peace in deceit' in
I Maccabees (1.30; cf. II Macc. 5.25), and serves to stress the wickedness of the enemy as was
done elsewhere in the book (see in detail pp. 485 and 490–1 below). As there is no real evidence
on Jason of Cyrene's use of another source for this episode, and the absence of the name of the
commander of the Mysians in I Maccabees is rather strange, we can deduce with a great
degree of certainty that Jason took the name Apollonius from I Maccabees and it was later
dropped in one of the reincarnations of I Maccabees.

Greco-Macedonians rather than compatriots of the troops they led,[19] and if so there was no obstacle to his appointment as governor of Samaria (cf. p. 133 above). His activity in Jerusalem preceded the promulgation of the coercive edicts, and the document of the 'Sidonites in Shechem', which refers to Apollonius as governor of the Samaritan region, dates from after the edicts. Having succeeded in suppressing the Jewish unrest in Jerusalem, Apollonius may have been appointed governor of the Samaritan region when the concentrations of opposition to the new measures had moved to two of the southern toparchies of Samaria which were populated by Jews (I Macc. 11.34): Ramathaim, which included Modein, and Aphairema (*'Afrayim*), which included the Gophna Hills to the west and the desert to the east.

Thus as governor of Samaria Apollonius' operations against the Jews did not go beyond the boundaries of the region he was in charge of. And this is enough to refute the hypothesis of a number of scholars who concluded from this episode (and from it alone) that Judaea was then administratively subject to Samaria.[20] As to Apollonius' formal authority, the meridarchs had both civil and military functions, as did the satraps in their satrapies, the largest administrative units,[21] and that accounts for Apollonius' active endeavour to suppress the Revolt. Attempts have been made on the basis of the I Maccabees statement on the appointment of Jonathan as *stratēgos* and meridarch (10.65) to infer that in the Seleucid kingdom the two posts were held by different people,[22] but that verse cannot be submitted as evidence, because the context shows that the author is trying to stress the honours conferred upon Jonathan by highlighting his military authority.

Gentiles and those from Samaria: ἔθνη καὶ ἀπὸ Σαμαρείας. Some scholars have accepted this syntactically deviant sentence.[23] Others have suggested the reading 'Gentiles from Samaria' (omitting the καί),[24] or the reconstruction ⟨מגליל ה⟩גוים ⟨ומשומרון – '⟨from Galilee of the⟩ Gentiles and those from Samaria'.[25] Samaria in the first two readings refers to either the Macedonian military settlement (later called Sebasteia)[26] or to the meridarchy as a whole. The latter interpretation is valid for the third suggestion. The expression

[19] See, e.g., Polybius 5.79.3,6, and perhaps also para. 12.
[20] Abel 1949: 55; Avi-Yonah 1966: 46, and others.
[21] On the functions of the *stratēgos* see the summary by Bengtson (1964: 2.188–93). On the meridarchy and meridarch see M. Stern 1965: 63–4; Bengtson 1964: 2.24ff. and passim.
[22] Contrary to Bengtson 1964: 2.172,188.
[23] Bengtson 1964: 2.173; Abel 1949: 55.
[24] Michaelis 1778: 67; see also Syncellus' paraphrase (p. 532, ed. Dindorff).
[25] Melamed 1951: 125.
[26] On Samaria as a military settlement see Tcherikover 1927: 73–4, and in Herod's time: Schalit 1969: 358–66; G. M. Cohen 1972: 83–95.

'Gentiles' appears *inter alia* as a pejorative epithet for the Samaritans in the early literature of the Second Temple period.[27] However, the position of the Samaritans at the time of the persecutions is quite obscure since the 'Sidonites in Shechem' who supported Antiochus Epiphanes (*Ant.* 12.258–64) may have been descendants of Phoenician settlers and not Samaritans. Be this as it may, 'Gentiles' can as well apply to the Macedonian settlers and (or) to mercenaries stationed in the region on garrison duty. In view of Apollonius' former position as the commander of the Mysian mercenaries, these garrisons may have been taken from the Mysian contingent. In any case, the Samaritans cannot be considered a military body of real ability, and the number of military settlers in Samaria together with the mercenaries in the garrisons was quite limited (see pp. 131–2 above).

A large army: The Greek is δύναμιν μεγάλην. The original Hebrew was ṣāv'ā (an army), and not ḥayil (a force) as Cahana translated.[28] For the phrase ṣāv'a gādōl (a large army) cf. Daniel 10.1, and its translation in the Septuagint. The word *dynamis* which appears in the singular in our verse serves to translate both ṣāv'ā and ḥayil in the Septuagint. In the battle descriptions of I Maccabees it denotes both the Jewish force and the enemy army. As it often appears with no qualifier or identification (e.g. 3.42, 4.4, 6.33,47, 9.11), it seems likely that the Hebrew original made some linguistic distinction between the forces of the two sides. I Maccabees makes frequent use of the plural *dynameis* to designate the enemy troops (3.27,34,37, 6.30,47, 7.2,4,14, 9.1; cf. p. 312 below). In the Septuagint that form is generally used for ṣāv'ā or the plural ṣevā'ōt and only in a few (doubtful) cases for ḥayil. Thus it may be suggested that the author used ṣāv'ā for the enemy force and ḥayil to designate Judas Maccabaeus' men.

To fight Israel: This definition of the purpose of the expedition is too general and flowery to permit any conclusions to be drawn. In view of the circumstances, it may be assumed that the purpose was to destroy the initial nucleus of rebels rallying round Judas Maccabaeus in the Gophna area by penetrating that area and conducting mopping-up operations there.

11 *And Judah knew and he went forth toward him*: καὶ ἐξῆλθεν εἰς συνάντησιν αὐτῷ. Cf. I Sam. 17.48: 'and he came and drew nigh to meet David'; and in the Septuagint: καὶ ἐπορεύθη εἰς συνάντησιν Δαυιδ.

---

[27] In Second Temple days the term גוים (= Gentiles) may have been used among others as a pejorative referring to Samaritans, like the term 'Cutheans'. It appears in Sirach ('a contemptible Gentile nation living in Shechem' 50.26), in the tradition on Samaritan settlement by the Assyrians in the Samarian Hills in II Kings (17.26,29,41; the Septuagint translation in 17.29 is ἔθνη, ἔθνη).

[28] Cahana 1957: 109.

The author says nothing about the site of the confrontation. Apollonius' position and the fact that the Seleucid force came from Samaria have suggested the possibility that the battle was fought at a point on the main road from Samaria to Jerusalem. On the assumption that it was an ambush, Avi-Yonah proposed locating the battle site on the Lebonah Ascent half way between Shechem (Nablus) and Jerusalem, south of the village of Lubban Sharqiya and near Khan Lubban, a steep winding ascent along which there are places of concealment and surface features ideal for setting an ambush for a force making its way up.[29] Another proposal has been Wadi Ḥaramiya, further south along the road, north of the village of Silwad, where the road is overlooked by ridges on both sides.[30] That the battle was an assault from ambush is likely: such a conclusion is based on an inference from the subsequent battle against Seron at Beth Horon, on the indirect tactics applied by Judas Maccabaeus in the battle of Ammaus, and on the general description in II Maccabees of Judas Maccabaeus' early operations as surprise attacks, ambushes, and the like (8.6–7). The location of the battle site, however, depends largely on the determination of the purpose of the expedition undertaken by the Seleucid force. If it was to capture the rebels in the Gophna Hills, the confrontation could be located at many points on the road from Shechem to the Gophna area, and within that area as well, and there is no sense in trying to arrive at a precise location.

And smote him and slew him: I Sam. 17.50 has exactly the same phrase. The application of phrases taken from the story of the David and Goliath confrontation creates the impression that there was a duel between Judas Maccabaeus and Apollonius. This is obviously impossible. Descriptions of the same 'Homeric' type regarding the Hellenistic period are to be found in Books 18–20 of Diodorus, but they are valueless and derive (directly or indirectly) from Duris of Samos and other pathetic sources of similar nature.[31] The conclusion that must be drawn is that the author did not witness the battle, and that the oral or written source he utilized knew very little about the episode. The only historical detail is apparently Apollonius' death in the battle.

And many fell dead: Cf. I Sam. 17.52. The Greek word is τραυματίαι (literally 'wounded'), here a translation of the Hebrew חללים (= fallen), the usual rendering in the Septuagint (see also I Macc. 1.19). Interpreting the word according to the ordinary Greek meaning, Josephus had difficulty in understanding why the enemy dead were not mentioned, and wrote: 'Many of them he

[29] Avi-Yonah 1964: 59.
[30] Avissar 1955: 104; see also Avi-Yonah 1972: 154.
[31] See Beloch 1912–27: 4(2).4–5.

killed...and wounded many more' (*Ant.* 12.287). As this is the only time Josephus refers to the wounded in a battle description, it is not a chance paraphrase, and Josephus' addition must have resulted from a misunderstanding of the Greek of I Maccabees. His mistake makes it unlikely that he had at his disposal the Hebrew original of I Maccabees (see p. 193 above).

12 *And Judah took Apollonius' sword and fought with it all the days*: The parallel to I Sam. 17.51,54 and 21.10,11 has already been noted by all commentators.

10

The ambush for Seron at the Beth Horon Ascent

The battle against Seron, like the confrontation with Apollonius, is described only in I Maccabees (3.13–26). As stated above, II Maccabees refers to this affair as well in the brief summary on Judas Maccabaeus' exploits at the start of his career, before the battle of Ammaus (8.1–7). The two battles are reported in I Maccabees in the narrative framework of the year 146 which is mentioned in connection with a domestic event, that is, between April 166 and April 165 B.C., and could have taken place any time between the summer of 166 and April 165 B.C. (see p. 200 above).

The description of the ambush for Seron is longer and more detailed than that of the battle that preceded it. The author locates the battle site in a general way, mentions the operational method of the Jewish force, and reports the number of enemy dead and the direction in which the vanquished retreated. At the same time, important details are missing on points dealt with in I Maccabees in regard to the other battles such as the number of Seleucid combatants, their tactical units, the number of soldiers Judas Maccabaeus had, the features of the terrain, and the precise location of the ambush. The author probably did not take part in the battle, but may possibly have had the assistance of an eye-witness account. The book exaggerated both the enemy numbers and Seron's status in the royal army and stressed the small number of the Jewish combatants, although presumably Judas Maccabaeus deliberately chose to use a small force to set the ambush (re verse 16). This presentation dictates the tenor of the pre-battle oration ascribed to Judas Maccabaeus, an oration which well serves the author's didactic purpose of indicating the hidden hand of God directing the course of events (verses 17–22). The timing of the speech does not, however, fit the situation as well as its contents (pp. 214–16 below).

Josephus' version of the battle in *Antiquitates* (12.288–92) is as usual a paraphrase of the description in I Maccabees. The attempt of a number of scholars to infer Seron's rank from the Josephus text is unacceptable (re verse 13). Certainly it cannot help to reconstruct the military operations. Contrary to I Maccabees, Josephus does not mention a surprise assault. He relates that Seron set up a camp at Beth Horon, Judas Maccabaeus attacked it, and after Seron fell in battle all his soldiers fled. The placement of the camp in the centre of events is based on the mistaken explanation according to its meaning in Classical Greek of the term παρεμβολή (= camp), which appears in I Maccabees (3.17,23), while in the language of the Septuagint (and of I Maccabees) it can also mean a mobile army, as does the biblical מַחֲנֶה which was in the original Hebrew. This adds weight to the conclusion that when writing *Antiquitates* Josephus did not have the Hebrew original of I Maccabees before him (see p. 193 above). The reference to Seron's death in the battle is a too literal interpretation of καὶ συνετρίβη Σήρων καὶ ἡ παρεμβολὴ αὐτοῦ ἐνώπιον αὐτοῦ ('and Seron and his camp were smitten before him', 3.23), which refers to Seron's defeat as a commander and not his death in the field.

I Maccabees 3.13–26

13 And Seron, (chief) commander of the army of Aram, heard that Judah gathered an assembly and company of adherents with him and (they are) going forth to battle.

14 And he said, I will make a name for myself and be respected in the kingdom, and fight Judah and those with him who scorn the king's word.

15 And he added and [took up] with him a heavy camp of sinners to help him take revenge on the children of Israel.

16 And he approached the Beth Horon Ascent and Judah came out toward him with few (warriors).

17 And seeing the camp coming toward them they said to Judah, How can we the few fight this strong throng and we are tired, we have not eaten today.

18 And Judah said, it is easy to deliver many into the hands of few, and there is no difference before Heaven to save us with many or few.

19 For not in a great army is victory in war, but from the Heavens (comes) valour;

20 They come to us full of pride and evil to destroy us and our wives and our children to despoil us.

21   And we fight for our lives and our Law.

22   And He will smite them from before us, and you need not fear them.

23   And when he ceased to speak, he came upon them suddenly and Seron and his camp were smitten before him.

24   And he pursued them on the Beth Horon Descent up to the plain, and of them some eight hundred men fell, and the remainder fled to the country of the Philistines.

25   And fear of Judah and his brothers began, and dread befell the Gentiles in their vicinity.

26   And his reputation reached the king, and all nations told of the wars of Judah.

COMMENTARY

13 *And Seron, (chief) commander of the army of Aram*: The name 'Syria' that figures in the Greek version is the usual rendering of *'arām* in the Septuagint, and in I Maccabees as well (cf. p. 247 below). Seron's title ἄρχων τῆς δυνάμεως Συρίας (head of the Syrian army) is identical with that of Naaman, the Aramaean general, in the Septuagint translation of II Kings 5.1. The reconstruction based on Naaman's title in the Bible should be *śar ṣevā 'arām*, which in Hebrew means chief of staff of the Aramaean (Seleucid) army. As already noted (p. 133), Seron seems to have been the commander of some Thracian garrison troops posted in the coastal plain. Seron's position was exaggerated because the author was not acquainted with his exact rank, although he was aware that Seron was not chief of staff (see verse 14).

Michaelis, the eighteenth-century scholar, followed by others, suggested that Seron's title as given in *Antiquitates* τῆς κοίλης Συρίας στρατηγός (= the *stratēgos* of Coele Syria, 12.288) originated in a misreading of *śar ḥeyl 'arām* (= commander of the troop of Syria) in the Hebrew I Maccabees as *śar ḥeylat 'arām* (= governor of Coele Syria).[1] The suggestion is made in support of the view that Josephus made use of the Hebrew original of I Maccabees. But Josephus could have arrived at his determination of rank on his own, from a realization that the position ascribed to Seron in the Greek translation of I Maccabees was too exalted, especially in view of the clear implication that the latter exceeded his authority (3.14), and because according to I Maccabees even in the battle of Ammaus the commander-in-chief of the Seleucid army was not personally involved, but only the *stratēgos* of Coele Syria and Phoenicia, Ptolemy son of Dorymenes (3.38). Furthermore, the assumption

[1] Michaelis 1778: 60.

that the Hebrew original had *śar ḥeyl 'arām* is not tenable, for there
is no biblical parallel for *śar ḥeyl*. Finally, as already noted (p. 204
above), *ḥayil* is used to denote the Jewish force, and *ṣāvā* to denote
the enemy troops.

*Heard that Judah gathered an assembly...and (they are) going forth to
battle*: Evidently this verse refers in general to the mopping-up
operations Judas Maccabaeus and his men carried out in the
Judaean Hills (I Macc. 3.1–9; II Macc. 8.6–7) and especially their
defeat of Apollonius. Although the wording seems to imply that
Seron had intervened in Judaea because of an unusual gathering of
the rebels there to plan a far-reaching operation – as for instance an
assault on the garrison of the Jerusalem citadel and the
concentration of the Hellenizers in the city – it is hard to imagine
that at such an early stage Judas Maccabaeus would have dared
provoke the authorities by launching an attack on the citadel, which
he and his brothers hesitated to do even at later stages (see pp. 458–9
below).

14 *And he said, I will make a name for myself*, etc.: This implies that Seron
exceeded his authority (cf. I Macc. 5.57; Gen. 11.4). As such an
implication does not fit in with the information about Seron's
position and the author's efforts to glorify the victory, it must be
viewed as a slip of the pen.

15 *And he added*: The Greek καὶ προσέθετο (cf. 9.1,72, 10.88) should be
reconstructed according to the Septuagint as ויוסף, which means
'to (do) again' or 'to add'. The first meaning, which was adopted
by the commentators and translators, is difficult because it implies
that Seron personally conducted an earlier expedition against Judas
Maccabaeus (cf. I Macc. 9.1). Grimm's suggestion that the
expression refers to the previous expedition led by Apollonius[2] is
contrived and unsuited to the meaning of the Hebrew word. The
Lucianic version, which has καὶ προσέθετο τοῦ ἀναβῆναι (= and he
continued to ascend), is even less acceptable, indicating not only a
former expedition, but a similar ascent to the Judaean Hills. The
redactors who also understood ויוסף as 'he (did) again' obviously
tried to solve the difficulty imposed by the next verb καὶ ἀνέβη (see
below). Other suggestions based on the same meaning involve
considerable emendments and additions to the text.[3] The meaning
of the verb should therefore be 'he added'.

---

[2] Grimm 1853: 54; Gutberlet 1920: 51.

[3] Schwabe and Melamed (1928: 202–4) and Zeitlin (1950: 58–9) believe that the original
had ויאסף את צבאו (= and he gathered [ויאסף] his army); the word ויאסף was garbled
to ויוסף, and the rest of the sentence dropped. The evidence from *Ant.* 12.289 ('gathering the
force at his disposal') is not compelling: Josephus seems to have added the sentence out of the
need to note the participation of the Seleucid force of Seron himself, which is not mentioned
explicitly in I Maccabees, besides the Hellenizers (= sinners) mentioned in the next sentence.
In any case, Josephus did not consult the Hebrew original of I Maccabees while writing his
paraphrase in *Antiquitates* (see p. 193 above).

And [took up] with him a heavy camp of sinners: The Greek has the verb ἀνέβη (= went up) with the 'camp of sinners' as its subject. However, Seron must be the subject, as he is of the preceding verb καὶ προσέθετο (he added). Goldstein rightly suggested that the Hebrew source had the word ויעל; the translator understood the word as being in simple form (*qal*),[4] while it actually was in the active causative form (*hif'il*), with Seron as the subject. Accordingly the verse states that Seron supplemented the army of 'Aram', indicated by his title, with the 'sinners'.

A heavy camp of sinners: From the word ἀσεβῶν (חטאים = sinners; perhaps פושעים = criminals) as well as the 'to help him' that follows, it appears that the author means the Hellenizers who helped Seron, and that was Josephus' understanding in *Antiquitates* too (12.289; cf. I Macc. 3.8, 6.21, 7.5,9, 9.25,73). The description of the Hellenizers' auxiliary as a 'heavy camp' is no clue to the numerical strength of the Hellenizer movement in Judaea, but only the same type of exaggeration that I Maccabees so frequently applies to enemy armies. For an estimate of the overall number of Hellenizers see p. 57 above.

To take revenge: The author refers to the desire to avenge the death of Apollonius or to repay Judas Maccabaeus and his men for their constant harassment of the Hellenizers and their supporters. The special effort made by Judas Maccabaeus to surprise the enemy in the Beth Horon Ascent (see p. 214) shows that the rebels aspired to prevent the enemy from regaining control of the main roads and reinforcing the Jerusalem garrison. If the purpose was to prevent Seron from invading the rebels' base, this could have been achieved more conveniently and more effectively within the Gophna region itself.

16 *And he approached the Beth Horon Ascent*: The reference is to the difficult steep part of the way from the northern part of the Aijalon Valley to the mountain plateau north of Jerusalem between the villages of Lower and Upper Beth Horon which gave the road its name. The fact that Seron chose to ascend via Beth Horon may indicate that the object of his expedition was to conduct a 'policing' operation in the region north of Jerusalem and perhaps also to penetrate the nearby Gophna mountains and clear them of the rebel nests.

The Beth Horon Ascent is located on one of the north-western interfluves of the Judaean Hills rolling toward the plain (see Map 10 on pp. 222–3). The start of the road, from the village of Beit Sira at the northern end of the Aijalon Valley to Lower Beth Horon, is rather easy, climbing gradually for about four kilometres on a moderate gradient over a relatively broad bed. The hard sector is the one between Lower and Upper Beth Horon, where the trail

[4] Goldstein 1976: 247.

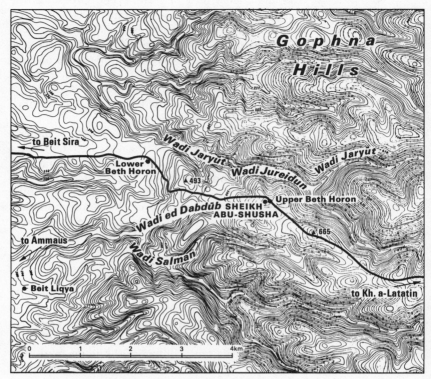

9 The Beth Horon Ascent

climbs 225 m over an aerial distance of 2.8 km (including one descent). The trail is extremely narrow and has intermittent steep slopes on either side of it. The path winds, and every bend has a hill overlooking it and a dangerously steep slope on its other side. A small force stationed on the heights at these points could prevent the passage of a large army making the climb, and hurl it down the mountainside. Today the road is wider, its construction having involved considerable earth-moving, so that the inherent difficulties are somewhat mitigated. The road in ancient times is described by a Beraita: 'Two camels that climbed the Beth Horon Ascent and met each other, if both were going up both would fall; if one after the other, they would go up.' (BT Sanhedrin 32b). A sector of the Beth Horon Ascent of Roman times which has survived on the western edge of the village of Upper Beth Horon east of the local graveyard exemplified the difficulties of that part of the route.[5] From Upper Beth Horon the road continues for 6 km to Khirbet a-

[5] On the Roman road see Thomsen 1917: 7–8; Alt 1925: 55; id. 1927: 23–6; id. 1929: 19; id. 1932: 18; Beyer 1930: 211. On the difficulties in ascending the road in the nineteenth century and early twentieth see Guérin 1868–80: 1.346–7; Wavell 1928: 159–60.

Latatin, where there are remnants of the Roman way station at the ninth mile from Jerusalem (τὸ ἐννάτον).[6] At this point the trail reaches the wide plateau north of Jerusalem. In the last section of it there is just one steep section going to the hill south-east of Upper Beth Horon (Hill 665). The ridge line is generally easy to advance along, although in three sectors it narrows considerably and has steep slopes on its north-eastern side.

Despite its difficulties and dangers, the Beth Horon Ascent was the main road from the west to Jerusalem and the northern part of the mountain range during the Second Temple era (*Bell.* 2.228) as well as earlier and later, because the other possible routes involved even greater difficulties. The alternate routes passing through gullies are longer, narrow and winding, full of pebbles, and subject to observation from both sides, while the terrain of the other ridge lines to the north of the Elah Valley is rough, broken up by gullies, and in places very steep (like the adjacent one north of the Beth Horon Ascent).[7]

And Judah came out toward him with few (warriors): According to II Maccabees, at that stage Judas Maccabaeus had about 6,000 regulars (8.1,16,22; cf. I Macc. 3.56, 4.6). While the figure is certainly rounded off, in view of the author's purposes and character it cannot be assumed that he inflated it. The force must have been considerably larger than Seron's. Owing to the propinquity to the Beth Horon Ascent of the Gophna area, where the rebels were concentrated and must have been always on the alert, Judas Maccabaeus was able to utilize this numerical potential for the confrontation with Seron though he seems to have had only short notice about the approaching expedition. However, there is little doubt that in the actual clash Judas Maccabaeus deliberately employed only a small number of combatants and consequently was numerically inferior. As verse 23 states and the terrain indicates, Judas Maccabaeus and his men surprised the enemy from an ambush. An attack of this sort is generally conducted with a small force to reduce the risk of early discovery and permit the maximum coordination. The author ignores this fundamental consideration and represents the small number of Jews involved as a tactical disadvantage (see also verse 17), in order to serve his religious–didactic purpose of demonstrating the indirect role of God in the course of events (see pp. 63–4 above).

17 *And seeing the camp coming toward them they said to Judah, How can we the few fight this strong throng*: The 'complaint' is the pretext for the 'battle oration' which follows. However, unlike the oration itself, the two parts of the 'complaint' may be genuine. Judas Maccabaeus' men may have expressed some anxiety in the face of the enemy's

[6] Avi-Yonah 1954a: 20 n. 55.
[7] On the Beth Horon Ascent road see also Oelgarten 1914: 73–89.

overwhelming numerical superiority, though their commander deliberately did not utilize all the manpower at his disposal.

And we are tired: The fatigue seems to have been the result of a forced march to the battlefield. Judas Maccabaeus could have had only short notice of Seron's advance, and had to move quickly with his select men along the 15 km from the Gophna area to Upper Beth Horon, if he intended to surprise the enemy in the ascent. The physical ability of his combatants to stand even longer forced marches (followed by pursuits) considerably improved shortly thereafter as indicated by the course of events in the Ammaus campaign (see pp. 261–2, 270–2 below).

We have not eaten today: Since ἀσιτοῦντες means 'not eaten' rather than 'fasted', evidently no ritual was involved (in contrast to the one on the eve of the battle of Ammaus: I Macc. 3.47); and seeing that the ambush was set in Jewish territory, it could hardly be attributed to particular logistic difficulties. It was the result of the need to reach the ambush spot as soon as possible and after arrival to remain on the alert and take care not to be discovered by the enemy and their advance patrols, and even not to attract the attention of local sympathizing passersby (which could be no less harmful). The Seleucid march may have taken longer than expected because of the difficulties of the route and the need to proceed cautiously for fear of a trap. All this kept the Jewish force penned down to its position for a long time, preventing it from getting any food or rest.

18 *And Judah said...there is no difference before Heaven to save us with many or few*: The Greek has the noun διαφορά which means 'difference'. The wording of the verse is influenced by Jonathan's comment to his armour bearer in I Samuel 14.6 ('For there is no restraint to the Lord to save by many or by few'), but in the Septuagint the translation of מעצור (= restraint) is συνεχόμενον, while διαφορά does not figure at all. As the translator of I Maccabees seems to have been extremely faithful to the Hebrew original even in cases where obvious difficulties resulted (see, e.g. pp. 323–4 below), the translation in this case cannot be his own free interpretation. The proposal to reconstruct the word as הפרש (= difference),[8] which is known in this meaning in the sages' language, is therefore possible, as well as (ה)הבדל. This case shows that the author of I Maccabees was not averse to rendering biblical verses in an interpretive paraphrase as did the authors of the Dead Sea Scrolls,[9] or by a slight change to adapt them to the particular situation (see p. 169 above).

19 *From the Heavens (comes) valour*: This statement is the clearest expression of the author's conception of the Divine role in the

[8] Alon 1958: 2.153.
[9] On this phenomenon in the Isaiah scroll see Kutscher 1959: 23–9,436.

events. God does not intervene directly, but only inspires the Jewish combatants to fight bravely and give the utmost of themselves. It means that if they do not take matters into their own hands, do not deploy a reasonable number of men in the circumstances, and do not employ proper stratagems, the Divine help will not appear, and nothing will save the day.

22 *And He will smite them from before us, and you need not fear them*: The word 'He' is a substitute for the Tetragrammaton (cf. I Macc. 2.60).[10] The contents of the verse must not be taken literally to mean that God would fight for the Jews. It can be explained by the request attributed to Judas Maccabaeus at Beth Zur: 'Give them dread and dissolve the courage of their strength' (I Macc. 4.32). In the same way as God inspires his believers with extraordinary courage, so he discourages the enemy and lowers its fighting spirit. The 'general' phrasing of the verse under discussion derives from its being in fact a summary of the speech of '(the Priest) Anointed for Battle' in Deuteronomy (20.3–4; cf. II Chron. 20.15; Sotah 8.1). It is not impossible that Judas Maccabaeus indeed did utter this verse (or something similar) on some occasion while awaiting the enemy, being influenced by a long tradition. But this still does not enhance the authenticity of the speech as a whole.[11] Impressive authentic statements were preserved here and there even in literary orations.

23 *And when he ceased to speak*: See Numbers 16.31 and cf. Job 1.16,17,18. The situation into which the oration was injected underlies its artificial, literary character. The basic framework required for setting an effective ambush does not allow for speeches, certainly not immediately preceding the assault.[12] Furthermore, there is a disproportion between the great length of the speech and the laconic description of the battle itself. A writer who had so little information on the military events would certainly have less on the contents of the orations and words of encouragement which are naturally harder to remember and preserve.

As far as the content of the speech is concerned, it stresses that the few can defeat the many thanks to their bravery, inspired by God, and their high motivation. All this could have been said in many wars, and there is nothing in this oration specific to the special circumstances of the ambush at Beth Horon. Viewing the long enemy column stretching along the precipitous ascent flanked

[10] See further examples in Stein 1970: 109–11. On other substitutes for the Tetragrammaton current at the time of the Second Temple (e.g. 'Heavens', verses 18 and 19 above) see Marmorstein 1927: 54ff.; Urbach 1975: 69ff.; Licht 1957: 15–16; Yadin 1962: 261. On the method of the author of the Letter of Aristeas see Hadas 1951: 5–6.

[11] Contrary to Baer 1968: 106.

[12] For a similar incompatibility between the delivery of an oration before the battle and a situation requiring absolute silence in Livy 7.35.2–12 see Walsh 1963: 229–30.

by chasms, while hidden in his commanding position, Judas
Maccabaeus would certainly have encouraged his men by stressing
their advantage in topography and surprise, as well as the
difficulties facing the enemy along the ascent. Moreover, there is no
indication that numerical inferiority was actually dictated by the
Jewish battle plan, and was, in this case, a tactical advantage.

He came upon them suddenly: The Greek is ἐνήλατο εἰς αὐτοὺς ἄφνω.
The uses of the verb ἐνάλλεσθαι in the Septuagint (Job 6.27,
16.5,11, 19.5) do not fit the context. The verb should be
reconstructed as בָּא עֲלֵיהֶם פִּתְאֹם (= came upon them suddenly), in
accordance with the description of the attack and pursuit of the
Amorite kings in the Beth Horon Descent which naturally
influenced the style of this verse ('And Joshua came upon them
suddenly', Josh. 10.9).

Suddenly: The utilization of the surprise element, the terrain, and
the pursuit in the Beth Horon Descent (verse 24) together with
parallels in other episodes in the same site show that the assault was
made from ambush. Where it was set exactly is a moot question.
Abel suggested it was on Hill 665 east of Upper Beth Horon, or on
the hill which is the location of most houses of present-day Upper
Beth Horon.[13] Sheikh Abu-Shusha, the ancient tel of Upper Beth
Horon, seems more appropriate. That hill provides an ambushing
force with considerable advantages. It rises about twenty metres
above the road, while a steep slope down to Wadi Jureidun flanks
the other side of the road. That slope, the most precipitous of all on
either side of the Ascent, was almost vertical in the past, though
nowadays it has been softened by the terracing of the local Arab
farmers. The passage there was extremely narrow as the remains of
the Roman road at the place prove. Signs of the later cutting to
widen the roadbed are discernible on the hillsides. An ambush at
Sheikh Abu-Shusha could easily force anyone passing at its foot over
the cliff. Moreover, the site is at the end of the most difficult section
of the Beth Horon Ascent (a climb of 110 m over an aerial distance
of 950 m). Close to the hill the road bends sharply right, so that the
ascending force could not see what was happening around it, a
situation which would increase its fear and hasten its retreat. If it
succeeded in overcoming that obstacle, danger awaited it further on
from Hill 665, and if it retraced its steps it would have to make its
way past other points on the descent where additional ambushes
could be stationed. According to Josephus it appears that it is here
that the Jewish rebels concentrated their great effort against the
army of Cestius Gallus who retreated down the Beth Horon Descent
in 66 A.D.[14]

[13] Abel 1924: 503; id. 1949: 57; cf. Avi-Yonah 1972: 157.
[14] Bar-Kochva 1976: 19–21.

One can hardly believe that the Seleucid–Thracian force moving up the Beth Horon Ascent fell into the trap without previously sending out patrols to check for ambushes (cf. Xenophon, *Hipp.* 4.4–6, *Lac*; 13.6; Polybius 10.29.4–6; Onasander 6.7–7.2, and in the Roman army–Vegetius 3.6; see also p. 333 below on the *prodromoi*). The ambushing force succeeded in evading them and avoiding discovery.[15] The absence of any mention of advance patrols in the description reinforces the impression that the author was not an eye-witness to the battle.

And Seron and his camp were smitten: The verb συνετρίβειν of the Greek version usually represents in the Septuagint the Hebrew לשׁבֹּר (= to break). However, this verb is used in the Bible in a military context only to designate the Lord's victory over the enemies of Israel (e.g. 'To break Assyria in my land', Is. 14.25; 'For I have broken Moab', Jer. 48.38). In I Maccabees, as in this verse, the verb συνετρίβειν appears many times with regard to Jewish victories, described in a realistic way.[16] The reconstruction should therefore be ויגֹּף (= was smitten), which refers to human as well as to divine victory, although the root נגף is only once translated in the Septuagint by the verb συνετρίβειν (Deut. 1.42).[17] Verse 22 should accordingly be translated 'and He will break them from before us'. Cf. I Maccabees 7.42 where it should be translated 'break this camp before us' and the following verse 'And Nicanor's camp was smitten'.

24 *And he pursued them on the Beth Horon Descent up to the plain*: The reference is to the Aijalon Valley, 4 km south-west of Lower Beth Horon.

And of them some eight hundred men fell: This estimate of enemy casualties is quite modest compared to those for other battles. It recalls the 500 dead in the Kafar Salama battle (I Macc. 7.32) where historical circumstances point to the participation of quite a small Seleucid force (pp. 44–5 above). A defeat on terrain like that of the Beth Horon Ascent could result in the annihilation of a good part of the force. At the same time one should not be too hasty in inferring the overall size of the force in this case from the number of casualties as the figure itself is doubtful.[18] The most it proves is that the author was aware that the enemy force was not especially large.

And the remainder fled to the country of the Philistines: The word

[15] Thus during the ambush set for Cestius Gallus the Jewish force was able to keep under cover until the light advance troops had passed and then attacked the heavier forces. See Bar-Kochva 1976: 19–20.

[16] I Macc. 4.14,36, 5.7,21,43, 7.43, 8.4,5,6, 9.15,16,68, 10.52,53,82, 14.13.

[17] Against Goldstein 1976: 248.

[18] The number of dead evidently provided the basis for the estimate made by Bévenot (1931: 66), who believes Seron had 1,000 men in his army.

'Philistines' appears in the Greek in transliteration Φυλιστιϊμ, while
in other verses of I Maccabees it is translated as ἀλλόφυλοι (=
aliens), as is the Septuagint practice from Judges on. The terms
'Philistines' and 'the country of the Philistines' refer to the residents
of the Hellenized cities in the southern coastal plain, although at
that time those terms were no longer used officially. However, the
use of the term in I Maccabees is not necessarily anachronistic as
some believe,[19] for quite possibly the area continued to be so called
popularly both by the local residents and their neighbours in the
Judaean Hills (cf. Sirach 50.38 (26)). This can be inferred also from
the ethnographic situation: there is no archaeological evidence of
the destruction or of the deportation of the Philistine population
from the coastal region during the Persian period.[20] The description
of the region in the Pseudo-Scylax (*GGM* I, p. 79) does not support
deportation either: it lists the political–administrative purtenance of
the cities to Tyre and Sidon (as indicated also in the Eshmunezer
inscription) and says nothing of the ethnic origin of the
population.[21] That is the case with Herodotus as well, who reports
that Caditis (Gaza) was ruled by the Arabs (3.5.1). On the other
hand the population on the coastal plain is designated as 'Syrians
who are called Palestinoi' (Herodotus, ibid.), their language as
'Ashdodian' (Neh. 13.24), and there are references to Dagon-
worship in the area (I Macc. 10.83, 11.4).

25 *And dread befell the Gentiles in their vicinity*: The reference is to
Idumaeans, Samaritans and residents of cities in the coastal plain
and Transjordania. The harm these people did the Jews in their
vicinity, and Judas Maccabaeus' inability to combat them until
after the purification of the Temple at the end of 164 B.C. (see 3.41,
5.3,9,14–15,23; II Macc. 10.14–23,12), prove that these concluding
statements are quite exaggerated and aimed at enhancing the
importance of the victory over Seron. This exaggeration is especially
obvious in the final verse: 'And all nations told of the wars of Judah'
(3.26; cf. Ps. 96.3; I Chron. 16.24).

[19] Contrary to Abel 1949: 60, and to others.
[20] On the continuity of settlement in the Azotos area see E. Stern 1973: 226,239–40.
[21] Galling (1964: 200–1) is unduly hesitant in this matter.

11

The ceremony at Mizpah and the Ammaus campaign

The battle at Ammaus took place sometime in September 165 B.C. (see p. 472 below), that is, at least half a year after the failures of Apollonius and Seron (p. 200), and about three years after the start of the religious persecutions. At that stage the suppression of the Revolt in Judaea did not have a prominent place in the plans of Antiochus Epiphanes, who was occupied with more serious problems. The Ammaus campaign was preceded by important events in the history of the Seleucid realm. Antiochus Epiphanes had gathered his whole army (apart from that of the Upper Satrapies) in Syria, and even displayed it at the famous festival at Daphne. When preparations were completed he set out on a great expedition to subdue the Upper Satrapies. The western part of the kingdom was put in charge of the regent Lysias. The new acting ruler began to turn his attention to the military situation in Judaea, and the initiative and supervision passed from low-ranking officers and officials to Ptolemy, son of Dorymenes, who was in charge of the satrapy of Coele Syria and Phoenicia, which included Judaea.

The background and phases of the battle of Ammaus are given in I Maccabees 3.38–4.25 and II Maccabees 8.8–29,34–6. The two sources differ in important points relating to the preparations before the battle: the hierarchy and staffing of the Seleucid command, the size of the contending armies, and the tactical division of the Jewish force. An examination of the differences indicates that in administrative details concerning the Seleucid army the information in II Maccabees is preferable, while I Maccabees is more accurate in regard to the organization of the Jewish force. This conclusion is supported also by the general impression that the author of II Maccabees has considerable information on external events connected with the Seleucid kingdom, whereas the author of I Maccabees was better acquainted with domestic affairs. As to the figures for the enemy armies, both books exaggerate as usual; in regard to the Jewish army, on the other hand, both seem to give quite acceptable figures this time, though II Maccabees reports the overall strength of the Jewish troops, while I Maccabees deals only with the picked men retained after the screening conducted at Mizpah.

As to the description of the campaign and the battle itself, the version in I Maccabees is extremely detailed and includes military manoeuvres and geographical points which paint a variegated and fascinating picture of the confrontation. The detail, the great precision, and the way the various movements and actions, and their timing, conform to the topography and terrain, lead to the assumption that the author himself participated in the battle. The general atmosphere is earthy and realistic, and Judas Maccabaeus overcomes the enemy thanks to a series of manoeuvres, diversionary movements, surprises, and the like. The author does hint at the hidden hand of God helping the Jewish camp, but the hint is confined to prayers, the commander's exhortation preceding the battle and thanksgiving after the victory, and is absent from the description of the actual military events.

In contrast, II Maccabees provides no real information on the course of the battle, and does not cite a single topographical point (not even the name Ammaus) compared to the many in I Maccabees. The description is extremely sketchy: Judas Maccabaeus gathers up his people, prays and exhorts, and then divides his army into four parts, sets out against the enemy, strikes, and pursues him (8.23–5). The pursuit is terminated because of the Sabbath (8.25). As is his wont, the author stresses direct and overt divine intervention in the battle, having a decisive effect on its outcome (8.24). He even adds that divine help was forthcoming because of the charitable acts and scrupulous orthodoxy of Judas Maccabaeus and his men. The need to justify the moral right of the rebels to the assistance of Providence was what motivated the insertion of the Sabbath into this episode (see pp. 486–9 below). The mention of the *synthēma*, the signal for battle (verse 23) does not add to the credibility of the battle description in this source. A *synthēma* is mentioned even in the II Maccabees imaginary confrontation near Modein in Lysias' second expedition (13.15), which did not take place at all (see pp. 197–8 and 294). The contents of the signal, in both cases (θεοῦ βοήθεια [= 'God's help'] and θεοῦ νίκη [= 'God's victory']), expressing trust in heavenly intervention, fits in with the pathetic description of the Jewish soldiers setting forth to battle with prayers on their lips (ibid., and 15.26–7), and is evidently a Jewish variation on popular pagan battle cries in the Greek world.[1] This variation, if not invented by the author, could well have been current among the Jewish soldier-settlers in Cyrene.

In *Antiquitates*, Josephus as usual provides a consistent paraphrase of the I Maccabees narrative (12.298–312), but the geographical background is deficient and therefore remains obscure. Thus he does not mention Mizpah, the assembly site and point of departure of the Jewish force, nor the bivouac south of Ammaus. Knowing very well that most of the orations are the author's invention, he allows himself to expand considerably the exhortatory speech that appears in I Maccabees when the force is assembled, and to attach to it motifs that are not mentioned in his source. He also adds that Judas Maccabaeus left lights burning in the camp in order to deceive Gorgias, a *stratēgēma* he was familiar with from literature and from Hellenistic warfare methods (see below, p. 263). The only value of his version is in providing some help in the reconstruction of the original sequence of events in the text of I Maccabees, which was somewhat garbled by the misplacement of I Maccabees 3.57 (see p. 259). Josephus' description of the battle illustrates that even a consistent word-for-word paraphrase cannot meticulously preserve all topographical details, and this provides further grounds for the impression that the author of I Maccabees actually participated in the battle.

I Maccabees 3.27–4.25

3.27 And when Antiochus heard these things he was wrathful and he sent and mustered all the armies of his kingdom, a very heavy camp.

---

[1] See Xen. *Anab.* 1.8.16 (Ζεὺς σωτήρ καὶ νίκη), *Cyr.* 7.1.10; Aeneas Tacticus 24.16 (Ζεὺς Σωτήρ); Plut. *Demetr.* 29.2 (Δία καὶ Νίκην); Appian, *Bell.* 2.76 (Ἀφροδίτη νικηφόρος); for other slogans see Xen. *Anab.* 6.5.25 (Ἡρακλῆς ἡγεμών); id. *Cyr.* 3.3 (Ζεὺς σύμμαχος καὶ ἡγεμών); Appian, *Bell.* 2.76 (Ἡρακλῆς ἀνίκητος); Lucian, *Pro lapsu inter salutandum* 9 (τὸ ὑγιαίνειν). The many *synthēmata* listed in Aeneas Tacticus 24.14–17 are not signals for battle but passwords for patrols, guards, etc. For the use of *nikē* with a proper name in inscriptions and on sling bullets see the summary in Gera 1985: 154–6. The slogans in II Maccabees have two parallels among the many tribal *signa* mentioned in the Scroll of the War of the Sons of Light (עזר אל נצח אל‎–4 [6] 13). However this late source, which was evidently well acquainted with Hellenistic and Roman military practices, cannot prove that the slogans were of Jewish origin, certainly not the reliability of their mention in II Maccabees (against Dupont-Sommer 1960: 102; Avi-Yonah 1954b: 3). It may be added that these parallels are inscribed on banners, while I Maccabees mentions only oral slogans (so rightly Yadin 1962: 58 n. 1), which in the Scroll are used (among other *signa*) only for the purpose of thanksgiving after the congregation returns from the battlefield, while in the preparation stage of and in the battle itself many other exhortation *signa* are hoisted, all in all 36 in number (see the table, Yadin 1962: 43,57).

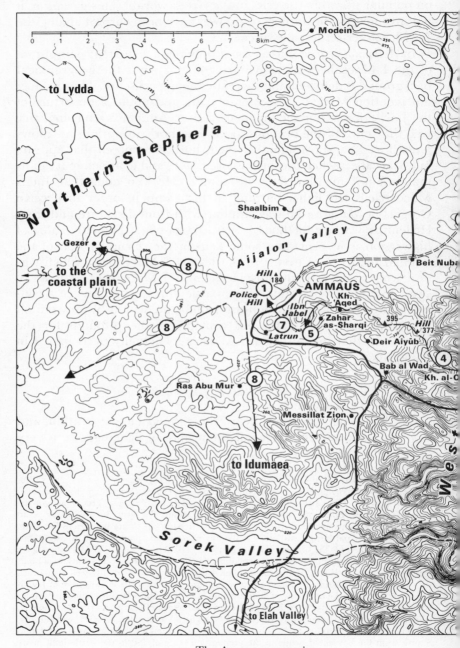

10 The Ammaus campaign

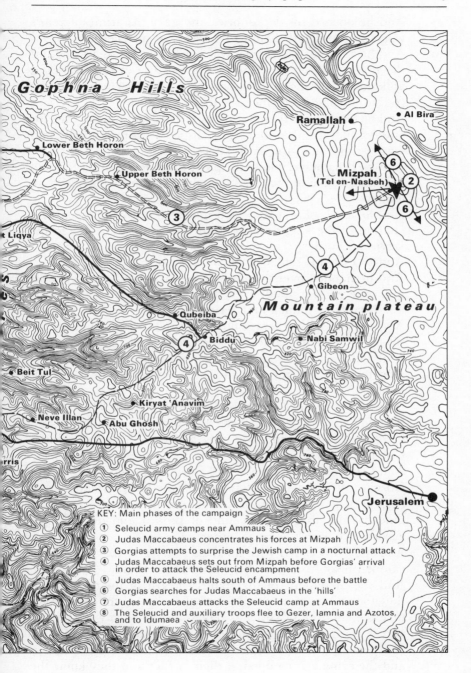

Gophna Hills

• Al Bira

Ramallah •

• Lower Beth Horon

Mizpah
(Tel en-Nasbeh)

Upper Beth Horon

③

② ⑥ ⑥

⑥

• Liqya

④

• Gibeon

Mountain plateau

Qubeiba

④ Biddu

• Nabi Samwil

• Beit Tul

★ Kiryat 'Anavim

• Neve Illan ★ Abu Ghosh

•rris

Jerusalem ●

KEY: Main phases of the campaign

① Seleucid army camps near Ammaus
② Judas Maccabaeus concentrates his forces at Mizpah
③ Gorgias attempts to surprise the Jewish camp in a nocturnal attack
④ Judas Maccabaeus sets out from Mizpah before Gorgias' arrival
    in order to attack the Seleucid encampment
⑤ Judas Maccabaeus halts south of Ammaus before the battle
⑥ Gorgias searches for Judas Maccabaeus in the 'hills'
⑦ Judas Maccabaeus attacks the Seleucid camp at Ammaus
⑧ The Seleucid and auxiliary troops flee to Gezer, Iamnia and Azotos,
    and to Idumaea

28   And he opened his depositories and gave his armies a year's wages and ordered them to be ready for any need.

29   And he saw that the money was gone from his treasuries and the taxes of the country were few because of the strife and affliction he brought in the country (seeking) to repeal the codes that had been since the first days.

30   And he feared that there would not be as from time to time for outlays and gifts that he used to dispense open-handedly and scatter more than the early kings.

31   And he became very low (in spirit) and took counsel to go to Persia and take the taxes of the countries and collect a lot of money.

32   And he left Lysias, a respected man and of royal descent, (in charge) of the king's affairs from the Euphrates river to the Egyptian border,

33   And to raise his son Antiochus until his return.

34   And he handed over to him half the army and the elephants and ordered him about everything he wanted and about the inhabitants of Judaea and Jerusalem.

35   And to send upon them a host to uproot and extinguish the strength of Israel and the remainder (of the people) of Jerusalem, and to erase their memory from the place.

36   And to settle foreigners in all their borders and to allot their land.

37   And the king took half the remaining army and left Antioch, his royal city, in the year seven and forty and a hundred, and he crossed to the Euphrates river and travelled in the Upper Countries.

38   And Lysias chose Ptolemy son of Dorymenes and Nicanor and Gorgias, men of valour from among the king's friends.

39   And he sent with them forty thousand men and seven thousand cavalry to go to the land of Judaea and devastate in accordance with the king's order.

40   And they proceeded with all their army and they came and camped near Ammaus in the land of the plain.

41   And the merchants of the country heard of their fame and they took much money and [chains] and came to the camp to take the children of Israel as slaves, and the army of [Edom] and of the Land of the Philistines joined them.

42   And Judah and his brothers saw that troubles had multiplied and the army was camped at their border and they knew the

king's orders which he commanded to be done to the people
to (the point of) annihilation and obliteration.

43 And they said to each other, Let us rebuild the ruins of our
people and fight for our people and the Temple.

44 And the community gathered to be ready for war and to pray
and ask for grace and mercy.

45 And Jerusalem was desolate as a desert,
None of her offspring came or went.
And the temple (was) trampled,
And aliens (were) in the Akra,
A dwelling for the Gentiles.
Joy has been banished from Jacob.
And pipe and harp are mute.

46 And they assembled and came to ⟨the⟩ Mizpah opposite
Jerusalem for there was a place of prayer in ⟨the⟩ Mizpah
formerly in Israel.

47 And they fasted on that day and put sackcloth and ashes on
their heads and rent their garments.

48 And they unrolled the Torah book[s] [on] which the Gentiles
[painted] the images of their idols.

49 And they brought the priestly vestments and the first fruits
and the tithes and they set up the Nazirites that had completed the days.

50 And they shouted in a loud voice to the Heavens and said,
What shall we do to these, and where shall we lead
them?

51 And your sanctities are trampled and defiled and your priests
are in mourning and low.

52 And lo the Gentiles assembled against us to destroy us, You
knew what they plot against us.

53 How can we withstand them if You do not help us?

54 And they blew the trumpets and shouted in a loud voice.

55 And after that Judah appointed officers for the people, commanders of thousands, commanders of hundreds, commanders
of fifties and commanders of tens.

56 And he said to the builders of houses, and the betrothers of
women, and the planters of vineyards and the faint-hearted,
to return each man to his home according to the Torah.

57 {And the camp set out}, and they camped south of
Ammaus.

58 And Judah said, Gird yourselves and become men of valour

and be ready by morning to fight the Gentiles who have
assembled against us to destroy us and our sanctities.

59   For it is better for us to die in the war than to view the evils
to our people and sanctities.

60   And whatever shall be the will in the Heavens, so shall be
done.

4.1   And Gorgias took five thousand men and a thousand picked
horse and the camp moved at night.

2   To assault the camp of the Jews and smite them suddenly, and
the Akra men were his guides.

3   And Judah heard and he and the valorous advanced to smite
the king's army at Ammaus.

4   As the army was scattered outside the camp ⟨and they
camped south of Ammaus⟩.

5   And Gorgias came to Judah's camp at night and found nobody, and sought them in the mountains, for he said, They
are fleeing from before us.

6   And as morning dawned Judah was seen in the valley with
three thousand men, but shields and swords they had not as
they wished.

7   And they saw a strong fortified Gentile camp and cavalry
circling it, and they (were) learned in war.

8   And Judah said to the men with him, Do not be afraid of their
multitude, and do not fear their wrath.

9   Remember how our forefathers were saved in the Red Sea
when Pharaoh chased after them with a ⟨great⟩ army.

10   And now let us cry to the Heavens, perhaps He will have
mercy on us and remember the ancestral covenant and destroy
this camp from before us today.

11   And all the Gentiles will know that there is a redeemer and a
saviour for Israel.

12   And the strangers lifted their eyes and saw them coming
toward them.

13   And they went out of the camp to war, and those with Judah
blew (the trumpets),

14   And they clashed and smote the Gentiles and they fled to the
plain.

15   And the last all fell to the sword and they chased after them
up to Gezer and up to the fields of Edom and Ashdod and
Jabneh, and of them three thousand men fell.

16   And Judah and the force returned from chasing after them.

17   And he said to the people, Do not covet the booty, for war is
     ahead of us.

18   And Gorgias and the army are in the mountain near us, and
     now stand up to our enemy and fight them and afterwards
     take booty confidently.

19   As Judah was uttering these (words), some part was seen
     reflected from the mountain.

20   And he (Gorgias) saw that they were beaten and they were
     burning the camp for the smoke that was seen revealed what
     happened.

21   And when they saw those (things) they were sore afraid.

22   And when they saw Judah's camp in the plain ready for battle
     they all fled to the land of the Philistines.

23   And Judah returned to loot the camp and he took gold in
     plenty and silver and blue and marine purple and great
     wealth.

24   And returning they sang and praised the Heavens, for (He is)
     good, for his grace (endures) forever.

25   And there was a great salvation in Israel that day.

COMMENTARY

3.27 *And when Antiochus heard these things*...: The reference is to the
     victories of Judas Maccabaeus over Apollonius and Seron. The
     author obviously tries to present a continuous narrative, and he is
     doing so in other cases, even when a relatively long period separated
     two events (see esp. 4.26–7, as against 4.28, and cf. p. 380 below).
     Apart from forming a literary sequence, it serves his aim to present
     events in Judaea as the most important in the life of the Seleucid
     empire (see below). As the two early victories took place sometime
     between summer 166 and April 165 B.C. (see pp. 201, 207), it is not
     impossible that in reality even more than a year elapsed between the
     Seron debacle and the expedition to Ammaus.
     He sent and mustered all the armies of his kingdom: The Seleucid army was
     made up of military settlers who were scattered throughout the
     kingdom, auxiliary forces of subject peoples, allies and vassals, and
     also mercenaries. They were not concentrated in one place, and it
     was necessary to summon them to northern Syria before any
     important military mission.[2] The author represents the mustering as
     aimed against Judaea, but in fact the purpose was to suppress the

---

[2] On the manpower sources and national composition of the Seleucid army, and on
the geographic distribution of the soldiers, see Bar-Kochva 1979: 42–3,48ff. Cf. above,
pp. 30ff., 92ff.

rebellions in the eastern satrapies (see below pp. 466ff.). This manner of presenting external events, making the crisis in Judaea the king's main concern, is even more obvious further on, especially in verse 31.[3]

Armies: τὰς δυνάμεις (the forces [of one side], the whole army). The Hebrew צבא (= army) was also used in this sense in the plural (see p. 204 above).

28 *And gave his armies a year's wages*: The term *opsōnia* in the Greek version denotes, in the Hellenistic military terminology, pay in the form of money, in contrast to reimbursement for current needs (food, clothing, etc.) which was called *sitōnion*, though the term sometimes refers to both types of soldier's pay, as does the vague *sitarkhia*.[4] In the Hellenistic world both types were paid not only to mercenaries, but to vassals, allies, military settlers, and regular soldiers of various categories.[5] Although we have no direct testimony, presumably as was the case in Ptolemaic Egypt, the regular soldiers and reservists also received some pay, albeit of a considerably smaller amount than the mercenaries. The wages were paid at the completion of a mission, or at the end of the month, while the subsistence allowance was paid in advance. In unusual circumstances, when it was necessary to encourage or win over the soldiers, the wages as well were paid in advance.[6] The expedition to the eastern satrapies justified such prepayment, though there is no other instance on record of a whole year's pay, the usual being two to six months.[7] It thus appears that the author, who connects the distribution of pay with preparations for the expedition to Judaea, is exaggerating in this matter as well in order to underline the importance of the mission.

29 *And he saw that...the taxes of the country were few*: The reference is to all types of taxes collected in the satrapies.[8] The Greek translation has the word φόροι, which in Hellenistic administration is the term for a levy on a national territory based on a fixed quota, the collection of which was the responsibility of the ethnarch, the leader of that nation, in contrast to individual land taxes (such as the *dekatai* [= tithes]). However, in the Septuagint, the word φόρος serves as one of the translations for *mas*, which the Bible reserves especially for forced labour. Evidently in the days of the Second

[3] See also Niese 1900: 42–3; Laqueur 1904: 345; Kolbe 1926: 223.
[4] Grote 1913: 80–9; Griffith 1935: 274–6; Launey 1949–50: 2.725ff.; Pritchett 1974: 1.3ff.; and see there also on the *sitomētria*-rations in kind, and *sitēresion*, which may refer to both *sitōnion* and *sitomētria*.
[5] See Griffith 1935: 264–5,294–308.
[6] Ibid. 265,270,277,292–3; Bickerman 1938: 95; Launey 1949–50: 2.725–75.
[7] The sources are given in Griffith 1935: 292 n. 3.
[8] On the tax system in the Seleucid empire in general and in Judaea in particular see Rostovtzeff 1940: 1.469–72; Mittwoch 1955: 352–60; Schalit 1969: 267–70; Bickerman 1938: 179; Alon 1954: 2.231–3; M. Stern 1965: 101; Préaux 1978: 1.384ff.

Temple, the Hebrew *mas* acquired a more general application (so too in I Macc. 1.4,29, 8.2, 10.33). In several instances in I Maccabees φόροι has the usual meaning in Greek, and there is no doubt that the original had the word מס in the singular or plural (10.29, 15.30,31, and also 8.4,7).

From the rest of the verse, according to which income was reduced because of the deteriorating security situation resulting from Antiochus' flouting of the 'codes', it appears that the author may be referring to revenue from Judaea.[9] It is, however, hard to assume that he was prepared to distort the proportion to the extent of representing the revenues from the meridarchy of Judaea as a crucial factor in the total Seleucid budget; thus 'the country' (the Hebrew הארץ) must certainly denote the entire kingdom, and especially the eastern satrapies (see verse 31).

Because of the strife and affliction he brought in the country: The internal strife was accordingly caused by the king's coercive edicts. The author thus obliterates the part played by the Hellenizers in initiating the cultural reform (see in detail pp. 302–3 below).

(Seeking) to repeal the codes: Obviously the reference is not to the religious decrees in Judaea only, but also to the well-known order regarding Hellenization, which the author says was sent throughout the kingdom: 'And the king wrote to his entire kingdom to all be one people; and for every man to abandon his codes, and all the people accepted as the king ordered' (1.41–2). The degree to which the order is historically credible, as well as its meaning, are a matter of dispute.[10] On the one hand, no information is available on any attempt by Antiochus Epiphanes to persecute any religion except that of the Jews,[11] and there is even literary and numismatic evidence that he respected Oriental deities (see especially Polybius 30.25.13–14) and did not interfere with the traditional cult in the cities of Phoenicia and Babylonia.[12] On the other hand, there are indications that he emphasized more than his predecessors the royal cult and the cult of Zeus rather than Apollo.[13] Consequently, some

[9] Gutberlet 1920: 53.

[10] See the summary of various views and the available material in Hengel 1973: 516ff.

[11] The evidence for the existence of a general order presented by Baer 1968: 118–19 (especially no. 46) from the document in II Macc. 11.23 is quite contrived. The purpose of the verse is not necessarily to announce the repeal of edicts supposedly applied to all the peoples in the empire, but to equalize the status of the Jews with that of the other nations, who were not harassed in regard to the fulfilment of their religious practices. In any case, the passage cannot stand up to the abundance of information indicating that, aside from the Jews, no peoples were forbidden to follow their traditional cults.

[12] A great deal of material on this question has been collected by Mørkholm 1966: 127–8,131–2; cf. also Bickerman 1937: 46–7; id. 1938: 128,231; Hengel 1973: 518–24. See also Nock 1952: 209–11.

[13] A comprehensive bibliography for Antiochus Epiphanes' reign appears in Hengel 1973. On king-worship among the early Seleucids see Habicht 1956: 82–108; Cerfaux and Tondriau 1957: 47–9,241–5; Taeger 1959: 1.318ff.; Nielsen 1961: 153,165–70,180–4; Préaux 1978: 2.54–6,238–71.

have proposed that the statement in I Maccabees is an exaggerated version of a 'recommendation' or even a royal edict (*programma*) to spread the royal cult throughout the kingdom, or to initiate a special celebration to mark the king's birthday and the like, which did not prohibit the retention of the local cults.[14] Such a *programma* may have been published, but its synchronization with the coercive measures taken in Judaea seems somewhat artificial. It appears more likely that I Maccabees, who was not very well acquainted with foreign matters, had only a very rough idea of Antiochus Epiphanes' efforts to introduce his own cult, and imagined that the order sent to Judaea prohibiting the local religion was a royal *programma* issued throughout the empire, and not limited only to Judaea. The author was inclined to believe that such was the case in view of the uncommon ease with which Hellenism was making progress among the eastern peoples (cf. I Macc. 2.19; this evaluation was not affected by sporadic popular uprisings against Hellenism[15]). The 'order' itself is worded in the legendary style and spirit of the Book of Esther (especially 3.8).[16] It is illuminating that II Maccabees, who had good information on events in the Seleucid empire, says nothing about a general edict of that nature. The well-known verses in Daniel 11.36–8 ('He will exalt and magnify himself above every god' etc.) does not necessarily mean there was a general suppression of other religions, but only that preference was given to the cult of the king and/or that of Zeus.

30 *And he feared that there would not be...for outlays and gifts that he used to dispense*: The extreme extravagance of Antiochus Epiphanes is noted by Polybius in the famous passage describing the king's strange behaviour. He scattered money among passersby in the streets of Antioch and distributed unexpected gifts to people he did not know; the gifts he sent to the Greek cities and temples were much costlier than those of his predecessors. Among others he contributed to the Temple of Zeus in Athens and the altar at Delos (26.1.8–11).[17] The Daphne ceremony, which was partially financed by plunder from Egyptian temples (Polybius 30.26.9), was another example of the wastefulness of Antiochus Epiphanes, shown by the vast quantities of spices, oil, opulent clothing and gold and silver utensils displayed at the feasts and banquets (Polybius 30.25 (especially 12–19), and

[14] Galling 1939: 228; Nock 1952: 210, and others.
[15] The evidence for this matter cited by Eddy (1961) does not testify to mass opposition to Hellenism for cultural–religious reasons. The great uprisings in Egypt had a chiefly national basis. The close collaboration between the authorities and the ancient Egyptian priesthood might have made outside elements such as the Jews feel that in Egypt, too, Hellenism had overwhelmed the local religion. On that collaboration see Otto 1908: 2.167–309.
[16] On the linguistic influence of the Book of Esther and the problem inherent in its distribution see p. 373 below re verse 49.
[17] Cf. Daniel 11.38; Livy 41.20; Strabo 9.1.17 (397); Vitruvius 7.15; Velleius Paterculus 1.10.1.

30.26.1–3). Other sources make mention of monumental construction projects the king financed in the Greek cities of Syria, in Asia Minor, Rhodes and Greece.[18]

31 *And he became very low (in spirit)*: The Greek ἠπορεῖτο should be reconstructed as וַיִּמֹךְ (= became low); see the Septuagint for Leviticus 25.47 (וְכִי יָמוּךְ אָחִיךָ = 'And thy brother...becomes low' (= poor)). The sentence should perhaps not be interpreted as pure rhetoric: the sources report the king's depression after being forced to withdraw from Egypt in 168 B.C. (Polybius 29.27.8, βαρυνόμενος καὶ στένων (= depressed and sighing); Daniel 11.30, וְנִכְאָה (= he shall be downcast)[19]), and on his instability, his erratic behaviour, inconsistency and tendency to drink a lot (Polybius 26.1, 30.26; Livy 41.20; Diodorus 29.32, 31.16). The extreme capriciousness in his attitude to people also indicates alternating moods, typical of a manic-depressive personality. Various scholars are of the opinion that his 168 B.C. failure in Egypt made him hysterical, nervous, melancholy and emotionally unstable.[20] Others say that there is no evidence of any change in his character after 'the days of Eleusis'. Since they appear mainly in Polybius, the stories about Epiphanes' eccentricities are even rejected by some as valueless popular gossip originating with some of the king's Ptolemaic and Seleucid rivals and foes, like Demetrius I who fraternized with the great Greek historian.[21] Be that as it may, the characterization of Antiochus in our verse, in the Book of Daniel and elsewhere in I Maccabees (6.4,8–9) and II Maccabees (5.21, 9.4), does not derive only from a hostile Jewish view, but also from the king's image in some circles of the Hellenistic intelligentsia.

And took counsel to go to Persia: The author is inconsistent, for while at the outset of the description the mustering of the army is intended for the suppression of the Revolt in Judaea, at the end the king sets out for Persia. He harmonizes the two rather tortuously: when Antiochus Epiphanes wished to pay the soldiers mustered for the expedition to Judaea, he opened his depositories and realized his treasures had diminished. Overtaken by fear of not being able to display his customary extravagance, he decided to leave for Persia

---

[18] Strabo 16.2.4 (750); Malalas 205; Livy 41.20.7–9; *OGIS* 249–50; *SIG*³ 644,645; Wiegand 1908: 95–9; and see Mørkholm 1966: 56–9,118; Downey 1961: 99–107.

[19] For the meaning of וְנִכְאָה cf. Isaiah 16.7; Proverbs 15.13, 17.22, 18.14; Psalms 109. 16, although the verse in Daniel might also be construed as 'he was smitten' or 'he was humiliated', and the like; cf. Ezekiel 13.22, and in Theodotion's translation – ταπεινωθήσεται (= humiliated). On the value of the Theodotion translation of Daniel see Montgomery 1927: 26–7,39–42; Wikgren 1932. For doubts regarding Theodotion's authorship of this translation see A. Schmitt 1966.

[20] Otto 1934: 35,84; Niese 1893–1903: 3.96; Bouché-Leclercq 1913–14: 1.245; and Bevan 1902: 2.129–30.

[21] Reuter 1938: 19,55; Welwei 1963: 74; Pédech 1964: 152 n. 278; Tarn 1951: 183ff.; Mørkholm 1966: 96,130,183–4.

where there was hope of raising a good sum of money. In this
manner the author turns the expedition to Persia into an outcome
of the crisis in Judaea, which is represented as the crucial event in
the life of the empire.[22] This tendency also dictates the explanation
of Antiochus Epiphanes' death as a result of a broken heart upon
learning of the retreat from Beth Zur and the purification of the
Temple (I Macc. 6.5–14).

To Persia: The Greek has *Persis*, one of the Persian satrapies which
comprised eastern Iran around Persepolis. According to external
sources, Antiochus Epiphanes died in the course of the expedition
after trying to plunder a temple in Elam (Polybius 31.9; Appian,
Syr. 66(252)), a district in the satrapy of Susiana. According to I
Maccabees he tried to plunder a temple 'in the city of Elam which
is in Persis' (6.1). Thus the term פרס (= Persia) should be
reconstructed in our verse, the reference being to the entire territory
of historical Persia with the various satrapies that it included, and
in fact that is the denotation of 'Persis' in another occurrence of the
word in I Maccabees (14.2) and regularly in the Septuagint. As to
the designation of Elam as a city, I Maccabees simply erred, as did
II Maccabees, generally better informed on foreign matters, in
stating that the temple concerned was in Persepolis (9.2).[23]

And take the taxes of the countries: The verse seems to imply that the aim
of the expedition was purely economic. But the very fact that it was
necessary to use troops from the western regions to collect taxes
indicates the difficulties inherent in controlling the Upper Satrapies.
And it may well be that the expedition also included Armenia, ruled
by the former *stratēgos* under Antiochus III, Artaxias, who proclaimed its independence (see p. 469 n. 16 below). Furthermore,
for the procession at Daphne no mention was made of light infantry
and cavalry units from the nations of the eastern regions who had
constituted a respectable proportion of the Seleucid manpower at
Raphia and Magnesia. A numerical analysis shows that the military
settlers from the eastern regions were likewise absent (see p. 38
above) indicating a state of unrest there. And finally, those eastern
satrapies had always been an Achilles' heel for the Seleucid authorities. They revolted during the First and Third Syrian Wars, early in
the reign of Antiochus III, later when Demetrius I acceded to the
throne, and during the power struggle betwen Alexander Balas and
Demetrius II. The accession of Antiochus IV likewise aroused a
certain amount of opposition in various regions since he was actually
a usurper (Diodorus 30.7.2; Daniel 11.21; John of Antioch, *FHG* IV,
no. 558, F58; Porphyry, *FGrH* IIB, no. 260, F49a). That opposition,

---

[22] See also Niese 1900: 41,53; Kolbe 1926: 156–7; Wellhausen 1905: 136.
[23] Against the harmonization attempt of Kugler (1922: 508). On the question of identification see Tarn 1951: 464ff.; Altheim and Stiehl 1970: 555–7.

together with his later diplomatic failure in Egypt and growing Parthian pressure, certainly operated to augment the constant ferment in the regions east of the Euphrates. Even if we reject the far-reaching hypothesis that Antiochus Epiphanes planned direct action against the Parthians,[24] it is hard to imagine that his protracted activity in the eastern satrapies was not somehow connected with Parthian attempts at advancement and influence in those regions. It should be noted that the Polybius fragment, reporting that 'in his desire to enrich himself with a lot of money' Antiochus decided to loot the temple of Artemis at Elam (31.9), is not intended to explain the aim of the expedition as a whole, but of just one episode of it, and cannot therefore support the conception of I Maccabees. The emphasis on the economic aspects of the expedition and the disregard of its military and political goals derive from the author's desire to relate the expedition to the situation in Judaea.

And collect a lot of money: Although it was not the chief aim, there is no doubt that Antiochus indeed intended to improve the financial condition of the kingdom through the expedition to Persia. It has been inferred from the statements of Pliny the Elder (*Nat. Hist.* 6.138–9,147,152) that Antiochus took certain steps to gain control of the maritime trade between the Tigris delta and India.[25] Other reports on his activities in the area refer to an attempt to plunder the temple of Nanaea in Elam (Polybius 31.9; *Ant.* 12.358; Appian, *Syr.* 66; Porphyry, *FGrH* IIB, no. 260, F56; and cf. I Macc. 6.1–3; II Macc. 9.2).

32 *And he left Lysias*: Lysias later played a central role in the confrontations near Beth Zur and Beth Zacharia (I Macc. 4.26–35, 6.28–63).[26]

A respected man and of royal descent: The Greek is ἀπὸ γένους τῆς βασιλείας, an epithet based on a well-known biblical phrase (מזרע המלוכה: II Kings 25.25; Jer. 41.1; Ezek. 17.13). Underlying it is the title of *syngenēs* (= kin), which was the highest Seleucid title of nobility.[27] Lysias is so referred to in II Macc. 11.1,23; cf. I Macc. 10.89. The author of I Maccabees misunderstood the term which he probably encountered in the Seleucid chronicle at his disposal, and translated it literally with the biblical phrase.[28]

(In charge) of the king's affairs: The Greek is ἐπὶ τῶν πραγμάτων τοῦ βασιλέως. Lysias was appointed to deputize for the king in the

[24] Tarn 1951: 171–87; see, on the other hand, Altheim 1947–8: 2.36; Le Rider 1965: 311–23; and especially Mørkholm 1966: 172–80.

[25] Le Rider 1965: 309–11; Mørkholm 1966: 167–70.

[26] A survey of his reign in Antioch and the sources where he is mentioned appears in E. Obst in *RE* s.v. 'Lysias' (9), cols. 2532–3.

[27] Corradi 1929: 281ff., esp. p. 284; Bickerman 1938: 42; Abel 1949: 63.

[28] Cf. Pfeifer 1949: 492; against Niese 1900: 51.

western districts (cf. Bacchides, I Macc. 7.8) and as regent (verse 33). There is no identity between that appointment and the well-known title of ὁ ἐπὶ τῶν πραγμάτων (= the (official) in charge of affairs), which in the Seleucid empire designated the chief minister or the second most exalted personage in the kingdom.[29] The title conferred upon Lysias on this occasion is inaccurately worded. Most probably Lysias had become chief minister earlier, and it should not be deduced from this verse that the position was functional only when the king was away from his capital, and the like. Heliodorus had the same title in normal circumstances during the reign of Seleucus IV (II Macc. 3.7).[30] The proof Mørkholm deduces from Andronicus' appointment as Antiochus Epiphanes set out for Tarsus (II Macc. 4.31),[31] is invalid: the text does not say that Andronicus was appointed 'in charge of affairs'. His assignment was to deputize for the king and, just as in the cases of Lysias and Bacchides, his official title is not given. The II Maccabees statement that upon acceding to the throne Antiochus V put Lysias in charge 'of affairs' (10.11) does not contradict the present verse and should not be interpreted to mean that Lysias did not fulfil the function before Eupator's reign. It undoubtedly signifies a formal reconfirmation by the new king (see also below, p. 535 n. 56).

From the Euphrates river to the Egyptian border: In the time of Seleucus I the kingdom was divided into two large administrative units that were governed separately (Appian, *Syr.* 59–62). Generally, the capital being in the west, the king himself directed affairs in the west, and was assisted by a governor stationed in the east. Sometimes two kings operated as co-regents in the two parts, or two governors, both directly answerable to the king. At first it was the Tigris and the Zagrus range that separated the two parts of the kingdom, but later, perhaps at the end of Antiochus III's reign, and certainly during Antiochus IV's, the Euphrates was the dividing line.

33 *And to raise his son Antiochus*: Antiochus Junior, later Antiochus V Eupator, was nine when his father died, and thus seven or eight at the start of the expedition (see p. 304 below). His appointment as co-regent is mentioned in the Porphyry fragment noting that Antiochus V reigned for 'one year and six months' during his father's lifetime (*FGrH* IIB, no. 260, F32, para. 13). On the basis of a cuneiform inscription, in the past various scholars were of the opinion that the joint reign of Antiochus Epiphanes and Antiochus V began in 170 B.C.[32] Wilcken consequently proposed correcting

---

[29] Contrary to Niese 1900: 49 etc. On this title in the Seleucid empire see Corradi 1929: 257–8,266ff.; Bevan 1902: 2.280,284; Bickerman 1938: 42,145,197,205.

[30] For the reign of Antiochus Epiphanes see also I Macc. 7.8, and Bengtson 1964: 2.78–89.

[31] Mørkholm 1966: 104–5.

[32] First Strassmaier 1893: 110, followed by others.

Porphyry's text to 'six years and a month'.[33] However, the list of the Seleucid dynasty published by Sachs and Weisman has made it definite that the co-regency of 170 B.C. was that of Antiochus Epiphanes and Antiochus the infant, son of Seleucus IV.[34] The list does not mention Antiochus Eupator as co-regent, but no conclusion can be drawn from the omission because the compiler of the list neglected also other co-regencies. As a matter of fact, Eupator's co-regency was meaningless, given the boy's age. On the other hand the co-regency of the son of Seleucus IV was recorded because he and not Antiochus IV was the legitimate heir. On the duration of the co-regency of Antiochus IV and Antiochus V see p. 466 below.

34 *And he handed over to him half the army and the elephants*: The Hebrew text said חצי הצבא והפילים (= half the army and the elephants), which in Hebrew may mean either 'half the army and half the elephants' or 'half the army and all the elephants'. The translator mistakenly chose the second alternative, while the verse should be understood to mean half the elephants, which is still quite a great exaggeration. The Seleucid army at Daphne which comprised troops available for long-range expeditions, numbered 41,000 infantry, 4,500 cavalry, and 36 or 42 elephants.[35] Antiochus certainly took with him on the eastward expedition much more than half this army. This sentence is an important link in the chain of distortions in the passage which aim to highlight out of all proportion the importance the events in Judaea had for the authorities, and so to enhance and glorify Judas Maccabaeus' victory in the battle of Ammaus. Josephus, who sensed the difficulty, wrote that Antiochus Epiphanes left Lysias 'part of the army and of the elephants' (*Ant.* 12.295).

34-5 *And ordered him ... to uproot and extinguish ... and to erase their memory from the place*: The phrasing of the verse shows that the author does not mean only religious obliteration but actual physical destruction. However, the wording of the order given to Lysias is not based on any official document, and seems rather extreme, as at the time Jerusalem was ruled by Hellenizers and the Seleucid garrison. In any case, a revolt on the scale of the one that broke out in Judaea was by no means rare in the Seleucid kingdom, and never led to such drastic measures.[36] Probably the author did not really know

[33] U. Wilcken in *RE* s.v. 'Antiochus' (28), col. 2476.

[34] Sachs and Wiseman 1954: 208–9.

[35] Polybius (30.25.11) reports thirty-six elephants arranged in a row at the end of the military part of the Daphne procession. They were preceded by two chariots, one pulled by four elephants and the other by two. The chariot elephants may for one reason or another have been unfit for military service and used only for ceremonial purposes. For the number of infantry and cavalry see pp. 30–2 above.

[36] On the avoidance of mass slaughter and destruction of towns by the Hellenistic armies see Kiechle 1958: 149ff.; Schneider 1969: 2.122–3. On sporadic massacres in small localities see Préaux 1978: 2.301ff.

exactly what the enemy's intentions were, and relied on popular rumours based on the nation's experience of the distant past, late in the period of the First Temple. Hence also the fear expressed in the next verse that the country would be settled by foreigners.

There is no justification for attempting to support the verse with the advice 'to annihilate the nation' given, according to Diodorus, to Antiochus VII Sidetes at the time of the siege of Jerusalem early in John Hyrcanus' reign (34–35.1.5; cf. Jos. *Ant.* 13.245). Antiochus Epiphanes' actions in Jerusalem and the Temple are presented in the words of Sidetes' 'advisers' as a model of the attitude that should be adopted toward Jews. The substance of the 'advice' should not, however, be considered a reflection of instructions given in his time by Antiochus IV. The extremely drastic approach to the Jews does not fit the situation at the time of Antiochus Sidetes, which in itself raises doubts regarding the reliability of the ascription of such an attitude to Antiochus Epiphanes. The 'punishment' proposed fits the gravity of the 'crime' attributed to the Jews in the same passage, which presents the notorious anti-semitic view of Jewish antiquity, morals and religion (ibid. 1–4). This accounts also for the imaginary description of the contempt for Jewish ceremonial in the Temple displayed publicly by Antiochus Epiphanes himself (ibid. 4), and its explanation in the king's 'shock' at the misanthropy and xenophobia of the Jews (ibid. 3).[37] The passage originates in Poseidonius of Apamea, the great Stoic philosopher of the early part of the first century B.C.,[38] and echoes the hostile attitude of the Hellenistic world to the Hasmonaean State because of its territorial expansion, destruction of Greek cultural centres, and forced conversions. It serves also to fulfil the moral need to explain the deviant nature of Antiochus Epiphanes' religious persecutions.

36 *And to settle foreigners in all their borders and to allot their land*: 'in all their borders' is used in the biblical sense of 'in their country' (cf. Deut. 16.4, 28.40; Jer. 17.3; Ezek. 45.1; Ps. 105.31). There is no connection between this instruction and the statement 'he will distribute land for a price' (Dan. 11.39). The sentence in the Book

[37] The fictional nature of the story of the defilement of the Temple was noted especially by Baer 1968: 109–10. For the sources of the hostile attitude see Friedländer 1903: 123ff.; Bickerman 1937: 22. The statements attributed to the 'advisers' are in the main a variation of Egyptian anti-Jewish accusations and libels known to us from the versions of Manetho, Lysimachus and Mnaseas (Jos. *Ap.* 1.237–50, 304–10, 2.112–14).

[38] On Poseidonius of Apamea as Diodorus' direct source see lately M. Stern 1974: 1.142–3,168,184, and the bibliography there, and pp. 142–3 on Poseidonius' objection to the anti-semitic version. Poseidonius' own view emerges also from Josephus' statement on the episode, based on Nicolaus (*Ant.* 13.236–47, especially 242–5). There are clear indications that Diodorus' source also served Nicolaus (ibid. 243,245,247). On Nicolaus as Josephus' source for that passage see Bar-Kochva 1977a: 182–4. Poseidonius' particularly favourable attitude to early Jews and Judaism, formulated in the Stoic vein (preserved in Strabo 16.2.35–7), makes it hard to believe that he accepted the anti-semitic argument (despite his severe criticism of the Hasmonaean state: Strabo 16.2.37). Cp. p. 561 below.

of Daniel refers to land that was confiscated and allocated to
Hellenizers at the start of the Revolt, and is not a forecast for the
future (see p. 441 below). If the content of this verse in I Maccabees
is accepted as reliable (and this does not depend on an acceptance
of the previous verse), it would mean that the king intended to set
up military settlements in Eretz Israel, which the Seleucids had
previously refrained from doing for fear that the military settlers
would offer their services to the Ptolemies. The persistent Ptolemaic
weakness since Panium would explain the Seleucid divergence from
the traditional policy (p. 444 below).

37 *And the king...left Antioch*: The Seleucid army generally set out from
Apamea-Pella, the site of a concentration of army camps, training
bases, stables and elephant cages, and not from the capital of
Antioch.[39] Possibly the verse shows that the Seleucid army started
on the expedition immediately after the procession and festival (see
pp. 469–73), or the author may have written 'Antioch' thinking
of the king himself leaving the capital.

His royal city: Antioch, now known as Antakya, lies in Turkish
territory not far from the Syrian border. Founded in 300 B.C. by
Seleucus I, it was the Seleucid capital from the reign of Antiochus
I (280–261 B.C.) until the Roman conquest. Its first residents were
5,300 military settlers, who were joined in the course of time by
other soldiers as well as civilians. The city retained its military
character and the settlers continued to fulfil their military
obligations in return for ownership of tracts of land (*klēroi*).[40]

In the year seven and forty and a hundred: An examination of the
chronology of the procession at Daphne before the expedition to the
east shows that the expedition should be set in mid August 165 B.C.
The battle at Ammaus followed shortly (see Appendix E, pp.
466ff.)

And travelled in the Upper Countries: The author means 'the Upper
Satrapies' (αἱ ἄνω σατραπεῖαι), which was the official term for the
satrapies east of the Tigris.[41] The Greek translation has 'the Upper
Countries' in the accusative as object of the verb διεπορεύετο, i.e.
'passed through the Upper Countries'. However, the Hebrew
reconstruction should be ויעבר ׀ בארצות העליונות (= and travelled
in the Upper Countries) as shown by the use of the same sentence
in I Maccabees 6.1; cf. Ezekiel 39.15 in the Septuagint.

[39] Polybius 5.50.1 and 59.1; Livy 37.18.6; Strabo 16.2.10 (752); and see Bar-Kochva 1979:
28–9,94.

[40] On the history of military settlement in Antioch and northern Syria ('Seleucis') see Bar-
Kochva 1979: 28–31,43, and especially pp. 29–30. See also p. 101 above. The history of
Antioch has been comprehensively treated by Downey (1961), and Liebeschuetz (1972).
Although the latter deals mainly with a later period, it is very illuminating on the Hellenistic
period as well; so also Petit 1955.

[41] Polybius 3.6.10, 5.40.5,7 and 41.1; I Macc. 6.1; II Macc. 9.25; and see Robert 1949:
5–22.

38 *And Lysias chose*: According to II Maccabees, the initiative for the expedition to Judaea was taken by the lower echelons: Philippus, who was appointed *epistatēs* of Jerusalem (II Macc. 5.22), namely a civilian official in charge of the city on behalf of the king,[42] appealed to Ptolemy son of Dorymenes, the *stratēgos* of Coele Syria and Phoenicia, whose satrapy included Judaea, and the latter sent there Nicanor, who had a high rank of nobility ('of the first friends'), and with him Gorgias, ('a very experienced military man', 8.8–9). In view of the elaboration in II Maccabees on the status and functions of the Seleucid officers and the chain of command (cf. also 14.12), that version seems preferable. Ptolemy's higher administrative position compared with those of the other two commanders (see below) also tips the balance in favour of II Maccabees. Furthermore, a triumvirate of commanders is hardly possible in the light of what is known of the command hierarchy in the Seleucid army.[43] Command triumvirates are well known from the Homeric age (*Iliad* 2.563–7, 12.85–107; *Odyssey* 14.470–1), but in later periods they appeared only in coalitions and alliances of various cities, kingdoms and satrapies (e.g. Diodorus 19.15.3, 21.1) and have no place in the army of a single state. The exaggeration in the presentation of the enemy command must be attributed to I Maccabees' inadequate knowledge of external affairs. This does not stand in contradiction to the conclusion stated above that the author of I Maccabees was an eye-witness of the battle itself, for the exact composition and hierarchy of the Seleucid command were not necessarily obvious to the Jewish combatants and to the author, who was not a member of Judas Maccabaeus' headquarters staff (cf. pp. 281, 335 below). It may be estimated that there was a rumour among the Jews that Ptolemy son of Dorymenes, the satrap himself, was in the camp. II Maccabees, on the other hand, seems to have drawn the information on the enemy's command from Seleucid sources.[44]

Ptolemy son of Dorymenes: He is mentioned in II Maccabees as the *stratēgos*, that is the civil and military governor of the satrapy of Coele Syria and Phoenicia (8.8),[45] which included present-day Israel, Jordan, Lebanon, and southern Syria up to the el-Kebir river north of Tripoli.[46] The name Dorymenes the Aetolian is mentioned as that of a field commander in the service of the Ptolemies in

---

[42] On the post of *epistatēs* see Szanto in *RE* s.v. ἐπιστάται, cols 200–2; Heuss 1937: 29–35; Bengtson 1964: 2.324,371, etc.; Griffith 1935: 156; G. M. Cohen 1976: 80–2.

[43] On the high command of the Seleucid armies see Bar-Kochva 1979: 85–93.

[44] On the preference for the II Maccabees version of the command system see also Niese 1900: 53; Wellhausen 1905: 136; Bévenot 1931: 68; Oesterly 1913: 79; Bengtson 1964: 2.168 n. 2; Dancy 1954: 93; Avi-Yonah 1972: 158; Bunge 1971: 232–3; Schürer... 1973–9: 1.160 n. 58; Schunck 1980: 311.

[45] On the term *stratēgos* after the battle of Magnesia see Bengtson 1964: 2.191–3.

[46] On its boundaries see Otto 1928: 37; Leuze 1935: 367,385; Bickerman 1947: 256–9; Seyrig 1951: 212ff.; Galling 1964: 201–4.

219 B.C. (Polybius 5.61.9) and he may have been the father of the Ptolemy referred to here.[47] If so, then the father, or Ptolemy son of Dorymenes himself, left the Ptolemies for the Seleucids, as did other high-ranking officers at the time (cf. Theodotus the Aetolian in Polybius 5.79.4 and Ptolemy Macron in II Maccabees 10.13). As a former Aetolian mercenary officer he could not have had much prior knowledge of Jewish matters. It was therefore easy for the Hellenizers to convince him to act in their interests in return for financial gains (II Macc. 4.45). As governor of Coele Syria and Phoenicia, Ptolemy son of Dorymenes was almost the only channel through which the king was fed information on developments in Judaea, and thus the king's chief adviser on Jewish matters. Antiochus Epiphanes spent most of his young manhood in Rome and had too little knowledge of Jewish affairs, so that Ptolemy son of Dorymenes' advice may well have been persuasive when the king decided to issue the coercive edicts. After the defeat at Ammaus, Ptolemy son of Dorymenes was dismissed and replaced by Ptolemy Macron (see pp. 535–7 below).

And Nicanor: According to II Maccabees, Nicanor son of Patroclus was 'one of the first friends' (8.9 – τῶν πρώτων φίλων). This respected noble title, and the fact that he is mentioned after Ptolemy son of Dorymenes, the *stratēgos* of the satrapy, and before Gorgias, the meridarch of Idumaea, suggest that Nicanor governed one of the important districts in the region, perhaps the coastal plain (*paralia*), which seems to have had a special status.[48] Consequently he is not to be identified with Nicanor the 'Cypriarch', who (as his title implies) commanded some Cypriot garrison troops in the region when Antiochus V Eupator acceded to the throne (II Macc. 12.2; perhaps the commander of the Jerusalem citadel – II Macc. 4.29). Even less likely is his identification with a medium-rank official by that name who held some financial post in Samaria when the religious persecutions began (*Ant.* 12.261).[49] Likewise to be rejected are the attempts to identify him with the meridarch of Judaea early in the reign of Demetrius I, who fought against Judas Maccabaeus in Kafar Salama and Adasa (I Macc. 7.26–50; see p. 352 below).

And Gorgias: He was the *stratēgos* of Idumaea in the period after the purification of the Temple (II Macc. 10.14). Idumaea-Mt Hebron was one of the meridarchies included in the satrapy of Coele Syria and Phoenicia. Gorgias' connection with the Idumaean area is

[47] See Launey 1949–50: 1.186 n. 8; Bagnall 1976: 10 n. 26.

[48] The special status of the coastal plain in the administration of Coele Syria and Phoenicia is evident from the designation of Kendebaeus in I Macc. 15.38 as *epistratēgos* (= chief regional officer; supreme *stratēgos*) and not simply *stratēgos*. The district may have had an intermediate status between a meridarchy and a satrapy, and been divided into meridarchies each of which was in charge of the usual *stratēgos*-meridarch. On the *epistratēgos* in Egypt as the superior of the *stratēgoi* of the *nomoi* see Bengtson 1964: 2.121–7; Van't Dack 1976: 177–84.

[49] Contrary to Grimm 1853: 59; Dancy 1954: 93.

reflected also in the account of the battle of Marisa (II Macc.
12.32).[50] According to II Maccabees, Gorgias was only a deputy
commander of the expeditionary force, the high command being in
Nicanor's hands (8.9). Contrary to their practice of naming only the
commander-in-chief, the sources mention Gorgias in this battle
because of his role in the special task force which played a crucial
role in the course of the campaign (I Macc. 4.1,5,18).

From among the king's friends: τῶν φίλων τοῦ βασιλέως is low on the
scale of noble titles in the kingdom. The Daphne procession featured
no fewer than a thousand 'friends' (Polybius 30.25.8). It is hard to
believe that Ptolemy son of Dorymenes, the *stratēgos* of Coele Syria
and Phoenicia, did not have a higher rank (cf. the rank attributed
to Nicanor in II Macc. 8.9). This too testifies to I Maccabees'
meagre knowledge of matters connected with the Seleucid
command hierarchy.[51] In the same way I Maccabees describes
Bacchides as no more than a 'friend' (7.8), despite his exalted post
in charge of the western satrapies of the kingdom early in the reign
of Demetrius I (see pp. 380–1 below).

39 *And he sent with them forty thousand men and seven thousand cavalry*: This is
an extemely inflated estimate based on association with the figures
for the Aramaean force in one of David's wars (I Chron. 19.18). II
Maccabees cites 20,000 Seleucid soldiers (8.9), but the number
derives from a garble in the text (see p. 41 above n. 41). It would
still be something of an exaggeration to estimate the royal task force
(excluding the local auxiliary troops mentioned in verse 41) at
10,000, though it is not impossible that the total strength of the
Seleucid camp reached 20,000 (see above, pp. 41–2 and n. 42).

The composition of the infantry force is not reported. II
Maccabees emphasizes the great ethnic variety in the Seleucid camp
(8.9). This feature, which was characteristic of the Seleucid armies,
was stressed in other sources as well (e.g. Livy 37.40.1). It is also well
reflected in the extant Seleucid tables of organization (especially
Polybius 5.79, 30.25; Livy 37.40; Appian, *Syr.* 32). The placement
of units of different nations next to each other was considered one of
the main weak points of the Seleucid army (Appian, *Syr.* 37(197)).
The deployment plan had to take into account not only tactical
considerations but also the complex of relationships between one
nation and another, as well as similarities in mentality and
language.[52] It was also necessary to employ interpreters to transmit
orders to the different units (Polybius 5.83.7). If the II Maccabees
statement is based on specific information and not merely on general
knowledge of the normal Seleucid army organization, or on the
presence of soldiers from Idumaea and the coastal plain, it may be

---

[50] So also Abel 1949: 411.
[51] On the 'friends' and the hierarchy of the titles of nobility see Bevan 1902: 2.276–80;
Spendel 1915: 17; Corradi 1929: 318–43; Bickerman 1938: 40–5.
[52] Bar-Kochva 1979: 58–60.

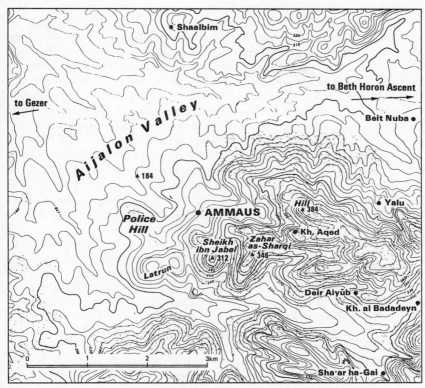

11 The hills of Ammaus and the 'Land of the Plain'

taken as testimony for the participation of a goodly proportion of
'lights' and 'semi-heavies' in the force that set out for Ammaus, for
ethnic heterogeneity was especially characteristic of them, in
contrast to the relative homogeneity of the heavy units.

To go to the land of Judaea and devastate: II Maccabees has 'to
exterminate all the seed of Judaea' (8.9). The real purpose, as
appears from the plan of the expedition was to conduct a mopping-
up operation against the rebels. At this stage there is no sign of an
encircling action against the Jerusalem citadel, so that the purpose
of the Seleucid expedition would not have been to break through to
the fortress and extricate its people.[53]

40 *And they ... camped near Ammaus*: The Greek is πλησίον Ἀμμαους; for
the translation of πλησίον as על יד (= near, by) see the
Septuagint, Joshua 15.46. It could also be translated as בקצה (=
at the edge of; cf. the Septuagint, Num. 33.37) or even אצל (= at;
see the Septuagint, Deut. 11.30). The reconstruction מול (=
opposite), proposed by Cahana,[54] is not supported by the

[53] Contrary to E. Meyer 1921: 2.206; Avi-Yonah 1972: 151.   [54] Cahana 1957: 111.

Septuagint and does not accord with the literal meaning of the Greek word. In view of the customary precision of I Maccabees in topographical indications, the Seleucid camp should be located very close to Ammaus itself, and there is no sense in the proposal to place it near Shaalbim, for example.[55] That location is unsatisfactory for other reasons as well: its proximity to the Jewish settlements in the Modein hills, its distance from the starting point of the Jewish attack, the directions of the pursuit, and the like. There is certainly no possibility of accepting the interpretation of Theodoretus (*PG* 81 cols 1532–3) that אהלי־אפדנו (= the tents of the *afdanō* (= pavilion)) in Daniel 11.45 refers to the Seleucid camp in the battle of Ammaus, which was set up near a place called Apedano. Avi-Yonah identified it with Kh. al-Badadeyn (grid reference 153/137).[56] However, the Daniel verse does not refer to this battle, *afdanō* is not a place-name, and Kh. al-Badadeyn is in a rugged mountain area north of Sha'ar ha-Gai (Bab al Wad).

Ammaus itself has been identified with the Arab village of 'Imwas in the Aijalon Valley north of Latrun, and with the ruins near it.[57] Destroyed in the Six Day War, the village was slightly to the north of the former United Nations building in whose courtyard there are remnants of a Crusader church. It was generally accepted that the Hebrew name of Ammaus was *ḥamāt*, because '*ḥamāt* (or in the Aramaic form *ḥamāt'a*) in Judaea' is mentioned in midrashic sources (*Lament. Rabbah* 1.48 (thus in the printing; see the Buber edition, 82); *Song of Songs Zuta* 6.9) and in a mediaeval collection (*Yalqut Shim'oni*, Joel 537). However, the form *ḥamāt* was obviously valid basically in the construct form. According to the Greek it appears that the place itself was called *ḥama*.[58] The Greek suffix was then added to the Hebrew (just as '*ḥamāt* of Tiberias' became Greek 'Ammathos'). But the expected Greek form *Ammaos* became for one reason or another *Ammaous* in the colloquial idiom. Be that as it may, the name indicates that there were hot springs there. This is supported by the tradition regarding Rabbi Eliezer ben 'Arakh, the disciple of Rabban Johanan ben Zakkai 'who went to Maus (Ammaus), a beautiful place and fine beautiful waters'.[59] Geological

---

[55] Contary to Avissar 1955: 135–6. On the I Maccabees method of locating battle sites see pp. 154–5 below, and p. 358 below re verse 31. For Shaalbim see Judg. 1.35; I Kings 4.9.

[56] Avi-Yonah 1963: 106.

[57] Guérin 1868–80: 1.293ff.; Conder and Kitchener 1881–9: 3.14; Riemer 1918: 34–43.

[58] Kutscher 1977: 225.

[59] *Avot de Rabbi Nathan*, version A, 14 (according to the Oxford manuscript); and version B, 29 ('Maūs'); *Eccles. Rabba* 7.15 has ''*Amaūs*, a place of beautiful water and beautiful pasture'. The later manuscripts of Avot de-Rabbi Nathan have *Demasit* or *Demōsit* (from the Greek *dēmosion* [*balaneion*] = public baths, medicinal baths) instead of Ammaus. Those versions are only explanations of the description of Ammaus as 'a place of beautiful water'. For an assessment of the various versions and manuscripts see Shechter 1945: xx ff.; on the variations in the tradition cited above see Finkelstein 1951: 187.

investigations have shown that there may well have been hot springs in the area in the past.[60]

As to the reconstruction of the form of the name in the Hebrew original of I Maccabees, although the translator sometimes gives Hebrew names in their Greek forms (Jabneh = Iamnia; Ashdod = Azotos) or with a Greek suffix in the proper case (Beth Zur, 4.29,61, 9.52, etc.; 'the land of ḥamat' [τὴν Ἀμαθῖτιν χώραν], 12.25), he evidently found the form 'Ammaous' in the Hebrew original. The place-name appears in this form alone in the Greek, with no change of ending for genitive, dative and accusative cases (see the verse under discussion, and 3.57, 4.3, 9.50), which indicates that the Greek suffix was not added by the translator. The use of the Hellenized form in Hebrew derives from the fact that the name 'Ammaous' was widely and popularly used in the author's time. This shows the Hellenized character of its population at the start of the Revolt. We have no early information on the ethnic origin of that population, but there are indications for a Jewish majority in 4 B.C. (Jos. Ant. 17.291; Bell. 2.71) and a Samaritan one in the Byzantine period.[61] As Ammaus was still within Judaea (see verse 42 below), it is not impossible that it was a 'mixed' settlement, including also a small Jewish community.

Ammaus was a camping place not only for the Seleucid army, but also for Vespasian's Fifth Legion which stayed there for two years, from spring 68 to spring 70 A.D., before breaking through to Jerusalem (Bell. 4.444–5, 5.67). The water in the area, its demography and rural status, and especially its unique geographical location, explain its selection: Ammaus is at the eastern end of the Aijalon Valley which constitutes a broad gap among the lowland hills, through which the western slopes of the Judaean Hills can easily be reached. It is only 10 km from the entrance to the Beth Horon Ascent, and close to the junction of alternative routes to Jerusalem. Although those routes were more difficult and dangerous than the Beth Horon Ascent and were not normally used, they could be utilized in case the Beth Horon Ascent was blocked or overloaded, or when it was desirable to separate into several parties.[62] In the light of their initial failures, the Seleucid forces were well aware of the difficulty of invading the Judaean Hills from the west. They consequently camped at Ammaus near the start of a number of routes. They intended to 'clean' them up gradually and ensure an orderly and convenient climb, with no surprises, to the plateau north of Jerusalem. The Seleucid commanders may also

---

[60] See Avnimelech 1933: 63.
[61] See Kutscher 1977: 59; S. Klein 1939b: 6.
[62] On the roads from the Aijalon Valley to Jerusalem that existed in the nineteenth century see Smith 1894: 149 n. 2.

have intended to divide the army and get to the Judaean Hills by several routes simultaneously, thus preventing Judas Maccabaeus from catching the whole army by surprise. Still, the Seleucid plan may have been based from the outset on passive tactics, the purpose being to tempt Judas Maccabaeus into skirmishes in the Ammaus area. This would explain Gorgias' return to Ammaus after losing track of Judas Maccabaeus at Mizpah (although other explanations are also possible). And it may be that the Seleucid force intended to operate in all the ways noted, in accordance with developments in the field. In every case Ammaus was an ideal place for the camp: the fertile valley provided a solid logistic base, the Hellenized locals were trustworthy, and as Ammaus did not have the status of a *polis*, its residents were required to supply the troops' needs as Hellenistic law stipulated for rural settlements, the *khōra* (see p. 58 n. 100 above). The convenient routes from the Aijalon Valley to the coastal plain ensured constant communication with the rear. And finally, the hot springs made the Seleucid soldiers' stay there pleasant, as they did Vespasian's at Ammathos after the battles of Iotapata and Tarichaeae, before the siege of Gamala (*Bell.* 4.11–12).

In the land of the plain: The Greek is ἐν τῇ γῇ τῇ πεδινῇ. The exact reconstruction of the Hebrew is important for locating the Seleucid camp, and for following the course of the battle. The Septuagint uses the word *pedinos* (and also *pedeinos*) to translate both *mishōr* (= plain) and *šefēlā* (= lowland), the hilly region between the coastal plain and the Judaean Hills.[63] But the translator of I Maccabees did not follow that practice. The world *šefēlā* appears once in transcription: Adid (*Ḥadid*) is 'in the *šefēlā*' (ἐν τῇ Σεφηλα, 12.38), 'opposite the plain' (κατὰ πρόσωπον τοῦ πεδίου, 13.13),[64] a description that fits its location at the edge of the lowland hills bordering the coastal plain. In all the places where the translation has *pedion*, *pedinē* and the like, the reference is unquestionably to a level area or the coastal plain.[65] As to the word *gē*, it is undoubtedly the translation for the Hebrew *'ereṣ* (= land), and it is in hundreds of verses in the Septuagint and many in I Maccabees.[66] In one case it renders the word *gevūl* (= border, Ex. 10.19) but this rare usage cannot be taken into account, especially since there it is not introduced as a literal translation of *gevūl* but as an interpretation of the meaning of a phrase ('and there remained not one locust in the border (= land)

[63] See references in Hatch and Redpath 1897: 2.1113. The term 'shefela' applying to the hilly region between the coastal plain and the mountains appears in Deut. 1.7; Jos. 15.33; Shebiith 9.2; *Tosefta Shebiith* 7.10; *PT Shebiith* 9.2(38d). See also S. Klein 1939a: 207–8.

[64] For the translation אל מול פני (= in the face of...) see Hatch and Redpath 1897: 2.1223–30, no. 15e; and see, e.g., I Macc. 4.61, 5.37,52,55.

[65] 3.24, 4.6,14,15,21, 5.52, 10.71,73,77,83, 11.67,68, 12.49, 14.8, 16.5.

[66] Hatch and Redpath 1897: 1.241–55.

of Egypt'). Furthermore, I Maccabees consistently uses the word
oros to translate *gevūl*.[67] The only possible reconstruction is therefore
'in the land of the plain'. Abel's proposal 'in the land of the *šefēlā*',
setting the Seleucid camp on the hills near Ammaus, must therefore
be rejected.[68] It should be noted that the phrase *gē pedinē* appears in
the Septuagint for 'land of the plain' (Deut. 4.43), while 'land of the
šefēlā' does not appear in the Bible at all (for 'land of the plain' cf.
also Jer. 48.21 and Ps. 143.10).

The placement of the camp in the 'land of the plain' means that
the Seleucid force did not camp within the settlement of Ammaus
which was in the low Latrun hills, nor in one of the interior valleys
of the hill district (such as the 'Valley of Springs' north-east of
Ammaus), but in the Aijalon Valley itself. As noted, 'near Ammaus'
indicates that the camp must have been adjacent to that settlement,
in other words, at the foot of the hill it was on. This conclusion is
supported by military and logistic considerations too. Polybius
reports that the Hellenistic armies, in contrast to the Roman legions,
set up their camps in places that were naturally fortified (6.42.2–3).
The area suggested for the Seleucid camp is flanked by two long
extensions from the hills to the east; one of them, the rise on which
the British-built Latrun police fortress stands today, starts out from
the ruins of Latrun, and the other, extending from Ammaus, has an
old olive orchard on it, and is now crossed by the new Tel Aviv–
Jerusalem highway (elevation point 184). The two extensions
together with the Latrun hills provided the camp with protection on
three sides, as well as excellent visibility in all directions, and the
western open side facing the coast plain was the least likely to be
attacked. It is true that the site is rather low, but in view of the
Hellenistic tendency not to bother much with fortifications, it is
understandable that the camp was not set up on one of the rocky
hills in the area. This does not mean that no artificial fortifications
at all were built around the camp (see below, pp. 265–6), but their
construction required much less effort than would have been
necessary in rocky hilly terrain. Furthermore, some of the water
sources of Ammaus were in the area noted.[69] Similar considerations
determined the placement of the Persian camp at Plataea on a site
similar in structure to the camp site near Ammaus (Herodotus
9.25).[70]

41 *And the merchants of the country heard*: The logistics in the Hellenistic
army camps was based on merchants and businessmen operating as
'service contractors'. The author, however, does not mention the
other dealings of these merchants, because their very inclusion was

[67] Ibid. 2.1017.   [68] Abel 1949: 66.
[69] On them see Clermont-Ganneau 1874: 149. Those sources existed till the beginning of
this century. Some wells on the northern ridge still supply water.
[70] On the terrain in Plataea see Grundy 1901: 460–1. See, however, Pritchett 1965: 1.109ff.

intended to stress the maliciousness of the enemy and their evil intentions.

And they took much money and [chains]: The Greek manuscripts have παῖδας (= youths; slaves). Apparently the copyist was influenced by the end of the verse where that word does properly appear. The Greek should be πέδας (= fetters, chains) as in Josephus (*Ant.* 12.299) and several manuscripts of the Syrian translation.[71] On the pre-battle accumulation of chains for captives, compare Herodotus 1.66. Josephus' version does not prove he had recourse to the Hebrew text of I Maccabees. The error is obvious, and the slight correction of the Greek word does not require enormous thought. Just as the translators into Syrian made the proper correction, Josephus could have done so without seeing the Hebrew original. It is also possible that the Greek manuscript at his disposal had πέδας.

To take the children of Israel as slaves: It is generally accepted that the ancient custom of selling prisoners of war into slavery was no longer common as a policy in the period (see esp. Diodorus 19.85.4), during which a decided trend toward a more humane attitude to a defeated foe is discernible in wars between Hellenistic powers.[72] However, the trend did not apply in wars against small rebellious peoples (cf. the merchants who arrived to take prisoners during the siege of Rhodes by Demetrius Poliorcetes in Diodorus 20.84.5–6), or in confrontations between Greek cities and alliances (e.g. Polybius 2.56.7 and 58.9), not to mention the selling of 150,000 people into slavery by the Romans after the conquest of Macedon, just a few years before the battle of Ammaus (Polybius 30.15; Plut. *Aem.* 29.1–3; Livy 45.34.1–7).[73] Two inscriptions from Delphi of 170–157 B.C. even note the liberation of Jewish slaves (*CIJ* 709,710). As Tcherikover speculated, they may have been brought from Judaea in the wake of battles with Judas Maccabaeus.[74] In view of all these points, there is no reason to reject the substance of this verse. II Maccabees further develops and elaborates the matter, stating that through the revenue from the sale of the slaves Nicanor intended to repay the debt of 2,000 talents to the Romans; he invited traders

[71] Grimm 1853: 60; Gutberlet 1920: 56; Abel 1949: 66.

[72] See, e.g., Tarn 1913: 209–10; Cary 1951: 242–3; Volkmann 1961: 71ff. On the practice in ancient Greece see Pritchett 1974: 1.53ff.

[73] See further Volkmann 1961: 61ff.; Ducrey, 1968a: esp. 337ff.; Préaux 1978: 1.299–301.

[74] Tcherikover 1961a: 291. See also the Letter of Aristeas 14, which records the fact (albeit in an exaggerated manner and in a clearly literary adaptation) of Jewish captives being sold into slavery in the reign of Ptolemy I. The second part of the Reiner Papyrus (*PFR* inv. 24,552 = *SB* 8008) may refer to the sale into slavery of the civilian population captured in the war; it may however be interpreted differently to refer to the ordinary sale of a number of slaves, the purpose of the royal edict being to ensure the Ptolemaic authorities a monopoly in the slave trade. For other explanations of the purpose of the *prostagma* see Liebesny 1936: 257–91; Westermann 1938: 1–30; Rostovtzeff 1940: 1.341–4.

from the coastal cities and promised to sell them ninety slaves for a talent (8.10–11). The dubious value of the information is evident in the number of slaves anticipated – 180,000 – according to that calculation. Furthermore, in 173 B.C. Antiochus Epiphanes remitted to Rome the last instalment of the indemnity imposed upon his father in the Treaty of Apamea (Livy 42.6.6–7). The exaggeration in the description of enemy machinations was designed to highlight the gravity of the danger and impart a moral dimension to the enemy's ignominious defeat. Cf. the II Maccabees version of the battle of Adasa (pp. 361, 489–91 below).

And the army of [Edom]: The Greek is δύναμις Συρίας (= the Syrian army), which is a translation of צבא ארם (= the army of Aram – see p. 209 above). This is how I Maccabees denotes the Seleucid army (3.13, 7.39). As that army was already mentioned in verse 39, Abel rightly conjectured that the original had אדם (= Edom), subsequently miscopied or misread as ארם (= Aram; cf. Jud. 3.8,10; II Sam. 8.13ff.; II Chron. 16.6; and the Septuagint for I Sam. 21.7[8]).[75] The correction is supported by the account of the enemy defeat stating that some of the Seleucid camp fled to Edom-Idumaea (4.15). That the Idumaeans, who were situated in the Hebron Hills, backed the authorities against the Jews is also deduceable from Judas Maccabaeus' military operations in that region after the purification of the Temple (I Macc. 5.3,63–5; II Macc. 10.14—23, 12.32–7) and from Lysias' expeditions to Beth Zur and Beth Zacharia (see pp. 284–5, 308). It is hard to evaluate the Idumaeans' standard of warfare. They were a source of manpower for Ptolemaic military settlements,[76] but are not mentioned even once in sources of the Seleucid royal army. There is no evidence, direct or indirect, to support the notion that they served as military settlers for the Seleucid authorities in the Hebron area during the Hellenistic period.[77]

Josephus (in *Ant.* 12.299) realized the difficulty in I Maccabees, and in order to avoid repetition wrote σύμμαχοι ἀπό τε τῆς Συρίας (= allies from Syria), which is merely a guess. This does not support the view that he consulted the Hebrew original. Even if the Hebrew manuscript already read ארם, he would have figured out the origin of the mistake and made the proper correction.

And of the Land of the Philistines joined them: The Greek has γῆς ἀλλοφύλων, literally 'the land of the aliens', which in the Septuagint usually renders the Hebrew 'land of the Philistines'. The residents of the Hellenized cities on the coastal plain are meant (see pp. 217–18 above). The numerical potential of the Idumaeans and

[75] Abel 1949: 66.
[76] See the list in Launey 1949–50: 2.1235–41; Cf. also Rappaport 1969: 73–82.
[77] Contrary to Gichon 1967: 30,35.

Philistines was not to be sneezed at (I Macc. 10.77), but since neither of them ever appears in the large Seleucid campaigns, adding them to the imperial army could not have improved its strength or chances very much. The state of the local militia is well reflected by the relatively quick and easy victories Judas Maccabaeus gained in his battles with the neighbouring peoples and cities after the purification of the Temple.

Josephus in *Antiquitates* says τῆς πέριξ χώρας (= from the nearby region, 12.299), apparently construing γῆς ἀλλοφύλων literally. He may have been influenced by verse 4.12 in which ἀλλόφυλοι does mean 'aliens'. In any case, had the Hebrew text been available to him, he would not have fallen into that error.[78]

42 *And Judah and his brothers saw that...the army was camped at their border*: 'At their border' means 'in their country' (cf. p. 245 above). Bacchides' list of forts shows that at the time Ammaus was part of Judaea (I Macc. 9.50). Evidently the Aijalon Valley up to and including Gezer was already within the administrative borders of Judaea in the Persian period.[79] Those arrangements did not change in the Hellenistic period despite the Hellenized character of Ammaus and the establishment of Gezer-Gazara as a Seleucid fort.

45 *Jerusalem was desolate as a desert*: The lamentation in this verse, influenced by those in Lamentations and Jeremiah, is designed to explain why Mizpah was chosen as the assembly and prayer site. Possibly 'desolate as a desert' refers to the destruction wrought by the Seleucid troops in the area close to the Jerusalem citadel (I Macc. 1.31,39). The exaggeration here can be ascribed to the poetic context (cf. Jer. 12.10; Joel 2.3, 4.19). But apparently the author is alluding to the city's being desolate of pilgrims (cf. Dan. 9.17), just as the much debated expression השקוץ משומם (= the desolating abomination: Dan. 9.27, 11.31; I Macc. 1.54) refers to the Temple's being 'desolate' of sacrifices and pilgrims, that is, the abomination is 'desolating', causing the Temple to be desolate (cf. I Macc. 4.38).[80] The latter interpretation accords well with the substance of the subsequent verses regarding the fulfilment at the Mizpah ceremony of precepts connected with the Temple.

And aliens: The garrison was made up of people from many nations, among them Cypriots (II Macc. 4.29), Mysians (II Macc. 5.24) and Thracians (p. 119 n. 12 above), who served in the citadel as mercenaries, and not military settlers (see below pp. 438ff.).

---

[78] See also Ettelson 1925: 337.
[79] Kallai 1960: 97–9; E. Stern 1973: 243–4.
[80] For the interpretation of השקוץ משומם see Herzfeld 1863: 2.430–1; Baer 1968: 112; Efron 1980: 64 n. 28. This interpretation is preferable linguistically as well as substantively on the identification with *Ba'al šamīn* first proposed by Nestle 1884: 248, and developed and expanded by Bickerman 1937: 111, and passim.

The verse as a whole is one of the poetic sections scattered throughout the book.[81] The notion that these excerpts were taken as they stand from existing anthologies, as a number of scholars believe, is unjustified,[82] although there is no denying the possibility that certain phrases were borrowed from such anthologies, just as others were clearly influenced by biblical verses. In all cases the excerpts fit the situations they react to, although they are at times somewhat exaggerated.

In the Akra: The Greek is *akra*, which in the case of Jerusalem meant a citadel, built on some higher ground, dominating the inhabited area (see p. 455 below). Cahana translates it as *meṣūdā* (= fortress),[83] but both *meṣūdā* and *mivṣar* (= fort), which certainly appeared many times in the Hebrew of I Maccabees, were translated as *okhyrōma*,[84] while *akra* in the Septuagint renders *milō'* (I Kings 9.15.24, and passim), which certainly does not fit the various contexts in which it occurs in I Maccabees.

It appears that the Hebrew source had *ḥaqrā*, and the translator merely restored its original Greek form. The word was adopted into Hebrew following its frequent use in daily life after the Hellenistic conquest of the country. The name is applied to the Seleucid citadel in Jerusalem (Scroll of Fasting, 23 Nisan), and to the Gush Halav citadel (Arakhin 9.6), and the form *ḥaqr'ā* appears in the Aramaic translations in the meaning of 'fortress' and even 'fortified town' (e.g. in the Jonathan translation of Num. 32.17; II Sam. 5.9). However, the suggested connection between *ḥaqrā* and *beēr ḥeqer* (Erubin 10.14; *Tosefta* ibid. 11.22)[85] is rather dubious: the version *bōr ha-qēr* is linguistically more acceptable (cf. Jeremiah 7.8), and even *ḥeqer* does not necessarily indicate its identification with *ḥaqrā*. On the location of the Akra at the northern part of the south-eastern hill, the biblical 'City of David', see Appendix D (pp. 445ff.).

46 *And they asembled and came to ⟨the⟩ Mizpah*: The Greek is εἰς Μασσηφα (= to Mizpah) which is customary in the Septuagint for the Hebrew המצפה and המצפתה (= '[to] the Mizpah' and 'to the Mizpah'; Judg. 11.34, 20.1,3, 21.5,8; I Sam. 7.5,6; Jer. 40.6,8,12,13). In biblical Hebrew the definite article was thus usually prefixed to the name Mizpah. The article is deleted here and in the Septuagint according to the common practice in the Septuagint with place-names.[86] Thus the article of Ai, Gilgal and

---

[81] See the list of passages, their reconstruction and interpretation in Neuhaus 1974a: 19–22.   [82] See the bibliography for this suggestion in Pfeifer 1949: 487.

[83] Cahana 1957: 112.

[84] References appear in Hatch and Redpath 1897: 1.1043–4.

[85] On the reading *ḥeqer* and its identification with the Akra see Epstein 1957: 322; Lieberman 1962: 468; Baer 1964: 313; and especially Schwartz 1985: 3–16.

[86] On the exceptional use of the definite article with place-names in the Septuagint see Abel 1927: 121–2. For the practice of the Greek *koinē*, aside from anaphoric sentences and meanings, see Mayser 1933: vol. II.2.1, pp. 13–16; Blass and Debrunner 1967: no. 261.

Ramata, which in Hebrew are inseparable from the name, is always deleted in the Septuagint.

Opposite Jerusalem: The Greek is κατέναντι Ιερουσαλημ. The Mizpah of the period of the First Temple is now definitively identified with Tel en-Nasbeh, seven kilometres north of Jerusalem near Kafr Aqab.[87] However, even scholars who do not question the location of the biblical Mizpah believe that the Mizpah mentioned here was located on the top of Nabi Samwil which was erroneously identified in the past as Samuel's Mizpah. Some even ignore the Septuagint practice, and claim that the absence of an article proves that the verse refers to another place, and that a distinction should be made between 'Mizpah' which they identify with Nabi Samwil, and 'the Mizpah' which is Tel en-Nasbeh.[88] All note chiefly that the expression 'opposite Jerusalem' is more applicable to Nabi Samwil which is close to Jerusalem and overlooks it, while from Tel en-Nasbeh no part of the city or its suburbs is visible. However, the vague Hebrew word נֶגֶד or מִנֶּגֶד (= opposite) which underlies κατέναντι[89] does not necessarily imply visibility.[90] Thus in Babylonian captivity, Daniel prays 'opposite (נֶגֶד) Jerusalem' (6.11). In describing the place chosen by Judas Maccabaeus for assembly and prayer the author may have been influenced by the occurrence of that phrase in the Book of Daniel which he knew well and which affected his style.[91] To support further the identification of Nabi Samwil, its relative proximity to Judas Maccabaeus' temporary camp south of Ammaus (I Macc. 3.57) has been noted, as also to the routes leading to the Aijalon Valley. Above all these considerations, however, is the fact that I Maccabees clearly implies that the place is identical with the Mizpah of Samuel's time. The character of the ceremony conducted there shows that the participants themselves identified Mizpah with the prayer-and-ceremonial site of the Judges period (see below). It cannot be assumed that the people of the generation of the Revolt were mistaken in the identification. Like other cities in the land of Benjamin, Tel en-Nasbeh had not been devastated at the time of the Babylonian conquest and exile,[92] and Mizpah in Nehemiah's time was the chief town of the northern district (פֶּלֶךְ) of the

[87] See Z. Kallai, 'Mizpah', in *Biblical Encyclopaedia*, vol. 5 (Jerusalem, 1958) cols 240–1 (Hebrew), and the detailed bibliography there.

[88] E.g. Albright 1923: 116–17; Abel 1923: 36off.; Bévenot 1931: 70; Avi-Yonah 1963: 101; id. 1972: 159–60; Kanael 1964: 111.

[89] Hatch and Redpath 1897: 2.749; and perhaps לפני should be reconstructed according to Numbers 17.19.

[90] So also Z. Kallai, 'Mizpah', in *Biblical Encyclopaedia*, vol. 5 (Jerusalem, 1958) col. 240 (Hebrew). Cf. also p. 311 below re verse 32.

[91] On the influence of Daniel on I Maccabees see Efron 1980: 25,50.

[92] McCown 1947: 1.58–9,165–7.

province of Yehud (Neh. 3.7,15). It was inhabited in the Hellenistic period as well, as the local archaeological finds indicate.[93]

For there was a place of prayer in ⟨the⟩ Mizpah formerly: On Mizpah in the past as an assembly and prayer site on the eve of a battle see Judges 20.1; I Samuel 7.6–9, 10.17 (cf. Judges 10.17, 11.11). As the text below itself conveys, the assembly, precisely in that place, was intended to inspirit the soldiers, for it could remind them of the nation's glorious past and the divine response to the people's entreaty at Mizpah in Samuel's time (cf. Taanith 2.4). At the same time the purely military factors that affected the choice of Mizpah should not be disregarded: Tel en-Nasbeh is close to the Beth Horon Ascent, with quick and free access to it, and not far from the Gophna region in the north-west or the roads to the east, in all of which a safe haven could be found in times of danger. The distance between Mizpah and Jerusalem enabled a force concentrated in the former to move around without being constantly observed and followed by the garrison of the Jerusalem citadel. Although there are other hills in the region with similar advantages, Mizpah was preferred because of its nostalgic significance and contribution to the morale of the men.

The assembly is not mentioned in II Maccabees nor is Mizpah. Niese, as usual eager to prove the superiority of II Maccabees, goes to the extreme of rejecting the event of Mizpah as a 'biblical anachronism'.[94] As will be shown below, the description of the campaign and course of the battle in I Maccabees are well anchored in the geographical background, and the details of the ceremony accord with the halakha of the time and the particular circumstances.

47 *And they fasted on that day*: Fasting the day before a battle is mentioned in the description of the ceremony Samuel conducted at Mizpah (I Sam. 7.6). It may be that the mishnaic passage 'For these things they warn (= מתריעין) in every place...wild beast and the sword' (Taanith 3.5) refers also to the fast before a battle. Another reason for the fast might be connected with the burning or defilement of the Torah scrolls (see below re verse 3.48). A fast before battle would reduce the physical strength of the soldiers when unusually great exertion was to be demanded of Judas Maccabaeus' men that night and the next day,[95] but the contribution to morale made by the fast and the accompanying ceremony was more significant for the success of the battle.

[93] See McCown 1947: 1.63.
[94] Niese 1900: 48,54; and also Elhorst 1905: 38.
[95] Cf. Vegetius stressing the need for nourishing food before battle (3.11), and the *Tosefta*: 'a city surrounded by troops...(they) are not allowed to torment themselves in fasting so as not to break their strength' (Taanith 2.12).

And put sackcloth and ashes on their heads and rent their garments: On fasting
and mourning customs see I Kings 21.27; Joel 2.12–13; Jonah 3.5;
Dan. 9.3; Neh. 9.1; II Macc. 10.25; Judith 4.9–15; and compare
Taanith 2.1.

48 *And they unrolled the Torah book[s]*: The Greek has the singular – τὸ
βιβλίον τοῦ νόμου – but the rest of the verse indicates that it should
be in the plural. There is not the slightest basis in the verse (nor in
II Macc. 2.14) for the hypothesis of a number of scholars that the
Holy Scriptures were canonized during the ceremony at Mizpah,[96]
and in fact it is the Torah books alone that are mentioned and not
the books of the entire Bible.

[On] which the Gentiles [painted] the images of their idols: The sentence
in the uncial manuscripts – περὶ ὧν ἐξηρεύνων τὰ ἔθνη τὰ
ὁμοιώματα τῶν εἰδώλων αὐτῶν (= about which the Gentiles sought
the images of their idols) – is certainly defective and led to some odd
interpretations and reconstructions.[97] Scholars have noted in
particular the addition τοῦ ἐπιγράφειν ἐπ' αὐτῶν (= to write on
them) appearing after the word τὰ ἔθνη (= the Gentiles) in a
number of the minuscule manuscripts. As they include all the
manuscripts of the q group, which is based on an invaluable ancient
uncial manuscript which has not survived,[98] the assumption was
that the addition was not merely a gloss, and attempts were made
to employ it (or part of it) to fill in what is apparently missing. Most
of the proposals, however, are not tenable, either because they
go against the rules of Hebrew grammar, or do not fit the
circumstances, or do not provide a proper explanation for the
phrase περὶ ὧν (= 'concerning them', 'about which...') which will
fit it to the verb.

Of all the proposals made to date, the most apt, with some
modification, appears to be that of the nineteenth-century Irish
scholar, Kirkpatrick, who thought the Hebrew original to have been
אשר חקקו הגוים עליהם את דמות עצביהם (= on which the Gentiles
had etched the image of their idols). The word חקקו (= etched)
was garbled to חקרו (= investigated), which led to the translation ἐξηρεύνων (see the Septuagint translation for I Chron.
19.3).[99] A similar error occurred in the Septuagint translation of
Judges 5.14 where מחקקים (= legislators; governors) was read as

---

[96] Klausner 1950: 3.22; and less lucidly Segal 1950: 4.865; id. 1951: 42; Tcherikover
1961a: 486 n. 33.

[97] See the survey of the various methods in Abel 1949: 68–9. Goldstein (1976: 261–2)
recently proposed the reconstruction 'They spread open the scroll of the Torah at the passage
where the Gentiles sought to find analogies to their idols'. The notion that Antiochus Epiphanes, who ordered the Torah scrolls to be torn, burned and forgotten (I Macc. 1.49,56),
would bother searching them for evidence of his faith is quite absurd.

[98] On this group of manuscripts see Kappler 1967: 30–5.

[99] Kirkpatrick 1884–5: 111–12.

חקרים, and consequently rendered as ἐξερευνῶντες (= investigators). Cf. also חקק and חקרי in Judges 5.15–16. The Kirkpatrick reconstruction is the only one that provides a solution to the difficulty imposed by the περὶ ὦν in the sentence as it came down to us, and explains its origin: the word attached to חקקו (= etched) was עליהם (= on which), which can also mean 'about which' or 'concerning them'. However, since the translator read חקרו (= investigated), he rendered it as περὶ ὦν (= about which).

One difficulty, however, still remains: the verb חקקו (= etched) can hardly refer to drawing or painting on Torah books, which were written on parchment scrolls, but only to etching on stone, clay tablets, and the like. It seems logical therefore to suggest that the original was חקו (= imitated, painted; see Ezek. 8.10, 23.14), which was read by the translator as חקרו (= investigated). The whole sentence should be reconstructed as follows:

אשר עליהם חקו הגוים את צלמי אליליהם·

Thus the verse means that the books unrolled during the ceremony were those that had been defiled, i.e. by painting of pagan images. The text does not say that the books were publicly read, in contrast to the usual practice in public fasts (Nehemiah 9.1–3; Taanith 2.1; *PT Megillah* 3.1[73d]). This would indeed not be expected with regard to defiled books. It therefore seems that they were displayed in order to arouse divine jealousy and wrath. The fasting itself and the garment-rending can also be explained as motivated by the defilement or burning of the holy books. On 'rending' because Torah books were burned see the Beraita *BT Moed Katan* 26a;[100] *Maseket Śmāḥōt* 9.19 (p. 175, Heiger ed.); *PT Moed Katan* 3.7[83b–c]; and see *BT* loc.cit., which applies the ruling to destroyed or torn Torah books.[101] A fast in connection with the burning (or desecration) of books is implied in *PT* loc.cit. ('whoever sees a learned man die is as one seeing a Torah book burnt...') and in *Maseket Sofrim* 21.1 (p. 354, Heiger ed.). On the burning of Torah books at the time of the religious persecutions see I Macc. 1.56; Diodorus 34–35.1.4 adds the hostile version regarding the sprinkling of pork juice on the sacred books (cf. p. 236 n. 38 above).

49 *And they brought the priestly vestments*: These were the vestments that were supposed to be used in the Temple in normal times.

And the first fruits: Some scholars assume on the basis of the first fruits mentioned that the ceremony took place during the Feast of Weeks

---

[100] There are versions like the Munich MS and others in which this matter appears in the Mishnah; see also Rabbinovicz 1896: 96.

[101] Possibly Rab Halabo's saying should be read as 'whoever sees a Torah burned' (instead of 'torn'); see also Rabbinovicz 1896: 90.

(= Shavuot; cf. Num. 28.26).[102] However, in the Second Temple period, first fruits were brought at either the Feast of Weeks or the Feast of Tabernacles, and some people even brought them to Jerusalem between the two feasts, arranging a special holiday for themselves. Others brought them as late as the end of Kislev (December), and there are conflicting traditions regarding the receipt of first fruits as early as Passover.[103] In any case, if the ceremony had taken place during the Feast of Weeks, the author would not have overlooked the opportunity of so noting, to highlight the solemn and nostalgic character of the occasion. In order to determine the date of the battle we must look to other data, and these indicate that the battle took place at the end of the summer (see pp. 466ff.).

And the tithes: According to the practice initiated early in the Second Temple period, all the tithes were brought to the treasury in Jerusalem, and not, as prescribed in some parts of the Pentateuch and customary in later halakha, allocated all over the country.[104] The existence of that modification is supported in this verse which indicates that following the desecration of the Temple the tithes were no longer collected, and Mizpah that day was a substitute for the Temple in regard to the tithes just as in regard to the other activities mentioned in the verse (and see the next verse). The allocation of the tithes is cited by Josephus together with the first fruits (*Ant.* 4.241; and perhaps also Tobit 1.6–7).[105] This was done for convenience because of the difficulty of the pilgrimage to Jerusalem. The deviation from the pre-Nehemiah practice shows that the details of the ceremony are not the 'biblical anachronism' some would have them but well grounded in the conditions and practice of the era.

And they set up: καὶ ἤγειραν – Hebrew: ויעמידו. The reference is to the presentation of the Nazirites to the community and to the Deity, as a preface to the appeal for help in the following verse ('What shall we do to these and where shall we lead them'). The verb ויעמידו is usual in this connection in the Bible (see, e.g., Lev. 16.7, 27.8,11; I Kings 12.32; II Chron. 20.21, 23.10, 29.25; Ezra 3.8) and

---

[102] Kugler 1922: 356–7; Cahana 1957: 2.112; Bévenot 1931: 70. Kugler's other arguments are unfounded.

[103] Alon 1958: 2.157; Safrai 1965: 225–6, and the sources there; also Blidstein, 1976: 80 n. 8. On the various occasions in which the first wheat, wine and oil respectively were brought to the Temple, as indicated in the Temple Scroll and a Qumran fragment, see Yadin 1978: 1.81–9, and 2.56–61. The oil was the last to be brought, on 22 Elul (ibid. 1.91,96).

[104] Malachi 3.10; Nehemiah 12.44, 13.5,12; II Chron. 31.5–12; Judith 11.13; Tobit 1.6–7; Philo, *De Leg. Spec.* 1.132–40; and see Alon 1977: 89ff.; Oppenheimer 1977: 30–2. The verse does not refer only to the Second Tithe, as Goldstein erroneously believes (1976: 263), but to all tithes. Consequently no chronological conclusions can be drawn from this reference (loc.cit.).

[105] Possibly the reading in Tobit should be ἀρχάς (= first fruits) rather than ἀπαρχάς (= donations).

very frequent in the books written during the Second Temple period. The reading καὶ ἔκειραν (= and they shaved) that appears in one of the minuscule manuscripts is therefore to be rejected.[106] *The Nazirites that had completed the days*: The reference is to a period of Nazirism whose length is determined by the vow of the person concerned (see Num. 6.13–21; Nazir 6.6–11). The mention of the Nazirites together with the main precepts connected with the Temple make it difficult to accept the view that Naziritism was widespread only around the time of the destruction of the Second Temple.[107] This is evident also from the well-known legend about the financing of the Nazirites' sacrifices on the initiative of Simeon ben Shatah in the reign of Alexander Jannaeus (*PT* Nazir 5.5 [54b]).[108]

50 *And they shouted in a loud voice … What shall we do to them and where shall we lead them*: According to the Torah precept, the Nazirite was supposed to cut his hair in the Temple and offer a sacrifice. Neither of these things could be done because of the desecration of the Temple.

The words τούτοις (= to these) and αὐτούς (= them), though they are masculine plural, refer to all the nouns in the preceding verse (which are not masculine in Greek) and not only to the Nazirites.[109] The Hebrew אלה (= these) and אותם (= them) refer grammatically to all the nouns in the previous verse – the priestly vestments, first fruits, tithes and Nazirites. As to the Greek translation, the pronoun in this case has the gender of the word Nazirites either because it is the only personal noun among those in the previous verse, or because it is the noun closest to the pronoun.

54 *And they blew the trumpets*: The Greek is σάλπιγξι, which can be reconstructed as either *ḥaṣoṣrōt* (= trumpets) or *šōfārōt* (= horns).[110] However, it may be assumed that if the Hebrew text had had the word *šōfārōt*, which has a ritual meaning and application, the translator would have written κερατίναις, which the Septuagint reserves for *šōfārōt*, to distinguish them from the trumpets mentioned in the accounts of the actual battles (I Macc. 7.45, 9.12).

Pre-battle trumpet-blowing is mentioned in Numbers, the stated purpose being to stir the Deity into providing help (10.9; and cf. Taanith 3.7). Presumably it was also intended to encourage the soldiers. Such a purpose is reflected in all the ritual practices mentioned above. Moreover, Numbers states that trumpets should

---

[106] Against Epstein 1957: 384.
[107] Büchler 1928: 420, and others.
[108] See also Efron 1980: 133; M. Haran, '*nāzîr*', in *Biblical Encyclopaedia*, vol. 5 (Jerusalem, 1958) cols 778–9 (Hebrew).
[109] Contrary to Gutberlet 1920: 58–9. So also Hunkin 1928: 44. Abel's contrived interpretation (1949: 70), is unnecessary.   [110] Hatch and Redpath 1897: 2.1258.

be blown on all feast and assembly days, as the sacrifices are made (10.10). And perhaps the trumpets were intended also to summon the men before the selection process mentioned in the following verses. This function, of 'summoning the congregation', is described in detail in Numbers 10.1–7.[111]

55 *And after that Judah appointed commanders of thousands, commanders of hundreds, commanders of fifties and commanders of tens*: II Maccabees (8.21–2) reports that the 6,000-man Jewish force was divided into four 1,500-man units (σπεῖραι; in Hellenistic terminology = a phalanx unit of 256 men) led by four of the five Hasmonaean brothers. In the absence of any biblical association for the numbers cited, some scholars have preferred the overall figure and tactical divisions cited in II Maccabees.[112] However, the numerical strength estimated in II Maccabees is affected by the number of men attributed in the book to Judas Maccabaeus at the start of the Revolt (8.1), while the tactical distribution described is based on the number of the Hasmonaean brothers (the fifth, Eleazar, being the 'priest') and has no parallel in either Jewish or Hellenistic military tradition. As in addition it is part of a description detached from real military and topographical background, it can hardly be considered more reliable than I Maccabees. Although its wording follows that of well-known biblical verses (Ex. 18.21,25; Deut. 1.15), the organization reported in I Maccabees is acceptable. Splitting the force into squads of at most ten men and combining those into larger units was essential for the efficient conduct of a long night expedition of the kind carried out in this battle. The adoption of the biblical model is understandable also in the light of the nostalgic nature of the ceremony, aimed at raising soldier morale. The type of organization described has parallels in the Jewish armies of the period of the Second Temple. The units of thousands are mentioned for Jonathan and Simeon's army (I Macc. 12.47, 16.19), and the 'biblical' division figures also in the Scroll of the Wars of the Sons of Light (2[4], 15–17), in the Scroll of the Rule of the Congregation (1.15) and in the Temple Scroll (p. 58), and even resembles that of the army Josephus prepared in Galilee (*Bell.* 2.577–8), though in general the latter followed the structure of the Roman army.[113] Units of ten, fifty and a hundred are known from the Ptolemaic

[111] Cf. the functions of the ceremonial trumpets in the Scroll of the War of the Sons of Light: see Yadin 1962: 86–7.

[112] Niese 1900: 53; Bévenot 1931: 71; Dancy 1954: 95; Avi-Yonah 1954b: 4.

[113] As Josephus does not mention a unit of fifty, he may have organized his troops according to the Roman rather than the Hellenistic system. The chiliarchs in charge of a thousand were actually tribunes, the commanders of the cohorts (of the size usual in the *auxilia*); the hecatontarchs in charge of a hundred were centurions; the decadarchs in charge of ten were decurions. The rest of the passage clearly indicates Roman influence (2.577–82) and Josephus' personal guard unit of 600 men (2.583) is similar in size to the cohort of the infantry guard in the Roman army, which was equipped differently from the cohort of the legion.

army as well, and those of a thousand appear in other Hellenistic armies.[114] The attempt made by various scholars to harmonize the versions of I and II Maccabees[115] does not work, and is in contradiction to the purpose of the authors and the contexts in which the division is mentioned in the two sources (see also pp. 171–2 above on the methodological question).

56 *And he said to the builders of houses, and the betrothers of women, and the planters of vineyards, and the fainthearted*: II Maccabees, which ignores the assembly at Mizpah, contains a pathetic description of the flight from, and abandonment of, settlements as the enemy advanced (8.13–14). Even if there is some truth in that report, it does not contradict the story of the voluntary 'screening' of the force at Mizpah, and it certainly does not impugn its credibility.[116] II Maccabees does not refer to a flight of soldiers from the camp, but to the familiar phenomenon of civilians in panic-stricken flight from the unknown. This is clear from the context of the verses and the 'information' on the sale of their remaining possessions by the fugitives (ibid. 14).

To return each man to his home according to the Torah: As indicated in this sentence, the list of those released from combat duty is based on the war code in the Pentateuch (Deut. 20.1–9). There is no justification for doubting the credibility of this verse as quite a few scholars have done, rejecting it as a 'biblical anachronism'. The force had to be reduced for tactical reasons; with the means at the disposal of the Jewish command, it was impossible to utilize a large force in a long night march and surprise attack. In order to thin out his army, Judas Maccabaeus made use of the criteria in Deuteronomy, which were quite suitable for the purpose. The adoption of the biblical practice was itself a morale-builder, and fitted the general atmosphere and intent. For the halakhic questions related to this verse see Appendix G, pp. 494ff.

57 {*And the camp set out*} {*and they camped south of Ammaus*}: The second sentence should be placed after the description of Gorgias' departure from Ammaus (between verses 4 and 5 in ch. 4), while the first one is merely a gloss. The amended reading of 4.3–4 is thus as follows: 'And Judah heard, and he and the valorous advanced to smite the king's army at Ammaus, as the army was scattered outside the camp, ⟨and they camped south of Ammaus⟩.'

The present location of 3.57 involves some difficulties. First, it

---

[114] On the Ptolemaic army see Lesquier 1911: 92–7; on the 'thousand' in the Seleucid army see Bar-Kochva 1979: 66 and 235 n. 43. A great deal of information on the commanders of those units in the Hellenistic armies – the decadarchs, pentacontarchs, hecatontarchs and chiliarchs (as well as pentacosiarchs) – appears passim in Launey (1949–50). For units of thousands and hundreds among the Jews of Elephantine in the Persian period see Porten 1968: 29–30.

[115] Especially Avi-Yonah 1972: 160.   [116] Contrary to Niese 1900: 54.

separates the description of the Mizpah ceremony from the
hortatory speech of Judas Maccabaeus, which is more logically
connected with the ceremony at Mizpah, whose main purpose was
to encourage the troops, and not with the end of a long and
exhausting march before striking camp and resting. Is it likely that
the Mizpah ceremony, which involved fasting, shouting and
trumpet-blowing, did not conclude with encouraging words by the
military commander before the exhausting march and campaign, or
that the author refrained from reporting them? Moreover, the
warfare code in Deuteronomy which dictated the details of the
ceremony, includes such an oration (20.3–4).[117] And above all, if we
accept the order of verses as it stands, that would mean that Gorgias
set out from camp after Judas Maccabaeus had already reached the
region south of Ammaus (3.57, 4.1) and the latter decided to fight
the following morning before he learned of Gorgias' march (3.58).
However, Judas Maccabaeus' battle plan, as appears from the
combination of the various manoeuvres and is even stated explicitly
(4.4), was based on surprise and taking advantage of the
complacency and overconfidence that prevailed in the Seleucid
camp at Ammaus owing to Gorgias' attempted night raid. It seems
clear that while still at Mizpah, Judas Maccabaeus intended to
conduct the battle under such conditions, for otherwise he would
have chosen to stay in the mountain area and confront the Seleucid
force trying to climb eastward in rugged terrain, rather than
challenge the full strength of the camp on level ground. The
stringent selection he conducted among his people also shows his
intention of carrying out a forced march in difficult conditions and
surprising the enemy. Gorgias' venture proved to be a decisive factor
in producing complacency in the Seleucid camp. Consequently it is
hard to consider accidental the occurrence within such a short time
of the two events, Judas Maccabaeus' departure from Mizpah and
Gorgias' from Ammaus. It looks as if Judas Maccabaeus intended
from the start to draw some Seleucid troops away from the camp at
Ammaus and so reduce the vigilance of the Seleucids remaining in
camp. In that case moving to a hiding place near Ammaus could
have jeopardized the whole plan by stopping Gorgias from leaving
the camp on the way to Mizpah, all the more so as Mizpah is said

[117] It would not help to appeal to the later halakhic distinction between an oration
attributed to the priest 'at the border' which gives just the list of the exempt, and one 'in the
battle array' which includes words of encouragement (*Tosefta Sotah* 6.18; *PT Sotah* 8.1(22b);
BT Sotah 42a–b; *Sifre*, Deut. 191). The distinction is theoretical and is basically questionable,
for it contradicts the order of things in Deuteronomy and in the Mishnah as well (Sotah
8.1–16). On the origin of this distinction see Rofé 1974: 153. There is no justification for the
change in order in Sotah 8.1–16 proposed by J. Brand (cited by Yadin in the Hebrew version
of *War of Sons of Light* 1955: 64 n. 17). The Mishnah interprets and explains the laws on war
in Deuteronomy in accordance with the verse order in the Bible, the usual practice of halakhic
Midrashim.

to have been evacuated (3.56–7, 4.5), and there is no indication that a 'bait' force was left there. The intelligence system at Judas Maccabaeus' disposal could not have been efficient and sophisticated enough to provide definite information on Gorgias' intentions and timing and permit Judas Maccabaeus to leave Mizpah with confidence and station himself south of Ammaus before Gorgias left the camp. The possibility that Gorgias did not look for Judas Maccabaeus in the distant and traversable plateau near Mizpah but tried to find him at night in the rough hills to the south of Ammaus does not explain the absence of a battle oration at Mizpah and imposes obvious difficulties. Special notice should be taken of the indication in I Maccabees that Gorgias knew exactly where the Jewish camp was located (4.5). Had it been near Ammaus, the failure to find Judas' men would certainly have alerted the Seleucid camp, and Gorgias would not have spent his time in a futile search in dangerous terrain, while his own camp was exposed to immediate danger (see also pp. 260–1 below). The displacement of verses and the resultant insertion of glosses is not surprising in a book which underwent a transformation from one language to another, aside from being recopied many times, and is not rare in I Maccabees.[118]

Josephus in *Antiquitates* describes the course of events in the spirit of the reconstruction proposed above (though he does not mention the name of Mizpah): Judas Maccabaeus set out at night from the place where his forces were assembled and the ceremony took place when information that Gorgias was on his way reached him, and he marched throughout the night to the Ammaus area (12.305–7). In the Josephus version the commander's oration concludes the ceremony (12.302–4), an indication that the version he relied on had an order of verses different from that available to us. Josephus would not have changed the order himself, for the mix-up in the text is not obvious, and nowhere else did complex considerations of the sort noted above lead Josephus to offer an interpretation of his own in paraphrasing I Maccabees.

Exegetes and scholars, who have dealt more extensively with the battle of Ammaus than with the other battles, have not realized the difficulty in the present placement of the verse. They have tended to reconstruct the course of the battle according to the present sequence of verses in I Maccabees, and assumed that Gorgias tried to surprise Judas Maccabaeus in the latter's bivouac south of Ammaus. Those who accept that Gorgias moved toward Mizpah, probably on the basis of Josephus' version,[119] ignore the textual difficulties in I Maccabees and do not justify their view.

[118] See 5.66–7 (cf. 5.55–62; II Macc. 12.32–45); 6.49–50 (cf. 6.31, and see pp. 308–9 below); 9.1 (cf. 9.12 and see p. 382 below); and 9.34 *versus* 9.43.
[119] Kanael 1964: 114; Avi-Yonah 1972: 159–60; id. 1974: 26 n. 32.

4.1 *And Gorgias took five thousand men and a thousand picked horse*: Considering that it was a long, hard night march in which the surprise element was vital, the figures ascribed to Gorgias' task force seem quite inflated, which is well in line with the general exaggeration in the estimate of enemy forces.

Picked horse: The number of picked horsemen noted fits either the *agēma* or the *hetairoi*, both picked cavalry units of the Royal Guard.[120] But it cannot be imagined that Antiochus Epiphanes did not take these units with him to the Upper Satrapies, for the Seleucid kings were accustomed to directing combat while fighting in the midst of a Royal cavalry unit.[121] I Maccabees indeed uses the word 'picked' quite loosely (see p. 284 below). Presumably the verse refers to the inclusion of mountain peoples such as Thracians, Mysians and perhaps even Galatians in the special task force Gorgias took with him on his way to Mizpah. As a Thracian horseman is mentioned among Gorgias' troops in the battle of Marisa (II Macc. 12.35), and Thracians always excelled in night assaults,[122] it is quite likely that Thracian mounted mercenaries played a central role in the special task force that ascended to Mizpah.

And the camp moved at night: The sequence of events implies that Judas Maccabaeus found a way to let the Seleucid command know of the concentration of the Jewish force at Mizpah in order to draw some of their forces up to the mountain plateau. This was done either through deliberate leakage, or through some conspicuous action, such as the mass ceremony, which would attract the attention of the Hellenizers and their supporters who collaborated with the authorities. Presumably Gorgias used the Beth Horon Ascent to climb to Mizpah.

2 *To assault the camp of the Jews and smite them suddenly*: It is possible that one of the Seleucid aims in camping at Ammaus was to bring about a concentration of the Jewish force in one place and then strike a surprise blow. Indirect methods of this kind and night attacks were by no means foreign to Hellenistic warfare.[123] What was special about this third Seleucid confrontation in Judaea was that both sides attempted indirect methods, and the winner was the side which could manoeuvre better in the rugged and confusing terrain. The Jewish troops had no alternative to indirect warfare. Thus the foe, though certainly preferring direct methods, was forced to choose

---

[120] On their numerical strength see Bar-Kochva 1979: 68–75.
[121] See p. 335 n. 70 and p. 392 n. 38 below.
[122] E.g. Herodotus 6.45.1; Xen. *Anab.* 7.2.22; Polyaenus 2.2.6,8,10; and see Best 1969: 52–3; Walbank 1972: 95; Pritchett 1974: 2.170–1.
[123] Polybius 5.47–48.10,52.13, 7.17–18; Polyaenus 4.9.2; Diodorus 18.40.3, 19.47.2,68.7, 92.3–4,93.2; Plut. *Dem.* 49.1–4. For Classical Greece see Pritchett 1974: 171–2.

indirect ones because of the conviction that the Jewish force would seek to avoid a frontal clash.

And the Akra men were his guides: The allusion is to scouts from the garrison of the Jerusalem citadel, who were presumably supported by their allies, the Hellenizers.[124] Josephus (*Ant.* 12.305) estimates that the reference is just to Hellenizers, probably because he assumed that only they could have been so familiar with the roads in the Judaean Hills and their surroundings.

3 *And Judah heard*: According to the proposal made above regarding the proper location of the end of 3.57 ('And they camped south of Ammaus'), Judas Maccabaeus left Mizpah that night after learning that Gorgias was moving in his direction. Judas Maccabaeus could not have learned that Gorgias was on the way to the Jewish camp and managed to reach the region south of Ammaus the same night if he had not had an efficient 'warning system', possibly signal fires, or fast riders.[125] Some such system was absolutely necessary given the overall problem facing the Jews – to block the enemy before he could reach the mountain plateau – and seems to have already been employed against Seron. In any case, the fact that Judas Maccabaeus did not try to stop the task force while it was making the difficult ascent, but set out for Ammaus to surprise the large camp, indicates that he had detailed information on the enemy's movements and intentions. It is not impossible that the sources who reported them were actually inside the Seleucid camp or very close to it. Presumably therefore Judas Maccabaeus left Mizpah for Ammaus as early as he could, just at nightfall.

And he and the valorous advanced to smite the king's camp at Ammaus: The adjective 'valorous' (οἱ δυνατοί) refers to the picked soldiers who remained in the Jewish camp after the strict screening at Mizpah (3.55–6).

Various proposals have been made as to the route Judas Maccabaeus followed from Mizpah to the temporary camp near Ammaus. Abel proposed the Biddu–Kiryat 'Anavim–Saris route, and Kanael the Biddu–Kiryat 'Anavim–Beit Tul–Deir Aiyūb route.[126] The first is long, hard and winding, certainly for the one-night march to Ammaus. The second is shorter (up to 25 km) but involves many steep ascents and descents and is too difficult for a rapid march of 3,000 men who had fasted for a day and were about to fight. Consequently it seems reasonable to propose the road from Biddu through Abu Ghosh, Neve Illan, Kh. al-Qasr (elevation

---

[124] Gutberlet 1920: 61 and others.

[125] On signalling methods and the transmission of information via messengers in the Hellenistic period see p. 279 n. 7 below. On the military use of signalling systems see esp. Diodorus 19.97.1 which is somewhat reminiscent of the situation in the battle of Ammaus; see further Polybius 10.43–4; Aeneas Tacticus 4,6; Phil. Byz. *mēkhanikē syntaxis* 95; and cf. Polyaenus 6.16.2.   [126] Kanael 1964: 112; Abel 1949: 71.

points 377,395) and Kh. 'Aqed, a road which is at present being thoroughly explored.[127] Milestones have been found on that route, as well as impressive remains of forts from the Hellenistic, Hasmonaean and Roman periods. The route during the Hellenistic period was certainly similar if not identical with that of the Roman period which is supported by natural conditions. For the most part the road passes along a ridge, which offers a good view of the neighbourhood. Here and there it goes below the ridge line, but movement is quite easy, and there is no need to cross gullies. The road to the Aijalon Valley goes downhill, and the descent is easy and almost regular. The distance from Mizpah to Ammaus via this route is 27 km. At the end of the summer, when the march took place (p. 472 below), there are about 10 to $10\frac{1}{2}$ hours of darkness. Judas Maccabaeus' men who set out as darkness fell could have reached the Ammaus area about 4 hours before sunrise and then they would have had enough time to rest and organize for the attack. The march testifies to the good mobility of the Jewish force, even more evident the next day in the approach to the camp, the assault, the pursuit, and the return to the battlefield. That ability is demonstrated also in Judas Maccabaeus' expedition in Transjordania (I Macc. 5.28–9) when in one night the Jewish camp of 8,000 men moved from Bosora (= Bozrah) to Dathema, which according to proposals for its location was about 50 km away.[128] A similar pace was usual in the Hellenistic armies of the period (see n. 131 below and p. 384).

4 *As the army was scattered outside the camp*: The reference is to the picked units which set out with Gorgias. It implies that Judas Maccabaeus' plan was based on the complacency in the Seleucid camp.
⟨*And they camped south of Ammaus*⟩: On the proper placement of the sentence see pp. 257–9 above. The identification of the bivouac site before the raid on Ammaus will help in understanding the progress of the operation. However, the site is a matter of conjecture. Kanael suggests it was the palm valley at the foot of Ras Abu-Mur (reference point 1475/1355).[129] The place is well hidden, has a spring, and a view of 'Police Hill', but since Judas Maccabaeus camped there at night and attacked at dawn, the advantages of the site for observation could not have weighed very heavily in the choice. And on the other hand, the valley site adds six to seven kilometres to the distance from Ammaus. Avi-Yonah proposes the valley south of the village of Mesillat Zion,[130] which is likewise rather far from the battlefield.
    The temporary camping place must be located close to the road

---

[127] See Gichon 1980: 235; M. Fischer 1979: 461–2; id. 1980: 235–7.
[128] On this identification see Abel 1923: 516–17. See also Map 21 on p. 509 below.
[129] Kanael 1964: 112.   [130] Avi-Yonah 1972: 160.

that the force took from Mizpah to Ammaus. The assertion that the force camped 'south of Ammaus' makes it necessary to assume that the Jewish force left the road to Ammaus somewhere near Kh. 'Aqed and turned southwards to one of the nearby valleys. It could be the valley separating the tomb of Nebi-Ayub on one side from Kh. 'Aqed and Zahar as-Sharqi on the other, or the valley between Zahar as-Sharqi and Sheikh ibn Jabel. The second possibility seems more likely because the structure and form of the valley were apt to provide cover for a force camping there. There was also a spring that dried up only recently.

5 *And Gorgias came to Judah's camp at night*: The distance between Ammaus and Mizpah through the Beth Horon Ascent is about 23 km. Gorgias, who was advancing up hill, arrived at Mizpah sometime before dawn and continued to search until daylight (see the map, pp. 222–3 above). Unlike the armies of Classical Greece, the Macedonians from the reign of Philip II onwards had excellent mobility, undergoing special training in long marches with full equipment.[131]

And found nobody, and sought them in the mountains: Josephus states that Judas Maccabaeus left lights burning in his camp (*Ant.* 12.306). That statement was not taken from any other source and is a free invention of Josephus', based on his knowledge of the deceptive methods current in the Hellenistic period (I Macc. 12.28–9; Appian, *Syr.* 16; Polyaenus 4.9.15; Onasander 10.13; Plut. *Luc.* 15.3–4; *Eum.* 15.6–7; Nepos, *Eumenes* 8.3–6). Camp fires were lit also to create the impression of a large force (Appian, *Syr.* 16).

For he said, They are fleeing\from before us: The author is trying to explain why Gorgias lost precious time searching on the mountain plateau. The Seleucid commander realized that his march had been discovered and the Jews had therefore left their Mizpah base in a hurry; he did not suspect that Judas Maccabaeus was already at that time about to attack the main Seleucid camp at Ammaus.

6 *And as morning dawned Judah was seen in the valley*: As the temporary Jewish bivouac was south of Ammaus, the Jewish force broke into the Seleucid camp from the south-east, which was the shortest and safest route to the presumed Seleucid camp site. From that direction they had to climb up to one of the three saddles between the Latrun hill and the Ammaus hill, where it was possible to observe the camp (see 4.7). It is not likely that Judas Maccabaeus circled the Latrun hill, entering the broad, open part of the Aijalon Valley to attack from the south-west; in that case he would have been visible from observation posts certainly set up on Police Hill and run the

---

[131] See Cary 1951: 237; Tarn 1930: 40–1; Bar-Kochva 1979: 95,125; and see especially Polybius 5.80.1–3, 10.49.4; on the training of the armies see Polyaenus 4.2.10. On the usual speed of advance in the Roman campaigns see Watson 1969: 54, and the bibliography there.

risk of a frontal clash on the level ground at the foot of that hill, which he could not have coped with at that stage. As the Jewish force was in a position to observe the entire Seleucid camp before raiding it, it was obviously in a place that overlooked the camp. This deduction is reinforced by the description of the flight of some of the enemy soldiers 'to the plain' (4.14), indicating that the initial battle contact took place in hilly terrain. And finally, some of the Seleucid troops fled toward Idumaea (verse 15), which would be hard to imagine if the attack came from the level terrain south or south-west of Police Hill, the shortest way to Idumaea.

The statement that Judas Maccabaeus 'was seen (ὤφθη) in the valley' at dawn contains nothing to contradict these conclusions. The Jewish camp, placed in one of the extensions of the south-eastern part of the Aijalon Valley, was apparently seen by the mounted Seleucid patrols (4.7) passing by. But the early warning was of little help to the sleeping, smug Seleucid camp (see below re verse 4.12). The time was too short to permit any reorganization, especially since Judas Maccabaeus and his men burst into the camp from the short and comfortable route through the saddle with the advantage of height, and the camp itself was too crowded for an 'orderly' battle. According to this conclusion the word πεδίον used to describe where Judas Maccabaeus was seen should be reconstructed בָּעֵמֶק (= in the valley) as it often is in the Septuagint, rather than בַּמִּישׁוֹר (= in the plain) as appears several times in I Maccabees. However, it is also possible that Judas Maccabaeus was not discovered before, and that the Seleucid camp was totally taken by surprise. Notice should be taken that the sentence 'And as morning dawned Judas Maccabaeus was seen in the valley' is preceded by 'And Gorgias came to the Jewish camp at night and did not find anyone, and he sought them in the mountains.' In both sentences there is clear contrast between 'night' and 'morning' as well as 'in the mountains' and 'in the valley'. Thus the intention of our verse may be to celebrate the cleverness and initiative of Judas Maccabaeus: while Gorgias searched for him in vain at night in the mountains, Judas Maccabaeus managed to appear in the valley in the morning. The word 'was seen' accordingly implies not his discovery by the enemy but his mere presence in the valley.

With three thousand men: The number of fighters in Judas Maccabaeus' force after the screening at Mizpah indicates the size of the entire force, probably no less than six thousand, as II Maccabees also estimates (8.1,16,21–2; see p. 48 and n. 68 above on the 3,000-man figure). A night march of three thousand soldiers on the hidden trail, 27 km long, from Mizpah to the area south of Ammaus, was quite a difficult operation requiring a high degree of excellence in the soldiers, an efficient command, and a first-rate sense of direction. They were select men out of quite a good-sized irregular army that had been living in guerrilla conditions for at least two years, and had doubtless been training for precisely such missions. Judas Maccabeus' plan of action, which was not at all accidental or improvised, had necessarily to be based on the availability of combatants capable of carrying out complicated operations.

But shields and swords they had not as they wished: The verse obviously indicates that at this early stage at least part of the Jewish force was equipped with swords and shields, and was fighting in the style of the classical peltasts. Two of the late minuscule manuscripts (nos 55 and 58) contain an interesting addition to this verse: καὶ περικεφαλαίας καὶ σφενδονὰς καὶ λίτους καὶ σκορπιδία καὶ ὅπλα καὶ θωράκας (= and also helmets and slings and stones and armour), but this is clearly a gloss to which no value need be attached.[132]

7 *And they saw a...camp*: Certainly standing on one of the three saddles between the Latrun and the Ammaus hill, and perhaps also appearing on more than one saddle. Upon reaching them, Judas Maccabeus' force was able to see the Seleucid camp in its entirety.

A strong fortified Gentile camp: The wording of the sentence makes it clear that the adjective τεθωρακισμένην refers not to the armour of the soldiers in the camp,[133] but to the fortifications of the camp itself.[134] The root does not appear in the latter meaning in the Septuagint, is not known as a verb or participle in that usage, and is not too common as a noun or adjective (see Herodotus 1.181; Dio Cassius 74.10 (θωράκιον); Suda s.v. θωρακεῖον).

Despite the fact noted above that the Seleucid camp was protected by natural obstacles, this verse undoubtedly refers to artificial fortifications. Like the practice of Classical Greece, the Hellenistic commanders generally protected their camps with a palisade (χαράκωμα).[135] Polybius notes that the Macedonians of the end of the third century actively engaged in a variety of excavation and fortification work (5.2.5), and the same may have been true in the Hellenistic armies. If necessary, at times more complicated fortifications were undertaken in Seleucid camps, such as at Thermopylae and Magnesia. The camp at Magnesia was

---

[132] For a general negative assessment of these manuscripts see Kappler 1967: 33.

[133] Keil 1875: 84; Gutberlet 1920: 63; Michaelis 1778: 82–3 refers to previous commentaries.

[134] So also Michaelis 1778; Grimm 1853: 66; Abel 1949: 75, and others.

[135] For ancient Greece see Liers 1895: 147–8; Anderson 1970: 6off.; Pritchett 1974: 2.133–46. On the Hellenistic period see especially Arrian, *Anab.* 3.9.1; Diodorus 18.13.1, 19.18.4,39.1, 20.47.1,83.4,108.7; Livy 33.5.5–12, 38.37.6; Polybius 2.65.6,9, 5.2.5,20.4,47.4, 6.42,73.10, 18.18; Polyaenus 4.6.19; Onasander 40.2. Cf. Phil. Byz. *mēkhanikē syntaxis* 93 (5.36–7). On the weaknesses and shortcomings of the Hellenistic palisade compared with the Roman see Polybius 18.18; Livy 33.5.6–12.

surrounded by a waterless moat six cubits deep and twelve cubits wide. Across the moat was a palisade with a series of watchtowers, and in front of the moat was a double palisade (Livy 37.37.10–11). At Thermopylae a moat was dug across the width of the pass and on the ridge dominating it, and behind it a double wall of stone was built (Livy 36.16.3; Appian, *Syr.* 18(78)). In addition forward posts were constructed around the Seleucid camps.[136] Given the stress in the verse on the fortifications and their strength, the Ammaus camp may have been surrounded by more than just a palisade.

And cavalry circling it: As early as the Classical period, camps were guarded by day by horsemen placed at prominent observation points, and by night by infantry (Xen. *Lac.* 12.2–3). Advance cavalry guards (προφύλακαι) that patrolled at night are mentioned in Alexander the Great's army (Arrian, *Anabasis* 5.23.5, and evidently also 2.8.2). Patrols of this kind circled the Aijalon Valley, and it may very well have been they who discovered Judas Maccabaeus and his men in their bivouac to the south of Ammaus.

Judas Maccabaeus did not follow the example set by Gideon (Judg. 7),[137] and refrained from attacking the Seleucid camp at night, being aware of the difficulty of controlling and coordinating 3,000 troops in the darkness in the large camp. His select force was ten times larger than that of Gideon, because his enemy was much more sophisticated and better trained than the nomads routed by Gideon.

8 *And Judah said... Do not be afraid of their multitude...*: The timing and contents of the oration attributed to Judas Maccabaeus in these circumstances provides further evidence of the artificial nature of the battle orations in the book. The Jewish commander's plan was based on exploiting the complacency of the Seleucids and launching a surprise attack. The plan was almost spoiled by the enemy's early discovery of the Jews in their bivouac, and Judas Maccabaeus most certainly speeded up the advance so as to prevent the enemy from getting organized. Under those circumstances, when any delay might have had serious consequences, there was no time to deliver a speech (cf. p. 215 above). Even if we accept the interpretation suggesting that there was no such early discovery, Judas Maccabaeus certainly would not have delivered a speech to a crowd of 3,000 combatants standing exposed to observation on the saddle overlooking the camp and thus jeopardizing the element of surprise. Furthermore, the oration contains no reference to the deliberate

---

[136] On the remnant of Antiochus III's wall at Thermopylae see Bequignon 1934: 20. Cf. Pritchett 1965: 1.73. On forward posts see Appian, *Syr.* 26(127), 36(184); Livy 36.11.4, 37.43.10; Polyaenus 4.9.2; Polybius 5.80.7, 7.17.2.
[137] On the military aspects of Gideon's raid see Malamat 1965: 110–23; Rösel 1976: 10–24.

release of a considerable proportion of the available manpower and the tactical advantage gained by the remaining small number which could have reinforced the morale of the soldiers selected.

The oration itself is a figment of the author's imagination, based on Deuteronomy 20.3–4, with the addition of a statement on the enemy's advantages and historical precedents. In structure it resembles that of the Priest 'Anointed for Battle' in the Mishnah (Sotah 8.1) and the pre-battle orations at Beth Zur and Adasa (I Macc. 4.30–3, 7.41–2). The precedent of the miraculous victory on the Red Sea is mentioned as well in one of the war prayers in the Scroll of the Sons of Light (11[14].10), which are similarly structured (see also pp. 287–8, 496). The Ammaus speech which II Maccabees attributes to Judas Maccabaeus follows the same pattern, although it is quite clumsy, like the other orations in that book, and lists as historical precedents the defeat of Sennacherib and a unique episode relating to the clash in Babylonia between Jews and Galatians in about 235 B.C. (8.19–20; see below pp. 500ff.).

12 *And the strangers lifted their eyes and saw them coming*: The Jewish force that climbed to the saddles overlooking the camp from the south-east, was fully visible to the Seleucid soldiers in the camp. Early sunbeams glaring from behind the back of the Jewish force on the south-east may have somewhat dazzled the enemy soldiers during the attack, and thus given the attackers an added advantage (cf. the advice of Vegetius 3.14). Even if the Seleucid camp had warning of an imminent attack a short time before, its ability to organize quickly for defence and counter-attack varied from campaign to campaign depending on the ability of the commanders, the circumstances, expectations, and estimate of the enemy's intentions and *modus operandi*. Sometimes the Seleucid army was on full alert, with the soldiers eating and resting in full battle equipment, but there are also known cases when belts were loosened.[138] The atmosphere in the Seleucid camp near Ammaus was apparently quite relaxed, for the camp commanders were convinced that Gorgias had succeeded in surprising Judas Maccabaeus at Mizpah, and in any case had no reason to be particularly uneasy because Judas Maccabaeus had always refrained from operating in level terrain. Even though the camp may have intended to take advantage of Gorgias' anticipated victory and climb to the plateau right after it or the next day, that was not reason enough to keep the men on the alert throughout the night as Seleucid commanders were wont to do when an attack was expected.

The strangers: The Greek is ἀλλόφυλοι, literally 'strangers',

---

[138] Polyaenus 4.9.1; Athenaeus 12.540b–c; Livy 37.20; Appian, *Syr.* 26(127); Polybius 5.45–6. For an analysis of these episodes see Bar-Kochva 1979: 96–100. On a surprise attack during the first watch cf. also Diodorus 19.93.2.

'foreigners', which in the Septuagint is the usual translation for
פלישתים (= Philistines; cf. p. 217 above). Only twice does the word
appear in its literal meaning (Is. 2.6, 61.5). In the present context
it is clear that the Hebrew source had נכרים (foreigners; in the
Septuagint ξένοι; ἀλλογενεῖς; cf. I Macc. 4.26, 11.68).[139] Abel's
proposal that the Hebrew was 'Aramaeans' (i.e. Syrians), which is
once translated in the Septuagint as ἀλλόφυλοι (II Kings 8.28),[140]
is less acceptable. The word 'Aramaeans' is always translated in I
Maccabees as 'Syrians'.

13 *And they went out of the camp to war*: The next verse ('and they fled to
the plain') shows that the first confrontation was in the hills.
Because of the crowded condition of the camp, the patrols and
guards (as opposed to the ἔσχατοι [= 'the last'], see 4.15), tried to
deal with the danger and fight Judas Maccabaeus on the slopes of
the Latrun–Ammaus ridge.
And those with Judah blew: The trumpets were sounded in this case in
order to encourage the men, to frighten the enemy, and perhaps also
to simulate a large force (cf. Judg. 7.19–20; Plut. *Sulla* 14.5;
Polyaenus, *Excerp.* 15.4; Leo (Byz.), *Stratagemata* 12.2) or convey an
order. For details on the role of trumpets in Hellenistic warfare see
p. 394 below.

14 *And they clashed and smote the Gentiles and they fled to the plain*: The clash
took place, as noted above, on the hills, so that when the forward
guards were beaten they took 'to the plain'. Judas Maccabaeus'
men exploited the advantage of height and numbers they had
compared with the enemy guards and whatever soldiers managed to
get organized. On the effect of an army appearing from above on
troops camped on a plain see Thucydides 4.36; Plutarch, *Sulla* 18;
Vegetius 3.13; and see Polybius 5.45–6 and Appian, *Syr.* 26(125–7)
on a force that breaks into a complacent camp.

15 *And the last all fell to the sword*: The Greek is καὶ οἱ ἔσχατοι, which
should be וְהָאַחֲרוֹנִים (= and the last), as in the Septuagint. The
translation מאסף (= rear) preferred by Cahana (based on the
Septuagint for Num. 10.25),[141] is unacceptable, for the verse does
not deal with an army on the march but with soldiers in camp. Nor
is ἔσχατοι the usual translation for 'rear' in the Septuagint. The
original version may have been וְהָאֲחֵרִים (= and the others), which
the translator read (or found in his manuscript) as וְהָאַחֲרוֹנִים (=
and the last). The allusion in any case is to the soldiers who were in
the camp and had not managed to get organized to take part in the
preliminary clash in the hills. As the advance guards were defeated
and fled back into the crowded camp, there must have been general
pandemonium which was utilized by Judas Maccabaeus' men who
burst into the heart of the camp and made themselves at home.

---

[139] Cf. Grimm 1853: 66; Keil 1875: 84, and others.
[140] Abel 1949: 74.   [141] Cahana 1957: 114.

12 The Ammaus battle area

Aerial view from south-east to north-west (see also Map 10 on pp. 222–3 above)

Key:

1 Ridge of the Ammaus–Latrun hills, descending to the Aijalon Valley from the east
2 Gezer ridge bounding the valley on the west
3 Shaalbim ridge bounding the valley on the north-west
4 Aijalon Valley and its branches
5 Sheikh ibn Jabel tomb
6 Former U.N. building (in the courtyard of the Byzantine-Crusader church)
7 Ruins of the village of Imwas-Ammaus
8 Canada Park
9 Hill 184
10 Police Hill and the Latrun police station
11 *Suggested site of the Seleucid camp*
12 Trappist Monastery
13 Latrun Hill
14 New road to Jerusalem – the presumed route from which the Seleucid camp was attacked
15 Gezer – the retreat route of part of the Seleucid force
16 Retreat route to Idumaea (southwards) and the egress of the southern branch of the valley leading eastward toward Sha'ar ha-Gai

And they chased after them up to Gezer: Seven kilometres north-west of Ammaus, Gezer was the closest Seleucid fort in the area (cf. I Macc. 7.45, and see 13.43–8).

And up to the fields of Edom: The Alexandrine Codex has τῆς Ἰουδαίας (= Judaea), instead of τῆς Ἰδουμαίας (= Idumaea) which appears in the rest of the manuscripts and translations. Some scholars prefer that version, and identify the place as the Arab village of el-Jehudiye (today Yahud) near Lydda.[142] But the routes from Ammaus to that place cross the lowland hills north-west of Shaalbim. Because of both the topographic and demographic features of that hilly area, it is hard to believe that the Seleucid force fled in that direction and not through the plain south of it. The area was in the toparchies of Ramathaim and Lydda which were annexed to Judaea in Jonathan's time (I Macc. 11.34), certainly because their population was chiefly Jewish even before that. Furthermore, I Maccabees speaks of the territories of Ἰδουμαία (or Ἰουδαία) in the same breath as 'the field of...Ashdod and Jabneh'. As the reference is undoubtedly to the rural areas (the *khōra*) of the Hellenistic cities of Ashdod (Azotos) and Jabneh (Iamnia), it may be deduced that the first place-name as well refers to a *polis* or a district. El-Jehudiye, if it was inhabited at all during the Second Temple period, could not have been more than a small hamlet, as it is not mentioned in the sources. Finally, on the basis of the practice in the Septuagint, the use of the article may show that the reference is not to a small settlement or even a town, but to a district (cf. on the deletion of the article from Mizpah, p. 249 above). There is certainly no justification for the reading 'the fields of Judaea'.[143] The reconstruction then should be 'the fields of Edom', meaning the territory of the meridarchy of Idumaea. Thus some of the force fled southwards. Idumaean auxiliary troops indeed took part in the campaign (I Macc. 3.41).

As the pursuit could not be very long, this is perhaps an indication that the territory of Idumaea extended to the Sorek Valley area (Wadi Sarrar) or perhaps even a little further north. We have no real data on the north-western border of Idumaea, except for some hints indicating that the Elah Valley and the ridges on both sides of it marked the south-western border of Judaea.[144] And it may be that the area west of the Latrun–Elah Valley road, south of the Sorek Valley, i.e. the southern Low Shephela, was also included in Idumaea.

[142] Eissfeldt 1931: 271; Abel 1923: 508; Avi-Yonah 1963: 109; Kallai 1960: 98 n. 9; Schunck 1980: 315.

[143] Against Keil 1875: 86–7.

[144] This can be inferred from II Macc. 12.38 and I Macc. 9.50; on the identification of Thamnatha with Kh. Tibna on Mount Sansan north-east of the Elah Valley see Avi-Yonah 1963: 113, and there also pp. 19–20 on the south-western border of Judaea in the Persian period.

And Ashdod and Jabneh: See Map 10, pp. 222–3 above. Ashdod and Jabneh, which apparently both had the status of *polis*,[145] had extensive rural areas attached to them and within their jurisdiction, as was the usual Hellenistic practice. As a result the territory of Ashdod extended to Gezer (according to I Macc. 14.34; and also 16.9,10[146]). The distinction between Gezer on the one hand and the 'fields of Edom, Ashdod and Jabneh' on the other, supports the general credibility of the topographic information given in I Maccabees. An author who is not precise in such matters would have characterized the pursuit as being 'to Jabneh and Ashdod'. Linguistically speaking this means that the Hebrew word עַד (= to, or: up to) which was in the I Maccabees original narrative (in Greek the preposition ἕως followed by a genitive) does not denote a general direction, but an advance up to the point noted (and see p. 398 below).

As to the reconstruction 'Edom, Ashdod and Jabneh', the Greek translation has the Greek forms: Idumaea, Azotos, Iamnia. Although they were the rule among the Hellenized residents and perhaps also among Jews, it is hard to believe that a Hebrew author with such a predilection for biblical phrasing did not use Hebrew names for places familiar from Scriptures. The use of 'Edom' rather than 'Idumaea' is indicated also by the garbling of *edōm* to *arām* in I Macc. 3.41 (see p. 247 above).

And of them three thousand men fell: The figure is inflated and is proportional to the inflated figure given for the Seleucid force as a whole. It is equivalent to the number of men attributed to Judas Maccabaeus, and the equivalence does not seem to be accidental. The author adjusted the estimate of the enemy dead to the number of Jewish soldiers, as if to say that every Jewish soldier killed an enemy soldier. The same equivalence between the number of enemy dead and the number of Jewish soldiers occurs in other places in I Maccabees (5.20,22,34, and perhaps also 11.44,74).

16 *And Judah and the force returned from chasing*: Even if Idumaean territory extended to the Sorek Valley, it is hard to assume that the unit that pursued the enemy as far as the Idumaean border returned to the Ammaus area. Nonetheless, the fact that Judas Maccabaeus was able to bring at least part of the pursuing force back to Ammaus indicates excellent control of the army, and remarkable mobility and physical fitness. These characteristics are well reflected in the long night march and the raid as well. The accomplishment of all these ventures shows that the Jews utilized to the maximum the two to three years they had had to organize. High moral and religious

145 Tcherikover 1961a: 94–5.
146 On the reading of *Kedron* as *Gedron* and its identification with Kh. Judeira at Kibbutz Nakhshon near Gezer see Naor 1959: 121–5.

devotion alone would not have made possible undertakings of the sort required in that battle.

17 *And he said to the people, Do not covet the booty for war is ahead of us* : Philip V's military code found at Amphipolis stipulates how booty should be handled and looting prevented.[147] Presumably similar practices were adopted in other Hellenistic armies. The Hasmonaean army, on the other hand, was not organized to deal with spoils, and this accounts for Judas Maccabaeus' warning.[148] On the danger of scrambling for booty before the total collapse of the enemy cf. Plut. *Luc.* 4.2–3; Polybius 5.48.1–3.

18 *And Gorgias and the army are in the mountain...* : This statement (and cf. the next verse) further indicates that Gorgias did not search for Judas Maccabaeus' men south of Ammaus (which was in the Shephela, the low hills) but in Mizpah, on the mountain plateau.

19 *As Judah was [uttering] these (words)* : Most manuscripts have πληροῦντος (= filling),[149] which is a garbling. The Lucian manuscripts followed by the old Latin translation have λαλοῦντος (= saying). Michaelis suggested that the Hebrew was מְמַלֵּל (= uttering) which was garbled to מְמַלֵּא (= filling).[150]

Part was seen reflected from the mountain: The Seleucid force may have come down from the mountain plateau by the same route it climbed up, the Beth Horon Descent. The ridge of hills north-west of Ammaus does not allow a view of the Beth Horon Descent from Ammaus and its vicinity. However, it can be observed from the northern part of the site proposed for the Seleucid camp, about a kilometre north of Ammaus (slightly north of elevation point 184), although it is doubtful whether the naked eye could distinguish figures coming down from the mountain. Judas Maccabaeus could have sent guards to the Beit Nuba sector, two or three kilometres east of the camp, from which it was possible to watch military movements on the various slopes leading to the Aijalon Valley. Gorgias might as well have returned via Biddu–Qubeiba–Beit Liqya so as to avoid encountering a possible ambush at the Beth Horon Descent. From that road they could see more clearly not just smoke but what was actually happening in the camp and its environs, and decide on a withdrawal.

20 *And he (Gorgias) saw that...they were burning the camp*: Setting fire to the camp at this stage, even before looting it, was probably aimed at making clear to the observer from afar that the camp was already

---

[147] Feyel 1935: 31, ll. 1–10. On the handling of the booty in general see Préaux 1978: 1.199–200,297–8.

[148] On arrangements for the distribution of booty and the units assigned to the task in the Scroll of the War of the Sons of Light see Yadin 1962: 141–2.

[149] For the reconstruction of πληροῦντος as ממלא see Hatch and Redpath 1897: 2.1147.

[150] Michaelis 1778: 87; cf. Grimm 1853: 69; Keil 1875: 87.

devastated and the battle lost, and perhaps also at creating the impression that the Jews had a large force. Apprehensive about joining battle with Gorgias' picked men, Judas Maccabaeus tried in this way to prevent them from joining battle.

For the smoke that was seen revealed what happened: Although part of the camp was invisible from the Beth Horon Descent, one of the possible return routes, the smoke was certainly visible. The reference to the smoke at this point seems a further indication that the author was an eye-witness and took an active part in the battle, as details of this kind do not generally appear in second-hand sources.[151] It cannot be denied, however, that the author may have wished to mention the smoke in order to make his description more pictorial.

22 *And when they saw Judah's camp in the plain*: The smoke was what first held the attention of the Seleucid soldiers. It was only later, as they advanced down the Descent, that Gorgias and his men became aware of the Jewish combatants waiting in the plain.

They all fled to the land of the Philistines: The Jewish troops were too exhausted at this stage to pursue the enemy, and they may have hesitated to clash with Gorgias' men, the elite soldiers of the Seleucid expedition. Judas Maccabaeus' aim was to prevent the Seleucid force from reforming near Ammaus, and that was why he again took up a position in the plain. However, when the enemy began to retreat, there was no need for further pursuit (on the special II Maccabees version of the pursuit see pp. 486–9 below).

23 *And Judah returned to loot the camp and he took gold in plenty and silver*: The Hellenistic army camps abounded in gold and silver, brought there by the traders (see 3.41) and the mercenaries, who sometimes carried their savings with them (Plut. *Eum.* 9.6; Justin 14.3). Often precious metals were brought along by the high command for bribing local groups or leaders to change their allegiance (Diodorus 30.16; cf. Zonaras 9.20.3). Also in the camps were silver and gold of different kinds, among them phalerae, tiny ornaments for the horses and the men's clothing,[152] shields, and the like (see pp. 320, 325–6). Two sources report that the Seleucid expedition that Antiochus VII Sidetes led against the Parthians in 129 B.C. carried a plethora of luxury items such as gold and silver cooking utensils and table ware, ornaments and clothing, including even gold-plated boots (Athenaeus 12.540b–c; Justin 38.10). Although there is no doubt that the atmosphere in the Seleucid army camps was quite different from the tough, rigid order prevailing in Roman army camps, these last sources appear to be exaggerating the luxuries and pleasures of Seleucid camps. Those reports were taken from the 'histories' of

---

[151] Cf. Thucydides 4.34; and on this Grundy 1948: 2.131.

[152] On phalerae in the material culture of the period see Allen 1971: 10–23. Cf. Rostovtzeff 1922: 137–8; Minns 1913: 271–3, and Pl. XIIa.

Poseidonius of Apamea (Athenaeus 10.439e, 12.540b), who deliberately exaggerated in describing the degeneration of the Hellenistic world, and even waxed satirical in his historiosophic purpose of explaining the rise of the Roman empire and its ascendancy over the Hellenistic kingdoms.[153]

And blue and marine purple: This phrase, like 'gold and silver', is common in the Bible, but cannot be considered pure rhetoric. It may refer to jewellery or precious stones brought along by the merchants and mercenaries, or to semi-precious stones with which the weapons were decorated (cf. Plut. *Luc.* 7.5). It might also refer to the clothing of the soldiers which, being caught by surprise, they had not managed to don, and left in the tents. The combination of light blue and wine-colour occurs in the clothing of a Macedonian horseman of the early third century (see the tombstone, Pl. V). The report on the Daphne procession shows that the outer clothing of the Seleucid soldiers was purple (Polybius 30.25.10; on the expression 'marine purple' referring to costly attire cf. Diodorus 17.70.3). For variety some of the soldiers in the Hellenistic armies also wore other colours such as blue, black and yellow-gold.[154] The horsemen's saddles were coloured as well, mainly purple.[155]

The author lists the colours rather than the objects so as to make his description more picturesque. But this does not explain his failure to report weapons that had been abandoned in the camp. The reason for that is his reluctance to disclose the gradual improvement in the Jewish armaments. It is only after Lysias' first expedition, just before the purification of the Temple, that the book mentions the strengthening of the Jewish army through captured arms, and that only incidentally as the author is carried away in his attempt to connect the death of Antiochus Epiphanes with events in Judaea (6.6; and see pp. 52, 68 above).

[153] Bar-Kochva 1979: 99–101. On discipline and the punitive system in Classical Greek camps see Pritchett 1974: 2.232–45.

[154] Cf. the armies of Perseus and Mithridates in Plut. *Aem.* 18,30, *Sulla* 16; and see also the painted gravestones from Alexandria and Sidon in Reinach and Hamdy-Bey 1892: pls. 34–7; Breccia 1912: vol. 2, pl. 23; Mendel 1912: no. 105; Pagenstecher 1919: 51, no. 45 and fig. 37. Similar colours appear in the gravestones of the soldiers from Demetrias, now in the museum at Volos in northern Greece. See Arvanitopoulos 1928: 140–1 and pl. 1.

[155] See, e.g., Breccia 1912: pl. 12.

12

Lysias' first expedition and the raid near Beth Zur

The failure of the expedition to Ammaus – an expedition initiated by Ptolemy son of Dorymenes, the *stratēgos* of Coele Syria and Phoenicia – marked a change in the military situation in Judaea. The Antioch authorities realized that as long as the main army was occupied in the Upper Satrapies, it would be rather difficult to effect a decision and turned therefore to negotiations which lasted about six months (see below pp. 533ff.). The failure of these negotiations brought about the direct intervention of the regent Lysias, who was also in charge of the western part of the kingdom. Lysias personally led the expedition to Judaea, the first of the two. Like the battle of Ammaus, it was conducted at a time when the majority of the Seleucid army stayed with Antiochus Epiphanes in the eastern satrapies, a situation which inevitably severely reduced the numerical strength of the troops sent to Judaea.

There is a certain similarity between the I Maccabees descriptions of Lysias' two expeditions (4.26–35, 6.28–54): in both Lysias broke into the Judaean Hills from the south, and in both a confrontation with the Jews took place in Beth Zur. However, contrary to the views of a number of scholars,[1] there is no justification for doubting that there were really two expeditions. The resemblance derives from the fact that in both expeditions Lysias tried to solve the problem of the ascent to the Judaean Hills in the same way, and in both he first of all had to break the blockade of Beth Zur, the southernmost fort in Judaea, which could not be bypassed. While the details concerning the first expedition are few, general, and quite ambiguous, it is clear that the confrontation with Judas Maccabaeus took place in Beth Zur itself, whereas in the second expedition the main battle was joined near Beth Zacharia.[2] The abbreviated

[1] Proksch 1903: 457–64; E. Meyer 1921: 233,459; Kolbe 1926: 78–81; Mørkholm 1966: 152–4; Schürer... 1973: 160 n. 59.
[2] See also Wellhausen 1905: 141–3; Tcherikover 1961b: 195–6; Zeitlin 1950: 60; Goldstein 1976: 268.

character of the description is attributable to the author's non-participation in the battle (see p. 161 above) and to the vagueness of the source he relied on. This vagueness may well arise from an attempt by that source to blur the capture of Beth Zur, the scale and nature of the confrontation, and the real reason for Lysias' retreat, thus further glorifying the achievements of the rebel leader (see pp. 134–5 above).

The II Maccabees version of the Beth Zur episode (11.1–15) has most of the defects typical of that source: it greatly exaggerates the size of the enemy army and the confrontation is decided with the help of divine intervention. The number of enemy casualties and the extent of the defeat are much greater than reported in the I Maccabees version. The author however locates Beth Zur five *skhoinoi* from Jerusalem (11.5).[3] The *skhoinos* could be equivalent of 30, 40 or 60 *stadia* (Strabo 17.1.24,41). If the first possibility is applicable in this case, the estimation of II Maccabees is surprisingly more or less accurate (28.5 km). As I Maccabees does not refer to the distance from Jerusalem, this information indicates the usage of an additional source. Such information is hardly to be expected in a Jewish source written in Judaea for the local population. This and the possible accuracy of the reference may point to a Seleucid source. The account of Lysias' preliminary siege of Beth Zur (11.5), which is not mentioned in I Maccabees either, could be taken from the same source.

Josephus in *Antiquitates* (12.313–15) consistently follows the I Maccabees description, adding no information of any value. Sensing properly the general tone of the account, he explains that Judas Maccabaeus clashed with only part of the enemy (in his view, the advance troops: 12.314), and that with some modification seems to be the right interpretation.

The sequence of events

One of the main differences between I Maccabees and II Maccabees that has engaged scholars concerns the chronological placement of this expedition. While I Maccabees sets Lysias' first expedition before the purification of the Temple, in II Maccabees the purification precedes the expedition. The sequence in II Maccabees must be rejected: the author of I Maccabees, a native of the country who experienced the events (though he was not an eye-witness to the

---

[3] On the preferred reading σχοίνους, which appears in the Alexandrinus, see Abel 1949: 423 and Hanhart 1959: 93. The amendment suggested by Nelis (1983: 39–42) is less plausible.

raid), could not have erred in connection with such a crucial matter concerning occurrences in the country itself, and would not have described Lysias' retreat as paving the way to the purification of the Temple (esp. 4.36) while that expedition actually took place much later.

Why did II Maccabees locate the expedition after the purification of the Temple? The reason is to be found in the author's tendency toward 'tragic' writing and in his religious–didactic purposes. The book describes the course of events in two stages: in the first, which preceded Judas Maccabaeus' appearance, the Jews suffered severely, were not able to defend themselves, and the situation seemed hopeless. The persecutions, and especially the defilement of the Temple, are explained by God's anger aroused by the sin of the Hellenizers and their followers (5.17–19). The self-sacrifice and the tortures of the martyrs, however, atoned for all the sins, appeased God (6.12–17, 7.38) and turned his rage into grace (8.5). This grace was revealed in all its strength with the appearance of Judas Maccabaeus, which designates the dramatic turning point (*metabolē*): the author opens with a short, general summary of the minor victories and operational methods of Judas Maccabaeus (without elaborating on the battles themselves – see p. 201 above), victories which invited a major Seleucid expedition and a decisive military confrontation (the Ammaus campaign, 8.8–36). After the great Jewish victory, religious and literary logic could not allow any further delay; God's rage being appeased, there was no justification for His letting his Temple go on being defiled, pending a further military victory. Accounts of further victories would only have diminished the effect of the *metabolē* and the impression of the omnipotent Divine ability to turn the tables at one stroke. This conception can be traced also in the false statement that part of the booty gained in the Ammaus campaign was brought to Jerusalem (8.31), and that the victory was celebrated 'in the city of the forefathers' (8.33), all these after a campaign which took place fifteen months before the reoccupation of the city and the purification of the Temple. However, Antiochus Epiphanes' death was placed between the Ammaus victory and the purification of the Temple (ch. 9), because Jason of Cyrene found in one of his sources that Antiochus' death preceded the purification, and being a sudden, quick event could not be seen as a delay in the implementation of God's wish to liberate his Temple. Moreover, Antiochus Epiphanes' bitter end, presented as the accomplishment of the divine vengeance, operated to emphasize the role of the Jewish God in the great *metabolē*.

In this connection another celebrated difference between the two books deserves clarification: II Maccabees places Antiochus Epiphanes' death before the purification of the Temple (9.1–10.9), while I Maccabees reverses the order of events (4.36–60, 6.1–17). Following a debate that lasted for many years, it became universally accepted in the 1950s that the sequence in II Maccabees is the right one: a Babylonian chronicle published by Sachs and Wiseman indicates that the information on Antiochus Epiphanes' death in Persia reached Babylonia in Kislev of 148 (20 November–18 December 164 B.C.).[4] The only date at our disposal for the purification of the Temple is recorded in I Maccabees (4.52), which notes 25 Kislev 148. As a 'domestic' date, it was based on the Jewish version of the Seleucid count which adhered to the Babylonian one. Accordingly, it has been argued that there was only a slight chance of Antiochus' death not preceding the purification of the Temple. In fact, the chronological calculations are not so simple as was assumed by scholars, and need further elaboration.

The Jewish calendar in the time of the Second Temple did not always run parallel to the Babylonian: while the Babylonians used a fixed cycle of intercalation, the Jews declared a leap year according to strict agricultural and astronomical observations carried out at the end of the month Adar (about March). Two out of three signs were required to intercalate the year (*Tosefta, Sanhedrin* 2.2; *BT, Sanhedrin* 11b).[5] As the two calendars were basically lunar, an intercalation by the Jews alone, for example, brought about a difference of one month between the two calendars, until it was redressed by a Babylonian intercalation. There is indeed no doubt that at the time of the purification of the Temple the Babylonian year was one month ahead of the Jewish: according to the dates provided by II Maccabees (11.30,33) and the Scroll of Fasting (s.v. 28 Adar) for the selective repeal of the religious decrees, the Jewish and Babylonian calendars ran parallel in Adar 164 B.C. (see pp. 526–7 below). Jewish Tishri (autumn) 164–Elul 163 was a Sabbatical year (see p. 544 below; on the different New Year 'for fallow and Jubilee years' see Rosh Hashana 1.1). As a rule, the year before the Sabbatical was intercalated, while the Sabbatical and the year after the Sabbatical were not (*Tosefta, Sanhedrin* 2.9; *BT, Sanhedrin*, 12a). Thus, a second Adar was certainly proclaimed by the Jews in 164 B.C. As the Babylonian year is known to have been intercalated only a year later in Addaru 163 B.C.,[6] the Jewish Kislev 164 B.C. must have fallen

---

[4] Sachs and Wiseman 1954: 208–9. For the exact date see Parker and Dubberstein 1956: 23,41.

[5] See further Schürer... 1973: 592–4; Herr 1976: 852ff., and bibliography there.

[6] See Parker and Dubberstein 1956: 41.

a month later than the Babylonian Kislev.[7] This means that Antiochus' death was known in Babylonia no more than 55 days and no
less than 25 days before the purification of the Temple. It can be
concluded now that the sequence of II Maccabees is undoubtedly
the correct one.

We have thus seen that the death of the king and Lysias' withdrawal both preceded the purification of the Temple. Is there any
connection between the first two events? The end of Lysias'
expedition is not dated, but I Maccabees clearly indicates that the
Temple was purified immediately after Lysias' retreat and as a result
of it ('And Judah said... Lo, our enemy was smitten, let us go up and
purify the Temple', 4.36). As the preparatory work for the
purification lasted just one day (4.52), and the news about the king's
death reached Babylonia so long before the purification of the
Temple, it is quite certain that Lysias was informed about the king's
death while he was still at Beth Zur. This vital information must
have been transmitted to Lysias, the regent, within a few days, and
the Seleucid postal service, modelled after the Persian, was indeed
capable of performing this task efficiently.[8]

The news about the king's death certainly led Lysias to the deci-

[7] Goldstein (1976: 274ff.) argues that since according to rabbinical sources intercalation
could be proclaimed only by the supreme religious authority, this could be done only after the
purification of the Temple, which means that by the time of the purification the Jewish
calendar was two months ahead of the Seleucid calendar. This assumption is challenged by the
evidence referred to above that Jewish Adar 164 B.C. ran parallel to its Babylonian counterpart.
Goldstein is therefore forced to suggest that the special day of 28 Adar, commemorating the
selective repeal of the decrees according to the Scroll of Fasting, which proved that equation,
was fixed at a later stage according to the newly intercalated calendar. If this were true, the
more important Hanukkah (the Feast of Dedication – 25 Kislev) would certainly have been
adjusted to the intercalated calendar, so that the date for the purification of the Temple at our
disposal was in any case calculated according to the ordinary leap years. The whole idea that
the year was not intercalated in the time of the persecutions does not by itself make sense: the
rebels who sacrificed themselves for the preservation of the Jewish law would not have violated
the Day of Atonement, nor eaten leavened food during Passover. The evidence of the rabbinical
sources, reflecting the period after the destruction of the Temple, attributes the intercalation
even to a court of three, and requires rectification by the President (Rosh Hashana 2.7,9, 3.1;
Sanhedrin 1.2; Eduyoth 7.7; *BT, Sanhedrin* 11a). However, in the time of the religious persecutions under Hadrian, the year was intercalated even by Rabbi Akiva in prison, and by
seven of his disciples in a Galilean valley (*Tosefta, Sanhedrin* 2.8; *BT, Sanhedrin* 12a; *PT, Hagigah*
3.1[78d]; for further details see Mantel 1969: 203ff.). Judas Maccabaeus must have likewise
established his own religious court (perhaps 'the court of the Hasmonaeans' recorded in *BT,
Sanhedrin* 82a; *Abodah Zarah* 36b) and authorized it to resolve such questions.

[8] For the Seleucid–Persian system see Rostovtzeff 1906: 249ff. He mentions only the slower
mail carried by horsemen through regular stations. Of the more rapid means, it was said that
it was capable of conveying information from Greece to Persia within two days by means of
criers stationed on mountain tops and couriers (probably horsemen: Herodotus 8.98; Cleo-
medes 2.73.15–25; for the system see Diodorus 19.17.7), and within a day from anywhere in
the Persian empire to the capital in Susiana or Ecbatana by means of fire signals and couriers
(Pseudo-Arist. *De Mundo* 398A, 27–35; see also Diodorus 19.57.5 on its adoption by Antigonus
Monophthalmus).

sion to leave before his mission was accomplished. He had to hurry to Antioch to take over the reign as regent for Antiochus V, the dead king's young son – hence the peculiar features of the confrontation at Beth Zur, especially the absence of any reference to a flight and a pursuit of the enemy (see pp. 134–5 above). The oral or written source used by I Maccabees did not record the death of the king because it wished to mask the real reason and turn it into another great victory for Judas Maccabaeus. I do not believe that the author of I Maccabees was responsible for this: elsewhere he mentions quite innocently that the news of Lysias' defeat at Beth Zacharia and of the purification of the Temple reached Antiochus Epiphanes while he was still alive (6.6), which indicates that he was not aware of the precise dating of Antiochus' death.

The dating of the termination of the expedition after the king's death has to be examined in the light of the information about the commencement and duration of the expedition. According to I Maccabees, Lysias mustered the troops for his first expedition a full year after the battle of Ammaus (4.28; see p. 283 below). The Ammaus campaign took place in late summer or early spring 165 B.C. (see p. 472 below), so that the expedition could have started in Tishri, the seventh month in the Jewish calendar, or somewhat earlier. As Antiochus died in Kislev of the Babylonian calendar, which in 164 B.C. ran parallel to Marheshvan, the Jewish eighth month, the expedition would have lasted one or two months. This is quite reasonable for an invasion which, in view of the lessons learned in the Ammaus campaign, should have been conducted carefully and slowly, as is indeed shown by the decision to ascend the Judaean Hills from the south. The siege of Beth Zur by itself could have delayed the advance for a few weeks.

Be that as it may, there was ample time for the news about the king's death to come to the knowledge of Judas Maccabaeus well before the purification of the Temple. This explains why the Temple was purified at that stage: it could not be simply the retreat of the enemy that convinced the rebel leader that the time was right for the liberation of the Temple, for he could have done it a year earlier, after the victory at Ammaus – all the more so as Antiochus and his army were then away on their march to the eastern satrapies. Judas Maccabaeus refrained from doing so then because he was aware that such a significant step would infuriate the king to the point where he might soon turn all his military force against Judaea (cf. the cautious handling of the Akra problem: pp. 458–9 below), and that the Jews were still unable to defend the Temple. The king's death raised hopes of a change of policy in Antioch, especially in view of the selective repeal of the religious decrees some months earlier, the earlier negotiations with Lysias (which were impeded by Antiochus Epiphanes) and the favourable attitude of Ptolemy Macron, the governor of Coele Syria and Phoenicia (see in detail pp. 533ff.). In these circumstances, it was indeed wise to try to 'establish facts'. In any case, the Jews could expect to have a breathing space to organize themselves for the defence of their new territorial gains while the regent was preoccupied in settling things and strengthening his position in Antioch.

The error of I Maccabees in dating the purification of the Temple prior to the king's death does not detract from his reliability in setting the Beth Zur raid before the purification. Living in Judaea and being a contemporary of the events, he must have known the sequence of the internal happenings and found it in the source at his disposal as well. The king's death, however, was an external event which occurred far away. Though the rumour somehow spread through the country, it was not taken by the public mind as the reason for the purification of the Temple. The victory (or rather the retreat) of the enemy troops was a closer and more attractive explanation. The author of I Maccabees, who did not belong to Judas Maccabaeus' close circle, and was not acquainted with his various political and tactical considerations (cf. pp. 238, 335), was not better informed than the general public, and his sources were not instructive either. As in his mind there was no substantive connection between the retreat of Lysias and the purification of the Temple on one side, and the death of Antiochus Epiphanes on the other, he did not remember many years later, in writing his book, the sequence of events. It requires a definite relation of cause and effect between internal and external events to recall the right sequence and exact dating of external occurrences. Thus, for instance, most Israelis (including professional historians), who are well acquainted with the Middle Eastern background and causes of the Suez campaign of 1956, have forgotten the right sequence of events and have no idea about the exact year of the Hungarian Rebellion, although its outburst on 23 October determined the D-Day of the campaign six days later. Finding in the Syrian–Seleucid chronicle he used that Antiochus died in the third month of 149 s.e. (see 6.16, where only the year is mentioned), the author of I Maccabees thought that the purification of the Temple, dated to 148 s.e., occurred earlier. Both dates are correct and refer to the end of 164 b.c. They differ because they are based on two different systems: the date for the purification

Table 3. *Chronology of Lysias' first expedition*

Date	External events	Internal events
End of summer 165 B.C.	Antiochus Epiphanes' expedition to the Upper Satrapies	**Battle of Ammaus**
October 164 B.C.		Lysias sets out on his first expedition to Judaea The siege of Beth Zur The conquest of Beth Zur and preparations for advancing
Kislev 148 S.E. in Babylonia (20 November –19 December 164 B.C.)	The death of Antiochus Epiphanes in Persia	**The raid near Beth Zur** Lysias' return to Antioch
25 Kislev 148 in Judaea (14 January 164 B.C.)		Purification of the Temple

of the Temple (which was an internal event) on the Seleucid–
Babylonian system that was used in Judaea and began in the spring
of 311, and the second on the Seleucid–Macedonian system used in
official chronicles, which began in the autumn of 312. For the same
reason the author of I Maccabees advanced the expeditions to extricate the Jews of Eretz Israel (ch. 5) which took place mainly at
the start of 163 B.C. – that is, according to the author's calculation,
the end of 148 and first months of 149 (by the Seleucid–Babylonian
count) – and put them before the death of Antiochus IV.

I Maccabees 4.26–36

4.26 And whoever of the foreigners escaped upon arrival told
       Lysias all the happenings.

27   And having heard he was alarmed and vexed that not as he
       had wanted had happened to Israel, and what the king com-
       manded him had not been done.

28   And after a year he gathered in arrays sixty thousand picked
       men and five thousand horsemen to fight them.

29   And they went to Edom and camped in Beth Zur and Judah
       met them with ten thousand men.

30   And he saw the strong camp and he prayed and said, Blessed
       be Thou, Saviour of Israel, who curtails the hero's ferocity
       through the hand of Thy servant David and gives the Phili-
       stine camp into the hands of Jonathan son of Saul and his
       armour bearer.

31 Deliver this camp unto your people Israel and let them be ashamed of their troops and their cavalry.

32 Give them dread and dissolve the courage of their strength so they will tremble in their calamity.

33 Fell them with the sword of those who love Thee and all who know Thy name will praise Thee in hymns.

34 And they charged and there fell some five thousand men of Lysias' camp {and they fell from before them}.

35 And when Lysias saw the blow that was to his army and the courage of Judah, and that they were ready either to live or die bravely, he rode to Antioch and hired a numerous army to come back to Judaea.

36 And Judah said to his brothers, Lo, our enemy has been smitten, let us go up and purify the Temple and dedicate it.

COMMENTARY

4.26 *And whoever... escaped, etc.*: The sentence seeks to give the impression that the main part of the enemy army was slain in the preceding battle at Ammaus. But the author is unaware that such an implication does not accord with the number and losses he himself attributed to the enemy in the later campaign.

From the foreigners: The word ἀλλόφυλοι should here be reconstructed according to its literal meanings, 'foreigners', which it has twice in the Septuagint (Is. 2.6, 61.5) and not 'Philistines' (cf. p. 267 above).

Told Lysias all the happenings: Antiochus V, the co-regent, was then only nine years old (see p. 304 below).

28 *And after a year*: After the defeat in the Ammaus campaign. According to the Lucian version, the old Latin translation, and *Antiquitates*, the text should be ἐν τῷ ἐχομένῳ ἐνιαυτῷ (אחר שנה = after a year; see, e.g., the Septuagint for II Sam. 21.1; that is, after a full year), and not ἐν τῷ ἐρχομένῳ ἐνιαυτῷ (בשנה הבאה = the following year; that is, within the next calendar year) as in the uncial manuscripts.[9] The first version seems preferable: the translator of I Maccabees uses the word ἐνιαυτός to denote a full year (3.28, 13.52) and ἔτος for a calendar year (e.g. 1.7,9,10,20,54), as is the practice in Greek.[10] If the Hebrew had been בשנה הבאה (in the next [calendar] year), he would have written ἐν τῷ ἐρχομένῳ ἔτει. Thus Lysias' first expedition began a full year after the battle of Ammaus. The defeat at Ammaus took place in late summer or

---

[9] Contrary to Hanhart 1964: 66.

[10] For the addition of the word ἔτος to the participle of ἔρχομαι cf. the Septuagint for Gen. 41.35.

early autumn of 165 B.C. (see p. 472 below), and Lysias' expedition must therefore have started around October 164.

He gathered in arrays: The source has συνελόχησεν, the literal meaning of which is 'formed units'. The word does not appear again in the Septuagint. In view of the frequent use of the term סדר in the Scroll of the War of the Sons of Light to mean a row of infantry soldiers and a unit of cavalry,[11] it seems likely that the Hebrew was אָסַף לִסְדָרִים.

Sixty thousand picked men and five thousand horsemen: As usual, II Maccabees gives more inflated figures (80,000 foot and 'all the cavalry' or 'thousands of cavalry' – 11.2,4) and even adds eighty elephants (ibid. 4). The figures are valueless in both sources as they exceed the overall table of organization of the elephant- and manpower of the Seleucid army, and the expedition was conducted while most of the army was pinned down in the eastern satrapies (see p. 42 above). The term 'picked' (ἐπίλεκτοι), applied to all the foot soldiers, is also an exaggeration, for only the units of the Royal Guard were officially designated as such. In the time of Antiochus Epiphanes they comprised about a quarter of the infantry and about a third of the cavalry,[12] and it may be assumed that they were with the king in Persia. On the exaggerated and free use of the adjective 'picked' in I Maccabees see also 4.1, 6.35, 9.5, and cf. Daniel 11.15.

29 *And they went to Edom*: Some of the manuscripts have εἰς τὴν Ἰδουμαίαν (= to Idumaea) and some have εἰς τὴν Ἰουδαίαν (= to Judaea). From the substantive point of view both are possible. The first is preferable because it is more likely that a copyist would change Idumaea to Judaea, which occurs frequently in the book, than vice versa.

This time the Seleucid chose to climb up to the central mountain ridge from the south-east through Idumaea-Mt Hebron. Previous attempts to suppress the Revolt had failed because of the difficulty of climbing up to the Judaean Hills from the west. The southern and south-eastern roads were not easy either, but they passed through a region populated by sympathizers. The Idumaeans enabled the Seleucid army to ascend to the plateau unhindered, and presumably provided support in intelligence and logistics. Idumaean help to the Seleucid authorities is mentioned elsewhere in I Maccabees as well (3.41, 4.61, 5.3,65).[13] Even if there was some sympathy for the Jews among the rural Idumaean population because of its antagonism to Hellenistic culture,[14] it certainly did not

[11] See Yadin 1962: 132–3.

[12] See the charts, pp. 34, 117 above. On the permanent table of organization of the infantry Royal Guard see pp. 415–18 below.

[13] See also Abel 1924: 209–11; Plöger 1958: 166–9; Avi-Yonah 1964: 60.

[14] That is the opinion of Rappaport (1980: 269–70).

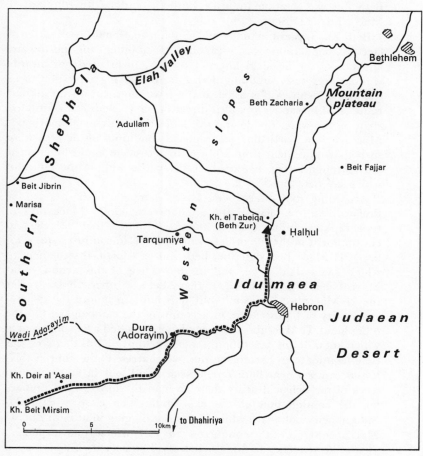

13 Lysias' first expedition

attain dimensions that could imperil the massive invasion by the Seleucid force through Mt Hebron. Lysias may have climbed up to Mt Hebron along the 'Adora road' mentioned in the story of Tryphon's campaign against Jonathan (I Macc. 13.20), that is, one of the roads joining the plateau near Dūra-Adorayim, although there are also other possibilities from the west.

And camped in Beth Zur: The place has been definitely identified as Khirbet el Tabeiqa, a tel at the north-western edge of the village of Ḥalḥul, about a kilometre from the main road. The ancient name has been preserved in the name of the ruin of a Mameluke watchtower near the road, known as Khirbet Beit Zur.[15] Ancient

---

[15] On the identification see Abel 1924: 209.

Beth Zur was then on Judaea's southern border with Idumaea (I
Macc. 4.61, 14.33).

Beth Zur was not actually on the main road, and as a matter of
fact its population was incapable of stopping the northward
advance of the Seleucid forces. However, to proceed northwards
without previously subduing Beth Zur and leaving a garrison there
was risky, for in case of a defeat the Jews could cut off the retreat
route (see Onasander's explicit directive, 11.4). Beth Zur is situated
right on the water divide and overlooks the entire neighbourhood.
Moreover, the particular geographical conditions of the area were
such that movement from Hebron to Jerusalem could be effected
only through a strip two or three kilometres wide in the centre of
which lay Beth Zur.[16]

According to I Maccabees, Lysias camped 'in Beth Zur' (ἐν
Βαιθσούροις); in view of the great precision of I Maccabees in
topographical indications, it may be assumed that he refers to
encampment in the site of Beth Zur itself (cf. in contrast 3.40, 5.27,
6.31). II Maccabees describes Beth Zur as a fortified settlement to
which Lysias laid siege, and in the course of this action Judas
Maccabaeus attacked him (11.5ff.). Abel and other scholars prefer
the II Maccabees version,[17] but it is hard to ignore the general
superiority of I Maccabees in accounts of the campaigns. On the
other hand, II Maccabees seems to have consulted a Seleucid source
which knew of this expedition (see p. 276 above). It is therefore this
time legitimate to harmonize the two sources. Quite conceivably,
Lysias camped near Beth Zur, besieged and took it, and stationed
some of the Seleucid army there to man the fortress and prepare
for the continuation of the expedition. The clash with Judas
Maccabaeus took place while Lysias was digging in at Beth Zur. II
Maccabees ignores the conquest of the fort, which is no surprise in
view of his tendency to disguise defeats. The siege itself was skipped
over in silence by I Maccabees because of the vagueness of the
Jewish source that he used for the expedition (see pp. 134–5 above).

The report in II Maccabees that Beth Zur was a fortified place
during Lysias' first expedition does not contradict other sources or
the archaeological findings. The fortification of the site is mentioned
only after the purification of the Temple (I Macc. 4.61),[18] but that
does not mean it was neglected until that time. Beth Zur was
certainly somehow fortified as it was already a border point of
Judaea and administrative centre in the Persian period (Neh. 3.16)
and, as indicated by the numismatic evidence, in the Ptolemaic
period as well.

[16] On the possibilities of movement in the area see Carmon and Shmueli 1970: 49–50.
[17] Abel 1949: 80–1.
[18] Despite the syntactic difficulty, there is no doubt that the first part of the verse also refers
to Beth Zur.

As to finds on the site, the remains of three forts have been discovered at Beth Zur, the first two of mixed Hellenistic–Oriental style, and the last purely Hellenistic. The archaeologists who excavated the hill sought to date the forts to various times in the Hellenistic period.[19] Thus, for example, Sellers attributes the three fortresses to Judas Maccabaeus, Bacchides and Simeon the Hasmonaean, while Funk and Albright ascribe the first to the Persian or the Ptolemaic period, the second to Judas Maccabaeus, and the third to Bacchides. Someone even assigns one of the forts to Lysias. The combination of the sources and the archaeological finds, however, points to another set of possibilities: the first fort was built by the authorities during the Ptolemaic or Seleucid period, abandoned by the local garrison and then taken over by a Jewish force when Judas Maccabaeus grew stronger. That fort was destroyed by Lysias in the course of his first expedition. The second fort was constructed on the initiative of Judas Maccabaeus (I Macc. 4.61), and the third by his brother Simeon (I Macc. 14.33). Lysias and Bacchides, to whom the construction of one of the Beth Zur forts has been attributed, only strengthened and improved the existing structure: during his second expedition, Lysias entered Beth Zur without having to breach its wall after the inhabitants surrendered because of starvation, and left a garrison in it (I Macc. 6.49–50). The list of Bacchides' forts has Beth Zur in the second group together with the Jerusalem *akra* and Gezer (I Macc. 9.52), that is, existing forts that were merely renovated, in contrast to the first group which included new forts (ibid. 50). The purely Hellenistic character of the third Beth Zur fort is the result of the profound influence of the Hellenistic art of fortification (and poliorcetics – I Macc. 13.43) in Simeon's time.

And Judah met them with ten thousand men: This figure is the highest the sources ever attribute to Judas Maccabaeus' army in a single engagement. Applied to a battle joined before the purification of the Temple, this estimate alone obliges us to assume that after the dramatic turning-point at Antiochus Epiphanes' death and the purification of the Temple, the numerical strength of the Jewish forces was considerably greater than the modest numbers (up to 3,000 men) cited by the sources for the later battles with the central authorities.

30 *And he prayed and said, etc.*: There is a certain resemblance between the structure and content of this address and that of the Priest 'Anointed for Battle' (משוח מלחמה) reported in the Mishnah: 'They come with the strength of flesh and blood, and ye come with the strength of the Almighty; the Philistines came in the strength of

[19] Sellers 1933: 11; Albright 1932: 227; Funk 1958: 11; id. 'Beth Zur', in *Encyclopaedia of Archaeological Excavation in the Holy Land* (Jerusalem, 1970) pp. 62–3 (Hebrew).

Goliath (and) what was his end? In the end he fell by the
sword...but not so are ye', etc. (Sotah 8.1). The resemblance arises
because both are sermonic paraphrases based on Deuteronomy
20.3–4, and because the victory over Goliath was often evoked as an
example and model of the divine hand guiding the wars of Israel.
Nothing about the antiquity of the mishnaic regulations on war can
be concluded from the similarity (see pp. 496ff. below), or about the
authenticity of the address as a whole. The length of the oration, out
of all proportion to the amount of information given on the battle
itself, suggests that it is merely the product of the author's
imagination.

*Blessed be Thou...who curtails the hero's ferocity through the hand of Thy
servant David*: A number of scholars have sought to support the
authenticity of the exhortation by claiming that the propinquity of
Beth Zur to the Elah Valley reminded Judas Maccabaeus of the
combat between David and Goliath. But the Elah Valley is not
visible from Beth Zur, and the Goliath story is not mentioned in the
oration at Ammaus which is closer to the entrance to that valley,
near Azekah, than Beth Zur is. The David and Goliath story
already inspired the author in his imaginary description of the battle
with Apollonius (3.10–13) which took place in a completely
different area.

And gives the Philistine camp into the hands of Jonathan: The mention of
the foray of Jonathan and his armour bearer into the Philistine
camp (I Macc. 4.30; cf. I Sam. 14.1–16) may seem an indication of
the true nature of that battle as a small-scale raid and assault. But
it is more likely that, just as in the other battle orations he presents,
the author's goal was to stress the enemy's numerical advantage,
and the reference to Jonathan's foray in connection with this episode
is merely coincidental.

34 *And they charged*: Behind the phrase συνέβαλλον ἀλλήλοις (= they
clashed with one another) stands the Hebrew verb *wa-yitgārū* (= and
they charged, clashed; see e.g. Deut. 2.9; Dan. 11.10,25 and the
Septuagint to II Chron. 25.19). The word ἀλλήλοις (= each other)
is the translator's clarifying addition. It appears several times in the
Septuagint, but never represents a word figuring in the Hebrew
source. The Greek translator thought the reference was to a frontal
clash, and therefore added ἀλλήλοις. The author of I Maccabees
may have initially intended to report only the raid of the Jews
against the enemy camp, and the grammatical subject of *wa-yitgārū*
is just the Jewish soldiers previously mentioned (verse 29), and not
the two sides (contrary to 7.43). As suggested above, the action was
probably a 'hit and run' raid against the Seleucid army encamped
at Beth Zur (p. 134). II Maccabees, on the other hand, elaborates on
the course of the confrontation. This time divine intervention plays
a decisive role not in direct fighting but in inspiring and boosting the

morale of the Jewish combatants (11.8–10; cf. Pausanias 10.23.2; Justin 24.8.3, and see p. 180 n. 92 above).

And there fell some five thousand men: The number of losses attributed to the enemy is inflated proportionately to the inflated numbers cited for the force as a whole (cf. the 3,000 dead out of 47,000 soldiers in the battle of Ammaus). So many dead would certainly have led to a panic-stricken flight, but there is no hint of a withdrawal of that nature. The estimates in II Maccabees are even more exaggerated – 11,000 infantry and 1,600 cavalry (11.11).

Of Lysias' camp: In line with our conception of the author's intentions and the course and circumstances of the clash, the word παρεμβολή in this context (as well as in verses 30 and 31), should be understood in its literal meaning as 'camp' (cf. 3.41,57,4.2,4,5, 7) and not 'army' (cf. I Macc. 3.3,15,17).

{*And they fell from before them*}: This sentence, found in most manuscripts, is superfluous and appears to be a gloss which a scribe inserted in order to emphasize the victory more strongly.

35 *And when Lysias saw the blow that was to his army*: The word τροπή, whose literal meaning is 'turning point', 'flight', and the like, is here to be translated as 'blow'. It appears three times in the Septuagint, rendering מַכָּה (= blow), אֵיד (= calamity), and חֲלוּשָׁה (= weakness). In the Greek version of Sirach (45.23), the word appears for the poetical פֶּרֶץ (= breach, misfortune) of the Hebrew original (45.42). Elsewhere in I Maccabees τροπή figures evidently in the meaning of 'blow' (5.61). In any case, the rest of the verse describing the return to Antioch as a planned, orderly operation undertaken in a calculated desire to prevent losses and accomplish the task more easily a short time later (and not as a hasty disorganized flight) is enough to show that it was not a military defeat that led to Lysias' retreat. The chronological analysis suggests that Lysias learned of the death in Persia of Antiochus Epiphanes and therefore hurried to Antioch to take over the reins of leadership as regent for Antiochus V, the dead king's young son (see pp. 279–81 above).

II Maccabees describes a panic-stricken flight: 'And most of them wounded, were saved naked, and Lysias himself was saved, fleeing in a shameful manner' (11.12). In view of the imaginary character of the battle description in that source, the statement is clearly valueless.

And that they were ready either to live or die bravely: This sentence may be an interpolation, as its Hellenistic style is distinctly different from the biblical style predominating in I Maccabees.[20] For the general conception, which is not necessarily non-Jewish, cf. 6.44, 9.10.[21]

[20] See Tcherikover 1961a: 486 n. 38, in the name of M. Schwabe.
[21] Against Zeitlin 1950: 104–5.

He rode to Antioch and hired a numerous army to come back to Judaea: This
is a reference to Lysias' second expedition, fifteen months later,
which was preceded by an extensive recruitment drive (I Macc.
6.29).[22] In the period immediately after the withdrawal from Beth
Zur, however, Lysias was preoccupied with internal problems more
serious than the Revolt in Judaea.

*And Judah said...Lo, our enemy was smitten, let us go up and purify the
Temple*: The verse implies that the Temple was purified immediately
after Lysias' withdrawal from Beth Zur and as a result of it.
However, the main reason for the purification of the Temple at that
time was the death of Antiochus Epiphanes (see pp. 280–1 above).

In this context, it must be added that the event mentioned in the
Scroll of Fasting on 14 Sivan (about June) – 'Migdal Zur was
captured' – is not connected with Judas Maccabaeus' victory over
Lysias as some believe. The event to be celebrated by then was
Lysias' departure from the country, which was much more
important than the reoccupation of Beth Zur. The reference is to its
capture by Simeon the Hasmonaean in 144 B.C., a while before
Jonathan's murder (see I Macc. 11.65–6, 14.33).[23] There is no basis
for reading 'Šūr Tower' and identifying it with the Šaršōn-Straton
Tower, the old Phoenician name of Caesarea Maritima.[24]

[22] See also Abel 1923: 511; Bévenot 1931: 75.

[23] See also Derenbourg 1867: 443; Schlatter 1891: 26; Lichtenstein 1931–2: 281ff., and
many others.

[24] See the objections to this view in Graetz 1888: 3(2).565, no. 7. Examination of the MSS
also indicates that the place should be identified with Beth Zur; see pp. 565–6 below.

13

Lysias' second expedition and the battle of Beth Zacharia

In the winter of 164 B.C., after the death of Antiochus Epiphanes and Lysias' retreat from Beth Zur, Judas Maccabaeus gained control of Jerusalem. The Temple was purified and the Hasmonaean brothers were now able to help the Jews scattered outside the Judaean Hills region, who were being pressed by their neighbours, the Idumaeans, the Samaritans and the Hellenized settlements in Transjordania and the coastal plain (I Macc. 5). The Seleucid crown passed to Antiochus V Eupator, son of Antiochus Epiphanes, who was just nine years old. The real power at Antioch, however, was wielded by the regent Lysias. That situation made the stability and continuity of the dynasty doubtful, for it was clear that Lysias aspired to the throne. Judas Maccabaeus' great successes in the expeditions against the neighbours, and the development of his military power on the one hand, and on the other the internal crisis in the Seleucid kingdom, encouraged the Jews to lay siege to the Jerusalem citadel, some time around April 162 B.C. (see the chronological discussion in Appendix K, pp. 543ff.). That step, designed to eradicate the last real symbol of Seleucid power in Judaea, immediately elicited a strong Seleucid reaction, surpassing in quantity and quality all the previous battles against the Hasmonaean brothers.

The Seleucid army invaded the country from the south-west, through Mt Hebron, as had Lysias on his first expedition. They laid siege to Beth Zur, and when it surrendered they proceeded northward toward Jerusalem. Judas Maccabaeus attempted to block them at Beth Zacharia at the end of May 162, but was roundly beaten in the battle there in which the Seleucid heavy formations and elephants distinguished themselves. The Seleucids continued on their way north and besieged the remaining rebels who had gathered in the Temple. Yet once again they were unable to destroy the rebels. Domestic events made it necessary to stop the operation and

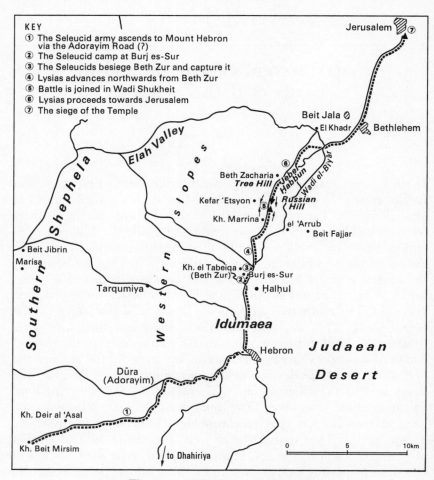

KEY
① The Seleucid army ascends to Mount Hebron via the Adorayim Road (?)
② The Seleucid camp at Burj es-Sur
③ The Seleucids besiege Beth Zur and capture it
④ Lysias advances northwards from Beth Zur
⑤ Battle is joined in Wadi Shukheit
⑥ Lysias proceeds towards Jerusalem
⑦ The siege of the Temple

14 The course of Lysias' second expedition

hurry the army to Antioch some time at the end of June or July of that year.

The main source for the reconstruction of the expedition and battle is I Maccabees (6.28–47). The description abounds in information on the size of the Seleucid army, the composition of the participating units, its deployment and advance under changing conditions of terrain, exact weaponry employed, the topographical structure of the battlefield, and various phases of the battle. The author provides many more details on the enemy army than in descriptions of earlier battles, because this time the appearance and external effect of the enemy had a vast impact on the fighting spirit of the Jewish troops and on the outcome of the battle. The elephants attracted special attention both because of their important role as a deterrent force, and because of their picturesqueness; mention is made of their location in the 'formations', of how they were trained and urged into battle, of the 'towers' and soldiers on their backs, and even of unimportant technical accessories like the metal sheathing of the wooden 'towers' and the straps to fasten them. The information in the main accords perfectly with other data we have on the Seleucid army and on the structure of the battlefield and the special conditions prevailing on it at the season and time of day of the invasion. Only the placement and special composition of the units deployed around the elephants (the 'formations') are not known from the history of the Seleucid army, but their credibility should not be doubted for they constitute an adaptation of the conventional Hellenistic deployment to the special nature of the terrain (see pp. 126–8 above). The uniqueness of the formation here eliminates the possibility that the author based his text on literary descriptions and theoretical treatises on military organizational and combat methods common in the Hellenistic period. As already noted, the description of the deployment of the Seleucid army while moving through the broad valley and in the narrow pass, of the rising sun and its effect on the impression made by the shields just before the army entered the defile, and the reference to the noise of the advancing enemy army only in the second stage when it entered the pass and altered its formation, all indicate that the author was an eye-witness to this battle (see pp. 159–60 above).

Despite the great detail and accuracy, the report is not complete. Aspiring to explain the Jewish defeat, the author omits various details on the composition, numerical strength and actions of the Jewish army, and exaggerates more than usual in his estimate of enemy numbers. He even glosses over the Jewish defeat in discreet wording. On the other hand, he omits the pre-combat oration he usually inserts, perhaps because this time it was not needed for the purpose of indicating the enemy's quantitative and qualitative superiority, which was obvious from the figures for the Seleucid army and the description of its deployment and advance in the field.

II Maccabees reports in detail the foe's advance to the Judaean Hills and the siege of Beth Zur which preceded the expedition to Beth Zacharia. The author also prefaces the account of the siege with a story of a successful night assault made by Judas Maccabaeus and his men, whom he describes as encamped at Modein, on the Seleucid

camp in the vicinity (13.14–17). If we ignore the mention of Modein
which Jason of Cyrene, who was unfamiliar with the locality, borrowed from the story on the start of the Revolt (see pp. 197–8 above),
it is not impossible that the assault story is a reflection, exaggerated
as it may be, of a certain raid on the Seleucid camp which occurred
before the start of the siege of Beth Zur or in the midst of it, and the
reference to the 'first (leading) elephant' in this episode (verse 15) is
a kind of muffled echo of the decisive role of the elephants in the Beth
Zacharia battle and of the death of Eleazar in the struggle with the
tallest and most impressive elephant, both of which were deleted by
the author (or the epitomist) in line with his efforts to efface the
Jewish defeat (see below). The great value of the elephants in emphasizing the enemy's power led him to retain their participation in
the expedition by inserting them in one of the early phases.[1]

The account of the siege of Beth Zur includes particulars whose
credibility there is no reason to question, noteworthy among them
being the episode of the Jewish traitor, Rhodocus (13.18–22a). In
contrast the rest of the expedition is described with extreme brevity
and confusion. The name Beth Zacharia does not appear, and
nothing is said about the siege of the Temple. The author compresses the decisive clash into a few words: 'And he assaulted the men
of Judah and was defeated' (13.22b). The sentence may refer to the
battle of Beth Zacharia with the defeat turned into a victory by the
author, but it may allude to the siege of the Temple after the defeat,
and the judgement 'and was defeated' is only an exaggeration of
Lysias' lack of success in breaking through to the besieged Temple.
If we accept the latter alternative, this would mean that the author
omitted the story of the battle of Beth Zacharia in order not to
mention the serious setback. Be that as it may, it is clear that he knew

[1] Bunge (1971:253) and Habicht (1976a:268) conclude from the absence in the description
of the nocturnal assault at Modein (II Macc. 13.14–17) of any reference to Eleazar and the
status of Modein as the cradle of the Revolt that Jason of Cyrene was hostile to the Hasmonaeans. But the very mention of Modein, being a pure invention, clearly indicates a special
attitude on the part of the author to places and events connected with the Hasmonaean family.
Moreover, the reference to the 'leading elephant' is inserted in a totally false context. If the
author had any special interest in consigning Eleazar to oblivion he would certainly have
refrained from inventing the participation of the elephant, the object of Eleazar's heroic deed,
in the Modein episode. Moreover, II Maccabees ascribes a ritual function to Eleazar in the
battle of Ammaus (8.23), while in I Maccabees Eleazar is mentioned only in the description
of the battle of Beth Zacharia. Finally, an examination of the passage in II Maccabees shows
that it is an abridgement, so that it is not impossible that Eleazar was mentioned in Jason of
Cyrene's original book in connection with Modein. On the character of the passage as an
abridgement see Büchler 1906:292ff., and cf. p. 197 above. The failure to mention Eleazar in
connection with the main confrontation derives from the desire to slur over the defeat. For that
reason II Maccabees (at least in its present form) devotes no more than half a verse to the
confrontation.

the truth, for he explains Lysias' withdrawal as motivated by fear that Philippus might gain control of the kingdom and not as the result of a military defeat. Furthermore, II Maccabees is also aware of Lysias' stay in Jerusalem, though he distorts the circumstances, saying 'and he gave in and swore and agreed to all the just (demands) and he brought a sacrifice, and he honoured the Temple and behaved generously in regard to the place' (13.23). In view of the abundant information on the early stages, there is no doubt that the original description of the battle in Jason of Cyrene's book was much more detailed, although it is hard to assume that the author was more accurate than the epitomist in reporting the progress and outcome of the battle.

Josephus' version in *Bellum Judaicum* (1.41–6) contains valuable facts and figures. The passage is part of the summary of the persecutions and Revolt which is extremely compressed and confused. However, in contrast to most of the summary, the passage describing the battle of Beth Zacharia is quite detailed and contains credible information which is missing from I Maccabees or contradicts it: the estimate of Seleucid military strength (para. 41) is not at all inflated, and more or less fits in with the recruitment possibilities then available to the court at Antioch (see pp. 42–3 above);[2] the sequence of events (para. 41) is logical (see p. 308 below); the information (proffered in this source only) on Judas Maccabaeus' flight to Gophnitikē–Gophna (para. 45), the district north of Jerusalem, after the battle, seems basically sound (see p. 337 below); the battle site was set in a 'narrow pass' (para. 41), a conclusion in fact inferable from a careful perusal of I Maccabees (6.40) but not explicitly stated there; there is mention of a Jewish 'phalanx' taking part in the battle (para. 45), referring to heavy or 'semi-heavy' infantry, which is not hinted at in any battle in the Books of Maccabees, but is deducible if the course of the battle of Elasa is carefully analysed (see pp. 72–6 above). Most of the additions and modifications cannot be explained as the interpretations of Josephus (or the source at his disposal) respecting I Maccabees; their rationality and precision lead to the conclusion that this version was not written on the basis of the author's memory, but was directly or indirectly derived from another source with quite reliable information. It cannot be denied that the Josephus version in *Bellum Judaicum* has glaring defects, such as the failure to mention Lysias' leading role in the expedition and battle, the absence of any intimation that the expedition took place

---

[2] On the exaggerated number of the elephants and its emendation see p. 307 below re verse 30.

immediately after a Sabbatical year (which affected its progress and outcome), and especially the attribution of the retreat of Antiochus Eupator from Jerusalem to a shortage of supplies, without any indication that it was necessary to direct the army against Philippus who was menacing Antioch (46); all these defects, however, can be ascribed to the general character of the passage as a summary. The distinctly Hellenistic features of the Eleazar episode – such as the view of his death as an 'omen' (κληδών) of the outcome of the battle (45), the help of Tyche extended to the royal troops (45),[3] and the presentation of the Jews as ἐπιχώριοι ('natives', 1.38,48) – prove that the source underlying the description in *Bellum Judaicum* was not Jewish. In the general discussion on the sources, we came to the conclusion that in regard to the battle of Beth Zacharia Josephus made direct use of Nicolaus of Damascus. Nicolaus in turn relied on I Maccabees and on some Seleucid source, while in relation to the Eleazar episode, on I Maccabees alone (see pp. 188–90 above).

The Josephus version of the Beth Zacharia battle in *Antiquitates* (12.362–81) is as usual a paraphrase of I Maccabees. Here and there, however, it adds valuable details, especially in regard to the deployment of the Seleucid army as it entered the pass (ibid. 371; see p. 330 below). A number of these additions can be attributed to Josephus' familiarity with the topography of southern Judaea and the information he had on Hellenistic warfare methods, as well as to his understanding of military notions. By the same token, it is conceivable that when attempting to make some details in I Maccabees clearer, he recalled a number of points on the battle from Nicolaus, the source he had used twenty years before while writing *Bellum Judaicum*, or even obtained help directly from his own earlier work (see also pp. 191–2 above).

I Maccabees 6.18–63

6.18   And the people from the Akra were besieging Israel around
        the Temple and continually seeking evils and backing for the
        Gentiles.

---

[3] For the various connotations of Tyche in Hellenistic literature, especially in Polybius, see Roveri 1954: 275–93; Walbank 1957–79: 1.16–25; id. 1980: 42–3,56–7. On Tyche in Josephus' works see Brüne 1913: 187–92; Michel and Bauernfeind 1962: 2(2).212–14, and further bibliography on p. 212; Lindner 1972: 42–8,85–94, esp. 89–94. In the context of the Hasmonaean–Seleucid confrontation (in contrast to the struggle against the Romans), the reference in Josephus to Tyche's intervention in favour of the Hellenistic side can be regarded as definite evidence for a Gentile source.

19   And Judah thought to annihilate them and called on the whole people to besiege them.

20   And they gathered together and besieged them in the year fifty and a hundred and made against them battering rams and (artillery) devices.

21   And some of them went out of the siege and several of the sinners of Israel cleaved unto them.

22   And they went to the king and said, Till when will you not do justice and avenge our brothers?

23   We wished to serve your father and follow his commands and comply with his laws.

24   {and the children of our people besieged it because of that} and they disclaimed us and even killed those of us they found and despoiled our land allotments.

25   And not only against us did they raise a hand, but also at your entire border.

26   And here they are camping today around the Akra in Jerusalem in order to capture it, and they fortified the Temple and Beth Zur.

27   And if you do not swiftly anticipate them they will do bigger things than those and you will not be able to stop them.

28   And the king raged upon hearing, and he gathered all his friends, the officers of his army and those in charge of the mounted (force).

29   And from other kingdoms and from islands of the sea mercenary armies came to him.

30   And the number of his armies was a hundred thousand foot and twenty thousand horsemen and elephants thirty-two trained for war.

31   And they went through Edom and camped around Beth Zur and they fought many days and made devices, and they went out and burned them in fire and they fought bravely.

32   And Judah moved from the Akra and camped at Beth Zacharia opposite the king's camp.

33   And the king rose early in the morning and in his fury moved the camp on the Beth Zacharia road and the armies armed for battle and blew the trumpets.

34   And the elephants they [saturated] (with) blood of grape and berries to rouse them for the war.

35   And they divided the beasts into the formations and with each elephant they positioned a thousand men armoured in chain and bronze helmets on their heads and five hundred picked horse were prepared for each beast.

36   These were beforehand in the place where the beast was, and
      wherever it went they went together not separating from it.

37   And wooden towers on them strong and covered on each beast
      strapped to it with [thongs] and on each one men of valour
      [four] fighting on them and an Indian to it.

38   And the rest of the horsemen they positioned on either side of
      the camp frightening and cover[ing] the formations.

39   And as the sun rose on the shields of gold and bronze the
      mountains glittered from them and blazed like torches of
      fire.

40   And a part of the king's camp spread out on the high moun-
      tains and many in the depression and they walked confid-
      ently and in order.

41   And all trembled who heard the sound of their throng and the
      strides of the throng and the clank of the weapons for the
      camp was very large and heavy.

42   And Judah and his camp approached the battle and of the
      king's camp six hundred men fell.

43   And Eleazar 'Eran saw one of the beasts armoured in royal
      armour and it was taller than all the beasts and it was seen
      that the king was on it.

44   And he gave his life to save his people and to make an eternal
      name for himself.

45   And he ran toward it courageously into the formation and he
      killed to the right and to the left and they parted from him
      there and there.

46   And he came under the elephant and struck it ⟨with a sword⟩
      and killed it and it fell down on him and he died there.

47   And they saw the might of the kingdom and the fury of the
      armies and they verged away from them.

48   And the men from the king's camp went up toward them to
      Jerusalem, and the king camped in Judaea and at Mount
      Zion.

49   And he made peace with the people of Beth Zur and they left
      the town for there was no bread there for them to (stay)
      enclosed in it for there was Sabbath for the country.

50   And the king captured Beth Zur and he put a garrison there
      to guard it.

51   And he camped around the Temple many days and he set
      battering rams there and (artillery) devices {and} flame-
      throwers and stone-throwers and scorpions to shoot arrows
      and projectiles.

52   And they also made devices against their devices and they fought many days.

53   And there was no food in the Temple because of the seventh {year} and those who fled to Judaea from the Gentiles ate the rest of the repository.

54   And very few remained in the Temple for hunger waxed upon them and they scattered each man to his place.

55   And Lysias heard that Philippus whom King Antiochus while alive charged to raise Antiochus his son to rule

56   Had returned from Persia and Media, and the armies that went with the king with him, and that he sought to inherit the affairs.

57   And he hurried and dissembled to return and he said to the king and to the army officers and to the people, We are (more) tired from day to day and we have little bread and the place we are camped around is strong and the affairs of the kingdom are on us.

58   And now let us give (our) right (hand) to those people and make peace with them and with their whole nation.

59   And now let us sanction them to follow their laws as in the beginning for only because of their laws which we broke did they rage and do all these (things).

60   And the word seemed good to the king and the officers and they sent to them to conciliate and they accepted.

61   And the king vowed to them and the officers and afterwards they left the sanctuary.

62   And the king came to Mount Zion and saw the citadel of the place and he retracted the oath he swore, and he commanded and destroyed the wall around.

63   And he moved hastily and returned to Antioch and found Philippus governing the city, and he fought him and took the city by might.

COMMENTARY

6.18 *And the people from the Akra*: The Jerusalem citadel was manned primarily by the Seleucid garrison, as was the case in the period preceding the persecutions. On the Seleucid garrison in the Akra later on see I Macc. 9.52, 10.6–9, 11.41, 14.36.

Were besieging Israel around the Temple: In view of Judas Maccabaeus' dominion in Jerusalem and of the general situation in Judaea and Jerusalem, there is no doubt that the meaning is not a real siege, but annoyances such as raids and artillery fire from the citadel on people approaching the Temple area and gathering there. The Temple, which was about 350 m away from the Akra, was within range of artillery placed in the fortress (see p. 461 below). The author chose the word 'besieging' under the influence of the mention of Judas Maccabaeus' siege in the following verses which likewise involved artillery. The intention seems to be to indicate that Judas Maccabaeus' action was preceded by some provocation of similar nature.

Continually seeking evils and backing for the Gentiles: The second part of the sentence indicates that the Hellenized Jews, who found refuge in the Akra (see re verse 21), participated in the harassment of the Temple.

19 *And Judah... called on the whole people to besiege them*: Judas Maccabaeus had been careful not to clash with the citadel people and left them a 'supply corridor' in order to avert a massive military reaction on the part of the central authorities (see p. 459 below). At this point, however, the Jewish commander decided to try to subdue the citadel, on the assumption that Lysias, who was preoccupied with establishing his position at Antioch and with domestic mopping up, would not again get involved in a military expedition to the Judaean Hills.

20 *In the year fifty and a hundred*: The date applies to an event connected with the Jews and should therefore be calculated according to the Babylonian variation of the Seleucid calendar which began in April 311. The year 150 thus started in April 162 B.C. and ended in March 161 B.C. As suggested in Appendix K (p. 545 below), the siege of the Akra began immediately in early spring of that year, and perhaps even before that.

And they...made against them: The reference is to the construction of battering rams and the assembly of the artillery devices which used to be brought to the siege site dismantled (cf. I Macc. 6.52, 9.64, 13.43).

Battering rams: The Greek is *belostaseis* (see also I Macc. 6.51), denoting platforms of compacted earth or of stone and the like upon which the artillery machines were set (Latin: *ballistarium*). The Septuagint has the word in the plural to translate *dayēq* (Ezek. 17.17, 21.27, 26.8), and that was the view of various scholars who reconstructed the Hebrew text of this verse.[4] *dayēq* in Hebrew means a peripheral wall built by besiegers in order to prevent help and supplies from going in, and people from coming out, like the Roman *circumvallum*. This is seen in II Kings 25.1 and Jeremiah 52.4 (where the Septuagint translation rightly has *periteikhos*). However, the

---

[4] On *belostaseis* see Droysen 1889: 202 n. 3; Garlan 1974: 165,350; and see Diodorus 20.85.4; Polybius 9.41.8; Phil. Byz. *mēkhanikē syntaxis* 81.19 (A.21a). For the reconstruction *dayēq* see Michaelis 1778: 131–2; Grimm 1853: 96; Cahana 1957: 1.126; Goldstein 1976: 319.

word *belostaseis* appears in the account of Lysias' siege of the Temple (verse 51) with the verb καὶ ἔστησεν (וַיַּעֲמֵד = and he set), which in biblical Hebrew could not mean building or a similar operation. Moreover, the time at Lysias' disposal was not enough for constructing a peripheral wall. The reconstruction should be *kārīm*: elsewhere in the Septuagint the word *kārīm* is translated as *belostaseis*, although the Hebrew *dayēq* appears in the same verse (Ezek. 4.2). *kārīm* is known in the Bible in a military context with the meaning of battering rams (see also Ezek. 21.27; for this word as a synonym of *'ēlīm* (= battering rams), Deut. 32.14; Ezek. 39.18). It seems that because of the other meanings of the word ('saddle' in Gen. 31.34; 'gentle hills' in Isaiah 30.23 and Psalms 65.14; and 'cushion' in the Mishnah), the word in the days of the Second Temple was also applied to artillery platforms, hence the translation *belostaseis*. However, as far as the meaning of the Hebrew word in our verse is concerned, the verb וַיַּעֲמֵד (= he set) which preceded it in verse 51 is again decisive and indicates that *kārīm* refers to battering rams and not to mounds. The mention of mounds is also strange in that context which does not specify the artillery devices.

And (artillery) devices: The Greek is *mēkhanai*, which refers both to artillery machines and complicated poliorcetic devices, The original was *ḥiśvōnōt*, which in the Bible refers to artillery pieces (see p. 319 below). This is what should be understood here also for it is hardly possible that the Jews had at their disposal at this stage any sort of siege towers. It is typical of the author that he does not name the kinds of artillery machines at the disposal of the Jews while providing great detail on the enemy artillery (6.51).

In Hellenistic warfare, artillery devices were generally used only in siege operations. Because of the limited number of these devices, their slow firing speed, inaccuracy and relatively short range, the scales could not be quickly tipped through their utilization (cf. 6.51–2) and the besiegers often had recourse to slow methods such as starvation (see 12.36, 13.49–50), the penetration of secret exits, the breaching of the walls with battering rams or undermining them by tunnels, etc. As a result the citadel people were able to alert Lysias in time. For the conclusion inferable from this verse in regard to the evaluation of the munitions and equipment of the Jewish army see pp. 81, 88–9 above.

21 *And some of them went out of the siege and several of the sinners of Israel cleaved unto them*: The Hellenizers found refuge in the Akra as can also be inferred from the wording of the complaint said to have been delivered in Antioch (verses 22–7, esp. 23–4).

22 *And they went to the king and said*: According to II Maccabees the delegation of the citadel people to Antioch was headed by Menelaus, who even seems to have participated in Lysias'

expedition to Judaea after which he was put to death at Beroea
(13.3–8; for the correct chronology and the exact circumstances of
Menelaus' execution see *Ant.* 12.383–5, and p. 541 n. 80 below). The
failure of I Maccabees to mention Menelaus in the context of the
delegation and the expedition is rightly ascribed to the disregard of
the activity and functions of the whole Toubias family in the events
preceding the religious persecutions. This disregard has been
explained by a number of scholars through the 'dynastic bias' they
attribute to the author of I Maccabees, contending that he avoided
reporting the events in order not to have to mention the firm stand
of Onias III against Hellenization, which might have dimmed the
glory of the Hasmonaeans as the only priestly family to hold out and
initiate the resistance movement, and even strengthened the claims
of the house of Onias to the high priesthood and represented the
Hasmonaeans as usurpers.[5] All this, however, does not justify the
consistent disregard of Menelaus' activity before the promulgation
of the decrees and certainly not at later stages. Menelaus could have
been touched on without a reference to Onias, for his involvement
actually began three years after Onias was relieved of the high
priesthood. The presentation of the position of Onias' brother Jason
could have contributed more to the 'dynastic bias' noted than the
deletion of Onias, and that could have been done without
mentioning Onias' name at all. Nor are there any signs of a real
power struggle between the Hasmonaeans and the House of Onias
on the question of the right to the high priesthood. It consequently looks as if the omission of any mention of domestic
developments in Jerusalem around the time of the religious
persecutions derives from the tendency of the author of I Maccabees
to represent the persecutions as primarily a confrontation between
Jews and Gentiles. The leading Hellenizers remain anonymous,
their activities are presented in a very general and vague way,
obvious negative manifestations in the Jewish people are glossed
over, all in order not to highlight the decisive role of the Jews in the
escalation of events that preceded the religious persecutions.[6] The
manner of presenting matters suited practical needs when the book
was written, in the early days of the Hasmonaean State. At that time
the struggle was against the Seleucid involvement in the country
and against the Gentile elements there, and not within the Jewish
people. National unity, the minimization of internal differences and
the rallying of all forces was essential in order to prepare for the
coming undertakings, especially the anticipated conquests and

[5] Niese 1900: 45; Momigliano 1930: 108–9; Tcherikover 1961a: 190; id. 1961b: 169; and
many others.
[6] This assumption is phrased somewhat differently by Pfeifer (1949: 496), who stresses the
theological conception of the author of I Maccabees; see also Bickerman (1937: 33), who
explains the deletion in the literary context.

territorial expansion. The transition to the framework of an orderly
state also required the participation of former Hellenizers in the
political and military administration.[7] It should be recalled that at
the height of the Revolt the Jewish army included soldiers from the
military settlements in Transjordania founded by the Toubias
family (see pp. 82–4 above). Although these were probably
supporters of Hyrcanus, the son of Joseph son of Toubias, the rival
of the other pro-Seleucid brothers, the mention of the important role
of the sons of Toubias in hastening the religious persecutions would
have reflected ill also on the settlers whose names were connected
with the same family. In any case, Hyrcanus son of Toubias himself
was one of the leading figures in the Hellenization of the country. In
contrast, there is no disregard of the activities of the high priest
Alcimus (I Macc. 7.5ff.), as they were unrelated to the actual
promulgation of the decrees, and less serious than his predecessors',
being based mainly on different political tactics from those of the
rebels, and not on a different far-reaching revolutionary religious–
cultural conception, and also because he was probably not a
member of a rich and influential Hellenized family.

Till when will you not do justice and avenge our brothers, etc.: The exact
words of the complaint by the citadel people, which were delivered
in Antioch, could not be known to the author. Verses 22–6 are thus
not an authentic quote but a reasonable summary of the situation of
the opposing parties.

24 {*And the children of our people besieged it because of that*}: This sentence is
out of place, and indeed is missing in the Alexandrian manuscript.
It may be only an alternative version of verse 26 relating the siege
of the citadel ('And here they are camping today around the
Akra'), or it may be a marginal interpretative note to verse 24,
which was interpolated in the text by one of the copyists.[8]

And despoiled our land allotments: κληρονομίαι. The reconstruction
should not be ורכושנו (= and our property) as Cahana has it
(p. 127). The word is used in the Septuagint to translate נחלה
(land allotment; cf. also I Macc. 2.56, 15.33,34). The Hellenizers'
estates were plundered not only because they were actually
abandoned while their owners found refuge in the citadel, but also

---

[7] On the possibility that even Eupolemus, Judas Maccabaeus' envoy to Rome, was an
adherent of Jason's see Wacholder 1974: 15,222. That suggestion does not seem acceptable,
however, in view of the favourable mention of Eupolemus in II Macc. 4.11 in a passage
censuring Jason most severely, and in the verse noting the contrast between Jason's despicable
actions and the great contribution made by Eupolemus' father, Johanan (and Eupolemus
himself), to safeguarding and reconfirming the Jews' right to live according to their ancestral
laws. On Hellenizers in the Hasmonaean administration at its inception see especially the
status and personality of Ptolemy son of Aboubus, early in Simeon's reign, according to I
Macc. 16.11–12; *Ant.* 13.228–35. See also p. 88 n. 54 above on the Greek names of the envoys
despatched by Jonathan and Simeon to foreign countries (I Macc. 12.16, 14.22,24, 15.15), and
of Rhodocus who betrayed the besieged at Beth Zur (II Macc. 13.21).

[8] For the last possibility see Goldstein 1976: 319.

because some of those lands had been confiscated by the Seleucid authorities and allotted to the Hellenizers (Dan. 11.39).[9]

25 *And not only against us did they raise a hand, but also at your entire border*: The Greek manuscripts have ἐπὶ πάντα τὰ ὅρια αὐτῶν (= at their entire border). Cahana's and Goldstein's proposal 'your...border', following the Latin translation,[10] is acceptable, for the Jews conducted actions beyond the boundary of Judaea after the purification of the Temple (I Macc., ch. 5).

26 *And they fortified the Temple and Beth Ẕur*: See I Macc. 4.60.1. Presumably other places as well were fortified after the purification of the Temple but the author does not list them because they were not involved in the main events in Judas Maccabaeus' time.

28 *And the King raged upon hearing*: According to Appian, Antiochus V Eupator was nine years old when his father died (*Syr.* 46 (236)) so that he was only ten or eleven at the time of the Beth Zacharia campaign. Porphyry's statement (*FGrH* vol. IIB, no. 260, F32, para. 13) that he was twelve when his father left for Persia cannot be accepted.[11] In any case, actual control was in the hands of Lysias, the regent. Although well aware of Lysias' status (6.17,55), the author of I Maccabees attributes a will of his own and even the high command to the boy-king. Thus he recognizes the formal aspect of Lysias' actions, taken officially in the name of the king.

Token or active participation of teenage kings and princes in military undertakings are well known in Hellenistic tradition. Thus Demetrius Poliorcetes, when only twelve or thirteen, headed at least formally the Companions, an elite cavalry unit in the army of his father, Antigonus Monophthalmus, in the battle of Paraetacene (Diodorus 19.29.4); and Antiochus Epiphanes, at fifteen, led the right cavalry wing of his father, Antiochus III, in the battle of Panium (Polybius 16.18.6). In general, it was the custom of the Macedonian kings to involve their sons in military campaigns at an early age (cf. Plutarch, *Pyrrhus* 9).[12]

And he gathered all his friends: On the friends (*philoi*), the lowest rank of nobility in the Ptolemaic and Seleucid aristocracies, see p. 240 above. The 'friends' frequently convened in a council (*synedrion*), see Polybius 5.41.6,49.1,50.6, 8.21.2, 18.50.5; II Macc. 14.5.[13]

---

[9] See further Appendix C, pp. 441ff. For the translation of κληρονομία see also Tcherikover 482 n. 17.

[10] Cahana 1957: 127; Goldstein 1976: 319, and see Goldstein's interesting explanation there for the source of the error in the Greek manuscripts.

[11] See the reasons given by U. Wilcken in *RE* s.v. 'Antiochus' (26), col. 2471; Jacoby 1923: 873; Mørkholm 1966: 48 n. 41.

[12] See also Bar-Kochva 1979: 148. For an explanation of this custom see Hammond 1981: 24–5.

[13] On the Seleucid council of 'Friends' see Bevan 1902: 2.280; Bickerman 1938: 40, 189.

The officers of his army: Perhaps the reconstruction should follow the Lucian manuscripts and old Latin translation and read 'his friends and the officers of his army' for the officers were not the only 'friends' and the cavalry officers are mentioned later separately.

And those in charge of the mounted (force): The reference is to the cavalry officers. The author interprets the biblical term רֶכֶב (literally: chariots) to mean 'horsemen' as it appears several times in the Septuagint and commonly in the Scroll of the War of the Sons of Light (see p. 41 n. 40 above). No chariots are mentioned in the I Maccabees description of the battle itself. II Maccabees notes 300 scythed chariots (13.2), many more than any estimate of chariots in the sources on the Seleucid army.[14] The information is in general worthless: like I Maccabees, Josephus in *Bellum Judaicum*, which as noted is based on a knowledgeable Hellenistic source, makes no mention of chariots. The condition of the terrain make it unreasonable to suppose that chariots were mobilized for this expedition, for there are relatively few level expanses in the Judaean Hills long enough for scythed chariots to develop the acceleration needed for effective operation (cf. Plutarch, *Sulla* 18).[15] And in general, the Seleucids were sparing in the use of chariots in their wars because of their vulnerability to archers and other light forces (see p. 19 above; cf. Xenophon, *Anab.* 1.8.19–20). That was how Antiochus III was beaten in 190 B.C. at Magnesia (Livy 37.41.5–42.1; Vegetius 3.24), and it cannot be supposed that after such a bitter lesson the Seleucids continued to use chariots. I Maccabees does report the involvement of chariots in Antiochus Epiphanes' expedition to Egypt in 168 B.C. (1.17), but it is hard to accept the statement in view of the sandy terrain in Egypt. The chariots mentioned in Daniel (11.40) are connected not with the expedition to Egypt, as some scholars believe, but to the apocalyptic 'end of days',[16] and cannot enlighten us about military realities in the author's time. The apocalyptic verses in the book are based among others on an association with Isaiah's prophecy on the Assyrian invasion in 701 B.C. and its failure,[17] and that accounts for the mention of chariots which played an important role in the biblical drama (see especially Is. 5.28). The 140 chariots that took part in the Daphne procession (Polybius 30.25.11) were not operational but were kept for ceremonies and competitions. It is illuminating that Polybius makes no mention of scythes, the war chariots' most characteristic and impressive accessory, despite detailed descriptions

[14] On the use of scythed chariots in the Seleucid army see Bar-Kochva 1979: 83–4.

[15] On other objections to the use of chariots in the expedition, and especially on their vulnerability to Jewish archers, see Abel 1949: 449; Dancy 1954: 65,114; contrary to Bickerman 1938: 164.

[16] For the background to Daniel 11.40–5 see p. 442 n. 20 below.

[17] On the influence of the Assyrian chapters of Isaiah on Daniel see Efron 1980: 114–15. See also Daniel 11.44 *versus* Isaiah 37.7.

of the arms and even the clothing of the other units that took part
in the procession. Some of the chariots mentioned were hitched to
six horses, some to four, and two chariots even to elephants, one of
them to four and the other to a pair, which in itself indicates the true
function of the chariots (cf. the display chariots in the procession of
Ptolemy Philadelphus in 270 B.C.: Athenaeus 5.200f).

29 *And from other kingdoms and from islands of the sea mercenary armies came
to him*: The allusion is to the recruitment of mercenaries in the
countries north of the Taurus. One of the provisions of the Treaty
of Apamea, signed between the Romans and Antiochus III after the
battle of Magnesia, forbade the Seleucids to recruit mercenaries in
the countries north of the Taurus which both sides recognized as
being in the exclusively Roman zone of influence (see Polybius
21.42.15; Livy 38.38.10; Appian, *Syr.* 39(202)). But this provision,
like others in the same treaty (especially the outlawing of elephants
in war), was violated by Antiochus IV as can be seen from the
participation of Mysians and Thracians in the Daphne procession
(Polybius 30.25.3–5) and in the battles in Judaea (II Macc. 5.24,
12.35). Probably an intensive recruitment drive was in fact
conducted prior to the battle of Beth Zacharia, although in view of
the greater difficulty of operating north of the Taurus, the paucity
of manpower sources there, the military needs of the allied states in
their conflicts among themselves and the Seleucids' reduced
financial resources, presumably the campaign did not have very
impressive results. Given the complex of relationships between
Rome and the various elements in the Mediterranean basin in those
years and the contacts between those same elements and the
Seleucids, the recruiting could have been conducted mainly in
Cilicia, Crete, the kingdoms of Pontus and Cappadocia, and
perhaps also in Bithynia. The composition of Antiochus IV's forces
at the Daphne procession suggests that it was possible to mobilize
Thracians, Galatians from Asia Minor, and also Mysians whose
settlement areas were only nominally under the control of
Pergamum.[18] Elsewhere in I Maccabees the term 'islands of the
Gentiles' is applied to the homeland of Demetrius II's mercenaries
(11.38) who were all exclusively Cretans (*Ant.* 13.86,129; Justin
35.2). On methods of recruiting mercenaries through local kings,
tribal chiefs, and prominent high-ranking officers sent throughout
the Greek world see Polybius 15.25.16, 33.18.14; Livy 31.43.5–7,
37.8.4,18.7,31.4; and also Plautus, *Miles Glor.* 72,75,947.

30 *And the number of his armies was a hundred thousand foot and twenty thousand
horsemen*: Most scholars believe the figure is grossly exaggerated.[19]
The data available on the Seleucid manpower potential in the

[18] See Griffith 1935: 146–7.
[19] The first to state this was Wernsdorff (1747: 118ff.).

western part of the kingdom at the time, and on the local auxiliary troops, allow the estimate of fifty thousand foot and five thousand horse reported by Josephus in *Bellum Judaicum* (1.41), though they are somewhat rounded off upwards (see pp. 42–3 above).

And elephants thirty-two: The figure seems exaggerated. Only thirty-six or forty-two elephants took part in the Daphne procession (Polybius 30.25.11). Most of them were taken along on the expedition to the eastern satrapies (see p. 235 above). Although some may have been sent back to Syria as part of the infantry and cavalry after Epiphanes' death (see pp. 546–7 below), they may have suffered some losses, the war elephant depletion rate being as high as 25% on long expeditions.[20] The replenishment of the elephant reserve was a difficult matter because at the time there was no land communication with India, the source of the Seleucid elephants, and elephants did not reproduce in captivity. II Maccabees reports twenty-two elephants (13.2), but as it almost invariably gives much inflated figures for the Seleucid forces, there is little reason to rely on the elephant figure. Josephus in *Bellum Judaicum* reports eighty elephants (1.41), an astonishing figure in view of the overall reliability of the description and especially of the relatively moderate numbers he attributes to the Seleucid army on that occasion. It seems reasonable to assume that the original version reported eight elephants: as numbers were commonly expressed by letters in Greek manuscripts, the letter H (eight) could have been miscopied as Π (eighty). A similar error occurred in I Maccabees in regard to the number of soldiers in the towers mounted on the elephants (see p. 322). The proposed number of elephants also fits the deployment of the Seleucid force according to the width of the battlefield (see p. 324 below). Even a few elephants were enough to cause a great confusion in the ranks of the opposing force (cf. Lucian, *Zeuxis* 9–11; Plutarch, *Eumenes* 18.2; Polyaenus 4.9.3; the last source notes eight elephants). No connection can be assumed between the eighty elephants mentioned in the II Maccabees version of the battle of Beth Zur (11.4) and the number in *Bellum Judaicum*. It has long been proven that Josephus was not familiar with II Maccabees (see p. 191 n. 124), and in any case the number in II Maccabees refers to Lysias' first expedition and not to the battle of Beth Zacharia. The identity of the numbers is merely coincidence.

Trained for war: In almost all their wars, the Seleucids used war elephants that were imported from India and kept at Apamea in northern Syria. See pp. 16–19 above for the military advantages of elephants, their drawbacks, and the way they were deployed and utilized in battle. Because of their great military value, the Romans

[20] See Bar-Kochva 1979: 78–9.

in the Treaty of Apamea forbade the Seleucids to use them in future battles. This prohibit on was disregarded more than once, as was the one dealing with recruiting forces north of the Taurus, but the Seleucids paid a heavy price: shortly after the battle of Beth Zacharia the Roman legate Gnaius Octavius arrived at Apamea, where he slaughtered all the war elephants, thus putting an end to one of the main foundations of the Seleucid military strength (on the chronology see p. 547 below). For subsequent years only a few elephants are reported in the Seleucid army, primarily in connection with breaching walls and fortifications.[21]

31 *And they went through Edom*: As he did on his earlier expedition (4.29), this time too Lysias solved the problem of climbing to the Judaean Hills by penetrating them from the south-west, through friendly Idumaean territory.

And camped around Beth Zur: On the fortification of the place see I Macc. 4.61 and p. 286 above. The hill is separated from its environs by steep cliffs on three sides, but is joined on the south-east to the Burj es-Sur hill by a rather convenient saddle (see Map 15 on p. 310). It may be assumed that the Seleucid army's greatest efforts were concentrated on that saddle and that the siege machines were placed there.

And made devices: On the reconstruction *ḥiśvōnōt* for Greek *mēkhanai* see p. 319 below. In this context the reference is first and foremost to various types of siege machines, the most noteworthy of which was the siege tower, the *helepolis*, whose function was to breach the city wall. It was equipped with a battering ram, and had archers and artillery machines positioned in its upper storeys which could reach into the heart of the city.[22]

And they fought bravely: According to the rest of the description, Beth Zur was not taken until after the battle of Beth Zacharia and the siege of the Temple (verses 49–50), and the impression is that the Beth Zur struggle went on inconclusively the whole time. The verses are, however, mixed up, and Beth Zur seems to have fallen before the battle of Beth Zacharia as can be deduced from *Bellum Judaicum* (1.41) and perhaps also from II Macc. (13.22; see p. 294 above), with which (as noted) Josephus was not familiar. The latter sources are to be preferred in this case[23] because the same considerations that motivated Lysias to besiege Beth Zur twice, namely to secure the rear in case of retreat (see p. 286 above), would have dissuaded him from proceeding northwards before taking it. Verses 49–50 should be inserted after verse 31. The misplacement in I Maccabees, attributable to an editor or copyist, arises from the resemblance

---

[21] On elephants in the Seleucid armies see ibid. 75–83,146–57.

[22] A detailed survey of the towers and the means of defence against them appears in Droysen 1889: 217–60; Kromayer and Veith 1926: 226,235; Marsden 1969–71: 1.50–4,101–15; Garlan 1974: 228–34.   [23] So also Abel 1949: 124; Dancy 1954: 138.

between the siege of Beth Zur and the siege of Jerusalem, and
especially from the mention of the Sabbatical year which in both
places made things difficult for the besieged and led to their
surrender (6.51–4). The insertion of the Beth Zur siege in those
verses also led to certain deletions in the description of the siege of
Jerusalem (see p. 340 below). Josephus in *Antiquitates* follows the
present text of I Maccabees and this indicates that the
misplacements in I Maccabees occurred at an early stage in the
history of the text. The information on this matter in *Bellum
Judaicum* was taken from Nicolaus, who relied on a much earlier
version of I Maccabees, and perhaps also on the Seleucid source
he consulted for the Beth Zacharia episode. Regarding the
phenomenon of misplaced verses in I Maccabees, compare p. 259
and n. 118 above.

II Maccabees provides more details on the siege of Beth Zur:
despite the heavy siege, Judas Maccabaeus managed to get food and
equipment to the defenders (13.20). A Jew named Rhodocus passed
'the secrets' (τὰ μυστήρια, 13.21) to the enemy, perhaps the paths
and methods by which supplies were carried into the besieged hill.
This revelation may have made the situation there worse and
compelled the defenders to surrender (13.22). It should be noted
that the shafts seen in the southern part of the hill are not 'secret
accesses' through which supplies were brought, as was suggested by
Sellers, the first of the excavators of the site,[24] for they are arranged
in a straight and symmetrical line, and one is even located outside
the wall. Nor is there any basis for the hypothesis of some other
scholars that the Seleucid force broke into the town through a
'secret access'. It is true that the method was as always common
during the Hellenistic period (Polybius 5.71.9; cf. 7.15–18) and the
word 'secrets' can be interpreted in that way, but the Books of the
Maccabees state that the defenders of the fort gave up because of
starvation (I Macc. 6.49–50; II Macc. 13.22). This is obvious also
from the imprisonment of the traitor Rhodocus by the defenders
before the surrender (II Macc. 13.21).

32 *And Judah moved from the Akra*: According to II Maccabees,
Judas Maccabaeus watched the progress of the Seleucid army before
it reached the mountain plateau and even stayed in the vicinity of
Beth Zur for a while to help the besieged (13.14–20). Although in
that book the geographical picture of Lysias' expedition is extremely
vague and doubtful (especially the mention of Modein in 13.14; cf.
p. 197 above), the information on the siege of Beth Zur is detailed
and quite reasonable (13.18–22a), and in any case it cannot be
assumed that throughout the siege of Beth Zur Judas Maccabaeus
continued to besiege the citadel effectively. Simeon followed the

---

[24] Sellers 1933: 272–8; and also Abel 1949: 116–17.

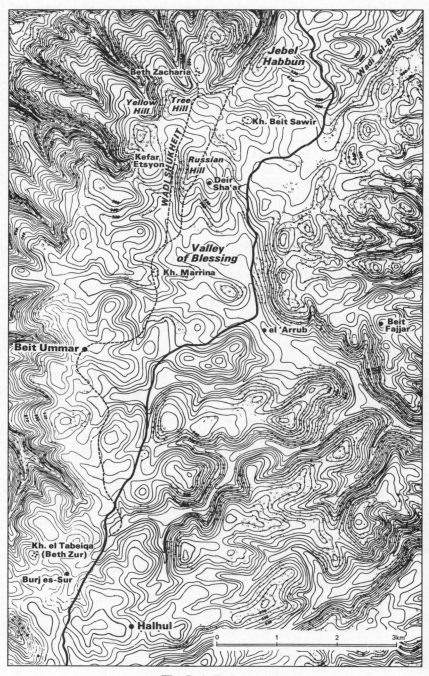

15 The Beth Zacharia area

movements of Tryphon in the same way in 143 B.C. (I Macc. 13.20).
If there is any truth in the II Maccabees story on the preliminary
clash with the Seleucid camp (13.14–17), it would mean that small-
scale raids were carried out against the enemy camp near Beth Zur,
but did not, it appears, do it much harm.

And camped at Beth Zacharia: εἰς Βαιθζαχαρια. For the translation of
εἰς as 'at' see p. 338 below. The site has definitely been identified
with the hamlet of Kh. Zakariya, about a kilometre north of
present-day Kefar 'Etsyon, nine kilometres north of Beth Zur.[25]

Judas Maccabaeus chose to make a stand at Beth Zacharia not
only for topographical reasons. The terrain in the area between Beth
Zur and Beth Zacharia is not significantly different from that
further on between Beth Zacharia and Jerusalem to the north. Judas
Maccabaeus was apparently concerned about the actions against
the population in the area south of Jerusalem (such as occurred later
during Bacchides' two expeditions: I Macc. 7.19, 9.2). At that stage,
after the purification of the Temple, when semi-independent forms
of military and civil authority were being organized, the new Jewish
leadership could not afford to sacrifice southern Judaea to Lysias'
initiative. Presumably its past victories and present enhanced
military power gave the Jewish command the illusion that it could
stop the Seleucid troops on their way to Jerusalem. After the fall of
Beth Zur on Judaea's southern border, Beth Zacharia was the
nearest place whose topography could be exploited to block the
advance of the enemy (see p. 329 below).

Opposite the king's camp: The original of the Greek ἀπέναντι was
נגד or מנגד (= opposite). This preposition in Hebrew need not
denote visual contact (see p. 250 above). Beth Zur is not visible from
Beth Zacharia, which is lower than the Tree Hill saddle. Even if the
Jewish force actually camped on the saddle (where the force finally
formed for battle) they could only discern the village of Ḥalḥul
adjacent to Beth Zur, without being able to distinguish people or
military movements even there.

33 *And the king rose early in the morning and...moved the camp on the Beth
Zacharia road*: The Greek is τὴν ὁδὸν Βαιθζαχαρια. The Roman
milestones and *PEF* maps show that of the two roads that went
north from Beth Zur only the westernmost reached Beth
Zacharia.[26] The verse thus cannot be assumed to apply to the other
(which in some parts covers the same route as the present-day one)
passing two kilometres east of Beth Zacharia. The western road
wound through broad valleys, defiles, slopes and ridges. The
topographical structure of the area dictated the Seleucid formation
as it advanced (see pp. 324, 329–30 below).

---

[25] Guérin 1868–80: 316–19; Abel 1924: 211.
[26] On that route see Thomsen 1917: 81–2; and *PEF* maps nos 17 and 21.

And the armies armed for battle: This does not mean that the troops of the two sides formed openly in sight of each other. The word δυνάμεις (= forces, armies), which is a plural, is used in I Maccabees to mean the Seleucid forces (2.31, 3.27,34,37,7.2,4,14, 9.1; cf. 10.36) as below in this chapter where 'the fury of the armies' (τὸ ὅρμημα τῶν δυνάμεων, verse 47) clearly refers to the enemy only. It was often used in official Hellenistic terminology (including the Seleucid) to mean 'army units' or 'the entire army'.[27] Similarly the Hebrew צבא (= army), which is frequently translated as δύναμις by the Septuagint, appears also in the plural to designate the troops of one side (Ex. 12.41; Deut. 20.9; Ps. 44.10; I Chron. 27.3). Josephus in *Antiquitates* describes a frontal deployment of both of the armies (12.370), but that is only a careless paraphrase of I Maccabees, possibly influenced by the word ἀπέναντι (= opposite) in the preceding verse.

As to the word διεσκευάσθησαν in the sentence: διασκευάζειν, literally 'equip oneself', appears in the Septuagint just once, to translate the word חֲמֻשִׁים (= munitioned, Josh. 4.12). According to the literal meaning, the original Hebrew may have used mishnaic language and the word can then be reconstructed וַיִּזְדַּיְּנוּ (= and they armed themselves). In any case, the verse refers to the stage of securing and preparing the weapons before leaving camp, for the formation stage is described in the following verses (35–8).

34 *And the elephants they [saturated]*: The Greek is ἔδειξαν (= showed). Wellhausen correctly deduced that the original was הִרְווּ (= saturated), and the Greek translator mistakenly read הֶרְאוּ (= showed).[28]

(With) blood of grape and berries: On various beverages administered to elephants to rouse them to battle cf. III Mac. 5.1–10; Aelian, *De nat. animal.* 13.8. For the phrase 'blood of the grape' see Deut. 32.14 and Gen. 49.11. It is hard to know how the author was privy to what the elephants were given to drink, and he may have simply assumed the usual. In any case this reference cannot provide any chronological verification proving that the expedition took place during the grape harvest season.[29]

35 *And they divided the beasts into the formations*: The Greek is εἰς τὰς φάλαγγας (= into the phalanxes). On the reconstruction *ma'arākōt* (= formations), see Appendix B, pp. 432ff. The word denotes the units stationed in the centre of the Seleucid array. Each of the units was composed of a war elephant, 1,000 heavy armed foot soldiers and 500 heavy cavalry.

The Alexandrian version has εἰς τὰς φάραγγας, 'to the valleys'

[27] E.g. Arrian, *Anab.* 3.5.3; Polybius 5.54.12,66.6; and Lesquier 1911: 99ff. Welles; 1934: 329.
[28] Wellhausen 1905: 161–2; I. Lévy 1955: 35; Maxwell-Stuart 1975: 230–3.
[29] Against Wellhausen 1905: 167. Bickerman 1937: 156; Bunge 1971: 351.

(defiles, canyons). According to that version, each of the elephants with its escorts was stationed in a different defile. Various scholars are of the opinion that Josephus was influenced in *Antiquitates* by this erroneous text and therefore included the defiles in his description of the march (12.370). However, the context in which they are mentioned by Josephus should be carefully examined: 'And Judah...stationed his camp near mountain defiles in the place called Beth Zacharia, 70 stadia away from the enemy.' And the king... led the army toward the defiles (ἐπὶ τὰ στενά) and toward the camp of Judah, and in the morning deployed the army. The elephants he arranged...'. What Josephus has to say is far from what the Alexandrian version indicates. He mentions the defiles as the target and destination of the march (along with Judah's camp), and not as places where each of the elephants and their escorts were stationed separately. Further on he even asserts that the elephants were all concentrated at one defile (para. 371). The distance noted between the Jewish camp and the defiles near Beth Zacharia, which is not given in I Maccabees, indicates that what Josephus reports is based on familiarity with the battle area between Beth Zur and Beth Zacharia where there are a number of mountain defiles. On the source for the rest of Josephus' description on the deployment of the army in the defile see below p. 330.

And with each elephant they positioned a thousand men...and five hundred picked horse: These figures should at the outset raise reservations in view of the gross exaggeration in regard to the overall strength of the Seleucid force and the difficulty that eye-witnesses had in assessing the size of the separate units in a battle array. However, the deployment of a 'formation' of 1,000 phalangites and 500 cavalrymen according to accepted Hellenistic standards would have enabled the 'formation' to operate in the most effective way in the narrow pass where the battle actually took place (see p. 330 below). Moreover, these figures accord with the size of Hellenistic infantry and cavalry units: the chiliarchy (the second largest tactical unit of the phalangites) numbered 1,024 men,[30] and the hipparchy (the second largest tactical unit of the cavalry) comprised 512 horse (Asclepiodotus 7.11; Arrian, *Tact.* 18.2–3, etc.). On 500 horseman units in the Seleucid army see Livy 35.43.5–6, 36.15.3,19.11; Appian, *Syr.* 17(75) and 20(90).

A thousand men armoured in chain and bronze helmets on their heads: The Greek is τεθωρακισμένους ἐν ἁλυσιδωτοῖς καὶ περικεφαλαίαι χαλκαῖ ἐπὶ τῶν κεφαλῶν αὐτῶν. Exegetes have customarily reconstructed the phrase τεθωρακισμένους ἐν ἁλυσιδωτοῖς as 'armoured in scales', based on the similarity of the verse to the one describing Goliath's

---

[30] See Rüstow and Köchly 1852: 236–7. The main sources are the Tacticians and references in Ptolemaic papyri, Polybius and Plutarch.

armour (I Sam. 17.5: 'And a bronze helmet on his head and in scale armour he is clad') according to the Septuagint (καὶ περικεφαλαία χαλκαῖ ἐπὶ τῆς κεφαλῆς αὐτοῦ, καὶ θώρακα ἀλυσιδωτὸν αὐτὸς ἐνδεδυκώς). However, the term ἀλυσιδωτός means 'made of chains' or 'rings'. The possibility that the translator of I Maccabees followed the erroneous translation of the Septuagint need not be rejected out of hand, but before making the decision we must ascertain whether scale armour was customary for the infantry of the Seleucid or any other Hellenistic army. Scale armour was well known from the Ancient East, the fringes of Greek culture in Cyprus and Crimea, the Parthian and Scythian civilizations and Rome in the early Principate, but there is no evidence of the use of armour of that kind by the infantry forces in the third and second century B.C. The Seleucid cataphract horsemen were apparently armoured in scale (see p. 13 above), but this present sentence refers definitely only to infantry. Probably scale armour was never adopted by phalangites because it was too thin to withstand the blow of a pike (in contrast to a suit of solid armour). For a similar reason scale armour was not popular in Archaic and Classical Greece in which hoplite combat was prevalent and the horsemen also engaged in hand-to-hand combat.[31] The Seleucid cavalry, on the other hand, adopted it because on horseback the men had to be flexible, and it was necessary to protect the horse as well, while the regular metal armour was too heavy for that purpose. Moreover, cavalry were more vulnerable to archers than phalangites were, and scale armour provided considerable protection against them.

On the other hand literary sources ascribe chain armour to the Galatians (Diodorus 5.30.3: σιδηροῦς ἀλυσιδωτούς; Varro, *De lingua latina* 5.116: *ex anulis ferrea tunica*), to the highest propertied class (*pedites*) in the Roman legion of the third and second centuries B.C. (Varro, loc.cit.; Polybius 6.23.15: ἀλυσιδωτούς...θώρακας),[32] and also to a picked Roman-type unit of the Seleucid army (Polybius 30.25.3). From these sources we learn that, influenced by Galatian equipment, the Roman army adopted chain armour (*lorica hamata*), and in turn later inspired the Seleucid army. The Pergamum reliefs show a number of instances of mesh-like chain mail. It can be assumed that they represent Galatian armour, just as a substantial part of the weapons carved in the temple of Athena Nicephorus are Galatian. The same can be traced in one of the Sidon Steles (see Plates IX, XI). The verse should therefore be reconstructed as שרשרות (= chains; cf. Ex. 28.14,22,39.15, etc.) or

---

[31] On the few references to scale armour in the Classical Greek armies see Snodgrass 1964: 86–94; id. 1967: 90–1; Anderson 1970: 23–4,142–4.

[32] On mail armour in the Roman legion in the second century B.C. see Grosse in *RE* s.v. 'Lorica', cols 1444–5; Daremberg and Saglio, s.v. 'Lorica', p. 1315; Couissin 1926: 268–70; Robinson 1975: 164ff.

perhaps עבתת (= thongs, Ex. 28.22, 24 – ἁλυσιδωτοί in the Septuagint). It should be noted that the biblical קשקשת (= scale) in the context of dietary laws on fish is translated λεπίς in the Septuagint (Lev. 11.9,10,12, etc.), and that the biblical sentence 'And in scale armour he is clad' in any case differs in structure and wording from the sentence in our verse, so that it should not be relied on too much in the reconstruction of the Hebrew.

The equipment of the infantry described as armoured in chain shows that they were part of the picked unit of the Seleucid army which had been retrained for Roman-style warfare some time before the Daphne procession (Polybius 30.25.3). That unit comprised 5,000 men and constituted half of the *argyraspides*, the Seleucid infantry Royal Guard (see p. 417 below). Polybius describes the equipment of that unit in the words 'equipped according to the Roman system with chain armour'. He stresses the chain armour because body armour was not regulation for Seleucid phalangites, apart from officers and members of the Royal Guard, and that of the latter was not of the chain type.[33] At the same time, in view of the limited number of soldiers in the 'Roman' unit, it is clear that the infantry in some of the 'formations' was composed of proper phalangites, which is inferable from the description mentioning shields typical of them (verse 39). The author found it necessary to put special stress on the presence of soldiers of the 'Roman' type partly because they were in the forward formations which entered the pass (see p. 330 below) and so caught the spectator's eye, and also because of the particular biblical association evoked. The second motive seems especially valid in view of the adjacent reference to 'bronze helmets' which were used by both phalangites and 'Roman' soldiers, although they were less important or impressive items than various types of offensive weapons, which are not mentioned at all in the episode.

In listing the contingent as 'Roman' Polybius refers just to its equipment and does not imply that the 5,000 Guardsmen were organized like a Roman legion of their time (divided into maniples and deployed on the battlefield in three lines, each six men in depth, etc.). In any case they certainly were not deployed in as dense and deep a formation as the phalangites; the intervals between their rows and lines must have been double those of the phalangites (given by Polybius 18.30.9), and the number of rows must have been smaller. Otherwise the change in equipment would not have made much sense tactically. Consequently the figure of 1,000 infantry in each of the 'formations' cannot refer to the 'Roman' troops: the width of the pass accords with the space occupied by a compressed 'formation' of 1,000 phalangites and 500 horsemen

[33] Griffith 1956–7: 3–10; Bar-Kochva 1979: 54–6.

(p. 128 above). This correspondence indicates that the conditions of the terrain were taken into account in the organization of the 'formations' and must have determined as well the number of 'Roman' infantry in a 'formation'. However, a 'formation' that included 1,000 'Roman' infantry could not have been positioned in any effective combat deployment in the narrow pass where the battle took place.

Bronze helmets on their heads: According to the Greek the helmet was made of *khalkos*, a term used like the biblical *neḥošet* for both copper and bronze, and the reference is no doubt to bronze helmets. Bronze, an alloy of copper and iron, is stronger than copper, and had replaced it for military purposes long since. The only Macedonian helmet from the Hellenistic period so far discovered is made of iron.[34] However, the helmets seen on the Sidon gravestones have the golden tinge characteristic of bronze (see, e.g., Plates IX, X). According to the Septuagint, the Hebrew must have been *neḥošet*, all the more so because of the clear association with Goliath's helmet (I Sam. 17.5,38). The particular biblical expressions נחושת ממרט, קלל נחושת and esp. נחשת מצהב (I Kings 7.45; Ezek. 1.7; Dan. 10.6; Ezra 8.27) probably refer to burnished bronze. Cf. the phrase מגיני נחושת מרוקה כמעשה מראת פנים (= shields of burnished bronze, like a face mirror) in the Scroll of the War of the Sons of Light (5[8] 4–5).

And five hundred picked horse: The adjective ἐκλελεγμένη (Hebrew: בחור = picked) has no implication as regards the unit the horsemen belong to (cf. pp. 260, 284 above, 388 below). Although some of them may have been among the cavalry Royal Guard composed of the best young sons of the military settlers, it should be noted that there were no more than about 2,000 men in that Guard,[35] while the number of horsemen in the 'formations' certainly exceeded that total. The word 'picked' which differentiates these from the horsemen at the far ends of the series of 'formations' (verse 38) is an allusion to the nature of their equipment: they were apparently cataphracts. At the end of the third century B.C., all the Seleucid cavalry in the Royal Guard and the reserves from the military settlements were converted into cataphracts, that is, 'armoured' (see p. 12 above). For the reconstruction 'horse' in the singular cf. p. 260 above.

Were prepared for each beast: The deployment of the 'formations' can be reconstructed in the light of the tactics and combat methods of the period, of the mention of an elephant in the centre of each 'formation', of a comparison with the Seleucid deployment at

[34] See Hatzopoulos and Loukopoulos 1980: 123,127.
[35] On the fixed complement in the Royal Guard cavalry units see Bar-Kochva 1979: 68–73.

Magnesia (Livy 37.40.2; Appian, *Syr.* 32(162)), and especially of the need to protect the sides of the elephants and the flanks of the infantry. In the centre of each 'formation' was an elephant, with 500 heavy infantry (in some 'formations' Roman-style soldiers, in others phalangites) on each side defending the elephant's flanks (see also below re verse 45). The heavy infantry was protected by cavalry, 250 on each side. Each of these formations thus reproduced in miniature the customary Hellenistic deployment, which normally featured tens of thousands of phalangites in the centre, protected on the flanks by thousands of horsemen. To them were added elephants, sometimes interspersed in the phalangite front line (as in the battle of Magnesia). On the purpose of the special deployment at Beth Zacharia see below, and pp. 126–8 above.

36 *These were beforehand*: The reference is to the deployment just prior to the march and the battle, and not to exercises or manoeuvres before that day.[36] The reconstruction of πρὸ καιροῦ (= beforehand) should be בטרם עת; compare Sirach 30.24, and its Septuagint translation.

In the place where the beast was, and wherever it went they went together...: The verse is influenced by the description of the 'beasts' in Ezekiel (1.19–21) which accounts also for the use of the word 'beast' from verse 35 on. The term *thēria* (= beasts), as a substitute for 'elephants', is not unusual in Hellenistic literature and appears mainly for reasons of variety and style.[37] The purpose of the verse is to stress the independence of the 'formation' and the ability of each one to operate without contact or reliance on what was happening in other sectors of the battlefield.

37 *And wooden towers on them*: The term *pyrgoi* used in this sentence was applied in literary sources to structures placed on the elephants' backs as shelters for soldiers who sat or stood on them. Sometimes they were even called *thōrakia* (Suda, s.v. θωράκιον). Towers of various designs appear on a considerable number of artifacts, noteworthy among which is the Capena bowl now in the Villa Giulia in Rome, the celebrated phalera from the Hermitage in Leningrad, and two terracotta statuettes from Pompeii and Myrina in western Asia Minor (see Plates XII–XIV). Most of them are constructed like Hellenistic towers or city walls, and are even crenelated (cf. also Jos. *Bell.* 1.42; Appian, *Syr.* 32(162)). It appears from the sources that the first one to use such towers was King Pyrrhus of Epirus in the 270s B.C. (Zonaras 8.5).[38] The use of these

---

[36] Contrary to Grimm 1853: 100; and see also Bévenot 1931: 92.

[37] E.g. Polybius 18.23.7 (the battle of Cynoscephalae), and especially Polybius 16.18.7,10, 19.1,3,5,11 *versus* 19.6–7 (the battle of Panium). In the latter description Polybius makes frequent use of the word 'beast', apparently because his version is a paraphrase of Zeno of Rhodes, whose style was reportedly particularly elegant and extravagant (Polybius 16.17.9, 18.2). [38] Scullard 1974: 104–5,240–1.

towers in the Seleucid army is explicitly noted in connection with the battles of Raphia and Magnesia (Polybius 5.84.2; Livy 37.40.4).

The available material does not help verify the I Maccabees statement that the towers were made of wood. The tower in the Leningrad phalera seems to be made of some metallic material while the Pompeii terracotta clearly shows courses of bricks in the form of headers and stretchers following the usual Hellenistic style (Plates XIIIa, XIVa). A fourth-century A.D. source speaks of 'iron towers' (Julian, *Orationes* 2.64ff.). Since a structure made entirely of metal would have greatly limited the elephant's speed and assault capacity, it seems reasonable to assume that only the plating or sheathing of the towers was metallic. The bricks on the Pompeii terracotta are only a decoration designed to accentuate the resemblance between the structures carried by the elephants and regular wall towers.

Strong and covered on each beast: As the towers known from the various finds had no roofs, the statement that the wooden towers were 'strong and covered' should be understood as referring to the metal sheathing mentioned above (see p. 334 below as well). The towers on the bowl from Capena, the Myrina statuette and the Pompeii terracotta even have round shields fixed to them which augmented their strength and added a decorative element, thus imitating the practice of soldiers of hanging their shields demonstratively on tower walls (Plates XII, XIIIa, XIVa; cf., e.g., Song of Songs 4.4).

Strapped to it: According to the pictorial testimony on African elephants, the tower seems to have been attached to the animal's body with three heavy ropes (the Capena bowl, see Pl. XII) or metal chains (the Pompeii terracotta, see Pl. XIVa) around the elephant's front, belly and rear. As the Indian elephants used by the Seleucids did not have a prominently curved rear end, the base of the tower was attached to a heavy rug which covered the elephant's back and sides, and the lower edge of the rug had three straps which went around the belly (the Myrina terracotta and the Leningrad phalera, see Pl. XIIIa, b).

With [thongs]: The Greek translation has *mēkhanai*, which in Greek and in some places in I Maccabees, including this chapter (verses 20,31,51,52; cf. 5.30, 9.64,67, 11.20, 15.25), is the general term for artillery as well as poliorcetic devices. Various commentators have assumed that I Maccabees preferred to write *mekōnōt* in Hebrew because of the phonetic resemblance to the Greek *mēkhanai*. However, in the Bible the word is used only in connection with ritual objects, and is clearly derived from *kan* (= base, pedestal).[39]

---

[39] E.g. I Kings 7.27 and passim; II Kings 16.17, 25.13,16; Jer. 27.19, etc. The Septuagint properly translates βάσις.

Moreover, the statement that the towers were tied to the elephants by artillery devices does not make sense, and both *mēkhanai* in its literal meaning ('machines') and the suggested Hebrew reconstruction *mekōnōt* would make it necessary to construe the meaning in this verse as a complicated (and quite superfluous) tying device, while as noted above the tying was quite simple. The context of the word together with the artistic finds compel us to assume that the source had a specific Hebrew word meaning 'thongs' or 'ropes' or the like. Besides, in the Septuagint, the Hebrew word *mekōnōt* is always transliterated exactly and not as *mēkhanai*.[40]

Presumably, then, the Hebrew original had *ḥišvōnōt* in our verse. It appears once in II Chronicles denoting artillery devices (26.15),[41] and is translated *mēkhanai* in the Septuagint. According to the popular etymology of the Hebrew word,[42] it means 'devices', and could have applied to poliorcetic machines as well. These two meanings fit all the other instances of *mēkhanai* in I Maccabees. As to this verse, *ḥēšev*, a word with the same root, does occur in the singular in the meaning of 'thong', 'rope', etc. (Ex. 28.8,27,28, 29.5, 39.5,20,21; Lev. 8.7). There is a striking resemblance between the suggested reconstruction 'strapped to it with *ḥišvōnōt* (= thongs)' and the verse in Leviticus (8.7) describing how the ephod

---

[40] The Hebrew original of I Macc. 13.29 undoubtedly had *mekōnōt*, meaning the pyramid bases. The Greek has *mēkhanēmata* (= artillery pieces; cf. IV Macc. 7.7). The proposal of Abel (1949: 240)–that the original Greek was a transliteration of *mekōnōt* as μεχωνώθ, as is usual in the Septuagint, and that a copyist garbled it to *mēkhanēmata* – is reasonable.

[41] We must concur with the accepted view that the *ḥišvōnōt* ascribed to Uzziah are an anachronism. In general, the II Chronicles story of Uzziah's exploits abounds in later post-Exilic Hebrew expressions ('for he waxed exceeding strong', 8; 'And his name spread far and wide', 15; 'But when he was strong, his heart was lifted up', 16, and the like). Less convincing is Yadin's explanation that the *ḥišvōnōt* were defensive structures erected on the wall towers (Y. Sukenik [= Yadin] 1947: 19–24; Yadin, '*ḥišvōnōt maḥševet ḥōšev*' in *Biblical Encyclopaedia*, vol. 3, (Jerusalem, 1955) cols 314–15 (Hebrew); id. 1963: 326–7). The verse literally states that the *ḥišvōnōt* were designed 'to shoot arrows and great stones'. It is hard to understand the phrase חשבנות מחשבת חשב (= devices invented by a cunning man), which points to an especially sophisticated device, if the reference is simply to shelters. Also the term *mēkhanai*, which the Septuagint uses to translate *ḥišvōnōt*, serves in Hellenistic (though not Classical) Greek mainly to designate artillery weapons (contrary to Y. Sukenik 1947: 22).

[42] The etymology of the word *ḥišvōnōt* is generally explained on the basis of the Hebrew root *ḥ(a)š(a)v* (= think) as a complex, complicated instrument or structure whose design requires a great deal of thought. This explanation is supported by the description of the devices as being 'invented by a cunning man'. The phrase as a whole is strange, however, for it is superfluous and also alliterative in a completely non-poetic context. On the other hand, the military application of the word in Chronicles is somewhat reminiscent of the Arabic *ḥusbān* which medieval dictionaries explain as small arrows of a certain Persian bow, or a hollow of a reed for shooting many arrows at the same time (see Lane 1863: 2.567 and Huari 1941: 105ff.). The military meaning of the word is not Semitic in origin, having no semantic connection with the root *ḥ(a)š(a)v*, and it may have come from some Persian dialect and undergone a modification in Hebrew and Arabic. Evidently the author felt it necessary to explain the foreign, unfamiliar word, and consequently added his own etymological explanation מחשבת חשב – which reflects his awareness of the complex structure of the weapon. This popular etymology is perhaps reflected also in Dan.11.24 (יחשב חשבנותיו; see below).

was attached (ויחגר אתו בחשב = And he girded him with the ḥēšev [= band]). All this indicates that the original had ḥišvōnōt and the translator, influenced by the meaning of the word in the other verses of the chapter, interpreted it as artillery devices, hence his translation mēkhanai. A similar error occurs in the translation of Symmachus and Theodotion for the ḥēšev of the Biblical ephod (mekhanōma = 'crane', 'hoist' or the like; see Ex. 28.27,28; Lev. 8.7).[43]

Why did the author, who generally (except in lyric passages and the story of Judas Maccabaeus' last battle – see p. 377 below) avoids a high-flown lexicon, here choose the word ḥišvōnōt, which is not common in the Bible, instead of, for example, the much more usual ḥagōrōt? The reason is that the ḥēšev described in the Bible had a special form and place. It was not an ordinary strap, but was decorated like the ephod in various colours such as gold, blue and purple (Ex. 28.6–8, 39.5; Sirach 45.10). As to its position, some scholars believe that it served to hang the ephod from the shoulders, while others suggest that it encircled the hips and helped fix the ephod to the body along with the shoulder pieces.[44] In Arabic the ḥēšev is a long strip of leather decorated with pearls and shells which women wear across the shoulders or around the hips.[45] The written and illustrative material from Mesopotamia is of no help in deciding between the two hypotheses on the placement of the ḥēšev. With regard to our verse, it may well be suggested that the straps that tied the tower to the elephant were decorated and bejewelled. The state of preservation of illustrative material on elephants that has survived does not show how the straps were designed, but since horses at the time were adorned with gold and silver phalerae[46] and the carpets on the elephants' backs were multi-coloured and ornamented (Plates XII–XIV), presumably the straps for the towers were not plain either, which is why the author used the word ḥēšev. If the ḥēšev of the ephod was an abdominal belt for the ephod rather than a shoulder strap, there is a further reason for the use of ḥēšev, since the straps in question were tied around the elephants' bellies.

[43] The singular of ḥišvōnōt and the plural of ḥēšev are not known from the sources. The former may be the plural of the latter, but following other declension patterns the forms could be ḥēšev–ḥašāvīm and ḥišāvōn–ḥišvōnōt. Even if the latter possibility is the right one, there are instances of identical meanings in two different declensions (e.g. 'eṣev–'aṣāvīm and 'iṣāvōn–iṣvōnōt. The mistake of Symmachus and Theodotion noted above shows that the translators considered ḥēšev to be the singular of ḥišvōnōt or at least similar in meaning. That is true also of the translator of I Maccabees.

[44] Shoulders: see the summary of H. L. Ginsberg, 'Ephod', in Biblical Encyclopaedia, vol. 1, (Jerusalem, 1952) cols 495–7 (Hebrew). Hips: see the summary of J. M. Grintz, 'Ephod', in Hebrew Encyclopaedia, vol. 5 (Jerusalem, 1953) cols 117–18 (Hebrew).

[45] Ben-Jehuda 1908: 4.1793–4.

[46] See, e.g., Minns 1913: 271–3; Rostovtzeff 1922: 137–8; Allen 1971: 20–3.

There might seem to be another possibility for explaining the erroneous translation. The root *ḥ(a)v(a)š* is used in the Bible in the sense of 'tie' (see Ez. 27.24, 'tied up with cords'). It could therefore be suggested that the author wrote its plural *ḥivšōnōt* to mean 'cords', and the word was metathesized to *ḥišvōnōt* under the influence of the frequent use of the word in the chapter. There are indeed parallels for the variants of *ḥ(a)š(a)v* and *ḥ(a)v(a)š*.[47] In this case, however, it is hard to understand why the author would opt for an unusual and poetic word. The fact that *ḥ(a)v(a)š* in the biblical occurrences is always a verb rather than a noun also makes it somewhat difficult to adopt this last alternative.

In any case, *ḥišvōnōt* should be reconstructed in the verses of this chapter that refer to artillery pieces (20,31,51,52). In the light of this conclusion, perhaps the enigmatic Daniel verse referring to one of Antiochus Epiphanes' expeditions (11.24) should read יחשב חשבנותיו (= shall devise [assemble?] his artillery machines) rather than יחשב מחשבותיו (= shall devise his thoughts). This interpretation, however, entails an understanding of the general background of the verse, which is not sufficiently clear.

And on each one men of valour: The text says nothing about the equipment of the soldiers on the elephants. According to the available literary and pictorial material, the towers seem to have sometimes carried archers (Strabo 15.1.52 and the Capena bowl) and sometimes spear-throwers (Aelian, *Nat. Anim.* 12.9 and the Leningrad phalera). If a clash with enemy elephants was anticipated, the soldiers were armed with *sarissai* so they could attack the soldiers on the enemy elephant towers and even the elephants themselves (Polybius 5.84.2). Presumably if there was a clash of a row of elephants supported by 'light' defenders against the enemy phalanx (as in the battle of Panium: Polybius 16.18.7,9–10), the soldiers on the towers were also supplied with *sarissai*. As the elephants in the battle of Beth Zacharia were placed among the 'heavy' units and advanced with them, probably the soldiers in the towers were archers. These kept an eye on the elephants' flanks and defended them together with the surrounding infantry. In battle their position on the elephants' backs provided the snipers with a good observation post having the advantage of height, and the towers provided some protection.

[four] fighting on them: Some of the manuscripts have τριάκοντα (= thirty), and some δύο καὶ τριάκοντα (= thirty-two), but these figures are unacceptable. Towers were filled with large numbers of soldiers only for royal processions (Philostratus 2.6: ten to sixteen) and not in military operations. The literary sources state that each

---

[47] See Yalon 1967: 47,79, with regard to the Scroll of Confessions, 3.31–3, the evolution of the phrase '*ḥešev ha-efōd*', and a fragment in Christian Aramaic.

tower contained three soldiers (Aelian, *Nat. Anim.* 13.9; Pliny, *Nat. Hist.* 8.22; cf. Plate XIVc) or four (Livy 37.40; Strabo 15.1.52). The Leningrad phalera and the Capena bowl have only two soldiers on one side of the elephant (Plates XII, XIIIa; cf. XIVb), but this does not mean that the towers were manned by only two. The composition in the two works is 'flat' without perspective, so that the artists found it hard to insert additional figures, especially since space was reduced by the crenellations in the towers. As the soldiers on the elephant were supposed to prevent its being injured on its vulnerable flanks and also to protect the mahout, it is hard to believe that only two were considered sufficient. The only information on that point in regard to the Seleucid army notes four soldiers in each tower for the battle of Magnesia (Livy, ibid.). Given the fact that the Seleucid army table of organization remained constant for several generations, it may be assumed that in this matter, too, nothing changed in the twenty-eight years between the battle of Magnesia and that of Beth Zacharia.

Various proposals have been put forward to solve the difficulty in this verse. Bochart is of the opinion that the author did not state a figure, and that thirty-two is a gloss inserted under the influence of the total number of elephants mentioned above (verse 30).[48] Abel believes the original had שְׁלִישִׁם, that is, picked 'mounted' soldiers (as per Ex. 14.7, 15.4; II Kings 10.25) which the translator misread as שְׁלֹשִׁים (= thirty). In the same line Zeitlin suggests that the original was שְׁנֵי שָׁלִישִׁים (= two picked mounted soldiers) which the translator misread as 'two and thirty'.[49] Michaelis reconstructs 'two or three', 'two-three' or the like (cf. II Kings 9.32; Is. 17.6).[50] Cahana speculates that the error occurred in the original Hebrew when שְׁלֹשָׁה (= three) was miscopied as שְׁלֹשִׁים (= thirty).[51] None of the hypotheses is entirely satisfactory. It is hard to believe that no figure was given for the soldiers on the elephants when the author is so generous with numbers for the various enemy units in this battle (esp. verses 30,35); as noted above, two men on the elephant was not customary and it is doubtful whether three was the Seleucid practice. The best explanation seems to be that of Rahlfs, who suggests that the error occurred in the Greek when the original Δ (= four) was miscopied as Λ (= thirty).[52] This seems especially likely in view of the correspondence with the number of fighters per elephant noted for the battle of Magnesia, and considering the obvious association of the description of the elephants in the preceding verse with the chariot vision in the first chapter of Ezekiel (see p. 317 above re verse 36), where 'four' is repeated many times in regard to the 'chariot' and the 'beasts' and their various

---

[48] Bochart 1893: 2.262.
[49] Abel 1949: 119; Zeitlin 1950: 130–1. See also Goldstein 1976: 321.
[50] Michaelis 1778: 139–40, apparently in the wake of Wernsdorff 1747: 119ff.
[51] Cahana 1957: 2.128.   [52] Rahlfs 1934; 78–9.

components (verses 5,6,8,10,16,17,18). The extra 'two' which appears in some of the manuscripts was inserted later in the wake of the total number of elephants (verse 30, 'thirty-two').

In the detailed paraphrase on the battle of Beth Zacharia in *Antiquitates*, Josephus does not make any mention at all of the combatants on the elephants, probably because he was puzzled about the number of soldiers reported in I Maccabees. This indicates that the error was already in the Greek text at the end of the first century A.D.

Fighting on them: The Leningrad phalera shows the soldiers seated, though not in a battle position. The Capena bowl depicts them on their feet during a battle, as does an etched amulet now in the Cabinet de France (Plates XII, XIVb).

And an Indian to it: The reference is to the mahout (*elephantagōgos*) seated on the elephant's neck and directing it (see Plates XII, XIIIa, b, XIVa, b). The mahout, who had no protection at all, was equipped with a long hooked rod for guiding the animal. The term 'Indian' was applied to the mahout because at the beginning of the Hellenistic age, the elephant trainers all came from India.[53] It is doubtful whether in our period the mahouts were actually from the Far East.

38 *And the rest of the horsemen*: According to their location during the deployment and their actions in battle (verse 40) these seem to have been lighter cavalry than those in the 'formations', at any rate not cataphracts.

They positioned on either side of the camp: The word 'camp' refers here to the enemy 'formations' advancing along a broad front. The horsemen were stationed on the flanks and covered the 'formations' on the extremities of the front line. The 'formations' were preceded by some mobile infantry or cavalry (*prodromoi*), see p. 333 below.

Frightening and cover[ing] the formations: The Greek is κατασείοντες καὶ καταφρασσόμενοι ἐν ταῖς φάλαγξιν (literally: 'frightening and covered by the formations'), the grammatical subject of the sentence being the 'horsemen' mentioned in the beginning of the verse. But in fact the horsemen stationed on the extreme flanks of the 'formations' defended those 'formations' and not *vice versa* as the end of the verse seems to imply, so that it is impossible to retain the text as it is.[54] The translator must have misread the verb מְכַסִּים

---

[53] On elephant trainers see Scullard 1974: 131, 237 and p. 281 n. 156. Trainers from India are seen in the silver phalera of the Hermitage and the terracotta from Myrina, both dating from early in the third century B.C. (Plate XIIIa, b).

[54] This is also the opinion of Grimm 1853: 104; Gutberlet 1920: 107; cf. Cahana in his translation (1957: 2.128); but they do not adequately support the proposed reconstruction. The Goldstein explanation of the error (1976: 38) does not hold water. If later copyists perceived the mistake in the word φάραγξιν, which supposedly appeared in all versions and properly corrected it to φάλαγξιν, they certainly would have noted the inappropriateness of the passive form καταφρασσόμενοι.

(= covering) as a passive, מְכֻסִּים (= covered), which he rendered as καταφρασσόμενοι, no doubt under the influence of the passive form of the same verb in verse 36. The noun phrase *la-ma'arākōt* which in the original verse had a direct object (accusative) relationship to the verb (i.e., covering [= protecting] the 'formations'), was understood as an indirect object (dative) by the translator on the basis of the more common meaning of the prefixed Hebrew *lāmed*, and the misread passive form of the verb, and consequently rendered as ταῖς φάλαγξιν (= to the formations). It was probably a scribe who later inserted the preposition ἐν because of the passive form of the preceding participle.

The frontal deployment described above was carried out in the Valley of Blessing south of the 'Etsyon Bloc on the road leading to Beth Zacharia, which can be seen very well from Tree Hill. The low hilly ridge which traverses the valley from Khirbet Marrina eastwards is no real obstacle and therefore did not require a change of deployment. The valley is 2.5 km from north to south and 1.7 km wide. On that area it was possible to place some eight 'formations' in a row with cavalry cover on the flanks, each 'formation' taking up 120 to 150 m in the width (every heavy soldier needed three feet, and the phalanx was sixteen rows deep; each heavy horseman also needed three feet or so, and the cavalry units were eight rows deep).[55] The purpose of such a deployment was to terrify the Jewish troops and undermine their morale (see details above, p. 127). The advance of the entire force along the hilly ridge bisecting the valley must have been especially impressive. The conclusion on the number of formations supports the correction proposed above regarding the number of Seleucid elephants mentioned in *Bellum Judaicum*; in view of the effect on morale that was the reason for using the elephants at all, the elephants that took part in the expedition would certainly have been positioned in the forward line. It may very well be that the deployment was planned even before Lysias left for Judaea, and a suitable number of elephants sent along, leaving 'surplus elephants' ready to defend northern Syria. The commander was well aware of the particular structure of the terrain which had been under Seleucid rule for dozens of years. Topographical details were recorded somehow or other, and there are signs of the existence of a mapping service in the Seleucid kingdom (Pliny, *Nat. Hist.* 6.63; cf. Vegetius 3.6).

Instead of ἐν ταῖς φάλαγξιν (= by the phalanxes, i.e. by the 'formations'), the I Maccabees Alexandrian manuscript has ἐν ταῖς φάραγξιν (= in the defiles), as it does in verse 35 (cf. also I Macc.

---

[55] On the spacing of heavy infantry and cavalry see Polybius 12.18, 18.29.2,30; and see Bar Kochva 1979: 168, on the Seleucid deployment in the battle of Magnesia. Cf. Pritchett 1974: 1.144–54.

10.82). This certainly does not make sense. The deployment of the
Seleucid force on the march was clearly designed to impress and
terrify the Jewish force. Concealment of the cavalry in the defiles
does not accord with the nature of the campaign, nor is it feasible
under the conditions of the terrain with which we are familiar. Abel
and Grimm, who had difficulty in understanding how the heavy
Seleucid force operated in a narrow pass, concluded that this
mistaken version led Josephus to locate the battle in the defile (in
both *Bell.* and *Ant.*), and in *Antiquitates* to describe the deployment
of the Seleucid force in a column, unit after unit, as it entered the
defile (see p. 330 below).[56] Josephus did use a particular version
of the Alexandrian text while writing *Antiquitates*,[57] but the
arrangement of the battle in the defile is clearly indicated in another
verse of I Maccabees (6.40), and explicitly stated in *Bellum Judaicum*
which is based on an entirely different source. That source, Nicolaus
of Damascus, was apparently familiar with I Maccabees and even
utilized it, but it was an early edition of the Greek translation in
which such a glaring garble is unlikely. Nicolaus, who was well
versed in Hellenistic warfare, would in this context in any case
certainly have realized the mistake in the word φάραγξιν. Besides,
Josephus in *Antiquitates* (12.371) explains that the Seleucid army
marched in a column and not in a broad formation because of the
'narrow space' (στενοχωρία), while from the Alexandrian
manuscript it seems as if only the cavalrymen in the furthermost
flanks made their ways separately in different defiles. See also p. 313
above re verse 35.

39 *And as the sun rose on the shields of gold and bronze*: The Greek χαλκᾶς
ἀσπίδας renders both copper and bronze shields. The sources, which
designate the regular 'heavy' forces as *khalkaspides*,[58] certainly
intend the stronger bronze. As noted above regarding 'bronze
helmets' (p. 316), in this verse too the Hebrew was *neḥošet*, meaning
bronze. Cf. מגיני נחושת (= bronze shields) in I Kings 14.27; II
Chron. 12.10. The standard shields of the heavy infantry units were
made of or covered with bronze.

As to 'gold shields', many scholars believe that is no more than
'a Jewish exaggeration'[59] or an invention based on a biblical
association. Indeed a clear resemblance to the 'golden shields'
mentioned twice in the Bible in contrast to bronze ones (I Kings
14.26–7; II Chron. 12.9–10) is discernible, and 'golden shields' do
not appear frequently in the sources. However, such shields were
most likely mentioned in the listing of the phalanx units that took

[56] Grimm 1853: 99; Abel 1949: 118; and see also Ettelson 1925: 338; Goldstein 1976:
320–1.   [57] Thackeray 1929: 85; and Melamed 1951: 122–3.
[58] Polybius 2.66.5, 4.67.6, 5.91.7, 30.25.5; Livy 44.41.2, 45.33.1; Diodorus 31.8.10; Plut.
Aem. 18.8, *Sulla* 19.4.
[59] So Grimm 1853: 102. Against him only Dancy 1954: 115–16.

part in Antiochus Epiphanes' procession at Daphne two and a half years before Lysias' second expedition (Polybius 30.25.5).[60] Golden shields are also mentioned in other sources (Plut. *Eum.* 14.8; Pollux 1.175; Onasander 1.20). The allusion is either to shields with gold decoration or plating (see p. 7 and n. 5 above), or more probably to shields made of or decorated with *orichalcum* (brass), which, at least from afar, closely resembles gold.[61] While a shield probably largely made of gold (on a wooden cross and round frame) was found at Vergina in a tomb attributed to Philip II, its varied decorations, including ivory, and in particular the fact that *in situ* it was protected by another shield made of bronze indicate that it was used exclusively for ceremonial purposes.[62]

The shield colours described in the verse indicate that the heavy units in the 'formations' were composed of phalangites (in addition to those made up of soldiers of the 'Roman' type – see p. 315 above): 'gold' (or rather brass) shields are mentioned only with regard to phalangites, and in any case it is hardly likely that other than these privileged troops would have been supplied with such expensive equipment. On the other hand, an obvious omission in the passage is the silver shields, the *argyraspides*, characteristic of the infantry Royal Guard which took its name from them. It has already been noted that about half the unit underwent 'retraining' in Roman combat methods before the Daphne procession (p. 120, and see p. 416 below). It may be that in the time elapsed since Daphne more of the *argyraspides* had been retrained, or perhaps a considerable proportion of those remained with Philippus in Persia (see p. 343 below).

In addition to shields of bronze, silver and gold, Hellenistic sources mention also white ones (*leukaspidai*) that were common in the armies of the Antigonus dynasty.[63] The shield colours were designed to astound the enemy and dampen their spirits. The sight was particularly impressive against the clothing of the Seleucid soldiers which included a burgundy tunic often embroidered in silver or gold (Polybius 30.25.10; see p. 274 above); for the effect of

[60] On the reconstruction of the text see p. 417 below, esp. n. 21.

[61] Chronological questions connected with *orichalcum*, its first fabrication, the production of zinc, its known deposits, production technique, its value and distribution are all controversial, and there is an extensive literature on the subject. I mention only two books which take opposite positions: Forbes (1950: 272–89), who sets production and distribution early, and Caley (1964: esp. 13–31), who believes that the use of *orichalcum* was rare before the first century. See also Hengel 1982: p. 47 n. 106. When the detailed metallurgical analysis of recent finds from Macedonia is published, it will certainly support Forbes's position. See, e.g., the fourth-century B.C. brass greaves found at Derveni in Hatzopoulos and Loukopoulos 1980: 64, no. 43.

[62] See Andronikos 1980: 220–4. The same is probably true of the golden shields in the imitations of Hellenistic painting at Pompeii: see Barnabei 1901: 57, fig. 12. See also the typical Macedonian shield in Pl. VIII there.

[63] Plut. *Aem.* 18.3, *Tim.* 27.3, *Cleom.* 23.1; Livy 44.41.2; Diodorus 31.8.10. On *leukaspidai* among the phalangites see Walbank 1957–79: 1.275.

the contrast cf. the white shields against the black uniforms of the
Thracians in the battle of Pydna (Plut. *Aem.* 18).

The mountains glittered from them and blazed like torches of fire: The
statement suggests that the glittering shields flashed like mirrors in
the sun and cast their reflection on the shaded hills opposite them,
which created a glow ('glittered') like sunshine. They may have
even caused some fires in the dry thorny vegetation ('blazed', etc.),
and evidently blinded the Jewish force with their glare. On the
astonishment and apprehension caused by polished Hellenistic arms
glittering in the sun see Plut. *Eum.* 14.8, *Sulla* 16.3–4; Onasander
1.28, 29; and compare also with the Roman army at Iotapata,
Bellum Judaicum 3.265–9. The Hellenistic armies used to polish and
burnish their arms for this purpose (Polybius 11.9.1–2).

The credibility of the information provided can be verified in the
field. We must ascertain whether a force advancing from south to
north in the Valley of Blessing and Wadi Shukheit, as the Seleucids
did (see p. 329 below), could create the effect described during the
season and at the time of day of the march. The campaign took
place in late spring 162 B.C. (see p. 545 below) when dawn comes
rather early. According to the text the Seleucid army left Beth Zur
early in the morning (6.33). It would thus reach the site of the clash
8 km from Beth Zur some two hours later. At that hour in late
spring, the sun rises slightly north-east of the village of Beit Fajjar,
i.e. north-east and east of the Valley of Blessing and south-east of
Wadi Shukheit. This means that the shields could glitter in the sun
only when the troops were rather close to the entrance to the defile,
and that their effect was less impressive in the defile itself.

And indeed an experiment carried out at the same hour and
season with mirrors the size of the *peltē*, the round phalangite shield,
placed in the Valley of Blessing facing the north, produced a
glorious spectacle: the mirrors flashed and glistened in the sun to a
distance of about two kilometres, their shapes were projected on the
hills opposite and the glare was blinding six to eight hundred metres
away. Moreover, the Seleucid shields, positioned on the left arm and
as usual angled to the right,[64] faced the sun in the east. The
thousands of shields massed together in long continuous rows,
among them the oblong Roman-type bucklers (*scutum*), certainly
produced a marvellous and astounding effect as they advanced, and
dazzled the stationary Jewish force.

All this is recorded by I Maccabees with admirable accuracy:

[64] On the definitely rightward inclination of the Classical Greek hoplites so as to obtain the
greatest possible protection for the unshielded right side of the body from the shield of the
soldier next to him see the celebrated statement of Thucydides 5.71. This state of affairs led,
among other things, to concentrating the picked units on the right, and making them the first
to attack (see also Kromayer and Veith 1926: 85). As a result, the shield itself naturally inclined
to the right. This was even truer in the Hellenistic phalanx formation because the hand the
shield leaned against also held the *sarissa*.

although he describes the enemy's equipment when outlining the first phase of the deployment and advance in the Valley of Blessing (verses 35–8), he mentions the flash of the shields just before the description of the entrance into the defile. In any case the distance between the south section of the Valley of Blessing and the place in the Tree Hill where most of the Jewish force was (see below), was too great for the shields to have any effect, but when the Seleucid troops came close to the beginning of Wadi Shukheit the reflection of their shields began to disturb the Jewish defenders. Attention should be paid also to the mention of the sunrise: the glitter of the shields in fact gradually intensified as the sun rose and the enemy advanced northwards from Beth Zur. The great accuracy in the timing of the visual effect produced, and the mention of the sunrise, a superfluous detail from the substantive point of view, support the conclusion that the description is based on the author's personal experience. It must be stressed that even if the chronology I propose for the battle, based on I Maccabees, is rejected in favour of the chronological information in II Maccabees according to which the battle took place at the end of summer or autumn 163 B.C. (see p. 543 below), the above conclusion is still valid. For the angle of the sun's rays, the hours of the sun's rise, strength, and advance at the end of summer are not significantly different from those noted for the end of spring.

Josephus in *Antiquitates* shifted the bedazzlement to the assault stage in the defile itself and detached it from the natural conditions of gradual sunrise and advance: he reports that after entering the pass, when the order to sound the battle cry was given (close to the start of the assault), the king bared (γυμνώσας) the gold and bronze shields of the soldiers and then a great glitter was reflected (para. 372; cf. Plutarch, *Lucullus* 27.6).

An interesting parallel is provided by testimony regarding the battle which took place in the 'Etsyon Bloc on 12 May 1948, a day before the bloc surrendered to the Jordanians. The Jordanian advance started at 7 a.m. The season, the hour, and the route of the advance correspond to those in the battle of Beth Zacharia. The Jordanian force, made up of about 600 men, proceeded from the Valley of Blessing to Russian Hill, confident of its superiority and victory, and therefore dressed and deployed as for a triumphal procession. The many brass buckles and buttons of the standard British uniforms, the bandoliers of cartridges on their chests, the metal parts of the rifles, the completely uncamouflaged steel helmets and the numerous bugles were all highly burnished and polished. According to the few survivors of Kefar 'Etsyon who observed the advancing troops from the trenches south and east of the village, the metal parts glistened in the sun and blinded the defenders. They also testify that although the parade contradicted the most elementary rules of modern warfare, it made an astonishing impression on the small, exhausted force defending the village.

40 *And a part of the king's camp spread out on the high mountains and many in the depression*: The verse implies a change of formation. While previously (verses 35–9) the Seleucid army had been moving across a broad, flat area, at this point most of the force continued in a valley ('depression') confined on two sides at least by ridges of hills ('the high mountains'). The need to assign troops to seize the ridges indicates that the valley was quite narrow. Josephus properly understood the I Maccabees description, and in *Antiquitates* reports that the Seleucid army went through a mountain pass. The same is noted in *Bellum Judaicum* following Nicolaus (cf. p. 325 above).

These data, together with the statement that the battle took place near Beth Zacharia and on the road from Beth Zur to Beth Zacharia, make it possible to locate the battle site: in the northern part of the Valley of Blessing, the road branches into two, one ascending to a ridge line (Russian Hill) and the other going through a kilometre-long pass (Wadi Shukheit), 100 to 150 metres wide, and up to the saddle between Baluṭat el-Yerza (Tree Hill) and the hill west of it (Yellow Hill) where it rejoins the other branch to continue northwards, close to the ridge line of Jebel Ḥabbun, the hill north-east of Beth Zacharia. Another natural possibility for moving northwards is the valley road between Russian Hill and Deir Sha'ar (the Russian monastery), but that way is narrow and steep compared to the more westerly one. Thus the only possible identification for the pass is Wadi Shukheit overlooked by the saddle, Tree Hill and Yellow Hill on the north, the Kefar 'Etsyon hill on the west, and Russian Hill on the east. Other proposals made for the location of the battlefield ignore some of the basic elements noted above. Thus Conder proposed Rās Sharifeh north-east of Beth Zacharia, which is neither on a road nor in a defile; Abel proposes the level terrain stretching east from the Tree Hill (Ḥalat Jamal); Avissar locates the battle at grid reference 1635/1199, on the modern eastern road; Avi-Yonah places the battle in a general way in one of the valleys in the neighbourhood of Kefar 'Etsyon.[65]

A part of the king's camp...on the high mountains: The reference is primarily to the horsemen stationed on the flanks of the frontal formation in the Valley of Blessing, and probably mainly to light infantry generally numerous in the Seleucid army, who fought as *promakhoi* (= skirmishers) in frontal battles, providing cover and cleaning-up operations during marches. At this stage these troops

[65] Conder 1875: 67; Abel 1949: 117; Avissar 1955: 236; Wibbing 1962: 163; Avi-Yonah 1972: 172.

were despatched to seize the ridges dominating the defile on the east
and west, which had certainly previously been occupied by the
Jewish forces. The author does not bother to describe them because
they made a lesser impression than the colourful massive formations
or the elephants. Still, presumably, semi-heavy units too could have
been despatched to the hills. Their participation was essential if the
hills were covered with high vegetation (see p. 333 below re verse
42) which provided cover for the defending forces and enabled them
to surprise ascending troops in hand-to-hand combat.

In the depression: The Greek ἐπὶ τὰ ταπεινά is to be reconstructed
בשפל (= in the depression). Cf. I Macc. 3.52. The reference is
undoubtedly to the defile.

And many in the depression: The Greek is καί τινες which can be
reconstructed according to the Septuagint as either אחדים (= the
few) or רבים (= the many). The latter seems preferable, because
there is mention below of the 'formations', the heavy units of the
Seleucid army, which could certainly not be described as 'few'. For
the reconstruction 'many', cf. the Septuagint for Gen. 37.34.

   Josephus in *Antiquitates* describes in detail the advance of the
'formations' in the defile: 'He arranged the elephants to proceed
one after the other, for because of the narrowness of the space they
could not be deployed in the width, and around each elephant 1,000
foot and 500 horsemen moved ahead together with it' (12.371).
Josephus may have recalled that description from the source he
utilized earlier in writing *Bellum Judaicum* (the latter does not
mention the structure or deployment of the Seleucid force, because
of the abridged and compressed nature of the description there). But
even if this is Josephus' own interpretation, there is little doubt that
it is apt. The division of the Seleucid heavy forces into small
independent units, each comprising all the elements in the standard
Hellenistic deployment, is explicable only by the need to cope with
the difficulty of using the force in the narrow battlefields of the
Judaean Hills. Each unit constituted a flexible and independent
structure capable of modifying its deployment in accordance with
the terrain, and facing the enemy on its own, and was in fact a
miniature version of the overall Hellenistic formation (with the
exception of the light skirmishers). A unit of the size of the formation
mentioned could compress itself into the 100-metre width at the
narrowest point of the defile by increasing the number of phalanx
rows to thirty-two (see the calculations on p. 324 above; for the
depth of the deployment cf. Polybius 2.66.9; Livy 37.40.2;
Asclepiodotus 2.1). The forward 'formations' probably included
'Roman' soldiers rather than phalangites, allowing greater
flexibility to the first 'formations' to make contact with the enemy,
enabling them to alter their formation swiftly according to conditions

of the terrain and operate efficiently on the narrow and confined battle site.

And they walked confidently and in order: The Hellenistic heavy formation had to maintain a uniform pace in order to prevent the development of gaps which enemy lighter forces could penetrate. Those were capable of breaking up the phalanx from within by hand-to-hand combat. If Judas Maccabaeus set an ambush (see p. 333 below), the expression may mean that the Seleucid army proceeded confidently despite the danger of ambush, knowing that thanks to its flexible structure it would be able to withstand a surprise attack. Cf. Polybius 10.30.9, παραπορευομένων [ἐν] τάξει καὶ βάδην (= as they marched in order and slowly). And see p. 124 above on the deployment of the Seleucid army in the Elburz pass.

41 *And all trembled who heard the sound of their throng and the strides of the throng and the clank of the weapons*: The verse describes various methods for increasing the din and deterring the foe customary in Hellenistic warfare: the war cry, the stamping of the soldier's feet and the galloping of the horses which were purposely accelerated, and the continual clank of offensive weapons on shields and armour. These were augmented by the trumpets, designed both to frighten the enemy and to signal various messages (see p. 394 below). The Mishnah sums up in a similar vein the sound effects accompanying the appearance of the Roman army: 'Let not your heart grow faint – before the neighing of horses and the polishing of swords. Do not fear – the slamming of oblong bucklers and the shuffling of boots. Do not panic – at the sound of the horns. Do not break down – at the sound of the yelling' (Sotah 8.1; for the question of the time and the meaning see pp. 498–9 below).

The author mentions the sound effects that accompanied the Seleucid advance only at this stage, in describing the entry into the defile, and not the wide deployment and march in the Valley of Blessing. The fact is that the Jewish force, which was in the main watching from Tree Hill, could hear the noise only when the enemy 'formations' entered the defile, whose opening is about a kilometre south of Tree Hill. Even if there were considerable Jewish forces stationed on the hills on both sides of the defile, they would not have heard the enemy advancing, for the acoustics on the open valley are very bad, chiefly because of the prevailing winds, and loud yells are swallowed up even at short distances. On the other hand, in Wadi Shukheit and the hills around it acoustical conditions are extremely good, as in a Greek theatre. A farmer's exhortation to his animal ploughing in the wadi echoes a great distance, and conversations between soldiers in the army camp on Russian Hill are easily heard in Kefar 'Etsyon, 600 m away as the crow flies. The noise and confusion produced by the tens of thousands of soldiers with Lysias was magnified by the special conditions of the defile, and as reported no doubt terrified the Jewish defenders. The absence of any mention of 'sounds' in the detailed description of the first stage of the advance (6.35–9), although it is packed with visual features of the enemy's appearance, shows a high degree of accuracy which is not usual in second-hand accounts and heightens the impression that the author was an eye-witness. It is not surprising that Josephus does not mention the din and clamour at the entry to the defile and attributes them to the battle itself, when the signal to attack was given (12.372; cf. Plut. *Crass.* 27.1).

The sound of their throng: War cries (*boē*) were designed to frighten the enemy as well as to increase the soldiers' self-confidence and enthusiasm for battle. See, for instance, Diodorus 19.30.1, 41.3; Livy 37.41.11–12 (the battle of Magnesia); Plut. *Eum.* 14.5, *Aem.* 18, *Sulla* 16,19; and especially Onasander 29; Polybius 2.29.6. Cf. also Thucydides 7.70–1, and in the account of the battle at Elasa in I Macc. 9.13.

And the strides of the throng: The Greek is ὁδοιπορία (= steps), a word which does not appear in the Septuagint. The Hebrew term מצעדי (= strides) may very well have had a military connotation in the author's day (see Daniel 11.43), which would make it preferable to the צעדי proposed by Cahana (p. 128).

And the clank of the weapons: The reference is to the knocking of the spears, javelins and swords against the shields and armour (*patagos*: see Onasander 29; cf. Herodotus 3.79.4, 4.211; Xenophon, *Anab.* 1.8.18, 4.5.18; Plut. *Eum.* 14.11). The form συγκρουσμός (= clash, etc.) which appears in this verse is not known from the Septuagint. The underlying Hebrew was probably ונקישת. This is supported by the verb συνεκροτοῦντο, which in the Theodotion translation is used to render the verse וארכבתה דא לדא נקשן (= and his knees knocked one against another, Daniel 5.6). The same root is common in the meaning noted in the Mishnah (cf. Bekhoroth 7.6: המקיש בקרסוליו וארכובותיו = knocking his ankles and knees).

42 *And Judah and his camp approached the battle*: On the participation of some heavy or semi-heavy units in the Jewish army at Beth Zacharia see pp. 76 above. Apparently the Jewish troops were located on the saddle, i.e. Tree Hill and its environs, and on the ridges on either side of the defile, and intended to force the battle in the defile itself.

The description does not clarify whether an ambush was set for the Seleucid troops or if Judas Maccabaeus prepared openly for a pitched battle (cf. p. 139 n. 2 above). The absence of any mention of the preparation of an ambush is not decisive. A description of a sophisticated military action carried out by the Jews in this battle

would have interfered with the author's didactic purpose. The sad
outcome of the battle raises the question why 'the hidden finger of
God' did not operate in this case, as it did in other battles. The
author answers the question in his own way. As noted above, the
religious–national conception in the book is that divine help is
provided only to those who have the determination, knowhow and
the capacity to defend themselves and fight back (see p. 64). The
setting of an ambush in a dominating position and indirect warfare
are the methods by which an inferior force can prevail, with help
from on high, against a greater army (3.18–24, 58–4.15). The
author of I Maccabees thus had sufficient reason not to be too
specific in regard to the Jewish defence measures, although it is
possible that no ambush was set. The terrain does not allow for
an unequivocal determination of the deployment of Judas
Maccabaeus' army: Jewish tactics in the battle of Beth Zacharia
were dictated by the facilities for concealment in the saddle and
ridges that overlooked the defile. The area was most likely an ideal
place for ambush if the slopes were forested, which is not impossible
in view of the discovery of signs of early forestation on Tree Hill and
its environs,[66] or if they were planted with olive trees and the like.
It is hard to believe that Judas Maccabaeus would have missed a
chance to surprise the enemy and sought to face them openly in that
kind of terrain: he could be sure that the enemy would choose the
western rather than the eastern road, for in the sector north of the
'Etsyon Bloc the latter passed through 5 km of canyon, in Wadi
el-Biyār, which was much more dangerous than the relatively short
defiles in the western road. If the hills were bare, however, or
covered with low-growing flora, Judas Maccabaeus must have
shown himself openly, aiming to derive the greatest advantage from
his preferential topographical position and the limitations that the
battle site set on the deployment and manoeuvrability of the heavy
Seleucid forces.

And of the king's camp six hundred men fell: In *Antiquitates* Josephus
describes these six hundred as *prodromoi* (12.372). The *prodromoi*
constituted cavalry or mobile infantry whose main function in the
course of an expedition was to locate ambushes and direct the
advance of the forces.[67] Josephus may have recalled the
participation of the *prodromoi* from the source he utilized in writing
Bellum Judaicum. This possibility is supported by the comparison of
Bellum Judaicum and I Maccabees: according to *Bellum Judaicum*,
Eleazar's assault preceded the clash of the 'phalangites' (1.42; cf. p.
76 above), while according to I Maccabees the 600 soldiers fell

---

[66] On them see Conder 1893: 64; Abel 1924: 214.

[67] On the function of the *prodromoi* see Pritchett 1974: 1.130–1 and 2.188–9; A. F. Pauli,
in *RE* s.v. 'Prodromos', cols 102–4; Brunt 1963: 27–8; and see the sources there, e.g. Aristotle,
Ath.Pol. 49.1; Xen. *Hipp.* 1.25; Diodorus 17.17.4; Arrian, *Anab.* 1.14.1,14.6, etc.

before Eleazar penetrated the 'formation' to reach the elephant. And indeed the despatch of phalangites (including men of the 'Roman' unit) into the defile without some vanguard of more mobile troops might have resulted in a catastrophe if the Jews had been able to storm the defile from all sides. The use of elephants alone made it necessary to have flexible forces in the van to remove any artificial obstacles placed in the elephants' path.[68] I Maccabees does not specify the equipment or affiliation of the 600 fatalities, just as he does not define the light forces that operated on the flanks of the frontal deployment (see p. 332 above re verse 38).

43 *And Eleazar 'Eran saw*: The epithet *Auran* (*Sauran* in the Alexandrian manuscript and likewise in the ancient Latin translation) has been accorded many strange interpretations and reconstructions. Some have connected it with the killing of the elephant (*ḥōran*, derived from *ḥōr*(= hole), etc.), but Eleazar had the name in his lifetime, just as the other brothers had theirs (I Macc. 2.5), and it is apparently identical with the name of one of Menelaus' chief supporters (II Macc. 4.40). The most reasonable interpretation is that of Abel, who derives the name from the root עוּר, making it 'Eran ('the alert', 'the vigorous'; cf. Num. 26.36).[67]

One of the beasts armoured: The sources testify that various pieces of armour were attached to war elephants for their greater protection. In his report on the battle of Magnesia, Livy speaks of metal strips to protect the forehead (*frontalia*; and see Pl. XIVd) and even protective helmets (*cristae*, 37.40.4). In Julius Caesar's time armour was used for other parts of the elephant's body (*Bell. Afr.* 72). In this verse the reference may also be to the metal sheathing of the tower and the shields that were attached to its sides (on which see p. 318 above).

In royal armour: θώραξι βασιλικοῖς. The intention is to stress that the elephant described was armoured more heavily than the others, or that its armour was especially shiny and ornate.

Josephus in *Bellum Judaicum* says nothing about the elephant's armour, although he notes that there was a high tower on its back and a series of gilded crenellations, Nicolaus of Damascus, Josephus' source for the Eleazar episode in that book, here based himself entirely on I Maccabees. As Nicolaus was far removed from the era of elephant warfare, like the modern reader he found it hard to understand the reason the elephant required armour, and the meaning of 'royal armour'. He therefore interpreted *thōrax* to mean the tower on the elephant's back, which is the meaning of the kindred word *thōrakion* (see p. 317 above re verse 37), and construed

---

[68] Cf. Diodorus 18.71.4–5, 19.84.1–4; Livy 44.41.4; Polyaenus 4.3.17; Curtius Rufus 4.13.36; Vegetius 3.24; and see Glover 1948: 7–8.
[69] Abel 1949: 31,121.

the crenellations on the tower to be gilded so as to add royal splendour.

And it was taller than all the beasts: The 'evidence' of that elephant's high status recalls a number of sources noting that the elephant on which the Indian king Forus fought Alexander was the tallest of the elephants in the battle near the river Hydaspes (Diodorus 17.88.4; Curtius Rufus 8.13.7; and perhaps also Plut. *Alex.* 60.12).

And it was seen that the king was on it: The impression those present had regarding the particular importance of the elephant and its rider was produced not only by its height and armour but by the sight of the special ornaments that 'outstanding' elephants were decorated with, such as gold and silver jewellery, lovely burgundy rugs, or unusually spectacular fabrics. See Pliny, *Nat. Hist.* 8.12; Diodorus 2.17.7; Plut. *Eum.* 14; the Leningrad phalera and the Villa Giulia bowl (Plates XII, XIIIa); and cf. most of the Seleucid horsemen at Daphne, Polybius 30.25.6–7; and Curtius Rufus 8.13.7. On the 'leading elephant' see also Diodorus 19.42.6.

Nevertheless it is hard to believe that Eleazar really expected to find the king on the elephant. While the Indian kings formerly fought on elephant-back as Forus did, the Hellenistic kings and supreme commanders led their armies riding in the ranks of the Royal Guard cavalry.[70] Eleazar, the commander's brother, should have known that, as well as the king's age, which was just 10 or 11 years at the time (see p. 304 above). The erroneous explanation of Eleazar's motivation can only derive from the impression made on rank-and-file Jewish soldiers who were not yet familiar with the practices in the Seleucid kingdom and army, and did not know the exact age of the king. All this strengthens the conclusion drawn from the accounts of some of the campaigns that the author of I Maccabees, an eye-witness to the action, was not part of the command echelon (pp. 238, 281). Eleazar's supposed motivation had become widely accepted, adding a dimension of great military insight to the glory of the act of self-sacrifice, and suppressing any new information the author may have acquired later, before writing his book.

Despite everything said above, I would not entirely rule out the possibility that Eleazar, though he was aware of the Seleucid military practice, in the heat of the battle mistakenly believed that this time Lysias, the commander-in-chief-(certainly not the young king), had chosen to fight on elephant-back. This was the first time that Eleazar had ever seen any pachyderms, and he was much impressed by their size and strength. The splendid accoutrements,

---

[70] See, e.g., Plut. *Dem.* 29.3; Diodorus 19.29.7, 30.4,9,83.1, and in fact in all battle descriptions of the period. For sources on the Seleucid army see p. 392 below, n. 38. On the tactical considerations that led to the practice see pp. 26–8 above.

too, may well have led him to conclude that the man on the elephant's back could not be a plain soldier. If so, Eleazar's act should be viewed as an attempt to win the battle by putting the enemy commander out of action and so making control of the troops difficult, much as happened later at Adasa and Elasa.

44 *And he gave his life to save his people*: If Eleazar did realize that the elephant was driven by an ordinary soldier, then the true purpose of the act was to prove that even the terrifying elephants could be injured and stopped, and thus to pull the Jewish troops out of the state of shock and feeling of helplessness which beset them at the sight of the powerful Seleucid 'formations' (cf. Plut. *Sulla* 16), and get them to assault the advancing units. Similar acts of self-sacrifice are attributed to Roman soldiers of the rank and file at Heraclea, Asculum and Thapsus (Pliny *NH* 8.7,18; Appian, *Hannib.* 7; Livy 37.42.5; Caesar, *Bell. Afr.* 72,84; Vegetius 3.24) and to Ptolemy I during Perdiccas' attempt to break into Pelusium (Diodorus 18.34.2).

And to make an eternal name for himself: The expression 'eternal name' does occur in the Bible (Is. 56.5, 63.12) and elsewhere in I Maccabees (2.51, 13.29).[71] It may have been inspired as well by the Greek–Hellenistic concepts of bravery. Cf., for example, Herodotus 7.220; Thucydides 2.43.

45 *And he ran toward it courageously into the formation*: The Greek is *phalanx*, For the reconstruction *ma'arāka* (= formation) see p. 433 below. The wording of the sentence is influenced by the well-known verse in the story of David and Goliath – 'And he ran to the formation toward the Philistine' (I Sam. 17.48).

And he killed to the right and to the left: Eleazar certainly came under the elephant from the side, so that he had to push his way through the rows of heavy infantry that protected the elephant. As this elephant was in one of the forward formations, and maybe even the very first, the infantry was equipped in the Roman manner and not as phalangites (see pp. 315, 330 above), which makes Eleazar's daring all the greater.

46 *And he came under the elephant and stuck it ⟨with a sword⟩*: As the elephant's head was also protected by armour, Eleazar could only aim for its belly. The word ξίφος (= חרב, sword) appears only in the Lucian version, two minuscule manuscripts and some of the manuscripts of the Old Latin translation and the Syrian. It is perhaps merely a gloss, but in the light of the resemblance to the well-known phrase in the story of Ehud son of Gera (Judg. 3.21), may well have been based on the original Hebrew.

And he killed it, and it fell down on him, and he died there: Eleazar was certainly crushed by the elephant, but it is doubtful whether the elephant was killed that way. As is shown by the experience of

[71] Adinolfi 1964: 177–86.

elephant hunters (cf. also Agatharcides in *GGM* 1, p. 146), the only way to kill an elephant instantly was an arrow shot directly to its brain or heart with an especially strong bow from a distance of no more than five metres aimed at its temple or the gap between its ear and the top of its front leg. An abdominal wound generally does not produce instant death because of the bones preventing access to the heart from there. An elephant wounded in the belly might fall, but could recover and then the mahout would lose control of it and the animal would be much more dangerous (although it would die from loss of blood some hours later). The statement that the elephant expired on the spot must be attributed to the 'fog of battle'. Josephus does not mention the death of the elephant in *Bellum Judaicum* although the abridgement actually highlights the Eleazar episode (1.42–5).

I Maccabees says nothing at all about the removal of Eleazar's body from the field (in contrast to reporting on the removal of Judas Maccabaeus' – see 9.19 and p. 399 below). That is enough to indicate the extent of the defeat. Since Eleazar seems to have been buried in the mausoleum that Simeon erected in Modein for the family (I Macc. 13.27–30), his body was perhaps returned under the terms of the agreement made when the siege of the Temple was lifted as Lysias was forced to make a hasty departure from the country (verses 57–61).

47 *And they saw the might of the kingdom and the fury of the armies*: The plural form 'armies' refers to the Seleucid army. See p. 204 above.
And they verged away from them: The verse does not elaborate on the details of the defeat and reports the retreat in delicate wording. It may be that the expression ויטו מעליהם (=verged away from them) was current at the time for denoting defeats, like euphemisms in all languages (e.g. the military idiom 'improving backwards' in modern Hebrew). On the other hand II Maccabees says: 'And he [Lysias] went and attacked Judah's men and was defeated' (13.22). The author may be referring to the battle of Beth Zacharia and transforming the defeat into a victory, though much more laconically than in other episodes. But it may be that in the verse he is referring to the siege of the Temple (see p. 294 above).

Josephus in *Bellum Judaicum* reports the flight of Judas Maccabaeus and his men to the toparchy of Gophnitike-Gophna (1.45) which was the chief stronghold of Mattathias and his followers at the beginning of the Revolt (see p. 196 above). But in Jonathan's day the toparchy was still called Aphairema (I Macc. 11.34), and only later, certainly by Herod's time, was its centre at Gophna.[72] This does not, however, cast doubt on the information given, for Josephus – or rather the source he relied on – could have

---

[72] A. H. M. Jones 1931: 78; Beyer 1931: 260; Avi-Yonah 1963: 52; id. 1964: 258–60; Schalit 1969: 196ff. For the dates of the sources see M. Stern 1965: 222–4.

substituted the name current in their time for the earlier one. The information seems to be authentic: had Judas Maccabaeus and his brothers taken refuge in the Temple, the author of I Maccabees would have reported their part in the heroic defence of the holy place (6.51–4), and perhaps even in the negotiations that the besieged conducted with Lysias (see p. 345 below). In the circumstances that developed after the defeat, withdrawal to one of the mountainous zones north of Jerusalem and digging in there was a reasonable alternative. From there it was possible to continue to harass the troops besieging Jerusalem. On the other hand, confinement of the entire Jewish force in the Temple, in the year after the fallow year to boot, would have meant keeping it in a trap. Josephus or Nicolaus had no reason to invent the flight to Gophna, both because they never had critical considerations of that kind and because the area is not even named in I Maccabees as the rebel haven at any stage.

48 *And the men from the king's camp went up toward them to Jerusalem*: The Greek οἱ ἐκ τῆς παρεμβολῆς τοῦ βασιλέως can also be translated without the definite article for 'men', i.e. 'men from the king's camp'.[73] The clause has accordingly been cited to prove that the siege of Beth Zur continued even after the outcome of the battle of Beth Zacharia was certain.[74] However, even if we adopt the version 'men' instead of 'the men', that does not mean that the rest were still occupied at Beth Zur, for various units had to be left to gain control of the areas north and south of Jerusalem, and clean out the rebel nest there, as is indicated by the verse itself ('in Judaea and at Mount Zion'), while garrisons were stationed in the places that had been captured (thus in verse 50).

And the king camped in Judaea and at Mount Zion: καὶ παρενέβαλεν ὁ βασιλεὺς εἰς τὴν Ἰουδαίαν καὶ εἰς τὸ ὄρος Σιων (literally: 'camped toward Judaea and toward Mt Zion'), should be translated as 'camped in Judaea and at Mt Zion'. The construction... ב ויחנו (= and they camped at...) is usually translated in the Septuagint παρενέβαλον εἰς τήν.... The literal meaning suggested by most translators and commentators is here impossible because the king was already in Judaea. Moreover, he could not have camped at the same time (even in two camps) 'toward' (i.e. outside) Judaea and 'toward' Mt Zion (which is in the middle of Judaea). In addition, the Hebrew אל (= to) and לקראת (= toward), the only possible Hebrew equivalents of εἰς τήν...in its literal meaning (לקראת is actually translated εἰς συνάντησιν),[75] do not appear (and do not

[73] So Grimm 1853: 103, and Cahana 1957: 129.
[74] Gutberlet 1920: 50.
[75] The reconstruction מול (= opposite) or נגד (= against) probably assumed by the various modern translators, and על (= on) suggested by Goldstein (1976: 322), are never translated by εἰς and therefore must be discounted at the outset.

sound right) in Biblical Hebrew with the verb לחנות (= to camp).
The prepositions 'to' and 'toward' are untenable with 'camped',
even on the assumption that the Hebrew version referred to Judas
Maccabaeus and not to Judaea (the two being written identically in
Hebrew), i.e. that Lysias besieged Judas Maccabaeus at Mt Zion
(the Temple).[76] This suggestion must be rejected also because the
developments during the siege of the Temple were numerous and
varied, and the author would have had to mention Judas
Maccabaeus in connection with at least one of them if the latter had
been in the besieged Temple. Josephus, who frequently erred in too
literal reading of the Greek of I Maccabees without noticing the
practices of the Septuagint (see p. 192 and n. 132 above), may have
been puzzled by the Greek version and tried to solve the difficulty
by assuming that the right reading should be 'Judas' and not
'Judaea' (*Ant.* 12.375, 382).

Mount Zion: In the language of I Maccabees, the expression
denotes the Temple Hill (cf. p. 461 below). Despite logistic
difficulties, part of Judas Maccabaeus' force was assigned to guard
the Temple, because of its symbolic importance for the national
morale, and also in order to tie down enemy forces at that fortified
area. The Temple occupied only part of Mount Zion.

49 *And he made peace with the people of Beth Zur*: Beth Zur surrendered
before the battle of Beth Zacharia. Verses 49 and 50 should actually
be inserted between verses 31 and 32 (see pp. 308–9 above).

*And they left the town for there was no bread there for them to (stay) enclosed
in it*: The word συνκεκλεῖσθαι (= to stay enclosed) is passive, and the
reference is to the people of Beth Zur (cf. the Septuagint for Josh.
6.1; I Kings 6.20,21). Some scholars interpret it in the medial
meaning – 'to close', 'to enclose', 'to store' – with 'bread' as its
direct object, in which case it would mean that after the discovery
of all the secret paths to the fort (see II Macc. 13.21) there was no
longer any food to store that would enable the town to withstand
further siege.[77] But a decision to surrender after a hard struggle is
made not when there is no bread to store but when there is none left
to eat.

For there was Sabbath for the country: The absence of a past perfect
tense in Hebrew makes the statement in our verse ambiguous. The
reference could be to either the year of the siege or the preceding
year. As noted in the discussion on the chronology of the expedition
(p. 544 below), in the circumstances of that time, scarcity of food in
the Judaean Hills could be acute in the year after the Sabbatical,
especially in the third quarter, and not in the fallow year itself. This
and considerations arising from the evaluation of the sources suggest
that the expedition as a whole took place in the second half of the

---

[76] This possibility is suggested by Goldstein 1976: 322.
[77] Abel 1949: 122–3; North 1953: 507.

year after the Sabbatical, and that Beth Zur fell sometime toward
the end of the spring of that year (see also re verse 53 below).

50 *And the king captured Beth Zur and he put a garrison there*: The Greek is
φρουρά (= garrison), which is mistakenly used in the Septuagint to
translate נציב (= governor).[78] But according to the context, there is
no doubt that in I Maccabees the word has its usual meaning (cf.
9.51, 10.75, 11.3,66, 12.34, 14.33), and the reconstruction should be
מצב. This term, which occurs repeatedly in the story of Jonathan's
battle at Michmash, was not properly understood by the translators
of the Septuagint where it was rendered several times as a place
name (I Sam. 14.1,6,11); in II Samuel 23.14 it was rendered
ὑπόστεμα.

51 *And he camped around the Temple*: The resemblance between the end of
verse 48 and the beginning of verse 51 may indicate that this verse
was preceded by others relating to Lysias' seizure of the area near
the Temple, which were inadvertently omitted when the sentences
on Beth Zur were mistakenly inserted as verses 49 and 50.
And he set battering rams there: *belostaseis*. For the reconstruction *kārīm*
and its meaning see p. 301 above.
And (artillery) devices: *mēkhanai*. In the Hebrew: *ḥiśvōnōt* (see p. 319
above). The word here can mean artillery as well as poliorcetic
devices. In view of the mention of the battering rams before the
ḥiśvōnōt, and the listing of artillery machines subsequently, it seems
more likely that the author is referring generally to the artillery
machines listed. The conjunction καί which follows should therefore
be deleted.
{*And*} *flame-throwers*: In Greek πυροβόλα. The word designates
burning arrows and red-hot iron projectiles (Plutarch, *Sulla* 9,12,
Antonius 66.3; Arrian, *Anab.* 2.21.3 and Diodorus 20.96.4 and 6, have
πυροφόροι, evidently referring to fire arrows shot by manual bows).
In our verse the reference is most probably to a type of catapult
adapted for inflammable missiles. We have no information from
other sources on the existence of a model of this kind, as the adaption
apparently entailed only the addition of metal sheathing to the
embrasures, but no real structural changes, except perhaps in the
form and materials of the winding box.
And stone-throwers: In Greek λιτοβόλα, the archetype of the
Roman *ballistae* (called also *litoboloi* and *petroboloi*); all of these
contrivances were capable of hurling stones, lead balls, etc., to a
distance of up to 500 m.[79] In the Septuagint the verb λιτοβολεῖν
serves to translate the Hebrew root רגם.[80] The reconstruction should

[78] The translation derives from the similarity of the roots for the words מצב and נציב. On
Hebraisms of this type in the Septuagint see the short survey of Tov 1978: 133ff., and the
bibliography in p. 134 n. 34.
[79] Droysen 1889: 187–8; Marsden 1969–71: 1.59ff.,75ff.,86–91; Gerlach in *RE* s.v.
'Petrobolos', col. 1050; Garlan 1974: 214–25.
[80] There are examples in Hatch and Redpath 1897: 2.876.

be רוגמי אבנים, or מרגמות (Prov. 26.8; in the Septuagint, σφενδόνη).

And scorpions: The term generally denotes strong semi-automatic hand bows resembling scorpions. As the verse deals with artillery, the reference here is primarily to a stationary artillery machine whose mechanism resembled that of a scorpion.[81]

52 *And they also made devices against their devices*: The reference may be to the artillery fire on the besieging forces. Cf. above p. 300 in regard to the Jewish *ḥiśvōnōt* mentioned in the siege on the citadel (6.20). However, it seems more likely that the reference is to *antimēkhanēmata* ('counter-machines', Aeneas Tacticus 32), devices to obstruct various siege machines and actions, such as wooden towers with baskets of earth to soften the blows of battering rams, devices to grasp the rams, to kindle fires, 'doors' to push away assault ladders,[82] and the like (ibid. 32–7).

And they fought many days: From the chronological analysis it appears that the siege could not last more than one or two months. The description 'many days' echoes the feelings of the besieged, who were in dire straits (see p. 549 below).

53 *And there was no food in the Temple because of the seventh {year}*: This sentence, which seems at first sight capable of indicating the date of the Sabbatical year and the chronology of events, presents several linguistic difficulties. The Hebrew behind the explanation διὰ τὸ ἕβδομον ἔτος εἶναι can be reconstructed in various ways: בהיות השנה השביעית (= being the seventh year) and כי היתה השנה השביעית (= for there was the seventh year), both indicating that the siege was laid during the Sabbatical year, or בגלל השנה השביעית (= because of the seventh year) and בגלל השביעית (= because of the seventh), which can also be construed to mean that the year preceding the siege was a Sabbatical one, as scarcity of food in the year after the fallow year usually caused even more hardship. The combination בהיות השנה השביעית has no parallel in the Bible. Moreover, its word order does not correspond to the Greek translation, nor does that of כי ו היתה השנה השביעית (on the retention of the Hebrew word order in similar clauses of cause see I Macc. 10.42,77, 14.35; in the present verse διὰ τὸ εἶναι ἔτος ἕβδομον was to be expected). The phrase 'because of the seventh year' in Hebrew lacks anything like the Greek verb εἶναι, but it is possible that the verb was added by the translator to complete the sentence, as was often done in the Septuagint (cf., e.g., the verb ἀνήκειν in I Macc. 10.42, which occurs in a similar construction). Another difficulty in the last proposal arises from the fact that the Greek

---

[81] On the *scorpion* see Droysen 1889: 191–2; Marsden 1969–71: 1.5–6; 2.44ff., 98ff.; and see Biton W.61ff., and Hero of Alexandria, *Belopoeica* 75–81. On the stationary scorpion see F. Lammert in *RE* s.v. 'Skorpion', cols. 585–7; Marsden 1969–71: 1. 14–16, 2. 51ff., 8off.; and see Hero, *Belopoeica* 84ff.; Biton W.43ff.   [82] On the 'doors' see Garlan 1974: 173ff.

reverses the order of the noun and adjective (ἕβδομον ἔτος) contrary
to the usual practice in the Septuagint which adheres to the Hebrew
syntax (ἔτος ἕβδομον). Thus it seems that the original must have
been 'because of the seventh' (cf. Ex. 23.11 for an instance of
'seventh' appearing alone) and the author added the explanatory
noun; there having been no corresponding noun in the Hebrew, the
translator allowed himself to use the customary Greek word order.
An identical interpolation was made in Exodus 21.2 – 'And in the
seventh he shall go out free for nothing' – where the Greek is τῷ δὲ
ἑβδόμῳ ἔτει (= in the seventh year). The possibility that there the
Septuagint added the word ἔτει (year) to make it clear that it was
not necessarily the Sabbatical year that was involved (but seven
years since the slave was sold) does not affect the similarity of that
verse to ours, inasmuch as both exemplify the Septuagint tendency
to depart from the Hebrew word order in cases where some
explanation or addition is included. The translator's addition
provides support for the hypothesis that the word εἶναι is also an
addition. Be that as it may, the verse does not affect the chronology
of events, which must be determined by other factors. As suggested
in Appendix K below, the siege of the Temple was laid at the
beginning of June 162 B.C., i.e. the year after the sabbatical, and was
lifted a month or two later (see pp. 545ff.).

In the Temple: The uncial manuscripts have ἐν τοῖς ἁγίοις (= in
the Temple; the plural is quite commonly used in the Septuagint –
e.g. Lev. 19.30, 21.12; Num. 19.20), and there does not seem to be
any justification for preferring τοῖς ἀγγείοις (= in the pits) which
emerges from the ancient Latin translation and two minuscule
manuscripts.[83]

And those who fled to Judaea from the Gentiles ate the rest of the repository:
The allusion is to Jews from Galilee, Gilead and the coastal plain
who were brought to Judaea after the rescue campaigns
immediately following the purification of the Temple (I Macc.
5.23,45). Even if there is some exaggeration in the author's
statement that they 'ate the rest of the stores', it indicates that the
number of refugees was not negligible, a situation which operated
to increase the military potential available to Judas Maccabaeus
(see p. 51 above).

54 *And very few remained in the Temple for hunger waxed upon them and they
    scattered each man to his place*: Outside the Temple in rural areas it was
    possible to find some food that had been stored, and some from the
    first spring harvest. Possibly a considerable number of the Temple
    defenders joined Judas Maccabaeus in his haven in the Gophna
    Hills. The verse does not support the hypothesis of a crisis and mass
    desertion from the camp of Judas Maccabaeus, certainly not of a

[83] Contrary to Kappler 1967: 89.

crisis that was the outcome of a profound ideological rift (see also below p. 345, re verse 60).

55 *And Lysias heard that Philippus whom King Antiochus while alive charged to raise Antiochus his son to rule*: See I Macc. 6.14–15. This Philippus may be mentioned in a Babylonian inscription (*OGIS* 253). In II Maccabees he is called σύντροφος (9.29), a title of nobility indicating that he was educated together with the king.[84] It is possible that Antiochus Epiphanes, who had been close to Philippus since childhood, did appoint him regent.[85] But it may well be that Philippus took matters into his own hands as leader of one of the repeated rebellions of troops stationed in the eastern satrapies. Philippus' earlier connection with those satrapies is indicated in the inscription referred to above.

56 *Had returned from Persia and Media, and the armies that went with the king with him*: Contrary to the implication in this verse that the forces that set out with Antiochus Epiphanes returned to Syria at the time that Lysias was besieging the Temple, there are reasons for believing that at least some of them returned home before that, especially the 'Roman' contingent, which belonged to the Royal Guard, and took part in the battle of Beth Zacharia (see p. 315 above, and p. 546 below). The author of I Maccabees did not know this, an ignorance by no means surprising in view of the incompleteness of the information that he had on imperial affairs and the Antioch court.

The army that advanced against Antioch with Philippus was probably composed mainly of military settlers from the eastern satrapies and local auxiliary troops. It was not an especially large force. Philippus dared to advance on Antioch, the capital, not because of the total number of soldiers under his command, but because of the superior horsemen at his disposal as the ruler of Media, the source of cavalry for the entire Seleucid kingdom, and also because of the dissatisfaction in Antioch with Lysias' attempts to remove potential rivals for the throne who were members of the royal family.[86] The hostility to Lysias was expressed later in the aid the Greco-Macedonians extended to Demetrius I, who fled almost alone from Rome and was welcomed in Syria with open arms (Polybius 31.11–15; I Macc. 7.1–4; *Ant.* 12.389). This was not enough, however, to tip the scales in Philippus' favour. At that stage the military settlers who generally supported the legitimate government in order to ensure the stability of the empire and their own survival in a hostile expanse, preferred to back the nominal king, Antiochus V, rather than Philippus who appeared to them as a potential usurper. The son of Seleucus IV, Demetrius I, who

[84] On this title see Bevan 1902: 2.283; Bickerman 1938: 43; cf. Polybius 5.82.8, 31.21.2.
[85] For speculations about the background to and reasons for this appointment see Th. Fischer 1980: 83 n. 202.
[86] On his activity in Antioch see p. 540 below, esp. n. 76.

landed in Syria a few months later, could be considered legitimate, as some of the settlers had once justifiably viewed Antiochus IV, his uncle, as a usurper.[87]

And that he sought to inherit the affairs: The Lucian version, τὰ πράγματα, seems more acceptable than the τὰ τῶν πραγμάτων which appears in the other manuscripts. The reference may be to the post ὁ ἐπὶ τῶν πραγμάτων (= *chargé d'affaires*; on which see p. 233 above), or to affairs of state in general as per the meaning of the word in Classical Greek.

57 *And he hurried and dissembled to return and he said...*: The Greek ἐπένευσεν, literally 'agree', 'nod', is rendered by Cahana (p. 129) as *wa-ye'ōt* (= and he agreed). In this meaning, however, the word is totally superfluous in our context. The Alexandrian manuscript has the plural form ἐπενύσσοντο, which is even stranger if reconstructed as *wa-ye'ōtū*. Grimm therefore proposed considering the word a gloss and deleting it.[88] But this is unnecessary. The verb ἐπινεύειν appears just once in the Septuagint to translate ינכר (Prov. 26.24), which, according to the synonymous parallel in the verse, means 'not tell the truth', 'pretend', etc.[88] If we alter the order of the verbs in the verse to 'And he hastened to return and dissembled and said: we are more tired from day to day', etc. it is clear that the author meant to say that Lysias did not tell his officers the real reason for lifting the siege, because he wished to conceal the news of Philippus' return and prevent disturbances and ferment at that stage while he was still in hostile territory. In fact the statement attributed to Lysias below makes no mention of an uprising among the forces in the eastern satrapies. The intention of the verse can actually be thus construed even without altering the order of the verbs, and this is also Josephus' interpretation in *Antiquitates* (12.379–81).

59 *Now let us sanction them to follow their laws as in the beginning*: The Greek καὶ στήσωμεν, which is to be reconstructed as וּקְיַמְנוּ (cf. Septuagint, Ruth 4.7; Esth. 9.21,27,31,32), means in this context 'to approve', 'to validate rights', and the like (cf. Dan. 6.8; I Macc. 11.34). This refers to the right to live according to ancestral laws which the Seleucid kings had always granted the Jews up until the coercive

---

[87] See esp. Mørkholm 1966: 47ff.

[88] Grimm 1853: 105; Gutberlet 1920: 112–13.

[89] An examination of the Septuagint wording shows that the translators used the verb ἐπινεύει in the meaning of 'agreed', 'promised' and the like (χείλεσι πάντα ἐπινεύει ἀποκλαιόμενος ἐχθρός, ἐν δὲ τῇ καρδίᾳ τεκταίνεται δόλους = a wailing foe promises everything with his lips and in his heart will plan deceptions' in contrast to 'with his lips will deceive an enemy and in his bosom place deception' as in the Hebrew original). The translator of I Maccabees, however, was likely not to have realized the inaccuracy of the translation of the Proverbs verse and concluded that the word ἐπινεύειν was a proper equivalent for the Hebrew *yinnākēr*. On the evolution of linguistic equivalents in the Septuagint see Tov 1981: 101ff. On the character of the Septuagint version of Proverbs as a free translation and sometime even a paraphrase see Thackeray 1913: 13; Gerleman 1956.

edicts (see *Ant.* 12.142; II Macc. 4.11). Lysias thus proposes repealing the edicts in their entirety. See further p. 524 n. 21 below.

60 *And they sent to them to conciliate and they accepted*: Some of the correspondence with the Jews figures in the second of the four well-known documents preserved in II Maccabees (11.22–6). There the king officially announces the repeal of the religious decrees and the return of the Temple to the Jews (see in detail pp. 523–5 below). Given the sorry plight of the besieged in the Temple and the limited scope of the treaty,[90] the conduct of the negotiations does not support the widespread view that there was a large group among the rebels who aspired to no more than religious freedom (see p. 59 n. 101 above).

61 *And the king vowed to them and...they left the sanctuary*: The word ὀχύρωμα, literally 'fort', 'citadel', is often used in that meaning in the Septuagint. Since the reference here is to the Temple, however, היכל (= shrine) as the reconstruction is possible, although there is only one parallel to this usage in the Septuagint (Prov. 30.28 [24.63]). The Greek translator apparently chose ὀχύρωμα because of the military function of the Temple at the time.

62 *And he retracted the oath...and destroyed the wall around*: The building of the Temple wall by Judas Maccabaeus after the purification of the Temple is recorded in I Macc. 4.59.

With Lysias' departure, control of Jerusalem returned to Judas Maccabaeus. There is insufficient support for the view proffered by some scholars that Alcimus already served as high priest during the reign of Antiochus Eupator and not just upon the accession of Demetrius I.[91] A verse in I Maccabees (7.6) explicitly denies such a possibility, and the author of I Maccabees is certainly more competent than any other source to report on domestic events at a relatively late stage of the Revolt.[92] As to the indication in II

---

[90] On the nature of the agreement see Efron 1980: 27.

[91] See the bibliography on this question in Mölleken 1953: 205–6, and Mölleken's view (ibid. 207–28). Recent followers of Mölleken are Bunge (1971: 257ff. and passim; 1975: 14ff.) and Goldstein (1976: 325). Mölleken's arguments would require stipulating that I Maccabees garbled his sources to an extent and in a manner which do not correspond to what we know about the quality of the book, nor to the time of writing, as demonstrated in the battle descriptions and the closing verse of the book. For further criticism see Kochabi 1983: 289–90.

[92] Goldstein's explanation (1976: 325) that the omission in I Maccabees of any mention of Alcimus' appointment during the reign of Antiochus V shows that 'our author reflects the Hasmonaean position that Antiochus V was an illegitimate ruler with no right to appoint a high priest' is rather strange. I Maccabees does not hesitate to report Alcimus' appointment by Demetrius I. Was the maintenance of the principle of transferring the power in Antioch from father to son so important for the Hasmonaeans that they recognized the authority of Demetrius I, that ruler who almost totally destroyed the rebel movement, to appoint a high priest, and on the other hand refrained from mentioning a similar deed of Antiochus Eupator who formally announced the return of the Temple to the Jews and permission for them to live according to ancestral laws?

Bunge (1975: 25) believes that the author of I Maccabees 'postponed' Alcimus' appointment because he wished to create the impression that the appointment was a 'prize' for the

Maccabees that Alcimus was high priest even before Demetrius I's accession (14.3 – προγεγονὼς ἀρχιερεύς), it allows only the inference that he was officially appointed by the Seleucid authorities after the execution of Menelaus at the end of the expedition (*Ant.* 12.383–5; II Macc. 13.3–9, and see p. 541 n. 80 below on the proper sequence). It cannot be assumed that Alcimus actually served in the Temple before the reign of Demetrius I. The lifting of the siege of the Temple left Lysias hard-pressed and incapable of changing the arrangements prevailing in Jerusalem and imposing Alcimus on the community. Josephus in *Antiquitates* (12.387, 20.235) is much too brief to provide a basis for contradicting the clear testimony of I Maccabees, especially since he drew on a source that abounded in errors in the names and sequence of the high priests.[93]

The fact that Judas Maccabaeus avoided being besieged in Jerusalem when Bacchides invaded the country and made Alcimus the high priest (I Macc. 7.10–20) does not prove that Judas Maccabaeus was not in control of the city before that. He simply refrained from confronting the enemy because his men had been roundly beaten at Beth Zacharia. The Temple wall had been destroyed, and the time left for recovery and preparations was quite short. Bacchides' army was large and strong, and the lessons learned at Beth Zacharia and the siege of the Temple were too recent to allow Judas Maccabaeus to risk another defeat. For that reason he did not confront Bacchides outside the city either.

63 *And he returned to Antioch...and took the city by might*: Regarding the end of the rebellion, II Maccabees adds that Philippus fled to Egypt and found refuge there (9.29). According to Josephus, Philippus was captured by Eupator and put to death (*Ant.* 12.386). It is hard to know whether the latter story is based on some external source or is simply a conjecture.[94]

murder of the Hassidim. However, I Maccabees notes explicitly that Alcimus was appointed before the murder of the Hassidim.

[93] On this list see Bloch 1879: 147–50; von Destinon 1882: 29–39; Hölscher 1940: 3–9.

[94] On external information of this type in Josephus' version of the Revolt period see pp. 191–2 above and p. 353 below.

14

The negotiations with Nicanor and the encounter at Kafar Salama

In the autumn of 162 B.C. there was a court insurrection at Antioch. Demetrius I (son of Seleucus IV and nephew of Antiochus Epiphanes), who was then twenty-three, attained the throne. He had been a hostage at Rome since childhood, in compliance with the terms of the Treaty of Apamea. Learning of the succession crisis in the kingdom that had developed in the wake of Antiochus Epiphanes' death, he had requested the Senate's permission to return to Syria and take over. When none was forthcoming he departed secretly with the active help of Polybius, the great Greek historian. In Syria he apparently gained the support and assistance of the Greco-Macedonian military settlers, the backbone of the Seleucid army and government. Because of their delicate situation within the native population, they were interested in putting the reins of leadership into stable, strong hands that would loyally represent the legitimate dynasty. Antiochus V Eupator was too young, and Lysias, who indeed aspired to the throne, was not a member of the royal family and could therefore not expect much support.

The accession of Demetrius met with the hostility of the Roman Senate, which did not forgive the new king for having fled from Rome. Suspicious, too, of his aggressive and dynamic personality, the Senate refused to recognize his authority and maintained contacts of various sorts with rebellious elements in the Seleucid empire. In contrast to the admiration that he was accorded in Syria, Demetrius was unable to win over the countries east of the Euphrates. The centre of resistance was Babylonia, led by Timarchus, the local satrap, and his brother Heraclides, the satrap of Media. In Commagene, north of the centres of the government in Syria, too, a revolt erupted under the leadership of the satrap, Ptolemaus. The political situation was exacerbated a year later as a result of diplomatic negotiations which Timarchus' envoys conducted in Rome. Although the rebels were not given any military aid, the very fact of the negotiations brought home to Demetrius the danger the revolt presented to the unity of the empire and the future of his rule in Syria.

Upon assuming the throne, Demetrius appointed Bacchides commander of a large army despatched to Eretz Israel (I Macc. 7.1–25). The numerical strength of the expedition is not reported and no military confrontation took place between the Seleucid troops and Judas Maccabaeus. We have no real data to support a decision as to whether or not the outbreak of the rebellion in Babylonia preceded the Bacchides expedition, for the Timarchus affair is not mentioned in the Books of the Maccabees. Presumably the extent and seriousness of that rebellion were not appreciated in Antioch at the start of Demetrius' reign when Bacchides was sent to Judaea. At that stage there were still contacts to ascertain the conditions and demands of the rebel satrap, so that it was possible to allow Bacchides a mighty force reflecting the military potential of the Antioch authorities at the time. In view of his bitter experience in the battle of Beth Zacharia in a confrontation with an army of comparable size, Judas Maccabaeus was now reluctant to engage the larger force. He did not face the enemy in the field, and also stayed out of Jerusalem to avoid the risk of being besieged there. Consequently, Jerusalem seems to have fallen to Bacchides without much resistance. Bacchides then elevated Alcimus, a moderate Hellenizer, to the high priesthood. This appointment awakened hope among some of Judas Maccabaeus' warriors, chiefly the Hassidim who believed that the time was ripe for negotiating with the authorities to obtain concessions and relief. Judas Maccabaeus, however, refused to conduct negotiations from a position of weakness (see p. 59 n. 101 above). His view proved to be correct: the representatives of the Hassidim were put to death, and Bacchides embarked upon deterrent and mopping-up operations on the edge of the Gophna–Beer Zayit area, the traditional haven of the rebels. He did not complete the task, however, and was unable to uproot the rebels from the region. He returned to Antioch with his army, probably because the troops at his disposal were recalled as a result of the deteriorating situation in Babylonia and the Upper Satrapies.

The military and civil governor (*stratēgos*) assigned to Judaea was Nicanor, who had previously served as commander of the Seleucid elephant force. Occupying the Jerusalem citadel with his troops, Nicanor was well aware of his numerical inferiority, and therefore sought to restrain the rebels through negotiation. At times he even resorted to tricks in an attempt to capture the rebel leaders, particularly Judas Maccabaeus. When these attempts failed, he went forth to fight Judas Maccabaeus at Kafar Salama. Conducted on the plateau near Gibeon, the battle ended in a Seleucid failure, though not a disastrous defeat, for Nicanor returned to Jerusalem and continued to control the city and the Temple.

The Sources

The I Maccabees description of the battle is short and dry, giving no details beyond the site of the battle, its outcome, and the number of enemy casualties (7.31–2). There is no doubt that the sources available to the author on the start of Nicanor's activity in the country were quite meagre, as is also indicated by the absence of any reference to the battle of Kafar Dessau described in II Maccabees (see below). Josephus in *Antiquitates* adds a few details that make the events more vivid, especially as regards the negotiations and the meeting between Judas Maccabaeus and Nicanor (12.402–5), but they are merely the fruits of the writer's imagination. Josephus also improperly identified Nicanor with a friend of Demetrius who helped him in his flight from Rome.

II Maccabees does not mention the battle at Kafar Salama. On the other hand, it describes a military clash between Simeon, Judas Maccabaeus' brother, and Nicanor near Kafar Dessau (Δεσσαυ; in some manuscripts Λεσσαυ), where the latter defeated the Jewish force. Only after that comes the story of the contacts between Nicanor and the leader of the Revolt (14.15–25), which according to I Maccabees preceded the battle at Kafar Salama. The absence of any reference to this episode in I Maccabees has led some to identify it with the battle that took place at Kafar Salama.[1] However, the name 'Dessau', whatever the place it refers to, bears no resemblance to 'Salama'. Others considered it a kind of duplication of the battle of Adasa, and still others questioned the basic credibility of the episode altogether. There is, however, no reason to insist that before the Kafar Salama battle there was no confrontation between Jewish troops under the command of Simeon, and Nicanor and his men.[2] As to the identity of 'Dessau', it is not unlikely that the name should be corrected to 'Adasa', as Ewald was the first to appreciate,[3] and that Nicanor fought twice in the same place. It is also possible that the

---

[1] Abel 1924: 375; S. Klein 1939a: 63; Dancy 1954: 124.
[2] In agreement are Plöger 1958: 180; Wibbing 1962: 66; and also Abel 1949: 138, 461–2.   [3] Ewald 1864–8: 4.418 n. 4.

epitomist (or even Jason of Cyrene) confused the site of Simeon's battle with that of Judas Maccabaeus' second battle against Nicanor (which is the only one of the two battles between Nicanor and Judas Maccabaeus that II Maccabees describes). This may account for the failure of II Maccabees to mention the battle site of the latter confrontation. As the II Maccabees version is as usual quite vague on topography, it is not possible to be definite.

In connection with the Kafar Dessau episode, we must reject the well-known hypothesis proposed by Geiger and his followers that II Maccabees reported the failure of Simeon because its author was hostile to the Hasmonaeans that succeeded Judas Maccabaeus, while I Maccabees omitted mentioning it because its author admired the dynasty started by Simeon.[4] I Maccabees may not have reported the battle because the author did not find any mention of it in his sources. As noted above, it is evident that the sources at his disposal for the start of Nicanor's activities were very scanty. In contrast, II Maccabees used quite detailed sources for the period, as is clear from the account of the meeting and negotiations between the two sides (14.19–25; and see especially the names of Nicanor's envoys to the negotiations in verse 19). With no possible 'anti-dynastic' purpose, II Maccabees also describes other battles that are not mentioned in I Maccabees (see 8.30–3, 10.24–38, 12.1–9).

This is true also in regard to the mention of Simeon in the war with the Idumaeans (II Macc. 10.14–23). It is hard to take seriously the attempt to prove the existence of an 'anti-dynastic' purpose in a verse reporting that a number of people under Simeon's command allowed the Idumaeans to flee during the siege in exchange for money (10.20). In the same vein it can be argued that II Maccabees designed the story of the battle of Marisa in order to diminish the stature of Judas Maccabaeus: he reports a defeat in a battle and the discovery of accessories used in idol worship in the clothing of the Jewish dead (12.39–40), while attributing the command of the battle to Judas Maccabaeus (12.36) who did not take part in it at all (see I Macc. 5.55–62,67, and cf. p. 52 above). Nor is there any basis for the argument of some scholars that the expression οἱ περὶ τὸν Σίμωνα appearing in II Maccabees 10.20 to designate the traitors means 'Simeon and his men'.[5] The meaning is certainly 'Simeon's men'. The construction οἱ περὶ τὸν δεῖνα, which is common in II

---

[4] Geiger 1875: 206–16,219–20; Meyer 1921: 2.457; as well as Wellhausen 1924: 81; Büchler 1906: 124ff., and many others.

[5] That is the view of Wellhausen 1905: 149 n. 2; Weierholt 1932: 69–70; and also Bunge 1971: 200 n. 98. The contrary view is held by Meyer 1921: 457 n. 1.

Maccabees, appears several times to denote 'so-and-so's men' (8. 30,32; 10.35) and not 'so-and-so and his men'. There are other verses where the latter meaning could be construed (11.6, 13.1, 14.1),[6] but if the intention was to mar Simeon's image, the sentence would have been worded unambiguously (e.g. Σίμων καὶ οἱ σὺν αὐτῷ, a construction which appears twenty-one times in the book, and cf. 8.1, 10.1; or even Σίμων καὶ οἱ μετ' αὐτοῦ, which is less common: 1.7, 5.27). Furthermore, according to the account all the people who took bribes were executed (10.21–2). For refutation of the opinions on the 'dynastic' and 'anti-dynastic' purposes of I and II Maccabees cf. pp. 52–3 (the battle of Marisa) and pp. 197–9 (the Modein episode).

II Maccabees reports at length on the talks and contacts between the parties after the Kafar Dessau clash. The descriptions of the stages of the negotiations, and of their purposes and results are also different in the two books. According to I Maccabees, Nicanor intended at the outset to capture Judas Maccabaeus through a trick; the latter found out, cut short the meeting (7.27–30), and this avoided the trap. According to II Maccabees, frank and substantive negotiations were conducted and led to the cessation of hostilities and the involvement of Judas Maccabaeus in the Seleucid administration in the country (14.18–26). It was only Alcimus' intriguing and his tattling to the Antioch authorities that impelled Nicanor to resume the campaign against the rebels (4.26–30). There is little doubt that negotiations did in fact take place for II Maccabees gives the names of several otherwise unknown people who took part in it (14.19); on the other hand, there is no basis for accepting the story of an agreement between Nicanor and the Jewish commander (see in detail, p. 354 re verse 27). The statement in I Maccabees that Nicanor tried to capture Judas Maccabaeus through a trick (7.27,29) has a parallel in II Maccabees stating that, when the relations between them deteriorated, Nicanor decided to operate with the help of a stratagem, but Judas Maccabaeus managed to evade it (14.29–31). It thus seems that the information from the two sources should be merged: after the initial contacts, realizing that Judas Maccabaeus was not inclined to make concessions, Nicanor decided to resort to guile and take him prisoner when he came to one of the meetings set up between the parties.

[6] By analogy with 13.10 and 14.16, the latter three references can be understood to mean 'Judah's men' rather than 'Judah and his men'.

I Maccabees 7.26–32

7.26   And the king sent Nicanor, one of his respected ministers and a hater and foe of Israel, and he ordered him to destroy the people.

27   And Nicanor came to Jerusalem with a large army, and he deceitfully sent to Judah and his brothers words of peace, saying:

28   Let there not be a quarrel between me and you. I will come with few men in order to see your faces in peace.

29   And he came to Judah and they greeted each other and the [ambushers] were ready to seize Judah.

30   And it became known to Judah that he came deceitfully, and he rushed to depart from him and did not wish to see his face any more.

31   And Nicanor knew that his plot was discovered and he set out toward Judah to war in Kafar Salama.

32   And of those with Nicanor some five hundred men fell, and they fled to the City of David.

COMMENTARY

7.26 *And the king sent Nicanor*: This Nicanor is not the Nicanor son of Patroclus who took part in the battle of Ammaus (I Macc. 3.38; II Macc. 8.9) as a number of scholars believe,[7] endeavouring thereby to explain his hostility to the Jews. The name is quite common in the onomasticon of the period, and if this Nicanor had taken part in the Ammaus campaign, I Maccabees would certainly have referred to his past. The epithet τρισαλιτήριος (= blackguard, scoundrel, literally = 'triple sinner') applied to both in II Maccabees (8.34, 15.3) shows at most that the epitomist of II Maccabees believed that they were one and the same. Nor can this Nicanor be identified with the Cypriarch Nicanor (II Macc. 12.2) who served in Coele Syria after the purification of the Temple (on him see p. 239 above).

One of his respected ministers: According to II Maccabees, Nicanor had been in charge of the Seleucid elephant force (ἐλεφαντάρχης, 14.12). He was free to take over a new job, since all the elephants were slaughtered at Apamea by the Roman legate, Gnaius Octavius, a short time before Demetrius came to power (Appian, *Syr.* 46; Polybius 31.2.9–11, and see p. 547 below on the chronology). For that reason he cannot be identified either with the Nicanor who was Demetrius' friend and helped him flee from

[7] Ewald 1864–8: 4.418 n. 4; Bevan 1902: 2.200; Gutberlet 1920: 121; Abel 1949: 137.

Rome (Polybius 31.14.4),[8] as Josephus says in *Antiquitates* (12.402). Josephus had no information on the identity of the two men, and he made the connection only because of the identical names.

A hater and foe of Israel: That is how Nicanor is described in II Maccabees as well (14.39). The concrete evidence for that evaluation in both books is the description of Nicanor's threats against the Temple (I Macc. 7.35; II Macc. 14.31–3). The physical rampage after the defeat at Adasa and the declaration of a holiday to commemorate the event too (I Macc. 7.47–9: II Macc. 15.30–6) are explicable in the same context. Nicanor may well have evinced more obvious personal hatred of the Jews than other Seleucid commanders, and his threats against the Temple noted in both books support that possibility. But it is also possible that Nicanor is represented as a Jew-hater not because he demonstrated unusual hostility, but because, in contrast to other commanders who came to Judaea on a one-time mission, Nicanor served as civil and military governor and to accomplish his task utilized various diplomatic and military methods which left a lasting impression. In an enterprise of that nature, there is room as well for psychological pressure in the form of threats, etc., all of which could lead to an extremely unfavourable view of the man.

And he ordered him to destroy the people: This is an exaggerated way of expressing the idea that the Revolt was to be suppressed. It should be remembered that this applies to the period after the repeal of the coercive decrees, and to the reign of a king who, because he was not a direct descendant, did not have to feel under any obligation to pursue the ambitions or policy of Antiochus Epiphanes, who himself did not intend to 'destroy the people' either (see p. 235). II Maccabees specifies the instructions issued to Nicanor in a more practical form: 'Giving him instructions to slay Judah, disperse those with him, and set Alcimus up as the high priest of the largest Temple' (14.13).

I Maccabees does not give Nicanor's official position, but II Maccabees states that he was appointed *stratēgos*, that is, civil and military governor of Judaea (14.12). Avi-Yonah speculated that Judaea became a meridarchy upon Nicanor's appointment, it having previously been part of the meridarchy of Samaria. He attributes the change to the recognition by the Antioch authorities of the importance and special nature of the Jewish community in the Judaean Hills following the success of the Revolt. But as noted above, there is no real evidence that Judaea and Samaria were regarded as one meridarchy before the accession of Demetrius I (see p. 203). The innovation was not the establishment of the post, but the high military rank of the incumbent.

[8] Contrary to Grimm 1853: 113; Bévenot 1931: 30; Abel 1949: 137; Schunck 1980: 329.

27 *And Nicanor came to Jerusalem with a large army*: The army sent with
Nicanor to serve as a garrison could not have been very large, in
view of the troubles that had developed at the time in the regions
east of the Euphrates.

And he deceitfully sent to Judah and his brothers; According to II
Maccabees, Simeon was defeated at the battle of Kafar Dessau
before negotiations between the two parties were initiated. That
battle is not mentioned in I Maccabees. Combining the two sources
makes it possible to reconstruct the course of events: the clash at
Kafar Dessau which took place shortly after Nicanor's arrival
preceded the negotiations, and when these failed, the opposing sides
clashed at Kafar Salama.

Words of peace: II Maccabees, on the other hand, states that
Nicanor sincerely intended to negotiate with Judas Maccabaeus.
The preparations and the meeting are described in detail, and the
author notes that, fearing a trap, Judas Maccabaeus had sentries
stationed at various places, but nothing happened. The parley
between the two commanders was substantive, Judas Maccabaeus
compromised with the enemy, took a wife on the advice of Nicanor,
and stopped his rebellious activity. In return he was appointed
diadokhos (heir? assistant? representative?). The high priest Alcimus,
fearing his position would be undermined as a result of the
rapprochement between Judas Maccabaeus and Nicanor, com-
plained about the latter to the Antioch authorities, who compelled
Nicanor to turn his back on Judas Maccabaeus and resume the
campaign against the rebels (14.18–30). The very fact that the
episode is presented in such detail in II Maccabees in contrast to
the extreme brevity of I Maccabees weighs at first sight in favour of
the former's version. The listing of the names of the Nicanor people
who made arrangements for the meeting (verse 19) is a telling
example. However, a distinction should be made between the
description of the preliminary contacts and the presentation of the
meeting or its outcome. It may also be that the meeting referred to
in II Maccabees is not the one in I Maccabees, for it is quite likely
that a number of preliminary meetings took place. As to the
outcome, the I Maccabees version is preferable: II Maccabees does
not explain (and indeed it is hard to imagine) what concessions
Judas Maccabaeus would have been prepared to make at that time;
the persecutions had stopped before then, and the repressive
religious decrees had been rescinded, but Alcimus remained the
high priest, the garrison stood fast in the citadel, and Nicanor, the
representative of Antioch, was still ruling Judaea from Jerusalem. It
is hardly likely that Judas Maccabaeus and his men would have
been prepared under those conditions to lay down their arms,
especially in view of the weakness of the kingdom at the time, and

the small force at Nicanor's disposal. It should be noted that in both sources the initiative for the negotiations was taken by the Seleucid governor. Judas Maccabaeus would have consented to negotiate with the enemy in order to obtain at least an autonomous status (such as was attained in the time of Jonathan, who was recognized as *stratēgos*, high priest and ethnarch) and possibly also the removal of the garrison. The presentation of Nicanor's actions – especially the 'appointment' of Judas Maccabaeus – as being on the Seleucid commander's initiative without the knowledge or permission of Antioch proves how contrived and unreliable the II Maccabees information is. Nor does the matter of the strange 'appointment' as *diadokhos*, whatever its nature,[9] add to the credibility of the II Maccabees version. It thus appears that what II Maccabees has to say about the success of the negotiations is only a literary invention intended to complicate the plot and make it more exciting in the manner of 'tragic' historiography. The 'romantic' padding added to the episode ('And he took a wife', etc. – verse 25) likewise serves this purpose, and is characteristic of the pathetic school as well. Within this framework perhaps came a detailed description of Judas Maccabaeus' hesitations about whether to go on with his rebellious operations, the influence of the woman who tries to persuade him (pro or con), and the like. All this was omitted by the epitomist.[10]

The description of Nicanor's favourable attitude to Judas Maccabaeus may as well derive from the 'tragic' approach to the characterization of heroes: the author tends to make the negative characters more human. On the one hand Nicanor is the epitome of evil, and on the other he manifests good intentions. The tendency is especially evident in the characterization of Antiochus Epiphanes (4.37–8, 9.11–27).[11] The author tries to balance the characters in accordance with the well-known rule of the poetics of tragedy, that characters are not to be complete scoundrels or complete saints, but

---

[9] An understanding of the nature of the 'appointment' requires the elucidation of the wording of II Macc. 14.26. On the question of the location of the word αὐτοῦ (= his) in the manuscripts, and on the reading ἑαυτοῦ (= of himself) and its location in the Lucianic version, see Abel 1949: 464, and the Kappler-Hanhart edition, p. 109. According to the Alexandrinus version, the epithet *diadokhos* (= heir, deputy) can be construed as an honorific title. The Venetian manuscript indicates that the reference is to the appointment of Judas Maccabaeus as deputy for Alcimus, the high priest (cf. II Macc. 4.29) or for Nicanor as *stratēgos* in Judaea. According to the Lucianic version, it would refer to his deputizing for Nicanor. Whether it was a title or a promotion to one of the ranks proposed, it would have had to be granted by the king, and not by Nicanor. The title of *diadokhos* as a rank of nobility (e.g. *OGIS* 100) is known from Ptolemaic Egypt but not from the Seleucid empire.

[10] The fact that the report in II Maccabees (14.25) is drastically abridged is discernible from its wording and grammatical structure: ἐγάμησεν, εὐστάθησεν, ἐκοινώνησε βίου, 'And he married and conducted himself peaceably (stably?) and took part in the (good?) life.'

[11] This feature of the book has already been noted by M. Stern (1960: 3 n. 9); contrary to the implication in Stern, however, I believe it does not represent a historical element but should be considered a purely literary embellishment.

average people (Aristotle, *Poetics* 1452b30–53a10). This statement must be modified, however , for the pathetic approach prevails, and in general the characters are black or white, probably because the author's hatred of people like Jason and Menelaus overcame his artistic considerations.[12] In dealing with a religious book like II Maccabees which also belongs to the tragic–pathetic school, it should be kept in mind that the author makes no effort to keep to historical fact, and is more concerned with his particular didactic and artistic purposes.

It is therefore more realistic to suppose that Nicanor tried to capture Judas Maccabaeus by trickery when it turned out that the negotiations were stalled. This was at quite a late stage of the Revolt, and the Seleucid authorities were aware of the central role and great influence of its leader, and therefore came to the conclusion that his capture or death would put an end to the uprising. The explicit instructions to Nicanor according to I Maccabees (14.13) also point in that direction. As Nicanor was to stay in Judaea permanently, he could try to take action to attain his goals, differently from the commanders of expeditions previously sent to the country.

29 *And the [ambushers] were ready to seize Judah*: The Greek is οἱ πολεμίοι (= the foes). According to the context, it appears that the original Hebrew was אורבים (= ambushers).[13] The translator mistakenly read, or the manuscript he worked from had, אויבים (= foes). Josephus' paraphrase in *Antiquitates* makes no reference to an ambush (12.404), indicating that his source was the Greek translation of I Maccabees. It is less likely that Josephus had at his disposal a Hebrew version in which the same garble occurred.

31 *And he set out toward Judah to war in Kafar Salama*: Most of the manuscripts have Χαφαρσαλαμα and the like, though the Alexandrinus has Χαρφαρσαραμα, and some of the minuscules have Χαφαρσαραμα. The majority of scholars have read the place-name as 'Kafar Salama'. As to the identification of the place, the name is quite common in the toponymy of Eretz Israel, but in view of the direction in which Nicanor was proceeding and the circumstances at the time, any proposal of an identification moving the place far from Jerusalem must be rejected.[14] Abel at first cited Ḥirbet Irhā (near Ar Ram), close to ruins of a Byzantine monastery called Deir Salam.[15] The only finds, however, have been Arab ones, and the same is true of two other sites with like-sounding names – Salmiya

---

[12] On the bias of the 'pathetic' school see Niese 1900: 36 and passim.

[13] See Cahana in his reconstruction, 1957: 2.132 (without further comment).

[14] Against Schürer 1901: 1. 217 n. 26; Goldstein 1976; 339–40; cf. Möller and Schmitt 1976: 126–7.

[15] Abel 1924: 373–6; J. Press, in *Encyclopaedia of Palestine*, vol. 3 (Jerusalem, 1946–52) p. 495 (Hebrew).

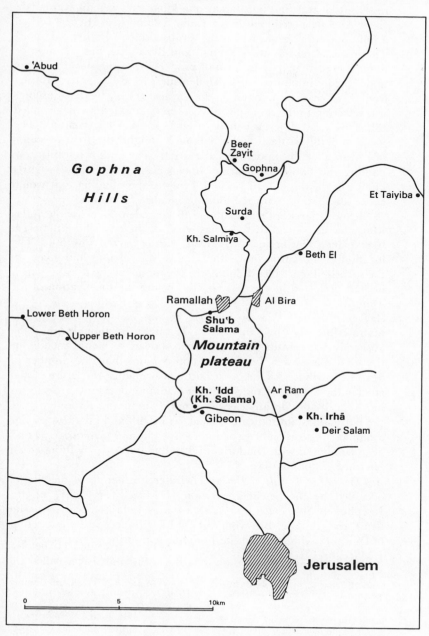

16 Proposals for the location of Kafar Salama

near Surda and Shuʻb Salama, one kilometre west of Ramallah. Later Abel proposed identifying Kafar Salama with Ḥirbet ʻIdd on a hill opposite Gibeon, which the Arabs also call Ḥirbet Salama.[16] The material on the site is Roman and Byzantine, but it should be remembered that only in a small proportion of the sites that were undoubtedly inhabited in the Hellenistic period has pottery dating from those years been found on the surface. It may be that Eusebius was referring to the same place when he mentioned a village called 'Shalem' west of Jerusalem (p. 152, l. 4, ed. Klostermann). The location of the battle at Kafar Salama highlights the great precision of I Maccabees in topographical matters. The author refrains from naming the battle for nearby Gibeon even though it was better known in the days of the Second Temple, and alluding to it would evoke associations with the glorious victories of biblical times.

Nicanor's territory was confined to Jerusalem alone, while Judas Maccabaeus controlled the areas north of the city where the clash took place. The area is a plateau with scattered low hills. The location of the battle shows that Judas Maccabaeus had given up the surprise tactics based on taking advantage of the terrain, which he had preferred in the early battles before the purification of the Temple.

32 *And of those with Nicanor some five hundred men fell*: Most of the manuscripts say 'five thousand'. It might be thought that the author is exaggerating in the number of dead, as he did usually for the total manpower, but since 5,000 is more than the number of dead he attributes to the great battle of Ammaus, the figure of 500 cited in the Sinaiticus and a number of minuscule manuscripts seems more acceptable. In any case, Nicanor's conduct in Jerusalem after the battle does not indicate that his army suffered great losses. For a similar substitution of 5,000 for 500 see Plutarch, *Demetrius* 5.2 and 28.3, compared with Diodorus 19.85.3 and 20.113.4 (both based on Hieronymus of Cardia).

And they fled to the City of David: The reference here is to the citadel occupied by the Seleucid garrison (I Macc. 1.33, 2.31, 14.36). Josephus in *Antiquitates* reports that it was Judas Maccabaeus who fled there (12.405). But we no doubt have to accept the correction of Dindorff, who adapted the Josephus text to the extant version of I Maccabees.[17]

---

[16] Abel 1949: 139.

[17] G. Dindorff 1865: 1.473; and see the reasons given by Grimm 1853: 114, for substituting καί for ὁ δέ.

15

The battle of Adasa and Nicanor Day

The victory of Judas Maccabaeus at Kafar Salama made it clear that the area north of Jerusalem was under his exclusive supervision. Nicanor, who from the base in the citadel controlled the Temple and the city, was in danger of being besieged. Aware of his difficult situation, he threatened the priests with the destruction of the Temple. According to the sources, the threat was designed to force them to turn over Judas Maccabaeus (I Macc. 7.33–8; II Macc. 14.31–6). However, since the latter did not recognize the authority of the Temple priests, and presumably most of them belonged to the high priest Alcimus' faction which in any case supported Nicanor, it appears that the threat was aimed mainly at deterring the rebels from making an assault on the city and regaining control of it, while the Temple was Nicanor's 'security'. Nevertheless, the threats against the Temple may also have been intended to persuade the Jewish rank and file, most of whom supported the Hasmonaeans, to hand over Judas Maccabaeus in order to avert the desecration of the Temple, the resumption of persecutions, and the reversion to the situation obtaining during the reign of Antiochus Epiphanes. Be that as it may, the sharp criticism of Nicanor voiced by the priests (I Macc. 7.36–8; II Macc. 14.34–6), if the wording in the sources is reliable, seems to testify to a change of heart in some of Alcimus' supporters. It would not be unprecedented for moderates to have second thoughts in the face of sudden harsh measures and threats by foreign elements.

The danger to the Temple did in fact deter Judas Maccabaeus from laying siege to the city. He also knew that a direct assault on the citadel might compel the king to despatch a large royal expedition without delay, as happened in Lysias' second expedition. He consequently preferred to wait for an occasion when Nicanor left Jerusalem and strike at him in the open field.

In March 161 B.C. some reinforcements were sent out from Antioch, though as the Timarchus revolt had not yet been suppressed, the central authorities were not in a position to help with numerous troops. Wishing to prevent Judas Maccabaeus from endangering the convoy on the steep winding road from the Aijalon Valley to the mountain plateau, Nicanor left the city for the Beth Horon Ascent in order to welcome the convoy and guide it to Jerusalem. It is illuminating that Judas Maccabaeus made no attempt to prevent Nicanor from proceeding toward Beth Horon, nor did he manoeuvre in order to force the confrontation to take place on the difficult ascent or in inconvenient sectors further on toward Jerusalem, but preferred to await the united force of the enemy at Adasa, at the edge of the level terrain on the plateau near Gibeon. That planning shows the extent of Judas Maccabaeus' self-confidence, which is explicable only on the assumption that he then had an overwhelming numerical advantage over the enemy and weapons of considerable variety. The battle on 13 Adar ended in a great Jewish victory: Nicanor himself was the first casualty (or among the first), and his death was the signal for a hasty and panic-stricken flight of the Seleucid soldiers westward, while the villagers in the area closed in on the Beth Horon Ascent and cut off the stragglers. Judas Maccabaeus returned and took control of Jerusalem, although the citadel remained in the hands of the garrison. The enemy commander's head and right hand were cut off and displayed 'opposite' Jerusalem, and a holiday known as 'Nicanor Day' was declared. The defeat of the enemy was so celebrated on that occasion because of the rejoicing at the salvation of the Temple from the destruction threatened by Nicanor and at Judas Maccabaeus' second return to Jerusalem, just as Hanukkah was initiated following the conquest of the city and the purification of the Sanctuary.

The battle description in I Maccabaeus is well anchored in reality and in the geographical conditions in the area, and the moves of the contenders appear to be realistic although reported in rather a general way without many tactical details. As is his wont, the author attributes a large army to the enemy and only 3,000 men to Judas Maccabaeus (7.39–50). The distortion in the figures does not, as we have noted more than once, carry over to the description of the battle itself and the events around it.

Following his usual practice, Josephus in *Antiquitates* adheres to the description in I Maccabees, although in this case his version contains an addition which is hard to explain as a mere paraphrase: while I Maccabees does not state a figure for the enemy troops, Josephus reports 9,000 men in Nicanor's camp (12.411), a figure which sounds reasonable. On the other hand, the figure of 2,000 which Josephus gives for the Jewish army (12.408) must be viewed as a typographical error. Other additions and changes, mainly in the sequence of events, derive from Josephus' tendency to interpret I Maccabees (see below re verse 43), and the same applies to the exact topographical location of Adasa (12.408).

II Maccabees is expansive regarding the battle of Adasa (ch. 15), among other reasons in order to justify for the Jews of the Diaspora the declaration of a holiday on 13 Adar (15.36). The description of the battle is clumsy, detached from the geographical background, and lacking any real tactical moves; it includes only a schematic deployment of the Seleucid army in which even elephants figure (perhaps following the mention of Nicanor's former post: 14.12), though the Seleucids no longer had war elephants at the time. The number of enemy casualties is grossly inflated to 35,000. Judas Maccabaeus and his men march to battle with prayers on their lips, implying divine intervention in the battle. That intervention is not actually described this time, but the author concludes by stating that the Jewish combatants 'rejoiced at the appearance (ἐπιφανεῖα) of God' (15.27).[1] The author's stress on Nicanor's wickedness and harsh punishment provides an opportunity to apply some of the literary principles of the 'pathetic' and 'tragic' schools to which he belongs.

I Maccabees 7.39–50

7.39   And Nicanor departed from Jerusalem and camped at Beth Horon and the army of Aram came toward him.

40   And Judah camped at Adasa with three thousand men, and Judah prayed and said:

41   When those who (came) on behalf of the king of Assyria blasphemed, Your angel went out and smote of them a hundred and eighty-five thousand.

42   So break this camp before us today and the survivors will know that he spoke evil against your Temple and judge him in his iniquity.

43   And the camps joined battle on the thirteenth of Adar and Nicanor's camp was smitten and he fell first in battle.

44   And when his camp saw that Nicanor fell they threw down their arms and fled.

45   And they pursued them a way of one day's distance from

---

[1] Benedictus Niese, the famous German Hellenist, who strove to prove the superiority of II Maccabees over I Maccabees, went so far as to prefer the II Maccabees version even for the battle of Adasa (1900: 85–7).

Adasa towards Gezer and they sounded the blaring trumpets after them.

46   And they came out of all the Judaean villages around and they encircled them and the ones confronted the others and they all fell by the sword and not one of them survived.

47   And they took the booty and the loot and they cut off Nicanor's head and his right (hand) which he had brandished arrogantly and they brought and impaled (them) opposite Jerusalem.

48   And the people rejoiced greatly and they made that day a day of great joy.

49   And they resolved to make that day on the thirteenth of Adar year after year.

50   And the land of Judaea was tranquil for a few days.

COMMENTARY

7.39 *And Nicanor departed from Jerusalem*: Jerusalem was ruled by Nicanor from the citadel. He requested reinforcements from Antioch and, since Judas Maccabaeus was in control of the area north of Jerusalem, Nicanor left to meet them, so that they would be able to reach the plateau unhindered.

And camped at Beth Horon: Nicanor camped at Beth Horon, probably Upper Beth Horon, in order to keep an eye on what was happening in the area of the ascent, and to prevent the Jews from surprising the reinforcements. Still, if Nicanor had been superior in manpower and weapons, presumably Judas Maccabaeus would not have failed to clash with him in the area of the ascent, which he would have preferred to the level terrain of the plateau near Adasa. On the way from Adasa to Jerusalem, too, there were a number of battle sites more convenient for an inferior force. Thus the choice of battlefield tells us something about the relative size of the opposing armies and about Judas Maccabaeus' equipment and methods in the second phase of the Revolt.

And the army of Aram came toward him: The reference is to reinforcements which had arrived from Syria. They could not have been very numerous, for at the time the Timarchus rebellion had not yet been suppressed. The size of the army is not given, but the prayer attributed to Judas Maccabaeus is intended to indicate a tremendous superiority in the enemy (verse 41). The figure of 35,000 dead out of Nicanor's force cited in II Maccabees (15.27) certainly has no historical value. In *Antiquitates* Josephus speaks of 9,000 Seleucid soldiers taking part in the battle (12.411). He may have recalled the figure from the book by Nicolaus of Damascus

which he utilized in writing his shortened version of the
Hasmonaean revolt in *Bellum Judaicum* (see p. 44 above). The figure
seems reasonable given the recruitment potential of the kingdom at
the time, and it may have included also locals from the coastal cities
and Idumaea.

II Maccabees does not even mention the approach of the
reinforcements. According to him, the initiator of the battle was
Nicanor, who wanted to surprise Judas Maccabaeus and his men on
the Sabbath 'in the places in (the region of) Samaria' (15.1, ἐν τοῖς
κατὰ Σαμάρειαν τόποις; for the translation cf. 12.2 and 14.1).
Because I Maccabees is clearly superior with regard to topographical data, as is evident also from the description of the
Seleucid retreat in this battle (see below re verse 45), and since there
is no doubt about the identification of Adasa within the confines of
Judaea, it is hard to assume that II Maccabees' contradictory
geographic information (itself very general and vague) is based on
any real knowledge about the battle location.[2] Apparently southern
Samaria, which included the Aphairema–Gophna district, was
mentioned in Jason of Cyrene's original book, or the source he relied
on, as the rebels' stronghold in previous phases of the Revolt (cf. pp.
196, 337 above) or close to the battle of Adasa (as in *Bell.* 1.45) and
that explains its appearance in the present context (cf. the insertion
of Modein in II Macc. 13.14: p. 197 above). Similarly, no value
should be assigned to the II Maccabees statements regarding the
special circumstances preceding the battle or its timing on the
Sabbath designed to stress the treacherous, vicious characteristics
attributed to Nicanor (see in detail pp. 490–1 below).

40 *And Judah camped at Adasa*: The Greek in all the uncial manuscripts
is *Adasa*. The accepted view that the Hebrew was חדשה seems
reasonable, it being also the name of a settlement known from
Hebrew sources (Josh. 15.37) which is *Adasa* in the Septuagint (see
also Erubin 5.6), although the biblical Hadashah is in the southern
Judaean lowland, while the location of mishnaic 'Hadashah in
Judaea' cannot be determined. Josephus locates Adasa 30 *stadia*
(5.7 km) from Beth Horon (*Ant.* 12.408), apparently from the upper
village. Eusebius in his *onomasticon* mentions a place by that name
near Taphnōn. Some have corrected this to Gaphnōn (= Gophna),[3]
but that correction is not necessary as the reference may be to
Tappuah in the southern lowland or the Mt Hebron area (see Josh.
15.34,37,53). In any case Eusebius' information is irrelevant for the
identification of our Adasa, which must be located north-west of
Jerusalem.

There are three ruins known as 'Adasa or some variant of it in the

[2] Contrary to Bunge 1971: 259, and many others.
[3] E.g. Melamed 1966: 11.

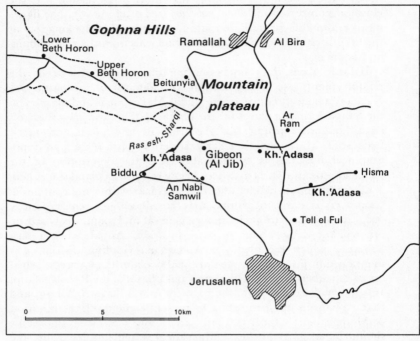

17 Proposals for the location of Adasa (cf. p. 61 above)

hilly region north of Jerusalem. Abel proposed identifying
Adasa with a Byzantine ruin of that name near the intersection
of the Gibeon–Ar Ram and Jerusalem–Nablus roads.[4] Another
proposal is the ruin on the way to Ḥisma, north-east of Tell el
Ful.[5] But on the basis of the exact correspondence with the distance
noted in *Antiquitates*[6] and the geographic context described,
Hadashah-Adasa should be identified with the 'Adasa at the
junction of the Beitunyia–Biddu and Gibeon–Ar Ram roads, close
to the end of the Beth Horon Ascent. There are three ruins there.
One, near the top of the Er Ras esh–Sharqi hill, is Arab, and the
lower two are mainly Byzantine. Wibbing, who surveyed one of
the lower sites, notes the discovery of Hellenistic pottery there.[7]

[4] Abel 1924: 377–8; and see also Kochavi 1972: 158.
[5] Wibbing 1962: 161.
[6] Drüner (1896: 42 n. 2) has reservations about the distances that appear in Josephus, but
the examples he cites merely show that Josephus gave accurate information on this. While in
three cases Josephus cites contradictory figures, in two the accurate figure appears in *Antiquitates* which he wrote later and with greater care (*Ant.* 5.140 *versus Bell.* 5.51; *Ant..* 7.283
versus Bell. 2.516). In the one case where two different figures are given in *Antiquitates* itself
(5.139 *versus* 7.312) the copyist is perhaps at fault. On the accuracy of the distances cited in
Bellum see Broshi 1982: 23.   [7] Wibbing 1962: 165.

If the place is identical with the 'Hadashah in Judaea' mentioned in the Erubin tractate, this only reinforces our appreciation of I Maccabees' precision in topographical matters, for according to the Mishnah Hadashah was a tiny settlement with only 50 inhabitants (cf. pp. 154–5 above).

With three thousand men: The potential manpower at the disposal of Judas Maccabaeus was much greater. The hypothesis that the rebel camp was then suffering a serious internal crisis does not hold water: it is not supported by the episode of the negotiations between Bacchides and the Hassidim (see p. 59 n. 101 above), nor by the II Maccabees story of a pact between Judas Maccabaeus and Nicanor. The latter tale has no foundation, contradicts I Maccabees, does not accord with the situation, and is only a literary embellishment (see pp. 354–5 above).

40–1 *And Judah prayed and said: When those who (came) on behalf of the king of Assyria blasphemed, etc.*: The Sennacherib expedition is mentioned in II Maccabees as well (15.22), but this does not prove the authenticity of the oration. The affair is also mentioned in II Maccabees (8.19) in an oration attributed to Judas Maccabaeus before the battle of Ammaus, in III Maccabees (6.5) and in the Scroll of the Sons of Light (11[14]11–12), and seems to be a regular literary cliché. The Books of Judith and Daniel also abound in allusions to that expedition. In any case, there is little doubt that Jason of Cyrene was acquainted with I Maccabees (see p. 183 above). The association with the fall of Sennacherib in this case was called forth by the blasphemies against God and the Temple attributed to Nicanor (I Macc. 7.34–5,42; II Macc. 14.33–6, 15.3–5,24; cf. especially Is. 10.7–15, 36.18–20, and ch. 37). Doubtless the statement is intended also to make the reader aware of the enemy's supposed enormous numerical advantage, or otherwise the verse would not stress the number of casualties in the Assyrian king's camp.

43 *And the camps joined battle*: This wording implies that the battle was a frontal clash between two formations facing each other, and eliminates the possibility that it was an ambush, a surprise attack, or the like. If Judas Maccabaeus had attacked the enemy in any unusual way, the author would have noted the fact, however briefly, as he did in describing the battles of Beth Horon and Ammaus, and perhaps also the confrontation at Beth Zur.

The location of the battlefield likewise indicates definitely that the battle was a conventional frontal clash. The short convenient route from the end of the Beth Horon Ascent to Jerusalem passed 2.5 km north of Adasa. Below Adasa stretched a broad easily traversable valley separated from the road by a low hilly ridge which concealed the valley from those using the road. It might be suggested that Judas

Maccabaeus gathered his forces in that valley below Adasa that provided cover, and slipped over the ridge to the north heading for the enemy expedition. Nicanor's men then quickly reformed, turning their marching order into battle order, which accounts for the expression 'And the camps joined battle'. However, the clear assertion that the pursuit was conducted 'from Adasa toward Gezer' (verse 45), and not 'from Gibeon' which is closer to that road, shows that the battle was joined below Adasa, that is, in the broad valley mentioned, and not on the road (regarding the author's precision in topographical matters, especially with reference to Adasa, cf. p. 155 above). Moreover, no army would have advanced on the road to Jerusalem without sending scouts ahead to observe the nearby valley. It appears then that the Seleucid force did not incur a surprise attack on the road, but deliberately left the road for the place where Judas Maccabaeus was located in order to do battle in the broad valley. Presumably Nicanor preferred to do so, despite his numerical inferiority, in order to avert more serious damage to his forces further along the road, such as Cestius Gallus later incurred *en route* to and from Jerusalem (*Bell.* 2.517–22,540–5) and perhaps also in order to use the opportunity finally to catch Judas Maccabaeus, his aim from the start of his governorship in the country. In general, for a military force moving in hostile territory it is always preferable to confront the foe directly as quickly as possible rather than take the risk of encountering unknown, unexpected situations and having the lines of retreat cut off.

The Seleucid deployment, which is not mentioned at all in I Maccabees, is described in detail in II Maccabees: 'And when the army was arrayed, and the animals (elephants) were stationed on an advantageous wing, and the horsemen in the wings' (15.20). This type of formation was standard for Hellenistic armies, but it is certain that no elephants took part in this battle for the entire Seleucid elephant force had been destroyed by Gnaius Octavius on the eve of Demetrius' accession (Polybius 31.2.11; Appian, *Syr.* 46 (240); for the chronology see p. 547 below). Consequently the II Maccabees description of the Seleucid deployment must be regarded as imaginary, based on a general knowledge of the practice in Hellenistic armies, but not on acquaintance with the course of this particular battle.

And Nicanor's camp was smitten: II Maccabees provides a detailed description of the battle, but it contains little of value, for its purpose is to show that the issue was decided by Providence: Nicanor's men set out for the battle to the sound of trumpets, and Judas Maccabaeus and his men to the murmur of prayers. The Jewish victory was achieved thanks to 'the manifestation (ἐπιφάνεια) of God' (15.25–7). However, both sides used trumpets and similar means to direct the movements of their forces on the battlefield (see below re verse 45). The II Maccabees account serves to highlight the book's didactic and literary character.

And he fell first in battle: This detail is not given in II Maccabees, which states only that after the battle Nicanor's body was found among the enemy dead (15.28). Josephus reports that when the battle began, there were many enemy casualties, and when Nicanor was killed the survivors threw away their weapons and fled for their lives (*Ant.* 12.409–10). This interpretation is apparently an attempt to explain the statement 'And Nicanor's camp was devastated' coming before 'and he fell first in battle'. Actually the sequence does not support Josephus, for 'Nicanor's camp was devastated' is merely a summary of the consequences of the battle, preceding the specific details (cf. Judg. 20.35ff.; I Sam. 4.2). Bévenot proposes translating the word πρῶτος (= first) as 'commander', so that the verse would mean that Nicanor the commander fell in battle.[8] This interpretation does not fit in with the vocabulary and syntax of I Maccabees. If we assume that the article was inserted before the word πρῶτος in the manuscript available to Josephus, he may well have understood the passage the way Bévenot did, which led to his mistaken version.

44 *And when his camp saw that Nicanor fell*: Judas Maccabaeus' tactical plan entailed striking at the enemy commander and thereby contributing to the headlong flight of the Seleucid army. As it was a small force and the Seleucid practice was for the commander to fight among the front line cavalry of the right wing (cf. p. 394 below re verse 14), it was no trouble to locate Nicanor in his colourful coat and insignia.

They threw down their arms: Cf. 5.43. The need to get rid of their arms in order to facilitate their flight suggests that at least some of Nicanor's army were heavies or semi-heavies. It is very likely that the reinforcements from Antioch included semi-heavy troops who were by nature 'all-purpose' and suited to the varied missions awaiting them in the Judaean Hills.

45 *And they pursued them a way of one day's distance from Adasa towards Gezer*: The distance from Adasa to Gezer via the Beth Horon Descent and the Aijalon Valley is about 30 km. Nicanor's men fled to Gezer, which was the closest Seleucid fort to the west (cf. 4.15). The way to the Jerusalem citadel was actually blocked as Judas Maccabaeus was in control of the plateau north of Jerusalem. The author does not write 'up to Gezer' (as in I Chron. 14.16; I Macc. 4.15), but 'towards Gezer' (ἕως τοῦ ἐλθεῖν εἰς Γαζαρα), indicating that Nicanor's routed soldiers did not manage to find refuge in the fortress of Gezer, but were annihilated before its gates (and see the

[8] Bévenot 1931: 106.

following verse). II Maccabees makes no mention of a pursuit because he is ignorant of the geographical background.

And they sounded the blaring trumpets after them: The Greek is ταῖς σάλπιγξι τῶν σημασιῶν (literally = 'signalling trumpets'). That is the Septuagint translation of the biblical expression חצוצרות התרועה (blaring trumpets) which appears several times in Numbers (cf. I Macc. 4.40).[9] The trumpets were sounded in order to alert the men of the nearby villages to block the path of the retreating foe.[10] For the role of the trumpets in the battle itself see I Maccabees 4.13 and 9.12.

46 *And they came out of all the Judaean villages around and they encircled them*: The reference is not necessarily to armed villagers of military age, so that the verse does not imply, as some have sought to suggest, that Judas Maccabaeus' army was small, and only if he was victorious did the masses of villagers appear and attack the stragglers.[11] Wounded and exhausted soldiers can be tormented and injured by men untrained in regular warfare, and even by children, women and elderly people, as was demonstrated in the same region in the Israeli retreat via the Aijalon Valley after the first assault on Latrun in Israel's War of Independence (25 May 1948). The steep, difficult Beth Horon Descent through which the Seleucid force fled to the Aijalon Valley was even easier to block, especially against despondent combatants who had discarded their weapons to facilitate their flight.

And they all fell by the sword and not one of them survived: This is somewhat of an exaggeration (cf. the contrary exaggeration in I Macc. 5.54), although there is no doubt that military and topographical conditions made it possible to slay quite a large proportion of Nicanor's army (cf. p. 217 above). II Maccabees reports 35,000 enemy troops killed in the battle itself (15.27), not counting the retreat and pursuit. This is a much larger figure than is given by II Maccabees for Seleucid losses in other battles (e.g. 8.24; 10.17,23,31; 11.11; 12.19,23,26); the more than customary exaggeration is affected by the earlier reference to the disaster that overtook Sennacherib's tremendous army (see above re verses 40–1), and derives from the need to augment the punishment meted out to Nicanor, whose iniquity the author previously stressed, and to present the victory as an extraordinary one justifying the declaration of a holiday.

47 *And they cut off Nicanor's head and his right (hand) which he had brandished arrogantly*: Decapitation and the amputation of the right hand was

---

[9] See Abel 1949: 82; Yadin 1962: 163 n. 74.
[10] Cf. Judges 3.27, and see Abel 1949: 143. See also Yadin 1962: 88, on the role of the 'pursuit trumpets' in the Scroll.   [11] E.g. Avi-Yonah 1964: 65.

originally a Persian punishment.[12] The dismemberment of Nicanor's body and its hanging was a retaliation for his provocation against the Temple. Probably a contributory motive was the fact that Nicanor was the first high-ranking officer killed in a battle with the Jews, and the display of his body would tend to raise morale. It was customary in the Greek and Hellenistic world to allow the foe to gather up their dead from the battlefield.[13] That is the reason Josephus' version of the battle of Adasa omits the barbarous treatment of the body, and mentions only the victory celebration (*Ant.* 12.411–12). Josephus sometimes 'neglected' to include reports of events which might hurt the feelings of the Greco-Roman readers or impair the image of the Jews (e.g. *Ant.* 6.203 *versus* I Sam. 18.27). It should be remembered, however, that there were cases in the Greek and Hellenistic world of the desecration, for a variety of reasons, of the bodies of enemy soldiers, especially high-ranking officers.[14] Acts of this kind became routine in the Roman period, and were carried out on the bodies of domestic rivals as well.[15] Some justification for Judas Maccabaeus' action from the point of view of Greek jurisprudence and the Hellenistic outlook can be found in the customary law stipulating that the body of a temple-robber should be thrown away unburied (Diodorus 16.25.2–3), although ultimately Nicanor only threatened harm to the Temple but did not carry out his intention.

A version similar to that in I Maccabees is preserved in the Palestinian Talmud: 'He severed his hand, and cut his head off, and stuck them to wood and wrote below them, the mouth that spoke faultily and the hand that was stretched out arrogantly, and hung them on a stake facing Jerusalem' (*Megillah* 1.6 (70c): *Taanioth* 2.13 (66a)). The Babylonian Talmud version is further removed: 'They cut off the thumbs of his hands and feet and hung them at the gates of Jerusalem and said, A mouth that used to speak arrogantly and hands that used to be brandished at Jerusalem...' (*Taanith* 18b).

[12] Xen. *An.* 1.10.1, 3.1.17; Plut. *Arat.* 13.2, *Crassus* 32–3; see also Plut. *Ant.* 20.2; Valerius Maximus 9.2.6.

[13] Examples are provided in Phillipson 1911: 275–9; Jacoby 1944: 37–66; Lonis 1949: 56–62; Ducrey 1968b: 231–43; Garlan 1972: 39–40; Pritchett 1985: 94–257; cf., e.g., Josephus' paraphrase of I Macc. 9.19 (*Ant.* 12.432) where, however, the explanation is erroneous (p. 399 below).

[14] See *Iliad* 24.14–21; Xen. *An.* 3.4.5; Plut. *Nicias* 27–8, *Cleom.* 38, *Mor.* 849a; Polybius 2.59–60, 5.54.5–7, 8.21.3–4; Arrian, *Anab.* 4.7.3–4; Pausanias 9.33.9; Diodorus 20.103.6; Curtius Rufus 4.6. 26–9; Hegesias, *FGrH* II, no. 142, F 5; Dion. Hal. *de comp. verb.* 18. The last three sources, which tell of Alexander's brutal treatment of the eunuch Batis, the governor of Gaza, are quite suspect, for they are essentially pathetic, inclined to dramatic descriptions and tales of horror, and based on some source who was hostile to Alexander. See Tarn 1948: 2.267–70; Pearson 1960: 247ff.

[15] See, e.g., Dio Cassius 33.109.4, 47.3.2,8.3,4, 48.14.3–4, 49.20.4, 51.5.5, 67.11.3, 73.13.6, 74.10.2, 76.7.3; and Plut. *Ant.* 20, *Cic.* 48–9 on the maltreatment of Cicero's body.

The later *scholion* for the Scroll of Fasting (s.v. 13 Adar) combines the
Palestinian and Babylonian versions: 'And they severed his head
and chopped off parts of his body...They said, a mouth that spoke
arrogantly and hand that was brandished...'[16] II Maccabees adds
to all these the cutting out of Nicanor's tongue (15.33), certainly as
punishment for his blasphemy (14.33, 15.5). Tragic–pathetic
literature repeatedly stresses the principle of measure for measure as
is customary in tragedy,[17] and II Maccabees does so in other verses
as well (4.38, 5.10, 13.8).

And they brought and impaled (them): the source is ἐξέτειναν. Of all the
words the Septuagint renders with this verb, וַיִּפְרְשׂוּם (= they spread
them out) seems most suitable. But it is doubtful whether the
Septuagint should be relied on in this case. It may well be that the
eye of the scribe was drawn by the singular (and similar) form of the
same verb used earlier in the verse – ἣν ἐξέτεινεν ὑπερηφάνως (=
which he had brandished arrogantly). Nor is it impossible that the
translator himself used the same Greek verb here to render two
different Hebrew verbs in order to stress the principle of 'an eye for
an eye'.

The most suitable reconstruction is וַיּוֹקִיעוּם (= and they impaled
them; cf. II Sam. 21.9). The mention of loot and plunder together
with Nicanor's head suggests that the Jews set up a trophy. As usual
in the Greek world it was composed of captured weapons hung on
a wooden cross that simulated a human form.[18] Instead of the
helmet and arm protectors, Nicanor's head and right arm were
impaled on the points of the cross. This may account for the
Palestine Talmud passage: ותחבן בעץ ··· ותלין בקונטס(= and stuck
them to wood...and hung them on a stake).

Opposite Jerusalem: The Greek is παρὰ τὴν Ιερουσαλημ. Following
the practice of the Septuagint, the preposition παρά with the
accusative can be reconstructed עַל־יָד, אֵצֶל, נֶגֶד and מוּל ('near',
'at', 'opposite' and 'across from'). The choice of the last is
supported by the wording in the Palestinian Talmud *Megillah* which
evidently was indirectly or directly influenced by I Maccabees and
may even have been familiar with the Hebrew original: 'and hung
them on a stake opposite (מוּל) Jerusalem' (the less accurate
Babylonian Talmud version has 'at the gates of Jerusalem'). The
reconstruction מוּל (= opposite) seems more reasonable in the light
also of the purpose of the display; hanging up the enemy's head in
public was usual among eastern peoples and is known from Roman

---

[16] That is the version in the Parma manuscript, which is the most reliable. The Oxford has
'and he disjoined his head', etc., while the Mantua printing has 'And they cut off his head
and chopped off the thumbs of his hands and feet', etc.

[17] See Ullman 1942: 39–40; and e.g. Polybius 7.7.1–2,6.

[18] For the *tropaion* and its design see F. Lammert in *RE* s.v. τρόπαιον, cols 669–73; West
1969: 7–19; Garlan 1975: 62–4; W. K. Pritchett 1974: 2.246–75. See, e.g., the coins in *BMC
Central Greece*, pp. 39,64.

history as well.[19] Nicanor's body was probably put in a prominent place in the hills which could be seen from inside the city.

II Maccabees on the other hand reports that Nicanor's body was brought to Jerusalem, his arm (and head?) was hung opposite the temple and displayed, his tongue was cut out and thrown away, and his torso was tied and dangled from the citadel in order to demonstrate to all the salvation of God and to intimidate the citadel people (15.30–5). This version is more vivid and illustrates concretely how the extent, form and locale of the punishment fit the character and quality of the sin. However, the absurd description of the hanging of Nicanor's torso on the wall of the citadel (the enemy's ominous and unvanquished fort!) and the statement that Nicanor's head and arms were displayed before the people gathered 'near the altar' (31–2), which would be contamination by an alien as well as by a corpse,[20] are enough to invalidate totally the II Maccabees version. It should be remembered that just bringing a corpse into Jerusalem is against the halakha.[21] The author may have been influenced by the story of Goliath's head being brought to Jerusalem (I Sam. 17.54). A study of some episodes in II Maccabees provides further grounds for rejecting the idea that the book can be relied on for information on the history of halakha practices in Eretz Israel, or that the book reflects a certain trend in Palestinian pietism (see p. 180 above).[22] The author's lack of familiarity with the customs there is indicated also by the fact that

[19] I Samuel 31.10; Judith 14.1; Herodotus 7.238; Xen. *An.* 1.10.1, 3.1.17; Plut. *Arat.* 13.2; Appian, *B Civ.* 1.71.

[20] On the defilement of the Temple by a Gentile see *Ant.* 12.145; Mishnah Kelim 1.8. On the antiquity of the conception see Alon 1977: 165–6; Rabello 1972: 267–81. The question of whether one is defiled by contact with a dead Gentile (e.g. *Tosefta Niddah* 9.14) does not affect our argument, which refers to the Temple.

[21] *Tosefta Negaim* 6.2; *Avot de-Rabbi Nathan*, Version A, 35; *BT Baba Kamma* 82.b: 'A corpse is not to be left there overnight, nor are human bones to be placed (or in other versions: 'transferred', 'stored') there'; and also Mishnah Kelim 1.7 and *Tosefta Kelim, Baba Kamma* 1.14. The latter Tosefta 1.8 (cf. *BT Sotah* 20b) is a minority opinion, and in any case does not refer to the altar. The arguments regarding the lateness and theoretical nature of the 'Jerusalem rulings' proffered by A. Gutman 1970. 251–75, certainly do not apply to טומאת מת (= defilement by a corpse) as shown especially by Kelim 1.7 (for the current reading of the Mishnah cf. *Tosefta Kelim, Baba Kamma* 1.14, 'circulate in it' (and not 'to it'), see Lieberman [1939]: 3.5, 190–1). Cf. also the tradition on the departure of Rabban Johanan ben Zakkai from Jerusalem (although suspect from the historical point of view).

[22] The earliest manuscript of the *scholion* to the Scroll of Fasting, the Parma manuscript, has 'and they hanged them opposite (כנגד) the Temple'. The Oxford manuscript has 'and they hanged him at the gate of Jerusalem', and the first printing (Mantua) has 'they hanged him opposite (נגד) Jerusalem'. In any case there is nothing in the text of the later *scholion* to prove that a rabbinic scholar – and it is doubtful whether the authors of the *scholion* can be so described – can err in this matter: the *scholion* is, after all, based on a combination of the Palestinian and Babylonian Talmuds, the former having 'opposite [מול] Jerusalem', and the latter 'at the gates of Jerusalem'. The version in the Parma manuscript is thus the error of the copyist who was misled by the mention of the Temple in the previous line ('a hand that waved against [כנגד] the Temple') or who wished to underline the principle of 'an eye for an eye'. Furthermore, the expression 'opposite the Temple' does not necessarily mean that the body was hung up within the walls.

he does not reproach the aliens for entering the Temple. Heliodorus is punished for his intention of robbing the Temple (3.13–40) and Nicanor for his threats against it (14.31–6, 15.34), but, though the author enlarges upon the iniquity of the Gentiles, he does not strongly deplore their having entered the Temple (e.g. II Macc. 14.31). It is illuminating that according to I Maccabees Nicanor did not set foot in the Temple, and it was the priests who went out to meet him (7.33). Noteworthy too are the pagan terms that II Maccabees uses to describe the Feast of the Tabernacles celebration and the 'three[!] species' in the Temple after its purification (10.7). The species of plants listed are not those known from the Pentateuch (Lev. 23.40) or Nehemiah (8.15), either in kind or in number. Similarly, the prayer and offering for the resurrection of the dead (II Macc. 12.43–4) has no analogue or root in Jewish tradition.

48   *And they made that day a day of great joy*: The day Nicanor was defeated was declared a holiday forever after, but not because the defeat was an amazing achievement. Nicanor was at a military disadvantage even before the battle, and the victory was the result of Judas Maccabaeus' definite superiority. It is hard to believe that personal revenge on Nicanor was the most important element in the decision to commemorate the day. The chief purpose of the holiday, like that of Hanukkah, was to mark the return of Judas Maccabaeus to Jerusalem following a military victory, after the city had been under enemy rule, and the Temple in grave danger. Possibly Nicanor's high rank and prominence in the kingdom enhanced the victory beyond its actual dimensions.

49   *And they resolved to make that day on the thirteenth of Adar year after year*: The date appears in II Maccabees as well (15.36) and in the Scroll of Fasting ('Adar – on the thirteenth of it Nicanor Day'). It is surprising that the author of I Maccabees does not mention that Purim comes the following day. II Maccabees does say that for future celebration the holiday was set for 'one day before Mordecai's day'. Zeitlin, who maintains that the celebration of Purim began in the fourth century B.C., hypothesized that the battle of Adasa took place during a leap year; Nicanor was defeated in First Adar and Purim that year fell in Second Adar, which accounts for the failure of I Maccabees to mention Purim.[23] It is indeed almost certain that the year 162/161 B.C. was a leap year;[24] however, the

---

[23] Zeitlin 1922: 82,118. This suggestion was already made by Michaelis (1778: 166) and Grimm (1853: 133), not, however, because of the absence of any mention of Purim, but in order to leave a gap between the battle of Adasa and Bacchides' second expedition, which both mistakenly believed to have taken place in 161 B.C. (see re verse 50).

[24] The year 165/164 was intercalated (see p. 278 above). The year 164/163 was a Sabbatical (p. 544 below). The sabbatical and even the year after the Sabbatical were usually not intercalated (*Tosefta Sanhedrin* 2.9; *BT, Sanhedrin* 12a). Adar 161 thus fell three years after the last Jewish leap year.

Mishnah says that Purim was commemorated also on the 14th of First Adar (Megillah 1.4). In any case, the difficulty remains, for the 13th of Adar appears in our verse not to indicate the time of the victory (which was dated in verse 43) but to establish a holiday for all time ('year after year'). Taking into account also the fact that Ben Sira makes no allusion to Mordecai and Esther in his 'Praise for the Forefathers of the World' (chh. 44–50), the absence of any reference to Purim in I Maccabees indicates that at least the holiday (as distinct from the Book of Esther) was still not recognized in Eretz Israel even in the generation following the Hasmonaean revolt.[25] 'Mordecai's day' is mentioned in II Maccabees either because Jason of Cyrene's book was composed later than I Maccabees, or because the holiday was popular among the Jews of the Diaspora before it was adopted in Eretz Israel.[26] The second alternative seems less likely, for a colophon of 113/114 or 77/78 B.C to the Greek translation of the book of Esther[27] speaks of its being brought from Eretz Israel to Egypt.[28] This can only mean that the Purim holiday, too, was then not yet celebrated by the Jews of Alexandria. None of this, however, is evidence that the book of Esther was a later composition,[29] and in fact there are signs that the author of I Maccabees was influenced by it (see, e.g., 1.1, 3.14, 5.27 *versus* Esther 1.3, 3.13) as the author of Daniel was (especially in ch. 6).

50 *And the land of Judaea was tranquil for a few days*: This final verse together with the statement above that the battle took place on the 13th of Adar are the only explicit references in the book that can help to date the battle. The account of it follows that of the accession of Demetrius I (I Macc. 7.1) in the autumn of 162 B.C. (p. 544 n. 3 below), and precedes that of the second Bacchides expedition which was undoubtedly undertaken in April 160 B.C. (see p. 385 below).

[25] Against Kaufmann 1937–56: 4.448. Also worth mentioning is Mantel 1980: 38–9, who hypothesizes that the Book of Esther and the Purim holiday were a point of dispute between the Pharisees and Sadducees, and that the Sadducees rejected them. Consequently I Maccabees – which is in his view a Sadducee book – ignored Purim, while the 'Pharisee' II Maccabees considered it proper to mention it. However, there are no grounds for assuming that the Sadducees rejected that holiday, nor that the author of I Maccabees was a Sadducee and the author of II Maccabees a Pharisee. On this last point, which for some reason is still made by many scholars, see pp. 571–2 below. Regarding the attitude to Sabbath warfare, which is cited as indication of the ideological adherence, see p. 484 below. Cf. also p. 180 n. 92.

[26] The original and peculiar form of the term 'Mordecai day' does not prove that II Maccabees did not officially recognize the holiday. The author chose that term, and not the usual 'Purim', which appears in the Book of Esther and the colophon noted below, in order to follow the form of 'Nicanor day'.

[27] On the dating and text of the colophon see Bickerman 1976–80: 1.225–45. On the dating see also Tcherikover 1960: 46 n. 119.

[28] Bickerman 1976–80: 351–5. Zeitlin's interpretation of the colophon (Zeitlin and Enslin 1972: 18–20) is unacceptable as it ignores most of the linguistic and substantive considerations proposed by Bickerman.

[29] On the lateness of the Book of Esther see, e.g., Pfeifer 1941: 742.

Thus the battle of Adasa was fought in March of either 161 or 160
B.C. The choice depends on the clarification of the time that elapsed
between the battle of Adasa and the battle of Elasa. Our verse
ostensibly points to the later date. However, if we accept the
sequence of events in I Maccabees, it appears that the despatch of
Judas Maccabaeus' delegation to Rome and its return to Judaea
(ch. 8), or at least the conduct and conclusions of the negotiations,
must be set in the period between the battles of Adasa and Elasa.
The location of the negotiations in the book, together with other
information independent of I Maccabees indicating that the
negotiations were already concluded in 161 B.C. (*Ant.* 14.233),[30]
show that the battle took place before 160 B.C. and should be set a
reasonable time before the battle of Elasa, that is, in March 161 B.C.,
and not in March 160 B.C., which would be a bare month before
that battle.

Most probably Jason of Cyrene's original book also put the report
of the delegation to Rome after that of Nicanor's defeat: II
Maccabees presents John son of ha-Kotz, who is mentioned in
relation to the internal struggle that took place in Jerusalem before
the persecutions, as the father of Eupolemus 'who carried out the
mission to the Romans regarding amity and cooperation' (4.11; cf.
I Macc. 8.17). The mission itself is not described in the book, which
ends with the downfall of Nicanor in the battle of Adasa. Thus it is
clear that in Jason's complete work the negotiations with the
Romans were reported after the Nicanor story (cf. p. 181 above).
Even if the hypothesis that Jason's original work covered a certain
period after Nicanor death is invalid, the absence of the negotiations
from the sequence of events up to the battle of Adasa shows that the
author knew they had taken place after the battle. It is not likely
that Jason of Cyrene, who deliberately parades his familiarity with
external developments and evidently knew of the contacts with
Rome, would have omitted that episode if it had taken place before
the battle of Adasa. It is hard to find a reason which could have led
the epitomist, who tended to abridge less toward the end of the
book, to leave out this Roman episode.

The final statement in the Nicanor episode – 'and the land of
Judaea was quiet for a few days' – is thus not to be taken literally.
The characters of the Hasmonaean brothers, and especially the
description of the final actions of the rebel leader, reflect quite a few
of the traits of the 'saviours' in Judges (e.g. 9.20–1,23,27,73; see also
p. 199 above). The sentence quoted is an antithesis to the well-
known refrain in Judges ('and the country was tranquil for forty
years') and means to say that unfortunately, despite the victory and

---

[30] On the dating and meaning of the document in *Ant.* 14.233 see Niese 1906: 817–29;
Timpe 1974: 143ff.; M. Stern 1965: 76–7,83.

Table 4. *Chronology of the battles of Kafar Salama, Adasa and Elasa*

Date	External events	Internal events
Autumn 162–autumn 161	'The year 151' (I Macc. 7.1)	
November 162	Demetrius I accedes to power	
		Bacchides' first expedition
Winter 162/161	Revolt of Timarchus in the eastern satrapies	Appointment of Nicanor
		Negotiations between Nicanor and Judas Maccabaeus
		Battle of Kafar Salama
		Nicanor threatens the Temple and priests
13 Adar 161		**Battle of Adasa and Nicanor's death**
Spring–winter 161		Negotiations and pact with the Romans
Early 160	Suppression of the Timarchus revolt	
Nisan 160–Nisan 159		'The year 152' (I Macc. 9.3)
Nisan 160		Bacchides' second expedition
		Battle of Elasa

the great hopes it generated (probably also owing to the growing dimensions of the Timarchus revolt and the prospects of Roman patronage and help), peace and serenity were not assured, the country did not gain a period of protracted calm, and Judas Maccabaeus' leadership did not achieve stability or longevity.

Still, it cannot be denied that there is another apparent difficulty in the chronology proposed above: Bacchides' first expedition and Nicanor's incumbency are crammed into a period of no more than six months, between the fall of 162 and the spring of 161 B.C. But as a matter of fact we do not have any real data on the duration of those operations. In that connection it should be recalled that the story of the reconciliation between Judas Maccabaeus and Nicanor and the cessation of hostilities in the country (II Macc. 14.23–30) have no historical basis (see pp. 354–6 above) and consequently it is not necessary to assume that Nicanor's incumbency lasted longer than a few months (see also p. 380 below on 'And Demetrius heard that Nicanor fell').

16

Bacchides' second expedition and the battle of Elasa

The victory in the battle of Adasa in March 161 B.C. again gave the Hasmonaeans dominion over all of Judaea. Judas Maccabaeus took control of Jerusalem and the Seleucid garrison was confined to its stronghold in the citadel. In the course of the following year Judas Maccabaeus took steps to strengthen his position at home and abroad. The high point of his efforts was the pact between the Jews and Rome, which contained among others the formal provision concerning mutual assistance in case of war and an explicit warning to Demetrius (I Macc. 8.24–32). The agreement did not ensure military intervention in practice, but it was a signal to the Antioch authorities of growing Roman interest in events in the country, and warned of the danger in the long run to the kingdom presented by the Revolt in Judaea. At the time Demetrius was preoccupied with the suppression of the uprising in Babylonia and the eastern parts of the empire under Timarchus, satrap of Babylonia, and his brother Heraclides, satrap of Media. Timarchus, who declared himself king, was able to establish ties with Rome, while the kingship of Demetrius I in Syria had not yet gained Roman recognition. However, at the beginning of 160 B.C. Demetrius seized control of Babylonia, and it appears that the local population and the military settlers east of the Euphrates gradually accepted his rule. The suppression of the opposition in the east enabled the king to divert part of the army to dealing with the war in Judaea, in the spring of 160 B.C. (see pp. 43–5 above).

Bacchides' expedition to Judaea, and the battle near Elasa in which Judas Maccabaeus fell, are described only in I Maccabees (9.1–22). II Maccabees concludes his account of events with the victory over Nicanor at Adasa.[1] The battle description in I Mac-

---

[1] On the question of whether Jason of Cyrene included the battle of Elasa in his book see p. 181 n. 95 above. Whether the deletion was the author's or the epitomist's, it was made in order not to detract from the book's religious–didactic message, and also in order not to upset

cabees is noteworthy for its great accuracy. Like the report of the battles at Ammaus, it contains many topographical indications making it possible to follow closely the progress of Bacchides' expedition and battle. The report of the deployment and movements of the Seleucid army is quite detailed, in the same manner as the description of the confrontation near Beth Zacharia, and includes also a classification of the principal contingents and their weapons. Like other military writers of antiquity, the author focuses on the deeds of the commander, and therefore reports nothing on developments in other parts of the battlefield, such as the struggle of the infantry in the centre and the movement of the Jewish right flank. This is not his practice in reporting the battle of Beth Zacharia, and not even the battle of Ammaus, where attention is paid also to moves in which the commander-in-chief was not involved. This time he concentrates on the movements of the hero of the book, as it was Judas Maccabaeus' last battle and he wished again to stress the unique and central position of the leading Hasmonaean brother. This emphasis in itself increases the sense of bereavement and loss caused by the hero's death on the battlefield. In order to maintain the tone of pain and sorrow the author even refrains from reporting the heroic efforts involved in the removal of the commander's body from the field (see below re verse 19). As usual, the author ignores the tactical composition of the Jewish force. In order to explain the defeat he reduces the Jewish force more than customarily. The author may have taken part in the battle, but the possibility cannot be entirely ruled out that he based his version on someone else's first-hand oral testimony (see pp. 160–1 above).

The language of I Maccabees in this episode contains many deviations from the conventional Greek of the Septuagint, which make it difficult to reconstruct the original Hebrew.[2] A persual of the vocabulary shows that the author inclined to a more poetic and exalted style than was his practice in regard to the previous battles.[3] The change in style arises from his desire to impart a lofty and heroic character to his hero's last battle, and this is apparent also in the contents of the dialogue between Judas Maccabaeus and his men, and in the concluding passage after the hero's death. This

---

the reader. From the artistic point of view, too, the deletion of the last battle was necessary. The two 'tragedies' that make up the epitome go from 'defeat to victory' and both end with the declaration of a new holiday (see p. 174 above).

[2] E.g. ἀνδρεῖα and χάριν in verse 10; πρωταγωνισταί (verse 11); συνημμένος (verse 13); στερέωμα and εὔψυχοι τῇ καρδίᾳ (verse 14).

[3] Verse 6: ἐξερρύησαν (= וַיִּשְׁלוּ); 7: ἀπερρύη (= נָבַל); 8: ἐξελύθη (= וַיָּעַף); 13: ἐσαλεύθη (= וַתִּרְגַּז), and συνημμένος (= וַתִּשֶּׁם).

special style presented some difficulties to the translator and forced
him to deviate from the vocabulary of the Septuagint.

In his version of the battle of Elasa in *Antiquitates*, Josephus relies
exclusively on I Maccabees (12.420–33); there is no evidence at all
that he utilized any other source. We emphasize this in order to
refute the attempts of some scholars to find support for Josephus'
statement that Judas Maccabaeus camped at *Bērzēthō* before the
battle (12.422). There is no doubt that the statement is simply a
result of a textual and substantive garble (see below re verse 5).
Josephus adds various explanations, such as the location (mistaken)
of 'Arbel' in Galilee (12.421), a sketchy description of Bacchides'
battle array (acceptable in this case – 12.426), and an explanation
(dubious) of the removal of the commander's body from the battlefield (12.432). As Josephus was not familiar with the Hebrew
version of I Maccabees, he is of no help in the reconstruction of a
number of the difficult topographical references in the passage, and
it appears that the three places mentioned in his version – Arbēl,
Bērzēthō and Mt Aza (᾽Αζᾶ) – figured in already garbled form in the
Greek manuscript at his disposal. In the description of the battle
there is no reference to the advance of the Seleucid phalanx against
the centre of the Jewish force, and instead Josephus reports in a
general way on a Jewish attack on the enemy army. As a result the
story has quite a general and casual character, and it is impossible
to trace the reasons for the tactical decisions of the belligerents, in
contrast to the detailed and illuminating report in I Maccabees. The
confusion of the order of the military manoeuvres together with the
errors in the location of the contending camps and the battlefield
itself clearly show the qualitative difference between a primary and
secondary source, and strengthen the positive impression made by
the report in I Maccabees, although, as stated above, they still
do not definitely prove that the author was an eye-witness of the
battle.

I Maccabees 9.1–22

9.1   And Demetrius heard that Nicanor fell and his armies in the
      battle and he went on to send Bacchides and Alcimus again
      to the land of Judaea {and the right corner with them}.

2   And they went on the Gilgal road and camped at the trails in
      [*har bēt 'ēl*] and they captured [them] and killed many human
      souls.

3   And in the first month in the year two and fifty and a hundred
      they camped opposite Jerusalem.

4   And they moved and went to Be⟨e⟩ra with twenty thousand men and with two thousand horsemen.

5   And Judah was encamped at Elasa and three thousand picked men with him.

6   And they saw the throng of the armies that it was numerous, and they were sore afraid and many vanished from the camp, no more than eight hundred men of them remained.

7   And Judah saw that his camp faded away, and the battle pressed him, and his heart broke for he had not the time to collect them.

8   And he tired and said to those remaining, Let us rise and go up to our enemies, perhaps we will be able to fight them.

9   And they answered him saying, We will not be able to, but if we save our souls now we will return with our brothers and fight them, and we are few.

10   And Judah said, Far be it from me to do that thing, to flee from them, and if our end is near let us die bravely for our brothers, and we shall not leave behind us an offence to our honour.

11   And the army departed from the camp and they went forward toward them, and the horsemen were divided into (the) two sides and the slingers and the bow holders went before the army and the first of the battle all the valorous.

12   And Bacchides was in the right corner and the phalanx approached from the two parts and they blew the trumpets, and those with Judah also blew the trumpets.

13   And the land raged from the sound of the camps and the battle was joined from morning to evening.

14   And Judah saw that Bacchides and the might of his camp were in the right and all the strong-hearted joined him.

15   And the right corner was smitten before them and he chased after them as far as the [slopes of] the mountain.

16   And those in the left corner saw that the right corner was devastated and they turned toward Judah's trail and those with him from behind.

17   And the battle grew harder and many fell dead of these and of these.

18   And Judah fell, and the remaining fled.

19   And Jonathan and Simeon carried Judah their brother and buried him in his ancestral tomb in Modein.

20   And they lamented him and all Israel eulogized him a great eulogy, and they mourned for many days and they said:

21   How is a hero fallen, the saviour of Israel.

22   And the rest of Judah's story and the wars and braveries he
      made and his greatness were not written down for they were
      very numerous.

COMMENTARY

9.1 *And Demetrius heard that Nicanor fell*: The news of Nicanor's defeat
reached Demetrius long before Bacchides was sent to Judaea (see p.
374 above). The verb 'heard' is no evidence that the expedition
occurred immediately after Nicanor's defeat. It is influenced by
biblical verses in which hearing about some event precedes an
expedition or a war (e.g. Jos. 22.11–12; I Sam. 7.7, 13.3; II Sam.
5.17, etc.), and appears in I Maccabees as a preface to military
expeditions (cf. 3.13,27). The account of Lysias' first expedition
conducted, according to I Maccabees, a whole year after the battle
of Ammaus (4.28), is also prefaced by 'And he heard' (4.27),
referring to the defeat in that battle. See also p. 227 on I Macc.
3.27.
And he went on to send Bacchides: During his first expedition to Judaea,
when Demetrius I acceded to power, Bacchides was 'governor in the
(region) across the river' (κυριεύοντα ἐν τῷ πέραν τοῦ ποταμοῦ, I
Macc. 7.8). This seemingly biblical title is not known from other
sources referring to the Seleucid kingdom, and its exact definition is
debatable. Some believe that Bacchides was in charge of the western
districts of the kingdom which stretched from the Euphrates to the
Egyptian border.[4] Avi-Yonah adds that it was a regular position
whose incumbent was called the *stratēgos prōtarkhos* ('the first of the
stratēgoi'), as he believes Lysias is called in II Maccabees (10.11).
But a substantive examination shows clearly that Lysias was put in
charge 'of affairs', and Protarchos is the name of an officer who was
appointed *stratēgos* of Coele Syria (see p. 535 and n. 56 below).
Wellhausen assumed that the reference in our verse was to Coele
Syria only,[5] but that notion was deservedly rejected by a number of
scholars.[6] In addition it must be stressed that I Maccabees uses the
expression 'Coele Syria' to define the position of Apollonius Daus
who was in charge of the area in Jonathan's time (10.69), and there
is no reason to assume that in regard to Bacchides the book defines
the same territory as 'the (region) across the river'. Nor would this
fit in with the author's great precision in respect of geographical
terms. Bengtson suggested that Bacchides was the governor of
Seleucis, the four satrapies in northern Syria where most of the
Greco-Macedonian military settlers were concentrated.[7] However,

---

[4] Abel 1949: 131; Avi-Yonah 1963: 32.
[5] Wellhausen 1905: 162; see also Kahrstedt 1926: 60.
[6] Laqueur 1927b: 533; Otto 1928: 32; Bengtson 1964: 2.182.
[7] Bengtson 1964: 2.181–5.

in an inscription found in Delos and dating from the time of
Demetrius I himself the governor of the area is described as 'the
satrap in charge of Seleucis';[8] and moreover, the area was for many
years previously referred to in official documents simply as
'Seleucis'.

Apparently Bacchides did deputize for the king in the districts
west of the Euphrates. This appointment was assigned to Bacchides
because Demetrius was preparing to stay in Babylonia in order to
suppress the Timarchus revolt. It was cancelled when the king
returned to his capital, and that may have been the reason that the
title is not noted in connection with Bacchides' second expedition
(although of course the author may have deemed the former
mention sufficient). In the same way, Lysias was put in charge of the
area between the Euphrates and the Egyptian border when
Antiochus Epiphanes set out to restore calm to the Upper Satrapies
(I Macc. 3.32). In connection with Bacchides, the author did not
cite his official title but only explained its connotation in biblical
terms (cf. Ezra 5.3,6, 6.6,13). Lysias' official title does not appear in
I Maccabees either (see p. 234 above), nor does that of Andronicus,
who fulfilled a similar function when Antiochus Epiphanes tarried
in Tarsus (II Macc. 4.31).

And Alcimus: This was the moderate high priest Bacchides forced on
Judaea during his first expedition, a short time after Demetrius'
accession at the end of 162 B.C. (I Macc. 7.5–25; on the question of
the dating of his appointment see p. 345 re verse 62). His Hebrew
name was Yakim (*Ant.* 12.385, 20.235). According to the Midrash,
he was the nephew of Yose ben Joaezer of Zeredah (i.e. Surda near
Gophna: *Genesis Rabba* 65.18), who was among the first 'pairs' of
sages (Aboth 1.4). An ossuary found in a burial cave near Gophna
(*CIJ* II, 1172) has an inscription reading Σαλώμη Ἰακείμου (=
Salōmē, wife [daughter?] of Yakeimos), and since there were many
priests in Gophna (*PT Taanioth* 4.8[79a])[9] it has been suggested that
the ossuary held the bones of Alcimus' wife.[10] The nature of
Alcimus' political and religious views is not sufficiently clear, and
has been the subject of some speculation. It is clear, however, that
he was close to the moderate Hellenizers and loyal to the Seleucid
authorities.

Josephus in *Antiquitates* does not mention Alcimus' participation
in Bacchides' second expedition because he previously reported the
priest's sudden death while trying to demolish the inside Temple
wall (12.413). The story comes from I Maccabees which sets the
event in Sivan of 159 B.C. (9.54–6), that is more than a year after the
battle of Elasa. It may be that the erroneous sequence in Josephus

---

[8] Durrbach and Roussel 1935: no. 1544.   [9] See also Sukenik 1933: 7–9.
[10] Vincent 1913: 103–6.

is not his fault, as many are inclined to believe, but is based on some
source to which he had recourse, since there is no doubt that for the
succession of high priests Josephus did rely on another source (see
also *Ant.* 20.235ff.).[11] Josephus' statement regarding the death of
the high priest Menelaus in Beroea (12.383–6) supports this
assumption, for the matter is not mentioned in I Maccabees but
only in II Maccabees (13.4–8) with which Josephus was not
acquainted (cf. p. 541 n. 80 below).

Again to the land of Judaea: As noted, Bacchides and Alcimus were
first sent to Judaea a short time after Demetrius' accession (I Macc.
7.5–25).

{*And the right corner with them*}: Both Greek *keras* and Hebrew *keren*,
which certainly underlies it, mean 'horn' and metaphorically
'corner'. In a military application it may denote 'flank' or
'column'.[12] In the description of the battle itself (verse 12) it clearly
signifies 'flank', and the sentence means that Bacchides personally
commanded the right wing. As this remark seems somewhat
superfluous in connection with the description of the expedition,
various scholars since Grimm have proposed a variety of
interpretations.[13] Explanations of the expression in a different sense
from the one that it has later in the description of the battle must be
rejected, however. Most of them do not accord with information
available on the usual terminology in the Seleucid army or its
regional concentrations and composition. The most reasonable
explanation was proffered by Dancy, who suggested that the
expression was simply a gloss under the influence of verse 12.[14] The
copyist or exegete who added the gloss probably wished to
emphasize the power of the enemy army and assumed that the elite
units were called 'the right corner' (and he may also have been
influenced by the frequent use of the word *keren* in Daniel). At the
same time, it cannot be ruled out that the expression is the author's,
and he meant to say that during the march as well the commander
was in the company of the picked horsemen whose traditional
position during the battle was in the right wing.

2 *And they went on the Gilgal road*: For a detailed analysis of the wording
of this verse, and the topographical indications, see Appendix L, pp.
552ff. The 'Gilgal road' led from the Jordan Valley to the mountain
plateau north of Jerusalem; it was so called because of the Gilgal
near Jericho at one end of it, and Beth ha-Gilgal near the village of
Rammun at the other.

And they camped at the trails: The Greek is Μαισαλωθ, a transliteration

---

[11] On the problem of the sources for the high priest list see p. 346 n. 93 below.
[12] See Roussel 1969: 337, and the Liddell–Scott dictionary.
[13] Grimm 1853: 132; Meyer 1921: 248; Abel 1949: 160; Bengtson 1964: 2.184; Goldstein
1976: 371.
[14] Dancy 1954: 131; so also Schunck 1980: 333.

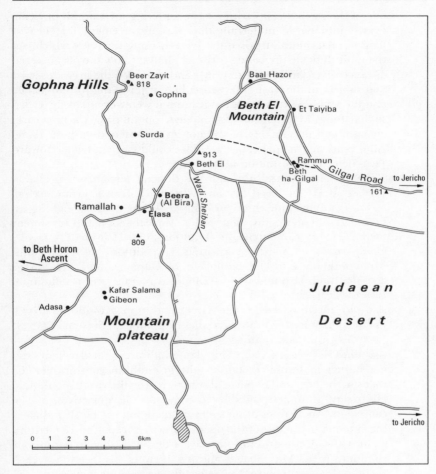

18 Bacchides' expedition and the battle area
(see also the topographical map on p. 73)

of the Hebrew מסילות (= trails) which the translator misconstrued
as a place-name. The preposition *epi* is a translation of '*al*, in this
context = 'at' (see p. 558 below). Bacchides camped at a junction
of several roads in the area.

In [*har bēt 'ēl*]: Mount Beth El, which is Αρβηλοις in Greek. For the
proposed corrected reading see pp. 556–7. The reference is to the
Baal Hazor–Beth El area, the high plateau north of Ramallah. The
choice of a route climbing from the Jordan Valley indicates a bold
but well-thought-out plan based on the experience that the Seleucid
commanders had gained in previous operations in the Judaean
Hills. The topographical problem they faced was how to climb up

one of the steep ascents without encountering an ambush or being drawn into battle in terrain that was inconvenient for 'heavy' fighting. Bacchides surprised the Jews by using the route which was the most difficult (involving a rise of almost 1,200 m over an aerial distance of 21 km in arid terrain), and thus also the least expected and subject to the least observation by the Jews: the Jordan Valley and the semi-desert zone east of Rammun were very sparsely settled so that Judas Maccabaeus was unable to obtain prior warning early enough, and presumably he did not set up observation posts there. After reaching the plateau, Bacchides could easily advance toward Jerusalem through the broad plateau.

The Seleucid march through this difficult terrain was probably very rapid. At the speed customary in the Hellenistic armies (see p. 263 n. 131 above) the climb probably took no more than eight to ten hours. It is noteworthy that Judas Maccabaeus adopted similar tactics in his campaigns in Transjordania (I Macc. 5.24,28). Compare the hard, surprising expedition of Antigonus Monophthalmus to the battlefield of Gabiene, and the similar considerations he put forward – Diodorus 19.37.2 (see also Plutarch, *Eumenes* 15.3).

And they captured [*them*]: The Greek has προκατελάβοντο αὐτήν (= they captured it) because the translator understood מסילות (= trails) as a place-name.

And killed many human souls: This clause indicates that Bacchides did not hasten to Jerusalem but sought to establish control over the roads in the area and in particular to terrorize the rural population. His delay is understandable in view of the objectives of the campaign. An analysis of the Seleucid tactics in the battle indicates that the main purpose of the operation was not to acquire territory or to win a decisive victory in the battle but rather to capture or eliminate Judas Maccabaeus and his disciples (see below re verses 12,15). At this point the Seleucids were well aware of the Hasmonaean family's vital role in the revolt movement, and imagined that they would be able to put an end to the Revolt by removing its leaders. Instructions to that effect were issued to Nicanor who tried to take Judas Maccabaeus through a trick and even demanded that he be handed over (I Macc. 7.27–30,35; II Macc. 14.33). Bacchides' actions in *har* Beth El seem to have been aimed at drawing Judas Maccabaeus into battle and forcing it to take place in an area where the qualitative advantage of the Seleucid 'heavies' allowed Bacchides free tactical manoeuvring to draw the rebel leaders personally into a trap. In the conditions which developed, Judas Maccabaeus had no choice but to report for battle: the capture of the roads and the 'neutralization' of the local population obviated any surprise attack on the Seleucid camp, and

Bacchides' systematic raids against the local people made it impossible for Judas Maccabaeus to stand idle. Aside from his concern for the well-being of Jews everywhere (cf. his measures after the purification of the Temple), he knew that inaction on his part might impair his status as leader of the people and tip the scales gradually in favour of Alcimus and his faction.

3 *And in the first month in the year two and fifty and a hundred*: Since the event in question is 'domestic', the date must be set on the basis of the Babylonian variation on the Seleucid calendar beginning in April 311 B.C. The first month of 152 on that basis started in April 160 B.C. That date also accords with the hypothesis of some scholars that the dating of the 'internal' events in I Maccabees is based on a mixed chronology, i.e. on the Syrian–Macedonian calendar beginning in October 312 B.C. for the year, and on the Hebrew calendar beginning in Nisan (April) for the months.

They camped opposite Jerusalem: The expression ἐπὶ Ιερουσαλημ does not imply that Bacchides attempted first to besiege the city before moving northwards toward Judas Maccabaeus.[15] The preposition ἐπί renders the Hebrew מול, which sometimes indicates visual contact rather than propinquity (see, e.g., Josh. 9.1, 22.11). In this context the verse means that Jerusalem was within sight of Bacchides. And indeed the city can be seen from the Beth El mountain, the highest ridge north of Jerusalem.

4 *And they moved and went to Be⟨e⟩ra*: Bacchides was advancing from the Beth El area to Jerusalem. The camp site of the Seleucid force is given as *Berea* in the uncial manuscripts, and has a number of variations like *Berethin* in the ancient Latin translation, *Birat* in the Syrian translation, etc. Abel, who suggests the reading *Bereth*, identified the place with Al Bira, the small town near Ramallah.[16] There are remnants of the ancient settlement in the *tel* in the middle of the place where parts of a mediaeval fortress have survived. As to the original Hebrew name, various suggestions have been made. Abel thought of *bīrat* and others have identified the place with the Gibeonite city of Beeroth.[17] The former is not known from any other source, and the last would have to be south of Ramallah.[18] The identification with Al Bira seems the most appropriate, and would be related to the Beera (באֵרא or בארה) mentioned in the Bible (Judg. 9.21; I Chron. 7.37),[19] and that is how I Maccabees should be read. It is not impossible, however, that in Second Temple days the place was called 'Beeroth', for in at least one manuscript of the

[15] Contrary to Abel 1949: 382; Plöger 1958: 182.
[16] Abel 1924: 383; id. 1949: 160; Avi-Yonah 1963: 160, and others.
[17] Avi-Yonah 1963: 99; Albright 1923: 114; id. 1924: 90–111.
[18] Kallai 1954: 111–15.
[19] The last verse is included in an ostensibly genealogical list that is in fact geographical. On that list see S. Yeivin in *Biblical Encyclopaedia*, vol. 1 (Jerusalem, 1952) col. 779 (Hebrew).

Hebrew source Bacchides' camp site was so designated (see below re verse 5; and there too re the reading Βερζητω = 'Beer Zayit'). The form Berea in the uncial manuscripts may be influenced by the name of the well-known Seleucid *polis* Beroea (present-day Aleppo) in northern Syria, which was one of the larger cities of Seleucis, the nerve centre of the kingdom. For the translator's and copyists' lack of familiarity with the toponymy of Eretz Israel, as shown in the description of Bacchides' expedition, see p. 557 below; cf. p. 396.

With twenty thousand men and with two thousand horsemen: In contrast to other figures given in the Books of the Maccabees for the Seleucid army, these figures seem to reflect more or less the true strength of the expeditionary force, although they may obviously be somewhat rounded off. The fear of Roman intervention, the defeat of Nicanor, and the advanced stage of the Revolt, necessarily impelled the authorities to a massive reaction. Bacchides' high rank, the special nature of the march, the course of the battle and the ring of fortresses prepared after the victory all indicate that the Seleucid reaction was more extreme than usual. And in fact the suppression of the Timarchus revolt made it possible to direct a considerable proportion of the troops to Judaea. This time the author gave the true figures for the enemy while drastically minimizing the strength of the Jewish force (see in greater detail in pp. 44–5, 48, 64 above).

5 *And Judah was encamped at Elasa*: The Greek is ΕΛΑΣΑ. An 'Elasa' is recorded in the genealogical lists of the families of the tribe of Judah (I Chron. 2.39–40) and Benjamin (ibid. 8.37, 9.43), which are partially based on the personification of place-names.[20] The place was identified by Abel with Il'asa at the southern approaches to Ramallah, south-west of Al Bira. The identification is based on the similarity of names, on the geographical context, and on the discovery of Hellenistic pottery in the place.[21] Khirbet La'asa in the Beth Horon Ascent, proposed by Conder and Klein,[22] has produced only Arab finds, can in no way be placed in a reasonable geographical context with any possible location of Bacchides' camp,[23] and is disqualified by its low site as well.

According to Josephus, Judas Maccabaeus concentrated his troops at *Bērzētō* (Beer Zayit, *Ant.* 12.422). Some scholars have tried to harmonize the two sources and suggested that the Jewish force was assembled and deployed first in the Gophna Hills, at Beer Zayit,

[20] See in general Klein 1927: 1–16; id. 1928b: 1–16; id. 1930; 14–30. And specifically on the Benjaminite list see S. Yeivin, s.v. 'Benjamin' in *Biblical Encyclopaedia*, vol. 2 (Jerusalem, 1954) col. 274 (Hebrew); id. s.v. 'Judah' in *Biblical Encyclopaedia*, vol. 3 (Jerusalem, 1955) col. 508 (Hebrew). Cf. B. Mazar, s.v. 'Elasa' in *Biblical Encyclopaedia*, vol. 1 (Jerusalem, 1952) col. 371 (Hebrew).

[21] Abel 1924: 383–4.

[22] Conder 1893: 157; S. Klein 1939a: 63–4.

[23] So also S. Löwenstamm, s.v. 'Elasa' in *Biblical Encyclopaedia*, vol. 1 (Jerusalem, 1952) cols 371–2 (Hebrew).

from which it moved to Elasa.[24] Some have also accepted Josephus'
statement as offering independent testimony that the battle took
place at Beer Zayit.[25] However, there is no evidence at all that in
describing the battle of Elasa Josephus used any source besides I
Maccabees, and consequently the explanation of the name *Bērzētō*
must be sought in the various transformations that the I Maccabees
text underwent. The identical form appears in the Lucianic version
and in one of the manuscripts of the Syrian translation influenced by
it as the place where Bacchides arrayed his army. The origin of the
form seems to be the palaeographic similarity between the Hebrew
form of the name בארות (Beeroth), which apparently appeared
in some Hebrew manuscript, and באר זית (Beer Zayit).[26] The
Lucianic version and the underlying pre-Lucianic version, which
were a proof copy of the Alexandrian version corrected from a
Hebrew original,[27] may have drawn on a Hebrew manuscript in
which 'Beeroth' was garbled to 'Beer Zayit'. The transformation of
'Beeroth' into *Bērzētō* may also have first occurred in the Lucianic
(or pre-Lucianic) version itself. In any case, the garbling may have
been caused under the influence of the reference to Beer Zayit in I
Maccabees as the place where Bacchides camped during his first
expedition (7.19). Josephus, who used the pre-Lucianic version,[28]
copied that wording and mistakenly made the Seleucid camp site
the assembly point of Judas Maccabaeus' men. This conclusion is
supported by the fact that Josephus does not mention the Seleucid
camp site at all. He may have assumed that Elasa and Beer Zayit
were adjacent and out of a desire not to encumber the Greco-
Roman reader with too many topographical details that were not
clear to him, confined himself to the mention of Beer Zayit which
was already familiar from an earlier episode. In any case, Josephus'
version should not mislead us to follow the Lucianic text and accept
Beer Zayit as the Seleucid camp site.[29] According to the story, the
Jewish force saw the Seleucid camp in all its glory (9.6), but from
Elasa it is impossible to see what is happening in Beer Zayit and its
environs.

As the camps at Al Bira and Elasa were only a kilometre apart,
it is possible to locate the battle site on the two-kilometre wide
plateau where the towns of Ramallah and Al Bira are situated and
in the valley below Elasa. The terrain does not exactly resemble a
table, but it is convenient enough to allow the satisfactory operation

[24] Abel 1924: 382; Yeivin 1941: 83–4; Avi-Yonah 1974: 30.
[25] Plöger 1958: 184.
[26] On the close resemblance of the letters ר and ד in the palaeography of the Hasmonaean
period see Avigad 1961: 120–1.
[27] Sweet 1900: 8off.; Jellicoe 1968: 163ff. See also Rahlfs 1911: 3.80–111.
[28] Thackeray 1929: 85–6; Melamed 1951: 122–3.
[29] Contrary to Ewald 1864–8: 4.422 n. 1; Schürer 1901: 1.222 n. 36.

of phalanx units, as becomes evident when it is compared with other
battlefields on which phalanx units of Hellenistic armies fought
quite effectively.[30] The approximately 8,000-man Seleucid phalanx
on the Elasa battlefield (see below) could have been arrayed on a
space of about 500 m in the centre of the area (see pp. 324, 330 on
the spaces and number of rows in the phalanx formation).

And three thousand picked men with him: The number is identical with
that ascribed to Judas Maccabaeus in the preceding battle with
Nicanor (7.40), and it appears more than once in I Maccabees in
the estimate of Jewish forces (4.6, 5.20, 11.44; cf. p. 48 above).

Picked: The Greek is ἐπίλεκτοι, in the plural; the Hebrew
combination איש בחור was in the singular; cf. 4.1 and 4.28. This
verse seems to point to prior selection and screening in the Jewish
force, leaving just 3,000 combatants in the camp, as was done before
the battle of Ammaus (4.6). However, since the battle of Elasa was
not conducted at night or by indirect methods, and since given the
terrain and the circumstances it is hard to believe that Judas
Maccabaeus planned an operation of that kind, this possibility must
be rejected. The author simply exaggerated and defined the Jewish
force as 'picked' in order to imply desertion from the camp even
before the deployment stage, as if to say that most of the soldiers
were reluctant to proceed to the battlefield, leaving only the
'picked', that is, the brave. As noted above, I Maccabees used the
word 'picked' very loosely (see p. 284). The possibility should not
be discounted that the adjective 'picked' in this verse was also
influenced by a biblical association – the 3,000 picked soldiers of
Saul who stayed with him for the regular operations (I Sam. 13.2,
24.2, 26.2; and cf. Josh. 7.3–4; Judg. 15.11). In any case in the
following verse I Maccabees states that even a large proportion of
the latter left the camp when they saw the power of the opposing
army. In this way the author stresses the grave situation facing the
Jewish commander and provides an alibi for the defeat. Just as
the figure of 800 given in the description of the battle itself is worthless (see below), no significance should be attached to the number
cited for the start of the deployment.

Josephus reports that the Jewish force numbered 1,000 men in the
formation stage (*Ant.* 12.422). This is obviously a scribal error, for
further on he states that most of the army fled and only 800 men
were left on the battlefield (ibid. 423).

6 *And they saw the throng of the armies that it was numerous and they were sore
afraid and many vanished from the camp*: The pre-battle ratio of Jewish
to enemy forces (3,000 *versus* 22,000) is no different from that
presented in previous battles. It might seem possible to claim that

[30] Cf. the battlefields of Cyrrhestica and Panium, and those in the battle against Molon and
at Beth Zacharia. On the first three see Bar-Kochva 1979: 111,117,146.

many soldiers quit the Jewish camp because they realized that there
was no chance this time of surprising the Seleucids with indirect
methods and because the choice of battle site was dictated by the
enemy. But the description of the battle shows that the number
attributed to the Jewish force is blatantly false (see pp. 48–9 above).
If there were some desertions from the camp, they were not more
numerous than was usual in similar circumstances.

Vanished: The Greek is ἐξερρύησαν, literally 'disappeared', 'melted
away', etc., which the Septuagint uses to render the root נשל
(= drop out, drop off; Deut. 28.40, 'thine olives shall drop off').

Eight hundred men of them remained: This estimate is far below the
number I Maccabees generally attributed to the Jewish troops,
which is never less than 3,000 men. The small number together with
the exaggeration of the dimensions of the desertion are designed to
explain why the commander was defeated and killed in battle. As
usual the author ignores the tactical composition of the Jewish force,
but an analysis of the battle shows that the Jews had cavalry and
infantry with heavy and semi-heavy equipment (see pp. 64, 70–6
above).

7 *And Judah saw…*: This verse belongs to the category of battle
orations. Its object, as usual with such orations, is to stress the
inferiority of the Jewish side. In the context of the last few verses it
is designed also to explain why Judas Maccabaeus was not deterred
from joining battle despite the desertions. Thus another halo is
conferred on Judas Maccabaeus in his last hour.

That his camp faded away: The word ἀπερρύη should be reconstructed
as the somewhat poetic נבל (= faded, withered). Compare the
Septuagint for Psalms 1.3. The root appears in a similar context in
Isaiah 34.4 ('And all their army faded away'). The reconstruction
נמס (= melt) proposed by Cahana has no precedent in the
Septuagint and no connection with the literal meaning of the Greek
word.

And his heart broke: The Greek is συνετρίβη τῇ καρδίᾳ. For the
translation, compare the Septuagint for Psalms 51.19, 147.3; Is.
57.15, 61.1.

For he had not the time to collect them: The author is referring to
gathering together again the various deserters and shirkers who
were scared off at the sight of the enemy both before and after its
formation.

8 *And he tired*: The Greek is ἐξελύθη, which the Septuagint uses to
translate various words; the most suitable for the contents and
language of the verse seems to be ויעף (= and he tired: see the
Septuagint for Judg. 8.15; II Sam. 21.15) or וילאה (= and he
wearied: Jer. 12.5). Cahana proposes וירך לבו (= and his heart
became faint) as per Deut. 20.3 (actually: לבבו), but that verse in

the Septuagint has καρδίᾳ (= in (his) heart) which I Maccabees
does not. From the substantive point of view as well, 'tired' or
'wearied' is preferable: the author keeps stressing Judas
Maccabaeus' courage, so that what he means here is that Judas
Maccabaeus was exhausted by his endeavours to persuade the
soldiers not to quit the field.

10 *And Judah said, Far be it from me...to flee from them...and we shall not
leave behind us an offence to our honour*: The argument that the author
has Judas Maccabaeus provide does not accord with the
commander's actions on other occasions. Judas Maccabaeus
avoided battle or fled for his life more than once. After the battle of
Beth Zacharia he retreated to the Gophna area, and only part of his
army stayed in the besieged Temple. During Bacchides' first
expedition he took care not to clash with the Seleucid army, and
needless to say in the earlier confrontations he avoided a clash until
he could dictate the choice of battlefield. The real reason Judas
Maccabaeus joined battle this time was, as noted above, because of
internal politics. The heroic motive cited by the author is designed
to enhance Judas Maccabaeus' image. The concern for posterity is
attributed also to Eleazar at Beth Zacharia – 'to make an eternal
name for himself' (I Macc. 6.44) – which is likewise an invention of
the author.

And if our end is near let us die bravely: The possibility of receiving help
from on high which would extricate his men from their dire straits
is not even hinted at here, in contrast to the orations before the other
battles.

11 *And the army departed from the camp and they went forward toward them*: The
words δύναμις (= army) and ἔστησαν εἰς συνάντησιν αὐτοῖς (=
went forward toward them) raise some difficulties. There are some
who think that 'army' refers to the Jewish troops, meaning that
Judas Maccabaeus and his men were the ones who advanced first,
while the grammatical subject of 'and they went forward toward
them' is the horsemen, archers and slingers mentioned thereafter,
that is, the Seleucid army.[31] This separation is supported by the
ancient Latin translation and the propinquity of 'and the horsemen
were divided...' to 'and they went forward toward them'. But the
Seleucid army was as usual in a well-fortified camp near the battle
site: if Judas Maccabaeus had taken the initiative and advanced
toward the enemy that was well protected inside its camp, it is hard
to assume that the Seleucids would have had enough time to deploy
themselves outside the camp in the classic manner that the verse
describes before the actual clash (verses 11ff.). It might be claimed
that the author simply omitted a description of the Seleucid
deployment stage and dealt only with that of the Jews, but that

---

[31] E.g. Grimm 1853: 134.

would not fit in with his strong desire to impress the reader through his description of the enemy army. Others interpret 'army' as applying to the Seleucid army, and 'they went forward' to the Jewish troops.[32] It seems more logical to view the verse as confined entirely to the movements of the Seleucid army, including its departure from the camp, its presenting itself on the battlefield, and its deployment and formation. From verse 6 on, the author strives to stress the elements that frightened Judas Maccabaeus and his men.[33] That is the way Josephus, too, understood the verse (*Ant.* 12.426). On δύναμις reconstructed in this context as *ṣāvā* (= army) rather than *ḥayil* (= force) see p. 204 above.

And the horsemen were divided into (the) two sides: The reference is to the usual division of the horsemen into two wings on the flanks of the phalanx units mentioned in verse 12. Thus the phrase εἰς δύο μέρη (the Lucianic version adds the definite article τά) can be translated 'to the two sides' or 'to two sides'. The reconstruction ראשים which Cahana proposes has no basis in the Septuagint, which translates the biblical ראש as ἀρχή (see also I Macc. 5.33). Nor does the biblical meaning of ראש (= head, column, file, etc.)[34] fit the context in the present verse.

And the slingers and the bow holders went before the army: The archers and slingers are the skirmishers (*promakhoi*) who were normally stationed in front of the phalanx. No units of slingers participated in the Daphne procession. In the only case in which slingers in the Seleucid army are mentioned, they were Orientals (Livy 37.40.9). In the Greek world, the men of Rhodes excelled in that art typical of mountain people, but Rhodian slingers and Rhodian units are not mentioned in descriptions of the campaigns of Hellenistic armies in the east (aside from individual soldiers, including some of high rank).[35] Furthermore, in view of the Rhodians' sensitivity about their relationship with Rome and their interest in improving it after the battle of Pydna,[36] it is hard to assume that the Seleucids could conduct an effective recruitment campaign on the island. The absence of slingers in Daphne may be connected with the unsatisfactory situation in the eastern satrapies at the time. The suppression of the Timarchus revolt made it possible to move forces of that type from the Upper Satrapies to Judaea and also to reinforce the archers who were below standard strength at Daphne.

And the first of the battle all the valorous: The title πρωταγωνιστής

[32] Gutberlet 1920: 142; Abel 1949: 161–2.

[33] As rightly pointed out by Goldstein 1976: 375.

[34] For an explanation of the word *rō'š* see Yadin 1962: 144–5.

[35] On the Rhodians in the Hellenistic armies see Launey 1949–50: 1.240–6; on the slinger tradition in Rhodes see F. Lammert in *RE* s.v. Σφενδονῆται, cols 1695ff.

[36] See Schmitt 1957: 151ff.

appears one other time in II Maccabees in the meaning of 'commander', 'head of the army', etc. (15.30), but nowhere else in the Septuagint. This can be reconstructed in our verse literally as either *ri'šōnē ha-milḥāmā* (= the first of the battle) or *rā'šē ha-milḥāmā* (= the heads [i.e. commanders] of the battle; the word *lōḥamīm* (= fighters) does not appear in the Bible). The first reading is not very satisfactory if 'the valorous' are construed as the lightly equipped skirmishers because the latter were not picked soldiers but national contingents of Orientals or Cretans, and the author of I Maccabees must have known it. The reference may, however, be to the soldiers in the front rows of the phalanx who, in order to prevent the formation from collapsing, were as a rule the bravest, tallest and strongest (see Asclep. 2.2, 3.1–3,6; Aelian, *Tact.* 13.1–2; Arrian, *Tact.* 5.6, 12.1–4). Their height and strength may have so impressed the observer that he described them as 'the valorous'. At the same time, I would not discount the second alternative reading in reference to the command, meaning that it was composed of bold and experienced military men. Ptolemaic tombstones show officers of enormous stature,[37] which is certainly exaggerated, but indicate their physical superiority over the rank-and-file. The comment on the enemy commanders may have led to the mention in the next verse of the place where the supreme commander, Bacchides, was to be found on the battlefield. It may be, too, that the connection between *rā'šē* (= heads), and *ha-gibōrim* (= the valorous) has an associative relation to the lists of David's heroes (*ha-gibōrim*), some of whom are also called *rō'š* (II Sam. 23.8,13,18; I Chron. 12.1,3,4,9,10,15,19,21–2). Yet I incline to the first reconstruction referring to the first rows of the phalanx, both because the verse clearly relates to the visual effect created by the deployment of the Seleucid army, and because a sentence like 'and the heads of the war all the heroes' is somewhat superfluous, as it only notes the usual practice in ancient warfare.

12 *And Bacchides was in the right corner*: The word *keras–keren* (= corner; see re verse 2) denotes the edge of the formation and thus certainly refers to a wing of the horsemen, whose division into '(the) two sides' is mentioned in the preceding verse. The supreme command customarily fought and took personal charge of the right-wing cavalry.[38]

And the phalanx approached: The Greek is *phalanx*. The Hebrew source had the Greek word in transliteration, probably פלנכס. The

---

[37] See Pl. II; cf. the stele of the Bithynian officer from the necropolis of Gabbari near Alexandria published by Rostovtzeff (1949: 1.288), and especially the mercenary from Sciatby in Breccia 1912: 12–13.

[38] See Kromayer and Veith 1903: 1.166; Bar-Kochva 1979: 85. Cf., e.g., Polybius 5.53.6,54.1,82.7–8,84.1,8,11–13, 10.49.7; Appian, *Syr.* 20(90); Plut. *Cato Maior* 14.6; Livy 36.18.4, 37.40.6,41.1,42.7–8,43; Asclepiodotus 3.1–12.

reference is to the heavy infantry unit of *sarissa*-bearing soldiers who were stationed in the centre of the formation (see Appendix B, pp. 432ff.).

From the two parts: The Greek is ἐκ τῶν δύο μερῶν. On the basis of the usual deployment of phalangites in the formation, the reconstruction should be משני החלקים (= from the two parts) and not משני הצדדים. (= from the two sides) as suggested regarding the division of the horsemen in the previous verse (both possibilities would fit in with the Septuagint vocabulary). For the division of a phalanx formation into two 'parts' (μέρη) see Arrian, *Tact*. 8.3. In view of the overall number of soldiers at the disposal of Bacchides and the proportion of phalangites in the Seleucid army, the 'two parts' apparently comprised two phalangarchies (*stratēgiai*) of 4,000 men each (see Asclepiodotus 2.10; Arrian, *Tact*. 10.5–7; Aelian, *Tact*. 9.8).

The description below indicates that the battle started with the 'skirmishers', followed by an attack by the phalangites, and not by the usual cavalry assault. The reason for the unusual tactics adopted by the Seleucid commander becomes clear in the subsequent developments; the feigned withdrawal of the right wing and thereafter the encirclement of the Jewish left wing by the cavalry of both wings (see below re verses 15–16) indicate that Bacchides planned to draw Judas Maccabaeus into a trap outside the battlefield in a manner that would leave no room for reinforcement or retreat, and so ensure the killing or capture of the rebel leader and his companions. Starting the battle with the advance of the phalanx was an important element in the plan. Had the cavalry of Bacchides' right wing assaulted that of Judas Maccabaeus, it might very well have carried the day, and the Jewish force would have been quickly defeated. However, Judas Maccabaeus and his men would have been able to flee through the open road to the south as they did after their defeat at Beth Zacharia. By refraining from attacking directly in the wings, Bacchides left the Jewish commander few options. As a leader who attained his status through military achievements, Judas Maccabaeus could not allow himself not to be involved in the battle. Since it was clear that sooner or later the Jewish infantry would break under the pressure of the Seleucid 'heavies', thus bringing the battle to a close, he had to choose between two possibilities. The first, to make a cavalry assault against the vulnerable flanks of the advancing Seleucid phalanx, was rejected because it would lay the Jews open to a flanking attack by Bacchides' horsemen. The second, to assault the right cavalry wing directly, seemed to have the better chance, in view of the assumption already proven in battles with Apollonius and Nicanor, that the death of the enemy commander was likely to tip the scales

(I Macc. 3.11, 7.43). Having previously spent some time in Judaea, Bacchides was doubtless acquainted with Judas Maccabaeus' methods, and expected a reaction of that kind. The despatch of the phalanx before the cavalry was thus designed to compel Judas Maccabaeus to attack Bacchides' right wing and fall into the trap.

And they blew the trumpets: The military use of trumpets was quite common in the Hellenistic armies from Alexander on, primarily for giving orders as the soldiers were forming for battle and in the battle itself. As the Hellenistic battlefields covered quite a large area, the officers found it difficult to transmit orders through visual signals. The din and clamour on the battlefield (see verse 13) made it hard for even the lower command echelons to transmit instructions and orders. The various tones and trills of the trumpet provided a satisfactory solution (see Asclepiodotus 12.10). The trumpet also operated to frighten the enemy (Onasander 17). In this verse the reference is to a signal to attack (cf., e.g., Diodorus 17.25.1,33.4,58.1 and 19.30.1,41.3).[39]

And those with Judah also blew the trumpets: For trumpets in Judas Maccabaeus' army and their function at various stages of the battle cf. I Macc. 4.13,40, 7.45.

13 *And the land raged from the sound of the camps*: On war cries and other means of increasing the din in the battlefield, and on their purpose in Hellenistic warfare, see pp. 331–2 above re verse 41.

And the battle was joined: The expression καὶ ἐγένετο ὁ πόλεμος συνημμένος in the Greek text is not known from the Septuagint. According to its literal meaning and a similar biblical idiom, it appears that the Hebrew original had ותטש המלחמה (= and the war was joined; cf. I Sam. 4.2).

From morning to evening: This shows that the battle, including the clash of infantry in the centre, lasted a long time. On the credibility of the statement see p. 72 above.

14 *And Judah saw that Bacchides and the might of his camp were in the right*: In the Hellenistic armies the right cavalry wing, led by the supreme commander, was ordinarily the strongest wing. This wing in the

---

[39] Yadin (1962: 111) states that trumpets were not common in Hellenistic armies, arguing that as the army as a whole fought in close formation it did not need signalling devices. This view ignores the variety of tactical and national contingents in the Hellenistic armies and the width of the battlefield. On trumpets in the Hellenistic armies see Asclepiodotus 2.9, 6.3, 12.10; Arrian, *Anab.* 3.18.7, 5.23.7,24.2; Diodorus 17.25.1,27.4,33.4,58.1,68.3, 19.30.1,10,41.3; Curtius Rufus 4.13.5, 5.2; Lucian, *Zeuxis* 9; Polyaenus 4.9.2, 7.39; Plut. *Dem.* 28.12, 49.1, *Pyrrh.* 22.9, *Sulla* 14.5, *Apopht.* 181; Polybius 2.29.6, 4.13.1,71.8, 10.31.4; Livy 33.9.1; and also I Macc. 6.33; II Macc. 15.25. The last verse by itself does not reflect the events of the battle of Adasa, but for that very reason throws light on the usual practice of the Hellenistic armies. For banners see Arrian, *Anab.* 7.14.10; Polybius 2.66.11, 5.84.1; Plut. *Philop.* 6.1–2; Livy 33.7; Asclepiodotus 2.9, 6.3, 12; Onasander 25–6, and the Dioscorides Stele from Sidon (Pl. X). For banners in Ptolemaic papyri see Meyer 1900: 96 n. 357; Lesquier 1911: 346.

Seleucid army generally included one of the thousand-man units of the Royal Guard, the *agēma* or the Companions, or both.[40] The Seleucid cavalry at Elasa numbered 2,000 horsemen. At least one of the Guard units also took part in the expedition to Judaea.

Judas Maccabaeus could have learned where Bacchides was through information he had on Seleucid warfare and formation in general, and because he noted that the Guardsmen of the cavalry among whom the supreme commander used to fight (see p. 335 n. 70 above) were posted in the right wing. At that stage he probably also had confirmed information on the types of units the Seleucids had, and their weapons and shield colours. Moreover, in view of the battle plan presumably the Seleucid commander made his position at the head of the right wing obvious in various ways. Cf. Diodorus 18.31, where Eumenes and Neoptolemus recognize each other according to their horses and *insignia*.

And all the strong-hearted joined him: When the position of the Seleucid commander was absolutely certain, and Judas Maccabaeus had come to appreciate the only course left to him, the main strength of the Jewish cavalry was concentrated in the left wing, opposite Bacchides' right wing.

15 *And the right corner was smitten before them*: It is doubtful whether Judas Maccabaeus' horsemen, whatever their origin, were capable of defeating Bacchides' experienced cavalry, much of which belonged to the Royal Guard. Furthermore, in most cases, beaten horsemen who had been put to flight would have been unable to reform and combat their pursuers unless the 'retreat' had been carefully planned in advance. It thus appears that Bacchides carried out a feigned withdrawal in order to draw Judas Maccabaeus away from the battlefield into a trap. Had he utilized his entire potential when his wing was attacked, he would in any case have defeated the Jews, but his prey might have escaped him for the road back was open to the Jewish commander, who did have horsemen at his disposal. The enthusiastic author of I Maccabees cannot be expected to have been aware of Bacchides' plans and the true nature of his 'retreat', but even if he had, he would not have reported it, in order not to detract from the partial success he attributes to the hero in his last hour.

And he chased after them: Judas Maccabaeus continued his pursuit and thus in fact abandoned the Jewish foot soldiers left on the battlefield, for Bacchides himself was not slain, and the Seleucid horsemen did not collapse, and he feared they would return to the battlefield.

As far as the [slopes of] the mountain: The wording in the Greek manuscripts – ἕως ᾿Αζώτου ὄρους (= up to [the] Azotos mountain)

---

[40] On the special status of the right wing in the Greek and Macedonian armies see Kromayer and Veith 1926: 84–5,93–4,142–4, and also Kromayer and Veith 1903–32: 1.166; Lévêque and Vidal-Naquet 1960: 294–308; Pritchett 1974: 2.191–2. On the *agēma* see Bar-Kochva 1979: 68–74.

is certainly garbled. No mountain or hill named Azotos is known, and the city Azotos-Ashdod was in the coastal plain, far from the battlefield.[41] Torrey proposed the reading ἕως ἄνω τοῦ ὄρους (= up to [the] ascent of the mountain),[42] but it is hard to believe that a copyist would turn an ordinary phrase of this kind into a place-name, and the substitution of ν for ζ does not make sense palaeographically or phonetically. In addition, the letter ζ occurs in the Latin translation (Gazara) and in *Antiquitates* (12.429, 'Αζᾶ ὄρος). Abel proposes the reading ἕως 'Ασώρου ὄρους (= up to [the] *Asōr* mountain), referring to Baal Hazor, the highest peak in the mountainous region north of Jerusalem, some twelve kilometres north-east of the battlefield.[43] This correction presents considerable difficulties: First, according to Biblical syntax the Hebrew should have been in this case עד הר חצור. The suggested Greek reading implies a departure from the practice of the I Maccabees translator to keep to the Hebrew word order in reading geographical names (see, e.g., I Mac. 4.36, 6.48: τὸ ὄρος Σιων, הר ציון (= Mount Zion); עד הר חצור would have been translated ἕως ὄρους 'Ασώρου). Secondly, the identification with Baal Hazor would mean that Judas Maccabaeus pursued the enemy's retreating flank for about twelve kilometres. Such a long pursuit is hard to imagine while the infantry was left on the battlefield, even if the aim was to strike at the enemy commander or capture the logistic camp or both. I would also rather doubt whether the concerted manoeuvre of the Seleucid flanks could be properly controlled and carried out over such a distance.

It thus seems preferable to accept the proposal of Michaelis and others, among them Abel himself in his later exegesis of the Books of the Maccabees, that the difficulty derived from a little mistake in the Hebrew copy, which had אשדוד (*Ashdod*-Azotos) instead of אשדות (*asdōt* = slopes).[44] This proposal accords with the topographical features of the battle area: in the Bible, the term *asdōt* when applied to western Eretz Israel refers to the eastern sharp inclines of the central mountain ridge (Josh. 10.40, 12.8). In view of the location of the battlefield and the placement of the opposing

---

[41] The recent attempt of van Henten (1983: 43–51) to defend the existing reading of the uncial MSS, suggesting 'into the borders of Ashdod', ignores the fact that I Maccabees does not describe here simply a pursuit (as in 4.15, 7.45), but a well-calculated sham retreat, the pursuing Jewish force being surprised from behind by another flank of the enemy, which was previously deployed in the original battlefield, and the decisive phase of the battle taking place at the site under discussion. Such a stratagem could be successfully performed only in a restricted area, where the advance of the troops could be controlled and disguised. Ashdod was, however, 60 km away from Elasa, and the border of its rural territory (the *khōra*) more than half that distance away (on the *khōra* of Ashdod, see p. 271 above).

[42] Torrey 1934: 32.   [43] Abel 1924: 386–7.

[44] Michaelis 1778: 193–4; Grimm 1853: 135; Abel 1949: 162–3; Dancy 1954: 132; Plöger 1958: 183; Avi-Yonah 1974: 30.

forces, Bacchides' withdrawal route had to be toward the eastern slopes. Therefore there is no room for the speculation that *ašdōt hāhār* refers to the Beth Horon Descent, certainly not for the opinion that the retreat was toward the Gophna Valley.[45] Well versed as he was in biblical terminology, the author of I Maccabees would not have used the term *ašdōt* to refer to the gentle incline leading to an inside valley of the mountain plateau. The suggestion that the place is to be located at some point on the way from the battlefield to Jerusalem[46] is certainly odd. Abel assumed that *ašdōt hāhār* still refers to the descent near Baal Hazor.[47] This is geographically possible, but unsuitable for other reasons: apart from the excessively long-range pursuit that this identification implies, why would the author use such a general expression for Baal Hazor, a mountain known, defined and familiar in the Biblical period as well as the Second Temple era?[48]

In the light of all that was said above, we must seek an area close to the battlefield, one that did not contain any well-known settlements or sites, that fits the biblical expression *ašdōt hāhār* in topographical features and direction, and that accords with the possible routes of retreat and pursuit in view of the deployment of the two armies. The point nearest to the battlefield which accords with the requirements is 1.5 km southeast of Beth El (at the junction south of Hill 887; see Map 4, p. 73 above). The road passes by the peaks of the mountain plateau, making a detour to avoid Wadi Sheiban. At the point mentioned, it starts to descend eastward to the Jordan Valley. That section contains no outstanding settlements or localities known from the Biblical or Second Temple periods, and that may very well have led the author to use the general term *ašdōt hāhār*. The distance from the battlefield to that point is about six kilometres. The retreat route passed close to Bacchides' first camp (see pp. 383–5), probably serving later as his logistic camp. He could thus roughly study the terrain and perhaps even train his sham retreat on the spot. Judas Maccabaeus on his part could have been tempted to take up the pursuit hoping to demoralize the enemy by the threat to his 'baggage'. A cavalry pursuit of 30 *stadia* (5.7 km) with the centre forces left in the field is known, for instance, from the battle of Paraetacene in 317 B.C. (Diodorus 19.30.4–10,31.2). The pursuit ranges of Demetrius Poliorcetes' cavalry wings at Ipsus (Plutarch,

[45] On the first view see Avi-Yonah 1964: 62; on the second see Yeivin 1941: 83–4.
[46] Goldstein 1976: 373–4.
[47] Abel 1949: 163. See also the Hebrew version of this book (Bar-Kochva 1980b: 78,303).
[48] See II Sam. 13.23; Neh. 11.33; Testaments, *Judas* 3.1; Genesis Apocryphon, p. 21, lines 8–9. While there is a difference of opinion on the identity of the Hazor mentioned in the second source, there does not appear to be any reasonable alternative, and the arguments against the identification are rather weak. As to the third mention, there is no doubt of the identity in view of the wording 'the Hazor plateau to the left of Beth El', and see also Avigad and Yadin 1956: 28,45.

Demetrius 29.3) and of Antiochus III's at Raphia (Polybius
5.85.11–13) are not known, but it is hard to imagine that they
exceeded the range noted above. As was already stressed, the fact
that Judas Maccabaeus followed Bacchides' cavalry for such a long
distance proves definitely that the Jewish force was likewise
composed of mounted soldiers (pp. 70–1 above).

Abel, believing in the identification with Baal Hazor, found it
difficult to understand how Judas Maccabaeus pursued the enemy
cavalry for twelve kilometres. He therefore suggested that the
pursuit did not actually reach the location referred to but only
proceeded in that direction.[49] However, the preposition ἕως with a
place-name or geographical term which appears numerous times in
I Maccabees indicates the destination reached, and that is the
meaning also of the עד. which certainly appeared in the Hebrew
original (see also p. 271 above, and 3.16,24, 4.15, 5.46,60, 7.45, 9.43,
11.7,8,59,62,73, 12.33, 16.9,10).

Josephus in *Antiquitates* (12.429) defines the final point of the
pursuit with the words μέχρι Ἀζᾶ ['Εζᾶ] ὄρους οὕτω λεγομένου
(= to the mountain of *Aza* [*Eza*] which is called thus). The
explanatory phrase, 'which is called thus', rather rare in Josephus,
shows that he himself had trouble identifying the place, and may
even have had doubts about the text at his disposal. It follows that
the Greek version he worked from was garbled.[50] Here again
Josephus' puzzlement refutes the view that he consulted the Hebrew
version of I Maccabees (cf. p. 193 above).

16 *And those in the left corner saw that the right corner was devastated*: The
reference is to the horsemen of the Seleucid left wing. Apparently a
Jewish cavalry force faced them; it is hard to believe that Judas
Maccabaeus concentrated all his horsemen in the left wing. Had he
done so, the infantry in the centre would have been vulnerable to an
assault by the enemy's left wing. If that had happened, he would
have refrained from pursuing Bacchides' cavalrymen, knowing that
those of the enemy left wing could attack him from the rear. It can
thus be deduced that not all the Seleucid left cavalry wing
participated in the encirclement, and at least part of it remained on
the battlefield to fight the Jewish right wing. The author says
nothing about this because he focuses on the action of the
commander, the hero of his book.

And they turned toward Judah's trail and those with him from behind: The
Greek is ἐπέστρεψαν, which should be translated ויהפכו (= and
they turned; cf. the Septuagint for Judg. 20.41). The time sequence

[49] Abel 1924: 386–7.

[50] The garbling in the version Josephus had does not support the correction to Ἀσώρου
proposed by Abel any more than it does the present reading of Ἀζώτου ὄρος. This is contrary
to the views of C. Möller and G. Schmitt (1976: 7).

in the description makes it difficult to determine when the cavalry of the Seleucid left wing followed Judas Maccabaeus. Was it only when the pursuers reached 'the mountain slopes' or was it immediately after the Seleucid right wing was 'beaten'? Presumably the intervention of the left wing was somewhat delayed in order not to reveal the trap that was set and to allow Judas Maccabaeus to put some distance between himself and the main part of his army fighting on the battlefield.

17 *And the battle grew harder*: Although not explicitly stated, there is no doubt that the retreating right wing about-faced toward their pursuers, and Judas Maccabaeus was caught in between. That is the way Josephus, too, reconstructs the events (*Ant.* 12.429); he even adds some details to the description, but they are only literary embellishments. The clause 'and the battle grew harder' does not indicate that the battle was long, but only that the situation of the Jewish force was desperate (cf. I Sam. 31.3; I Chron. 10.3).

18 *And Judah fell and the remaining fled*: It can be assumed that almost all the left flank headed by Judas Maccabaeus, being surrounded by the enemy's cavalry, fell to the sword. The survivors belonged to the Jewish centre and to the right flank, which were presumably commanded by Jonathan and Simeon, Judas Maccabaeus' brothers (cf. pp. 78–9 above), whose escape route to the south remained open.

19 *And Jonathan and Simeon carried Judah their brother*: Josephus explains that Judas Maccabaeus' body was removed from the field 'by agreement' (ὑπόσπονδον) with the enemy (*Ant.* 12.432). Permission to remove the dead was quite commonly granted in Ancient Greece and to a smaller extent in the Hellenistic world in battles between Hellenistic armies (see p. 369 n. 13 above). It is hard to believe, however, that the Seleucids followed this practice in the case of a rebel, especially in view of Judas Maccabaeus' mistreatment of the body of Nicanor whose defeat led to the Bacchides expedition. Antiochus III, the father of Antiochus Epiphanes, was extremely harsh to the rebels Molon and Achaeus, and the latter's body was horribly defiled (Polybius 5.54.5–7, 8.21.3–4;[51] for further examples see p. 369 above). Nor can the suggestion that Judas Maccabaeus' body was turned over to his brothers in return for a promise to keep the peace be accepted.[52] There are no signs that rebel activity diminished after Judas Maccabaeus' death, and in the year after the battle of Elasa Bacchides conducted a series of operations aimed at capturing Jonathan and Simeon (I Macc. 9.23–53; and see the

---

[51] For an explanation of the various phases of the defilement of Achaeus' body and their origins see Walbank, 1957–79: 2.97, and the bibliography there.

[52] Oesterly 1913: 97; Abel 1949: 163; Plöger 1958: 185; Goldstein 1976: 375.

chronology in 9.54). Josephus' statements are only an unsuccessful
explanation of I Maccabees based on the practice and terminology
known from Classical literature, especially from Thucydides and
from Xenophon's *Hellenica*.[53]

The body of Judas Maccabaeus was apparently somehow
removed from the battlefield, either in the middle of the battle
immediately after he was killed,[54] or later. It is hard to determine
definitely why I Maccabees disregards the story of the extrication of
the body which would itself have contributed an additional heroic
component. It may be that the author was so bereaved at the death
of his beloved hero that he wished to maintain a minor key. The
heroic tale of the removal of the body would not have fitted in with
the mournful tone of the description, and would have distracted the
reader from the essential point (cf. the story of the removal of
Leonidas' body in Herodotus 7.225, which imparts a kind of solemn
atmosphere to the Thermopylae disaster). It may also be that the
author wished to terminate the description of the battle with the
death of the hero, writing *finis* to a period in the history of
the Revolt, even though the end of the battle (and the removal
of the body) actually occurred later.

And buried him in his ancestral tomb in Modein: After Jonathan's death,
Simeon put up a magnificent structure composed of a podium on
which there were seven pyramids, probably containing the tombs of
Mattathias, his wife and sons, and around them columns decorated
with carvings of weapons and ships (I Macc. 13.27–30; cf. 2.70).
The exact site of the grave is not known. In any case it has no
connection with the late Roman–Byzantine graveyard called Kabur
al-Yahud near the village of El-Midya (see Map 8 on p. 195). A
number of scholars have proposed the Sheikh el-Gharbawi hill
north of El-Midya,[55] where in the last century the foundations of a
large Byzantine building were found, one room of which contained
burial crypts in the Hellenistic style.[56] It has been noted also that the
Madaba mosaic map shows a Byzantine-style structure at Modein.
The crypts are no proof, however, because similar ones were found
on other hills in the neighbourhood, and in any case the brothers'
tombs were pyramids. As to the general location, I Maccabees
reports that the ships were carved on the columns so that they
'could be seen by all seafarers' (13.29). Since the reliefs of the ships
could not be distinguished from afar, there is little doubt that the
word order of the verse was confused and the reference was to the
columns themselves. The columns on the podium probably rose 30

---

[53] On the influence of Thucydides on Josephus see Thackeray 1929: 110ff.
[54] That is also the assumption of Michaelis 1778: 194; Grimm 1853: 135; Zeitlin 1950:
157.
[55] Abel 1924: 499–500, and the bibliography there.
[56] On the finds see Clermont-Ganneau 1896: 2.358–74.

to 40 metres above the ground and could be seen from the coastal region. The Sheikh el-Gharbawi Hills would make this possible, as would a number of other hills scattered throughout the region of Modein.

22 *And the rest of Judah's story and the wars and braveries he made...were not written*: The verse is a paraphrase of the regular closing formula for the history of the kings of Israel and Judaea in I and II Kings. Various opinions have been expressed about the object of the verse and especially about the meaning of the last part of it. Some scholars believe that the sole purpose is to compare Judas Maccabaeus to the kings of Israel and Judaea.[57] However, it should be noted that the author has modified the formula from positive to negative and supplemented it as well. Furthermore, as has been pointed out more than once, I Maccabees does not normally make use of biblical terms indiscriminately and without a factual basis. Grimm's suggestion, that the author was seeking to deride the oral traditions that had developed around Judas Maccabaeus' personality,[58] is not acceptable because the verse actually pays its respects to the oral tradition by admitting that the book does not cover all the accomplishments and struggles of Judas Maccabaeus. Some scholars are inclined to believe that the verse is directed against other written works that were current in the lifetime of the author. However, the statement that the rest of the exploits of Judas Maccabaeus were not written down is not enough to denigrate such works which probably concentrated on the principal battles described in I Maccabees. In the author's time, a generation after Judas Maccabaeus' death, there were still people alive who had taken part in the battles, and writers could claim that their work was based on eye-witness accounts. There would be no reason in that generation for the author of I Maccabees to criticize written traditions, for they were undoubtedly panegyric in character and only added glory to the hero so admired by our author. Nor is there any basis for the assumption that the author hoped to give his own work some exclusivity in future generations by disparaging works likely to be written in his own time or later. The reference in the final sentences of the book to Hyrcanus' official chronicle (16.23–4) is not relevant (for its meaning and purpose see pp. 162–4 above). And if the author had wished to boast of the special value of his own work he would have done so clearly, providing information on himself and his sources, and stressing the first-hand knowledge he had of the events described.

Various conclusions have been drawn from this verse also in regard to the sources that the author utilized. Niese tried to deduce that I Maccabees is an abridgement, an epitome, of a large work, as

[57] Ewald 1864–8: 4.605; Pfeifer 1949: 485.   [58] Grimm 1853: 136.

II Maccabees is,[59] while others concluded that the author of I
Maccabees had no written sources at all.[60] On the other hand, most
scholars claim on the basis of this same verse that for his book the
author used written sources and refrained from relying on oral
testimony.[61] The contents of the verse do not support any one of the
above proposals. An examination of the descriptions of various
episodes in the book, however, refutes the suggestion that I
Maccabees is an epitome, as well as the contradictory suggestions
that the book relied exclusively on either written or oral sources.
The book is not an epitome, and includes some episodes based on
written sources, and some described on the basis of the author's
personal visual and auditory impressions.

It appears that in this verse, the author is trying to apologize for
some lacunae in the description in cases where he did not witness a
number of central events, and for the omission of some of Judas
Maccabaeus' battles and deeds. The descriptions of the battles with
Apollonius and Nicanor, as well as of Lysias' first expedition, have
considerable gaps, and the condensation or absence of other
episodes is obvious in comparison with II Maccabees (see, e.g. II
Macc. 8.30–3, 10.14–38, 12.1–9,32–7). In the closing verses of the
book the author refers his readers to the chronicle of John Hyrcanus
for further information on his reign (16.24). As there is no similar
reference in our verse, it indicates that his statement applies not only
to the coverage in I Maccabees, but also to that of other sources
known to him. This is also implied by the change of the celebrated
formula from the Books of Kings. The statement in our verse thus
refutes the suggestion that the additional episodes in II Maccabees
were drawn from a common source used by the two books (see
pp. 183–4 above).

[59] Niese 1900: 40ff.
[60] Knabenbauer 1907: 163; E. Meyer 1921: 458 n. 1; Dancy 1954: 4.
[61] Grimm 1853: xxii; Schürer 1901: 3.192; Abel 1949: xxvi; Schunck 1954: 53; id. 1980:
321; Goldstein 1976: 375.

Conclusion

A re-evaluation of the battles that Judas Maccabaeus led against the Seleucid troops — in the light of the historical circumstances, the information we have on the Seleucid army, and our familiarity with the battlefields – indicates that I Maccabees describes the course of most of the battles with considerable accuracy, and suggests that the author was an eye-witness of some of them (Ammaus, Beth Zacharia, and perhaps Elasa). The final passages of the book testify to its having been written a generation after the events. On the other hand, an examination of the book's character and purposes, hints, 'slips of the pen' in the two Books of the Maccabees, as well as external information on the size and movements of the Seleucid army, and an analysis of the course of some of the battles according to the conditions of the terrain, can repudiate absolutely most of the information contained in the book on the relative strength of the two sides. The same negative evaluation applies also to the battle orations attributed to Judas Maccabaeus. The great discrepancy in credibility between the figures of the armies as well as the battle orations on the one hand, and the descriptions of the course of the battles on the other, is well known from the historiographic literature of antiquity.

The pattern of the Hasmonaean Revolt is identical to that of revolutionary wars and struggles for freedom, as analysed by military theoreticians on the basis of the experience in such wars in the twentieth century. Like them, it is divisible into two main stages. In the first stage, during which the rebels had a small territorial foothold, the struggle had the character of guerrilla warfare. In the second stage, when part of the territorial aspirations had been achieved, the force organized to stop great royal expeditions, and defended its gains in some major battles utilizing up-to-date methods, weapons and battle formations of the period.

The Revolt began with Mattathias' charismatic feat at Modein which united round him a group of supporters and probably also inspired kernels of opposition that developed in other places. The first step was the establishment of a small territorial stronghold in the rugged mountain region of Gophna where it was possible to find shelter and organize small forces. The first actions were directed within, in an effort to create a united front against the outside authorities. Terror and intimidation were employed against the Hellenizers and others reconciled to Seleucid authority. This activity, together with raids on small government convoys, disrupted life in the country, undermined the authority of the Seleucids and served as a warning. The Seleucid governors tried at first to reinforce their garrisons in the country, then sought to penetrate the rebel strongholds and, following their initial failures, tried to draw out the rebel forces or surprise them in a sudden attack. During this stage Judas Maccabaeus defeated the enemy using guerrilla methods and the indirect approach.

The second stage came with the purification of the Temple, the death of Antiochus Epiphanes and the ensuing domestic crisis in Antioch, when Judas Maccabaeus seized control of Jerusalem and most of the Judaean Hills. The purpose of the struggle was now altered. Judas Maccabaeus now had to safeguard his territorial gains, the welfare of the population, and his own position as leader of the people. Guerrilla warfare by small groups no longer suited the new circumstances: 'hit-and-run' tactics certainly could not ensure the Jewish achievements in a small country like Judaea. Judas Maccabaeus adapted his army in preparation for the expected invasion by the Antioch authorities. The numerical strength of the army increased considerably, its weapons became heavier and as a result there was a change as well in the military tactics that Judas Maccabaeus applied. In addition he carried out fortification work and preparations for withstanding a protracted siege, and so forth. The confrontation with the Seleucid troops at this stage took the form of frontal battles with large numbers of men equipped rather like the enemy. In one case Judas Maccabaeus avoided battle, when Bacchides arrived in the country with a particularly large army, and then he lost some of his earlier territorial gains, mainly his control of Jerusalem. There is no indication that he attempted at the time to revert to indirect operational methods. Armies that have become used to conventional combat methods find it difficult to resort to the guerrilla warfare they previously were experienced in.

The principal conclusions relating to the historical–military evaluation of the battles can be summarized as follows:

(1) *Manpower*: The Jewish army before the purification of the Temple numbered 6,000–10,000 and after it at least 22,000. In his last years, Jonathan had at his disposal about 40,000 combatants. The Seleucid forces participating in the various battles ranged from a few hundred (Apollonius, Kafar Salama (?)), a few thousand (Beth Horon (?), Adasa), 20,000 (Ammaus, Beth Zur (?), Elasa) and reached up to 50,000 in Lysias' second expedition to Judaea. In two of the battles (Kafar Salama, Adasa) the Jews had the numerical advantage, in others (Ammaus, Beth Zur, Beth Zacharia) the Seleucids did, and in one (Elasa) they were more or less evenly matched. In three of the battles (Beth Horon, Ammaus, Beth Zur) the Jews preferred for tactical reasons (ambush, a long march, a raid on the enemy camp) not to use all available troops. Thus the accepted view of the war of the Jews against the Seleucids as a 'war of the few against the many' is an oversimplification as regards the relative strength of the forces on the battlefield.

That description is even less apt if the recruitment potential of the two sides is taken into account. The fact that the Seleucid kings ruled a large empire should not mislead us: after the Treaty of Apamea their rule in the western part of the empire was based on no more than 30,000 military settlers of Greco-Macedonian descent, only half of whom were available for long-distance expeditions, and an elite corps of 10,000 Guardsmen recruited from among their sons. The Seleucid mobilization potential was rather limited as well because of the refusal to accept indigenous Orientals in their 'heavy units', and Syrians and Babylonians even in their 'light' units. As to mercenaries, their employment was restricted for both economic and political reasons. And finally, the whole of the Seleucid army could operate on the Eretz Israel front only on rare occasions, because of the simultaneous missions which the army was called upon to fulfil in the far-flung empire.

(2) *Jewish equipment*: The Jewish army, at first equipped mainly as archers, and partly somewhat like the Classical peltasts, grew stronger after the purification of the Temple, apparently through the assistance of and instruction by a limited number of Jewish volunteers with military experience who came from outside the frontiers of Judaea. At that point it included semi-heavy and perhaps even heavy infantry and cavalry as well, although the numbers of these troops were most certainly smaller than those of the enemy. By the time of Jonathan's leadership the army included real phalanx units. The Jews had artillery devices available even earlier, as the sources explicitly indicate.

(3) *The Seleucid phalanx*: In the reign of Antiochus Epiphanes, the Seleucid army had not degenerated at all. The phalanx which was the spearhead of the imperial army was made up not of native Orientals but of soldiers of Greco-Macedonian descent. These soldiers were not unmotivated foreigners but an elite of citizens defending strategic interests which enabled them to retain the extra privileges their ancestors had acquired with great difficulty within the Oriental expanse. As to the operational capacity of the phalanx, it was by no means much inferior to that of the glorious Macedonian armies of the fourth century B.C. Furthermore, half of the infantry Royal Guard, the elite unit of phalangites, was retrained to fight in the Roman style, which made it much more flexible and effective than the traditional Macedonian phalanx.

(4) *Mountain warfare*: The Seleucid army suffered no lack of light and semi-heavy soldiers capable of and well trained in mountain warfare. The sources mention a number of such units operating in Judaea. Moreover, not those units alone, but the army as a whole, including the phalanx, was well trained in combat in mountainous, difficult terrain. This ability was displayed in the battles that took place in Judaea, especially that of Beth Zacharia.

(5) *The Jewish success*: Most of the Jewish victories were gained in confrontations with small forces of local garrison troops and commanders. Only in the case of Ammaus can it be said with some certainty that it was a victory over a relatively large force. The Jews confronted royal armies on three other occasions, at Beth Zur, Beth Zacharia and Elasa. In the last two campaigns where they faced large imperial armies, they lost, while the Beth Zur confrontation must probably be described as a nuisance raid which Judas Maccabaeus and his men conducted against the Seleucid camp. In any case, Lysias' retreat in that expedition was not forced upon him by Judas Maccabaeus, but was the result of events and developments in the eastern satrapies or the capital, Antioch. Judas Maccabaeus' main achievement in the struggle with the Seleucid empire lay not in victories wrested from its army, but in the organization and establishment of a large, strong Jewish army through which, in the course of time, it was possible to obtain strategic–political advantages.

(6) *The Jewish tactics*: In the first stage of the Revolt, Judas Maccabaeus utilized guerrilla warfare methods, executing quite complicated and sophisticated indirect combat manoeuvres taking maximum advantage of the difficult, rugged mountain terrain. In the second stage, however, after the purification of the Temple, the

Jews were not deterred by level battle arenas, and were victorious in frontal clashes approached directly and openly, and not only indirectly. At that stage, when the Jewish force had a considerable number of soldiers equipped and trained for Hellenistic warfare, and had from time to time a local advantage over Seleucid troops (the battles with Nicanor), Judas Maccabaeus did not hesitate to wage war in the open field by the conventional methods. Even in cases in which the Jews were vastly inferior in number or armament, he does not seem to have reverted to his old, indirect methods. In one case he avoided battle (Bacchides' first expedition), but for domestic reasons he was forced to accept the challenge in two other cases: at Beth Zacharia he at least tried in choosing the battlefield to limit the deployment possibilities of the enemy, but in his last confrontation (at Elasa) he joined battle on a site dictated by the enemy. We have no information on the *stratagēmata* adopted at this stage except for the tendency to concentrate great power opposite the enemy's right wing where its commander was to be found.

To sum up, it can be said that as a rule the Jewish forces did not always oppose the enemy as the few against the many, and after the purification of the Temple they had adequate weapons at their disposal. On the other hand, the Seleucid troops had by no means deteriorated, and were well motivated and capable of fighting properly on mountainous terrain. The two sides were basically composed of farmers, rightly regarded in antiquity as the best and most skilful recruits (see e.g. Vegetius 1.2). The outcomes of the battles were decided by the objective situations of the contenders, and there were no great 'surprises'. The Jews were victorious against armies smaller than theirs, at first in guerrilla and indirect warfare, and later, after the purification of the Temple, when their numbers had increased considerably and some units had become heavier, in open frontal combat as well. They suffered defeat at the hands of large imperial armies substantially superior to theirs in weapons and experience, and at Beth Zacharia in numbers as well. The battle at Ammaus, where a small but picked Jewish force overcame the large 'mixed' force, is in fact the only 'surprise', and stands out as a unique tactical gem among Judas Maccabaeus' battles.

The greatness of Judas Maccabaeus, however, lies not in local military–tactical achievements, but mainly in the construction and development of a great and powerful army which could not be destroyed by isolated failures. Even the defeats suffered by the Jewish commanders brought the independence they aspired to closer: to the enemy, unable to leave a large garrison in the country, they underlined the vast potential in the Jewish army, and the need to compromise with it, and later, in Jonathan's time, as the wars of succession in Syria grew more intense, also the possibility of benefiting from its help in domestic matters, in exchange for political concessions.

Finally, a few words on the motivation and fighting spirit, and the influence of these on the outcome of the battles conducted by Judas Maccabaeus. There is no doubt that these factors played a crucial role in the fighting capacity of the Jewish army. Judas Maccabaeus himself devoted a good deal of attention to them as the Mizpah ceremony shows. Belief in resurrection, if it did not originate in the Revolt generation, certainly acquired greater currency then and affected the willingness of the warriors to undertake daring exploits and to sacrifice their lives. At the same time, there is no reason to belittle the motivation of the Seleucid soldiers. The unmotivated mercenaries comprised only a quarter to a third of the army. The military settlers, its hard core, were a Greco-Macedonian minority among the Orientals. Established mainly in northern Syria within and near the centres of government, they shared the concerns of the ruling dynasty and were well aware that Judaea as part of Coele Syria was important as a 'warning zone' in respect of a Ptolemaic attack on the centres of government and military settlement in northern Syria, particularly after Judas Maccabaeus had begun to operate on the coastal plain as well. They also knew that a revolt in neighbouring Judaea could lead to trouble in their own bailiwick, and focus on themselves and their families, as the spearhead of foreign rule, the ire of the local population. A people fighting on its own soil generally exhibits a greater tendency to self-sacrifice, but this cannot be the only explanation for Jewish victories. That advantage was not sufficient to ensure a Jewish victory on the battlefield at Beth Zacharia and Elasa when the enemy had a decided superiority in numbers or weapons.

In a military–historical perspective, these conclusions do not diminish the appreciation that earlier commentators expressed of Judas Maccabaeus' achievements. On the contrary, some victories of the unarmed few, utilizing guerrilla methods in mountainous terrain, over a large, but degenerate and unmotivated army composed mainly of Orientals, which was extremely inflexible and able to fight only on level ground, as scholars universally accepted, deserve far less admiration than the notion suggested: a consistent struggle against a large, strong and well-motivated army, which preserved the exclusive Greco-Macedonian descent of its heavy troops, and was well adapted and trained to operate on rugged battlefields. With regard to the Jewish force and tactics, the efforts of Judas Maccabaeus to modify his operational methods to conform to the new circumstances after the purification of the Temple and organize his army accordingly, building an up-to-date large army, were much more demanding than the initial guerrilla war. And it takes no less personal courage, certainly greater leadership ability and military skill, to coordinate and command scores of thousands in a protracted action on the battlefield than a few combatants in a sudden raid from a safe ambush. Moreover, if Judas Maccabaeus fought his last battle at Elasa with just a tiny army, this means that he failed at the end of the day, and his brother Jonathan had to start the Revolt again from scratch. In our view, however, Judas Maccabaeus lost his last battle, but paved the way to the victory in the war as a whole by developing a large and well-equipped army, which, though defeated at Elasa, later on by its very existence forced the Seleucids to come to terms with, and concede to, the Jewish demands. The real test of military leaders has always been in the endurance of their achievements rather than in brilliant one-time stratagems.

APPENDICES

A

The infantry Royal Guard in the Seleucid army

The Seleucid phalanx, the backbone of the army, was mobilized for the big wars primarily from among the military settlers of Greco-Macedonian descent who were called to the colours in time of need.[1] However, the possibility of utilizing military settlers was not unlimited. As farmers, they could not leave their settlements for very long periods, and their mobilization itself was a lengthy process because of the great distances between settlements, and between the settlements and the governmental centres and the battle sites. To fulfil basic military needs and supply manpower for ordinary guard duties and police functions as well as extinguish small local conflagrations, the Seleucid kings had a Royal Guard. Like all royal armies even to the present day, the Guard was at the disposal of the king at all times in peace and in war, and in battle the kings always took their place in one of the Royal Guard units. As might be expected, most of the Seleucid Royal Guard were foot soldiers, only a minority being mounted.[2] We shall deal here solely with the infantry Royal Guard.[3] This investigation can illuminate not only the matter of the regular arrangements for the security of the Seleucid empire, but also the way that the military settlements were organized, and in particular the manner in which the military capability of the heavy infantry forces in general was preserved.[4]

Among the various units of the Seleucid army mentioned in the sources, three – the *argyraspides*, hypaspists and peltasts – refer at different times to units of the Royal Guard in the armies of Alexander, the Diadochs, and the Antigonid dynasty. Before examining the meaning of those terms for the Seleucid army, it is worth considering the available information on them in the other armies.

The origin, development and dimensions of the hypaspists at the time of Philip II and Alexander the Great has been the subject of a serious and

---

[1] On this matter see p. 36 n. 22.

[2] On the cavalry Guard see Bar-Kochva 1979: 68–74.

[3] The discussion below is a revised version of the one on the infantry Royal Guard in Bar-Kochva 1979: 58–67. Because the matter is so important for the subject of this book, I have rewritten it, adding many new comments and evidence that did not appear in the previous version.   [4] See pp. 96–100 above; cf. also pp. 31–40 above.

lengthy controversy.[5] It is generally agreed, however, that they constituted a small, select unit around the king in the reigns of Philip II and Alexander, and perhaps even earlier. The concept expanded in the course of time and designated the Royal Guard as a whole, but a small, picked unit detached from it and known as 'the *agēma* of the hypaspists' was especially close to the king. The hypaspists, or some of them, changed their name to *argyraspides* in Alexander's lifetime or shortly thereafter.[6] In any case, a certain contingent carried the new name in some of the Diadochian armies.[7] In third and second centuries B.C. Antigonid Macedon, the infantry Guard, numbering a few thousand troops, were known as 'peltasts', although they were 'heavy', evidently because the shield used was smaller and less concave than the traditional *hoplon* of the classical Greek heavy infantry and occasionally called *peltē*.[8] Part of them formed the *agēma*, and the term 'hypaspists' was applied to a much smaller unit of a few hundred men, which was the Royal Guard *par excellence*, and was also called *basilikoi hypaspistai* (= the royal hypaspists) or *sōmatophylakes* (= body guards).[9] In Antigonid Macedon the term 'hypaspists' acquired again the meaning that it had in Philip II's time.[10] It should be noted that such an authority as Polybius attached the term 'peltasts' also to a certain unit of the Ptolemaic guard,[11] although it is doubtful if in this case he used official terminology.

The *Argyraspides*: armament, status, descent, numerical strength and organization

To return to the Seleucid army, the *argyraspides* are specified in descriptions of the Seleucid deployment at the battles of Raphia (Polybius 5.79.4)

[5] Berve 1926: 1.104–29; Tarn 1941: 173; id. 1948: 2.137–42,153 n. 3; Milns 1971: 186–96; id. 1975: 87–136; Bosworth 1973: 245–54; Griffith 1979: 2.414–27; Hammond 1981: 24–8.

[6] On the start of the *argyraspides* in Alexander's time see Spendel 1915: 44–5; Berve 1926: 1.128; Launey 1949–50: 1.297; Strassburger 1952: 210; Schachermeyer 1973: 14; Hammond 1981: 28. Others, however, reject the information on the *argyraspides* in Alexander's time as anachronistic: Tarn 1948: 2.116–18,151; Milns 1971: 189; see especially Lock 1977: 373–8. Despite all the arguments, I find no justification for considering as anachronistic what Appian says (7.11.3) about a unit by that name after the suppression of the revolt at Opis in 324 B.C. See also recently Bosworth 1980: 8 n. 64.

[7] Spendel 1915: 46–53; Lock 1977: 374,376–7. The first of these two studies is the more comprehensive.

[8] On 'peltasts' see Griffith 1935: 319; Walbank 1940: 292–3; id. 1957–79: 1.278,518. On their shield see p. 7 n. 4 above. Walbank's later reservation (1979: 772) is unjustified: *ephodon* in Polybius 5.24.3 refers to the successive offensive of both the 'peltasts' and Illyrians, as contrasted with the defensive posture of the lighter mercenaries (5.24.2).

[9] On the *agēma* see next note. On the 'hypaspists' see Walbank 1940: 290–1; id. 1957–79: 1.560–1; Feyel 1935: 63–4.

[10] In the Antigonid army there is mention of another unit, the *agēma*, which included 2,000 picked soldiers out of a total of 5,000 'peltasts'. The hypaspists were fewer in number than the *agēma*, and there is no way of knowing whether they were part of the *agēma* (and thus among the 'peltasts') or a completely separate unit. On the *agēma* see Walbank 1940: 292; id. 1957–79: 1.558–9.

[11] Griffith 1935: 119, 319; Walbank 1940: 290; id. 1957–79: 1.590–1. See Polyb. 5.65.2.

and Magnesia (Livy 37.40.7 and Appian, *Syr.* 32(164) – both based on Polybius[12]) and in the Daphne procession (Polybius 30.25.4). That they were equipped as phalangites is clearly indicated by Polybius' statement in connection with the battle of Raphia that they were 'armed in the Macedonian style' (5.79.4,82.2). Their positions at Raphia beside the Seleucid phalanx and confronting the Ptolemaic phalanx (ibid. and 5.85.10) and at Magnesia confronting the Latin *ala* that was composed and equipped like the Roman legion (Livy 37.39.8,40.7),[13] clearly indicate their equipment, deployment and tactical function. As Polybius does not mention *argyraspides* in the battle against Molon or the expedition to the Elburz,[14] although he specifies the Seleucid deployment in both cases (5.53, 10.29), probably they were included in the general phalanx line.

The use of 'argyraspides' for infantry Guard units in the armies of Alexander and the Diadochs suggests that the term was applied to similar units in the Seleucid army. The name itself, meaning 'bearers of silver shields', indicates a particularly respected status. Polybius' assertion that its soldiers were chosen 'from all over the realm' (5.79.4) shows that it was an elite unit. Elite forces had always served in imperial armies as Guard units; at Magnesia the *argyraspides* were positioned near Antiochus III,[15] and Livy describes them as the *regia cohors* (= royal cohort, 37.40.7). Livy certainly did not invent the epithet, but evidently as usual reworded an assertion of Polybius', the only source at his disposal, on the status of that unit, or rather tried to translate a term used by Polybius.[16]

Royal Guard units in the armies of antiquity, like similar units in modern

---

[12] See p. 33 n. 13 above.

[13] On the deployment of forces in the battle of Magnesia see Bar-Kochva 1979: 168–9 (and map no. 14 there); and see further in detail pp. 567–8 below. On Appian's mistaken presentation of the *argyraspides* as cavalry (*Syr.* 32(164)) see n. 33 below.

[14] On these campaigns see Bar-Kochva 1979: 117–23,142–5.

[15] According to Appian (*Syr.* 33(170)), the king commanded the right cavalry wing (cf. Livy 37.41.1). It cannot have been the Dahae (the Scythian horsemen at the edge of the wing), but must have been the 1,000-man *agēma*, one of the two cavalry units of the Royal Guard, who were placed in the right wing immediately to the left of the *argyraspides*. The mention of 'auxiliaries' by Livy (37.42.7–8) likewise refers to the *agēma* (see Bar-Kochva 1979: 170,237 n. 56). On the Seleucid monarch's practice of fighting with the Royal Guard cavalry in the right wing see p. 392 n. 38 above; see also pp. 26–8.

[16] Most probably Polybius wrote σύνταγμα βασιλικόν (= royal *syntagma*), with the word *syntagma* used in the general sense arising from its etymology to mean simply a unit (e.g. Polybius 9.3.9, 10.22.6). As he did not mention the number of *argyraspides*, Livy understood the word in its specific meaning, denoting the smallest tactical unit of heavy infantry consisting of 256 men (see p. 9 above) and translated it as *cohors*, just as Polybius did the contrary elsewhere: because of the similarity in numbers, Polybius uses *syntagma* to denote three maniples (*speirai*) combined into a *cohors* (11.23.1; for a discussion of Polybius' meaning see also Walbank 1957–79: 2.302). Similarly, the word *cohors* appears in Livy in other places to denote an infantry unit when the Greek probably had *syntagma* (see Livy 31.24.10,39.12, 32.40.5, 34.30.6–7, 42.57.8, 43.18.11). For the phrase *regia cohors* see also 40.6.3, 43.19.11, and cf. Curtius 8.6.7,8.20, 10.7.16,8.3 for the fifty *paides basilikoi* (Diodorus 17.65.1; Curtius 5.1.42). In any case, it cannot be assumed that Livy meant to say that the unit was the size of a Roman infantry *cohort* (1,000 men in his time). In the parallel in Appian (*Syr.*32 (164)) there is no indication of the numbers of the *argyraspides*, so that evidently Polybius said nothing about the size of the unit either.

armies, were based on a fixed number of soldiers. Changes might be introduced from time to time in response to unusual circumstances, but in general the numerical stability of the units was maintained. That was the case with the Seleucid cavalry Royal Guard which numbered 2,000 horse,[17] and all signs suggest that the infantry Royal Guard too had a fixed complement, set at 10,000 men. At Raphia the *argyraspides* constituted the majority of the 10,000-man contingent. It was said of the contingent that its soldiers were chosen from all over the empire and fought as phalangites (Polybius 5.79.4). As noted above, its designation as 'chosen' (ἐκλελεγμένοι) itself indicates that the unit acted as a Royal Guard. Thus all the components of the contingent, not just the *argyraspides*, comprised the infantry Guard. We shall see below that the rest of the contingent was made up of hypaspists, the elite infantry Guard unit which apparently numbered 2,000 men.[18] As the hypaspists are not mentioned in the battle of Magnesia or the Daphne procession despite the detailed lists of units provided, they were presumably counted as part of the *argyraspides*, the largest of the infantry Royal Guard units. At any rate, for the moment suffice it to say that the data on the battle of Raphia indicate that the entire infantry Guard numbered 10,000 men. In the whirlwind campaign carried out by Antiochus III in Bactria in 208, he took with him, in addition to horsemen and 'lights', a force of 10,000 'peltasts' (Polybius 10.49.3). In this case Polybius used the term 'peltast' familiar to him from the Antigonid army which he knew better – to designate the Seleucid infantry Royal Guard as he had done with regard to the Ptolemaic one.[19] Neither Livy nor Appian, the sources for the battle of Magnesia, provides any information on the size of the *argyraspides* unit in that battle, but a comparison of the totals that they give for all troops with the breakdown by units, as well as an analysis of the actual space probably occupied by the units on the battlefield, suggests that their number stood around 10,000 troops.[20]

The Daphne procession included two infantry Guard units, one of *argyraspides* and the other of picked young men 'in the prime of life' (ἀκμάζοντες ταῖς ἡλικίαις) armed in the Roman style (Polyb. 30.25.3, 4). No doubt this second unit too was a Guard unit: the age of the soldiers, the selectivity in their recruitment and the need for lengthy training in the new combat style all point to its being an infantry Royal Guard unit. The number of those 'Roman' soldiers comes to 5,000. As to the *argyraspides*, the sentence on their number in the procession is generally considered to be defective. The most acceptable reconstruction is Kaibel's: Μακεδόνες δισμύριοι ⟨χρυσάσπιδες μὲν μύριοι⟩ καὶ χαλκάσπιδες πεντακισχίλιοι, ⟨οἱ⟩ δὲ ἄλλοι ἀργυράσπιδες (= twenty thousand Macedonians, of them ten thousand bearing gold shields [*khrysaspides*], five thousand bearing bronze

---

[17] See Bar-Kochva 1979: 68–72.   [18] See pp. 428–30.
[19] See p. 414 above, and nn. 8, 11.
[20] See Bar-Kochva 1979: 8–9,168–9, and pp. 567–8 below.

shields [*khalkaspides*] and the rest bearing silver shields [*argyraspides*]).[21] The *argyraspides* at Daphne seem thus to have numbered 5,000 so that the two infantry Guard units, the 'Roman' and the *argyraspides*, together had 10,000 men. The complement of the infantry Guard remained, then, numerically stable from the battle of Raphia in 217 B.C., through the expedition to Bactria in 208, the battle of Magnesia in 190, and up to the Daphne procession in 165 B.C. in the reign of Antiochus Epiphanes.

It appears from the data cited above that the 'Roman' unit included half the soldiers of the infantry Royal Guard who were retrained in Roman combat methods replacing the phalanx-type. And indeed these soldiers described by Polybius as being at the peak of their physical condition must have been 'selected from all over the realm' as Polybius describes the infantry Guard troops at the battle of Raphia (5.79.4). The retraining of half the infantry Guard in Roman combat methods can be credited to

[21] See the various proposals in Büttner-Wobst 1904: 301, and in Droysen 1889: 167 n. 1. The sentence as it stands reads as follows: Μακεδόνες δισμυρίοι καὶ χαλκάσπιδες πεντακισχίλιοι, ἄλλοι δὲ ἀργυράσπιδες (= twenty thousand Macedonians and five thousand *khalkaspides* [bronze shield bearers], and the rest *argyraspides*). The present reading is certainly corrupt. The conjunction καί between 'twenty thousand Macedonians' and 'five thousand *khalkaspides*' raises the possibility that the latter unit and the *argyraspides* were not included in the 20,000 Macedonians, while the phrase ἄλλοι δέ (= and others) that precedes '*argyraspides*' shows that both they and the bronze shield bearers were part of the Macedonians. Without at this stage going into the historical considerations relating to the estimate of the overall strength of the Seleucid heavy forces at the time (and all the terms referred to above apply to heavy infantry), it appears that the words ἄλλοι δέ are a solid element in the sentence that cannot be deleted, if only because no number is cited for the *argyraspides*, while Polybius specifies the size of all the other units that took part in the procession. On the other hand, the conjunction καί could easily have been added by a copyist, or may have been preceded by mention of a third unit. Consequently there is no doubt that the *khalkaspides* and *argyraspides* were both included in the 'Macedonians'. In order to decide whether only those two units appeared in the sentence or some third unit should be added before the conjunction καί, it must be borne in mind that as the *argyraspides* were an infantry Guard contingent, they could not have comprised most of the phalanx force, and that their introduction as the 'rest' and their position at the end of the sentence suggests that they could not be larger than the bronze shield bearers. The last unit had a total of five thousand men out of the twenty thousand Macedonians, so that preceding the conjunction καί there must have been another unit characterized by a shield (or colour) different from the bronze and silver shields of the other two units mentioned. The only other type of shield in Antiochus Epiphanes' time reported in the sources and not mentioned in the procession is the shield of gold (I Macc. 6.39); Kaibel's proposal of *khrysaspides* should therefore be accepted. As to their number, it might be between 10,000 to something less than 15,000. Kaibel's proposal of 10,000 is reasonable because that leaves 5,000 of the Macedonians for the *argyraspides* unit. The last figure together with the 5,000 'Romans' who were also infantry Royal Guard brings the count of the infantry Guard up to 10,000, which is the complement of that contingent as suggested by the data on the battles of Raphia, Bactria and Magnesia, and the numerical stability characteristic of units of this sort has already been noted.

For other opinions on the construction of the sentence see Griffith 1935: 146; Launey 1949–50: 319; Walbank (1957–79: 3.450, para. 5) rejects Kaibel's reconstruction mainly on the grounds that the gold shields were mentioned in only one lexicographical source (Pollux 1.175), but he ignores the above-mentioned report of the battle of Beth Zacharia and the references in Onasander 1.20 and Plutarch, *Eumenes* 14.8. The large number of gold shield bearers should not be marvelled at: The shields were not actually of gold but of brass. See pp. 325–6 above.

Antiochus Epiphanes, and it may be presumed that their appearance in the grandiose procession that he organized at Daphne was their first public exposure. Such a step accords very well with the admiration Antiochus Epiphanes developed for the Roman empire in the course of his long stay at Rome as a hostage, with his well-known inclination to emulate some of its customs and institutions (see especially Polybius 26.1.5–8),[22] and with his sense of inferiority in the face of the military power of the rising western empire as expressed in particular in 'the Days of Eleusis'. However, a purely tactical motive was involved as well: the Daphne procession preceded a great expedition to the eastern satrapies. Antiochus Epiphanes needed a crack force more flexible than the phalanx so that the army would be less restricted by topography and able to move quickly and operate more effectively in the difficult, rough terrain in the Upper Satrapies. Antiochus IV perhaps intended to have the entire Royal Guard retrained in the Roman system, but did not manage to do so because of his untimely demise on the expedition to Persia.

With regard to the descent of the foot Guardsmen, some scholars are of the opinion that they were Orientals,[23] deducing this from the phrasing of Polybius' definition 'selected from all over the realm and armed in the Macedonian style (καθωπλισμένοι δ' εἰς τὸν Μακεδονικὸν τρόπον), ten thousand men, most of them *argyraspides*' (5.79.4; cf. 82.2,10). The argument is that if they had been Macedonians, Polybius would have described them as such and not as 'armed in the Macedonian style', and that 'selected from all over the realm' indicates their autochthonous descent. The latter argument is rather arbitrary, however, as the Greco-Macedonian military settlers were also scattered all over the empire. As for the expression 'armed in the Macedonian style', it is not enough to prove that they were not Macedonians (or rather Greco-Macedonians). In the lexicon of Polybius and of Hellenistic historiography, the term 'Macedonian style' is a synonym for 'phalanx combat'. In some cases it does indeed describe 'mixed' or Oriental troops (Diodorus 19.14.5, 27.6, 40.3) or a non-Macedonian phalanx (Polybius 2.65.3, the Megalopolitan; id. 5.65.8, 82.4, the Libyan). But Livy – who, as has been mentioned above, draws solely on Polybius – provides the identical explanation ('armed in the Macedonian style') for the 16,000 Seleucid regular phalangites in the battle of Magnesia (37.40.2) who were of Greco-Macedonian ancestry and who originated in the Macedonian military settlements.[24] Livy's statement is evidently an accurate translation of Polybius.[25] Polybius himself called the Seleucid phalanx

[22] On this matter see Reuter 1938: 38ff.; Mørkholm 1966: 35–6,38–41,93–101; Goldstein 1976: 104–5.

[23] Tarn 1913: 428; Rostovtzeff 1940: 1.497; Launey 1949–50: 1.313; Bickerman 1938: 56. But see Bengtson 1964: 2.68 n. 1.

[24] See pp. 36 n. 22, 100–11. Even the scholars who are of the opinion that Antiochus Epiphanes' phalanx was 'Asiatic' believe for the most part that in Antiochus III's time its Macedonian character was still retained.

[25] Livy writes: 'There were sixteen thousand infantry armed in the Macedonian style, who are called *phalangitae*' (37.40.1), while Appian, in his description of the battle of Magnesia

forces that took part in the Daphne procession 'Macedonians' (30.25.5), and in describing the battle of Magnesia here and there he used the phrase 'the phalanx of the Macedonians' or 'Macedonians'.[26] Regarding the battle of Thermopylae that took place two years earlier Polybius probably also described the Seleucid phalanx as 'Macedonians'.[27] It has already been noted that Polybius does not use the term as a pseudo-national designation for phalangites.[28]

As to the Seleucid infantry Royal Guard at the battle of Raphia, Polybius employed the phrase 'armed in the Macedonian style' because the name *argyraspides* required some qualification in regard to the combat method used. In Polybius' day, only the Seleucid army had a contingent with that name. The army of the Antigonids with which the great Megalopolitan historian was certainly more familiar never included any *argyraspides*, and it goes without saying that Polybius' Roman readers required an explanation regarding the combat methods of that contingent. Moreover, the component *aspis* (= shield) in the name caused some confusion, for the phalangite shield was more similar in size to the small, round *peltē*, and in any case not the much bigger *aspis*[29] and, as already mentioned, the Royal Guard of the phalangites in Hellenistic Macedon and Egypt were even called 'peltasts' by Polybius,[30] as was at least once the Seleucid infantry Guard.[31] This quandary regarding the armament of the *argyraspides* is

which is also taken from Polybius, says: 'The phalanx of the Macedonians...arranged in the system of Alexander and Philip' (*Syr.* 32(161)). Thus Appian's ending, too, shows that Polybius' original version was a definition of the combat method of the force mentioned. Appian's version, however, clearly seems to be an independent paraphrase by this late author-elaborator (cf. in his version of the battle of Thermopylae, *Syr.* 19(83)). Polybius was aware of the difference between the Hellenistic phalanx and that of Philip and Alexander. He could be expected to restrict himself to the use of 'armed in the Macedonian style' and the like, referring to the Antigonid combat method with which he was very familiar, and indeed that is how he described the *argyraspides* in the deployment for the battle of Raphia. The beginning of Appian's introduction of the phalangites cannot be accepted as it stands, since for stylistic reasons it is hard to assume that Polybius wrote 'the phalanx of the Macedonians armed in the Macedonian style' (cf. nn. 34–5 below). The word 'Macedonians' in that sentence is therefore Appian's addition. The phrase 'the phalanx of the Macedonians' recurs constantly in his version of the battle of Magnesia (see *Syr.* 34(177), 35(178,183), 37(190,194)) under the influence of Polybius who doubtless used the phrase in the course of his description (though not in the instance under discussion, as he did in describing the battle of Thermopylae and the Daphne procession (see below). Polybius must have written '16,000 phalangites armed in the Macedonian style'. The last part of the passage in Livy – 'qui phalangitae appellabantur' (= who were called *phalangitae*) – recalls the structure of the sentence in his description of the *argyraspides* in the battle of Magnesia (37.40.7: '*argyraspides* a genere armorum appellabantur' = *argyraspides* so called from the type of their arms) and the 'peltasts' – *argyraspides* at Thermopylae (36.18.2 and see pp. 569–70 below: 'tum Macedonum robur, quos sarisophorus appellabant' = then the corps of Macedonians whom they call *sarisophoroi*). In both cases Livy tries to explain the Greek words that appeared at the beginning, and he does the same in the sentence under discussion for the Greek work *phalangitae*.

[26] See the preceding note. It is worth bearing in mind that Appian consistently says 'the phalanx of the Macedonians' and not 'the Macedonian phalanx', which may indicate that in the author's view (or rather that of Polybius, his source) the phalanx units were composed of Macedonians and not referred to on the basis of their combat style.

[27] Livy 36.18.2,3.5; Appian, *Syr.* 19(84) and see p. 569 below. [28] See p. 100 above.
[29] See p. 7 n. 4 above. [30] See p. 414 above. [31] See p. 427 below.

revealed in the two versions of the battle of Magnesia based on Polybius. Livy explains the name as follows: 'argyraspides a genere armorum appellabantur' (= they were called *argyraspides* from the kind of armament, 37.40.8). The sentence, phrased by Livy,[32] does not help much in clarifying the armament of the *argyraspides* and their style of warfare, and merely indicates that Livy himself was puzzled about these questions. Appian on the other hand erred and described the *argyraspides* as cavalry (*Syr.* 32 (164)).[33]

For obvious stylistic and substantive reasons, Polybius refrained from using the term 'phalanx' in his description of the *argyraspides* at Raphia. In the following sentence he listed the main body of the phalanx which was positioned next to the *argyraspides*: 'The phalanx was about twenty thousand strong and was under the command of...' (5.79.4). If he had described the *argyraspides* with, for instance, the words 'ten thousand phalangites selected from all over the realm, most of them *argyraspides*', the result in the ensuing sentence would have been a stylistic conglomeration of the kind Polybius consistently avoided.[34] Furthermore, the reader would have found it difficult to distinguish between the two phalanx units.[35] In

[32] For the sentence structure cf. Livy's presentation of the phalanx contingents at the battles of Thermopylae and Magnesia (see n. 25 above).

[33] This assertion of Appian's does not accord with all the other sources on the *argyraspides* and is therefore definitely unacceptable. Besides, Livy would not write *cohors* for an *ilē* in Polybius, and he uses *cohors* regularly of infantry and not cavalry (cf. n. 16 above). It should be noted also that the large number of Seleucid horse – 12,000 according to Livy (37.37.9) – corresponds to the breakdown of the cavalry units and does not allow for any additional ones (as rightly noted by Kromayer 1926: 2.210 n. 1). The error may have arisen from Appian's mistaken interpretation of the term *syntagma* which he found in Polybius (see n. 16 above), a term which denoted a cavalry unit as well (see Polybius 9.3.9, 10.22.6), but it is also possible that the mistake is not Appian's and that the conjunction καί should precede '*argyraspides*', or that '*argyraspides*' is a separate noun rather than an adjective modifying 'horsemen'. The sentence specifies the units positioned in the Seleucid right wing as follows: 'in addition to these (the Galatians, cataphracts and the *agēma* mentioned in para. 163) the right wing had a few "lights" and the rest cavalry *argyraspides* and two hundred mounted archers' (164). A look at the parallel in Livy shows that the 'lights' referred to are the regular complement of the elephants positioned in the same wing next to the *agēma* and behind(?) the *argyraspides* in the reserve (see Livy 37.40.6), which is why they are described as 'a few' (on the escort for the elephants see Bar-Kochva 1979: 82 and 8). The cavalry mentioned before the '*argyraspides*' is actually the part of the *agēma* which included soldiers who were not Medes but men from the Upper Satrapies (see Livy 37.40.6: 'et eiusdem regionis mixti multarum gentium equites'). Appian mistakenly considered them a separate unit. On the deletion of the conjunction see also in Appian in the present version in para. 163, Γαλάται τε κατάφρακτοι (= and Galatian cataphracts) – compared with Livy 37.40.5.

[34] On Polybius' avoidance of frequent repetitions of the same word see Foucault 1972: 205ff. On this stylistic feature in Greek historiographic literature see also Tarn 1948: 2. 136.

[35] As in the reference to *argyraspides* in the description of the deployment of forces in the centre in the same battle (Polybius 5.82.2): 'Both of them [i.e. Ptolemy and Antiochus] placed phalanxes and the selected troops armed in the Macedonian style confronting each other in the centre'. Here too the phalanx appears separately. The second part of the sentence applies both to the Seleucid *argyraspides*, whose armament is not clear to the reader, and to the Ptolemaic phalanx of Egyptian natives. Later on Polybius, in describing the placement of a light unit commanded by Battacus (5.82.10), says: 'between them [i.e., the Greek mercenaries

any case, it should be noted that in the lost chapters of Book 21 of his *Histories*, Polybius evidently described the Seleucid phalanx at the battle of Magnesia both as 'Macedonians' and as 'phalangites armed in the Macedonian style',[36] after having, in Book 18, described the operation of the Hellenistic phalanx in detail in the celebrated excursus to the battle of Cynoscephalae (ibid. 28–32). His version of the battle of Raphia precedes that excursus by thirteen books. If the Macedonian phalanx at Magnesia needed to be so explained, how much more so the equipment and combat methods of the *argyraspides* at Raphia. Thus, the phrase 'armed in the Macedonian style' does not constitute proof that the *argyraspides* were not of Macedonian descent.

The same conclusion applies to the designation of the contingent as οἱ...ἐπίλεκτοι τῶν Συριακῶν (= the select [troops] of the Syrians – Polybius 5.85.10), in the clash of the phalangites. It cannot mean that the soldiers were selected from the Syrian population, because in the list of the Seleucid troops in the same battle they are described as 'selected from all over the realm' (Polybius 5.79.4). 'Syrians' thus refers to the whole Seleucid side, or at least to all its phalanx troops whose defensive struggle against the Ptolemaic phalanx is reported in the same sentence. The Seleucid army was multi-national, and the phalanx of the military settlers Greco-Macedonian. 'Syrians' in this context was therefore used merely to distinguish between the Seleucid and Ptolemaic centre-phalanx. Polybius this time refrained from calling them, as was his practice, 'Antiochus' select (troop)' or the like, presumably because he stressed in the same chapter that Antiochus pursued the enemy with his right wing (comprised of his mounted guard, the select cavalry – 84.1) and left the force in the centre (to which these select troops belonged) to their fate (5.85.7,11–12). Another possibility, designating the contingent by the name of Theodotus, its commander, would have made reading of the account less understandable, since this reference is rather far from the introduction of the units of the Seleucid army and their commanders. In view of the composition of the Seleucid centre (20,000 'phalanx' and 10,000 'selected...most of them *argyraspides*') and the opposing Ptolemaic phalanx (20,000 Macedonians and 25,000 Egyptians) recorded in that introduction (79.4–5), any other description which would not have repeated the detailed definition of the contingent (79.4) might have been misleading or inaccurate (such as 'the select [troops] of the Macedonians', 'the select phalangites', 'Antiochus' select phalangites', 'argyraspides' and even 'Antiochus' select *argyraspides*').

mentioned in the previous sentence] and those armed in the Macedonian style he stationed the 5,000 under (the command of) Battacus'. The phrase 'those armed in the Macedonian style' goes back to the description of the infantry Guard in 79.4 and 82.2. They were positioned on the right edge of the Seleucid centre (composed exclusively of phalangites). Battacus' light unit was deployed between them on the left and the Greek mercenaries on its right. As the latter were also phalangites (see ibid. 84.9), any tactical description of the infantry Guard other than 'armed in the Macedonian style' would also in this instance have impeded the reader in understanding the deployment and developments, which are in any case hard to follow.

[36] See n. 25 above.

The assignment of an Aetolian rather than a Macedonian commander to
lead that unit at Raphia (Polybius 5.79.4) does not prove the Asiatic descent
of the soldiers either. As noted above, the term 'Macedonians' included
Greeks as well.[37] Among the Macedonians of the military settlements there
were Greeks too, and the differences between them became blurred in the
course of time so that entrusting the command to an Aetolian was not at all
offensive to the Macedonians. The Aetolians were a constant, reliable
source of manpower for the Hellenistic armies,[38] and the Aetolian officer
Scopas led the Ptolemaic army at the battle of Panium (Polybius 16.18.2,
4). Moreover, the Aetolian Theodotus had formerly served the Ptolemies as
governor of Coele Syria (Polybius 5.40.1–3). His familiarity with the terrain
in the southern part of Coele Syria and with Ptolemaic combat methods
was the reason for his being preferred to other commanders of pure Macedonian descent. His character was indicated also by his attempt to decide
the battle in advance by slaying Ptolemy IV in a daring personal operation,
evidently on his own private initiative (Polybius 5.81). It is therefore not
surprising that the picked infantry unit was placed under his command.

There are reasons that completely rule out the possibility that the *argyraspides* were Asiatics. To begin with it is unthinkable that native Orientals
would compose the infantry Royal Guard which was primarily charged
with defending the king and court, who represented the Macedonian minority, against the masses of Orientals. Furthermore, the Seleucids avoided accepting Orientals into ordinary phalanx units and were cautious
about arming native Syrians and Babylonians even with light weapons.[39] Is
it conceivable, then, that they would surround themselves with an Oriental
Guard armed with *sarissai*? Even the Ptolemaic rulers who did accept
native Egyptians into their armies, first as 'lights' and later as phalangites,[40] did not enlist indigenous Egyptians in their Royal Guard.[41] In addition, if the phalanx – the reserve force made up of military settlers – was
entirely Greco-Macedonian, is it possible that the *argyraspides*, the picked
elite of the phalanx, were not Macedonians too, but Orientals lacking a
national tradition and experience in phalanx combat?

Direct, definite evidence of the *argyraspides'* Macedonian descent is provided by their inclusion among the Macedonians in the listing of forces
taking part in the Daphne procession (Polybius 30.25.5).[42] Moreover,
Polybius described the Seleucid infantry Royal Guard at Thermopylae as
'Macedonians' (according to Livy 36.18.2).[43] That composition is also
indicated in the sources on events in northern Syria during the reign of
Demetrius II and Diodotus Tryphon's rebellion against him (145–144

[37] See p. 92, and n. 5 above.
[38] On the Aetolians in the Hellenistic armies see Launey 1949–50: 1.176–200.
[39] See pp. 103–5 above.   [40] See pp. 96–8 above.
[41] On the Ptolemaic Royal Guard see Griffith 1935: 114ff.; Fraser 1972: 1.80–1; against
Lesquier 1911: 21–4.
[42] On the wording of the sentence, see pp. 416–17 above and n. 21.
[43] See below, pp. 569–70. On 'Macedonians' in Polybius and its application to the Greco-
Macedonian population in the East see pp. 92, 100 above.

B.C.),[44] and it is those events which illuminate Polybius' assertion in connection with the battle of Raphia that the *argyraspides* came 'from all over the realm' (5.79.4), proving that it refers to their recruitment from the military settlements.

Demetrius II rose to power in Syria with the help of Cretan mercenaries led by Lasthenes. I Maccabees reports that after gaining control of the kingdom he sent the regular troops 'every one to his own place' (11.38). In his paraphrase of I Maccabees, in which he clearly had recourse to other sources, in particular in relation to the internal struggle in Antioch,[45] Josephus adds that the army was demobilized and its pay, which it used to get in peace time as well, was stopped and diverted to the Cretan mercenaries (*Ant.* 13.129–30). Both sources state that the anger of the soldiers who had been dismissed was exploited by Tryphon, who with their help removed Demetrius and seized control of the realm (I Macc. 11.55; *Ant.* 13.131,144; and see also Diodorus 33.4a). There is no doubt that the soldiers concerned were mainly the Royal Guard which was permanently stationed in the government centres, rather than the ordinary reserve army whose members were normally at home, being engaged in agriculture in peace time and earning their livelihood from it. They certainly could not have been mercenaries from outside the borders of the kingdom, for how could Tryphon have remobilized the same mercenaries in order to unseat Demetrius II if they had previously been sent 'every one to his own place' abroad?

I Maccabees and Josephus say nothing about the ethnic origin or place of residence of the demobilized soldiers, but the information on the disturbances and rebellions against Demetrius provides testimony on the origin of those soldiers. According to Strabo, the city of Apamea played a crucial role in Tryphon's rebellion, and was aided by neighbouring Apollonia, Megara, Cassiana and Larissa (16.2.10 (752)). Apamea was the largest and most important Macedonian military settlement in northern Syria,[46] and that is how Strabo describes it in connection with the Tryphon rebellion (ibid.). Diodorus stresses the role in the rebellion of the Larissans, who according to him were military settlers originating in Thessaly who served in the Seleucid cavalry (33.4a). The other three cities mentioned, two of which are named after places in Greece and Macedonia, may well have been military settlements as well. Tryphon himself, a Macedonian who was a high-ranking officer in the service of Alexander Balas (*Ant.* 13.131), was born in Cassiana (Diodorus 33.4a; Strabo 16.2.10 (752)). The sources also report Demetrius' disarmament of the people of Antioch (Diodorus 33.4.2) and the hard fight of the citizens against him that ensued (I Macc. 11.44–51; *Ant.* 13.135–44; Diodorus 33.4.2–3).[47] Antioch, too, was

[44] On this affair see especially Bevan 1902: 2.223–35. Cf. also Will 1967: 340ff.; W. Hoffmann in *RE* s.v. 'Tryphon', cols 715ff.
[45] See, e.g., *Ant.* 12.242–4,246,386, 13.36,60–1,86,88 (Apollonius' epithet),117,120, etc.
[46] See also Avi-Yonah 1971: 241–9; Bar-Kochva 1979: 29.
[47] On this matter see Downey 1961: 123ff.

basically a Macedonian military settlement.[48] The Macedonian character
of Tryphon's rebellion and his subsequent rule are well attested by his
coinage on which the typical Macedonian helmet is prominently featured.[49] The opposition to the rule of Lasthenes and the Cretans thus
erupted in the strongholds of the Macedonian military settlement in northern Syria. That information proves that the soldiers sent home each 'to
his own place' were Greco-Macedonians recruited from the military settlements that were spread throughout the empire.[50]

The conclusion that the soldiers of Demetrius II's Guard came from the
Macedonian military settlements explains Polybius' statement that the
argyraspides were 'selected from all over the realm'. They came from the
Macedonian military settlements that were spread throughout the empire.
The principle behind the selection of these military settlers for the Royal
Guard can be deduced from the information available on the composition
of the 'Roman' unit whose soldiers belonged to the infantry Guard. According to Polybius, they were 'men in the prime of life' (ἄνδρες ἀκμάζοντες
ταῖς ἡλικίαις, 30.25.3). As they had in the past been armed as phalangites,
it seems reasonable to assume that the other picked Royal Guard soldiers
who continued to fight as phalangites were also 'men in the prime of life',
and that age and fitness were the chief criteria for their selection. However,
these conclusions regarding the provenance and youth of the Guard soldiers
raise a number of practical questions and difficulties. For one, how was it
possible for settlers to be attracted into the royal service far from their land
allotments, and yet maintain a connection with the settlements, a connection demonstrated so well by the Macedonians sent home by Demetrius
II? The problem can at first sight be resolved by suggesting that recruits to
the Guard were given high salaries, and that they retained their allotments
in the distant settlements, which provided them with another source of
income, or that they were perhaps even allotted enlarged tracts of land (cf.
the phalangites on garrison duty at Palai-Magnesia, *OGIS* 229, line 101).
All the arrangements proposed above are by nature tentative and unsure,
and would involve practical difficulties such as frequent changes in the land
ownership and agrarian organization in the settlements, the need to find
replacements on the farm, etc. Secondly, the Seleucid military settlement
was constructed layer upon layer in the wake of various waves of recruitment and military events that occurred at considerable intervals.
The number of settlers that could be mobilized for specific missions even before
the Treaty of Apamea did not exceed 32,000–34,000 and their total number
was not more than double that.[51] It is hard to imagine that it would have
been possible to mobilize from within such a small population of varied ages
a group of 10,000 picked young men of high physical capacity, proprietors
of lands inherited from their fathers, and also to 'freshen' the unit peri-

[48] See Bar-Kochva 1979: 29–30.
[49] E.g., *Sylloge Nummorum Graecorum* (Royal Danish Museum, Copenhagen), pl. 9, no. 311.
[50] See also (without specification) Griffith 1935: 162.
[51] See pp. 36–40, 100–3 above.

odically with young men of the same origin, status and fitness. The selection of Guard soldiers from among the landowners in the military settlements would therefore have led to social and economic difficulties and prevented the maintenance of a proper standard in respect of both the age and physical fitness of the soldiers.

The Seleucid military settlement as well as the Royal Guard units can, however, be considered a success story in comparison with corresponding institutions in other places in the Hellenistic world. This is indicated by the persisting recruitment by the Seleucids of the reserve heavy troops as well as the Royal Guard from the military settlements, by their maintenance of the Greco-Macedonian character of these heavy contingents and retention more or less of their fixed complements, and above all by the impressive operational ability demonstrated by their troops – all these at least during the long period between the battle of Raphia and the Daphne procession.[52] How then is it possible to resolve the difficulties arising from the conclusion that the Guard soldiers came from the military settlements?

Since it is hard to imagine that the Guard troops were recruited from among the military settlers themselves, that is, from among the land-owning reserve soldiers, and since on the other hand there is clearly a connection between the Guard soldiers and the military settlement, and information is available on their youth, the presumption is that the Guard soldiers were the sons of the settlers, young men who had not yet been allotted tracts of land or been included in the reserves. Typologically the description of the men of the 'Roman' unit recalls the famous resolution of the Thera assembly of the seventh century B.C. regarding the settlement of Cyrene (*SEG* IX.3, ll. 10ff.).[53] Available to us in an adapted fourth-century B.C. version,[54] the resolution stipulates that each household was committed to send *one* of its adult sons (ήβῶντας = in their prime, l. 12) to settle Cyrene. According to the parallel in Herodotus (4.153), if a family had more than one son of suitable age, they were to draw lots.[55] It stands to reason that a similar arrangement existed between the Seleucid monarchs and the military settlers. It was evidently compulsory service on an individual basis. The military settlers' sons were called to the colours on reaching maturity.

It is not likely that the service was voluntary: the numerical relation between the Guard soldiers who were the settlers' sons and the reserve soldiers, i.e. the settlers themselves, makes it hard to believe that the Guard was manned by volunteers. For the same reason a collective levy would not have worked among farmers who needed their ablest sons as a labour force. The most probable arrangement, therefore, is that each settler was required

[52] See pp. 36–40, 90–115 above.

[53] A great deal has been written about that inscription. See a comprehensive bibliography in Seibert 1963: 9 n. 1, and on the passage mentioned in the decision, ibid. 36. For further discussion see Graham 1964: 41–68,224–6.

[54] On the question of authenticity see Graham 1960: 94ff.; Jeffery 1961: 141ff.

[55] On the Herodotus version and its reading and the reconstruction of the lines under discussion in the inscription see the various proposals in Graham 1960: 98–9,111; Jeffery 1961: 139–40.

to send one of his suitable sons to serve in the Royal Guard. Presumably the future prospect of obtaining the father's *klēros*, the farm unit allotted in return for reserve service, was an incentive to join the service for the sons who were more gifted for military functions. The constant numerical strength of the corps and the indication about the age of the troops suggest that soldiers served limited terms so as to allow the admission of fresh, new, young recruits. It is probable as well that after the basic training, young men found to be unfitted physically or psychologically were released, leaving those who had proven adequate to serve in the unit for a certain period as their age permitted. In the course of time discharges were gradually issued to soldiers whose fitness had diminished, to troublemakers, and most likely as well to young men whose fathers had died or become incapable of hard farm work and service in the reserve. All these were continually replaced by promising young recruits in order to maintain the total number at 10,000. In that way, the elite standards of the unit were maintained, and that is how the description of its soldiers as 'picked' and 'in the prime of life' should be understood.

The system may perhaps be illustrated by Diodorus' anecdote about Diophantes' hermaphrodite daughter (32.10.2–9). His only son died young, and when the girl, called Heraïs, turned into a man renamed Diophantes, the young lad enrolled in the cavalry and is reported to have followed Alexander Balas in his flight to Abae. The permanent nature of his service in the cavalry during peace time and the fact that his unit was attached to the king indicate that Diophantes junior belonged to the Guard. His father, a Macedonian living in Abae on the edge of the Syrian desert, could well have been a military settler; the Greek name of the place is not sufficient evidence,[56] but Macedonians living in that area – and Diophantes was certainly not the only Macedonian at Abae – are likely to have been settled by the authorities for military purposes. Alexander Balas' attempt to find refuge among them in his flight from the Ptolemaic army and Demetrius' Cretan mercenaries supports this possibility. Diophantes was then called up to the Guard in his father's lifetime like other male heirs of military settlers. Diophantes was a horseman, but there is no reason to assume that the organization of the mounted Guard differed from that of the infantry Guard.

'Peltasts' and Hypaspists

As noted above, the sources on the Seleucid army refer as well to 'peltasts' and 'hypaspists' familiar from the Antigonid dynasty as units of the infantry Guard. The former are mentioned twice in connection with the army of Antiochus III: in Polybius' description of the forced march against Euthydemus in Bactria in 208 and in Appian's version of Thermopylae in 191.

---

[56] On Abae in Phocis see *RE* s.v. 'Abae', col. 11, and on the dangers in relying on the place-name as sole evidence of a military settlement see Bar-Kochva 1979: 27–8. See also p. 438 n. 4 below.

Polybius' allusion to the 'peltasts' in the Bactrian expedition is the most interesting. Here they consisted of 10,000 troops (10.49.3), although no contingent of peltasts of this size or smaller can be detected in any of the great campaigns and not even in the references to the main units crossing the Elburz in the same expedition to the Far East (10.29–31). Their absence on the last occasion suggests that they were counted in with the phalanx. The selection of the 'peltasts' for the special Bactrian undertaking, the participation of the cavalry Guard in the same march (10.49.7), and the numerical strength of these 'peltasts', all taken together suggest that they should be identified with the infantry Guard. Polybius is thus applying Antigonid terminology to the Seleucid Guard in the same way as he does to a certain Ptolemaic guard unit.[57] The participation of these troops in the forced march does not refute the suggestion that they are to be identified with the heavily-armed infantry Guard. It is to be expected that the young, well-trained Guardsmen should have been selected for any unconventional and demanding venture in the same way as some phalanx and Guard units were in Alexander's and Philip V's armies.[58] The heavy equipment would not have impeded them in a forced march: the 6.7 kg *sarissa* and the even lighter shield, together with the coats of armour (the use of which is in doubt)[59] were no more of a burden than the equipment of the Roman legionary which is considered, even at the lowest estimate, to have been not less than 20 kg,[60] and there is no reason to suspect that the Seleucid Guard was not trained in route marches like Philip's army (Polyaenus 4.2.10) and the Roman legionaries, as can be deduced even for the Ptolemaic army.[61] In any case, since the 2,000 horse that participated in that expedition were not yet cataphracts,[62] they could have carried at least part of the infantry's equipment.

The same conclusion applies to the 'peltasts' of Thermopylae. A comparison of the descriptions in Appian and Livy of the deployment of forces and course of the battle shows that the 'peltasts' referred to by Appian (*Syr.* 18 (83)) were termed '*sarissa*-bearers' and 'the core of the Macedonians' by Polybius (Livy 36.18.2).[63] Thus the 'peltasts' operated as a phalanx in every way, and they can be identified only with the infantry Royal Guard, the one contingent in that battle (apart from the phalanx composed of reservists from the military settlements) equipped with *sarissai*. This con-

[57] See p. 414 above.
[58] See some references in Walbank 1940: 292–3; Tarn 1948: 2.149–50; see also pp. 428–30 below on the equipment and performance of the Seleucid hypaspists in mountain and urban warfare.
[59] On the weight of the *sarissa* and coats of armour see Pls. I, III. On the use of the latter p. 8 above.
[60] See the summary of the different views by Watson 1969: 62–3. Watson's conclusion that the sixty pounds of equipment Vegetius noted for route marches (*Epit. rei. milit.* 1.19) was carried only in exceptional circumstances does not accord with the emphatic nature of Vegetius' statement and underestimates what could have been expected of a well-trained soldier. [61] See p. 263, 384 above.
[62] On the first appearance of cataphracts in the Seleucid army see p. 12 above.
[63] See pp. 569–71 below.

clusion is strengthened by their description as 'the core of the Macedonians'. The status of this corps as a crack force explains its deployment in front of the rampart as a defensive spearhead (Livy 36.18.5).[64]

As to the hypaspists, they are first mentioned in the blocking action Seleucus I directed against Demetrius Poliorcetes in Cyrrhestica in 285 B.C.: the bravest among them accompanied the king in his courageous and surprising outflanking manoeuvre (Polyaenus 4.9.3).[65] Dionysius, the commander of the hypaspists, is described as one of the three ablest officers in the army besieging Sardis in 214 B.C. (7.16.2). At Panium in 200 B.C. the hypaspists, defined by Polybius as 'the best unit' (τὸ κάλλιστον σύστημα), were posted around the king, together with the 'Companions' (16.18.7, 19.7),[66] one of the 1,000-horse battalions of the cavalry Guard.[67]

There is no uncertainty in the description of that unit as a Guard force: the name 'hypaspists' itself, which means 'shield bearers',[68] testifies to a particular connection with the king. The infantry Guard functions of a unit by that name in the Alexandrian and Antigonid armies suggest its function in the Seleucid army. References to the unit in the battles of Cyrrhestica and Panium indicate its status as the best unit, and at Panium it was even described explicitly as such. In the first of these references the king is positioned among its soldiers, and in the second in their vicinity, among the cavalry Royal Guard.

Was this unit absolutely identical with the *argyraspides*,[69] or was it a

---

[64] The term 'peltasts' appears also in Lucian of Samosata's rhetorical description of the 'elephant victory' against the Galatians in 273 B.C. (*Zeuxis* 8–11). The text says that the force at the disposal of Antiochus I in the battle was composed of 'mostly peltasts and lights (*psilikon*), and the lights (*gymnētes*) made up half of the army' (10). Lucian is obviously trying to stress, by the use of the word 'peltasts', that the Seleucid army in that battle was unconventionally composed of an overwhelming majority of non-heavy troops. The wording of the sentence and its rhetorical style (e.g. ψιλικόν; γυμνῆτες) may be his own, but he could well have taken the term 'peltasts' from his source, possibly the epical narrative of the poet Simonides of Magnesia, who may have applied it in the old meaning referring to semi-heavy infantry. At any rate, no conclusions should be drawn from this reference with regard to the Seleucid 'peltasts' in Polybius. On Simonides as Lucian's possible source see Bar-Kochva 1973a: 1–3.

[65] On this battle and the activity of the hypaspists see Bar-Kochva 1979: 111–16.

[66] On the position and deployment of the hypaspists in the battle of Panium see ibid. 155, and on the Companions, ibid. 68–70.

[67] Hypaspists are mentioned also in Antisthenes' fragment on the battle of Thermopylae. He described the 500 warriors who fled with Antiochus III as 'hypaspists' (in Phlegon, *FGrH* 257, F 36 III 1), but Appian (*Syr.* 20(91)) explicitly says they were cavalry. Livy (36.19.11) says nothing of their tactical classification, but the inability of the Roman pursuers to catch up with Antiochus III and his 500 men (ibid. 10) indicates that the latter were mounted. And indeed in view of the defensive character of the battle, the Seleucid inferiority in manpower, the lack of room for manoeuvring in the narrow battle arena, and the prospect of a headlong rout, Antiochus' best course would have been merely to observe the battle with the virtually passive cavalry around him. Antisthenes' reference to 'hypaspists' is thus an error, and if this peripatetic philosopher is to be identified with the Rhodian historian Antisthenes (which is not certain), it would be appropriate to recall Polybius' comment on the latter's lack of precision (16.14ff.; on the identity of Antisthenes see Walbank, 1957–79: 2.518, and the bibliography there).

[68] See Kalléris 1954: 271ff.; Griffith 1979: 2.415–16; Hammond 1980: 28.

[69] That is the view of, e.g., Bickerman 1938: 52–3,64–5; Walbank 1957–79: 2.64.

component of them, or was it a separate unit and yet part of the infantry Guard? I tend to view the Seleucid hypaspists as the elite unit of the infantry Royal Guard which was especially close to the king and sent on special missions like the 'royal hypaspists' of Antigonus' army. The substantive relation between them and the *argyraspides* was like that between the *agēma* or the 'royal hypaspists' and the 'peltasts', the infantry Guard units in the army of Philip V of Macedon.[70] The hypaspists were generally listed with the *argyraspides*, sometimes as part of them and sometimes separately. As already noted, in his description of the deployment of the infantry Guard at the battle of Raphia, Polybius says that of the 10,000 troops, the majority were *argyraspides*. The remaining unit was thus significantly smaller. The sources on the Seleucid army make no mention of any infantry Guard unit that would fit the description aside from the hypaspists. Their absence from the listings of the Seleucid army at Raphia, Magnesia and Daphne is enough to suggest that they constituted a smaller unit lumped as a rule with the *argyraspides* or with the infantry Guard as a whole. The rank of the hypaspist commander at the siege of Sardis also suggests that it was a relatively small unit whose commander was subordinate to the commander of the larger contingent. He is described as a *hēgemōn* (Polybius 7.16.2), a title denoting commanders of units the size of chiliarchies, while the higher rank, *stratēgos*, was usually confined to commanders of independent, larger contingents.[71] Indeed there was a natural need for the establishment of a restricted, picked unit of soldiers out of the large 10,000-man Guard, to undertake special missions and fight alongside the king when for tactical reasons he chose to take his place amid the infantry rather than in the cavalry as was his wont.

The numerical strength of the hypaspists is not recorded explicitly. Alexander's infantry *agēma* numbered 1,000 troops.[72] On administrative grounds, the Seleucid hypaspists may be considered to have consisted of double this figure: the footguard, totalling 10,000, would have allowed two *stratēgiai* (the largest tactical unit of the phalanx), to the ordinary *argyraspides*, thus leaving 2,000 troops, i.e. two chiliarchies, to the hypaspists.[73] And indeed, the picked infantry force (ἀκολουθήσοντας, Polybius 7.16.6) that started the attack on Sardis in a bold and complex operation and was doubtless composed of the elite troops of the infantry Royal Guard, numbered 2,000 men (ibid. and 18.3). The identification of those two thousand as soldiers of the infantry Royal Guard and as hypaspists is supported by the fact that Lagoras, the Cretan, initiator of the special stratagem by which Sardis was conquered, asked Antiochus III for the help of two commanders – Dionysius, described as the commander of the hypaspists,

[70] On them see p. 414 above. The *agēma* in the Antigonid army in any case numbered 2,000 men out of 5,000 'peltasts' (see the references, p. 414 n. 10 above).

[71] See Bar-Kochva 1979: 92, and the bibliography in n. 24 there.

[72] See Tarn 1948: 2.148–9.

[73] On the *stratēgia* and *khiliarkhia* in the Seleucid infantry units see Bar-Kochva 1979: 66–7.

and Theodotus the Aetolian (ibid. 16.1–2), who at the battle of Raphia commanded the entire infantry Guard. It stands to reason that the request for the aid of the two generals referred not merely to their persons but also to some force under their supervision. In the assault itself these three officers led the decisive part of the stratagem, executed by forty-five extremely strong and courageous men, together with the 2,000 select infantry.

The phalangite equipment of the hypaspists in the large battles does not obviate the conclusion that they played the crucial role in the Sardis campaign which required steep climbs and face-to-face combat in a built-up urban area. The Royal Guard was certainly trained in combat of this kind and equipped accordingly. It is not reasonable to suppose that soldiers who regularly carried out guard and security missions at court, and had at their disposal an unlimited amount of time and resources for training and exercises would be capable of fighting only as phalangites and would be unable to adapt to changing conditions. Even the rank-and-file phalangite was trained in face-to-face combat in case his formation was broken up. It is true that his equipment for such combat was inferior to that of the semi-heavy Hellenistic soldier. His shield was smaller, his sword shorter, and it is doubtful whether he had body armour, but these deficiencies may well have been advantageous in a fast, surprise operation such as the one conducted on the steep, densely populated hill of Sardis. And, as stated above, presumably there must also have been an *ad hoc* adaptation of the infantry Guard's equipment to the needs of that particular operation. It should be noted that Philip V's hypaspists–peltasts, too, were assigned to set an ambush (Polybius 5.13.5–6; Livy 31.36.1) and to break through in a siege operation (Polybius 5.4.9) in difficult terrain.

Summary and conclusion

The above analysis shows that the infantry Royal Guard included 10,000 soldiers. The contingent as a whole was generally called the *argyraspides*. Eight thousand of them were *argyraspides* proper, while the remaining two thousand composed the elite unit of the Guard that was called 'hypaspists'. Influenced by the terminology in the Antigonid army, Polybius sometimes calls the entire infantry Guard 'peltasts'. The infantry Guard operated as a phalanx to all intents and purposes. During the reign of Antiochus Epiphanes, however, half of its complement was retrained and taught the combat methods of Roman legionaries. The Guard soldiers were all of Greco-Macedonian descent and came from Seleucid military settlements. They were the picked young sons of the military settlers, each of whom was required to send one of his sons to serve in the Guard. New blood was constantly supplied to the unit by the young recruits replacing soldiers who were or had become unable to meet the high standards of the Guard. The *argyraspides* served to guard government centres and were ready at a moment's notice to undertake defensive and offensive missions throughout the empire and abroad, being able to adapt their equipment and combat methods to changing circumstances.

This conception of the organization of the Guard units also illuminates the way the military settlements and the army reserve units were organized, and is the key to understanding the success of the system. It supplies answers to a series of important questions that arise in view of how widely scattered the settlements were and how far they were located from each other and in many cases also from the centres of government.[74] How were the military settlers who composed the reserve units trained for phalanx combat? How was the numerical stability of those units maintained?[75] How was it possible to ensure their loyalty to the central authorities? After completing their service in the Royal Guard, the discharged Guardsmen would return to their villages and presumably were then enlisted in the reserves as phalangites. It may well be that in most cases they took their father's place in the reserves, and the *klēros*, the tract of land that was the compensation for service in the reserves, was then transferred to the returning sons. The discharged servicemen thus became military settlers with all attendant privileges and duties. The obligation each military settler had to send a son to the Royal Guard was what ensured the numerical stability of the reserve forces as well. The corollary was that all the military settlers had at one time served in the Royal Guard. That term of service, whether long or short, made it possible for the military settlements to succeed in the task assigned to them – to supply efficient phalangites for the reserve forces. During their service in the Royal Guard, the future military settlers received their initial training, some practical experience and what is no less important, a good deal of indoctrination in identifying with the dynasty to see them through the long years of their service in the reserve.[76]

If Antiochus Epiphanes really intended to have the entire Royal Guard gradually retrained in the Roman style of combat, in less than a generation this would have led to the retraining as well of all the reserve soldiers, the military settlers. The process was halted by Antiochus' sudden death and the ensuing dispute over the succession.

---

[74] See ibid. 28ff. [75] See pp. 36–40 above.

[76] On the effect of the organization of the infantry Royal Guard had on the preservation of the phalanx force in the reserve army see also pp. 98–9 above.

B

maʿarākā (formation) and *fālanḵs* in the Hebrew original of I Maccabees

The term *phalanx* appears five times in the Greek text of I Maccabees, three times in the description of the battle of Beth Zacharia (6.35,38,45), once in that of the battle of Elasa (9.12) and once more in that of Jonathan's confrontation with Apollonius near Azotos (10.82). An accurate reconstruction of the Hebrew original term is essential for an understanding of the deployment and operation of the Seleucid army at least in the last battle, and consequently for an appreciation of the tactical composition of the Jewish force as well. The clarification of this question has significance also in regard to the domestic policy of the Seleucid kingdom in the second half of the second century B.C. The reconstruction in this case is especially difficult because the word *phalanx* does not appear in the other books of the Septuagint. It is therefore necessary to examine the context and possible renderings in each of the episodes noted.

In two of the three instances in the Beth Zacharia story (6.35,38), the word appears in the plural (*phalangai*), and clearly refers to the composite units placed in the centre of the Seleucid array. These units were capable of operating independently with great flexibility, and each included a war elephant, 1,000 heavy infantry (which in some units were phalangites, and in others soldiers armed in the Roman style) stationed on its flanks, and 500 cavalry deployed on each side of the infantry (6.35–6). In the initial phase, when moving through the broad valley, the units spread out side by side in a wide row, and as they entered a pass they altered their formation and advanced in a column, one after the other (6.40).[1]

Cahana believes that these units were called *gedūdim* (= battalions) in the original.[2] This would fit the context, but *gedūd* was translated in many other ways in the Septuagint (δύναμις, ἰσχυρός, σύστρεμμα, ἐξοδία, etc.),[3] and it will not fit the context of the word *phalanx* in the descriptions of the battle of Elasa and of Jonathan's battle near Azotos (see below). These arguments, of course, are not decisive, and it is not impossible that the rendering of a biblical term in I Maccabees is different from that in the Septuagint, or that

---

[1] See in detail pp. 126–7, 312ff. above.
[2] Thus in Cahana's translation, and also in my article, Bar-Kochva 1974b: 173 n. 44 and 175 n. 52.
[3] See references in Hatch and Redpath 1897: 2.227 (appendix).

the Greek text uses one term for a variety of Hebrew ones. However, the doubts raised make it necessary to present further evidence on the applicability of the word *gedūd* in the contexts of the verses. Lexical suitability alone is not sufficient for the reconstitution of the text, all the more so as it is easy to find other words that would fit (דגלים , צבאות , מערכות , ראשים and maybe even מחנות).

Other scholars, especially translators into modern European languages, have apparently accepted as self-evident that in the Hebrew original the Greek word appeared in transliteration.[4] However, in the two instances above the word refers to independent units each composed of soldiers of different kinds (not just heavy infantry). The author of I Maccabees keeps very close to the biblical vocabulary and departs from it to introduce Greek words in Hebrew transliteration very rarely, only when he needs to render properly a technical term peculiar to his time for which Hebrew has no adequate equivalent.[5] Here, as noted before, he had at his disposal a number of biblical words to define these composite units. Since he gives details of the internal composition and weapons of each unit, the use of a biblical term would not have interfered with the understanding of the matter. Furthermore, I Maccabees was written toward the last quarter of the second century B.C. when the Greek term 'phalanx' was for the most part restricted to a specific and well-known military formation, the overall massive dense structure of the *sarissa*-bearers. It was also used, though infrequently, to denote a heavy formation of infantry with shorter spears like the Carthaginian infantry men, or the Roman legionaries.[6] At any rate, at the time it was not used to signify individual units of heavy soldiers, certainly not units which included also cavalry and elephants, and it generally appears only in the singular to indicate the overall formation of the *sarissa*-equipped soldiers.[7] It is hard to imagine that the author of I Maccabees would include a Hebrew transliteration of a Greek word, which he did in only isolated instances, in a form and with a meaning that were not usual in his time.

An examination of the third instance of the word in the Beth Zacharia episode, in the verse describing Eleazar's bravery (6.45), suggests that the Hebrew original had *ma'arākā*. Considering the verse on its own, it could be interpreted as meaning an assault against the infantry defending the elephant's flanks, who were armed like phalangites or in Roman style, and not against the unit as a whole. Therefore at first glance it might be thought that the Hebrew original was a transliteration of the Greek *phalanx*. But as noted above, this is not possible for the other two instances of the word

---

[4] See the various translations (including Abel's) and especially Grimm 1853: 99,134,167.
[5] See p. 169 and n. 48 above.   [6] P. 76 nn. 23–4 above.
[7] Polybius consistently uses the singular (except for heavy troops of two sides, e.g. 5.82.2) and when distinguishing between phalanx units composed of various national groups, etc., prefers the term *phalangitai* (e.g. 5.82.6 and passim). Polyaenus 4.6.4 apparently reflects the later usage: the *stratēgēma* based evidently on Hieronymus of Cardia is reworded with great brevity by the compiler of the second century A.D.

(6.35,38); it is not likely that in such proximity to the verse under discussion the translator would use the same Greek word to render a different original Hebrew one. In view of the author's tendency to use not only single biblical words but even phrases from the Bible, attention should be paid to the great similarity between the clause 'and [he] ran into the *ma'arāḵā* toward the Philistine' (I Sam. 17.48), and the wording used for Eleazar's assault against the elephant, καὶ ἐπέδραμεν αὐτῷ...εἰς μέσον τῆς φάλαγγος (= and [he] ran toward him...into the *phalanx*). It cannot be dismissed as a coincidence: the David and Goliath story had considerable influence on the author of I Maccabees, particularly in his version of the confrontation between Judas Maccabaeus and Apollonius (3.10–12), and its impact is also discernible in the listing of the Seleucid infantry's equipment in the Beth Zacharia battle itself (I Macc. 6.35).[8]

The meaning of the word *ma'arāḵā* in the Bible is 'battlefield' or 'confrontation' (I Sam. 4.2,16, 17.20,48), the whole alignment of one side (ibid. 17.21), and a tactical unit or group of units, etc. (ibid. 8,10,22,36,45; according to the root of the word *ma'arāḵā*, in the last two meanings it should be translated as 'formation'). The first two meanings cannot apply to the references in I Macc. 6.35,38. The third one is a proper description of the composite units. And indeed evidence for this meaning and the frequent use of the term *ma'arāḵā* in the Second Temple period is to be found in the Scroll of the War of the Sons of Light where it denotes every one of the heavy units in the centre (with or without the word *ha-pānīm* = face, front).[9] According to the Scroll, those units are mobile and flexible (9[13].10), and are sometimes deployed alongside each other (6[10].8ff.), sometimes one behind the other (5[9].15), which recalls the composite units that took part in the Beth Zacharia campaign. There is, by the way, one place where the Vulgate renders the plural *ma'arāḵōt* as *phalangas* (I Sam. 17.8).

While the Greek for *ma'arāḵōt* in the Septuagint is *parataxeis* (literally = line of battle, front formation, or even = the battle itself), as has been noted more than once, the author of I Maccabees diverges from time to time from the usual Septuagint vocabulary, especially when he has substantive or associative reasons for doing so. The literal meanings of *parataxeis* certainly do not suit the context of the verses in question. By some stretch of the imagination they could be construed as several parallel lines of deployment, but even this is far from a proper description of the composite units that were placed in the centre, side by side, or one behind the other. The choice of *phalangai* itself was influenced by the description given in I Maccabees 6.35,39 of the equipment supplied to the heavy soldiers in the units. Or it may be a case of *pars pro toto* designed to stress that the soldiers who fought as heavy infantry were the backbone of the units described. The use of the term *phalanx* in the plural to designate units of phalangites or of heavy troops in general is not very usual in the middle of the Hellenistic period,

[8] See pp. 154, 204–6, 313–16 above.   [9] See Yadin 1962: 163ff.

but was quite common earlier and later.[10] We have no decisive evidence for dating the translation of I Maccabees, but it may well have been made at the end of that period (certainly not later)[11] when, as the Hellenistic armies and *sarissa*-bearing infantry waned, the word *phalanx* recovered a broader and more general application.

The general sense of the word *phalanx* in the description of the battle of Elasa (9.12) is clear from the context: it begins with the deployment of the Seleucid army (ἡ δύναμις, 9.11), goes on to describe the assault of the *phalanx* which was followed by a frontal confrontation between the sides (9.12), and only then reports on the cavalry operations on the flanks (9.14–16). It thus appears to mean all the troops placed in the centre, and not the army as a whole or the flanking cavalry. As was already noted, the literature of the Hellenistic period has the term *phalanx* in the singular usually to designate the overall formation of heavy *sarissa*-bearing infantry, which was usually in the centre of the battlefield. The various units of the phalanx, when not mentioned by name (as σπεῖρα, τέλος and the like – Polybius 11.11.6, 18.28.10, etc.), are called 'parts' (μέρη, e.g. Polybius 18.24.7; Arrian, *Tact.* 8.3; Livy 37.40.2 and Appian, *Syr.* 32(162), both based on Polybius[12]). The translator of I Maccabees indeed uses the same word in reporting the advance of the centre units in the battle of Elasa (9.12, καὶ ἤγγισεν ἡ φάλαγξ ἐκ τῶν δύο μερῶν = and the *phalanx* approached from the two parts).

The word *ma'arākā* cannot be considered for the reconstruction of the Hebrew, since none of its three meanings fits the context. The reconstruction *gedūd* (= battalion) proposed by Cahana must also be rejected out of hand: in addition to the reservation cited above to the association of the word *gedūd* with *phalanx*, the author who was well versed in biblical terminology and was able to apply it correctly would not have used a word which in the Bible denotes an irregular force of nomads, or an isolated tactical unit of the regular army,[13] to describe the alignment of heavy infantry placed in the centre. As the context clearly indicates that the word under discussion refers to the centre, composed of phalanx troops, and there does not seem any Hebrew word which could have led the translator to opt here for *phalanx*, it seems highly probable that the author used the current Greek term *phalanx* in some Hebrew transliteration. Whatever the reconstruction, there is no doubt that the author meant to describe the *sarissa*-bearing troops who occupied the centre of the battlefield.

[10] See in detail F. Lammert in *RE* s.v. 'Phalanx', cols 1626–7,1633,1642. The best examples of this usage occur in abundance in Homer, as well as in Xenophon (*Cyropaedia* 7.1.24), Arrian (*Anab.* 1.14.2–3; 3.9.6 – apparently following a later usage), in the lexicon of Suidas (s.v. φαλαγγας), and in the writings of the Tacticians (especially Asclepiodotus).

[11] On Nicolaus' acquaintance with the Greek version of I Maccabees see p. 189 above, esp. n. 118.

[12] On Polybius as the source for the accounts of the battle of Magnesia in Livy and Appian see p. 33 n. 13 above.

[13] For the interpretation of the word *gedūd* see A. Malamat,'*gedūd*', in *Biblical Encyclopaedia*, vol. 2 (Jerusalem, 1954) cols 432–4.

The word *phalanx* appears in the singular also in the description of the second phase of Jonathan's battle against Apollonius near Azotos (10.82). In the first phase of the confrontation Jonathan staged a defensive formation to withstand and absorb the intensive barrage of Apollonius' mounted archers (79–81). In the second phase his brother Simeon advanced toward the 'phalanx',[14] and the enemy flank cavalry is said to have collapsed shortly (verse 82). This context indicates that the word 'phalanx' can refer either to the enemy force as a whole, or only to the heavy troops in the centre.

The reasons cited above for the unsuitability of *gedūd* as a reconstruction are valid for this reference as well. The reconstruction *ma'arākā* in this context may mean either 'battle', 'confrontation', or the total alignment of the Seleucid forces. However, it is hard to believe that the author of I Maccabees, who applied the term *ma'arākā* three times to designate a unique composite unit, an application which was quite common in his time, would have selected it later for either of those different and somewhat vague meanings. Moreover, both meanings would have been rendered by the translator as *parataxis*, as was done for the word 'war' in I Maccabees (3.26, 4.21, 6.42, 12.41), and usually in the Septuagint for the general alignment of the troops and for the word *ma'arākā* itself. In contrast to what was said above about the references to the composite units in the battle of Beth Zacharia, the account of the second phase of the battle near Azotos does not make it obvious that phalangites were included in the term under discussion. On the contrary: the description of the collapse of the cavalry immediately after Simeon's advance would have convinced the translator that the reference was to the total alignment or to the battle itself, had the Hebrew source been *ma'arākā*.[15] As there does not seem to be any Hebrew word here either that could have been translated as *phalanx*, we can only repeat the conclusion reached in the discussion on the use of the term at Elasa (which itself can be considered supporting evidence), that the Greek word 'phalanx' appeared in Hebrew transliteration. Since in the time of the author of I Maccabees the term had a specific technical meaning, and the author of I Maccabees employed Greek words only when dealing with concepts that had no Hebrew equivalent, we can deduce that the reference was to the *sarissa*-bearing infantry deployed in the centre of Apollonius' array.

If the practice of the sages has any bearing on the system of transliteration used in I Maccabees, it can be assumed that *phalanx* was transliterated פלנבס; cf. פרידבסוס for παράδοξος, אלבסנדרוס for 'Αλέξανδρος. אבסניה for ξενία, אבסיריא for ἐξορία and אבסדרה for ἐξέδρα. However, פלנקס is

---

[14] The sentence καὶ συνῆψε πρὸς τὴν φάλαγγα should be reconstructed in this case as···ה אל ויקרב (= and he approached the...): see p. 78 n. 33 above.

[15] This did not happen to the translator in the account of Eleazar's assault on the elephant, despite the similar wording ('and [he] ran toward him...into the *ma'arākā*') because the occurrences of the word in the preceding verses (35,38) made it obvious to him that it was not the battlefield or the total alignment that was meant but only one of the special 'formations'.

also a possibility; cf. פֶּנְקֵס for πίναξ, פֶּנְקְרִיסִין for πάγχρυσος, גְלוֹסְקָא for κόλλιξ and אֲנְקְלִסְיָא for ἔγκλησις. Less likely is פְּלַנְס; cf. פְּלַנְס for πάλληξ, πάλλαξ, פֶּנֶס, for φέναξ, נִסְטְרָא for *castra*.

To sum up, the word *phalanx* in the Greek translation of the Beth Zacharia episode stands for *maʿarākā* (= formation) which appeared twice in the Hebrew source in the plural (6.35,38) and once in the singular (6.45). It denotes the special independent units put together specifically for that campaign, each deployed around a war elephant. In the descriptions of the battles of Elasa (9.12) and near Azotos (10.82), on the other hand, the Greek word *phalanx* in the singular appeared in Hebrew transliteration (probably פְּלַנְבַּס), denoting the formation of *sarissa*-bearing infantry in the centre of the battlefield. As a result, an analysis of the battles compels us to assume that at Elasa Judas Maccabaeus' army was not limited to light soldiers,[16] and that Jonathan had at his disposal a considerable force armed and deployed according to the practice of Hellenistic phalanx troops.[17] In addition, the latter episode indicates a significant change in the attitude of the authorities to the local population: the force that set out with Apollonius and served Demetrius I against the supporters of Alexander Balas was made up of 'the army of the cities' (10.71), that is, of people from the coastal towns of Coele Syria.[18] While Seleucid domestic policy in the past had been consistent in refraining from developing the military potential of the nations of Syria, and especially from making them privy to the secrets of heavy fighting,[19] the various rivals for supremacy in Antioch now encouraged the eastern Hellenized populations to equip themselves for, and perfect themselves in, phalanx warfare so that they could be of assistance in the struggle for the throne.[20]

[16] See pp. 72–5 above.
[18] See Bar-Kochva 1975: 85–6.
[20] Cf. p. 115 above.

[17] Pp. 76–81 above.
[19] See pp. 98–104 above.

C

Was a Seleucid military settlement established in Jerusalem?

Numerous scholars anxious to explain the background and contributory factors that led to the religious persecution and the Hasmonaean Revolt are of the opinion that Antiochus Epiphanes established a military settlement in Jerusalem composed of soldiers of the Seleucid garrison stationed in the Akra, the local citadel. The military settlers were given allotments (*klēroi*) confiscated from residents of the city.[1] Tcherikover even made this view the keystone of his well-known theory stipulating that the coercive laws were in fact a response to a general revolt of the Jewish population. In his opinion the uprising came in the wake of the confiscations of land which usually preceded the establishment of a military settlement.[2] Some scholars even attempted to explain that the citadel people later on held their own logistically, despite the protracted rule of the Hasmonaean brothers in the city, because their supplies were based on the agricultural produce of the settlement.[3]

This opinion about the change in the agrarian and municipal position of Jerusalem is based not only on considerations of historical probability, but also on two sources which seem to imply that a military settlement of Seleucid soldiers was founded in the city (I Macc. 1.38) and that land was confiscated and allocated to the troops (Daniel 11.39). Before examining the theory as such, it would be advisable to have a close look at these sources.

In the course of the lament on the bitter fate of Jerusalem after its capture by Apollonius, the Mysian commander, and the assignment of soldiers in the citadel, the city is said to have become an ἀλλοτρίων κατοικία ('*katoikia* of foreigners', 1.38). In the Seleucid terminology of Asia Minor, *katoikia* refers to a rural military settlement which has not achieved the status of *polis*.[4] However, the same word – which in Classical Greek means 'house',

---

[1] Montgomery 1927: 463; Bickerman 1937: 85–6; id. 1938: 85; U. Wilcken, *RE* s.v. 'Antiochus' (4), col. 2474; Bentzen 1952: 83; Tcherikover 1961a: 189–90; Hengel 1973: 512–13,515; Th. Fischer 1980: 32, etc.

[2] Tcherikover 1961a: 194–5 and passim; id. 1961b: 172–4.

[3] For an explanation of the survival of the garrison in the Akra see pp. 458–9 above.

[4] On the *katoikia* in the Seleucid empire see Bar-Kochva 1979: 22–48. A detailed discussion of the Seleucid military settlement is given in G. M. Cohen 1978. While contributing a great deal on the internal arrangements within the settlements, the author does not distinguish between military settlements founded by the Seleucids and civilian settlements started in the

'domicile', 'place of residence' and the like – appears dozens of times in the Septuagint in apposition to the Hebrew word *mōšāv* (= residence).[5] That is the way the Hebrew original should be reconstructed in the passage noted, especially in view of the fact that even the Jewish inhabitants of Jerusalem were termed *katoikoi* in the same verse.[6] Although there is no doubt that the author of I Maccabees mixed Greek terms into the Hebrew text,[7] he would not have done so in a purely lyrical passage such as this one.

The evidence cited from the Book of Daniel deserves more attention. The survey of the reign of Antiochus Epiphanes in ch. 11 states: 'And he shall make for fortresses of strongholds a nation of a foreign god, whom he acknowledged he shall increase honour to, and shall make them rule over the many, and he shall allocate land for a price' (verse 39). Porphyry, the pagan philosopher and scholar of Tyre of the third century A.D., explained the words 'and he shall allocate land for a price' as referring to the distribution of land to the Jerusalem garrison.[8]

A superficial examination of the context shows that it refers to a period of time after the defilement of the Temple, the religious persecutions, and the beginning of the Revolt, all of which are described in earlier verses (11.31–5). Thus, the location of the passage appears to refute its utilization in support of the view that confiscation of land for military settlers played a central role in the escalation of events which led to the coercive edicts. However, it seems that the author did not maintain a chronological con-

---

Hellenistic period, or older ones which merely changed their names. Only a small proportion of the places with dynastic or Greco-Macedonian names were actually Seleucid military settlements. Reliance on the names can be misleading, and places should be identified as military settlements only if it is possible to prove the Macedonian origin of the settlers or their military duties (see Bar-Kochva 1979: 27–8). As a result, the description of the distribution of the settlements, their purpose and their ethnic composition is inaccurate. Cohen errs also in applying the term *katoikia* to all Seleucid military settlements (p. 4).

[5] See Hatch and Redpath 1897: 2.755.

[6] Despite the linguistic resemblance to 'our inheritance is turned to strangers' (Lam. 5.2), I do not believe the original was *naḥlat zārīm* (= inheritance of strangers). In the Septuagint the word *naḥalā* is usually translated *klēros* or *klēronomia* (= inheritance, allotment) and never *katoikia*. So too in I Maccabees (2.56, 15.33,34). It cannot be assumed that the translator preferred *katoikia* to render *naḥalā* because the word *katoikoi* appeared in the same verse. The opposite is true: he adopted the word *katoikoi* under the inspiration of the word *katoikia*. Outside of this verse, the Septuagint uses *katoikoi* to translate the plural of *yōšēv* or *tōšāvīm* ('residents' or 'inhabitants') only in Genesis 50.11 (in four other places it seems to prefer the participial form of *katoikein* which appears in some manuscripts, rather than the adjective *katoikoi*; references and alternatives in Hatch and Redpath 1897: 2.756). The usual translations are καθήμενοι, ἐνκαθήμενοι, οἰκοῦντες, κατοικοῦντες. The Alexandrian translators may have avoided *katoikoi* because it had a clearly administrative significance in Ptolemaic Egypt, all the more so as there were suitable alternatives in Greek for the word *tōšāvīm*. On the other hand, there was no adequate translation for the Hebrew *mōšāv*, and they were therefore compelled to use *katoikia*. On *katoikia* and *katoikoi* in Egypt see P. Oertel in *RE* s.v. 'Katoikoi', cols 13–25.

[7] See p. 169 above, and n. 48.

[8] See the translated quotation from Porphyry's κατὰ χριστιανῶν in the Hieronymus exegesis to Daniel: *PL* 25, col. 572. Porphyry was followed by many modern commentators, among them Montgomery 1927: 463; Delcor 1971: 246; Hartman and Di Lella 1978: 272.

tinuity between verses 31–5 and the next passage (verses 36–9); the latter passage depicts the deification of Antiochus Epiphanes, which actually antedated the religious persecutions, in order to show where the king found the courage to provoke the God of Israel. Verse 39, about the construction of fortifications and distribution of land, probably deviates from the framework, and may have been placed in the second passage by association of the beginning of verse 38 ('and to the God of strongholds') with the beginning of verse 39 ('and he shall make for fortresses of strongholds'), a common occurrence in the Book of Daniel.

The literal meaning of the verse does not bear out that the lands referred to were allocated to soldiers. The first part – 'And he shall make for fortresses of strongholds (למבצרי מעזים) a nation (עם) of a foreign god' – speaks of the building of forts or the strengthening of them through added construction or manpower.[9] The use of the plural indicates the erection of fortresses or their reinforcement not only in Jerusalem but also in other places in the country. Presumably it was the main fortresses of Gezer (Gazara), Beth Zur, Jaffa and Iamnia that were strengthened.[10] The problem of how the Hebrew עם should be vocalized and understood ('with' or 'nation') makes no difference to our point.[11] The sentences 'whom he acknowledged he shall increase honour to, and make them rule over the many' obviously refer to the benefits accorded to the Hellenizers and their ascendancy over the residents of Judaea, matters about which nothing was said in the first passage.[12] There is no sense in the interpretation that the reference is to the distribution of bonuses to soldiers stationed in the fortresses, and to the imposition of their authority over the land of Judaea. The phrase 'whom he acknowledged' (אשר יכיר) and the statement 'and make them rule over the many' (בָּרַבִּים) sound quite strange if they refer to Seleucid military forces. It should be added that the word רבים (= many) in Daniel refers to the majority of the Jewish nation.[13] Some of these considerations operate to reject as well the proposal made by various scholars that the verse refers to the intensive settlement drive and estab-

---

[9] The last possibility emerges according to a proposal of Di Lella who believes that the Aramaic source had ויעבר, which the translator into Hebrew read as ויעבר, hence his version ועשה (= and he did) rather than ויעבר (= and he transferred), all this based on Ginsberg's assumption that the whole book was originally written in Aramaic. The Hebrew text should then be ויעבר למבצרי מעזים עם אלוה נכר (= and he shall transfer to fortresses of strongholds a nation of a foreign god). See Hartman and Di Lella 1978: 272.

[10] On the fort at Gezer-Gazara see I Macc. 4.15, 7.45, 9.52, 13.43–8. On Beth Zur see I Macc. 6.7; on Jabneh-Iamnia see I Macc. 5.58–9.

[11] The correction עַם (= people) accepted by many (following Hitzig 1850: 213) is not inevitable. According to all the translations, the reading should be עִם (= with). On the other hand most of the translations of Daniel (in particular the Septuagint) are unreliable and cannot properly serve to reconstruct the original text. On the Septuagint free translation of Daniel see Montgomery 1927: 26,36–9.

[12] Cf. I Macc. 9.25. While the verse reports on the period after Judas Maccabaeus' death, it points to the same practice. Hitzig, too, believes that the reference is to the Hellenizers (1850: 214).

[13] See 8.25, 11.14,34, 12.3,4,10. For the interpretation of the word בָּרַבִּים (= over the many) see an analysis of the various possibilities in Rappaport 1965: 23–4; id. 1980: 68–9.

lishment of cities throughout the realm undertaken by Antiochus IV, and the subordination of the local population to the Greek cities. The view attributing the founding of many cities in the East to Antiochus Epiphanes is itself not sufficiently well grounded, and raises many doubts.[14]

The end of the verse, 'And he shall allocate land for a price (במחיר)', should naturally be interpreted in the light of the object in the two preceding sentences ('whom he acknowledged he shall increase honour to, and make them rule over the many') and not in reference to the beginning of that verse ('he shall make for fortresses of strongholds a nation of a foreign god'). Hence it can be construed as referring to the distribution of land confiscated for the benefit of the supporters of the Hellenistic reform. The Books of the Maccabees do not explicitly report the confiscation of land and its distribution to the Hellenizers, but probably the later despoilment of their estates (I Macc. 6.24 and 7.7) should be understood against that background. The Seleucid authorities presumably did not abandon the ancient Eastern custom of confiscating the lands of rebels and turning them over to supporters of the regime. This would justify the term 'for a price'. If we suggest that the subject is military settlement, it must be interpreted as 'in return (for military service)',[15] but that meaning is alien to the biblical word במחיר which means 'in return (for money)' and the like. However, if the verse refers to the distribution of land to the Hellenizers, the word would denote the payment they gave for the land. The custom is well known from the Seleucid empire: generally a low price was asked for royal lands which were handed over to people whom the king wished to reward.[16] It may also mean the sale of land not to private individuals, but to the Hellenistic *polis* established in Jerusalem, in order to increase its income.[17]

Some scholars connect this passage in Daniel with the orders said to have been given to Lysias just before Antiochus Epiphanes' campaign to the Upper Satrapies and before the battle of Ammaus, to encircle the Judaean Hills with military settlements (I Macc. 3.36).[18] The reliability of the information on the 'order' in general is questionable.[19] In any case, the plan was not carried out because of the defeat of the royal army in the Aijalon Valley, and there is no possibility of connecting the verse with the above order: the Book of Daniel says nothing about the concentration of the Seleucid army in Syria, the festival at Daphne, the campaign to the

[14] For particulars see Mørkholm 1966: 115–18.

[15] That is the interpretation of Montgomery 1927: 463; Delcor 1971: 246; Hartman and Di Lella 1978: 272. Theodotion translates: καὶ γῆν διελεῖ ἐν δώροις, and the Septuagint: καὶ χώραν ἀπομεριεῖ εἰς δωρέαν (= and he distributed land as a gift). This is certainly wrong. For the evaluation of Theodotion's translation of Daniel see p. 231 n. 19 above, and for the Septuagint see n. 11 above.

[16] Cf., e.g., Welles 1934: no. 18, esp. p. 96, nos 10–11; *OGIS* 335, ll. 133–4. See Rostovtzeff 1940: 1.493–4; Atkinson 1972: 45–72; Kreissig 1978: 40–6.

[17] On the practice of selling confiscated land in the *khōra* to cities see Rostovtzeff 1910: 248–56.

[18] Recently also Delcor 1971: 246. [19] See p. 235 above re verse 35.

Upper Satrapies and the battle of Ammaus, and it is therefore certain that it was written and closed before that. Despite its position near the last passage in the chapter (verses 40–5) referring to the future on the basis of fragmentary rumours regarding the plans of Antiochus Epiphanes,[20] it should not be assumed that verse 39 too refers to the future and is based on information the author had about the king's intentions; the phrase 'and at the time of the end' (verse 40) clearly separates the description of the past in the chapter from the detailed vision of the future from verse 40 on.

The sources discussed above thus do not show that a military settlement was founded in Jerusalem and that lands were allocated to the garrison. The very idea about the establishment of a military settlement in such a place is not particularly acceptable. Military settlements were established in places where it was possible to develop ties between the soldier–farmers and the land and place. Their attachment to their land helped the authorities to ensure the existence and availability of a permanent reservoir of European manpower for their great wars, and to rely upon it as a stabilizing force in everyday life in various sectors of the realm. These basic conditions were absent in Jerusalem: the cultivable land was too far from the citadel, and the soldiers stationed in the fortress did not have the leisure to engage in agriculture, especially not in the shaky security situation in Jerusalem in the sixties of the second century B.C.

Similarly the possibility must be rejected that land was distributed to the soldiers not in preparation for a military settlement but as part of the wages of the local garrison, an arrangement known from literary and epigraphic sources on Palai-Magnesia in Asia Minor and the Babylon fortress.[21] In such cases the soldiers continued to stay in the citadel as mercenaries or regular soldiers; they did not become farmers, and the land was cultivated by serfs. But the situation had to be peaceful for the land to be worked by tenants or serfs. Such an arrangement in the Jerusalem of 168 B.C. might have helped balance the imperial budget, but would have in fact reduced the soldier's income, diminished their goodwill and affected their operational capability.

The term *katoikia*, which scholars apply to the alleged Jerusalem military settlement, is even less possible. As has been already mentioned, the term was common in Seleucid Asia Minor to designate military settlement without the rights of a *polis*. The rural military settlements on the other side of the Taurus were called simply *kōmai* (villages).[22] Moreover, if there was a

[20] A summary of the various views on verses 40–5 appears in Montgomery 1927: 464–8; Bentzen 1952: 83; Plöger 1965: 166; Delcor 1971: 246–9; Hartman and Di Lella 1978: 303–4. The verses contain no allusion to a campaign to the east. They describe an additional campaign against Egypt which will, in the author's opinion, end up on the soil of Eretz Israel. The visionary description, undoubtedly influenced by the story of Sennacherib's campaign (e.g. Is. 7.17–25, 14.25) and other biblical associations (Ezek. 38.18–23) was apparently based on unfounded rumours disseminated in Coele Syria on Antiochus Epiphanes' intention of setting out on another campaign southward to Egypt and regaining the honour lost in the 'days of Eleusis'. For the influence of Isaiah on the Book of Daniel see Efron 1980: 45,63,114ff.

[21] On these fortresses see Bar-Kochva 1979: 31–2,213 n. 12.   [22] See ibid. 32–5,37–9.

military settlement in Jerusalem, it is hard to understand how it was not granted the status of a *polis*. The citadel garrison was made up of soldiers of European origin (see below). In the satrapies south of the Taurus the Seleucids used to grant the settlements composed of such soldiers the status of *polis*.[23] Only in western Asia Minor did the Antioch authorities refrain from doing so for reasons deriving from the geopolitical and cultural conditions in the region and the political tradition that characterized it.[24] The establishment in Jerusalem of a foreign *polis* rather than a *katoikia* was likely to contribute to the politico-cultural goals of Antiochus Epiphanes more than such a step anywhere else. And finally: as Tcherikover already proved, Jerusalem was indeed granted the status of *polis* in 175 B.C.[25] The transformation of the *polis* into a *katoikia* would have been a significant demotion, and we have no example of any *polis* whose privileges were withdrawn and which was turned into a *katoikia*. It is hard to understand what sense the king could have found in such a measure, for cancellation of the city's status would have been a blow to the promoters of the cultural reform who were his principal supporters in Judaea. Nor is there any precedent for the suggestion that the *polis* continued to exist alongside a newly established *katoikia*. Such a situation would have meant that the European soldiers would have enjoyed fewer privileges than the Hellenized local Jewish population.

In the course of the above discussion we deliberately avoided the question of the origin of the soldiers in the Akra and any attempt to learn their status from it. The reason is that the only reference that might be relevant is unacceptable: Josephus states that Antiochus Epiphanes settled Macedonians in the citadel (*Ant.* 12.252). A settlement of Macedonians is supposedly a good indication of a military settlement. However, in this matter, as in his whole account of the persecutions and the Revolt, Josephus relies exclusively on I Maccabees (1.33–4), and his version is only an interpretive paraphrase deriving from the later tendency to call the Hellenistic armies 'Macedonian'.[26] The definite information at our disposal indicates that the soldiers were Cypriots and Mysians and perhaps also Thracians.[27] Thracian and Mysian soldiers are known from the Seleucid empire as mercenaries as well as military settlers.[28] No decision on the status of those soldiers can therefore be made on the basis of information on their ethnic origin.

[23] On the urban military settlements see ibid. 28–32,37–9.

[24] See ibid. 22–7,37–9.

[25] Tcherikover 1950: 61–7; id. 1961a: 161–9,404–9; id. 1961b: 146–55. See also Le Rider 1965: 410–11; Habicht 1976a: 216–17. Even Bickerman, who believes that 'Antioch in Jerusalem' had the status of a *politeuma* only (1937: 59ff.), agrees that when the coercive decrees went into effect, Jerusalem was made a *polis* (p. 86). Bickerman's new evidence for his method (1978: 112) is not relevant for the years 175–168 B.C. that are the subject of the dispute. See additional bibliography in Th. Fischer 1980: 20 n. 53.

[26] On the use in later sources of the term 'Macedonians' in a general sense see Edson 1958: 13. On the reasons for the use of this term see Bar-Kochva 1979: 224 n. 94.

[27] See pp. 116–20 above, and p. 116 n. 2 on Porphyry, *FGrH* IIB, no. 260, F50.

[28] On the Myso-Macedonians and Thracian settlers in Persia see the bibliography above, p. 119 n. 9 and p. 120 n. 15.

Finally, it should be noted that the Seleucids apparently refrained from setting up military settlements in the Land of Israel. Settlements founded by Alexander and the Ptolemies, like Samaria and the Toubian settlements and perhaps some of the Decapolis cities in Transjordania,[29] were left to their previous status, but the Seleucids did not add to them. Despite the availability of a large number of sources for the period of Hellenistic rule in the country, we have no substantial information on the establishment of Seleucid military settlements there (except for the 'orders' given to Lysias which were not carried out anyhow).[30] This is in contrast to the situation regarding other satrapies, for which there is some information on such settlements even in the few fragmentary sources that have survived. The reluctance to establish military settlements can be explained by the special geopolitical status of the country during the Hellenistic period: military settlers developed particular affection for their land, and did not like to be cut off from it. During the Hellenistic period, Eretz Israel passed from hand to hand many times. The Seleucids refrained from establishing military settlements in border countries for fear of losing indispensable manpower of 'European' extraction in case those areas fell into hostile hands. The defence of border regions was entrusted to regular army or mercenary garrisons which were mobile and could easily be moved from place to place.[31] If indeed the order said to have been given to Lysias is to be deemed credible, Antiochus Epiphanes was evidently less cautious than his predecessors, because in the wake of his campaigns to Egypt in 169–168 B.C there was an impression that the Ptolemaic kingdom had ceased to be a significant factor likely to return and vie for the hegemony of Coele Syria.

[29] On Samaria and some of the Decapolis cities as military settlements see Tcherikover 1927: 73–4; Jones 1971: 237,448. On 'Macedonians' in the Decapolis see also Syncellus, pp. 558–9 (ed. Dindorff). On the Toubian settlements see pp. 82–4 above. They were controlled by Hyrcanus in his independent principality and fell into Seleucid hands only after 168. The way they were handled thereafter is anyone's guess.

[30] There is no implication that the soldiers in the forts built by Bacchides in the Judaean Hills after Judas Maccabaeus' death in the Elasa battle (I Macc. 9.50–2) were military settlers, and it appears that they served as regular soldiers or mercenaries, as was usual in the Seleucid realm at points of tension and in border regions.

[31] See Bar-Kochva 1979: 36–7.

D

The location and history of the Seleucid citadel (the Akra) in Jerusalem

The exact location of the Seleucid fortress in Jerusalem, which is of great importance for the understanding of the events in the city during the period of the persecutions and the Revolt, has been a matter of dispute for many years. The question is regarded as the most difficult in the geographical history of Jerusalem, and the identifications proposed are scattered over almost the entire area of city that was inhabited during the Second Temple period.[1]

The evidence of the sources

The sources in fact give clear indications of the placement of the Akra: I Maccabees places the citadel in the City of David (14.36), and states more than once that the Seleucid garrison was concentrated in the City of David (1.33,[2] 2.31, 7.32), while Josephus puts it in the Lower City (*Bell.* 1.39, 5.137; *Ant.* 12.252), both of them referring to the south-eastern hill, south of the Dung Gate.[3] This location, however, does not seem to fit in with the tradition that the citadel hill dominated the Temple, and that only in the time of Simeon the Hasmonaean was it levelled so that the Temple hill would tower above it (*Ant.* 12.252,362, 13.215,217; *Bell.* 1.50, 5.139). The top of that hill is about 40 metres lower than the Temple Mount, and for archaeological–topographical reasons it is impossible to assume that until Simeon's time any part of it was considerably higher than it is today.[4] It has

---

[1] See the detailed bibliography in Tsafrir 1975: 503. The most comprehensive and profound discussion appears in Simons 1952: 131–56. Following are some bibliographical items that have appeared since Tsafrir's article: Schürer... 1973–9: 1.154–5; Laperrousaz 1975: 241–59; Mazar 1975: 216; Avi-Yonah 1975: 231–2; Goldstein 1976: 213–20 and passim; Tsafrir 1977: 295–7; id. 1980: 17–40; Avigad 1980: 64–5; Ben-Dov 1980: 22–35; Luria 1981: 31–41; Schwartz 1985: 3–16.

[2] On the reconstruction of the Hebrew original of this verse and its meaning see pp. 463–4 below.

[3] The identification of the biblical City of David is not disputed and is unanimously accepted; the term Lower City in Josephus refers only to the south-eastern hill and does not include the slopes of the Coenaculum: see *Bell.* 5.137–40 (also *Ant.* 7.62 as compared with 7.67).

[4] The excavations in the north-eastern part of the City of David at the ridge line of the narrow extension uncovered buildings of the First Temple period (see Kenyon 1974: 197–8

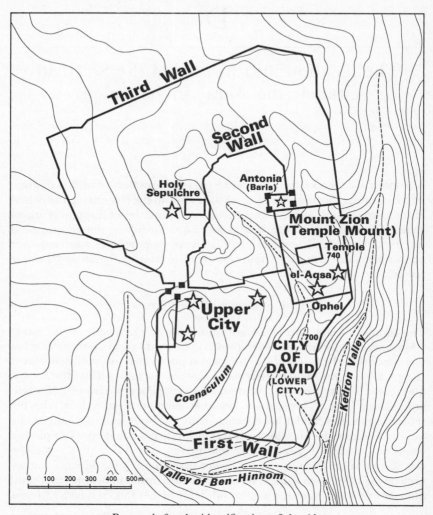

19 Proposals for the identification of the Akra
(Jerusalem in the time of Josephus)

consequently been suggested that I Maccabees used the term 'City of
David' improperly and applied it to the entire area of Jerusalem, as
happened in Josephus' paraphrase on the biblical story of the conquest of
Jerusalem in David's time (*Ant.* 7.66–7).[5] Josephus' location of the citadel

('site H')), and there is no sign in the immediate vicinity of the removal of a large quantity
of earth which would support the tradition mentioned. See also II Samuel 24.18; I Kings
8.1,4, 9.24; II Chron. 5.2, 8.11, all indicating its low position.
   [5] Although Josephus mistakenly locates the Jebusite citadel in the Upper City (*Bell.* 5.137),
he does not restrict the City of David to that hill, as some scholars think. According to him,

in the Lower City has been explained as a mistake resulting from his distance from the Hasmonaean period. This has led to the placement of the Akra in various sections of the city that overlook the Temple Mount or where some find was excavated that can be interpreted as belonging to a Hellenistic fort, and the like. Unfortunately the investigation of this matter has often tended to ignore the basic rules of historiographic criticism, especially the need to clarify the sources of information, the nature and time of the literary sources and their interconnection.

It is hard to imagine that, like Josephus, the author of I Maccabees used the term 'City of David' improperly. As the latter is extremely accurate in the use of biblical expressions and in giving topographical indications,[6] he was certainly well aware of the topographical denotation of the name 'City of David'. Its location on the eastern hill is clearly indicated in numerous biblical verses with which he generally showed considerable familiarity (e.g. Neh. 3.15; II Chr. 32.30, 33.14; and the various references to the tombs of the House of David). That hill continued to be popularly known as City of David in Nehemiah's time (Neh. 3.15), and it certainly continued to be called so, since the period from then to the author's time was one of uninterrupted Jewish residence in the city. The actual and formal use of the name at the time of the Hasmonaean Revolt is indeed shown in an official document of Simeon's era, the treaty between him and the people (I Macc. 14.27ff.), whose credibility is indubitable (see, e.g., verses 48–9), and which, like the other documents in the book, is not worded in strictly biblical style. Moreover, that treaty specifically states that the citadel was in the 'City of David which is in Jerusalem' (ibid. 36). The addition of 'which is in Jerusalem' shows that the reference was not to the entire area of Jerusalem in Simeon's time but to a particular, explicit part of it. Finally, from the time of the Restoration until the beginning of John Hyrcanus' reign, when I Maccabees was composed, the community was in the main concentrated on that hill and on the Ophel.[7] The author, a contemporary of the events,

Jerusalem as a whole was called City of David, which included the Lower City as well as the Upper City (including the former Jebusite citadel, *Ant.* 7.61–2,66). In addition there is no basis for the proposal that Josephus located David's tomb, said in the Bible to be in the City of David (e.g. I Kings 2.10, 14.31, 15.24), on the Coenaculum (at present the so-called 'Mount Zion'), i.e. in the Upper City. He does not say that anywhere, and the location of David's tomb in the City of David appears from Nehemiah (3.16), a location which was certainly preserved in the living tradition in the time of the Second Temple which refers to the tomb as a well-known place (*Ant.* 13.249, 16.179; Acts 2.29). Clear evidence for the identification of David's tomb on the Coenaculum is known only from the early Arab period. The question of the graves on the Coenaculum has recently been studied by Barkai (1977: 11–28).

[6] See pp. 154–5 above and passim.

[7] On the absence of any settlement on the western hill dating from early in the Second Temple period until the reign of Simeon or John Hyrcanus see Avigad 1970: 129–40; id. 1972: 193–200; Avi-Yonah 1971b: 168–9; Kenyon 1974: 179ff.; Tsafrir: 1975: 507–8; id. 1980: 25; Avigad 1980: 61–72; Geva 1983: 58–61. The recent discovery of a structure outside the City of David, near the Siloam Pool (Shiloh 1984: 29–30), does not change the picture; see Shilo himself n. 145. Tsafrir and others have difficulty in explaining the discrepancy between the archaeological finds and the information in the treatise 'On the Jews' attributed to Hecataeus of Abdera (Jos. *Ap.* 1.197) and in the Letter of Aristeas (para. 105) on the great dimensions

would not have applied the name 'City of David' to some hill that had been uninhabited by the local population. He even states clearly that the Seleucid garrison was quartered in a place where houses had been demolished in the city (1.31,33). The Ophel must be excluded as a possible identification of the Akra: its mention as a known quarter throughout the Second Temple period, separate from the City of David – the Lower City (Neh. 11.21; *Bell.* 5.145,253, 6.354) – makes it necessary to narrow the concept of the 'City of David' down to its biblical dimensions.

Thus, the use of the expression 'City of David' in I Maccabees is by no means anachronistic[8] and was still current in the Hellenistic period in regard to the south-eastern hill. The term 'the Lower City' which is familiar from Josephus, replaced the older name only during the period of the Hasmonaean State, when the Upper City was built west of the Temple Mount. It is possible that as the city grew during that period the term 'City of David' was occasionally applied to the entire Jerusalem area in patriotic contexts and for morale purposes, accounting for Josephus' celebrated mistake with regard to David's conquest of the city.

Josephus' assertion that the citadel was in the Lower City cannot be disregarded either, and resolved as a mistake resulting from unfamiliarity. It is not based on I Maccabees, for Josephus erred in locating the biblical City of David. This statement appears in the summary of the coercive edicts and the Hasmonaean Revolt in *Bellum* (1.50), in the description of the Jerusalem hills during the Great Revolt against the Romans (*Bellum* 5.139), in the account of the Hasmonaean Revolt in *Antiquitates* (12.252,362) and in the story of Simeon's period there (13.215,217). In the first two instances Josephus based his account on his memory, which was influenced by I Maccabees and Nicolaus of Damascus.[9] The story of the Hasmonaean Revolt in *Antiquitates* is a paraphrase of I Maccabees with the addition of marginal information chiefly from Nicolaus and Polybius.[10] The account in the last source of Simeon's time, however, is drawn entirely from Nicolaus.[11] It emerges from all these that according to Nicolaus of Damascus, Herod's court scribe, the Akra was located in the Lower City. Nicolaus took the information on events connected with the Akra before Simeon's time from I Maccabees and from Hellenistic sources.[12] As he was no biblical scholar, his location of the Akra in the Lower City could not be based on an interpretation of the term 'City of David' in I Maccabees, but on the current use of the latter name in his own time, on some specific information in Seleucid sources, and on the preservation of the name 'Akra' in the living local tradition. Of all these possibilities, only the third, however, can be definitely proved.

The name Akra in its Hebrew form *ḥaqrā*[13] was preserved even two or

and relatively large population of the city. However, these two sources do not antedate John Hyrcanus' reign. See p. 53 n. 83 and p. 74 n. 19 above.

[8] Against Niese 1900: 48–9; Pfeifer 1949: 486; Ettelson 1925: 304, and others.

[9] See p. 190 above.   [10] See pp. 190–3 above.

[11] See p. 452 below.   [12] Pp. 189–90 above.   [13] See p. 249 above.

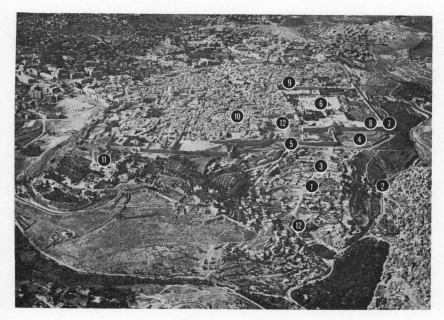

20 The City of David and the hills of Jerusalem.
    Aerial view from south to north

    Key:
     1 City of David–Lower City
     2 Gihon Well
     3 700-metre contour line
     4 Ophel
     5 Dung Gate
     6 Temple Mount–Mount Zion
     7 'Joint' in the Temple Mount wall
     8 Courtyard of the al-Aqsa mosque
     9 Site of the Fortress of Antonia
    10 Upper City
    11 Coenaculum (present-day Mount Zion)
    12 Course of Tyropoion gully

three generations after Nicolaus in the vernacular of the period before the
destruction of the Temple in reference to the south-eastern hill as a whole,
and Josephus, a Jerusalemite himself, uses the term naturally in reporting
domestic events and in identifying zones of control of the various commanders in the city at the time of the Roman siege. Because of the importance
of those references, they merit being examined one by one.

   It is reported of Simeon Bar-Giora that in addition to the Upper City he
also held 'the well [i.e. the Gihon] and parts of the Akra, that is, the Lower

City, up to the Helene palace' (*Bell.* 5.252–3), while Johanan of Gush Halav held the Temple and Ophel (ibid. 254). The identification of the Akra with the Lower City and the mention of it together with 'the well' and separately from the Temple, Ophel and Upper City, allows us to locate the Akra only on the south-eastern hill. Elsewhere the Akra is mentioned separately from the Ophel, and the palace of Helene is set in the centre of the Akra (*Bell.* 6.354–5).

In the detailed description of the layout of Jerusalem and its walls (*Bell.* 5.136–41) Josephus reports that the city was composed of three hills: the Upper City hill; the Akra hill 'supporting' (ὑφεστώς) the Lower City; and opposite the Akra hill, a third hill that was separated from it by a broad ravine and was originally lower than the Akra hill (paras. 137–8). However, the Hasmonaeans lowered the Akra hill so that it would not block the view of the Temple and filled the ravine in order to join the city to the Temple. With regard to the shape of the Akra hill, Josephus states that it was ἀμφίκυρτος (para. 137), which is 'convex on each side (like the moon in its second or third quarter)'.[14] This last statement caused difficulties for students of Jerusalem archaeology, some of whom even tried to find signs of an earlier crescent-shaped hill or something of that nature.[15] The crescent moon is convex only on one side, however. The description ἀμφίκυρτος does to a certain extent fit the south-eastern hill, the convex sides being on the west and on the east.

The elaborate topographical excursus does not indeed allow any room for doubting that Josephus in the passage under discussion too means the south-eastern hill. He states explicitly that the Lower City was on the Akra hill. Its place in the eastern ridge is indicated by the statement that a broad ravine (φάραγξ), that is, the Tyropoion (para. 140), separates it from the Upper City. Its more precise location on the southern hill of the ridge can be deduced from the description of its relation to the third hill (paras. 138–9). 'The third hill' is certainly that of the Temple: the Tyropoion is not said to have separated it from the Akra – the Lower City – which shows that it is located on the eastern ridge, while the elimination of a ditch that according to Josephus once separated it from the Akra-Lower City made possible the unification of the city and the Temple (para. 139). The Akra hill, which is the second hill, cannot be located north of the Temple Mount, but only south of it: further on Josephus lists a fourth hill, the Bezetha hill, along the eastern ridge north of the Temple Mount opposite the Antonia (para. 149), which shows that his list of the hills of the eastern ridge proceeds from south to north. Moreover, the area to the north is even today higher than the Temple Mount, while Josephus states that after the change made by the Hasmonaeans, the Temple Mount topped the Akra hill. Thus all details of his description fit the location, shape and relative height of the

[14] See Liddell-Scott's dictionary, s.v. and references there.
[15] E.g. Guthe 1882: 324; Simons 1952: 53 n. 1 (cf. p. 36); Ben-Dov 1980: 28.

south-eastern hill as known to us today.[16] In all these sources relating to the time of the Great Revolt, Josephus calls the entire Lower City 'akra', while for the period of the Hasmonaean Revolt he notes that the Akra was 'in the Lower City', that is, was part of it. The name of the Akra (which no longer existed) in the course of time became *pars pro toto* and was applied to the entire south-eastern hill. This type of development is well known from the toponymy of the Holy Land and not limited to antiquity.

This naïve use of the name 'akra', arising from a living tradition transmitted from generation to generation, testifies more than anything else to its location on the south-eastern hill, and there are no grounds for imagining that this was a later mistaken identification based on the I Maccabees statement that the Akra was in the City of David. As noted above, in the generation of the Great Revolt (and even earlier) the original meaning of the term 'City of David' had already been garbled. For about half the period between the destruction of the Akra up to the Great Revolt, the city was ruled by the Hasmonaeans who were interested in perpetuating memories of the bravery of the founders of their dynasty, and during the rest of the period, about a century, various groups looked back nostalgically to the lost period of independence.

The story about the decapitation of the Akra hill

The only obstacle to the identification of the Akra on the south-eastern hill remains Josephus' repeated statement that at the time of the Hasmonaean Revolt the hill towered over the Temple, and that it was levelled after the occupation of the citadel by Simeon. I Maccabees does not deal directly with the matter of the height of the Akra but only mentions in passing that Nicanor 'ascended' (ἀνέβη) from his stronghold in the Akra in the City of David to Mount Zion, which is the Temple Mount (7.33). It cannot be argued that the author used that verb for reasons of reverence for the Temple, disregarding the topographical situation which was well

---

[16] The description of the ranges of hills itself raises some difficulty at first sight. The statement that the first two hills, the Upper City and the Lower City, were opposite each other with the Tyropoion separating them, with no mention of the Temple which was also separated from the Upper City by the central valley – all these may create the impression that the Lower City includes the entire eastern ridge, and pave the way for the identification of the citadel in other places on the same ridge, north of the south-eastern hill (as per Luria 1981 : 35). However, this does not accord with the information on the relation between the second and third hills. The special nature of the description results from the fact that Josephus did not intend to describe the Temple Mount in that chapter. This is clear from the way he begins: 'The city was fortified by three walls', etc. (5.136) – the city, not the Temple. After that comes the specification of the hills, the walls and towers. As to the hill of the Temple, it is not even mentioned by name, but called 'the third hill', and mentioned only to explain the changes in the height and form of the second hill, that of the Akra, and in the alleged ditch north of it. Nothing is said about the walls and towers of the Temple. These, and the structure of the Temple hill and its environs, are described in a separate chapter (paras. 184ff.).

known to him. The author is too precise in topographical matters, and the
same description appears in the Bible (II Sam. 24.8; I Kings 8.1,4), in one
case even before the erection of the Temple with reference to the way from
the City of David to the threshing-floor of Araunah the Jebusite, the future
site of the Temple (II Sam. 24.18). Josephus in his consistent paraphrase of
I Maccabees 'corrected' the text in line with the tradition at his disposal
about the height of the two hills, saying that Nicanor descended from the
Akra to the Temple (12.406).

The tradition about the higher position of the Akra hill at the time of the
Hasmonaean Revolt originates from the detailed story about the hard work
done night and day during Simeon's incumbency, for three full years, to
demolish the citadel and 'straighten' its hill so that the Temple would
dominate it. The main story appears in the account of Simeon's time in
Antiquitates (13.215–17), and is alluded to in the parallel summary in *Bellum*
(1.50). The summary in *Bellum* (1.50–6) on Simeon's leadership does not
seem to be based on Josephus' memory like the distorted epitome on the
Revolt.[17] As it does not differ in nature from the account of the other
Hasmonaeans in the same book, which is universally acknowledged to have
been drawn only from Nicolaus, the same source stands behind the *Bellum*
abridgement on Simeon's time as well. As for the expanded story in *Antiquitates*, Josephus' account (from 13.213 onward) is not a paraphrase of I
Maccabees, but follows another source, and is similar to that of *Bellum* from
the viewpoint of basic contents, sequence of events[18] and at times even
vocabulary. There is therefore little doubt that Josephus' version of
Simeon's time in *Antiquitates* is also taken from Nicolaus.[19] Consequently

[17] On the problem of Josephus' version on the Revolt in *Bellum* and its sources see pp. 186–90
above.

[18] Sievers (1981: 159ff.) followed by Feldman (1984: 809) argue that according to *Bellum*
Simeon was appointed high priest and 'liberated the people' only after the victory over
Kendebaeus (1.53), while according to *Antiquitates* the battle came only later (13.213,255–7).
However, *Bellum* (1.53), similarly to *Antiquitates* (13.213) and I Maccabees (13.41–2), dates
Simeon's appointment and the liberation to the year 170 (142/141 B.C.), said by the two latter
sources to have been his first year. All this preceded the battle against Kendebaeus which
according to the detailed and consecutive account of I Maccabees (16.1–10) took place not
before 174 (138/137 B.C.; see 15.10). As the statement about Simeon's appointment and
liberation appears in *Bellum* at the end of the account of his leadership, on the eve of his murder,
its purpose seems to be to highlight Simeon's main achievements as a conclusion of the account,
which is not unusual for an abridged and compressed version.

[19] The consecutive historical description in *Bellum* (1.50) includes just one short sentence
reporting that Simeon completely destroyed the Akra (κατέσκαψε δὲ καὶ τὴν ἄκραν). Although
the sentence appears literally to refer to the fortress alone, in such an abridged account it may
possibly mean the destruction of the hill as well, which, as noted, Josephus likewise termed
'Akra'. In any case, the attribution of the destruction to Simeon, its placement immediately
after the defeat of the garrison, and the reference to a total demolition – these points are
identical to *Antiquitates*. It is only natural that *Antiquitates*, being a more expanded version,
includes greater detail. Although of the opinion that the description of the Simeon period in
Antiquitates comes from Nicolaus, Hölscher believes that the story of the destruction of the Akra
hill is not from Nicolaus but from some folk legend (1904: 11). He points out the apparent
discrepancy between the epitome in *Bellum* and *Antiquitates* on the destruction of the Akra and
the alternate utilization of expressions like οἱ 'Ιουδαῖοι (= the Jews) and τὸ πλῆθος (= the

Josephus' statement in his geographical excursus on Jerusalem on the eve of the Great Revolt, that the height of the Akra hill was reduced by the Hasmonaeans (*Bell.* 5.139), must also be regarded as ultimately based on Nicolaus, and the same refers to similar allusions in *Antiquitates* (12.362,406).

The very statement that the citadel was destroyed in Simeon's time presents some chronological difficulty. In the account in *Antiquitates* (13. 215) and *Bellum* (1.50), the destruction of the Akra appears immediately after the report on its conquest, while the author of I Maccabees says nothing about the destruction of the citadel. Moreover, according to I Maccabees (13.51) the citadel was conquered in the month of Iyyar (May) 141 B.C. (cf. Scroll of Fasting, s.v. 23 Iyyar), and the covenant between Simeon and the people, signed in Elul (September) 140 B.C. (14.27), more than a year after the conquest, includes a paragraph praising Simeon for fortifying the Akra and even for installing a Jewish garrison there (I Macc. 14.37). Furthermore, three or four years after the conquest of the Akra Antiochus VII Sidetes demanded its return (I Macc. 15.28; the chronology in verse 10) which means that it was then still in existence. In addition, in the description of Jerusalem, its hills and fortresses during the Great Revolt, Josephus testifies that the height of the Akra hill was reduced by the Hasmonaeans 'when the Hasmonaean kings ruled' (*Bellum* 5.139). Accordingly it has been argued that the Akra was not destroyed in Simeon's time, but was demolished or abandoned during the reign of one of the Hasmonaean rulers who followed him.

However, the disappearance of the citadel can only be understood against the background of the particular circumstances at the end of Simeon's reign when Antiochus Sidetes put pressure on Simeon to station a Seleucid garrison in the citadel once again.[20] Presumably the citadel was then destroyed for the purpose of establishing a *fait accompli* and putting an end to Antiochus Sidetes' claims to the Hellenistic fortress. Simeon understood that if the citadel was left as it was, the enemy would have not only a claim on the diplomatic plane but also a challenging reason to try to conquer Jerusalem and again station a garrison in the citadel. If on the other hand the Akra was destroyed, and the enemy conquered the city, they would not have a fortress they could man immediately with little effort. This consideration clearly emerges from the words by which Simeon is said to have urged his men to destroy the fortress: 'Reminding them what they are likely to suffer if a foreigner again conquers the country and stations a garrison in it' (*Ant.* 13.216). In fact the action taken was vindicated shortly thereafter: when Antiochus Sidetes subdued the city, Hyrcanus was able to reject his demand to leave a garrison there (*Ant.* 13.246–7). Antiochus, who insisted and attained all his other demands, was ready to give in on this

multitude) in *Antiquitates*, as proving that Josephus used two sources. The later argument must also be rejected: Josephus' style is never so dull as to allow the repetition of the same noun so closely. [20] See also Tsafrir 1975: 502 n. 5.

point presumably because there was no ready place to billet the troops. A
similar reason inspired the population of Heraclea Pontica to raze the local
akropolis after the death of King Lysimachus of Thrace in the battle of
Curupedion in 281 B.C. (Memnon, *FGrH* no. 434, 6.2 (9)).

The failure of I Maccabees to mention the event was evidently owing to
the fact that the covenant between Simeon and the people, actually the
constitution of the Hasmonaean State, lauds Simeon for strengthening and
manning the citadel, and as a reward for that achievement (and others)
grants him the authority to rule. Reporting on the destruction of the citadel
(which was done some years later under pressure of circumstances), after
quoting that document in full, would have been in questionable taste. On
the other hand, the author of I Maccabees could not delete the mention of
the Akra from the text of the treaty which was well known and was incised
on tablets placed publicly in the Temple area (14.48–9).

As to the dating in *Antiquitates* of the destruction immediately after the
conquest, Simeon's achievements and period are not reported there in
perfect chronological order, but in two parts, one dealing with domestic
developments (13.213–17) and the other with events in Syria (including
Simeon's involvement: 13.218–24) and the Kendebaeus expedition to
Judaea (13.225–7). The destruction of the Akra, which presumably occurred in the wake of that expedition, could be regarded by the author as
an internal event, or merely negligently attached to the account of its
conquest. The same sequence is followed in the compressed epitome in
Bellum, both being based on the same source. Finally, the assertion in *Bellum*
5.139 that the fortress was destroyed 'when the Hasmonaean kings ruled'
is only generally and briefly mentioned as part of a topographical survey,
not a historical one. In such a context, it cannot have the same weight as
the statement about the destruction in Simeon's days which appears twice
in the consecutive historical account.[21] In a geographical excursus Josephus
could have allowed himself to be somewhat negligent (or inexact) with
regard to Jewish constitutional history. The period of Simeon's presidency,
in which independence was declared and expansion campaigns were conducted could be regarded in such a context as belonging to the period of the
Hasmonaean kingdom with little detriment to the essence of the information
given or the reader's perception of it.

With regard to the exact contents of the information: from the context
of the full version of this story in Book 13 of *Antiquitates*, it is clear that the
statement on the height of the citadel hill was made in order to serve as
background for the description of Simeon's energetic action to destroy the
Akra and the hill it was on. The two elements of the tradition should not
therefore be separated. To accept them as credible means the refutation of
all the proposals for locating the fortress on sites higher than the Temple
Mount today (like the Antonia and the Upper City).

A study of the details of the story raises some substantive difficulties: the

[21] Contrary to Simons 1952: 54,157. See also n. 23 on the characteristics of *Bell.* 5.139.

information on the scope and duration of the work and of the reason for 'straightening' the hill seems rather odd and exaggerated. There are not really sufficient grounds for denying the likelihood that the Akra was razed to its foundations by Simeon; the declared purpose of the operation – to 'establish facts' and make it difficult for the Seleucids in the future – does sound logical. But for that purpose it was enough to destroy the citadel itself. There could be no sense in diverting all national resources, including people, for so long, to making the hill lower in a period of pressing national tasks. The levelling of the hill would have been useless if political and military circumstances had enabled the Seleucids to rebuild the fortress. If the aim was to control the inhabited area, a fortress in the Lower City, even at its present height, would have overlooked it sufficiently. And if the main purpose was to control the Temple, the south-eastern hill was in any case too far away for close control and supervision of the Temple, while in the north it was possible to find a more suitable place. Moreover, it is hard to imagine that the author of I Maccabees, who lived at the time of the Revolt and wrote such a detailed book, would have completely ignored an operation of such magnitude if it had really taken place. And a distinction should be drawn between the mere destruction of the fortress itself, which the author of I Maccabees could have avoided mentioning for the reason given above, and an operation so complex and protracted as the levelling of the hill described by Nicolaus. If therefore the difficulty that Nicolaus' dubious story imposes on the identification of the location of the Akra on the south-eastern hill is weighed against the definite and contemporary testimony of I Maccabees (shared by Josephus–Nicolaus) locating the Akra in the south-eastern hill, against I Maccabees' indication of the lower position of the Akra at the time of the Hasmonaean Revolt (which the Bible says of the City of David), as well as against the preservation of the name Akra for the south-eastern hill till the destruction of the Second Temple, by all the rules of historical research we must conclude that the information contained in that story of Nicolaus' must not be utilized in attempting to locate the Akra and cannot refute the identification suggested by all historical sources.

At the same time, we cannot evade the obligation to ascertain the origin and evolution of Nicolaus' story about the decapitation of the Akra hill. Nicolaus, who was well acquainted with Herodian Jerusalem, knew that the Seleucid fortress had been in the Lower City, and reiterated it in his writing. Yet the use of the term 'Akra' for the Lower City hill must have sounded quite strange to Nicolaus and to his contemporaries. The word *akra* means the highest point (of a city, settlement, hill), upper city, and a citadel (usually on a hill or some rise dominating the neighbourhood or the inhabited area, and the like). The Jerusalem Akra was certainly built on the highest point of the south-eastern hill, i.e. at its northern end close to the Ophel. It was originally so termed because it overlooked the City of David, then the settled section of Jerusalem, although the Temple towered above it. When the Akra was built, sometime in the Ptolemaic period (see below), the Ophel was at least partly inhabited (Neh. 3.26,11.21). Be this as it may, from its other side the fortress (not the hill) could also have dominated the Ophel as well.[22] Whoever gave the Akra its name obviously envisaged the purpose for which it was built, and therefore named it on the basis of its position in relation to the dwellings of the city rather than to the Temple which was beyond the confines of the city. Nicolaus (and Josephus in his wake) thought that the Upper City which clearly topped even the Temple was inhabited during the Hasmonaean Revolt (*Bellum* 1.39). How then could the name 'Akra' be applied to a location that was considerably lower than quite a proportion of the inhabited city? The Greek reader, too, who had no notion of the historical geography of Jerusalem, would probably have found this matter hard to understand, if only because of the statement that the Akra was in the Lower City. It may be suggested therefore that the whole point of the story about the levelling of the hill was to resolve the difficulty arising from the name Akra.

Nicolaus expanded and elaborated the correct original information on the destruction of the fortress, and added a number of elements in order to adapt the name Akra to the hill concerned. To the destruction of the citadel – which may have involved the removal of the stones it was built of and some 'cosmetic' levelling or rather ploughing of the ground in the area – he added the operation of 'decapitating' the hill and the total mobilization of the people for three years. In addition to the security reason, Nicolaus may have given another explanation for the levelling of the hill: Josephus elsewhere states that it was done so that the Temple would tower above the Akra hill and be visible beyond it (*Bellum* 5.139).[23] In any case,

[22] See p. 460 below on the exact location of the fortress at the edge of the City of David, close to the Ophel. The Ophel hill today is between 720 and 725 m high, that is, about 15 m higher than the highest point in the City of David, which borders the Ophel. However, part of the face of the hill is artificial, created by structures from the Herodian period, as the most recent excavations show. In any case, a massive structure erected between elevation points 700 and 710 could tower above the Ophel and could certainly observe what was going on among its houses.

[23] The full version of the story of the destruction of the Akra in *Antiquitates* 13 states only that the purpose was to prevent a foreign garrison from being stationed there again (13.215). However, at the end of the episode it is said that as a result of that destruction the Temple towered over the entire vicinity (13.217). Nicolaus may well have presented this result also as another reason for the action taken, and Josephus only 'compressed' matters. The *Bellum* description of the layout of the city during the Great Revolt against the Romans does not have the reason deriving from the political–military situation during the Hasmonaean Revolt, and gives only the second reason (5.139) which accords better with the historical context and character of that topographical excursus, since it relates to the status and altitude of the Temple during the whole Second Temple period.

The relatively expansive version in *Antiquitates* of the story of the destruction of the Akra does not necessarily include all the details that appeared in Nicolaus' original presentation. As first noted by von Destinon (1882: 12), quite often the *Bellum* epitome of the history of the Hasmonaean State and the Herodian dynasty contains more information and explanations than the more expanded treatment in *Antiquitates*, although both are based on Nicolaus, and in his latter book Josephus used other sources as well. In regard to the absence of explanations in *Antiquitates* see, e.g., the story of John Hyrcanus removing the treasure from David's tomb:

the reader concluded that the Akra hill – the Lower City – was formerly higher than at present and towered over the Temple, and also (although this was not explicitly stated) over the Upper City, which accounted for its being called *Akra*.[24]

The story of the decapitation of the hill must have raised a new difficulty: where did the quantities of earth removed from the hill disappear to? This was an enigma for the ancients no less than for some modern scholars who accepted Nicolaus' story. Nicolaus knew that there were no serious signs of earth-moving in the area, just as he knew that the south-eastern hill was lower than its neighbours. This is the background for Josephus' statements – in his description of the plan of Jerusalem during the Great Revolt – that in the past the Akra was separated by a broad ravine (πλατείᾳ φάραγγι διειργόμενος) from the Temple hill, and that the Hasmonaeans filled in the ravine as they levelled the Akra hill, in order to facilitate movement from the city to the Temple (*Bell.* 5.138–9). Just as the topographical and archaeological data make it impossible to concede that the hill was ever higher than the Temple Mount, they also do not support the possibility that in the time of the Hasmonaean Revolt there was a broad ravine on the north that separated the City of David from the rest of the eastern ridge.[25] Presumably, like the story of the destruction of the Akra, this information too contains a grain of truth but was blown up tremendously: the Hasmonaeans certainly filled in the moat that protected the Akra to the north, while in the story the moat became a broad ravine capable of explaining the whereabouts of the earth taken from the Akra hill. The obvious substantive connection between the story of the decapitation of the hill, which comes from Nicolaus, and the story of the filling in of the ravine and their mention in the same sentence by Josephus, suggest that the latter story too originates in Nicolaus.[26] All in all, Josephus' inventive talent, as

---

Antiquitates says only that the silver was used to hire mercenaries (13.249) while *Bellum* states that the initial purpose was to lift the siege on Jerusalem; for that purpose 300 talents were given to Antiochus Sidetes, the surplus going to hire mercenaries (1.61). On the story of the removal of the silver, its source and historical value, see Bar-Kochva 1977: 181–5. Cf. also on the outlet of the 'Jannaeus trench' in *Bellum* 1.99 ('from the mountainside above Antipatris') *versus Ant.* 13.390 ('from Kefar Saba, called Antipatris').

[24] Simons too, rejecting the credibility of the story, believes it was invented by Josephus to stress the heroic struggle of the Hasmonaeans and perhaps to explain the presence of rock and ash detritus in the Tyropoion valley (1952: 154). The first part of the explanation is not tenable because the source of the story is Nicolaus. As to the second explanation, actually the original form of the valley of Tyropoion was better preserved at the foot of the south-eastern hill than in the northern sector where the valley separated the Temple Mount from the Upper City. Furthermore, it appears that no ash dumps of any significant size were seen in the vicinity of the Lower City, and that was the background for the story of the existence of a broad trench north of the Akra that was supposedly filled in by the Hasmonaeans (see below).

[25] On the futile attempts of archaeologists to trace the trench see Simons 1952: 111–14.

[26] The existence of the ravine and its being filled in are not mentioned in the description of the destruction of the Akra in either *Bellum* or *Antiquitates*. In the former book, which is only an abridgement, Josephus devotes only one sentence to the whole matter of the Akra (cf. n. 19 above). As to the more detailed version in *Antiquitates*, it does not necessarily include all the components that figure in Nicolaus' original account (see n. 23 above).

we can assess it today, would not go so far. On the other hand, elaborate
revisions, adaptations and additions which depart for various reasons from
the basic historical kernel are typical of Nicolaus' version of the Hasmonaean State, especially as regards the reigns of John Hyrcanus and Alexander Jannaeus.[27] I would not rule out the possibility that the imaginary
destruction of the hill was inspired as well not only by the puzzling name
Akra, but also by an obscure statement in the source utilized by Nicolaus,
which could be interpreted, by some stretch of the imagination, as implying
that the hill itself was razed to the ground. Whether Nicolaus believed in
his explanation or only strove to satisfy the reader is anyone's guess. The
second possibility is not surprising for a Hellenistic author. Thus Josephus
did not refrain from inventing a false linguistic–ethnographic explanation
for the *gamma* in the name Gamala (*Bell.* 4.5), although as a Hebrew and
Aramaic speaker he knew perfectly well that this was nonsense.

Some additional arguments

In the debate on the location of the *akra*, the argument has been proffered
that the garrison would not have held out so long if the citadel had not been
located in a commanding position well away from the Jewish inhabitants,
which is not true of the south-eastern hill.[28] But it must be remembered that
the garrison held out for about thirteen years, during ten consecutive years
of which Jerusalem was ruled exclusively by the Hasmonaean brothers
(164–162, 161–160, 152–142 B.C.). Even if the citadel had been on the
highest and most isolated peak in the immediate vicinity, it would have
been rather easy to overcome its occupants by laying a siege to cut off
supplies.[29] And indeed the citadel fell to Simeon after he besieged and
starved its inhabitants for not very long a time – no longer than a year and
perhaps just a few months (I Macc. 13.42, 49–51). It was only because the
Hasmonaeans, for political reasons, generally refrained from trying to
starve out the garrison (as I Macc. 12.36, 13.49 implies). Most of the time
the Seleucids were preoccupied with difficult problems much more serious
and important than the rebellion in Judaea. As long as the citadel in
Jerusalem, symbolizing Seleucid sovereignty over the country, remained
under the control of the garrison, the suppression of the rebellion did not

[27] See Baer 1969: 39–40; 1980: 141ff.; Bar-Kochva 1977: 183,193. For an evaluation of
Nicolaus' version see also M. Stern 1972: 390–4. On the 'inventive genius' of Nicolaus see
especially the variation on the Oedipus myth in *Ant.* 13.322–3. On geographical–military
matters note the inclusion of an imaginary story on the digging of 'the Jannaeus trench'
between Antipatris and the Mediterranean (ibid. 390), a project entirely superfluous and
absurd given the existence of the broad Yarkon river and adjacent swamps along that line. The
negative evaluation obviously refers to the trench, not to the line of towers attributed to
Jannaeus.
[28] See Abel 1926: 518–26; id. 1949: 17; Vincent 1934: 205–36.
[29] On the ineffectiveness of siege devices and artillery against a fortress as strong as the
Jerusalem citadel see p. 301 above.

have top priority, and the forces sent to Judaea comprised only part of the army, which was in the main assigned to other theatres. In the first generation of the Revolt, when the overall military power of the kingdom was superior to that of the Jews, the Hasmonaeans preferred to come to terms with the existence of the Seleucid enclave in Jerusalem and allow it to obtain regular supplies rather than to provoke the Antioch authorities unnecessarily and lead directly to a punitive expedition of considerable scope, especially since, as the Jewish army took shape, the garrison was no longer able to interfere with the Hasmonaeans' freedom of action. The Hasmonaean brothers preferred to wait until there was less danger of massive reprisals. On only two occasions, on the eve of Lysias' second campaign and before the clash between Jonathan and Tryphon, are we informed about efforts to besiege the Akra and starve out its inhabitants (I Macc. 6.26, 12.36, 13.21). In both those cases, by overestimating the weakness of the central authorities at the time, the Hasmonaeans provoked immediate vigorous responses which were quantitively and qualitatively far greater than any earlier military campaign. On another occasion Jonathan sought to exploit the internal crisis following the death of Alexander Balas and the succession of the fourteen-year-old Demetrius II. Jonathan decided to breach the citadel and for that purpose assembled a large number of siege machines (I Macc. 11.20). The vigorous diplomatic intervention of Antioch, however, probably compelled him to desist, and lift the siege a short time later (I Macc. 11.20–4). It stands to reason that at certain times such as during the struggles Demetrius I and II had with Alexander Balas (152–145 B.C.) the matter of the citadel was settled in an explicit agreement between the Hasmonaeans and the rivals in Antioch (see also Jonathan's request, I Macc. 11.41). During Simeon's reign, the time was ripe for taking over the fortress, thanks to new developments and far-reaching changes in the realm. The great enthusiasm engendered by the fall of the citadel reflected in various sources derived more from past memories and its symbolic significance as representative of Seleucid rule than from any actual difficulty that the garrison created for daily life in Jerusalem and the security of the country at the time of Simeon's leadership.

There are also scholars who attempted, on the basis of the term 'acropolis' which in II Maccabees denotes the place where the Seleucid garrison was stationed and where the Hellenizers took refuge in the period before the coercive edicts (4.12,28, 5.5), to claim that only the sector north of the Temple Mount, which was higher than the site of the Temple, could be so designated. However, the tragic–pathetic II Maccabees simply called the Akra that he came across in his sources (primarily I Maccabees) by the more impressive and picturesque term 'acropolis'. Jason of Cyrene and the epitomist, both of them having rather vague and distorted ideas of the elementary geography of Eretz Israel, must certainly be avoided as evidence for the exact topography of Jerusalem. The same is true in regard to various attempts to find the gymnasium according to II Maccabees (4.12). The statement in the Letter of Aristeas that 'the *akra* of the city' (ἄκραν τῆς πόλεως) is 'on the highest place' (para. 100) and is supposed to protect the Temple (para. 104), is not relevant here for it refers to the *Baris*, the fortress built by John Hyrcanus north of the Temple Mount not long before the 'Letter' was composed.[30]

The location of the fortress and its purpose

The exact placement of the Akra cannot be ascertained before a careful, thorough and comprehensive archaeological study is made of the entire northern section of the south-eastern hill. Even then it is doubtful whether archaeology would offer much support as the fortress was totally demolished, its stones taken away, and its ground ploughed (though far from the extent described by Nicolaus–Josephus). As the City of David stretches down the gentle slope southward, it must be assumed that the fortress was built at the highest spot on the hill, i.e. the northern end bordering the Ophel, between the 695 m and 705 m contour lines.[31] Recent excavation in the celebrated G area on the eastern slopes of the City of David indirectly proved the location of the Jebusite and Davidic fortresses to be somewhat to the south of the place suggested above for the Akra.[32] It seems natural for the Hellenistic citadel to have been adjacent to the former fortresses. The excavations carried out close to that section by Macalister and Duncan in 1923–5 do not help much, being notoriously unreliable; new ones are unfortunately impossible because the area is now inhabited.

That location of the citadel was meant to oversee the inhabited Jewish parts of the city and not the Temple. Supervision of the religious site could be accomplished through watches and patrols. But it was necessary to have a commanding view of the city itself twenty-four hours a day. It can be understood from this how Judas Maccabaeus was able to gain control of the Temple so easily in 164 B.C., shortly after Lysias' retreat from Beth Zur (and see also I Macc. 4.41 on a diversionary move in the direction of the Akra in the course of the purification of the Temple). References to difficulties the garrison of the citadel caused 'around the Temple' (κύκλῳ τῶν ἁγίων, I Macc. 6.18,[33] 14.36) do not require it to be actually adjacent to

---

[30] See p. 53 n. 83 above.

[31] We do not have precise data on the southern boundary of the Ophel, aside from the statement that the Gihon was in the City of David, not the Ophel area (II Chron. 33.14; *Bellum* 5.254). The archaeological investigation has focused on the identification of the 'Ophel wall' (II Chron. 27.3; Neh. 3.27). The wall discovered by Warren extends southward to slightly beyond elevation point 710 and there disappears (see the summary of the material in Simons 1952: 138ff.). Mazar (1975: 56,215), on the basis of a re-examination of earlier excavations, places the boundary line halfway between elevation points 710 and 700. Shiloh's suggestion that the Ophel should be located on the site of the Jebusite fortress (1984: 27) is unwarranted by the sources and findings.

[32] Shiloh 1984: 17,27.

[33] On the meaning of the phrase 'were besieging Israel' in this verse see p. 299 above.

the Temple. It was quite possible to annoy the crowds near and inside the Temple by sorties from the Akra (as in 14.36) and to harass the throng by means of artillery machines set up in the City of David. The distance between the edge of the place suggested for the Akra and the Temple itself was not more than 330 m, and less than that to the Temple's southern courtyards, while the artillery machines of the period had an effective range of 450 m.[34] Certainly no special propinquity is inferable from the poetic description of the evils committed by the occupants of the City of David (I Macc. 1.36–7).[35] I Maccabees only states that the Seleucid garrison did as it wished in the city and the Temple.

In the light of all that has been said above, there are no grounds for the suggestions recently made by a number of Israeli archaeologists to locate the Akra within the courtyard east of the al-Aqsa mosque (near Solomon's Stables),[36] or on the Ophel hill, somewhat south of the south-eastern wall of the Temple Mount.[37] In the final days of the Second Temple, the plateau east of al-Aqsa was within the confines of the Temple Mount (see *Bell.* 5.145).[38] Although the area was raised and straightened by Herod in the course of his project to enlarge the Temple grounds (*Bell.* 1.401),[39] the structure of the area suggests that during the Hasmonaean Revolt the sector was on the slope of the Temple Mount. The author of I Maccabees consistently calls the Temple Mount 'Mount Zion' (4.37,60, 6.48,62, 7.33, 10.11, 14.27).[40] In one place I Maccabees explicitly uses the expression 'Temple Mount' and distinguishes between it and the Akra (13.53; cf. 14.36, 16.20). In any case, the Ophel separated the Temple from the City of David, and if the area east of al-Aqsa was not included in the Temple Mount, it was included in the Ophel.[41] As to the Ophel, it has already been noted that sources from the beginning and the end of the Second Temple period distinguish clearly between the Ophel on one hand, and the City of David (where the Akra was located according to I Maccabees), or the Akra hill – the Lower City (the location of the fortress according to the living

[34] See Marsden 1969–71: 1.15,37–9,86–91,131ff., esp. 91.

[35] On the location of the subjects of these verses in the City of David in general, not just in the limited area of the Akra, see in detail on pp. 463–4 below.

[36] Tsafrir 1972: 125–6; id. 1975: 501–21; id. 1980: 17–40. See also the arguments of Laperrousaz 1975: 241–59, and the answer of Tsafrir (1977: 295–7). Cf. further Schwartz 1985: 3–16, and p. 249 above on *be'ēr ḥeqer – bor ḥaqēr*.

[37] Mazar 1975: 216; Ben-Dov 1980: 22–35. Ben-Dov's hypothesis is based to a large extent on a misunderstanding of the word ἀμφίκυρτος which figures in relation to the Akra in *Bellum* 5.137 (see p. 450 above).

[38] On the northern boundary of the Ophel see Mazar 1975: 213–15.

[39] On the expansion see Kenyon 1974: 114, and Simons 1952: 346–9.

[40] In the Bible, Mount Zion (as opposed to Zion) refers exclusively to the Temple Mount; contrary to Simons 1952: 50,60 and passim. I Maccabees does not use 'Mountain of the Lord' or 'Mountain of the House of the Lord', which are also common in the Bible, in order to avoid the divine name (cf. p. 215 above re verse 22).

[41] The remnants of the Hellenistic wall visible north of the 'joint' in the south-eastern corner of the Temple Mount wall are thus not the lower courses of the Akra as Tsafrir suggests. They should perhaps be related to the improved wall built by Jonathan around Mount Zion-Temple Mount (I Macc. 10.10), but that possibility still requires archaeological verification.

tradition and Nicolaus) on the other (Neh. 11.21; *Bell.* 5.145,253, 6.354).
I Maccabees, which is so precise in topographical indications, would not
have set the Akra in the City of David if it was located anywhere on the
Temple Mount or in the Ophel. It should be added that the various
proposals of identification of the citadel in the Ophel concentrated on
the sector near the Hulda Gates and the south-eastern wall, which was
undoubtedly in the Ophel area during the Hasmonaean Revolt period.[42]

The Ptolemaic Akra

To conclude this discussion, it is desirable to consider also the location of
the Hellenistic fortress in Jerusalem in the period prior to the promulgation
of the coercive edicts. Even the scholars who agree that the Akra of the
Revolt period was south of the Temple in the City of David believe that the
fortress there was built only when the edicts were promulgated, and that
before that, during the Ptolemaic period and part of the Seleucid period,
there was a fortress in Jerusalem of the same name located north of the
Temple where the *birā* stood in Nehemiah's time (Neh. 2.8, 7.2), the *Baris*
in John Hyrcanus' (*Ant.* 15.403, 18.91), and the later Antonia (*Bell.*
5.238–47). In their view, that fortress is mentioned in Josephus' background
remarks for the battle of Panium (*Ant.* 12.133), in Antiochus III's charter
for the Jews (ibid. 138) and in the story of the internal events in the city that
preceded the coercive edicts (II Macc. 4.12,28, 5.5). The main evidence for
separating the northern from the southern Akra appears in a verse at the
beginning of I Maccabees which was taken to imply that the Akra in the
City of David was built only after the assault made by Apollonius, commander of the Mysian mercenaries, in 167 B.C. (1.38).

This assumption raises serious difficulties. The 'disappearance' of a
northern fortress and the absence of any mention of one in the detailed
sources for the Revolt period is incomprehensible. While the authorities
might have preferred to concentrate their military endeavours around the
southern fortress that overlooked the dwellings of the city, it is hard to
believe that they would have entirely abandoned a fortress that overlooked
the Temple, which also represented a danger at various times because of its
fortified construction (see, e.g., I Macc. 4.59, 6.19,51–4). One may suggest
that the northern fortress was destroyed in one of the uprisings that possibly
broke out in Jerusalem just before the coercive edicts were promulgated,
and that Jewish sources refrained from reporting this, just as they omitted
mention of rebellions in accordance with their desire to present the edicts
as a wicked, arbitrary, unprovoked measure.[43] It must be borne in mind,
however, that the fortress was a Hellenistic one that served both the

[42] See n. 31 above on the southern boundary of the Ophel, and n. 38 on its northern
boundary.

[43] That was my assessment in the Hebrew edition of this book (Bar-Kochva 1980b: 320 n.
11). On the uprisings that preceded the religious decrees see Tcherikover 1961a: 190ff.

Ptolemies and the Seleucids, and during the period of the 'Syrian Wars' withstood protracted sieges more than once. To destroy such a fortress, it would have been necessary first of all to starve out the garrison, and then assign a great many labourers to the task of demolishing (or rendering unusable) the massive, extensive structure. This was beyond the capabilities of the conservative Jews in that period, and would in any case have required more time than they would have had before the inevitable intervention of the central authorities. And finally, Josephus calls the Ptolemaic fortress 'Akra' (*Ant.* 12.133) and that name also figures once in an official document (*Ant.* 12.138). Is it reasonable to suppose that the same name was applied to two fortresses in different sectors of the city, the second constructed shortly after the destruction of the first, a name that in the case of the first fortress indicates its topographical position overlooking the Temple, and in the case of the later one only its control over the residential area of the city (since it was lower than the Temple)?

These difficulties compel us to re-examine the key verse in I Maccabees: 'And they built the City of David in a great, strong wall and it became an *akra* for them' (1.33). Conventional exegesis assumes that the second half of the verse means that the area described became a fortress called 'Akra'. But that raises a further difficulty. It would mean that the Akra included the entire territory of the City of David, and indeed some scholars have described the Akra as a fortified zone occupying all of the south-eastern hill.[44] That conclusion seems to be supported by Josephus' description of the city during the Great Revolt which implies that the entire hill was called Akra.[45] However, as the archaeological findings indicate that the western hill was not yet populated at the time,[46] where did the Jerusalemites live between the purification of the Temple and the liberation of the Akra? They could not all be concentrated in the Ophel. Furthermore, according to the description of Jonathan's siege of the Akra (I Macc. 12.36–8), Jonathan put up a physical barrier between the city and the Akra in order to isolate the fortress. The author does not say that the barrier separated the Temple from the Akra or the Ophel from the Akra, but the city from the Akra. This suggests that the barrier was located south of the Akra and that the area south of the eastern hill was inhabited by Jews loyal to the Hasmonaeans. It is also hard to believe that the garrison in Jerusalem, together with the Hellenizers who were not very numerous,[47] needed such a large fortified area. In any case, it could be a serious tactical drawback as it would have been difficult to defend and various parts of it would have been exposed to attack and invasion. As already explained, Josephus' statements about the period of the Great Revolt reflect the later developments when the term 'Akra' was applied to the south-eastern hill as a whole.[48]

As to the I Maccabees verse in question, the poetic tone of the entire

---

[44] So Simons 1952: 146–7,157; Shotwell 1964: 10–19.   [45] See pp. 448–51 above.
[46] See p. 447 n. 7 above.   [47] See p. 57 above.   [48] P. 451.

passage (see verses 31–2 in particular) makes it necessary at the outset to accord preference to the prose testimony on Jonathan's reign, and to the settlement and military considerations noted above. A more careful examination of the end of this poetic verse – καὶ ἐγένετο αὐτοῖς εἰς ἄκραν (ותהי akra- להם ל = and it became an akra for them)᠆ reveals its true meaning. The word 'akra' in the passage is a simple noun rather than a place-name (cf. the same construction in Gen. 11.3: ותהי להם הלבנה לאבן (= And the brick served them as stone); Job 13.5, ותהי לכם לחכמה (= It would be considered wisdom on your part)). It should be understood in the sense of a fortified zone. The Hebrew had *mivṣār* or *meṣūdā* (stronghold, fortress); the translator wrote *akra* and not the usual *okhyrōma*,[49] under the influence of the location of the Akra in the City of David emerging from the rest of the story. This conclusion is supported by the fact that the translator did not use the definite article with *akra* as he did more than twenty times in the other instances of the word.[50]

Thus the intention of the author was only to say that when buildings and walls in the city were destroyed (1.31), its inhabitants removed (1.38) and foreigners and 'sinners' settled there (1.34,38), the entire area of the City of David was encircled by a large, strong wall. Towers were added and the entire hill became a stronghold for the enemy and his backers. The area is not equivalent to the fortress known as the Akra, which was located in a limited space at its northern edge and served as a base for supplies and arms, quarters for the garrison, and as a refuge for the Hellenizers in times of stress. When Judas Maccabaeus gained control of the city, the garrison and the Hellenizing Jews withdrew into the Akra.

A provision in the pact between Simeon and the people regarding the removal of the garrison from the City of David contains wording resembling that of the verse under discussion: 'For in his time he succeeded in expelling the Gentiles from their country, and those in the City of David, which is in Jerusalem, who had made themselves an *akra*, from which they issued and polluted around the Temple and did great evil in the holy place' (I Macc. 14.36). Here too the definite article is missing and the reconstruction should be ויעשו להם מצודה (= had made themselves a fortress). However, in this case it does not affect the meaning and comprehension of the verse: Simeon expelled the Gentiles who had built a fortress 'in the City of David in Jerusalem'. The verse thus establishes that the fortress, that is the Akra, was in the City of David, which was a part of Jerusalem. It certainly does not mean that all of the City of David was fortified, for it was written in Simeon's time when the garrison was forced into the fortress. I would not conclude from the clause 'who made themselves a fortress' that it was built at the start of the Hasmonaean Revolt. The subject of the clause, the soldiers

---

[49] On the translation of the word *meṣūdā* or *mivṣār* in I Maccabees to *okhyrōma*, and on the use of the word *ḥaqr'ā* to render *meṣūdā* and *mivṣār* in the Aramaic translations of the Bible, see p. 249 above.

[50] 3.45; 4.2,41; 6.18,24,26,32; 9.52,53; 10.6,7,9,32; 11.20,21,41; 12.36; 13.21,49,50,52; 14.7; 15.28. For the only exception (14.36) see further below.

expelled from the citadel in 141 B.C., were certainly not the same ones who were there in 168, and could not have been its builders even if it was built in the early days of the Revolt. The verse speaks in general of the removal of the 'Gentiles', that is, the Hellenistic soldiers, from the fortress, the same fortress built by the 'Gentiles' some time in the past, not necessarily at the start of the Revolt, and not necessarily by the Seleucids.

The Akra – the citadel of the city of Jerusalem and abode of the foreign garrison – was thus located even before Antiochus Epiphanes' reign, certainly by that of Ptolemy V, on the south-eastern hill. If it is true that the *birā*, the fortress built by the Persians before Nehemiah's time, was north of the Temple on the site of the *Baris* and Antonia,[51] presumably the location was chosen by the Persians because of the centrality of the Temple in the Samaritan–Jewish conflict, and the Samaritan tale-bearing on secret Jewish plans within the Temple building (Ezra 4). The City of David, on the other hand, was wide open, and the settlement in it sparse, until it was reinforced in Nehemiah's time. Circumstances were entirely different in the Hellenistic period. The conflict subsided following the construction of the Samaritan temple toward the end of the Persian period, while the Jerusalem community that was concentrated in the City of David was surrounded by a wall and displayed great ambition in the inter-power political struggle.[52] The Hellenistic rulers considered it more important to keep an eye on what went on in the daily life of the city than on the sacrificial offering and ceremonial assemblies. The northern fortress was probably destroyed in the turmoil of the start of the Hellenistic period. The report of its destruction, however, has not survived in the sources on the period, because they are scanty and extremely fragmentary. One speculation is that the *akra* was erected by Ptolemy I as a measure of precaution after his harsh treatment of the city early in his reign.

[51] The chief evidence for the location of the *birā* north of the Temple is the absence of any mention of this fortress in the description of the construction of the city wall of Jerusalem (i.e. the wall of the City of David) in Nehemiah's days, and the use of the same name (graecized as *Baris*) for the fort that John Hyrcanus built north of the temple (*Ant.* 15.403, 18.91; *Bellum* 1.75,118). For other less valid evidence see Klein 1939a: 13–14.

[52] On the Jewish political involvement see p. 476 below.

E

The chronology of Antiochus Epiphanes' expedition to the eastern satrapies

In order to determine the exact date of the battle of Ammaus, it is necessary to clarify the time of the start of Antiochus Epiphanes' great expedition to the eastern satrapies which preceded it. The exact chronology is vital for the reconstruction of the timetable of the various phases of the campaign conducted at Ammaus and its environs, and in its wake for the dating of the Beth Zur battle and the evaluation of its outcome.[1]

In the primary sources the only direct data on the date of the expedition is the statement in I Maccabees that Antiochus Epiphanes set out in the year 147, on the eve of the battle of Ammaus, *en route* from Antioch to the Upper Satrapies (3.37). As the date relates to an external event, the Macedonian–Syrian version of the Seleucid calendar was the one applied. Thus that year began in autumn 166 B.C. and ended at the beginning of October 165.

The season when the expedition to the Upper Satrapies took place must be postponed to the second half of that year, that is, between the spring and autumn of 165 B.C., and probably to the last quarter, i.e. the summer of 165:

(a) Porphyry, quoted by Eusebius, states that Antiochus V served as co-regent together with his father for 'one year and six months' (*FGrH* 260, F32, para. 13). The combined rule was initiated according to the Seleucid tradition to avoid uncertainties in case something happened to the king during his eastern adventure (reflected in II Macc. 9.23–5), and presumably it began somewhat before the king's departure in order to get the public used to the position of the child-king, and his court (and regent) used to practising its new role. Since Antiochus IV died in Persia in late November or December 164 B.C[2] the expedition got under way no earlier than June or July 165 B.C., and probably later.

(b) According to I Maccabees (2.69), Mattathias died in 146; his death being an 'internal' event, that year must be construed as beginning in the spring of 166 and ending in early April 165. The patriarch of the rebel family died when the Revolt was just beginning to get

---

[1] See pp. 262, 280, 284 above.   [2] See Sachs and Wiseman 1954: 208.

organized. But the quality of the combatants, the standard of intelligence work, the mobility and control of the troops displayed in the battle of Ammaus, clearly indicate at least a year of preparations. And between Mattathias' death and the battle of Ammaus there were also the confrontations in which Apollonius and Seron were repulsed. Consequently the battle of Ammaus must be deferred to a date as far removed as possible from the initial organization of the Revolt and Mattathias' death,[3] in other words, as close as possible to the end of the year I Maccabees gives for Antiochus' departure for the east – 147 in the Syrian version of the Seleucid calendar, that is, late summer of 165 B.C.

Among the scholars who attempted to arrive at a more precise date for the start of the expedition were some who concluded from what Porphyry had to say that the expedition began exactly a year and a half before Antiochus Epiphanes' death, that is, between the end of May and the end of June 165.[4] But, as already noted above, there is reason to believe that the official announcement of the co-regency was made some time before the expedition set out, within the framework of the general preparations for it, and not exactly on the day it left. Other scholars sought support from a statement in Josephus' *Antiquitates* which may suggest that the expedition began in early spring (12.293).[5] But this view has been rejected by others who rightly noted that Josephus refers to early spring not as the start of the expedition, but as the time when Antiochus Epiphanes intended to attack Judaea, while the expedition to the eastern satrapies, according to Josephus, set out only after Antiochus became aware of his difficult financial straits which prevented him from undertaking to attack Judaea just then (12.294).[6] Even if Josephus originally meant to say that the expedition to the east began in the spring, nothing can be learned from him as his passage is only an interpretative paraphrase of I Maccabees containing nothing on the expedition not taken from that source. The mention of early spring originates in the practice that was common in Eretz Israel of beginning the 'military season' in the spring, and perhaps one should accept the suggestion that Josephus was also influenced by the statement in I Maccabees that Antiochus paid his soldiers a year's salary in advance (3.28), which can mean from the start of the 'military year'.[7]

In order to arrive at a precise dating of the expedition to the east within the period between the spring and late summer of 165 B.C. it is necessary to clarify the purpose and date of the celebrated procession that Antiochus Epiphanes arranged at Daphne near Antioch. It has been agreed by scholars that the procession took place in the middle of the summer of 166 B.C.[8] It

---

[3] The clause 'And when Antiochus heard' (I Macc. 3.27) does not constitute proof that the expedition to Ammaus took place immediately after Seron's defeat, See p. 227 above (according to I Macc. 4.26–8), p. 380 on I Macc. 9.1.

[4] See Goldstein 1976: 251.   [5] See Kahrstedt 1926: 122; Bevan 1902: 2.158.

[6] E.g. Bunge 1971: 401 n. 101.   [7] See Goldstein 1976: 251.

[8] See, e.g., Holleaux 1957: 5.180ff; Bunge 1976: 63 n. 61.

would be advisable to separate the question of the season from that of the
year. With regard to the season it is possible to arrive at an approximate
date: the procession was a part of an annual festival in honour of Apollo[9]
that was celebrated at a specific time. We have some information on the
annual Daphne games in 195 B.C.: Livy reports that Hannibal, after es-
caping from Carthage, arrived at the island of Cercina in the middle of the
summer, sailed from there on the same day, and reached Tyre after a
'prosperous voyage' (*prospero cursu*), probably meaning uneventful and
speedy, and then proceeded to Antioch, where he met the son of Antiochus
III at Daphne during the festival (33.48.4–6,49.6). Under such conditions
the trip lasted no longer than ten to twelve days.[10] It may therefore be
assumed that the festival at Daphne took place at the beginning of August.
It should be added that there is no identity between the *kharistēria* which
was held in Babylonia in Hyperberetaeus 146 S.E. (= 14 September 166 B.C.;
OGIS 253, ll. 3–5) and the Daphne festival, as some scholars believe.[11] The
former was an annual celebration to mark the anniversary of the king's
accession to the throne in 175 B.C.,[12] while the Daphne festival preceded
Antiochus IV's reign and was dedicated to Apollo.

However, contrary to the agreement on the season when the procession
took place, the year 166 B.C. is not acceptable. It raises the serious question
of the purpose of the military part of the procession, and of the reason that
the forces were mobilized, the mercenary troops in particular. Various
solutions have been proffered. Some scholars believe that the procession
was held to mark a military success, but if it took place in the summer of
166 B.C. that would be too remote from any victory of Antiochus Epiphanes'. Tarn, who realized that difficulty, proposed a bold hypothesis regarding an alleged involvement of Antiochus Epiphanes in events in Bactria
around the time of the procession, but this proposal was rightly rejected.[13]
Others claim that the only purpose of the procession was to imitate the
ceremonies Aemilius Paullus conducted at Amphipolis in 167 B.C. after his
conquest of Macedon.[14] They argue that Athenaeus states at the beginning
of a passage based on Polybius that having heard of the victory celebration
of Aemilius Paullus, Antiochus wanted to outdo him in splendour and
magnificence, and so sent envoys to the cities of Greece to invite them to the
games at Daphne (Athenaeus 5.194c = Polybius 30.25.1). However, the
recruitment and mobilization exclusively for the procession of 16,000 mer-

---

[9] See the term *solemne ludorum* in Livy 33.49.6, and cf. 48.5; cf. Athenaeus 12.540a; *OGIS*
248, ll. 52–3.

[10] On the average speed of sailing vessels in the Mediterranean, which under normal
conditions was about 4–6 knots, see Koster 1923: 177ff., esp. 181. Cf. F. Miltner in *RE*, s.v.
'Seewesen', col. 917.

[11] Esp. Bunge 1976: 63; id. 1974b: 50 n. 45.

[12] See Tarn 1951: 193–5; Mørkholm 1966: 100.

[13] Tarn 1951: 183–224, esp. 187–91. Against Tarn: Mørkholm 1966: 172–3; Altheim and
Stiehl 1970: 2.39ff.

[14] E.g. Rostovtzeff 1940: 2.69; Downey 1961: 98, and many others.

cenaries, a number exceeding the total number of mercenaries that Antiochus III recruited for his great wars,[15] is simply not conceivable even for so extravagant a character as Antiochus IV. The tremendous financial burden of maintaining the mercenaries, the political complications involved in recruiting some of them in areas where recruitment was forbidden by the Treaty of Apamea, and the great effort required to transfer them all to Antioch are enough to eliminate the notion that all Antiochus Epiphanes meant to do was to surpass Aemilius Paullus' festival. Furthermore, the various reports on the Amphipolis festival do not include the slightest hint of a military parade (Livy 45.32.8–33.7; Plutarch, *Aem.* 28.3–5; Diodorus 31.8.9). And if the suggestion is that the mercenaries were recruited anyway earlier and stationed for security purposes in extensive regions of the Seleucid kingdom, the marginal propaganda value in the procession could not justify endangering the security of the empire in distant sectors, in particular in view of the shaky situation in the eastern satrapies and Judaea.

Athenaeus' statement, which is not presented as a quotation from Polybius, may very well be his own interpretation intended to connect the festival with the preceding long passage on Antiochus Epiphanes' other strange deeds which derived from his desire to ape the Romans (5.193d–194b; the passage is explicitly credited to Polybius and quoted in direct speech). Suspicion of Athenaeus' intervention in the contents of the extract is supported by the fact that the report on the banquet at the Daphne festival is worded differently in the two Athenaeus books citing it and each of the reports contains some phrases missing in the other (5.195d–f *versus* 10.439b–e). The opening of the parallel in Book 10 even lacks the comparison with the celebration of Aemilius Paullus (though that might be explained by the fragmentary nature of that parallel). And above all: Athenaeus himself had devoted a separate work to the history of the Syrian kings (5.211a) and, considering himself particularly knowledgeable on the subject, was inclined to add interpretations of his own. In any case, it may also be that the intention was to explain the expense and magnificence in that year's festival, and not the reason for its arrangement or components.

In view of all that is said above, the assembling of the soldiers at Daphne must be connected with a crucial military operation that had either just ended or was about to begin close to the time of the procession. The military operation that preceded the procession was the second expedition to Egypt (168 B.C.).[16] However, many months had passed since the expedition,

---

[15] On the number of mercenaries see pp. 34–6 above.

[16] Antiochus Epiphanes' expedition to Armenia (Diodorus 31.17a; Appian, *Syr.* 45,66; Porphyry in *FGrH* IIB, no. 260, F38 and 56) is not definitely dated. According to Porphyry (fragment 56), it may seem that the Armenian campaign opened Antiochus' expedition to the East: see Otto 1934: 86; Mørkholm 1966: 167. The latter points out that Antiochus III did the same (Polybius 8.23). Indeed it is reasonable to assume that Antiochus Epiphanes did not return the entire army to Antioch after his Armenian triumph but continued south-eastwards. In any case, the fact that the rebellious Artaxias was left in Armenia (see Otto 1934: 86 n. 3)

and it ended in a diplomatic defeat, which was no reason for celebration. The only possibility is that the concentration of forces and the procession were arranged within the framework of preparations for the great expedition to the east.[17] And indeed a military display on the eve of an expedition or battle was not a rare occurrence in Macedonian tradition.[18] This explanation is suggested by Diodorus' note that Antiochus Epiphanes displayed at Daphne all his power, contrary to other kings who 'tried to conceal their intentions' (31.16.1). The sources are too fragmentary to offer more evidence.

This unavoidable conclusion is beset with difficulties arising from the generally accepted chronology: according to the date agreed on by scholars, the procession took place sometime in the summer of 166, that is, at least ten months before the earliest possible date for the expedition itself. The mobilization of mercenaries such a long time before the operation, and the enormous expense of supporting them for that period were an inconceivable waste of money, especially since the main purpose of the operation was the improvement of the difficult financial situation of the royal treasury. The salaries and allowances for 16,000 soldiers for such a period would certainly have exceeded a thousand talents, the amount of the annual reparations payment to Rome that so burdened the Seleucid empire a few years earlier.[19] Furthermore, if at the time all these mercenaries were standing idle in Syria, it is hard to understand why there are no signs of their being despatched to Judaea instead of the meagre forces that seem to have taken part in the initial confrontations. These considerations compel us to re-examine the assumption that the procession took place in 166 B.C., and see whether it is based on solid grounds.

Polybius' description of the procession is preserved in the *Deipnosophistai* of Athenaeus (5.194c–195f), who elsewhere attributes the passage to Book 31 of Polybius (10.439b). All editors, however, have rightly accepted the view that Athenaeus' original text referred to Book 30.[20] This book covered the four years of the 153rd Olympiad, that is, autumn 168 B.C. to autumn 164 B.C.[21] As is Polybius' practice, the events of each of the four years are

suggests that the victory there was not so decisive as to justify so grandiose a military procession as at Daphne.

[17] The procession as a prologue to the expedition to the Upper Satrapies was briefly commented on by Will (1979: 290), and treated at greater length by Bunge (1976: 56–7,71), but the latter considers the event to be simultaneously a celebration of the victory in the sixth Syrian War (similarly to Mørkholm 1966: 97f.), and also a celebration to mark the day the king acceded to the throne. The notion that an expedition that ended in the gloomy 'days of Eleusis' was celebrated with so much fanfare is inadmissible. As to the connection with the day the king assumed power, that proposal is based on a dubious interpretation of inscription *OGIS* 253; see p. 468 above.

[18] See, e.g., Diodorus 16.3; Arrian, *Anab.* 1.11.1–3,18.2,8,24.6, 3.6.1; Plut. *Alex.* 29,31; Curtius Rufus 3.7.2–5. The 'catalogue' in Diodorus 17.17.3–5 may be taken from the procession organized at the time. For victory parades see Arrian 2.5.8,24.6, 6.28.1.

[19] On the salaries in the Hellenistic period see Griffith 1935: 294ff.; Launey 1949–50: 2. 750ff.; and see p. 228 above on the distinction between salary and allowance.

[20] Metzung 1871: 10,29; see lately Walbank 1957–79: 3.33.

[21] The Olympic count began in July/August 776 B.C. In order to avoid cutting up descriptions of military campaigns which extended beyond a single year, however, Polybius

reported separately, beginning in Italy and proceeding eastwards to Asia and Egypt. The excerpt on the procession had been assigned to Olympic year 153.2 (autumn 167 to autumn 166 B.C.).[22] The only grounds for this are the order of the Polybius fragments in the chrestomathy entitled *De legationibus gentium ad Romanos* which is part of a general anthology, *Excerpta historica*, collected during the reign of Constantine VII Porphyrogenitus.[23] Polybius' fragment 87 (= Polybius 30.27) reports on the Roman survey delegation headed by Tiberius Gracchus which reached Antioch shortly after the games at Daphne. Since fragments 88 (= Polybius 30.28) and 89 (= Polybius 30.29) cover events in Italy and Greece, the assumption is that a new year began before them. As the events in the two latter fragments can, on the basis of various counts, be dated with a great deal of certainty in Olympic year 153.3 (autumn 166 to autumn 165 B.C.), the time covered by fragment 87 is construed as Olympic year 153.2 (autumn 167 to autumn 166).

However, there is no assurance that the order of the Polybius fragments in the Byzantine chrestomathies corresponds to the original one. In respect to *Excerpta antiqua*, which contains fragments from Books 1 to 17, the order can be checked, and it appears that the original order was indeed occasionally disrupted.[24] As the chrestomathies included in *Excerpta historica* contain fragments not from Polybius alone like those in *Excerpta antiqua* but from many writers, there is a likelihood that many more errors occurred. Such a conclusion is suggested in particular by the possibility noted by several scholars that *Excerpta antiqua* was only a preliminary stage for *Excerpta historica*.[25] Doubt about the proper placement of fragment 87 arises also because its inclusion in a chrestomathy dealing with delegations to Rome is inappropriate: the fragment deals with a Roman delegation that went to Antioch, and as such should have been included in another chrestomathy of the *Excerpta historica* entitled *De legationibus Romanorum ad gentes*.

The determination of the time of the Daphne procession is therefore based on a datum for which the likelihood of error is quite high. If we place one against the other, on one side the location of the passage in question in the Byzantine chrestomathy, and on the other the substantive considerations suggesting that the procession took place as close as possible to the expedition to the Upper Satrapies in 165, we will have to give preference to the latter. The location of fragment 87 has therefore to be rejected and

adopted the Olympic system with a modification, concluding with the close of the military season, that is sometime in the autumn. On this see Walbank 1957–79: 1.35–7 and 2.628, and the bibliography there; Samuel 1972: 194 n. 2.

[22] On 166 B.C. as the year of the procession see Metzung 1871: 30; Niese 1893–1903: 3. 215; Kolbe 1927: 238; Otto 1934: 83; Koperberg 1919: 99 n. xxv; Tarn 1951: 193; Mørkholm 1966: 98,166.

[23] The fragment numbers below are according to the edition of De Boor 1903. The discussion in Metzung is based on the fragment numbers in the V. Ursinus edition (Antwerp 1582).

[24] See examples in Walbank 1957–79: 2.1–28.

[25] Krumbacher 1897: 261; Moore 1965: 55.

Table 5. *Chronology of Antiochus IV's expedition to the Upper Satrapies*
(principal dates and relevant events)

Beginning of August 195 B.C.	Games and celebrations at Daphne
	Hannibal's arrival at Daphne
September 175	Antiochus Epiphanes comes to power
168	Battle of Pydna and conquest of Macedon
	Retreat of Antiochus Epiphanes from Egypt after the 'days of Eleusis'
167	Aemilius Paullus' victory celebration at Amphipolis
Autumn 168–autumn 164	Period covered by Polybius' Book 30 (years of the 153rd Olympiad)
Autumn 167–autumn 166	Olympic year 153.2
	Second annual cycle in Polybius' Book 30
September 166	The *kharistēria* in Babylon, celebrating the king's rise to power
Spring 166–spring 165	The year 146 of the Seleucid count in Babylonia and among the Jews in Eretz Israel
	The death of Mattathias
	The defeat of Apollonius and Seron
Autumn 166–autumn 165	The year 147–the date of Antiochus' expedition according to I Maccabees (3.37)
	Olympic year 153.3
	Third annual cycle in Polybius' Book 30
	Fragments 88 and 89 in *de legationibus gentium ad Romanos*
Spring 165	Early preparations for the expedition to the east, as per Josephus
End of May or June 165	Start of co-regency of Antiochus I and Antiochus V as per Porphyry
Beginning of August 165	**Procession at Daphne**
End of summer 165	Tiberius Gracchus' supervisory delegation at Antioch
	Antiochus Epiphanes leaves for the eastern satrapies
	The expedition to Judaea and the battle at Ammaus
Autumn 164–autumn 160	Period covered by Polybius' Book 31 (years of the 154th Olympiad)
November–December 164	Death of Antiochus Epiphanes in Persia

be moved to Olympic year 153.3 (autumn 166 to autumn 165). As the procession took place at the beginning of August, the appearance of the Roman delegation in Antioch should be dated sometime later, and the start of the expedition to the east after that – according to the date in I Maccabees – before October 165. Antiochus Epiphanes thus left for the east sometime in September 165, and that is also the time of the battle of Ammaus.

Finally, it should be noted that the timing of the start of Antiochus' expedition within only three months of the start of the rainy season does not refute the above conclusion. The expedition to the eastern part of the empire was not designed as a *blitzkrieg* that was to be completed in one blow before winter. Antiochus Epiphanes meant to stay in the Upper Satrapies a long time in order to consolidate his rule and improve the tax collection.

And indeed, from the start of the expedition to his death at least fifteen months elapsed. Furthermore, the crossing of rivers, the main climate-related obstacles to troop movements, was most convenient in September and October, while in spring the rivers are highest. Antiochus III set out in February on his campaign against Molon in the Zagrus mountains not far from Elam where Antiochus Epiphanes died.[26]

[26] See Schmitt 1964: 133, esp. n. 5.

F

Defensive war on the Sabbath according to the Books of the Maccabees

Students of the history of the halakha, the Jewish Oral Law, have generally agreed on the assumption that defensive warfare on the Sabbath was not permitted until early in the Hasmonaean Revolt.[1] This assumption became a basic point in the theory on the development of the halakha. The few dissenters, some of whom came from the ranks of the orthodox rabbinate,[2] were disregarded, either because of a dogmatic approach to the source and antiquity of the Oral Law, or because of unsystematic and incomplete consideration of Hellenistic sources.

The accepted view is based on the story of Agatharchides of Cnidus quoted by Josephus that the Jews did not defend themselves when Ptolemy I son of Lagus overcame Jerusalem on the Sabbath (*Ant.* 12.6), and on the tradition in I Maccabees (2.29–37) concerning the devout who took refuge in caves and did not defend themselves when attacked on the Sabbath. According to this view, the change took place with the declaration of Mattathias and his company, who in response to that incident demanded to fight on the Sabbath (I Macc. 2.38–40). And indeed from then on the Jews defended themselves on the Sabbath; so it was in the time of Jonathan (I Macc. 9.43–8), Alexander Jannaeus (*Ant.* 13.337) and at the height of the Great War with Rome.[3] This array of evidence is augmented by various references in II Maccabees (5.25–6, 6.11, 8.25–6, 15.1–5) from which there

[1] See Geiger 1875: 217ff.; Büchler 1897: 72–3; Weiss 1904: 1.73; Krochmal 1924: 69; Moore 1932: 2.63; Tchernowitz (Rav Tzair) 1935–50: 4.299; Albeck 1954: 1.9–10; id. 1959: 19–20; Epstein 1957: 278; Herr 1961: 242–56; A. F. Jones 1963: 482–6; Helfgott 1974: 47–70; Oppenheimer 1976: 34–42; Goldberg 1979: 430–4. There is variety among all these, especially in regard to the evaluation of the stand of II Maccabees.

[2] Orthodox Rabbis: Halevy 1901: 338–44; Goren 1958: 149–89; Neria 1959. Other scholars: Radin 1915: 178–81; and recently: Efron 1980: 38 n. 55, 39 n. 63; Ben-Shalom 1980: 217, and see pp. 218–22 for his view that even offensive war was allowed; Mantel 1983: 103–7.

[3] A comprehensive treatment of the various sources on Sabbath combat during the Great Revolt appears in Herr 1961: 254–5; Hengel 1961: 294–6; M. Stern 1974: 1.510. Herr's explanation of the Josephus passages which seem to indicate that self-defence on the Sabbath was still forbidden (especially in the oration attributed to Agrippa: *Bell* 2.390–4,456,517–18) fails to notice, however, that those passages, fabricated by Josephus, were designed to make clear to the non-Jewish reader that the debacle was the result of the Jewish God's wrath against the zealots, a point that is repeatedly stressed by Josephus (in these passages as well). This accounts for the deliberate distortion or ambiguity in the wording.

was an attempt to deduce that its author opposed defensive warfare on the Sabbath. Also cited were various restrictions and reservations regarding war on the Sabbath demonstrated in various incidents during the period of the Second Temple (especially *Ant.* 14.63–5, 18.323) and in sectarian sources like the Book of Jubilee (50.12), which seem to indicate that the uncertainty regarding permission to fight on the Sabbath persisted.

The above conclusions derive from and are connected with the general method of nineteenth-century scholars regarding the spiritual–theocratic nature of Jewish life in Eretz Israel and abroad from the time of Nehemiah up to the Hasmonaean Revolt. According to their view the Jewish community in the Persian and Hellenistic periods had no interest in the achievement of national freedom or even in the establishment of some independent political entity in Judaea. All this became a theoretical wish for the unforeseeable future, involving the appearance of the Messiah descended from the House of David. The Jews contented themselves with the existing religious freedom, and were consequently indifferent to the military and political developments in the region. The change came only during the religious persecutions when the traditional right to live according to the laws of the forefathers was curtailed. The Jews turned for the first time to armed resistance.[4] When Jewish life during that period is conceived in such a spirit, it is not difficult to explain the statement of Agatharchides: after Nehemiah adopted severe measures concerning strict observance of the Sabbath, the notion took root that repose on the Sabbath must be absolute and total, in emergencies as well, for wars and military matters were remote from the consciousness of the Jewish community. The Jerusalemites of the period of Ptolemy I behaved accordingly. In the reign of Antiochus Epiphanes, however, when conditions had changed, and opposition to the religious restrictions involved danger in daily life, Mattathias and his followers recognized the unrealistic character of the traditional restriction. Life thus did its work and led to the relaxation of the halakha. Doubts nevertheless continued to be expressed for a long time, and various reservations limited the application of the amendment.

A number of facts and figures on Jewish life in Eretz Israel and abroad do not fit in with the conception presented above of Jewish indifference to military and political life, and by themselves raise serious doubts about the above reconstruction of the development of the halakha with regard to the Sabbath. The constant conflict with Samaritans, some of whom certainly did not observe the Sabbath, as well as with Gentile neighbours from the early days of the Return to Zion onwards, makes it difficult to accept that before the Hasmonaean Revolt the Jews were not faced with the need to

[4] The conception was expressed in the most impressive and comprehensive way by Wellhausen 1924: 8ff. The origin is to be found in the writings of previous scholars, and it has been repeated since in many variations by historians as well as theologians. The main evidence was the alleged internal rift in the Rebel camp. On this see p. 59 n. 101 above. Against the application of this conception to the understanding of the internal strife in the Hasmonaean State see Bar-Kochva 1977: 173ff.

fight on the Sabbath. This is well illustrated by the way that the Jerusalem wall was built in Nehemiah's time. A project of that kind, which lasted fifty-two days (Neh. 6.15) with 24-hour guards (4.3,12,15–17), cannot be envisaged without the preparedness and willingness to fight on the Sabbath. Even if Nehemiah's נערים (= bodyguards; literally = 'young men') who participated in the building and guarding (4.10) were foreigners (indicated perhaps in 2.9, 5.15; but see 4.10) the defence was not assigned exclusively to them, and they were joined by the rest of the builders, 'the people in families' (4.7), 'the nobles... the rulers and the rest of the people' (4.8), and also Nehemiah and 'his brothers' (4.17). Furthermore, Jewish settlement and expansion in border regions such as the northern toparchies, the distant enclaves on the coastal plain, the Mount Hebron area, the Negev and Galilee could not have taken place in the absence of any ability to defend them and fight back if war broke out on the Sabbath.

As to the Hellenistic period, the tradition in the Letter of Aristeas regarding the deportation of Jews to Egypt by Ptolemy son of Lagus (paras. 12–13), despite exaggerated figures, testifies both to the strength of Jewish resistance to the Ptolemaic conquest and also to the community's aspirations and involvement in current events.[5] This happened in the short period between the Gaza battle (312 B.C) and that at Ipsus (301 B.C), when Eretz Israel (including the Judaean Hills) passed from hand to hand some half a dozen times. We have information on a Jewish active role in the struggle between the Ptolemies and the Seleucids in the third, fourth and fifth Syrian War.[6] Moreover, there is a relative abundance of information on the military activity of Jews, from the outset of the Hellenistic period on, in the armies of the great powers as military settlers, mercenaries and border guards, stationed in Egypt, Cyrenaica, Babylonia, Syria, Asia Minor and even eastern Transjordania. Information on the participation of Jews in foreign armies has survived from the Persian period as well. Aside from the Jews of Elephantine, there were Jewish soldiers in the Northern Negev. It can be proved with regard to at least some of these Jews that they served in units of their own, under Jewish commanders, and were officially granted the right to conduct their lives according to their ancestral laws.[7]

In view of this varied picture, it is hard to imagine that Jews did not come

[5] The tradition in the Letter of Aristeas is confirmed by Agatharchides (cited in Jos. *Ap.* 1.209–11; *Ant.* 12.6) and Josephus (*Ant.* 12.4,7), who bases himself on an internal Jewish source (see further below). The story of voluntary emigration ascribed to Hecataeus (cited in Jos. *Ap.* 1.185–9) is not reliable. It is designed to legitimize and justify the existence of the Jewish Diaspora in Egypt. On Pseudo Hecataeus cf. p. 74 n. 19 above.

[6] The Third Syrian War: M. Stern 1963: 43; the Fourth Syrian War: *Ant.* 12.130, and perhaps also the trilingual stele from Pithom, 1.23 (see Gauthier and Sottas 1925: 54–6; but see the opposing view of Spiegelberg 1928: 10; Otto 1928: 80–5; Thissen 1966: 19,60–3); the Fifth Syrian War: *Ant.* 12.131,133,135,136; Daniel 11.14.

[7] On Jews in military service see pp. 82–6 above. The existence of Jewish units is obvious from the Elephantine papyri and the edict about the establishment of Jewish military settlements in Phrygia and Lydia (*Ant.* 12.148–53). For Babylonia see below pp. 500ff., and for Ptolemaic Egypt see Kasher 1978: 57–67. On the privilege of living according to their laws see *Ant.* 12.150 and cf. *Ant.* 11.339; I Macc. 10.37.

up against the need to fight on the Sabbath until the Hasmonaean Revolt, and that a strict theoretical approach prevailed. Nor can it be argued that before the persecutions Jews were never faced with the choice of death or apostasy, and therefore preferred surrender and conquest and even captivity and slavery to the 'desecration' of the Sabbath. Fighting in antiquity was by no means fair and kid-gloved, and unconditional surrender on the Sabbath already signified mortal peril before the time of Antiochus Epiphanes. The accepted view makes the service of Jews in foreign armies even less understandable. The realities of daily life necessarily dictated sanctioning self-defence on the Sabbath even before the Revolt, if indeed it had ever been disallowed. And the people who throughout the generations delved deeply into the Bible could easily find support in the story of the seven-day siege of Jericho (Jos. 6.3–5) to legitimize war on the Sabbath. It is thus incumbent upon us to deal with the information transmitted in the sources with all the critical tools at our disposal, and ascertain whether it necessarily compels us to agree that until the Hasmonaean Revolt Jews in Eretz Israel and the Diaspora refrained from defending themselves on the Sabbath despite the fact that as professional soldiers and members of a community with political and military involvement they were doubtless confronted more than once with such a situation.

The occupation of Jerusalem by Ptolemy I

The Agatharchides' account is quoted twice by Josephus. The version mostly mentioned by scholars on our subject appears in *Antiquitates* within the narrative on the Successor period: 'There is a nation called Jews who, having a strong and great city called Jerusalem, allowed (suffered, περι-εῖδον) its falling into the hands of Ptolemy, since they refused to take up arms, and through their untimely superstition submitted to having a hard master' (12.6). There is no reason to reject the basic reliability of the information on Ptolemy's capture of the city on the Sabbath.[8] The intention of that passage may be thought to imply that Ptolemy succeeded in conquering the city because the Jews did not defend themselves on the Sabbath. Before conclusions are drawn from the Agatharchides' statement, however, the second version of Agatharchides' account, as well as another description of the event should be investigated.

The quotation in *Antiquitates* is preceded by an account of the event by Josephus himself: 'And he (Ptolemy I) seized Jerusalem by resorting to cunning and treachery: for he entered the city on the Sabbath as if to sacrifice, and the Jews did not oppose him – for they did not suspect him of any hostile intention – and because of the lack of suspicion and because they passed the day in idleness and ease, he became master of the city without difficulty and ruled it harshly' (12.4). The literal meaning indi-

---

[8] See esp. M. Stern 1976: 1121; against Radin 1915: 179–81; E. L. Abel 1968: 253–8.

cates that the Jews were accustomed to defending themselves on the Sabbath, or why else was Ptolemy I compelled to resort to a trick? Furthermore, the abstention from fighting is explained on the mistaken assumption of the city's residents that the king came to offer a sacrifice, and not because there was a prohibition to fight on the Sabbath ('they did not suspect him of any hostile intention'). The same thing could have happened on any other day of the week. The statement 'they passed the day in idleness and ease' is included only in order to clarify why Ptolemy 'became master of the city without difficulty' even after his true purpose was revealed. The implication is that the king entered Jerusalem on the Sabbath peacefully, and then took advantage of the Jews' lack of preparedness when acute danger was not imminent, and their custom of not carrying weapons on their day of rest, a practice well known from the subsequent history of the Second Temple and the halakha.[9] This custom may also have been known to the Hellenistic ruler who could have planned from the outset to take the fullest advantage of it, aside from the trick he played. At any rate, when Ptolemy entered the city and made his hostile intentions known (by a demonstration of force, occupying key positions, arresting influential citizens, and the like) the inhabitants had insufficient time to arm themselves and get organized, and the city fell to him like a ripe fruit. The difficulty of turning immediately to the defence in a similar situation is well illustrated by the Tosefta: 'At the beginning they used to lay down their arms in a house next to the wall; one time (the enemy) came back upon them (חזרו עליהם), and (they) pushed on to take up their arms and killed each other' (Erubin 3[4]6). Josephus' version is not a commentary on Agatharchides, as it includes clearly independent elements such as the pretext used by the king, and at the end of the story the deportation of Jews along with Samaritans. Also the introduction to the quotation from Agatharchides, which follows Josephus' story, should be noted ('Agatharchides too testifies to this'); the need to support his narrative with the testimony of a Hellenistic historian implies that Josephus obtained his information from some Jewish source.[10]

[9] On the prohibition against carrying weapons on the Sabbath see Herr 1961: 248–9, 354–6. The main sources: *Tosefta Erubin* 3.5–6; *PT Erubin* 4.3 (21d); *BT Erubin* 45a; cf. Mishnah, Sabbath 6.3–4; Jos. *Vit.* 161.

[10] Cf., e.g., Josephus' version of the Fifth Syrian War (*Ant.* 12.132–5) and the 'evidence' he states that he found in Polybius (ibid. 135–6), the internal source on the relations between Antiochus VII Sidetes and the Jews (*Ant.* 13.250) and the 'support' from Nicolaus (ibid. 251). Herr's claim (1961: 243 n. 5) that 'if he [Josephus] had any comments to make on what Agatharchides stated regarding the prohibition against arming and fighting on the Sabbath, he would certainly have made them', may apply to a rabbinical scholar and not to a Hellenistic historian like Josephus, whose works abound in 'adaptations' of this kind, and the utilization of contradictory sources side by side (e.g. *Ant* 13.247–8 *versus* 13.249–50; 13.301–17 *versus* 13.318–19; 14.34 *versus* 14.38; *Ap.* 1.184ff. *versus* 1.205–11). Anyone aware of the internal contradictions in the *Vita* and between it and corresponding chapters in *Bellum Judaicum*, would not expect that kind of critical–historical thought of Josephus. Cf. also the uncritical acceptance of the information that the Jews refrained from fighting during the fallow year (*Ant.* 13.234) and that there was a fast day during the third month (*Ant.* 14.66). See also n. 18 below.

A more detailed version of Agatharchides appears in *Contra Apionem*: 'Those (people) called Jews, inhabiting the most strongly fortified city of all, called by the locals Jerusalem, are accustomed to abstain from work every seventh day, neither to bear arms nor to engage in agricultural work, nor in any {other} form of public service, but to pray with outstretched hands in the temples until the evening; when Ptolemy, son of Lagus, entered the city with his force, the people, instead of guarding the city, kept to their folly, the fatherland received a cruel master, and the (defect of the) law which contains a thoughtless custom was exposed' (1.209–10). This excerpt is fuller and more accurate while the quotation in *Antiquitates* ascribed to Agatharchides seems obviously a compressed and abridged summary.[11] We should therefore rely only on the full version. From what it says, there is no need to assume that the narrator meant that the Jews were aware of Ptolemy's hostile intentions and nonetheless refrained from defending the city. As Agatharchides was extolled as a historian who in clarity of expression surpassed even the great Thucydides,[12] attention should be paid to his exact wording. He does not state that the Jews do not fight on the Sabbath, but that they do not bear arms on the Sabbath (μήτε τὰ ὅπλα βαστάζειν), and does not say that they did not finally fight when Ptolemy was inside the city, but that at the outset they did not guard the city (ἀντὶ τοῦ φυλάττειν τὴν πόλιν...). His story could therefore be understood as follows: Ptolemy entered the city in peace, and the inhabitants, who in their 'folly' had removed the armed guards the day before, and did not bear arms as there was no apparent serious danger, had to pay dearly when the enemy's true intentions became known. All this corresponds with the Jewish source cited by Josephus.[13]

The summary of Agatharchides in *Antiquitates* is thus worded in a careless manner likely to mislead.[14] The differences in contents between Agath-

[11] Thus rightly noted by M. Stern 1974: 1.109. Josephus abridged Agatharchides in *Antiquitates* because background material on the affair is provided there by the version of the Jewish sources appearing in the course of the historical narrative, which is not the case in *Contra Apionem*. To the evidence that the original text was reported in *Contra Apionem* and not *Antiquitates* must be added the information in the former on Jews praying in their temples on the Sabbath with outstretched hands, and the stress on the fact that they refrain from λειτουργίαι (= public service) on the Sabbath, reflecting the Hellenistic milieu in which the writer moved. The absence of any explicit mention of the seventh day in the 'quotation' in *Antiquitates*, no doubt in reliance on what was said in the version preceding it, likewise shows that the text in that source is an abridgement made by Josephus himself.

[12] Photius, *Bibl.* 213 (*FGrH* IIA, p. 206, no. 86 T 2.6). For the proper understanding of the sentence see Walbank 1965: 10 n. 69. See also Fraser 1972: 1.540ff.

[13] Plutarch's comments on the Sabbath (*De superstitione* 8) are not connected with the conquest during the reign of Ptolemy I (contrary to M. Stern 1974: 1.549), and cannot therefore help to understand Agatharchides. The reference to the carrying on of siege operations on the Sabbath recalls the story of the siege by Pompey (*Ant.* 14.64–8; Strabo 16.2.40). The placing of the ladders (διαβάθραι; κλίμακαι) and the assault on the city wall are mentioned in Plutarch and in Strabo's version of the siege of 63 B.C. On the other hand there is not the slightest hint in the Agatharchides quotations (certainly not in Josephus' account) that the city gates were bolted and the enemy was obliged to scale the walls or breach them.

[14] Josephus may have been influenced in one way or another, like modern scholars, by his own view of the affair of the fugitives slain in the cave and of Mattathias' reaction, as indicated

archides' original account preserved in *Contra Apionem* and that of the Jewish internal source are understandable in light of the context of the former version. The story of Ptolemy and the Jews is not related as part of the chronological historical description in either of Agatharchides' great historico–geographical works,[15] but as an illustration of the inherent danger of superstitions in the context of the story of the tragedy such beliefs brought on Stratonice, the daughter of Antiochus I, who would not leave Seleucia although her life was in danger (*Ap.* 1.206–7).[16] Agatharchides, whose main concern here was not reporting on the Jews, could have 'simplified' the original complicated story in order to adapt it better to the Stratonice episode. Perhaps he wished to emphasize the 'peculiarity' of the Jewish custom and thus impress his readers more. Even if Agatharchides' under-lying intention was to tell his readers that Jews do not fight or defend themselves under any circumstances on the Sabbath, his statement should not be given weight equal to that of the internal source reflected in *Antiquitates*. The possibility must not be ruled out that Agatharchides, who wrote a century and a half after the event, failed to grasp the exact meaning of the original story at his disposal and was influenced by the deliberately distorted, derisive notions about Jewish festivals and holy days that were current in the Hellenistic world.[17] Just as nothing can be learned from statements scattered throughout Hellenistic and Roman historiography and ethnography about fasting on the Sabbath, or the prohibition of war and all work during fallow years,[18] so nothing should be learned from

in the *Antiquitates* paraphrase of that affair (12.273–7; and see n. 23 below). The Jewish source on the other hand provided greater detail, so that Josephus' contribution when reporting it was very small. On the lack of correspondence between citations in Josephus, sometimes even when they appear consecutively, see n. 10 above. At the same time, it is of course possible that in *Antiquitates* Josephus reported Agatharchides' account negligently, without attention to its precise meaning.

[15] The story appeared in Agatharchides' history of Asia or history of Europe. See Jacoby, *FGrH* IIc, p. 154.

[16] Joshua Gutman's explanation of the purpose of the story (1958: 1.68) – that Agath-archides meant to answer the question of whether it was permissible to break the laws of justice in order to avert subjugation to others (cf. Cicero, *Rep.* 3.28) – does not take into account the context and is therefore unacceptable. On the background and special circumstances of the Stratonice affair see Bar-Kochva 1973a: 7, and n. 3.

[17] The mocking character of the stories on the Jews' avoidance of fighting on the Sabbath has already been pointed out by Tcherikover 1961a: 364–5; Sevenster 1975: 126–7; Efron 1980: 39 n. 63, and 152 n. 55. Tcherikover even describes them simply as an anti-semitic joke. Josephus actually viewed the matter similarly at the start of the presentation of Agatharchides (*Ap.* 1.205: 'although he mentions us only to ridicule our folly'). Josephus' statement may well be based on some remark of Agatharchides' on the subject that has not survived. On the other hand, Friedländer (1903: 363) and also M. Stern (1976: 1124) believe that Agatharchides had no anti-semitic intentions. Some indirect support for this view may perhaps be found in Agatharchides' career in Egypt: he served at the Ptolemaic court during the reign of Ptolemy Philopator, the patron of the Jews, and left it, or was dismissed, upon the accession of Ptolemy Physcon (see Jacoby, *FGrH* IIc, p. 152) who persecuted the Jews harshly at the start of his reign. At the same time the possibility that Agatharchides was not hostile to the Jews does not necessarily apply to the sources he used while writing about the event in question.

[18] Suetonius, *Augustus* 76; Strabo 16.2.40 (cf. Dio Cassius 37.16; the question of the exact dating of Pompey's conquest of Jerusalem (*Ant.* 14.66) does not affect our point because there

Agatharchides about fine points of the halakha. Similarly a contemporary of Josephus, Frontinus, relates that Vespasian attacked and defeated the Jews on the Sabbath, a day 'on which no business may be conducted' (*quicquam seriae rei agere*: *Stratēgēmata* 2.1.17). Since the quotation comes from a collection of stratagems, it may be deduced that Frontinus intended to imply that the Jews do not defend themselves on the Sabbath. This, however, contradicts the reliable information given by Josephus on the Great War with Rome.[19] Would it enter anyone's mind to prefer the Frontinus version and derive from it the halakhic rulings prevailing at the time of the Great War?

The death of the martyrs in the cave and Mattathias' reaction

Let us now turn to the episode of the death in the desert cave of the devout refugees and the response of Mattathias and his people (II Macc. 2.29–41), the second main support for the conventional view. A careful scrutiny of the episode itself shows that it was not a prohibition against fighting on the Sabbath that prevented the escapees from defending themselves. As to the response of Mattathias and his men, the first part was not meant to allow defence on the Sabbath, and the second can be interpreted in a way that is more, and certainly not less logical than the usual interpretation. In order to analyse the episode, what the refugees in the desert said must be considered separately from what Mattathias and his men said, and only then should the connection between them be clarified.

The refugees' statements occur in two separate parts. The first is a reply to the enemy's demand to profane the Sabbath ('Come out and obey the king's command and your lives will be spared' 2.33; and see 2.34 on the contents of that command). The enemy considered that a sign of compliance with the king's coercive edicts. The profanation of the Sabbath was one of the chief demands, as explicitly stated by I Maccabees ('to profane Sabbath and feast-days', 1.45) and the document of the 'Sidonites in Shechem' (*Ant.* 12.259–60), and suggested also by the fact that keeping the Sabbath is mentioned in Hellenistic literature as one of the four main characteristics of the Jewish faith. Similarly, the Jewish food restrictions, likewise among the four restrictions mentioned, led the central authorities to make a special effort to force the Jews to eat pork (I Macc. 1.48,62; II Macc. 6.8,18, 7.1). The faithful decided not to comply with the king's demand: 'We will not come out and will not obey the king's command to profane the Sabbath day' (2.34). Only then did the enemy start to attack them ('And they hastened to make war on them', 2.35). The martyrs' response constitutes

is no doubt that the Sabbath was considered a fast day in certain circles of the Greek and Roman world; see M. Stern 1974: 1.276,307). On the question of war during the fallow year see p. 546 and n. 10 below.

[19] See the bibliography in n. 3 above. For an explanation of the Frontinus statement see M. Stern 1974: 1.511.

the second part of what they said: 'Let us all meet death in our innocence, witness heaven and earth that you execute us without trial' (2.36); they acted accordingly: 'and they did not answer them, and they neither hurled a stone at them nor barricaded the hiding places...and they died, they, and their wives and their children and their cattle, some thousand people' (1.35,37). That is, the refugees took no defensive action at all, not even the slightest ('they neither hurled a stone at them') in order to prove to all ('witness heaven and earth') their innocence. They wished to show clearly that harming them would be a terrible unprovoked iniquity ('without a trial') that would reveal to heaven on the one hand their rectitude (cf. 2.29, 'justice seekers'), and on the other the malice and evil of the enemy, and eventually lead to divine intervention and vengeance. These people were therefore martyrs (cf. I Macc. 1.63)[20] who chose to be passive and refrain from all defensive action, and made no preparations from the outset to fight. It is typical that they brought their 'women, children and cattle' with them, a combination certainly unsuitable for military action.[21] According to II Maccabees, it was the acts of the martyrs, these and others, which ultimately led to the active intervention of the deity and the sharp turn in the course of events.[22]

The description of the episode in the cave thus contains not one word on the prohibition of fighting on the Sabbath. The martyrs would have refrained from doing so on a weekday as well. The episode took place on the Sabbath because the enemy sought to compel them to profane the day. It must be kept in mind that what the refugees, all of whom died, said to each other ('and they did not answer them') could not have been known to the author, and he designed their statements in accordance with the information he had and the principal response of Mattathias and his men to the episode which he doubtless knew of (though probably expressed in his own words). If Mattathias had intended to abolish a previous prohibition and allow defensive action on the Sabbath, the author would have shown, in the words he attributed to the martyrs, their objections in principle to a defensive war on the Sabbath, and not only their objection to resistance in general at any time.

As to the response of Mattathias and his men, it appears in two separate sections, each one of which begins with 'and they said': *And they said* to one another, if we all do as our brothers have done and do not fight the Gentiles for our lives and laws, then they will soon wipe us off the face of the earth. And they consulted that day, *and they said*, anyone who will come upon us

[20] The martyrological character of the episode was already noted by Klausner (1950: 3.17), who also pointed out the use of the word μαρτυρεῖ in the episode (verse 17). Nevertheless he states that the martyrs refrained from defending themselves because of the Sabbath (pp. 17–18).

[21] Halevy (1901: 3.340–2), Radin (1915: 180–1) and Mantel (1983: 103–4) rightly state that the fugitives were unable to fight, but they fail to deal properly with the second component in Mattathias' reaction.

[22] See in detail p. 487 below. See also n. 32 on the explanation offered by I Macc. 3.8 to the change in the divine attitude.

in war on the Sabbath, we would fight him back lest we all die as our brothers died in hiding places' (2.40–1). A cursory examination shows that the two sections contain two assertions dealing with two different problems, or else the passages exhibit a verbosity and repetitiveness quite foreign to the author's condensed, forceful style. The first part of the response clearly relates to the policy of restraint and the question of self-defence in general. The speakers express their fear that the way chosen by the martyrs may become a symbol and example, and might lead to the total annihilation of all the faithful ('if we all do as our brothers have done... they will soon wipe us off the face of the earth', 2.40). No hesitation is apparent, and there is a consensus ('and they said to one another') regarding the need to fight.

The second part of the response (2.41), however, is given after Mattathias and his men have 'consulted', that is, following a certain quandary. What was it about? As noted above, if Mattathias were referring to so basic a question, so decisive for the future of the campaign, as self-defence on the Sabbath, and he intended to institute a reversal of the existing practice, the author would certainly have indicated this in the words attributed to the martyrs as an additional reason for their refusal to fight and for the catastrophe that overtook them, and such an indication would have clearly demonstrated the need for an immediate change in the law and justified that change in the opinion of all. It is therefore hard to accept the premise that the quandary concerned the basic permission to self-defence on the Sabbath. On the other hand, the author stresses the choice that the enemy offered the martyrs: to profane the Sabbath or die. This suggests that Mattathias and his men were faced with the specific question of whether it would be proper to fight in a special and deviant situation similar to the one in the cave, and whether that would not besmirch the image of the faithful for the authorities. It was a difficult choice: the enemy did not delve into the fine points of religious law. Fighting on the Sabbath after the Jews had been commanded (and refused) to profane the Sabbath might itself have been interpreted by the enemy as profanation of the Sabbath and result in public mockery of the God of the Jews. There was also perhaps reason to suspect that the enemy's entire purpose in such situations was to ridicule observing the Sabbath, and demonstrate the illogicality in the Jewish faith. In other words, if you are not prepared to profane the Sabbath you will be forced to fight, and in fighting, will you not be profaning the Sabbath? The question facing Mattathias and his men was therefore whether in such a situation of deliberate provocation on the enemy's part in regard to one of the precepts considered to be a prime characteristic of the Jewish people, the response should be postulated on the basis of the accepted custom, or more strictly than required by the law so that God's name is sanctified in public. The decision was that one should fight even in such a situation: 'Anyone who will come upon us in battle on the day of the Sabbath we shall fight against him', 1.41). The stress on 'anyone' indicates that the dilemma refers to an exceptional case: defensive action should be taken on the Sabbath even if that action should (unjustifiably) be damaging to the honour, the image and the credibility of the Jewish faith and its adherents.[23]

All this does not eliminate the possibility that the refugees in the desert belonged to some sect which did forbid defensive war on the Sabbath along with other prohibitions it subjected its members to, as was the custom of reclusive sects during the Second Temple period.[24] However, as noted above, the question of defence on the Sabbath is not mentioned in the utterances ascribed to them, and presumably never even arose on that occasion, since they refrained from all resistance, on weekdays as well. Consequently Mattathias was not required to deal with the underlying principle of defensive war on the Sabbath.

Some references in II Maccabees

The question of fighting on the Sabbath figures several times in II Maccabees in a form that may allow the inference that the author opposed defensive war on the Sabbath. A comparison and clarification of the contradictions between the mentions of the Sabbath in II Maccabees and parallel passages of I Maccabees has led to various conclusions. At first many followed Geiger,[25] explaining that the author of I Maccabees allowed Sabbath warfare because of his Sadducee views, while the author of II Maccabees, whom they deemed a Pharisee, forbade it as the Pharisees did. However, it has already been noted that no source mentions Sabbath warfare as a matter of dispute between Sadducees and Pharisees, and that according to the strict Sadducee position holding that the Torah should be taken literally, they should have been the ones to forbid Sabbath defensive warfare as covered by the prohibition against 'any work'.[26] On the other hand the Pharisee halakha allowed defensive war on the Sabbath, as I Maccabees did. The very definition of I Maccabees as Sadducee and II Maccabees as Pharisee is fundamentally dubious.[27] Some have explained that the author of II Maccabees, who was a Diaspora Jew, suppressed the matter of permission to fight on the Sabbath in order not to provide an argument against the right of the Jewish soldiers in the Hellenistic armies to be exempt from military duties on the Sabbath.[28] Others are of the opinion that the author of I Maccabees represents a strict sectarian view

[23] On the II Maccabees version of the episode see p. 491 below. Josephus' report in *Ant.* 12.272–6 is only an explanatory paraphrase of I Maccabees, and is not based on any other source. It merely shows that Josephus assumed that a defensive war was permitted only from Mattathias' time on.

[24] See below, p. 493. Described by many scholars as 'devout' (Hasidim; by comparing I Macc. 2.29 with 7.12–13), their exact sectarian affiliation is still unknown.

[25] Geiger 1875: 217ff.

[26] See esp. Kugler 1922: 246; Efron 1980: 25.

[27] See Büchler 1906: 341; Kugler 1922; 345–6; Gutberlet 1927: 7–8; Bévenot 1931: 7; Pfeifer 1949: 491,515; Churgin 1949: 191 n. 3; Hengel 1973: 178–9; Efron 1980: 25–6. (See further in detail p. 571 below on the belief in resurrection.)

[28] See Büchler 1906, followed by Efron 1980: 38 n. 55.

which refused to recognize the halakhic regulation which, in the accepted
opinion, Mattathias and his company initiated. Recently there had been
a tendency to assume that the author of II Maccabees, too, permitted
defensive war on the Sabbath, and consequently an attempt has been made
to harmonize the two sources, and to explain that II Maccabees refers to
military activity that does not involve any saving of life (פיקוח נפש) or the
like.[29]

A separate survey of each episode shows that it is impossible to prove that
II Maccabees objects to fighting defensive war on the Sabbath. On the
other hand, the harmonization of the historical events in the two sources
is extremely contrived, and unacceptable to anyone familiar with the
characteristics and sources of information of the two books. Consequently
there is cumulative importance in the presence of stringent references to
the Sabbath in II Maccabees, and that in itself indicates, at first glance,
a difference in the halakhic approach of the two authors. Moreover, no
positive evidence has been cited as yet to show that the author of II
Maccabees does approve defensive war. We shall therefore attempt below
to examine the various episodes in II Maccabees where the Sabbath is
mentioned, paying special attention to the question of the historical
credibility of the information, and to the literary and didactic purposes of
the author. A combined study of this kind may throw light on the halakhic
question.

The first mention of the Sabbath in II Maccabees appears in the report
on the Mysian commander's incursion into Jerusalem. The author states
that Apollonius 'introduced himself as having peaceful intentions and
waited until the holy day of the Sabbath, and finding the Jews abstaining
from work, he ordered his men to (array for a) review, and all who came
out for the show he put to the sword. Then charging into the city with his
armed men, he killed a great multitude' (5.25–6). I Maccabees says that
the Seleucid commander did 'speak peaceful words in deceit' to the Jews,
and took advantage of their trust in him to make a surprise attack on the
city (1.29–30), but not that this took place on the Sabbath. The version in
II Maccabees fits in perfectly with the Jewish version in *Antiquitates* of
Ptolemy I's entrance into Jerusalem. As stated above in regard to the
Ptolemy I episode, it only indicates that defensive war on the Sabbath was
not forbidden, and this is the view of the author as well, for otherwise
Apollonius would not have needed to employ deceit and peaceful words.
That the Jews did not suspect him of any hostile intention, and therefore
did not carry arms, is proved by the fact that some of them went out of the
city to view the military parade. As to the essence of the historical event,
the author of II Maccabees may very well have dated the event on the
Sabbath in order to stress the wickedness and treachery of the enemy (see
in greater detail below in the discussion of Nicanor's disaster and death at
Adasa).[30]

[29] Esp. Herr 1961: 242–56.
[30] On the question of the source for II Maccabees' version and its connection with the
version of I Maccabees, see p. 202 n. 18 above.

The description in II Maccabees of Judas Maccabaeus' campaign against Nicanor and Gorgias tells that the pursuit of the enemy was discontinued because the Sabbath had begun (8.25–8). The parallel version in I Maccabees on the battle of Ammaus (4.14–25) makes no mention of the Sabbath, and the interruption of the pursuit is explained by the need to confront Gorgias' select detachment which was returning from its searches in the mountain region. No pursuit of Gorgias himself was undertaken, and the Jewish force set about looting the camp. In order to explain the discrepancies between the two sources, it has been claimed that the pursuit took place on the eve of the Sabbath, and the approach of the Sabbath was just an additional reason for abandoning it. As to the halakhic question, the explanation given was that pursuit does not constitute self-defence, and was therefore prohibited on the Sabbath.

From the historical viewpoint, no weight should be given to the reason II Maccabees proffers for the termination of the pursuit. The I Maccabees description of the course of the campaign is vastly more reliable than that of II Maccabees, and everything points to its being based on the author's personal observation. It describes at length, with careful topographical indications as well as a detailed timetable, the progress on both sides, while the II Maccabees version is 'general' and vague, and could be adapted to any arena. Moreover, I Maccabees elaborates on the pursuit itself, its direction and special circumstances, which are not mentioned at all in II Maccabees. And especially, the reasons I Maccabees gives for the suspension of the pursuit are well anchored in the various phases of the campaign in general, and derive from them. In contrast, the artificiality of II Maccabees' incorporation of the Sabbath into the historical nucleus of the story is very obvious: the assertion that the pursuit was called off 'because they were short of time, for it was the Sabbath eve' (8.25–6) does not fit in with the subsequent verse telling of the collection of arms and the onslaught on the spoils after the pursuit ('And after having collected the enemy's weapons and stripped the booty they occupied themselves welcoming the Sabbath', 8.27). Warriors compelled to stop a pursuit of the enemy because the Sabbath was approaching would certainly have refrained from collecting spoils and plundering just then.

There is no utility in the various attempts at harmonization, such as suggesting the possibility that the battle took place on a Friday, and the approach of the Sabbath was also taken into account when the pursuit was interrupted.[31] An omission in connection with such a crucial matter in I Maccabees does not fit with its attention to detail as regards the course of the battle in general, and the timetable and the pursuit in particular. It is hard to conceive of a reason that could have led the author to delete such

[31] See Herr 1961: 244 n. 11; Oppenheimer 1976: 36. Objection must be made as well to the comments of Goren (1958: 162), indicating that the abortive pursuit was aimed at merchants and not enemy soldiers. The pursuit in I Maccabees involved the entire army, and a pursuit of civilian merchants was superfluous, and in any case would have been rather short.

a point. What was noted above regarding the incongruity in II Maccabees between the termination of the pursuit because of the Sabbath, and the subsequent plundering of the camp is even more valid as regards the harmonization of the sources: I Maccabees related clearly that Judas Maccabaeus and his men looted the camp very thoroughly immediately after Gorgias' departure from the battlefield (4.23). And if it is argued that it was the same embarrassing difficulty which led the author of I Maccabees to delete the matter of the Sabbath, it should be remembered that looting on the Sabbath, or even very close to the start of the Sabbath, does not accord with the religious fanaticism of the Jewish soldiers as demonstrated in the ceremony the evening before the battle (3.46–60) and on other occasions. The author himself reports gleefully on the looting, and there is no intimation that he is in the least disturbed by it. And finally, the detailed timetable cited by I Maccabees makes it impossible to believe that the interruption of the pursuit had any connection with the Sabbath: the raid of the camp at Ammaus began at dawn, the camp fled in a panic, and the pursuit which covered a distance of seven to ten kilometres was stopped in order to confront Gorgias. All the operations had to end in the early morning.

The absolute superiority of I Maccabees in the description of the campaign, the impossibility of harmonizing the sources, and especially the obvious grafting of the Sabbath onto the episode of the pursuit and plundering in II Maccabees, show that the incorporation of the Sabbath into the episode is merely the product of Jason of Cyrene's literary imagination. Like the other additions and elaborations in II Maccabees, the incorporation of the Sabbath is to be explained in the light of the literary–artistic tendencies and the religious–didactic purpose of the book. The author describes the persecutions and the Revolt in two stages: at the outset of the persecutions, the Jews are in a state of despair and hopelessness; they suffer torture and torment but they do not counter-attack, while the enemy has boundless strength. As happens in tragedy, there is the sudden dramatic turning point (*metabolē*) when the hero, Judas Maccabaeus, appears in the arena and the initiative passes to him. The turning point is given ethico–religious justifications which serve the general didactic purposes. The changed situation is explained by the suffering of the martyrs on the one hand, and on the other by the good deeds of the warriors and the enormous care they took to preserve the sanctity of the precepts and the Sabbath; by their suffering the martyrs atoned for the sins of the people, appeased the ire of God, and impelled Him to shed once again His grace on His people (7.38).[32] After the torments of the martyrs, beginning in ch. 8 in which

---

[32] Cf. also Niese 1900: 5; Zeitlin 1952: 51ff.; Nickelsburg 1971: 523; Efron 1980: 54–6. Regarding the sin see also 4.16–17, 5.17–19, 6.12–17, 7.18,32,35, 10.4. In I Maccabees, on the other hand, it is the destruction of the wicked by Judas Maccabaeus that appeases God's wrath (3.8), which corresponds to the 'active' approach of the author. Despite some superficial resemblance to the Songs of Yahweh's Slave in Isaiah (esp. ch. 53), I am not sure that the author of II Maccabees was influenced by the Bible in this matter, and it is more likely that

Judas Maccabaeus also starts his military activity, 'the Lord's anger changed to mercy' (8.5; and cf. 8.27). The Lord's goodwill was reinforced then by the great righteousness and noble qualities of the combatants, indicated by their interruption of the pursuit toward the start of the Sabbath, and by their distribution of the spoils first of all to the wounded and then to widows and orphans (8.28). The influence of the fighters' behaviour on the change that took place in the situation is explicitly stressed in the last verse of the story and chapter: 'And the man [Nicanor], who had undertaken to settle the tribute to the Romans by the captivity of the inhabitants of Jerusalem, declared that the Jews had a champion (= ὑπέρμαχον) and were therefore invulnerable, because they adhered to the laws given by him' (8.36). In assessing the credibility of the information, it must be reiterated that Jason of Cyrene does not hesitate to add elements from his fertile imagination in order to serve his religious–didactic and literary–artistic ends. As an adherent of the Pathetic school, he is of the opinion that all these, along with the readers 'pleasure', are more important than pure historical truth.[33]

Thus the pursuit episode does not prove that II Maccabees opposes defensive war on the Sabbath. But is it possible to deduce from the episode that pursuit on the Sabbath was forbidden, or that II Maccabees reflects some sectarian strictness, or perhaps that the author was not familiar with the halakha regulation on pursuit, and simply derived the point by analogy with other Sabbath strictures? None of these possibilities is very reasonable. In the military conditions of the time, giving up a pursuit in the heat of the battle imperilled the outcome of the confrontation, for the enemy (especially cavalry units) could reform and counter-attack. On a battlefield like that of Ammaus, for instance, such a termination could have resulted in the total annihilation of the Jewish force which was not yet capable of fighting on level ground, and based its plan on a raid and surprise attack on the complacent camp. At any rate, there is no evidence that pursuit on the Sabbath was ever forbidden. The other restrictions known from the sources do not concern us here, for they apply to activities which are not carried out in the heat of the battle.[34] As to the possibility that this was an extremist sectarian restriction, before attributing strict views and meticulous compliance to Jason of Cyrene, we should examine his position on other more basic halakhic questions. As appears from the story of the 'Succot celebration' in the Temple and the list of 'the species' (10.6–7), from the imaginative description of the ill treatment of Nicanor's body in the Temple

the themes of self-sacrifice and martyrdom to atone for sins in his book originated in Greek tragedy and tradition. See the summary of material on the 'atoning sacrifice' in Greek culture in Hengel 1981: 19–28. See also Musurillo 1954: 236ff.; Kellermann 1978: 46ff.

[33] For the effect of the author's literary and religious conception see also pp. 354–6 above and pp. 491–2 below.

[34] It should be noted that the II Maccabees description of the battle of Marisa (12.38) does not deal with the cessation of the pursuit, as suggested by Herr 1961: 244, but with flight and debriefing after defeat, as becomes clear from a comparison with I Macc. 5.60–2. On that episode cf. pp. 50–3 above.

(15.30–5), and from the absence of any critical comment on the very presence of Gentiles in the Temple (3.13–40, 14.31ff.), the author had very little knowledge of the halakha current in Eretz Israel, and especially little in matters of defilement and purity which characterized the various strict sects.[35] His careless reference to the plundering after the interruption of the pursuit does not help us to view him as a conscientious representative of a strict sect. And finally, Jason's residence in Cyrene, where there was a considerable concentration of Jewish military settlers, eliminates the possibility that he was not familiar with the practice in regard to pursuit. The military settlers in Cyrene must have had a clear and accepted code on questions connected with fighting on the Sabbath.

The mention of the righteousness and charity of the Jewish fighters next to the pursuit episode, immediately after the Sabbath was over (II Macc. 8.28), and the motivation noted above for explaining the interruption of the pursuit by the start of the Sabbath, lead to the conviction that the author was well aware of the permission to fight on the Sabbath, and even to engage in a pursuit. His sole purpose was to present Judas Maccabaeus' men as conforming to the precepts more strictly than required, to the extent that they were ready to jeopardize the outcome of the battle. Thus the author explains even more emphatically the change that took place in the Divine attitude to His people, and provides an additional reason for his frequent open intervention in the future in the course of the events and battles themselves.

Another episode connected with the question of defensive war on the Sabbath is the story of Judas Maccabaeus' second confrontation with the governor Nicanor which ended in the great victory at Adasa. II Maccabees relates that Nicanor actually intended to attack Judas Maccabaeus and his men in their concentrations 'in Samaria' on the Sabbath, and that even his Jewish supporters attempted in vain to deter him. However, 'he did not succeed in carrying out his cruel plan' (15.1–5). I Maccabees makes not the slightest mention of such a matter (7.39ff.).

As with the pursuit episode at Ammaus, II Maccabees' mention of the Sabbath in connection with the decisive battle against Nicanor has no informational value. It is impossible to harmonize his version with that of I Maccabees: the latter indicates that the initiative in the battle was Judas Maccabaeus', and that the battlefield was not the Samarian Hills, but Adasa in Judaea, in the mountain plateau near the eastern end of the Beth Horon road. The I Maccabees version is to be preferred in regard to this battle as well. Although his account is not as detailed as the one on the Ammaus campaign, the author provides topographical information on the enemy movements before and during the battle, and in the course of the retreat, while the II Maccabees version is divorced from any geographic

---

[35] For further details see pp. 371–2 above. II Macc. 12.38 is not contradictory evidence: purification before the onset of the Sabbath was not a custom of a particular sect, nor peculiar to Eretz Israel. On the halakhic background see Alon 1977: 203–4.

background (even of Samaria), does not include real military actions, is anachronistic with regard to the Seleucid deployment and replete with prayers, dreams, miracles and epiphanies.[36] Had the planning and timing of the campaign been connected with the Sabbath, the author of I Maccabees would not have failed to mention that, as he did in regard to Bacchides in his war against Jonathan (9.34,43-4).

The story in II Maccabees of the campaign against Nicanor does not adequately clarify the author's position on Sabbath war. The text does not state whether or not the battle took place on the Sabbath, but just that Nicanor did not succeed in 'carrying out his evil plan' (15.5). The author's meaning can be interpreted in two ways:

(a) Defensive war on the Sabbath was forbidden. Nicanor wanted to take advantage of that, but for one reason or another did not manage to attack the Jews on that day, perhaps because of Divine Providence which prevented him from doing so, and the battle took place on a weekday.

(b) Defensive war on the Sabbath was not forbidden. Nicanor wished to take advantage merely of the Jews' well-known reluctance to carry weapons on the Sabbath when there was no imminent danger, and to launch a surprise attack. His plan was discovered, and Nicanor was not able to surprise the Jews, who were ready for battle and counter-attack on the Sabbath.

The second interpretation is supported by some precision in the wording of the verse. Further on we are told that Judas Maccabaeus decided not 'to remain in camp',[37] that is, not to remain inactive, but to 'charge manfully and clash with all their strength and decide the issue' (15.17). As previous battle descriptions in II Maccabees say nothing about a stationary stage, or about any qualms regarding the timing or conduct of the battle, the intention of the verse can only be to point out that Judas Maccabaeus did not recoil from a clash, despite the Sabbath. The lack of clarity in regard to the time of the battle can be blamed on the epitomist's careless work.

As noted above, the incorporation of the Sabbath into the episode is no more than a literary device. Just as in the case of the Sabbath in the Ammaus pursuit, it can be explained by the motives and nature of the book. Nicanor's downfall, and in particular his punishment after death, are described extensively in accordance with the 'pathetic' Hellenistic literary tradition favoured by the readers of the time. The author believes in tit for tat and loses no opportunity to illustrate that theological principle (in some

[36] See pp. 361, 363 above.

[37] According to the context, it is clear that the wording of Lucian, στρατοπεδεύεσθαι (= to camp), is preferable to στρατεύεσθαι (= to set forth to battle) that appears in the rest of the manuscripts. This is also the view of Abel 1949: 475; Katz 1960: 24; Habicht 1976a: 278, against Hanhart who chose the reading στρατεύεσθαι in his edition of II Maccabees (1959: 113). Despite Hanhart's detailed explanation, I do not see any essential difference required by the structure and contents of the verse between 'not to set forth to battle' on the one hand, and 'assault bravely' and 'wage war with all might' on the other.

measure also a poetic device of the 'tragic' school he belonged to), which in his opinion governed the world.[38] He therefore had to justify and explain Nicanor's bitter end. That was why he inserted the episode of Razis' horrible martyr's death shortly before the battle against Nicanor (14.37–46). That episode resembles the description of the agony of the martyrs in chapters 6 and 7, which among other things provides an introduction and explanation for the miserable death of Antiochus Epiphanes (9.5–18,28–9; see in particular verse 28: 'in suffering the most horrible things as he did to others'). Nicanor's 'evil plan' adds an important element to his adverse characterization and thus justifies his harsh punishment. It underlines more sharply his arrogance, wickedness and treachery, traits which were somewhat blurred as a result of the 'artistic balance' of his personality during negotiations with the rebels (II Macc. 14.13–28).[39] The author stresses that aside from his earlier evil deeds, especially his threats against the Temple and audacity toward heaven (14.33–6), the Seleucid commander employed unfair tactics in the campaign itself by seeking to exploit the Jews' abstention from bearing arms on the Sabbath when not under attack, and their diminished vigilance owing to the sanctity of the day. The plot attributed to Nicanor also provides the author with a further opportunity to mention Nicanor's sin of pride and his denigration of the God and holy things of Israel (15.4–5). It is noteworthy that the author explains the terrible punishment of Antiochus Epiphanes as well by his pride and his defiance of the God of the Jews (9.8,10,12), which resembles Nicanor's haughty talk. These two traits, the *hybris* and *theomakhia*, characterize the tragic hero, as they do some biblical figures.[40]

In conclusion, it is worth considering the version in II Maccabees of the story of the fugitives in the cave. It accounts for their death in slightly different words from I Maccabees: 'because of refraining (διὰ τὸ εὐλαβῶς ἔχειν) from helping themselves in accordance with the fame of the most holy day' (6.11). The wording does not indicate that the author is opposed to defensive war on the Sabbath: the phrase εὐλαβῶς ἔχειν actually means refraining from carrying out a particular activity because of excess piety and reverence. The epithet εὐλαβής in the Septuagint and New Testament also means *ḥasid*, 'devout', 'partisan', 'admiring', etc. Refraining from self-defence on the Sabbath in the eyes of the author was therefore perhaps an exceptionally pious approach and not the standard one. However, various scholars noting that the author does not refer at all to the reaction of Mattathias and his comrades to the story, concluded that the author opposed defensive war on the Sabbath. But it was already pointed out that for some literary reasons Mattathias' deeds and accomplishments (and even his name) were omitted in II Maccabees,[41] so there is little wonder his reaction to the episode does not figure in the book. It is necessary to add what can be deduced from the ideological and artistic framework of the

[38] See 4.16, 26, 38, 5.9–10, 8.34–5, 9.6–10, 10.35–6, 13.8, 15.32–3.
[39] See pp. 355–6 above.   [40] See p. 176 above.   [41] See pp. 197–9 above.

book: the episode appears in II Maccabees as part of a series of acts of
arbitrary brutality on the part of the authorities and martyriological sacrifice on the part of the Jews, which reached their climax in the story of the
mother and her seven sons. Mentioning the reaction of the 'activists'
would not fit in with the book's characterization of Jewish policy and
conduct (up to the turning point in ch. 8), which stresses the passivity and
suffering of the Jews, with not the slightest hint of any active resistance or
acts of provocation.

Summary

The military activity of the Jews and their involvement in political affairs
in Eretz Israel and the Diaspora during the period preceding the Hasmonaean Revolt makes it difficult to believe that the problem of self-defence
on the Sabbath arose only with the religious persecutions, and that no
practical regulations were developed before that. A critical comparative
examination of Agatharchides' account of the conquest of Jerusalem by
Ptolemy I does not prove that, and the Jewish source incorporated in
Antiquitates even shows that Ptolemy did in fact expect the Jews to defend
themselves on the Sabbath. What was actually forbidden was to bear arms
when the danger was not in sight and imminent. I Maccabees does not say
that the fugitives who fled to the desert refrained from defending themselves
because of a prohibition against fighting on the Sabbath, but because they
wanted to sacrifice themselves as martyrs. The first part of Mattathias'
reaction does not refer to the general question of defence on the Sabbath,
and the second can be explained in the light of the dilemma with regard to
fighting in special circumstances when the enemy is trying to force the
desecration of the Sabbath or may intend to ridicule the logic or sincerity
of Sabbath-observers within the overall policy of religious coercion.

The various statements of II Maccabees do not indicate a stricter
approach, and one or two of them even imply that self-defence on the
Sabbath was acceptable to the author. The restrictions mentioned in later
sources, such as the prohibition against transporting or bearing arms on the
Sabbath, or against interfering with the enemy's preparations to lay siege,
do not indicate any quandary regarding self-defence itself. In our own time
as well, when observant orthodox young Israelis have no doubt about the
permission and even obligation to carry out military duties on the Sabbath,
doubts and hesitations still arise regarding certain activities in various
circumstances.[42] The only source that reports doubt and uncertainty about
the principle is Josephus in the story of the scouts of Asinaeus the Babylonian

[42] On the hesitations see, e.g., the interview with an Orthodox company commander,
reported in the Israeli popular newspaper *Ma'ariv*, in the *Yāmīm we-Lēylōt Supplement* of 21
October 1977, p. 40: 'If I have any doubt about the crucial necessity of the patrol, and if it
would indeed justify desecrating the Sabbath, I instruct one of the platoon commanders [i.e.
the non-orthodox [B.B.]] to go with the company and I do not.' Such a practice does not
accord with the directives of the Chief Military Rabbinate. See Rabbi S. Min ha-Har 1973:
139.

(*Ant.* 18.322).[43] However, no proof can be cited from the hesitations of weavers in a distant Diaspora who joined a social revolutionary movement and had never before taken part in political and military affairs, and were faced with an unexpected situation. In any case, those events transpired after there was in Eretz Israel, as everybody agrees, no question about the right to defend oneself on the Sabbath, as indeed was clear also to the leader of the rebels in Babylonia, who instantly reacted accordingly (ibid. 323). Nor is there any sense in drawing halakhic conclusions from later writings of marginal, fanatic and ascetic sects, [44] who adopted strange and extremist restrictions in other areas as well, such as a prohibition against sexual intercourse and defecation on the Sabbath, and on weekdays within Jerusalem.[45] We would not after all venture to conclude from such sources that normative Judaism or its mainstreams ever had any doubts about such day-to-day functions.

[43] On Josephus' sources for this special affair and the background see Schalit 1965: 163–88; N. G. Cohen 1976: 30–7.

[44] The statement in Jubilee 50.12 is itself rather hazy, and might be interpreted as referring to offensive warfare, but the strict tone of the passage as a whole makes it more likely that the author is prohibiting warfare of any kind.

[45] See Jubilee, especially 50.8 (lying with a woman), and the corresponding passage in the Scroll of the Damascus Covenant, especially 11.16–17 (forbidding the rescue of a person who has fallen into a well or pool on the Sabbath). On the prohibition of evacuating and copulating in Jerusalem according to the Temple Scroll (45.11–12,17–18) see Yadin 1978: 1.218,223–4,228–35. *Bell.* 2.147 notes that the Essenes refrained from moving their bowels on the Sabbath. See also Alon 1977: 190–234; Herr 1980: 175 n. 83.

G

The ceremony at Mizpah and the chapter on '(the Priest) Anointed for Battle' in the mishnaic tractate Sotah

On the eve of the battle of Ammaus, as the Jewish force gathered at Mizpah, a religious ceremony was conducted there which included fasting and lamentation, precepts connected with the Temple and also practices of purely military significance such as the appointment of commanders and the granting of leaves (I Macc. 3.46–60). The account of the ceremony at Mizpah is the most detailed of all the descriptions of preparations for war in the historiographical literature of the period of the Second Temple. Consequently an attempt has been made to compare it with the reporting for war in the chapter on '(the Priest) Anointed for Battle' (משוח מלחמה) in the tractate Sotah (ch. 8), which is based on Deuteronomy 20.1–9, and to learn from this comparison something about the history of the halakha in general, and about the historical sources of the mishnaic rulings on war in particular.

Some of the activities carried out at Mizpah were peculiar to the circumstances and are not mentioned in the mishnaic chapter. The fasting, accompanied by practices like tearing garments and putting on sackcloth, was declared in order to lament the destruction of the city, the defilement of the Temple, and the profanation of the Torah scrolls. The display of the Nazirites, the priestly vestments, the first fruits and the tithes, were aimed at reminding those present of the day-to-day meaning of enemy rule in Jerusalem. Most of these accord with the later halakha reflected in the Mishnah.[1] The granting of releases, however, to those who were building houses, or who had plighted their troth and planted vineyards, as well as to 'the faint-hearted' (3.56), is somewhat surprising. According to the halakha, releases are granted only in an offensive war outside the borders of the Holy Land and do not apply to an offensive war within it or to a defensive operation anywhere (Sotah 8.7).[2] Since the battle of Ammaus was

---

[1] See in detail above, pp. 251–6. On the early halakha reflected in the display of the tithes at Mizpah see p. 254 above.

[2] According to the more acceptable comment of Rav'a in the Babylonian Talmud (Sotah 44b), this was the majority opinion (ḥakāmīm) in contrast to that of Rabbi Yehuda. But according to the explanation of Rav Ḥisd'a in the Palestinian Talmud (Sotah 8.9[23a]), Rabbi Yehuda thinks that there are no exemptions in a defensive war. The attempts to harmonize the two Talmuds are unsatisfactory; contrary to Alon 1959: 2.41; Lieberman 1973: 696; Ben-Shalom 1980: 222,300–1.

undoubtedly in the latter category, it has been suggested that in the Hasmonaean period the halakhic distinction between מלחמת מצוה ('war of [religious] duty') or חובה (= obligation) and מלחמת הרשות (= a war of free will) did not yet exist, and that the rules for exemption specified in the Torah were interpreted for, and applied to, all kinds of war.[3]

However, an examination of the course of the battle shows that the episode cannot indicate that the basic distinction evolved later. The classification and selection were made first of all for practical military reasons, and not halakhic ones. Judas Maccabaeus was preparing to embark upon a long night march of 27 km along a narrow hilly trail to the Seleucid camp at Ammaus, and make a surprise attack at dawn. The participation of too many soldiers would hinder progress and lead to the discovery of the task force by enemy patrols.[4] Judas Maccabaeus therefore had to reduce the size of the large army at his disposal. For that purpose he could have applied better criteria, but he preferred those of Deuteronomy as likely to contribute to morale by recalling the nation's glorious past and laws, just as he preferred to collect the army in Mizpah, although he could have found hills that provided a better view and closer and faster access to the Seleucid camp at Ammaus.[5]

The impression that the selection made on the eve of the battle was a result of the special circumstances of the campaign, and not of halakhic rulings, is supported by the fact that there is not the slightest hint of such exemptions in the other battles conducted by Judas Maccabaeus and his brothers, although the preparatory stage for a number of them is described in relative detail (I Macc. 3.15–23, 4.28–33, 5.16–20, 9.5–10, 13.1–11, 16.1–4). The absence of accounts of a ceremony like the one at Mizpah on the eves of other battles is no excuse: the fasting and carrying out of the precepts connected with the Temple were by nature unique and had no place before the major battles, most of which took place after the purification of the Temple. However, if the exemptions applied to any kind of war, they would have had to be carried out before each battle. In any case, the large number of soldiers in the simultaneous expeditions and confrontations after the purification of the Temple[6] obviated the possibility of exemptions of the type noted (for their wide application see Sotah 8.2–5; *Tosefta* Sotah 7.18–24). The description of the battle of Elasa even tells of the desertion of Jewish soldiers when the camps reported (I Macc. 9.6). Although there is considerable exaggeration in the story of the desertion,[7] it indicates that the command did not willingly and officially release the 'frightened and faint-hearted' as required in Deuteronomy.

The Scroll of the War of the Sons of Light, too, backs up the assumption of the antiquity of the distinction between the types of war in regard to exemptions. In the course of a description of preparations for the war which

---

[3] E.g. Baer 1952: 7; Yadin 1962: 67–70.
[4] See pp. 257, 261–2 above.
[5] P. 251 above.
[6] See pp. 48f. above.
[7] Pp. 48–9, 62, 388–90 above.

can certainly not be defined as a 'war of free will',[8] the Scroll (10[14].2–4) quotes the words of the priest about the rules of war from Deuteronomy (20.3–4), though it fails to mention releases for the betrothed and those building houses or planting vineyards. The release of the 'faint-hearted' mentioned soon thereafter (10[14].5–6) was no doubt effected in practical consideration of the likelihood that the damage they could do to the morale of their comrades would be greater than any contribution they might make (cf. Deut. 20.8). It is hard to accept Yadin's hypothesis that other releases are not mentioned because they were arranged earlier, in the preliminary muster of the forces, while the Scroll describes only the actual deployment stage.[9] If indeed the members of the Judaean Desert Sect understood the Pentateuch literally, as Yadin asserts, arguing that therefore they did not distinguish between wars of various types,[10] they would have had to relate the granting of the releases and the list of exemptions right after the priest's address in the same order as the Pentateuch (Deutr. 20.2–8).[11] At the same time it must be admitted that the assumption regarding the antiquity of the distinction between a 'war of obligation' and one of 'free will' still lacks decisive proof, even though it is hard to assume that the exigencies of daily life had no effect even in the early days of the Second Temple. Unfortunately, even the Temple Scroll does not illuminate this point (pp. 58–9,62).

Although there is no contradiction between the exemption rules in the Mishnah and the releases granted at Mizpah, and despite a general correspondence between most of the other actions taken on that occasion and the later halakha, no conclusion can be drawn as to the antiquity of the 'Anointed for Battle' chapter. Isaac F. Baer, in one of his important methodological articles on the relation between halakha and reality early in the period of the Second Temple, suggests that most of that chapter is a 'relic' from the days of Judas Maccabaeus, and preserves the war practices initiated by him. These 'regulations' are expressed chiefly in the ceremony at Mizpah.[12] As evidence, Baer proffers a number of parallels between the statements in the Mishnah and details of the ceremony, the activities of Judas Maccabaeus in other battles, and the method of warfare and military milieu of the period.

The similarities between the preparations described in the Mishnah and the ceremony at Mizpah (the granting of releases, the exhortatory oration,[13] etc.) are quite superficial and derive from reliance on the same source in

[8] For a definition of the type of war in the Scroll see Yadin 1962: 65,67.
[9] Ibid. 67–70, esp. 70.   [10] Ibid. 64,65.
[11] On the theoretical character and later dating of the Tosefta distinction between the ceremony בספר (= on the border), and the oration במערכי מלחמה (= in the battle deployment), see p. 258 n. 117 above.
[12] Baer 1952: 1–55. On this matter see pp. 7–8; cf. id. 1956: 60; and Albeck 1958: 228; Urbach 1984: 12.
[13] On the necessity of associating the exhortatory oration (I Macc. 3.58–60) with the ceremony at Mizpah and not with the temporary encampment south of Ammaus see p. 258 above.

Deuteronomy (20.1–9). The differences, however, are striking and fundamental: the ceremony at Mizpah did not involve the Priest 'Anointed for Battle'[14] who plays a central role in the preparations described in the Mishnah and makes the exhortatory oration, and it is Judas Maccabaeus himself who delivers it; the historical references to victories over famous heroes in biblical times which figure in the oration in the Mishnah (Goliath, Shobach: ibid. 8.1) are not identical with those in Judas Maccabaeus', and the same holds true for other points in the oration. The similarity in the general structure of the two orations (see especially I Macc. 4.30–3) is because both are sermonizing paraphrases of the priest's speech in the Pentateuch; the task of announcing the releases is assigned to the 'policemen' according to the Mishnah (44–5), while at Mizpah 'policemen' are not mentioned, and Judas Maccabaeus himself talks to those eligible (I Macc. 3.56); the Mishnah describes at length the coercive measures used by the policemen (8.6), but these are absent from the ceremony at Mizpah. Baer does point out the mention of 'the policemen'[15] who spurred on the soldiers during Judas Maccabaeus' expedition to Transjordania (I Macc. 5.41) and the sentence being carried out on the αὐτομολήσασι (= compliers; Baer erroneously translates as 'deserters')[16] after Alcimus and Bacchides arrived in the country (I Macc. 7.24). However, the 'policemen' there deal not with malingerers but with soldiers having a natural desire to stop and rest a while in the middle of an exhausting campaign and march, and the punitive action during Alcimus' high priesthood (which in any case is not said to have been carried out by 'policemen') was not against deserters from the battlefield but against civilians who supported Alcimus. Be that as it may, there is no mention even in the description of the battle of Elasa (I Macc. 9.5–10) of coercive actions to prevent shirking in the course of preparations in the field while watching the enemy deploying. On the other hand, the Mishnah does not elaborate on the division into officers over thousands, hundreds, fifties and tens (I Macc. 3.55), but says only 'and they shall appoint captains of the hosts at the head of the people' (8.6); furthermore in I Maccabees the appointment of officers precedes the granting of releases, while in the Mishnah the police measures, including the screening of the soldiers, comes first. Above all, the granting of releases on the eve of the Ammaus battle was, as noted above, a deviant case which evolved from the special conditions and requirements of the operation,

[14] The Priest 'Anointed for Battle' is not the high priest (*BT* Sotah 42a) and not identical with the commander of the forces. Eleazar, the brother of Judas Maccabaeus mentioned in II Macc. 8.23, does not carry out the functions of that priest.

[15] The word γραμματεῖς (literally 'scribes') should be thus reconstructed, as is usual in the Septuagint. The word does appear there in its literal meaning as well, to translate the Hebrew *sofrīm*, and is also known to have applied in the Hellenistic administration to various functionaries in the financial field including military finance, but there is no doubt of the proposed reconstruction in the present context. For the meaning of the term in the Hellenistic kingdoms see Schulthess in *RE* s.v. Γραμματεῖς, cols 1777ff.

[16] The expression ἐν αὐτομολήσασι stands for the Hebrew במשלימים ('compliers') and not בעריקים ('deserters') as Baer believes: see p. 59 n. 102 above.

while most of the other battles occasioned a maximal mobilization dictated
by the gravity of the situation, as is usual in a defensive war. A considerable
proportion of the Mishnah passage is devoted to defining those exempt
from serving. Would 'Judas Maccabaeus' regulations' (as Baer terms the
chapter in the Mishnah) have concentrated in the main on a development
that was unusual and anomalous for the period?

The military milieu described in the Mishnah is not supportive of setting
the regulations in Judas Maccabaeus' time: some of the returnees 'repair
the roads' (8.2), a task which does not fit in with the duties and needs of
an army of rebels, and even runs counter to them, and indicates an orderly,
independent political existence; 'the clashing of shields (*trīsīn*) and the
rubbing (noise) of tramping shoes (*šif'at ha-qalgasīn*)' (8.1) do not reflect
Hellenistic military equipment and terminology: according to the Mishnah,
these are mentioned by the priest 'Anointed for Battle' who encourages the
combatants facing the enemy's equipment and vocal effects on the battlefield. The *trīs* is the *thyreos*, which denotes either the oblong shield or the
scutum, the rectangular cylindrical shield of the Roman legions in the
Imperial Period. The characteristic shield of the Hellenistic army was the
round one carried by the phalangites. The oblong shield and the *scutum*
were used only by the semi-heavy mercenaries and the Seleucid 'Roman'
Guard contingent respectively. All these comprised less than a third of the
Seleucid infantry in the generation of the Hasmonaean Revolt.[17] Anyhow,
the long phalangite pikes were certainly more frightening and impressive,
and the priest would certainly have mentioned them if the enemy described
was Hellenistic. The word *qalgasīn* cannot be explained by the Greek
klageros or *klanktos* ('scream'), as Baer suggests on the basis of the Levy
dictionary.[18] They do not allow *šif'at* (i.e. *šifat* 'rubbing') any reasonable
meaning in that construction,[19] and in any case further on in the mishnaic
passage there is a reference to battle cries ('neither be ye frightened at the
sound of the yells'). The origin of the word, as already proposed, is *caliga*,
the hobnailed sandal of the Roman legionnaire.[20] So there is no doubt that
the Mishnah refers to the equipment of the Roman legions.

The 'Anointed for Battle' chapter is halakhic Midrash for the war
regulations in Deuteronomy.[21] It includes intimations of an early distinction
according to which releases from military duty were not granted in all
cases, but the exact definition of the distinction had been blurred, and was
in dispute. Most of the chapter consists of interpretations based on knowledge of the practices of the Roman army, together with theoretical rulings
and the dissenting views of Rabbi Akiva and his disciples. The theoretical

[17] See the table p. 117 above.
[18] J. Levy 1876–84: 4.306.
[19] For the reading *šīfat* and the meaning of *šīfat ha-qalgasīn* see also Albeck 1958: 389. Cf.
pp. 331–2 above re verse 41.
[20] Krauss 1898–9: 2.418; Jastrow 1886–1903: 2.1372; A. Kohut 1878–92: 7.97; and see
also Epstein 1957: 43.
[21] On the question of the relationship between it and the *Sifri* see Epstein 1957: loc.cit.

character is obvious in the description of coercive measures to prevent running away: 'they placed guards in front of them and others behind them, and they had axes of iron in their hands, and if anyone sought to turn back, he was empowered to cripple his legs' (8.6). Most of the chapter has no parallel even in the Scroll of the War of the Sons of Light,[22] which does not facilitate its dating to a period prior to the destruction of the Second Temple.

[22] The Scroll does not mention the Priest 'Anointed for Battle'; the oration assigned to 'the chief priest' (10[14].2–16) includes very little in common with the chapter the 'Anointed for Battle', and there is no sign of the coercive measures for preventing desertion which are mentioned in the Mishnah. On the other hand, the Mishnah lacks a number of the components of the ceremonial deployment for battle which appear in the Scroll of the War of the Sons of Light, first and foremost the bugles and their function (7[12].11ff.; cf. I Macc. 3.54) and the blessing of the priests and elders (13[17].1–20). On the absence of the Priest 'Anointed for Battle' in the Scroll see also Yadin 1962: 210–12.

H

The Babylonian Jews and the Galatians

In the II Maccabees version of Judas Maccabaeus' battle oration at
Ammaus in the campaign against Ptolemy, son to Dorymenes, and Gorgias,
the speaker refers to great victories in the nation's past against foes much
greater in number than the Jewish force, such as occurred with Sennacherib's famous expedition and in the battle of the Babylonian Jews against
the Galatians. The latter reference, which is not known from other sources,
is worthy of special attention. Since we are not oversupplied with data on
the Jews of Babylonia during the Hellenistic period, every crumb of information acquires added importance. Moreover, this information, if confirmed and set against its proper historical background, can supplement the
various sources on the early military tradition in the Jewish Diaspora. As
repeatedly noted above, there is no doubt that this particular speech was
not made by Judas Maccabaeus and, like the other orations in the Books
of the Maccabees, reflects only the views of the author. That does not mean,
however, that the historical references in the speeches should be denigrated.

Regarding the war against the Galatians, the author says (8.20):

καὶ τὴν ἐν τῇ Βαβυλωνίᾳ τὴν πρὸς τοὺς Γαλάτας παράταξιν γενομένην, ὡς
οἱ πάντες ἐπὶ τὴν χρείαν ἦλθον ὀκτακισχίλιοι σὺν Μακεδόσι τετρακισ-
χιλίοις—τῶν Μακεδόνων ἀπορουμένων οἱ ὀκτακισχίλιοι τὰς δώδεκα μυριάδας
ἀπώλεσαν διὰ τὴν γενομένην αὐτοῖς ἀπ' οὐρανοῦ βοήθειαν καὶ
ὠφέλειαν πολλὴν ἔλαβον.

(= And the war in Babylonia against the Galatians, how all of them as they
went forth to battle (numbered) eight thousand together with four thousand
Macedonians, and when the Macedonians lost (or: were helpless) the eight
thousand struck the hundred and twenty thousand thanks to the help they
had from Heaven and took great booty.)

We learn from this of a campaign in Babylonia in which 8,000 Jews and
4,000 Macedonians fought 120,000 Galatians. While the Macedonians
were losing, the Jews succeeded in beating the superior foe.[1]

[1] Although II Maccabees does not explicitly indicate that the 8,000 warriors were Jews,
there is no doubt that is what he meant (against Wellhausen 1905: 137). The structure of
verses 19 and 20 shows definitely that the two examples refer to Jewish armies. Verse 19 begins

Attempts have generally been made to connect the information in II Macabees with Antiochus I's celebrated campaign against the Galatians, known as the 'elephant victory'[2] (273 B.C.[3]), but it is impossible to transfer the latter episode from its natural background near the Ionian cities of western Asia Minor. Although Lucian, the only source describing that battle (*Zeuxis* 8–11) says nothing of the site, and sources from the Roman period report only that the battle was conducted in 'Asia'[4] (referring perhaps to the boundaries of the Roman province of Asia), there are clear indications that it did take place in western Asia Minor. Thus the proclamation of the city of Ilium during the reign of Antiochus I noting that the king crossed the Taurus and saved 'the cities' (*OGIS* 219, ll. 11–15) apparently refers to that same campaign.[5] The fact is that the Galatian invasion of Asia Minor six years earlier was disastrous for the old Ionian cities, as quite a number of epigraphic sources indicate, and the campaign was designed to save those cities; to help finance the war, the king levied the 'Gallic tax' on them.[6] It is not impossible that Babylonian Jews serving in the Seleucid army took part in the 'elephant victory' as a Babylonian chronicle reports the despatch of reinforcements from Babylonia before the battle,[7] although the reference may be to garrison troops stationed in Babylonia. II Maccabees, however, deals with a battle in Babylonia itself, and not outside it. The textual correction proposed by Isidor Lévy – Βαγαδαονίᾳ (between Lycaonia and Cappadocia on the way to the Taurus mountains)[8] – does not help to identify the campaign under consideration with the 'elephant victory' because that region is too far from the Ionian cities.

with τὰς ἐπὶ τῶν προγόνων (= on what happened to preceding generations) and is immediately followed by two examples, one being τὴν ἐπὶ Σενναχηρειμ (= the (campaign) against Sennacheri[b]) and the second being καὶ τὴν ἐν τῇ Βαβυλωνίᾳ...παράταξιν (= and the campaign...in Babylonia). Furthermore, in II Maccabees 'help from Heaven' is never granted to Gentiles, and in any case it is not reasonable to suppose that the author of II Maccabees would insert an episode demonstrating the bravery of Gentiles (Seleucids!) in an oration on the eve of a battle against the Seleucid enemy. The epitomist may have neglected to stress the Jewishness of the 8,000.

[2] Moffatt 1913: 1.142 n. 20; Abel 1949: 390; I. Lévy 1950: 681ff.; Edson 1958: 168; Hengel 1973: 29, among others.

[3] On the chronology of the 'elephant victory' see details in Bar-Kochva 1973a: 3–5. That article, however, contains an unfortunate mistake in regard to the absolute chronology of the First Syrian War. It should read (p. 5): 'The "elephant victory" is to be dated shortly after April 273: the Egyptian invasion was repelled some time in the year 38 of the Seleucid era, before the reinforcements were despatched in the month of Adar, i.e. between April 274 and March 273; the elephants were sent from Babylonia in March 273 and the Babylonian troops a month later; the rebellion may have been put down in that month and followed immediately by the expedition against the Galatians.'

[4] Appian, *Syr.* 65; Memnon 11.3–4 (*FGrH* IIIB, no. 434, p. 436); Pompeius Trogus, *Prologi* 25.

[5] See Tarn 1926: 157ff. Perhaps the expression σωτὴρ τοῦ δήμου (= the saviour of the *dēmos*) in the inscription (ibid. ll. 37–8) should be connected with the title of Soter (= the saviour) bestowed on the king after the 'elephant victory'.

[6] For a summary of the episode and a detailed bibliography on it see Will 1979: 1.124–5. On the tax see Welles 1934: no. 15, l. 28, and p. 81; *OGIS* 223, l. 29 and passim.

[7] See Smith 1907: 156, ll. 11–13.   [8] I. Lévy 1950: 681ff.

In an article on this specific subject Arnaldo Momigliano suggested that the II Maccabees passage reflects a campaign against the Galatians during the reign of Antiochus III, between 197 (the year that Antiochus invaded Media in Momigliano's opinion) and the battle of Magnesia in 190 B.C.[9] The assumption that there was a battle between Antiochus III and the Galatians is based on the Suda entry for Simonides:

Σιμωνίδης Μάγνης Σιπύλου, ἐποποιός. γέγονεν ἐπὶ ᾿Αντιόχου τοῦ Μεγάλου κληθέντος, καὶ γέγραφε τὰς ᾿Αντιόχου τοῦ Μεγάλου πράξεις καὶ τὴν πρὸς Γαλάτας μάχην, ὅτε μετὰ τῶν ἐλεφάντων τὴν ἵππον αὐτῶν ἔφθειρεν.

(= Simonides of Magnesia on Mt Sipulum, a poet. Lived in the reign of Antiochus called the Great, and also wrote of the deeds of Antiochus the Great and of the war against the Galatians in which with the help of elephants he overcame their cavalry force.) Since Antiochus III was accorded the epithet 'the Great' after his anabasis to the East (see, e.g., Appian, *Syr.* 1(1), etc.), the Suda evidently refers to that king. The chronology proposed by Momigliano is based on the analysis of an elegy, found on an Alexandrian papyrus, in which a Hellenistic king whose name is not given expresses his disappointment at the failure of negotiations with the Galatians, stating that he will put an end to the insurrection of 'the Galatian' just as he subdued the Medes.[10] The battle with the Galatians thus took place after the defeat of the Medes, which occurred in Momigliano's view in 197 B.C., and it is logical to date it before the battle of Magnesia in which Antiochus III lost control of Asia Minor, the seat of the Galatians.

There is no doubt, however, that although the Suda refers to the king who defeated the Galatians as 'Antiochus the Great', the reference is to Antiochus I and not Antiochus III. The mention of the 'elephant victory' over the Galatian cavalry, described in detail by Lucian in his treatment of the 'elephant victory' of Antiochus I, eliminates any possibility of ascribing the episode to Antiochus III. Although Lucian's description is definitely rhetorical in character and not distinguished for accuracy,[11] his attribution of Antiochus I's celebrated victory over the Galatians to the elephants can be believed: the episode is recorded on the Myrina terracotta from that period,[12] and the Babylonian chronicle mentioned above stresses the despatch of twenty elephants from Bactria to the aid of Antiochus I some time before the campaign against the Galatians, while according to Lucian sixteen elephants actually took part in the battle.[13] Momigliano's proposal, that the Suda's mention of 'elephant victory' is just a gloss inserted by an

[9] Momigliano 1929–30: 151–6.
[10] See the elegy in von Wilamovitz-Moellendorff 1918: 736–9; Powell 1925: 131–2.
[11] On the character of Lucian's description see Tarn 1926: 157ff.; Bevan 1902: 1.143; Droysen 1877–8: 1.167 n. 168; Stählin 1907: 12 n. 2; Wernsdorff 1744: 41–4. But see Bar-Kochva 1973a: 2–3.
[12] See Pl. XIIIb and the bibliography in the caption.
[13] Smith 1907: 156, l. 12; Lucian, *Zeuxis* 9; and see Tarn 1926: 157ff.; contrary to Otto 1928: 23 n. 4.

editor familiar with Lucian's version, might be entertained if we had any information on a campaign of Antiochus III's against the Galatians. But the various sources for the period of that king, which generally provide quite comprehensive coverage, do not contain the slightest hint of any military action of his against the Galatians, and even if there was a clash that did not survive in the sources, it could not have been of large dimensions and would certainly not have been noted by Simonides as the outstanding accomplishment of Antiochus III, who was the most vigorous and active of the Seleucid kings (with the possible exception of Seleucus I). The Suda's epithet 'the Great' can be considered as one of those applied to Antiochus I, for in the Babylonian chronicle of the Seleucid kings published by Sachs and Wiseman (British Museum no. 35 603) both Antiochus I and Antiochus II are described as 'the great king',[14] while no other Seleucid monarch is so described, not even Antiochus III. That epithet was applied to Antiochus I in addition to Soter and Callinicus, because of his military achievements.[15] But even if 'the Great' was confined to Antiochus III and Simonides wrote in that king's time, he could very well have recorded the event of Antiochus I's war against the Galatians which occurred three generations previously, for it had left a deep impression on Greek civilization for decades and occupied a central place in the art of Pergamum, most of which dates from the beginning of the second century. The epithet 'the Great' could also have been applied mistakenly in the Suda to the Antiochus who defeated the Galatians, in the wake of the reference to Antiochus III with whom Simonides was contemporary.[16] Moreover, only one manuscript calls the king who defeated the Galatians 'the Great'. The Suda refers in any case to the 'elephant victory' of Antiochus I.

As to the elegy which serves as the basis for Momigliano's suggestion, in addition to the absence of a reference to any confrontation of Antiochus III with the Galatians, Momigliano's assertion that in 197 B.C. Antiochus III defeated the Medes is not supported by any evidence. On the contrary: we have definite information of the king's presence north of the Taurus during that year. Furthermore, Antiochus III did not engage in any war in Media except the war against Molon (220 B.C.), and even that campaign was aimed mainly at the military settlers (see Polybius 5.54.8), most of whom were of Greco-Macedonian descent,[17] and not against native Medes as the elegy indicates.[18] The elegy should be connected with Antiochus I's war against the Galatians. To my mind it reflects the negotiations con-

---

[14] Sachs and Wiseman 1954: 206; cf. Aymard 1955: 106.

[15] On the title Callinicus see Lucian, *Zeuxis* 11; on the title 'Soter' see Niese 1893–1903: 2. 71 n. 1; Bouché-Leclercq 1913: 1.65; Head 1911: 639.

[16] In the opinion of Wernsdorff 1744: 41; Niese 1893–1903: 2.80 n. 4.

[17] See Griffith 1935: 150; Bar-Kochva 1979: 32–5.

[18] Appian, *Syr.* 1.1, reporting the expeditions to Media and Parthia, is referring to the 'anabasis' of 210–206 B.C. directed against the Parthians and Bactrians and their allies, the Tapurians and the Hyrcanians, but not the Medes (on this venture see Polybius 10.28–31,48–9).

ducted by Antiochus I with the Galatian invaders in the throes of his siege
of one of the rebel cities in Seleucis, the stronghold of the Macedonian
military settlers in northern Syria, not long before the 'elephant victory'.[19]
By 'defeat of the Medes' the king apparently means the subjugation of
the Upper Satrapies which was effected during his co-regency with his
father, Seleucus I,[20] or perhaps various revolts in those regions during his
own independent reign, which led to the reinforcement of the Greek elements in the region through the establishment of Antioch in Persis and
other *apoikiai* (see *OGIS* 233,. ll. 14ff.). In any case, to turn to the verse in II
Maccabees, a Galatian invasion of Babylonia between 197 and 190 B.C. is
not tenable in view of the solid position of the Seleucid kingdom in Asia
Minor, the Galatian base, and its great stability in other districts, including
Babylonia, at that time.

It seems to me that the information in II Maccabees should be connected
with the second stage of the 'War of the Brothers' between the legitimate
king, Seleucus II Callinicus, and his brother Antiochus Hierax (229/8
B.C.),[21] who benefited from Galatian help.[22] A 'stratagem' by Polyaenus
(4.17), apparently taken from Phylarchus,[23] describes Hierax's attempted
invasion of Babylonia:

Antiochus Hierax: when he revolted against his brother Seleucus,
Antiochus fled to Mesopotamia. *En route*, in the mountains of
Armenia,[24] he was (hospitably) received by Arsamenes, an old friend.
Seleucus' commanders (στρατηγοί), Achaeus and Andromachus,
pursued him with a large force, and a great battle took place. Finally,
after Antiochus was wounded, he escaped to the foot of the mountains
overlooking (the area) (εἰς τὴν ὑπερκειμένην ὑπώρειαν) while his army
camped on the plain (ἐν ὁμαλεῖ) between the ridges (ὑπὸ ταῖς λαγόσι
τοῦ ὄρους). He spread the rumour that Antiochus had been killed and
ordered quite a large part of his army to seize the foothills at night.
At dawn Antiochus' soldiers sent Phileteiron, the Cretan commander,

[19] For details see Bar-Kochva 1973a: 7–8.
[20] On rebellions in those regions see, e.g., Polyaenus 7.39–40; on the background of the
affair see Eddy 1961: 75ff.; Schmitt 1964: 46–51; von Gutschmid 1888: 27–8; Altheim
1947–8: 1.272ff.
[21] On the chronology and background see Will 1979: 1.298, and the bibliography there.
The sources are Pompeius Trogus, *Prologi* 27; Justin 27.2.10,3.1,5; Eusebius (Schoene ed.), vol.
I, p. 251, l. 19; *OGIS* 269,271,274,275,280; *Inscr. Perg.* no. 247; Plutarch, *De frat. amor.* 18(489);
Phylarchus, fr. 30 (*FHG* I, p. 341); Polyaenus 4.9.6. And see Stählin 1907: 18–29.
[22] See also Bar-Kochva 1973: 6–7; id. 1977b: 55–61.
[23] That is the view of Melber (1885: 640); although he lived in the second century,
Polyaenus quite accurately preserved information from primary sources. On his value in
general see ibid. 415ff.
[24] That is the way the Greek ὅθεν καὶ τοὺς μὲν Ἀρμενίων ὄρους διελθόντα...should be
understood. Seleucus' commanders confronted Hierax when he attempted to invade Mesopotamia, not when he withdrew from there; see Pompeius Trogus, *Prologi* 27. Cf. a similar
reconstruction in Droysen 1877–8: 3.304–5; Niese 1893–1903: 1.159; Bevan 1902: 1.202;
Beloch 1924–27: 4(1).685.

and Dionysius of Lysimachea as envoys to request the body of
Antiochus by agreement (ὑπόσπονδον), (promising) to give up
themselves and their arms. Andromachus said that Antiochus' body
had not yet turned up, and it was necessary to look (for Antiochus)
dead or (to bring him captive) in chains. He also said he would send
a force to accept the arms and soldiers (who were surrendering).
There set forth four thousand men who were not ready for battle but
(only) prepared to accept captives. When they reached (the plain)
between the mountain ridges (ὑπὸ ταῖς λαγόσι τοῦ ὄρους), those who
had previously seized the foothills (τὰς ὑπωρείας) 'flooded'
(ἐπιχυθέντες) them from above and did great slaughter among them.
And Antiochus took his royal robe, appeared and presented himself
not only alive but also victorious.

If we sum up the essence of the passage, the purport seems to be that
Antiochus Hierax, after being defeated by Attalus I, tried to surprise his
brother Seleucus by invading Mesopotamia via Armenia. In a hard battle
between Hierax and the Seleucid commanders Achaeus and his son Andromachus which apparently took place in northern Mesopotamia, at first
Hierax was defeated and took to the nearby mountains, but shortly
after succeeded in trapping four thousand enemy soldiers in his mountain
refuge by means of an unfair trick. Although the nationality of Hierax's
soldiers is not specified, there is little doubt that the Galatians who were the
backbone of his army accompanied him on that adventure as well.[25] The
numerical similarity of the 4,000 soldiers trapped by Hierax, according to
Polyaenus, and the 4,000 Macedonians defeated by the Galatians according
to II Maccabees, is striking, and it may be said that only during the
Brothers' War did the Galatians have both the opportunity and a reason to
invade Babylonia. The discrepancies between the two sources are not
crucial or unbridgeable: according to Polyaenus, the battle was conducted
in two stages, the imperial forces winning in the first, and Hierax succeeding
in capturing 4,000 soldiers in the second; the inference from II Maccabees
is that there was just one battle in which at first the Macedonians were
defeated and later the Jews were victorious. But the II Maccabees version
does not necessarily refer to incidents in the same battle, and may combine
some that took place at different times in the same campaign. The author or
the epitomist who was not familiar with details of the events may have
changed the order, and the victory ascribed to the Jews actually could have
taken place before the entrapment of the 4,000 Macedonians. But it is even
more logical to suppose that by the reference to the victory of the Jews, II
Maccabees meant a later clash with the Galatians that took place after the
capture of the 4,000 soldiers. And indeed a decisive battle conducted in
Babylonia, in which Antiochus Hierax was defeated and forced to flee to

[25] So also Droysen 1877–8: 3.305.

Cappadocia, is mentioned by Pompeius Trogus (*Prologi* 27) and Justin (27.3.7). As Seleucus II was then occupied east of the Tigris,[26] there were no large armies stationed in Babylonia, a situation which must have tempted Hierax not to content himself with the capture of the 4,000 men but to go on advancing into the heart of Mesopotamia. Being a collector of stratagems, interested only in military exploits, Polyaenus ignores later developments which did not involve any unusual tactics, and thus did not report the later battle in which Babylonian Jews took part. For the same reason he says nothing about the nationality of the units concerned. Furthermore, it should be remembered that in dealing with this stratagem, Polyaenus abridged and abbreviated his sources, as is shown by his concise wording and the large number of participial forms.

As to the inflation of the Galatian numbers, the crediting of the Jews alone with the victory, and the designation of the 4,000 defeated soldiers exclusively as Macedonians (which is hardly likely considering that the king and the imperial army were engaged in the Upper Satrapies), none of these detract from the overall historical credibility of the testimony of II Maccabees. As reiterated above, the author does his best to demonstrate divine intervention in events, as the conclusion of this very verse shows ('thanks to the help they had from Heaven'), and it is natural for a military victory in which Babylonian Jews took part to be attributed to the Jews alone. Nor can a fair and accurate report of the relative sizes of the opposing forces be expected in a speech that Judas Maccabaeus is supposed to have made on the eve of a battle in which the Jews were definitely numerically inferior. In this context the term 'Macedonians' refers to the Seleucid army as such, as was customary in the Jewish literature of the late Hellenistic period.[27]

If my hypothesis is accepted, the verse in question can be added to the sources reporting the participation of Babylonian Jews in foreign armies, first and foremost Antiochus III's letter on the transfer of Jewish soldiers from Babylonia to Phrygia and Lydia (Jos. *Ant.* 12.147–53; cf. 17.24ff.).[28] This hypothesis also helps to refute the usual assumption that Jews began to serve in Hellenistic armies only after the revolt of Judas Maccabaeus when the Hellenistic kings had become aware of their military gifts.[29] Jews served in both the Seleucid empire and Ptolemaic Egypt as individuals and in their own units long before the Hasmonaeans appeared.[30] As to the credibility of II Maccabees in regard to external knowledge and the extensive information imparted, these need no further proof. Yet the

[26] Thus Beloch 1922–7: 4(1). 685 n. 1. It should be noted that the summary of Agatharchides' account preserved in Josephus (*Ap.* 1.206) implies that the revolt of Stratonice in Antioch erupted while Seleucus was *en route* to the east, which facilitated Hierax's invasion. A number of scholars have sought to date the revolt in the stormy reign of Seleucus II, but that is a matter of dispute.

[27] Thus Abel 1949: 390; Edson 1958: 163ff.

[28] On the letter and the question of its authenticity cf. p. 85 n. 49 above.

[29] See, e.g., Tcherikover 1973: 32–5; Launey 1949–50: 1.150.

[30] See p. 85 n. 47 above.

preservation of an event connected with the Jewish community in Babylonia by a Jewish writer residing in remote Cyrene is quite astonishing. The connections among the various Jewish Diasporas (and not just those of each with Jerusalem) were apparently closer than has habitually been recognized, unless Jason of Cyrene got this information from a Jerusalem source.

I

The geographical background and chronological sequence of the clashes with Timotheus in the Second Book of the Maccabees

The Books of the Maccabees report several confrontations between Judas Maccabaeus and a military commander named Timotheus. In the I Maccabees description of the expeditions Judas Maccabaeus conducted to rescue the Jews of Transjordania, Timotheus is the leader of the enemy camp defeated three times by the Jews. The first campaign, to Ammanitis, is described only briefly: Judas Maccabaeus defeated Timotheus, conquered Iazer, and returned to Judaea (5.6–8). In the second expedition, to Gilead (Galaaditis), the Jewish commander made a surprise assault on Timotheus' men, who were besieging the 'fortress' (apparently Dathema, see 5.9–13) and threw them into a panic (5.29–34). After Timotheus reorganized his forces, another clash between the sides took place near Karnayim; Timotheus' army was defeated, his men took refuge in Karnayim, and Judas Maccabaeus conquered the place (5.36–45). Timotheus is mentioned in three separate places in II Maccabees as well. He first appears together with a commander named Bacchides in an episode that became interposed in the description of the battle against Nicanor and Gorgias, that is, the battle of Ammaus (8.30–3). According to the text, the battle ended with a decisive victory, the death of one of the enemy sub-commanders, the capture of forts, and the distribution of spoils and their transfer to Jerusalem. The second episode comes later, after the report on the purification of the Temple (10.24–38): Timotheus gathered some mercenaries and 'Asian horses' in order to conquer Judaea (10.24), Judas Maccabaeus prayed 'before the altar' and set out to meet the foe 'very far from the city' (10.27). With the help of an epiphany he won the battle, and Timotheus fled to the fortress of Gazara (10.32). After a siege of twenty-four days the fortress fell, and Timotheus was put to death (10.33–7). The third instance occurs within the description of the rescue expeditions that Judas Maccabaeus conducted throughout Eretz Israel (12.10–25): after a series of conquests, including a victory over Timotheus' men in a 'fort' (12.17,19), a big battle is fought with Timotheus near Karnion (12.21–3) which ends with Judas Maccabaeus as the decisive victor. Timotheus is released from captivity on his promise to exert his influence to liberate Jewish hostages, and subsequently the Jews besiege Karnion and take it (12.24–6).

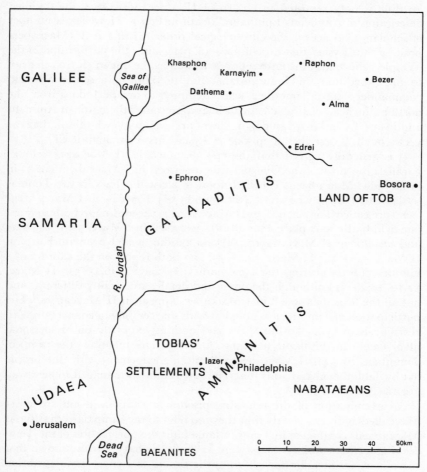

21 Judas Maccabaeus' expeditions in Transjordania

Many scholars have asserted that the three episodes in II Maccabees refer to Judas Maccabaeus' expeditions in eastern Transjordania, and that the episode on the battle against Timotheus and Bacchides was mistakenly inserted into ch. 8.[1] There is no disputing the fact that the last episode is out of place. It is artificially inserted between the story of the battle against Gorgias and Nicanor and its outcome (8.8–29) and the report on Nicanor's personal fate (8.34–6), and it contains a hint of Judas Maccabaeus' rule over Jerusalem (8.31), while the conquest of Jerusalem by the religious

---

[1] This is also the view of Grimm 1857: 143; Ewald 1864–8: 4.406; Büchler 1906: 323–4; Laqueur 1904: 74–7; Wellhausen 1905: 137–8; Kolbe 1926: 130ff.; Bickerman 1937: 149; Abel 1949: 394–5; J. Regner in *RE* s.v. 'Timotheos' (8), cols 1330–1.

loyalists is only reported in ch. 10 of II Maccabees, after the detailed description of Antiochus Epiphanes' death in Persia. However, a number of scholars who accept the chronological order existing in II Maccabees positing that Lysias' first expedition took place after the purification of the Temple believe that the latter episode as well as the one in ch. 10 refer not to the expeditions in Transjordania but to those of a senior Seleucid commander named Timotheus who attempted to invade Judaea from the north at the head of a royal expeditionary force after the battle at Ammaus and before Lysias' first campaign. There are even some who think that the verses in ch. 8 describe an episode in Lysias' first campaign itself.[2]

It is generally agreed that the episode noted in II Maccabees ch. 12 parallels the story of the Gilead battle described in I Maccabees ch. 5: in both Judas Maccabaeus is called upon to assist the Jews in the Toubias settlements ('those who are in [the country of] Toubias' in I Macc. 5.13; 'who are called Toubiaēnoi' in II Macc. 12.17); according to both sources, one field battle took place near a 'fort' (okhyrōma in I Macc. 5.29; okhyrōma and kharaka[3] in II Macc. 12.17, 19) and another near Karnayim-Karnion (I Macc. 5.37–44; II Macc. 12.21–5), and both report on the capture of a number of forts bearing the same names (I Macc. 5.36,45–51; II Macc. 12.12–18,26–31) although the order and details are slightly different, and not all the forts mentioned in I Maccabees appear in II Maccabees.[4] The participation of Timotheus is noted in both sources only in connection with Karnion-Karnayim. I Maccabees says nothing explicitly on his personal involvement in the battle near the 'fort' but does mention 'the camp of Timotheus' (5.34). II Maccabees tells of an engagement with 'the people left by Timotheus' and adds that Timotheus himself managed to get away (12.18–19).

An examination of the relevant episodes in chapters 8 and 10 of II Maccabees indicates clearly that they too refer to the campaigns that Judas Maccabaeus conducted in Transjordania after the purification of the Temple. Let us first consider the passage in ch. 8. We have already shown that there is no justification for rejecting the timing of Lysias' first expedition whereby it took place before the conquest of Jerusalem and the purification of the Temple, as described in I Maccabees.[5] According to II Maccabees, the confrontation with Timotheus and Bacchides took place when Jeru-

[2] Niese 1900: 55; Ed. Meyer 1921: 2.208; Kugler 1922: 361ff.; Cahana 1957: 2.205–6; Bunge 1971: 280ff.

[3] The proposal of Abel, Avi-Yonah and others, that kharaka is a place-name must be rejected. The word, whose original and usual meaning is a protective wall for a camp or field deployment (vallum) or a siege wall (circumvallum), also sometimes means (in the wake of the Aramaic) a fortress, a fortified city, and the like. See M. Streck in RE s.v. 'Charax', Suppl. I, col. 288; Robert 1963: 79. In all manuscripts, the word is preceded by an article, showing that it is not a place-name. In II Macc. 12.19 the battle was joined at the okhyrōma (fort), and similarly in the parallel I Maccabees passage (5.29). On the identification of the fort with Dathema, see p. 83 above n. 42.

[4] On the reason for the great detail of II Maccabees in the story of the battle of Kaspin (12.13–16) see p. 513 below. [5] See pp. 276–82 above.

salem was already in the hands of the rebels. That battle would then be after Lysias' first expedition. Even if we ignore the matter of the timing of Lysias' first expedition, the great resemblance between the episode in II Maccabees 8.30–3 and the clashes with Timotheus in Transjordania after the purification of the Temple is obvious: Timotheus is mentioned in both I Maccabees 5 and II Maccabees 12 as commander of the various ethnic troops that Judas Maccabaeus fought against in Gilead after the purification of the Temple; the enemy casualty total, 'more than twenty thousand men' (II Macc. 8.30), is reminiscent of the exaggerated toll II Maccabees attributed to the Gilead campaign (12.19,23,26,28); and in particular, there is mention of 'fortresses' (II Macc. 8.30) which characterized that campaign (I Macc. 5.5,9,27,29,46; II Macc. 12.19,21,27) and does not fit in with the repulsion of an attempted invasion by the royal army in the Judaean Hills. According to ch. 8 of II Maccabees, Timotheus himself was not killed in the battle, which is what is stated in ch. 12 too, and in ch. 5 of I Maccabees (contrary to ch. 10 of II Maccabees; see below), And finally, in I Maccabees the conclusion of the Gilead campaign was marked by a festive return to the Temple, by rejoicing and sacrifice (5.54), and in ch. 12 of II Maccabees by the celebration of the Feast of Weeks (31–2). This is also stated in II Maccabees: 'and when they celebrated the victory in the city of the forefathers...' (8.33). Other special festive ceremonies after victory are mentioned in both books only after the purification of the Temple (Hanukkah) and the battle of Adasa (Nicanor Day).

Some scholars have argued that the word *phylarkhēs* (literally 'tribal head'), applied in II Maccabees 8 to one of the commanders in Timotheus' army (verse 32), means 'commander of the cavalry' and therefore refers to a royal army which arrived from Syria.[6] That title has such a meaning only in Classical Athens, referring to the cavalry commander of each of the Athenian *phylai* (Herodotus 5.69; Aristotle, *Ath. Pol.* 61.5). During the Hellenistic period, however, it has the literal meaning, and is applied to Arab sheikhs and the like, which fits in with the composition of Timotheus' army in the Transjordania campaigns, and with the forces that cooperated with him (I Macc. 5.4,6,39; II Macc. 12.10–11). According to the context and the structure of the sentence it may also be the name of one of the sub-commanders in Timotheus' camp.[7]

It thus appears that the passage in II Maccabees 8.30–3 is a summing up of Judas Maccabaeus' accomplishments in the Gilead campaign which are described in detail in ch. 12. The mention of a commander named Bacchides together with Timotheus (and presumably Phylarches) is to be explained by the relatively numerous particulars on the participants in the episode (among them the Jewish sub-commanders, 12.19, 24) in Jason of Cyrene's book (cf. below on Timotheus' brothers in II Macc. 10.37).[8] The insertion

---

[6] Herzfeld 1863: 2.269; Bunge 1971: 280 n. 158; Th. Fischer 1980: 63.

[7] So Grimm 1857: 144; and see esp. Richnow 1968: 121.

[8] Abel (1949: 394) believes the name Bacchides was injected into the episode from the military campaigns conducted by Bacchides, 'governor in the (region) across the river', early

of the passage into the description of the battle of Ammaus should not be
explained simply as a scribal error for, according to the book, word of
Timotheus' defeat reached Antiochus Epiphanes on the eve of his death
(9.3) and the passage in ch. 10 presents Timotheus as having been previously defeated by the Jews (verse 24), obviously referring to the episode
in ch. 8. It seems therefore that the story of the war against Timotheus was
drawn into ch. 8 because of its similarity to the II Maccabees version of the
battle of Ammaus: both tell of the division of the spoils and their equal
distribution to the wounded, to widows, and to orphans (8.28,30), and in
both the plundering was stopped, at Ammaus because the Sabbath was
approaching (8.26), and in the battle against Timotheus because the Feast
of Weeks (12.31) was approaching and it was necessary to go up to Jerusalem (8.31,33). Presumably Jason of Cyrene combined these passages in
order to stress that the lofty qualities of the Jewish soldiers, and their
strictness in observing the precepts which led to the drastic change in events
beginning with the battle of Ammaus,[9] were discernible in other battles as
well. For that purpose he here summarized the episode of the war in Gilead
described at greater length and in greater detail later in his book, emphasizing the qualities noted. Associative writing of this kind is not alien to
the author of the book.[10] The epitomist, failing to understand the author's
intention, added the notice of Timotheus' defeat to the bad news communicated to Antiochus Epiphanes in Persia, and in reporting the first clash
with Timotheus explained that he 'had previously been beaten by the
Jews' (10.24). The didactic purpose and associative character of the
insertion were somewhat masked by the epitomization, which gives the
impression that the passage just reports the military confrontation which
immediately followed the battle against Gorgias and Nicanor.

The passage in ch. 10 of II Maccabees should be connected with Judas
Maccabaeus' campaign against Timotheus in Ammonite territory (I Macc.
5.6–8), the first of the three confrontations with Timotheus or his army. It
was undertaken after he was already in control of Jerusalem (II Macc.
10.26–7), that is, after the purification of the Temple. Timotheus fled to the
fortress of Gazara, which Judas Maccabaeus then besieged. As many
scholars have already determined, that fortress obviously should not be
identified with Gezer in the Judaean shephela, which fell only in Simeon's
reign (I Macc. 13.43–8), but rather with Transjordanian Iazer which
according to I Maccabees (5.8) was conquered right after Timotheus' first
defeat on the battlefield in Ammanitis.[11] The proposed identification follows
also from the synchronization of the events in the two books: in I Maccabees
the campaign to Ammanitis and conquest of Iazer preceded the expedition
to Gilead and the conquest of Karnayim, while the last expedition is

in the reign of Demetrius I (I Macc. 7.8–20 and 9.1ff). He thinks that the figure of Bacchides
became a symbol for hostile deeds (cf. Jos. *Bell.* 1.35). This explanation seems dubious in view
of the detail given by Jason on the enemy commanders.   [9] See pp. 487–9 above.
[10] See p. 541 n. 80 below on II Macc. 5.7–10, 13.4–8.
[11] See Wellhausen 1905: 141; Abel 1949: 415, among others.

described in II Maccabees 12. Thus Timotheus' earlier campaign which ch. 10 of II Maccabees reports is the expedition to Ammanitis and the conquest of Iazer.

It is true that the end of the episode in ch. 10 speaks of the death of Timotheus, which made scholars conclude that there was a mix-up in the order of the chapters, and that the sequence of the episodes should be changed, or that there were two people named Timotheus, but we should give greater weight to the remarkable correspondence with I Maccabees. The author of II Maccabees may have believed for one reason or another that the Timotheus who opposed Judas Maccabaeus at Iazer was not the same commander who fought him at Karnion. It is even more likely that the 'slaying' of Timotheus in that chapter had literary and didactic motives: the author aspires to enrich and vary the narrative and in each case show that the wicked received the penalty they deserved. Since he reported before that on the blasphemy which Timotheus' men heaped on God (10.34,36), the reader next expects the harsh punishment that fits the sin. The inclusion of blasphemy in this episode derives from the author's utilization of the dramatic devices of tragedy.[12] The need to vary the description and the desire to incorporate 'tragic' motifs such as blasphemy is especially obvious in the pathetic, pictorial description of the campaign against the town of Kaspin in the Gilead venture (12.14) which has no parallel in the I Maccabees version of the same expedition (5.36). The listing of the names of Timotheus' brothers (II Macc. 10.37) shows that Jason of Cyrene elaborated on the fate of the enemy commanders, and eliminates the possibility that the report on Timotheus being 'put to death' originates in an epitomist's mistake. Substantively, it is hard to accept the hypothesis that the two episodes deal with two different people. If that were so, a statement to that effect would certainly figure in I Maccabees which in several adjacent verses tells of two campaigns and three separate clashes with Timotheus' men. Timotheus was apparently the Seleucid *stratēgos* in the meridarchy of Gilead (Galaaditis), and should perhaps be identified with the man mentioned in the list of *stratēgoi* in the area (II Macc. 12.2).[13] Hence his involvement in all the conflicts of Transjordania.

II Maccabees does ascribe to Timotheus the intention of conquering Judaea (10.24), but it must be remembered that the geographical background was not clear either to the author or the epitomist. The lack of familiarity with the material connected with Transjordania is obvious from the vague location of the battle in question 'far from the city' (10.27), in the confusion of the geographical order in the Gilead campaign (II Macc. 12.13–21 *versus* I Macc. 5.28–37), and in the location of the war against Arab tribes in Transjordania at a distance of nine *stadia* (1.7 km) from

[12] On the ascription of the derision of God to the wicked and to enemies of Israel, in accordance with the 'tragic' design of II Maccabees, cf. p. 176 above, and see the references in n. 73. See there too on the special punishment of the 'blasphemers', in particular Antiochus Epiphanes and Nicanor.

[13] For the identification of Timotheus see also Rappaport 1980: 264.

Iamnia (II Macc. 12.10–12).[14] At the same time it is not impossible that
Gazara, mentioned by II Maccabees as Timotheus' place of refuge (10.32),
which as we have said is a garble of Transjordanian Iazer (I Macc. 5.8),
misled the author into thinking about Gezer in the Judaean shephela and
consequently to describe the affair as an attempt by Timotheus to conquer
the Land of Judaea.

As for Timotheus' troops, the mercenaries mentioned (II Macc. 10.24)
do not indicate a campaign by a royal army. I Maccabees too mentions
mercenaries working with Timotheus (though in the Gilead campaign, I
Macc. 5.39). Nor is the participation of 'Asian horses' (II Macc. 10.24) any
proof of the royal character of the campaign.[15] The best war horses of the
period were imported from Media, or at least were of Median stock,[16] and
all the author wants to say is that Timotheus had at his disposal real war
horses. There is no reason to suppose that horses of this breed were not
available to the militia of the eastern Transjordanian cities and to other
local elements.

To sum up, the passage in II Maccabees 10.24–38 parallels I Maccabees
5.6–7, and describes Judas Maccabaeus' expedition to Ammanitis and his
clash with Timotheus near Iazer, shortly after the purification of the
Temple. The passage in II Maccabees 12.10–31 describes the second expedition to Transjordania, which focused mainly on northern Gilead, and
parallels I Maccabees 5.24–54. The separation and distance between the
two descriptions in II Maccabees occurred because of the mistaken location
in the book of the battle of Beth Zur at a time after the death of Antiochus
Epiphanes and the purification of the Temple. The passage in II Maccabees
8.30–3 is a summary of the Gilead campaign, referred to by Jason of Cyrene
in the course of his description of the battle of Ammaus in order to stress

[14] It may well be that the epitomist, not Jason of Cyrene, is responsible for this latter error,
for he states in the same passage (12.9) that Jerusalem is 240 *stadia* (*ca.* 45 km) from maritime
Iamnia and that a fire lit in the Iamnia harbour could be seen in Jerusalem. Some episode
connected with another place was deleted between verses 9 and 10, and the distance of nine
stadia applied to that place. The reference to the fire being visible in Jerusalem shows what a
vague idea of the geography of Eretz Israel Jason of Cyrene had. The straight-line distance
between Jerusalem and Iamnia harbour is 55 km, but the road distance was twice as long as
the 240 *stadia* estimated by II Maccabees. Further on the book says that Beth Shean is 300
stadia (57 km) from Jerusalem (in reality, at least 105 km) which confirms the above conclusion.
[15] The translation of τοὺς τῆς Ἀσίας γενομένους ἵππους should be 'Asian horses' and not
'Asian cavalry' as some commentators propose (e.g., Grimm 1857: 162; Bunge 1971: 283). In
the Septuagint ἵπποι may mean 'cavalry' (Ex. 14.17,18; Jos. 24.6; III Kings 3.1, 10.26; I
Chr. 18.4; II Chr. 12.3; Is. 22.6; I Macc. 6.30, 10.81), but in II Maccabees it means only
'horses' (5.3; 10.29). For 'cavalry', the form in II Maccabees is ἱππεῖς (5.2, 10.31, 11.4,11,
12.10, 20, 33, 35, 13.2). However, the singular ἵππος (= horse) is used by II Maccabees, as
was common in Greek, also for 'cavalry' (11.2, 15.20). The vocabulary and grammar of the
Septuagint cannot be projected on to a rhetorical work, originally written in Greek, such as
II Maccabees. I Maccabees, for instance, even employs the singular ἱππεύς (= rider, cavalryman) to mean 'cavalry' in general (3.39, 4.1,7,28,31, 6.35,38, 8.6, 9.4,10, 10.73,77, 79,82,
13.22, 15.13, 16.7).
[16] On the breeding of war horses during the Hellenistic period, and on the Median stock,
see Tarn 1930: 76ff.

religious–didactic points. It was the epitomist who confused the original purpose and presented these verses as a battle in itself which supposedly took place shortly after the battle of Ammaus. Timotheus' forces were not regular Seleucid armies but local militia, nomadic mercenaries, and perhaps a small garrison. Timotheus, the enemy commander, was the Seleucid *stratēgos* in Galaaditis.

J

The negotiations between the Jews and the Seleucid authorities in the reigns of Antiochus Epiphanes and Antiochus Eupator

The contacts between various elements among the Jews, including the rebels, and the Seleucid authorities at the start of Demetrius I's reign have been discussed above in a variety of contexts. The understanding of the aims and course of those contacts affected the assessment of the rebel recruitment and resistance capability during the second phase of the Revolt.[1] Indeed during the reigns of Antiochus Epiphanes and Antiochus Eupator there were already diplomatic contacts between the Jews and the Antioch authorities. An accurate identification of the parties involved, the establishment of the exact timing, the way they evolved, their progress and outcome can illuminate Judas Maccabaeus' diplomacy at the end of the first phase of the Revolt, and contribute to the understanding of the nature of the contacts during Demetrius I's reign. They help also to clarify the political tactics of the Hellenizers and the internal struggle for power in Antioch in which the Jewish question played quite an important role.

The documents in II Maccabees 11

The information on the negotiations during the reigns of Antiochus Epiphanes and his son Antiochus Eupator is included in the four documents inserted in the eleventh chapter of II Maccabees. These documents have been the subject of much research in the last century, mainly because they present many fundamental difficulties which have attracted the attention of philologists as well as historians. The documents follow the description of Lysias' first campaign, but it is impossible to fit the contents of some of them into the situation that developed immediately after that expedition. Furthermore, while according to II Maccabees that campaign was conducted after the death of Antiochus Epiphanes and the purification of the Temple, the dates on three of the documents precede the death of Antiochus IV. The order in which the four documents appear in II Maccabees does not seem logical either. Consequently, their present placement and sequence has customarily been ignored, and they have been arranged and dated in

[1] See pp. 59–60, esp. n. 101 and pp. 146–7, 351, 354–6.

accordance with their contents and the dates that figure in them. The dates mentioned themselves present some difficulties. Thus the month in the first document is not known from the Macedonian calendar, and in the third and fourth documents an identical date is given, which does not fit in with the contents of the two, while the second document bears no date at all. The contents of the documents present even greater difficulties and make it hard to order and date them. In particular, according to the third document, it was Menelaus, the leader of the extremist Hellenizers, who conducted negotiations on the relaxation of the repressive measures, whereas for various reasons it would be difficult to attribute the contacts described in the first and fourth documents to the Hellenizers. These difficulties and others led on the one hand to attempts to deny the authenticity of the documents, and on the other to the proposal of an abundance of interpretations of them. Before reviewing these, it behoves us to look at the texts of the four documents.

Document 1 (verses 16–21)

(16) Lysias to the multitude (τῷ πλήθει) of Jews, greetings. (17) Johanan and Absalom who were sent (οἱ πεμφθέντες) from you delivered the attached document and requested (an answer) on the things noted on it. (18) The things that it was necessary to bring to the king we clarified, and what it was possible (to approve) I approved.[2] (19) If you retain (your) good thought regarding the affairs (of the kingdom) I will try to be a seeker of favour (for you) in the future too. (20) As to details, I authorized them and my envoys to confer with you. (21) Greetings. The year 148, the 24th of Dios Corinthios.

Document 2 (verses 22–6)

(22) King Antiochus to his brother Lysias, greetings. (23) After our father ascended to the gods we want all in the kingdom to be undisturbed in dealing with their private matters. (24) Having heard that the Jews do not agree with our father in regard to conversion to Hellenic customs, and preferring their (ancient) way of life ask to allow them their codes, (25) and wishing that this people too should be outside the whirlpool (ἐκτὸς ταραχῆς) we resolve that the Temple be returned to them and that they should be governed (πολιτεύεσθαι) according to the customs (ἔθη) of their forefathers (τῶν προγόνων). (26) And you will do well to send them (emissaries) and give (them) the right (hand), so that when they see our policy they will be cheerful and turn with pleasure to take up their affairs.

---

[2] It has already long been agreed that the reading συνεχώρησα (= I approved) is preferable to συνεχώρησεν(= he approved). See the recent Bunge 1971: 391; Habicht 1976b: 9 n. 16.

Document 3 (verses 27–33)

(27) King Antiochus to the Council of Elders (τῇ γερουσίᾳ) of the Jews and to the rest (τοῖς ἄλλοις) of the Jews, greetings. (28) If it is well with you, so we wish. And we too are in good health. (29) Menelaus informed us that you want to descend to your private affairs. (30) To those who return by the thirtieth of Xanthicus our right hand is (hereby) extended with no fear. (31) The Jews may use their foods[3] and laws as it was previously, and none of them will be bothered in any way because of the mistakes (of the past). (32) And I sent Menelaus to appeal to you. (33) Greetings, the year 148, the 15th of Xanthicus.

Document 4 (verses 34–8)

(34) Quintus Memmius, Titus Manius, the Romans' ambassadors (πρεσβευταί) to the *dēmos* of the Jews, greetings. (35) To the things that Lysias, the relative (συγγενής) of the King, conceded to you, we too agree. (36) As to the things that (he) decided to bring before the king, after you study the matter, send someone so that we can express our opinion as befits your (matter), for we are going to Antioch. (37) Therefore hasten and send several (emissaries) so that we too will know what your opinion is. (38) Be well! The year 148, the 15th of Xanthicus.

When systematic research on the Books of the Maccabees began, and also in the 1920s, a number of Protestant scholars were inclined to dismiss the documents altogether and label them forgeries.[4] At the same time, when it was proven that the formulas appearing in the documents stand the test of comparison, and that their contents do not correspond to the predilections and inclinations of the author of II Maccabees, the belief that the documents as a whole are authentic became entrenched. Nevertheless, attempts were made to 'cleanse' them of 'suspect' words and sentences, redundancies, extrapolations and glosses, and here and there doubts about the authenticity of one document or another were voiced. From that point on efforts were devoted to reconstructing the correct order, establishing their definitive chronology, and clarifying the historical background. The various combinations proposed cover almost all the theoretical possibilities.[5]

[3] This should be read διαιτήμασι (= in foods) and not as in the existing version of δαπανήμασι (= in expenditures). See especially Wilhelm 1937: 22. See also Habicht 1976b: 11 and the bibliography in n. 19 there. Contrary to them, Bickerman (1937: 180 n. 5) accepts the existing reading in the sense of 'foods'. This is a deviant usage incongruous for a legal document. The proposal of Bunge (1971: 397–8; implied also by Schlatter 1891: 29 n. 2) that the reference is to expenses of the Temple must be rejected.

[4] Wernsdorff 1747: 100–5; Grimm 1857: 172–4 (and earlier references there); Schubert 1926: 324–47; Willrich 1924: 30–6; Kolbe 1926: 74–107.

[5] Unger 1895: 281–300; Schlatter 1891: 28–31; Niese 1900: 63–78; Laqueur 1904: 30–51; Wellhausen 1905: 141–5; Ed. Meyer 1921: 2.212–16; Kugler 1922: 375–86; Laqueur 1927a:

Because of their quantity, we shall content ourselves with surveying the two outstanding pieces of research representing opposite approaches and stressing the historical significance of the documents. One of them, by Tcherikover, appeared some fifty years ago in its first version, while the other, by Christian Habicht, appeared a decade ago.

Tcherikover believes that the first, third and fourth documents all reflect negotiations conducted with the Hellenizers. The first document contains Lysias' letter to the Hellenizers and it belongs before his first expedition to Judaea (which Tcherikover deemed to have taken place in April 164 B.C.). It reports on the mission of Johanan and Absalom, representatives of the Hellenizers, and the negotiations they conducted in Antioch. The nature of the Jews' requests becomes clear, in his opinion, from the third document, which is later. The Hellenizers wanted to attract the masses of people to their side and weaken the power of Judas Maccabaeus by arranging an amnesty and the repeal or moderation of the religious coercive measures. At the same time the Hellenizers and their emissaries heard about a Roman delegation on its way to Antioch, and requested its help in persuading the Seleucid authorities. The fourth document contains the reply of the Roman envoys promising their support, and it belongs immediately after the first document, before the third. The date in this fourth document, identical with the one in the third, is simply a copying error. The outcome of the negotiations appears in the third document, sent in April 164 B.C., in Tcherikover's view in the middle of Lysias' first campaign in Judaea. In that document the Seleucid commander informs the *gerousia*, the governing body of the Hellenizers and the Hellenistic *polis* in Jerusalem, that it has been agreed to declare an amnesty and grant permission to live according to ancestral practice for people who return to their homes within fifteen days. That concession, however, did not produce any practical results because Lysias was defeated shortly thereafter and forced to withdraw from Beth Zur, control of the country passed to the rebels, and the concessions of the authorities no longer appealed to the Jewish population in general. The second document is chronologically the last. In it Antiochus Eupator repeals his father's repressive measures. It bears no date but should be set in 162 B.C., at the end of Lysias' second expedition to Judaea, when Philippus was advancing toward Antioch, thus obliging Lysias to abandon the struggle and allow the Jews to live in accordance with their code (I Maccabees 6.58–9).

Contrary to Tcherikover, Habicht believes that only the third document reflects negotiations with the Hellenizers. Like Tcherikover, he thinks it was sent in the wake of Menelaus' request, and its contents include a procla-

229–52; Gutberlet 1927: 158–64; Bickerman in *RE* s.v. 'Makkabäerbücher', cols 789–90; Tcherikover 1930: 31–45 (1961b: 181–98); Bévenot 1931: 223–7; Bickerman 1937: 179–81; Abel 1949: 426–31; Zeitlin 1952: 63–4; Schunck 1954: 103–9; Abel and Starcky 1961: 289–92; M. Stern 1965: 67–73; Zambelli 1965: 213–34; Mørkholm 1966: 162–5; Tcherikover 1961a: 213–19; Bunge 1971: 386–436; Schürer... 1973–9: 1.161–2; Habicht 1976a: 179–85, 256–60; id. 1976b: 7–17; Goldstein 1976: 254,270–1; Th. Fischer 1980: 64ff.; Bringmann 1983: 40–51; Gruen 1984: 2.745–7.

mation of amnesty and permission to practise their religion for people who
demonstrate loyalty to the regime and lay down their arms within a limited
period. But he differs in regard to the chronology, contending that the third
document antedates all the others, and was written not in April 164 B.C. as
appears from the date it bears, but prior to that. The 15th of Xanthicus
date is not credible, and is influenced by the 30th of Xanthicus noted as the
date of the expiration of the amnesty mentioned in the same document. In
Habicht's opinion, there had to be a longer period between the proclamation of the amnesty and its expiration. Thus he believes the offer preceded Lysias' first expedition and was designed to facilitate the planned
campaign against Judas Maccabaeus. Contrary to the accepted view, Habicht holds that the offer was directed primarily at the followers of Jason,
Onias' brother, and not at the conservative masses who were sticklers for
the Law. On the other hand, the first and fourth documents reflect negotiations carried on by Lysias with Judas Maccabaeus' men. Both documents report contacts made in the mutual desire to arrive at a solution, but
do not report any practical results whatsoever. The negotiations were not
concluded because of the difficulty in obtaining the response and reaction
of Antiochus Epiphanes who was then far away in the eastern satrapies.
The months in the dates noted at the end of the two documents (in contrast
to the years) are not reliable. Such negotiations between Lysias and the
rebels were possible in Habicht's view only after the failure of Lysias' first
expedition, which he sets between April and September 164 B.C.: according
to the third document, April 148 of the Seleucid calendar was the expiry
date of the amnesty period announced by Lysias, which Habicht reckons
was intended to prepare the way for his first expedition, while the date of
the first and fourth documents is 148 of the Seleucid calendar, which ended
in September 164 B.C. Habicht sets the dateless second document announcing the cancellation of the religious repressions at the end of 164
B.C., right after the death of Antiochus Epiphanes. For after the king's
death, Lysias as the regent was able to conclude the negotiations successfully
without having recourse to the approval of superiors.

Since the evaluation of the documents involves complicated chronological and historical considerations, the reader will not be burdened with a
complete treatment of the two proposals. Each document is now dealt with
separately, and its contents, the questions of its date, the relevant circumstances and causes surveyed, with the various scholarly views taken into
account. Thereafter an attempt is made to establish the order of the
documents and the events that inspired them.

Document No. 1

The document reports on negotiations between the Jews and Lysias
(verse 16). Two Jewish emissaries named Johanan and Absalom submitted
the Jewish requests or demands (17). Lysias acceded to some of them (18)

and is leaving the clarification of details to negotiations at a lower level (20). Other requests that he has no authority to decide on he is passing on to the king now staying in the eastern part of the empire (18).

With what Jews were the negotiations described in the document conducted? Some scholars (among them Tcherikover, as noted), on the basis of the mention of Menelaus in the third document and its contents, assumed that Johanan and Absalom were representatives of the Hellenizers, members of Menelaus' faction, and that their main interest was to obtain conditional amnesty that would tip the scales in their favour in the internal power struggle. However, for the view objecting to the assumption that Menelaus and his people were the addressees of this document, two main reasons are proffered. First, Lysias addresses the Jews as *plēthos* (= multitude, verse 17), while in the third document he addresses the governing body, the *gerousia* (verse 27), proving that the negotiations reflected in the first document were conducted with a group lacking any official status in the Hellenistic administration.[6] Second, the emissaries to the negotiations with Lysias had Hebrew names, which does not fit Hellenizers, who usually bore Greek names (see II Macc. 3.11, 4.7,23,29,49,14.3,19).[7] Some scholars have also noted that the names ascribed to those emissaries were common among the leading members of the rebel camp (I Macc. 2.2, 9.38, 11.70, 13.11).[8] In addition, it should be borne in mind that the Hellenizers who did all they could to prove to the authorities their devotion to the new culture would certainly not have despatched as their representatives people with Hebrew names, that the Hebrew names appear in an official document written in Greek by the authorities themselves, and that one of them – Johanan – is even theophoric in nature. Furthermore, the representatives of the Jews are called 'delegates' (οἱ πεμφθέντες, verse 17) which also suggests the absence of official recognition by the Seleucid authorities, while the Roman representatives in the fourth document are referred to as 'ambassadors' (*presbeutai*, verse 34).[9] Finally, as will be seen below (and is agreed on by all scholars), the fourth document was sent by the Roman ambassadors in the wake of an approach by the Jewish group which

[6] This was already noted by Niese (1900: 68) and Meyer (1921: 2.213); see also Bunge 1971: 389,420, and Habicht 1976b: 10. On the use of the term *dēmos* in Document No. 4 see p. 531 below (and n. 45). Goldstein (1976: 270–1) argues that after the massacre perpetrated in Jerusalem by the Mysian commander in 167 (I Macc. 1.29) the Jewish community in Judaea was no longer recognized as an *ethnos*, and consequently the use of the term 'multitude' is not an indication that the document was not sent to Menelaus and the Hellenizers. However, the mention of the *gerousia* in Document No. 3 (verse 29) shows that if it had been addressed to the Hellenizers they would have been referred to as *dēmos*, citizens, or *gerousia*, but not as 'multitude'.

[7] As appears in II Maccabees (3.4), the name of Menelaus' brother Simeon acquired the Hellenized form Simon, well known from the Greek onomasticon. While Mattathias does appear as the name of a Hellenizer in Nicanor's service (II Macc. 14.19), it seems to be no more than the equivalent of Theodotus mentioned before it. The source probably had 'Mattathias called Theodotus' or the like. Owing to some garbling, Jason of Cyrene or the epitomist assumed that two people were involved.

[8] Niese 1900: 68–9; Bévenot 1931: 223; Abel 1949: 427; Bunge 1971: 389–90; Habicht 1976b: 10. [9] For the last argument see Habicht, ibid.

initiated the first document. Is it reasonable to suppose that Hellenizers would have operated behind the backs of the Seleucid authorities and tried to win over the Roman ambassadors? All this points to the conclusion that Johanan and Absalom were representatives of the rebels, and that the negotiations in question were conducted between Judas Maccabaeus and the Antioch authorities.

The document is dated 148, the Macedonian-Seleucid year that began on 2 October 165 B.C. and ended on 22 September 164.[10] The day and month given are the 24th of Dios Corinthios. The month presents a certain difficulty, for in the period under discussion Dios was the first Macedonian month,[11] and the second element, 'Corinthios', is not known in the Macedonian calendar. For that reason, some scholars have proposed accepting the forms 'Dioscori' or 'Dioscoridis', which appear in most manuscripts of the Latin translations, while others have proposed correcting to 'Dystros'.[12] 'Dioscoridis' recalls the Cretan month Dioscouros, the equivalent of the Macedonian Xanthicus, while 'Dystros' is the fifth Macedonian month.

However, the correction Dioscouros does not solve the difficulty arising from the use of a non-Macedonian month name in an official Seleucid document, while the adoption of a Cretan name is by itself less explainable than that of a Greek month-deity. Moreover, the date of the document would accordingly have fallen a few days after the date of the third document. This is impossible under any interpretation of these documents, their parties and addresses, for the first certainly records two negotiating sides in the midst of the process, the third – a final decision. As to the proposal 'Dystros', it is unsatisfactory from the textual point of view: the Macedonian month names were utilized and well known in the Roman period as well.[13] A copyist could not have garbled the well known 'Dystros' to 'Dios Corinthios', but only the opposite. Some scholars have properly noted that precisely because of the deviant adjective 'Corinthios', which is a *lectio difficilior*, the term 'Dios' should not be disparaged, and that Antiochus Epiphanes introduced names of Attic months into Syria (*Ant.* 12.264; cf. Daniel 7.25), and the name Corinthios should perhaps be explained against that background.[14] We have no other example of the use of the addition 'Corinthios' in Seleucid writing of Antiochus Epiphanes' time, but relatively few remnants of that period have survived. Similarly, the document of the 'Sidonites in Shechem', from the time of Antiochus' religious decrees, preserved the curious epithet 'Hyrcanios' attached to Hecatombaios (*Ant.* 12.264), the Athenian equivalent of the tenth month in the

[10] For the exact dates see Parker and Dubberstein 1956: 41. The dates of the months listed there for the Babylonian version of the Seleucid count are applicable to the Macedonian–Seleucid months, since the latter were equated with the Babylonian calendar; see Bickerman 1968: 25; Samuel 1972: 140–1.   [11] On this see ibid. 140–3.

[12] Grimm 1857: 169; Niese 1900: 71–2 (objecting); Gutberlet 1927: 159; Bévenot 1931: 224; Bickerman 1937: 179; Abel 1949: 427–8.

[13] See Samuel 1972: 171.

[14] Niese 1900: 70; Ed. Meyer 1921: 2.211; Schunck 1954: 104; Tcherikover 1961b: 191; and esp. Hanhart 1961: 473–4.

Macedonian calendar. Thus, there is not sufficient evidence to deny the credibility of the version 'Dios Corinthios' that appears in all the Greek (including the uncial) manuscripts.

In the light of all these considerations, the date of the document should be at the end of October 165. As noted above, the battle of Ammaus took place at the end of the summer of 165 B.C.[15] Even if that conclusion is inaccurate, there is no disagreement about the battle having taken place between April and September 165. Negotiations with the rebels at the end of October 165 must thus have evolved from the results of the battle of Ammaus.

Document No. 2

The document is undated. In it Antiochus informs Lysias about the repeal of the coercive edicts and the return of the Temple to the Jews. While in the past some scholars tried to remove the reference to Antiochus Epiphanes' death from the document, today almost nobody doubts the authenticity of that sentence or of the document as a whole, or its application to the period after Antiochus Epiphanes' death.[16]

There are, however, differences of opinion on the exact time and circumstances of the writing of the document. At first some scholars dated it immediately after Epiphanes' death.[17] but later the notion developed that it was written after Lysias' second expedition to Judaea.[18] Recently Habicht has returned to the earlier view and tried to prove with a series of well-formulated points that the document is actually a *philanthrōpa*, a declaration of rights as the new king came to power, which, instead of confirming the current policy, proclaims its cancellation.[19]

A comparison of the contents of the document with the situation that developed after Epiphanes' death and Lysias' second expedition makes it clear, however, that the document was written after Lysias' second expedition to Judaea which was terminated in the middle of the summer of 162 B.C.[20] The statement attributed to Lysias at the end of his second expedition indicates that the coercive edicts were repealed totally only after that campaign ('and now let us sanction them to follow their laws as in the

---

[15] P. 472 above.

[16] Laqueur (1904: 37ff.), Wellhausen (1905: 142) and Ed. Meyer (1921: 2.212) doubted the reference to Epiphanes' death; against them see esp. Tcherikover 1961b: 183–4. Only Schunck (1954: 104–5) still questions the authenticity of the document, but his arguments are unfounded. For example, he wonders how the Jews knew about the king's letter to Lysias. But the letter was a *prostagma*, of the kind common in Hellenistic times, worded as a letter from the king to the chief minister, a copy of which was sent to the Jews. Cf. the letter of Demetrius II, who like Eupator was then a minor, to Lasthenes the Cretan (I Macc. 11.32ff.), the dominant figure in the kingdom as Lysias was.

[17] Clinton 1834: 3.572–3; Schlatter 1891: 29; Niese 1900: 74–5; Zeitlin 1952: 66,203–4.

[18] Laqueur 1927a: 233ff.; Bickerman 1937: 156–7; Tcherikover 1961b: 189–90; Abel and Starcky 1961: 39; M. Stern 1965: 60; Mørkholm 1966: 163; Bunge 1971: 437ff.; Hengel 1973: 178 n. 3 and p. 530; Schürer... 1973–9: 1.167.

[19] Habicht 1976b: 15–17, followed by Doran 1981: 66.

[20] On the chronology of Lysias' second expedition to Judaea see pp. 543–50 below.

beginning', 6.59).[21] The text does not justify the claim that Lysias' words only confirm an earlier repeal, for he tries to persuade the king and ministers of the need to allow the rebels to live according to their laws. Moreover, Lysias explains that 'only because of their laws that we violated did they rage and do all those (things)' (ibid.). In other words, a change of policy on the Jewish religion would lead to the pacification of the Jews and a willingness on their part to be reconciled to the authorities. The document likewise notes that the Temple should be returned to the Jews (verse 25). That concession does not fit the period around Antiochus Epiphanes' death either, but only the end of Lysias' second expedition: both Books of the Maccabees report the seizure or capture of the Temple by Judas Maccabaeus which led to its purification (I Macc. 4.36; II Macc. 10.1), and contain no suggestion that this was accomplished with the permission of the authorities or was retroactively confirmed by them. On the other hand, the Temple was under Lysias' control at the end of his second expedition (I Macc. 6.61–2), allowing for a proclamation on the return of the Temple to the Jews. In addition, the accession of Antiochus Eupator (and in effect of Lysias) meant a harsher governmental attitude to the Jews. II Maccabees indicates that Ptolemy Macron, the *stratēgos* of Coele Syria and Phoenicia, who tried to befriend the Jews, was upon Eupator's accession compelled to commit suicide because of his favourable attitude to the Jews (10.12–13).[22]

It is worth examining Habicht's argument that the document contains no hint of immediate hostile acts or negotiations in whose wake the document was composed, and therefore cannot be connected with Lysias' second expedition. The sentence 'and give (them) the right (hand),...they will be cheerful and turn with pleasure to take up their affairs' (verse 26) suggests the cessation of hostilities. As to the absence of explicit reference to negotiations, according to I Maccabees' account of the end of Lysias' second expedition, there were no negotiations, and because of the urgent need to return to Antioch, Lysias just issued the proclamation on the repeal of the edicts and the return of the Temple (6.57–60). Finally, the mention of Antiochus Epiphanes' death is no proof that the document was written close to the time of that event. The authorities tried to get the Jews to trust the seriousness of their intentions by creating the impression that they had been misled in the past and simply continued a policy initiated by the preceding king and his advisers. And now that the reasons for the Revolt and the Jews' complaints were clear to them, they realized that the Jews were right. For that reason they also hastened to execute Menelaus at the

---

[21] The expression στήσωμεν αὐτοῖς (= let us maintain, sanction, certify) can be construed to mean that Lysias issued a new permission or that he merely confirmed one that he had given earlier. The correct meaning should be decided according to the context and historical circumstances. Even if the author meant 'confirm', it may apply to the religious privileges the Jews had received during the reigns of the Seleucid kings who preceded Antiochus Epiphanes, which are referred to in the verse ('as in the beginning'), and not to previous concessions by Lysias himself.   [22] See further pp. 535ff. below.

end of the campaign.[23] The desire to deny responsibility for the anti-Jewish measures adopted early in Eupator's reign led to the rather general wording of the document and to a certain blurring of the actual background. 'Diplomatic' wording of this kind deliberately veiling recent negative events (on both sides) is plentiful in Hellenistic writings, and occurs also in letters of the Seleucid kings to Jonathan (notably in the letter of Demetrius I in I Macc. 10.25–7) and even in the (fabricated) letter attributed to the dying Antiochus Epiphanes (II Macc. 9.19–27).

Document No. 3

This is the most detailed of the four documents. It includes two dates, the names of the sender, the addressees, and the initiator of the negotiations, as well as some significant concessions and their recipients. The reference to Menelaus as the initiator of the concessions has always been quoted as a decisive argument in favour of the authenticity of this document. It has been pointed out that Jason of Cyrene would not have forged a document which attributed a positive development to the man whom he loved so much to deplore and hate.

The document, dated 15 Xanthicus 148 s.e. (10 March 164 b.c.), is addressed to the *gerousia* (verse 27). In response to Menelaus' request (29, 32), Antiochus (Epiphanes) announces the following concessions: (a) People are allowed (or called upon) to return peacefully to their homes within fifteen days (30,33); (b) The Jews would be allowed to practise the laws of their religion (31); (c) No one would be prosecuted for the crimes committed beforehand (31).

The general meaning and purpose of the declaration appears from the first and third concession. It offers an amnesty, limited in time, to rebels who will lay down their arms and resume normal life, certainly also to dissident sects who preferred an unarmed resistance and escaped to the deserts. The purpose was obviously to weaken the rebel camp by peaceful means.

The main stumbling-block for an understanding of the document is whether the second and most significant concession, which refers to 'the Jews', means a general and unconditional repeal of the coercive decrees. This question has actually been ignored by most commentators. The difficulty arises from the contents and language of the second document, from the time of Antiochus V, which announces that the Jews are entitled to live according to their laws. This proves that the decrees were still in force at the time of Antiochus V. And there is no room for arguing that the second document merely confirmed former concessions. The document, which also mentions the return of the Temple, makes it clear that it changes the existing situation and dissassociates itself from the steps taken by the previous king: 'Having heard that the Jews do not agree with our father in regard to the

---

[23] See p. 541 n. 80 below on the dating of Menelaus' execution.

conversion to Hellenic customs...and...ask to allow them their codes...we
resolve that the Temple be returned to them and they should be governed
according to the customs of their forefathers' (verses 24–5). Moreover, the
second document was initiated by Lysias in summer 162 B.C., about a year
and a half after Antiochus Epiphanes' death. It was too late for a formal
rectification of national and religious rights usually made on the occasion
of the accession of a new king; and the deliberations of Lysias with the king
and ministers quoted in I Maccabees (6.57–9) definitely show that the
concessions were new and not a confirmation of former ones granted by
Antiochus IV or V.

On the other hand, it is impossible to interpret the withdrawal of the
decrees as conditional upon the return of all (or most of) the rebels to
normal life – i.e. the cessation of hostilities on the Jewish side – and that
because the rebels carried on the military struggle, the religious decrees
were not revoked. An entry in the Scroll of Fasting indicates that this
concession indeed became valid. In the list of the special days of the month
Adar, it reads: 'On the twenty eighth thereof the good news reached the
Jews that (they did not) have to pass (away) from the Torah' (דלא יעדון;
מן אורייתא). It has generally been accepted that the event took place in
the generation of Judas Maccabaeus and not in the Roman period. The
date – early spring – shows that the Scroll does not refer to the proclamation by Antiochus V at the end of Lysias' second expedition
(midsummer 162). On the other hand, the Macedonian month Xanthicus,
dating the third document, was parallel to the Babylonian Addaru,[24] the
counterpart of the Jewish Adar. We can therefore conclude that the new
méasure commemorated by the Scroll is identical to that proclaimed in the
third document and, as the special day was preserved for generations, the
king's undertaking certainly was not revoked.

The identity of the events reflected in the two sources calls for further
chronological comment. As the Jewish and Babylonian months were lunar,
and the declaration of both sources is actually dated in Adar, the Jewish
Adar 164 B.C. must have run more or less parallel to the Babylonian Addaru,
and there was not then a month's difference between the two calendars as
occasionally arose because of the different systems of intercalation. That
can also be proved by the fact that the Jewish year was intercalated in the
following month, and the Babylonian a year later.[25] This conclusion
clinches the argument in the long-disputed question as to the sequence
of events close to the purification of the Temple, in the chapter on the
raid near Beth Zur. For the present matter, however, a closer look at the precise
date in the two sources is required. 28 Adar, recorded in the Scroll of
Fasting, fell on exactly 30 Xanthicus, the deadline set for the return of the
rebels to their homes in the third document: the Jewish month was still
determined solely by careful observation of the new crescent, while the
Babylonian calendar was by then already precalculated. While the astro-

---

[24] See p. 522 n. 10 above.　　　　[25] See pp. 278–9 above.

nomical New Moon of Adar 148 s.e. occurred on 24 February 164,[26] the Babylonian Addaru in that year is known to have commenced only two days later.[27] There is therefore no choice but to understand that, despite the statement of the Scroll that 28 Adar commemorates the day on which 'the news came', it was distinguished for generations afterwards because in fact it became clear on that day that the new measures were valid. The phrasing of the provisions and the reference to 30 Xanthicus could have caused much ambiguity as to the commencement date of the concession, and whether it would come in to force even if the rebels (or most of them) did not return to normal life, a question which would also have puzzled modern readers.

How, then, can the apparent discrepancy between the third and second document be reconciled? There is no indication of new religious decrees in the nine months left of Antiochus Epiphanes' reign nor under his son, and this is virtually impossible in view of the commemoration of the repeal for generations in the Scroll of Fasting. The only remaining alternative is to suggest that the repeal of the coercive decrees by Antioch IV, though referring to all Jews, was conditional in its application to the rebels and dissidents to their returning to normal life. The declaration of Antiochus V was, on the other hand, applied unconditionally to the rebels and dissidents as well. According to the motives behind the declaration elaborated in I Maccabees, it was meant from the outset to appease the rebels besieged in the Temple (6.57–61).

This interpretation does not contradict the wording of the third document: the third concession which declared the amnesty was certainly relevant mainly to the rebels. However, its grammatical subject ('no one of them') goes back to that of the second concession ('the Jews'), which means that it applied to all Jews. As there is no doubt that the amnesty was offered only to those rebels who would desert the camp within the time limit defined in the first concession, it can be deduced that the religious freedom promised to the rebels also depended upon compliance with the provision listed in the first concession. It may well be that the first concession (or perhaps I should say 'paragraph') does not stand by itself, and the second and third explain the practical meaning of the vague commitment of the king in the first concession – 'our right hand is (hereby) extended with no fear' (verse 30). Thus the two main worries of the rebels – the religious persecutions and the pending prosecution for rebellious actions – are eliminated. As an explanation of the first, the two later concessions were obviously dependent upon its provision, and did not have to repeat it. This reading draws support from the absence of any conjunction in the second concession (verse 31), which indicates that it serves as a specification of the first.

In addition to the consideration mentioned above, the general purpose of the move must be examined. Even if Menelaus and the extreme Hellenizers were not the active inspirers of the coercive edicts, at this stage they

[26] See the astronomical table in Bickerman 1968: 127.
[27] See the Babylonian chronological table in Parker and Dubberstein 1956: 41.

could not have any interest in the repeal itself, but in its contribution to the lessening of the rebels' pressure. They could expect that releasing the civilian population and the deserters from the religious persecutions would have isolated the rebels and weakened their camp from inside. As will be shown later, in reality the expectation of the Hellenizers did not come about, but there must have been some logic in their initiative. An unconditional repeal of the decrees, on the other hand, certainly was not enough to encourage the combatants to desert the ranks: the Temple was still defiled, the leadership held by the hated Hellenizers, and the goal of national independence far from achieved. For the general public it would have meant a royal recognition of the legitimacy of the violent methods used by the rebels, and an unreserved recognition of their success in the war for the preservation of the Jewish religion, which could only strengthen their influence.

A distinction between groups in the application of religious decrees (or rather discrimination in exemption from them) must not surprise us. The very declaration of the coercive measures had been motivated by political considerations and was adapted to the political goal and circumstances. Accordingly, the Jews in the Land of Israel alone were subject to discrimination – as against all the other nations in the empire, who were not forced to abandon their former religious practices, and it seems quite certain that the decrees did not apply to Diaspora Jews.[28] The discrimination against the rebels and dissidents, which was also designed to achieve a political–military aim, was not therefore unprecedented.

The date 30 Xanthicus, quoted by the document for the expiration of the amnesty, is above suspicion. In addition to the equation with the Scroll of Fasting, it should be noted that the end of Xanthicus ran parallel to the end of the year by the Jewish–Babylonian version of the Seleucid count that was current in the country. The beginning of the new year, in early spring, also marked the start of the 'military year' in the region. Having the expiration of the amnesty at the end of the year is thus very reasonable and its dating on the eve of the new season of military activity has an interesting parallel.[29] Doubts were raised, however, about the 15th of Xanthicus, the dating of the document itself. Thus it has been claimed that the fifteen-day period allowed for those wishing to return to their homes is too short to be real, and that the date of the document cited in the book is influenced by the date of the expiration of the amnesty.[30] All these are not sufficient reason to reject the date given for the writing of the document. Sent from Antioch, the document was the outcome of protracted negotiations with Menelaus and the Hellenizers, and could have been made public in Eretz

[28] See also p. 87 n. 52 above.
[29] See also Dancy 1954: 20; Habicht 1976b: 13; and esp. Wilhelm (1937: 22), who cites in comparison the document in Diodorus 18.56.5 of 319 B.C. which likewise gives 30 Xanthicus as the termination date for the amnesty of the exiles from the Greek cities.
[30] Laqueur 1904: 39–40; Abel and Starcky 1961: 40; M. Stern 1965: 71; Mørkholm 1966: 156–7; Schürer... 1973–9: 1.162; Habicht 1976b: 13; Doran 1981: 65.

Israel within a day or two.[31] The time left was enough for word of the amnesty to reach the rebels in the small area of the Judaean Hills. The short period allotted for deciding and the individual nature of the return are well suited to the probable aims of Menelaus who inspired them. He hoped to cause a scurried desertion of the rebel camp and prevent the rebel leaders from dragging the matter on by entering into negotiations on details and submitting additional demands as they did immediately after the battle of Ammaus with the support of Ptolemy Macron, governor of Coele Syria and Phoenicia.[32] A lengthy amnesty period was likely to lead to an orderly abandonment of the mountain strongholds and a rebel reorganization on the internal plane against the Hellenizers. Even if the date of 15 Xanthicus is not authentic, in view of Menelaus' probable aims in proposing the amnesty, it is unlikely that he would have been prepared to allow the rebels a long period before the expiration of the amnesty.

Some scholars assumed that the document was sent at the time of Lysias' first campaign in Judaea,[33] others that it came subsequently,[34] and still others that it preceded the campaign.[35] However, the expedition to Beth Zur began in the autumn of 164,[36] so that there is no real connection between Lysias' first campaign and the document. Even if the dating of that first expedition is incorrect, its start cannot be set before April 164.[37] The document cannot therefore be dated to the time of the expedition or after it.

To whom was the document sent? The references to the Hellenizer-controlled *gerousia* as the addressee, and to Menelaus as the inspirer of the document and agent of the authorities, clarify beyond any doubt that the document was sent to the Hellenizers and the official municipal body of Jerusalem. As noted, that fact misled many scholars into believing that the first document too was connected with the Hellenizers. Although of the opinion that the first document was sent to the rebels, Stern, who like others is concerned about the relation between the first and third documents, considers that the third communicates the final decision of the authorities following the negotiations with the rebels reflected in the first document. In order to formalize the decision, the letter was sent to the *gerousia*, the Jewish governing body.[38] It is, however, impossible to ignore Menelaus' central role in the negotiations as reflected in the document. It was he who inspired the conditional amnesty, and was sent to announce it to the potential

---

[31] On the Seleucid postal service see p. 279 n. 8 above.

[32] See pp. 535ff. below on Ptolemy Macron's favourable attitude to the rebels.

[33] Tcherikover 1961b: 194, and to a certain extent also Goldstein 1976: 271.

[34] Niese 1900: 66; Zeitlin 1952: 66–7; Dancy 1954: 19; Schunck 1954: 108; Bunge 1971: 432; Schürer... 1973–9: 1.164.

[35] Habicht 1976b: 15; Doran 1981: 65–6.   [36] See pp. 383–4 above.

[37] Antiochus Epiphanes' expedition to the Upper Satrapies could not have developed before April 165 (see pp. 466–7 above). The battle of Ammaus took place some time later, and Lysias' first expedition a full astronomical year after that battle (p. 383 above). Even if I Macc. 4.28 refers to a calendar year, that expedition could not have started until after April 164.

[38] M. Stern 1965: 58,71.

beneficiaries. The third document can only be the outcome of discussions
with the Hellenizers, not with the rebels. As to the formal aspect, in order
to publicize a proclamation of amnesty, it was not necessary to address it
to the *gerousia*. The proclamation could be issued by means of a royal
prostagma or *programma* without reference to any Jewish body. The five-
month period between the first and third documents makes it possible to
consider them the outcome of Seleucid negotiations with two different
prominent groups in Judaea at different times, without requiring the
establishment of a direct connection between the two.

At whom was the amnesty aimed? It has been generally agreed that it is
addressed to observant Jews who had left their homes and joined the rebel
camp. Habicht, on the other hand, considers it to be directed at the
supporters of Jason, Onias' brother, for the purpose of unifying the Hellenizer camp in preparation for a struggle with Judas Maccabaeus.[39] Though II
Maccabees considerably exaggerates in the characterization of Jason's personality, and the cultural–religious conception of his supporters seems to
have been more moderate,[40] the stress on the permission to eat kosher food
and live according to the Jewish law (verse 31) indicates that the proclamation was tailored to meet the requests and principles of the Jewish
public in general, and the religious fanatics in particular. In any case,
Jason's followers were too small in number[41] to justify such a significant
departure from Seleucid policy in Judaea. The amnesty and concessions
proffered could only have been directed at the entire community of Torah
followers, who at the time were rallied around Judas Maccabaeus.

Document No. 4

In the document dated 15 Xanthicus 148, the two Roman envoys inform
the Jewish *dēmos* that they approve the concessions obtained from Lysias
and request clarification of points which Lysias decided to submit to the
king, so that they can assist in those matters when in Antioch.

The authenticity of this document was questioned a great deal in the
past, and is still sometimes challenged by scholars who accept the other
three documents as authentic.[42] The doubts are based on the names of the
emissaries, the chronology, the identity of the addressees, and the nature of
the Roman intervention. As we shall see none of these is sufficient to refute
the credibility of the document. Another claim proffered is that I Maccabees indicates that contacts with the Roman empire took place only at a
later stage, during the reign of Demetrius I (ch. 8). However, the text there
speaks of a delegation that went to Rome and appeared before the Senate,

---

[39] Habicht 1976b: 14–15.
[40] This can be inferred especially from 4.16,19. The moderate Hellenistic reform attributed
to Jason described in II Macc. 4.11 involved the establishment of the *polis* constitution, but
that constitution may well have included references to Torah laws in matters of vital importance.
[41] P. 57 above.   [42] Mainly Mørkholm 1966: 163–4.

which was an innovation of a sort. This present document reports contacts at a lower level. And in general, for its own reasons, I Maccabees does not report the contacts between Judas Maccabaeus and the Seleucid authorities in the reign of Antiochus Epiphanes which are mentioned in II Maccabees, and consequently no mention is made either of rebel contact with the Romans at this stage which is connected with negotiations with the Antioch authorities. In support of the authenticity of the document, it has recently been pointed out that the exceptional usage of ὑγιαίνετε (= be well) at the conclusion of it (11.38) is merely a translation of Latin *valete*.[43]

To whom is the document addressed, and to which negotiations is it a reaction, those between Lysias and the rebels (the first document) or those between Lysias and the Hellenizers (the third document)? The resemblance of this fourth document to the first is quite striking. Both mention Jewish demands accepted by Lysias, and others passed on for the king's decision. The two documents also resemble each other in wording.[44]As already pointed out above, it is unthinkable that Menelaus and his people would turn to Roman envoys for help behind the backs of the Seleucid authorities, who were their only support. Roman intervention was definitely a consequence of rebel overtures. The despatch of the document to the Jewish *dēmos* does not refute this. The Romans recognized the rebels as a political community[45] or as the true representatives of the Jewish *dēmos*, and in any case were not necessarily familiar with the polarization that had taken place in the Jewish community in Eretz Israel or with its internal arrangements. The author of I Maccabees, a member of the Revolt generation, demonstrates poorer knowledge of the internal organization of the Roman empire, although it was certainly more widely known than the organization, status and factions of the small Jewish community in Judaea.

In most manuscripts this document is dated 15 Xanthicus 148 (10 March 164 B.C.), exactly like the third document, and this identity itself suggests that the date on one of the two documents represents a scribal error. Some scholars have also pointed out that the use of Seleucid dating in an official Roman document of the mid second century B.C. is very unlikely.[46] The epistle clearly suggests that Lysias' reply to the rebels was issued very close to the time the Roman envoys' letter was sent, for they ask the Jews to examine his reply and forward their reaction as soon as possible (verses

[43] See Habicht 1976b: 12 n. 24, citing J. Strugnell and B. Knox.

[44] Cf. 11.18 τῷ βασιλεῖ προσενεχθῆναι...συνεχώρησα with 11.35,36 – συνεχώρησεν... προσανενεχθῆναι τῷ βασιλεῖ. And see Bévenot 1931: 233; Bunge 1971: 386–7; Habicht 1976b: 11–12.

[45] See also Ed. Meyer 1921: 2.213. Niese (1900: 70) prefers the Venetus which has *plēthos* (= multitude) in this verse as well. The same is true in some of the old Latin manuscripts. However, the Venetus version of the Roman document has other differences and some redundancies, and caution is necessary (see also n. 47, and the discussion on the names of the Roman envoys).

[46] Schlatter 1891: 30; Tcherikover 1961b: 191–2. The explanation of Kugler (1922: 379) that this is not an official senatorial document and that the reference is to the Seleucid letter does not stand the test of analogy. For the dating of *senatus consulta* and *epistulae* up to the first century B.C. written in Greek see Sherk 1969: 14 and passim.

36–7). Probably the rebel Jews who met with the Roman envoys were not sure of their leadership's response to Lysias' reply, and were also awaiting instructions on the conduct of practical negotiations regarding the requests that had been approved. It is also possible that they did not meet with the Roman envoys at all, and simply managed to inform them of the negotiations with the help of Diaspora Jews. At any rate, since the date of the first document is the end of October 164, the Roman document should be dated close to that time.[47]

As to the names of the Roman envoys, according to the document they were Quintus Memmius and Titus Manius. A delegation of that composition is not known. Niese has pointed out the *cognomen* Ernios attached to Manios in the Venetian uncial manuscript, and proposed considering it a garble of Manius Sergius, the name of one of the two emissaries sent to Greece, Pergamum and Antioch (Polybius 31.1.6–8). With him was Caius Sulpicius.[48] Some scholars have suggested that the latter stayed in Pergamum while Manius Sergius went on to Antioch and was joined by Quintus Memmius, and this solution in some variation or other was accepted by most scholars.[49] It is, however, untenable from the chronological point of view. Polybius' passage on the delegation certainly fits into the Olympic year 154.1 which extended from the autumn of 164 B.C. to the autumn of 163.[50] Evidently its exact time is very close to the time of Antiochus Epiphanes' death at the end of 164.[51] This document then antedates the delegation noted by Polybius by more than a year.

As a matter of fact the difficulty presented by the emissaries' names is more apparent than real. We do not have information on all the delegations sent from Rome to Antioch. On the year 165/164, the final year in the cycle covered by Book 30 of Polybius, only a few fragments have come down to us, and not one of them deals with Asian affairs. Before Antiochus Epiphanes set out for the eastern satrapies following the Daphne procession at the end of summer 165,[52] a delegation headed by Tiberius Gracchus appeared in Antioch (Polybius 30.27). The next delegation we know of was the one headed by Manius Sergius and Caius Sulpicius at the beginning of 163. It is highly probable that in the fifteen months between those two delegations, when practically speaking a new ruler in the guise of Lysias was reigning, and the developments in Antiochus' anabasis were not

[47] Niese (1900: 71) believes that the original date was preserved in the Venetus: 'the year 148 Xanthicus, 15 of Dioscorides'. However, the Venetus version of the sentence is simply a mixture of versions, as is evident from the very mention of two different months (Xanthicus and Diocorinthios). The word 'Dioscorides' itself is a garble of Dios Corinthios, mentioned in the first document (see p. 522 above), and setting the date at 15th of the month is clearly influenced by the date of the third document. It does not jibe with Document No. 1 which precedes it and is dated 24 Dios Corinthios. And the main thing, as noted above, is that the use of a Seleucid date in a Roman document is extremely suspect.

[48] Niese 1900: 72–4.
[49] Bibliography: Bunge 1971: 393 n. 80; Habicht 1976b: 13 n. 25.
[50] See Walbank 1957–79: 3.35,463.
[51] See ibid. 464–5.   [52] See pp. 470–2 above.

regularly reported, a Roman delegation was despatched to explore the intentions of the man in Antioch.

Taking all these points into account, the order of the documents and diplomatic contacts should be reconstructed as follows:

1. Document No. 1: end of October 165 B.C. (24 Dios, 148 in the Seleucid calendar); negotiations between Lysias and the rebels shortly after the battle at Ammaus.
2. Document No. 4: a short time after Document No. 1 (the date on the document is an interpolation from Document No. 3); the Roman emissaries ask the rebels for a report on the course of their communication with Antioch.
3. Document No. 3: early spring of 164 B.C. (15 Xanthicus 148); Menelaus' initiative and the proclamation of a conditional amnesty limited in time (to 30 Xanthicus), and a selective withdrawal of the religious persecutions, six months before Lysias' first expedition.
4. Document No. 2: at the end of Lysias' second expedition (late spring or early summer of 162 – the document is undated); announcement of the return of the Temple and the unselective repeal of the coercive edicts.

Ptolemy Macron

The negotiations between Judas Maccabaeus' people and Lysias were thus conducted at the end of October 165 B.C., some time after the Seleucid defeat in the battle of Ammaus in the late summer of 165. How did the contact between the two sides actually start? In other words, how were the rebels, who were concentrated at the time in the Gophna Hills, able to present their case to the authorities who had long been subject to the exclusive influence of the Hellenizers? It would be an oversimplification to solve the problem by assuming that the contact was made primarily through a lobby of Antioch Jews, or the like. We have no evidence at all of any such influential lobby, despite the relatively plentiful information available on the activities in Antioch of delegations of various Judaean bodies at all stages of the relations with the Seleucids (esp. II Macc. chh. 3–4). Though the persecutions were apparently never applied to the Antioch Jews, their intervention on behalf of a rebellious movement at such an early stage would have been tantamount to treason which would have endangered the local community. At most, however, they could have tried to persuade the authorities to ease the restrictions, or taken advantage of their physical proximity to the centre of government, to provide various services after the first contact was made. Given the communications in the ancient world, long-distance mediation could not have initiated direct contact between belligerents imbued with hatred for each other, certainly not at such an early intense stage of the conflict, when the parties were not yet exhausted.

Contacts of this kind have their own brand of dynamics: they are initiated to begin with at a low level as a result of various military and human circumstances and pressures, they enable each party to appreciate the character of its opposite number, promote a basic mutual trust of a sort, and evolve into actual negotiations at a higher level.

The available documents and information do not directly report the circumstances leading to the contacts, nor the people involved. In view of the fact that the negotiations took place immediately after the resounding Seleucid defeat at Ammaus, it seems that the only way any initial contact could have developed between the rebel Jews and the authorities was from the Seleucids' need to bury their warriors who had fallen in the battle. Although Judas Maccabaeus did not control the Aijalon Valley, he did pursue fleeing enemy soldiers for a considerable distance, and the Seleucid commanders would have had to come to an agreement with him in order to arrange the immediate burial of their dead. The Greek and Hellenistic world placed a high value on the burial of dead warriors left in territory controlled or supervised by the enemy, and the defeated party made every effort to reach an accord on the matter with the victors. That effort also constituted a kind of official admission of defeat. Such an accord did not necessarily involve substantive concessions, for the victor too recognized his obligation to cooperate.[53] The situation was naturally somewhat different when the victorious party was a nation alien to Hellenistic tradition. In the present case, permission to locate and bury the bodies without interference may have been given in exchange for various pledges. And even if nothing was actually promised, a first contact was established with representatives of the enemy, enabling the rebels to have their say.

Contacts of that sort were naturally conducted at a local, low level on the part of the Seleucids. How could the Jews' point of view traverse the various echelons of the Seleucid hierarchy in Coele Syria and reach Lysias? Ptolemy, son of Dorymenes, the *stratēgos* of Coele Syria and Phoenicia, who was directly responsible to the central authorities for what went on in Eretz Israel, had once played a vital role, for a heavy bribe, in tipping the scales in favour of Menelaus and his faction (II Macc. 4.45–7), and his testimony may well have had considerable influence on the decision to issue the coercive edicts.[54] According to I Maccabees, he was even in personal command of the expedition to Ammaus (3.38), although the version in II Maccabees whereby the expedition was undertaken simply on his initiative seems more acceptable (8.8–9)[55] In any case, it is hard to expect a man of his ilk to change his views and cut himself off from his Hellenizer protégés. Who then passed the rebels' request on to Lysias? Presumably it could not have been done against the will of the governor, who could prevent the transmission of information of this type.

The passage introducing the reign of Eupator in II Maccabees reports

---

[53] On the duty of burying those fallen in battle and the agreements involved see p. 369 n. 13 above.   [54] See p. 239 above.   [55] P. 238 above.

the appointment of Lysias 'on the affairs' (referring, no doubt, to the extension of his appointment from the time of Antiochus Epiphanes) and of a man named Protarchus as *stratēgos* of Coele Syria and Phoenicia (10.11).[56] After noting the appointment of Protarchus, the text says:

> For indeed (γάρ) Ptolemy Macron, who had taken the lead in preserving justice in regard to the Jews because of the injustices that had been done to them, tried to settle (matters) in regard to them peacefully;[57] he was therefore accused before Eupator by the Friends, and when he heard that at every opportunity they called him a traitor because he had left Cyprus which Philometor entrusted to him and gone over to Antiochus Epiphanes, and that he holds[58] his post in a dishonourable way, he poisoned himself and departed from life (10.12–13).

A number of scholars have already surmised that Ptolemy Macron served as the *stratēgos* of Coele Syria and Phoenicia,[59] and the wording of the above passage confirms this. The appointment of Protarchus is explained in the words 'for indeed', meaning that Protarchus was appointed when Ptolemy committed suicide because doubts were voiced regarding the latter's loyalty and policy. The connection that Ptolemy Macron had with the Jewish problem as cited in the passage and his earlier experience as governor of Cyprus also provide support for that conclusion.

The battle of Ammaus, during which Ptolemy son of Dorymenes was the governor of Coele Syria and Phoenicia, preceded Ptolemy Macron's suicide, which occurred shortly after Antiochus Eupator became sole king of the

[56] Many scholars are of the opinion that *prōtarkhon* in II Macc. 10.11 is a modifier of *stratēgos* and not a person's name, and construe *stratēgos prōtarkhos* as 'head *stratēgos*'. That would mean that even before being put 'in charge of the affairs' (chief minister) by Eupator, Lysias served as *stratēgos* of Coele Syria and Phoenicia, or that Eupator made him responsible for 'the affairs' in Antioch and *stratēgos* of Coele Syria and Phoenicia at the same time. The suggestion that Protarchus is not a name was rejected for both lexical and syntactic reasons by Habicht, who noted also that there was no precedent or rationale for having a single person fill the two positions (1976a: 251, and see also the bibliography there). As to the possibility that Lysias was the *stratēgos* of Coele Syria and Phoenicia only before Eupator's time, according to I Maccabees Lysias occupied the position of regent and deputized for the king in the western part of the kingdom when Antiochus Epiphanes went on his eastern expedition (3.32), and this is clearly indicated in Documents Nos 1 and 4 in II Macc. 11 (verses 17,35). It seems probable that he served as chief minister even earlier (see p. 233 above re verse 32). It is not likely that the author of II Maccabees, who was so excellently informed on what went on at the Seleucid court, should have erred in regard to such an important position. The word *prōtarkhon* must therefore be understood as the accusative case of the name Protarchus, the *stratēgos* put in charge of Coele Syria and Phoenicia at the start of Eupator's reign. Lysias' appointment on the other hand was merely the reconfirmation of the appointment he already held, a reconfirmation that was normal practice upon the accession of a new king.

[57] Grimm (1857: 159) rightly compares the sentence ἐπειρᾶτο τὰ πρὸς αὐτοὺς εἰρηνικῶς διεξάγειν in our verse to Polybius 18.24.10.

[58] The text is difficult. See the proposal made by Risberg 1918: 24, followed by Katz 1960: 15–16; Habicht 1976a: 252.

[59] Mitford 1957: 184; M. Stern 1965: 43–5; Habicht 1976a: 251; Th. Fischer 1980: 206.

realm, by only a year and a quarter. It is thus reasonable to assume that Ptolemy Macron was Ptolemy son of Dorymenes' successor as governor of Coele Syria and Phoenicia.

When was Ptolemy Macron appointed to the post? While we have no explicit data, the most logical reason for the dismissal of Ptolemy son of Dorymenes is the failure of the Ammaus campaign undertaken on his initiative. Considering the composition, armament, pretensions and complicated stratagems of the Seleucid forces, in contrast to the few troops of Judas Maccabaeus who took part in the battle and their then still meagre weaponry, it was the most excruciating military defeat of the Seleucids in Judaea until the ultimate liberation of the region at the time of John Hyrcanus. The failure was a severe blow to the prestige of Lysias, who was responsible for the state of the western part of the empire to the king then in Persia and to the Macedonian military settlers in northern Syria, the main support of the regime. Ptolemy son of Dorymenes probably paid for the failure with his post. And indeed nothing is said of him in any connection in the description of events after the battle of Ammaus. In any case, there was no other event between the battle of Ammaus and Antiochus Epiphanes' death to which his dismissal could be ascribed. The very fact that the Jewish rebels were able to submit their views to Lysias shortly after the battle of Ammaus itself suggests that Ptolemy son of Dorymenes was no longer governor at the time.[60]

What led to the appointment of precisely Ptolemy Macron as governor of Coele Syria and Phoenicia? The appointment was certainly approved, if not originated, by Antiochus Epiphanes. In view of what is known of Ptolemy Macron's descent, personality and past history, certain considerations suggest themselves. Ptolemy Macron is mentioned several times in Polybius and in epigraphical findings,[61] and those references help explain what II Maccabees says of his past: his real name was Ptolemy son of Ptolemy son of Macron. His grandfather's name became his regular nickname.[62] Between 180 and 168 B.C. he was governor of Cyprus for the Ptolemies. His desertion is known only from II Maccabees. Since at the beginning of 169 B.C., when the *anaklētēria* marking Ptolemy Philometor's majority was celebrated in Alexandria (Polybius 28.12.8–9), he was still serving in Cyprus (Polybius 27.13.3), there is an inclination to ascribe his defection to the Seleucid conquest of Cyprus in 168 B.C. (see especially Polybius 29.27.9).[63] His post in Cyprus was the most important one in the

---

[60] In the past various scholars identified Ptolemy Macron with Ptolemy son of Dorymenes (Grimm, Abel, Avi-Yonah, Bengtson, et al.). However, the different policies on the Jews, the way Ptolemy Macron is presented in II Maccabees, and mainly recently available information on Ptolemy Macron from inscriptions, his name, the date of his defection from the Ptolemaic service, all operate categorically to reject this identity. On this matter see also Mitford 1957: 176–7.

[61] On Ptolemy Macron see I. Lévy 1950: 688–99; Peremans and Van't Dack 1954–5: 338–45; Mitford 1957: 163–87. See also the summary of Bagnall 1976: 256–7.

[62] See Mitford 1957: 182–4,186 (according to *OGIS* 105; *Syll.*[3] 585).

[63] See Otto 1934: 78; Mitford 1957: 184.

Ptolemaic administration outside Alexandria. A person in that position must necessarily have had a great deal of military and administrative experience and have advanced to that post through the whole *cursus honorum*.[64] All of this prepared him for the job of governor of Coele Syria and Phoenicia which at least in the western part of the Seleucid empire was then equivalent to Cyprus. Except for Seleucis, the main concentration of Seleucid military settlers in northern Syria and the nerve centre of the realm, Coele Syria and Phoenicia was most important from the point of view of the security in that part of the kingdom. Ptolemy Macron's outstanding success as governor of Cyprus, particularly in financial matters (Polybius 27.13) and his strong personality (see below) led to expectations that he would be able to deal adequately with the complex problems of the satrapy. Ptolemy Macron also had a special relationship with the Seleucid garrison in the country, which included soldiers who had defected from Cyprus even before he himself had (II Macc. 4.29), and perhaps also quite a few who had defected with him (cf. II Macc. 12.2). In Cyprus he already had decisive influence on them and their commanders as shown by the honours they accorded him.[65] And primarily, in contrast to his predecessor Ptolemy son of Dorymenes, who had no previous training in handling Jewish affairs,[66] Ptolemy Macron was no doubt familiar with Jewish issues and in particular with relations between the Ptolemies and the residents of Coele Syria and Phoenicia. He was a member of a prominent Alexandria family.[67] His origin and extended service in the administration (and perhaps also in the army) had put him in direct touch with many Jews, enabling him to understand their way of life and mentality. This prepared him to govern the satrapy at a time when the Jewish problem was salient. The connections that some of the Transjordanian Jews and the sons of Onias, leaders of the conservatives before the rise of the Hasmonaeans, had with the Ptolemies and their followers,[68] and the constant Ptolemaic interference in the affairs of Coele Syria gave an advantage to a person who was familiar with the Judaean connections of the Ptolemaic regime from inside. The three-year 'cooling off' interval during which Ptolemy Macron proved himself loyal to the Seleucid authorities was enough for the purpose and did not deviate from the norms of the period.[69]

The appointment of Ptolemy Macron as governor of Coele Syria and

[64] See Bagnall 1976: 46–7.

[65] See Mitford 1957: 177–84 (*OGIS* 105; *BMI* 388; *JHS* 12 (1891) no. 16).

[66] See p. 239 above re verse 38.

[67] See Mitford 1957: 182–4,185 (*OGIS* 105; *Syll.*³ 585).

[68] On the relations between Onias III and Hyrcanus son of Joseph son of Toubias, the chief Ptolemaic supporter in the country, see II Macc. 3.11. On the stand of the military settlers in Transjordania see pp. 82–3 above. The flight of the sons of Onias to Egypt was doubtless also connected with their earlier pro-Ptolemaic stand.

[69] Cf. Theodotus the Aetolian who defected from the Ptolemaic army in 219 B.C. (Polybius 5.61.3ff.) and only two years later at the battle of Raphia was put in command of the Seleucid Royal Guard (Polybius 5.79.4), the elite contingent of the Seleucid army, charged among other things with safeguarding the personal safety of the king. It is quite possible that Ptolemy son of Dorymenes was also a 'defector' (see p. 239 above).

Phoenicia led to a change in the attitude to Jews on the local level. Familiar
with Jewish matters and knowledgeable about eastern religious fanaticism
from Egypt, Ptolemy Macron realized that the coercive edicts and the
desecration of the Temple were not the proper way to pacify Judaea. It
should be borne in mind that in his generation the general attitude of the
Ptolemaic court toward the Jews was very favourable. The man also had
complex connections with the extra-Ptolemaic world,[70] attesting to his open
mindedness, innovative initiative, and sense of public relations by no means
characteristic of administrators in monarchic regimes.

According to II Maccabees, Ptolemy Macron 'sought to settle (matters)
in regard to them peacefully'. In the first phase at least Lysias was prepared
to heed his advice, particularly in view of the previous governor's failure
and the fact that most of the army was pinned down in the Upper Satrapies.
Thus presumably following the contact made with lower-ranking officials
and military in connection with the burial of Seleucid dead after the battle
of Ammaus, the rebels' point of view was communicated to the new
governor. As he kept an open mind while studying conditions, and had
already at the outset shown an understanding of the Jewish problem, he
supported their demands and willingly passed them on to Antioch with his
favourable recommendation.

No direct information is available on whether at that stage the negotiations were at all fruitful. It is clear only that Seleucid military activity
ceased, and was resumed a year later (I Macc. 4.28).[71] The demands
approved by Lysias could have related to the day-to-day points of conflict
between the sides, such as the activity of the garrison in the Jerusalem
citadel, and so forth. It is not likely that at this stage the coercive edicts were
actually implemented in Judaea. They could not have been enforced
militarily, and Lysias may have been willing to allow a temporary
relaxation. However, the basic rebel demand for official permission to keep
the laws of the Torah, the return of the Temple, and the removal of the
Hellenizer leadership in Jerusalem were beyond Lysias' authority and were
forwarded to the king who was in the eastern satrapies.

The character of Antiochus' reply can be deduced from the third
document written six months later. The fact that it was published on the
initiative of Menelaus, specifies only conditional amnesty for a limited time,
repeals the coercive edicts only selectively and makes no mention of the
Temple or the internal leadership of the Jewish community indicates that
on the important substantive matters no agreement was reached with the
rebels. Antiochus Epiphanes rejected their demands and insisted that
contacts should be made only with Menelaus and the Hellenizers. Aware
that their position and security were diminishing day by day as the rebels
grew stronger, the Hellenizers, who supported the persecutions, understood

---

[70] See Peremans and Van't Dack 1954–5: 338–45; Mitford 1957: 185–6 (*OGIS* 117;
*Syll.*³ 585, l. 138; *I Cret.* IV. 208).

[71] See p. 283 above on the meaning of the expression 'after a year'.

what Ptolemy Macron had earlier realized – that the religious persecutions were the secret of the rebel strength, and the way to weaken Judas Maccabaeus was through concessions in the area of religion. Unlike the Seleucid governor, they continued to be concerned for their own narrow interests and did not request a definite public cancellation of edicts, but confined themselves to asking for a selective permission to practise the Jewish religion and an amnesty with a time limit. As noted above, the object was to prevent the internal reorganization of the rebels, and the rise of the rebel commanders to national leadership.

There are no indications that the proposed amnesty achieved the expected results. The commemoration of the declaration in a special day recorded by the Scroll of Fasting does not prove that many combatants responded to the amnesty offer and deserted the rebel camp: the rebel army even at its peak, did not comprise more than 15 % of the Jewish population.[72] Most of the inhabitants of the Judaean Hills accordingly remained in their villages. Being exempted from the religious decrees, they had good reason to rejoice. The active rebels could also regard the new move as a step forward toward the accomplishment of all their demands. The fact is that the number of warriors with Judas Maccabaeus at the Beth Zur confrontation was greater than at the battle of Ammaus even according to I Maccabees, who usually minimizes the size of the Jewish force, and continued to grow after the purification of the Temple.[73] The experiment thus failed, and led to Lysias' first expedition to Judaea several months later.

Those developments were doubtless distressing for Ptolemy Macron, who tried to turn matters in the direction of the Jews but failed because of the decision of the king, who was far from the scene of events. No doubt the Hellenizers worked against him at Antioch, making accusations of the kind later levelled by the king's friends: Ptolemy Macron's defection from the Ptolemies after many years in the royal service made it possible to impugn his personal loyalty and perhaps even suggest that he was a Ptolemaic agent. His support of the rebel requests was described as abuse of office and anti-Seleucid activity designed to promote Ptolemaic interests. Menelaus and his cohorts condemned the rebels as pro-Ptolemaic, which was certainly true of the Onias faction and some of the Transjordanian Jews. At a later period, Alcimus too is said to have accused Nicanor of treachery for trying to compromise with Judas Maccabaeus (II Macc. 14.26–7).[74] Lysias' first expedition to Judaea undertaken against Ptolemy Macron's advice certainly led to the deterioration of the relations between the two men. Nevertheless the main motive for Ptolemy Macron's suicide was not neces-

---

[72] See pp. 56–7 above.

[73] See p. 48 above. On the significance of this matter in understanding the so-called 'rift' in the rebel camp, p. 59 above n. 101.

[74] Although the episode itself is not historical (see pp. 354–6 above) it indicates a similar train of thought; and perhaps the Hellenizers' intervention against Ptolemy Macron, which was known to Jason of Cyrene, inspired him to ascribe similar intervention to Alcimus against Nicanor.

sarily connected with the Jews but with changes in the government in Antioch after the death of Antiochus Epiphanes. II Maccabees does present the suicide as the result of the opposition to his pro-Jewish policies, but that is simply the practice of the author, who also describes Andronicus' execution by Antiochus Epiphanes as punishment for the former's murder of Onias III (4.38) rather than as an attempt to disguise Epiphanes' complicity in the slaying of his official co-ruler, Antiochus son of Seleucus IV (Diodorus 30.7.2).[75]

With the death of Antiochus Epiphanes, Lysias became the sole ruler in the kingdom thanks to his function as regent. From the start he made every effort to establish his reign on solid foundations, and cruelly removed potential rivals within the royal family (Polybius 31.7.2–4).[76] Ptolemy Macron was certainly deemed to be one of the most dangerous of the potential rivals: the available information shows him to have been a very strong, gifted person. He reached the highest pinnacles in the military and administrative service of the Ptolemies, was the first of the Cyprus governors to earn the noble rank of *syngenēs* (= kin to the king),[77] corresponding to that of Lysias in the Seleucid empire (I Macc. 3.32; II Macc. 11.35). He was very successful on the economic plane, and had the courage to take his own decisions which were contrary to the opinion of the *dioikētēs*, the Minister of Finance in Alexandria (Polybius 27.13).[78] Although he had joined the Seleucid staff only shortly before, he had an important power base: the soldiers from Cyprus who were absorbed in the Seleucid army were probably loyal to him, since they had shown great admiration for him when he was governor of Cyprus.[79] The danger in those relations is illustrated by the case of Lasthenes, the Cretan, who with the help of Cretans in the Seleucid army gained control of Antioch as a regent not many years later. Ptolemy Macron's support of the Jewish cause was likely to assure him of the help of the Jewish soldiers in the kingdom, and of the Jews in Judaea who had already proved themselves a potent military factor. The connection which Macron established in the Greek world, too, could assure him of diplomatic backing if necessary and recruitment sources as well. Thus Lysias could not avoid viewing him as a most dangerous potential rival. He removed the *stratēgos* 'democratically' by inciting the council of Friends against him through the same accusations that the Jewish Hellenizers had hurled at Ptolemy Macron earlier. We can only guess at the manner in which he was 'persuaded' to take his own life.

The great change in the attitude of the Antioch authorities to the Jews took place as Lysias' second expedition to Judaea ended, early in the summer of 162 B.C. Despite his overwhelming military success, Lysias realized that internal developments in the empire, and most urgently

---

[75] On the last matter see also M. Stern 1960: 2–3.

[76] See Niese 1893–1903: 3.220. E. Obst in *RE* s.v. 'Lysias' (9), cols 2532–3; H. H. Schmitt 1964: 24–5; Walbank 1957–79: 3.471–2.

[77] See Mitford 1957: 182,184 (*OGIS* 105); Bagnall 1976: 256.

[78] On this episode see Bagnall 1976: 225,250.   [79] P. 537 n. 65 above.

Table 6. *Chronological background of the four documents in II Maccabees Ch. 11*

September 165 B.C.	The expedition to the eastern satrapies
	The battle of Ammaus
Late September–October 165	Dismissal of Ptolemy son of Dorymenes
	Appointment of Ptolemy Macron
	Negotiations with the rebels
Late October 165	**Document No. 1**: Interim summary of negotiations by Lysias
	Document No. 4: Roman willingness to help in the negotiations
Winter 165/164	Antiochus Epiphanes' rejection of the main demands and refusal to negotiate with the rebels
Early spring 164	Menelaus' request for the proclamation of a conditional amnesty
Mid-March 164	**Document No. 3**: Proclamation of the conditional amnesty by Lysias
October–November–December 164	Lysias' first expedition to Judaea and the siege of Beth Zur
	The raid near Beth Zur
20 November–18 December (Kislev) 164	Death of Antiochus Epiphanes in Babylonia becomes known
	Lysias returns to Antioch
End of December 164	Purification of the Temple
April–July 162	Lysias' second expedition to Judaea
July 162	**Document No. 2**: Official repeal of the coercive measures and return of the Temple to the Jews by Antiochus Eupator

among them Philippus' approach to Antioch, would make it impossible to maintain a large force in Judaea to eradicate the rebels and prevent the resumption of guerrilla warfare. Having concluded that the Judaean situation was not amenable to a military solution, he decided to employ the diplomatic option. He proclaimed officially the overall repeal of the coercive religious measures which the authorities had long been unable to enforce, and the return of the Temple to the Jews. At this point, as though to write *finis* to the former policy, Menelaus was executed,[80] and Alcimus appointed

---

[80] Josephus took his material from some Jewish source and not from II Maccabees (see p. 191 above). In contrast, II Maccabees reports the execution of Menelaus in the introduction to Lysias' second expedition. Menelaus encouraged the authorities to undertake the expedition, and Lysias blames him 'for all the evils' and has him executed in Beroea (13.3–9). In fact there seems no good reason for his execution at this stage. If his way did not please Lysias, the latter had only to make an earlier announcement of the concessions contained in Document No. 2 and thus contribute greatly to facilitating the expedition to Judaea. Menelaus could have been blamed for 'all the evils' only at the end of the second expedition when the policy changed. He may have continued vociferously to oppose unconditional concessions to the rebels, as did the residents of Acre (II Macc. 13.25) and probably other cities as well, and thus intensified anger. In any case, setting the story of his execution in the framework of preparations for the expedition does not make it necessary to think that II Maccabees must mean that the execution was earlier. The author may have included the execution episode by association, since he had previously mentioned Menelaus' encouraging the king to embark upon the expedition. This

high priest and ethnarch (*Ant.* 12.383–5). Even now, Lysias was unwilling to hand over autonomous authority to the rebels, preferring to entrust it to a 'semi-Hellenizing' high priest. However, events in Antioch and his own short reign before the arrival of Demetrius I in Tripolis prevented Lysias from putting Alcimus in complete charge in Judaea.[81]

type of non-chronological associative writing deviating from historical continuity is well known in II Maccabees. Thus, in describing the fate of evil-doers he gleefully diverges to their deserved end without paying attention to the time order. In describing the fate of Jason, for instance, the author reports his seizure of Jerusalem in 168 B.C. and his evil deeds there (5.5–6) and, as he wants to relate the punishment also, adds that Jason fled to the land of the Ammonites, was captured by Aretas king of the Arabs and exiled to Egypt, went from there to Sparta, and when he died did not have a traditional burial or eulogy (5.7–10). All these things certainly happened long after the event reported subsequently – the reoccupation of Jerusalem by Antiochus IV in 168 (5.11). On the predilection of II Maccabees for associational order see also p. 512 above. Abel (1949: 450), and others in his wake, also defer Menelaus' execution. However, Abel's explanation, that the execution preceded the start of the expedition in order to show it was the result of divine intervention and not of the political military development, is questionable.

[81] On the question of when Alcimus' actual rule and high priesthood began in practice see pp. 345–6 above.

K

The chronology of Lysias' second expedition

The dating of Lysias' second expedition differs in the two principal sources. According to I Maccabees (6.20), it took place in the year 150 Seleucid era (S.E.). As a date relating to Jewish matters, it must be set between April 162 and March 161 B.C. According to II Maccabees (13.1), the expedition took place in the year 149 S.E. As that book uses only the Macedonian–Syrian variation of the Seleucid calendar,[1] the count of which started in October 312, the reference is to the year between the autumn of 164 and the autumn of 163 B.C.

An examination of the possibilities based on II Maccabees' chronology indicates that the beginning of the expedition must be dated later than midsummer 163 B.C., that is, close to the end of the year 149 in the Seleucid –Syrian calendar variation: Antiochus Epiphanes died at the end of 164 B.C., the Temple was purified, and then Judas Maccabaeus set out on protracted expeditions all over Eretz Israel. The only chronological clue regarding the end of those expeditions is the statement in II Macabees (12.31,32) that the expedition to Transjordania ended on the eve of the Feast of Weeks–Shavuot (Sivan–June). According to I Maccabees, Judas Maccabaeus continued with his military operations in Mt Hebron and the coastal plain thereafter too (5.63–8). The siege of the Akra, which was the pretext for Lysias' second campaign (I Macc. 6.20), began only after the completion of all these expeditions. It was followed by the Hellenizers' delegation to Antioch (6.21–7), Lysias' expedition (6.31), and the siege of Beth Zur and its surrender (6.31,49–51).[2] The battle of Beth Zacharia (6.32ff.) took place accordingly at the end of the summer or beginning of the autumn. After his victory Lysias besieged the Temple (6.48ff.). The siege was lifted only when Philippus was approaching Antioch (I Macc. 6.55ff.; II Macc. 13.23), which according to this chronology must have been later than the beginning of October 163, i.e. already in the year 150 by the Seleucid–Syrian count.

As to the date of 150 S.E. that appears in I Maccabees, it does not refer directly to the expedition itself but to the siege Judas Maccabaeus laid to

---

[1] See p. 167 above.
[2] For the misplacement of I Macc. 6.49–51 see pp. 308–9 above.

the Akra, in the midst of which a delegation of Hellenizers arrived at Antioch to seek help. This was followed, as mentioned above, by Lysias' expedition. Here, too, additional data are of help: Demetrius I acceded to the throne sometime in November 162 B.C.,[3] and the expedition must have been terminated earlier.

The date can be determined even more precisely: I Maccabees states that the besieged in Beth Zur and the Temple had to surrender as the granaries were empty (6.49,53) because of the Sabbatical year. The year commencing in Tishri (about October) 164 and ending in Elul (about September) 163 B.C. (i.e. the year equivalent to 149 in the Seleucid–Syrian count), was a fallow year.[4] This may at first sight decide the question in favour of the date of II Maccabees. A close examination of the wording of I Maccabees, however, shows that it does not state that the siege was carried out in the fallow year, but only that it was affected by it.[5] This permits setting the siege in the year after the Sabbatical year (מוצאי שמיטה). As a matter of fact, there should not be shortage of supplies in the Sabbatical year itself. The experience and tradition of many generations must have taught the Jewish farmers to prepare enough wheat in the previous years and store it in the granaries for the Sabbatical year. Moreover, they had to prepare supplies also for the year after the Sabbatical, until the wheat harvest in the second half of that year. A shortage of bread is therefore unlikely, unless the country suffered from drought in the years before the Sabbatical, or was severely devastated in the fallow year or the year before, or there was an unusual number of refugees. A drought would have been mentioned, no less than the Sabbatical, as a reason for the shortage if it indeed occurred. As for possible devastation, the invasions by Ptolemy son of Dorymenes and Lysias' first expedition, which preceded the Beth Zacharia battle, were stopped at Ammaus and Beth Zur, on the western and southern borders of Judaea. The refugees moved by Judas Maccabaeus from Galilee and Transjordania (I Macc. 5.23,45) were not so numerous as to exhaust alone all the granaries containing at least a six-months' supply; otherwise they would have been able to defend themselves and would have been left in their native regions. The absorption of these refugees (as indicated in I Macc. 6.53) could have begun to have an impact only toward the end of the first half of the year after the fallow year.

[3] For setting the date of Demetrius' abrupt departure from Rome and the start of his rule in Syria some time in November 162 B.C. see Bickerman in *RE* s.v. 'Makkabäerbücher', col. 783; Aymard 1953–4: 62; Schürer... 1973: 1.129. The main sources: I Macc. 7.1; II Macc. 14.1–2; Appian, *Syr.* 47(241–2); Polybius 31.11–15; Eusebius, *Chron.* 1. 253–4 (ed. Schöne); Obsequens 15, and esp. the Babylonian chronicle cited by Aymard.

[4] For the determination of the Sabbatical cycle in the time of the Second Temple see Schürer 1901: 1.34; Zeitlin 1950: 254–7; Dancy 1954: 113–14; and see also Akavia 1974: 302,654. The main data are Josephus' comments on the siege of Sossius (*Ant.* 14.475) and the Talmudic tradition regarding the date of the destruction of the Temple (*BT Arakḥin* 11b; Taanith 29a; *PT Taanioth* 4.8 [68d]). The doubts raised about the chronology of Sossius' siege are not valid; see Schürer 1901: 1.358 n. 11; Zeitlin 1950: 254–9; Schalit 1969: 764–8. See further pp. 545–6 on the siege of Dōk by John Hyrcanus.

[5] See p. 339 re verse 49, and p. 341 re verse 53.

The beginnings of the wheat harvest in the Judaean Hills took place early in June. The only Jewish region in which wheat ripened earlier was Jericho, but one can assume that – being celebrated for its expensive fruits and medicinal plants – the area did not produce much more wheat than needed for its own consumption. In any case, a dry desert wind, which is rather common at the beginning of April, could have burned the wheat while the spikes were still green, or late rain could have caused fungus to develop and spoil the crop. As for barley, the only known substitute for wheat in the country, its harvest began in mid April, but it was cultivated mainly in the northern Negev, separated from the Judaean Hills by the Idumaeans who collaborated with Lysias, and in the hostile coastal plain, and could equally be affected by the natural disasters mentioned above with regard to wheat.[6] All this means that the references to the effect of the Sabbatical year on the military operations indicate that those were carried out in the year after the fallow year rather than in the fallow year itself, and that the later siege, that of the Temple, cannot be deferred too long after the beginning of June 162. The shortages became acute as the siege dragged on (I Macc. 6.52–4).

Hence we can conclude that the expedition started some time in April, the siege of Beth Zur took place in May, and the battle at Beth Zacharia toward the end of May or in early June. The siege of the Temple was laid at the beginning of June. The compression of all these events into the period immediately after the siege of the Akra does not impose particular difficulties. It may be assumed that the siege of the citadel by starving it out began in one way or another even before 150 S.E. (i.e. before April 162 B.C.), so that the Antioch authorities had some warning of the need to intervene and mobilize troops before the delegation of the besieged arrived. At the beginning of 150 S.E. the siege became tighter, as siege machines were introduced, and that inspired the despatch of the delegation to Antioch. Besides, more than a year had passed since Antiochus Epiphanes' death and the purification of the Temple, and at least six months since the completion of Judas Maccabaeus' campaigns against the neighbours, so that the Seleucid army must have prepared itself much earlier to crush the revolt in Judaea.

A goodly number of scholars have preferred the II Maccabees date,[7] in particular because it falls in the fallow year. It is interesting to mention on this occasion the somewhat similar case of John Hyrcanus' siege of Dōk–Dagon, at the beginning of 134 B.C. (I Macc. 16.14), which was the

---

[6] On the kinds of crops in the various regions of the Land of Israel, the harvest seasons and the risks involved according to ancient sources, see Feliks 1963: 187–203.

[7] See esp. Wellhausen 1905: 150–2; Bickerman 1937: 156–8; Dancy 1954: 113–14; Schaumberger 1955: 430; Goldstein 1976: 315–19. Among those preferring the I Maccabees date are Bornstein 1921: 238–9; Bévenot 1931: 221; North 1953: 506; Schürer... 1973–9: I. 167 n 14. On the other hand, Bunge (1971: 351, following Hanhart 1964: 64) tries to settle the differences on the assumption that II Maccabees has adopted the Seleucid–Babylonian system and I Maccabees the Seleucid–Syrian one (for a domestic date!), but this does not accord with the methods of the two books.

year following the Sabbatical year. Josephus states that the siege was lifted because the Sabbatical year had begun (*Ant.* 13.234; *Bell.* 1.60), and various scholars have sought to rely on his statement and move the fallow year calendar forward one year, thus proving as well that 163–162 B.C., the date that emerges from I Maccabees for Lysias second expedition, was fallow,[8] but this has been completely refuted.[9] Nicolaus of Damascus, the Gentile source used by Josephus for the siege of Dōk, did not properly interpret the information he had, as is indicated also by his statement that the Jews rest in the seventh year (ibid.), implying that the siege was stopped because Jews do not fight then.[10] The siege was lifted not because the fallow year began, but because it was laid in the eighth year. It began in the second half of the winter, and the longer it dragged on, the greater the logistic difficulties became.

Another point has been raised in favour of the II Maccabees chronology: the expedition in Judaea ended suddenly because of Philippus' drive toward Antioch together with the troops left in Persia by Antiochus Epiphanes (I Macc. 6.55–6). If the II Maccabees chronology is accepted, that would mean that roughly ten months elapsed between the death of Antiochus Epiphanes and the return of the troops, while on the basis of the I Maccabees chronology about eighteen months elapsed. It is hard to understand why Philippus waited so long before making for Antioch, and how he was able to hold the military settlers from northern Syria in the Upper Satrapies for so long. Yet ten months (as per II Maccabees) is an extended period as well and raises the same questions. Moreover, there are reasons for believing that at least part of the forces that set out with Antiochus Epiphanes returned to Syria much earlier, and even took part in Lysias' second expedition to Judaea: the 'Roman' unit, which comprised half of the infantry Royal Guard, was involved in the battle of Beth Zacharia.[11] The Royal Guard units were the elite troops of the Seleucid army and accompanied the kings on the great campaigns. It is hard to believe that any of them would have been left behind when Antiochus Epiphanes left for the east, especially not the 'Roman' troops who were retrained in Roman combat methods which would make them more effective on the terrain and against the foe that Antiochus was going to confront in the eastern satrapies. In addition, the attachment of the entire force at Lysias' disposal to the

---

[8] Marcus 1943: 7.196 n.a; Wachholder 1973: 163–5, 187–8; id. 1976: 8–13, and also Schürer... 1973–9:1.19 and 167 n. 14; Bunge 1971: 683–6.

[9] See esp. the detailed reasons of Dancy 1954: 114.

[10] On Nicolaus as Josephus' source rightly Hölscher 1904: 11 (according to the parallel in *Bell.* 1.56–60). On the halakhic question and the attempts to explain the garbling see Herr 1961: 352–3. Even if the prohibition against offensive warfare and conquest during the Sabbatical year as noted in the Scroll of the War of the Sons of Light (3[2]6, 8–9) reflects the usual practice during the period of the Second Temple (which is itself doubtful), it is certainly not relevant to the problem of the siege of Dōk-Dagon, for Hyrcanus sought to extricate his mother and two brothers, and this definitely involved saving lives (פיקוח נפש), a precept which supersedes all others. See also Schürer 1901: 1.36; H. Levy 1960: 122 n. 32.

[11] See pp. 313–16 above.

long campaign in Judaea, when the main part of the Seleucid army was still in the eastern satrapies and preparing to attack Antioch, seems rather unlikely. I Maccabees on this point is therefore not accurate, as is often the case when the author refers to an external event. A certain proportion of the force that had accompanied Antiochus Epiphanes must have returned shortly after his death, and Philippus lingered in the Upper Satrapies to solidify his control and gain the support of the military settlers in those regions.

Surprisingly enough, in discussions of the chronological problem, little notice has so far been taken of the information about the destruction of the Seleucid elephants at Apamea by the Roman legate Gnaeus Octavius (Polybius 31.2.11; Appian, *Syr.* 46(239–40); Pliny, *Nat. Hist.* 34.25; Obsequens 15; Zonaras 9.25). As Lysias used elephants in the battle of Beth Zacharia, the animals were evidently executed only after his return from the Judaean expedition and the pacification of Antioch after Philippus' revolt. The passage in Polybius reporting the despatch of Gnaeus Octavius (31.2.1–14) is generally considered as belonging to Polybius' description of Olympic year 154.1 (autumn 164–autumn 163[12]). As the passage, which opens with the rejection of Demetrius' request to return to Syria (31.2.1–8), hints at the death of Antiochus Epiphanes (31.2.2,6) at the end of 164 B.C., Octavius' despatch was dated by many scholars to early 163 B.C., in the wake of the change in ruler in Antioch.[13] The Roman legate arrived in Syria only some months later for he inspected *en route* the situation in Macedonia, Galatia and Cappadocia (Polybius 31.2.12–14,8.4–5). That would mean that the elephants were slaughtered some time in the spring or summer of 163.

This dating does not accord with the dates for the end of Lysias' second expedition which can be derived from I Maccabees (July 1962 B.C.) or II Maccabees (no earlier than October 163 B.C.) either. However, if we reject the suggested connection between the despatch of the embassy to the death of Antiochus IV, the dating of the passage to the Olympic year 154.1 could allow the possibility of dating the destruction of the elephants itself a few months later than October 163, the date of Lysias' return to Antioch according to II Maccabees. The chronology of the Roman embassy in any case needs to be re-examined.

The date suggested for the slaughter of the elephants ignores its explicit dating by Julius Obsequens (ch. 15) to 592 'since the foundation of the city', i.e. 162 B.C. As for the Polybius passage 31.2.1–14, it includes nothing requiring the event to be attributed to a time immediately after Antiochus IV's death. The expression Ἀντιόχου δὲ μετειληφότος τὴν βασιλείαν (= after Antiochus [Eupator] succeeded to the throne, para. 2) recalls the

---

[12] On the special system for the Olympic year used by Polybius see p. 470 n. 21 above. In this case there does not seem any reason which could have led Polybius to deviate from his usual practice.

[13] See, e.g., Niese 1900: 83; Bevan 1902: 2.185–7; Walbank 1957–79: 3.465; Will 1967: 2.307.

words Ἀντιόχου διαδεδεγμένου...τὴν...βασιλείαν which appear in Demetrius' second appeal to the senate (Polybius 31.11.8) on the eve of his escape from Rome (November 162 B.C.[14]), almost two years after Eupator's accession to the throne. The timing of Demetrius' request to the Roman senate to be returned to Antioch is explained not by the king's death but by Demetrius' having reached adulthood (31.2.4). Moreover, some time after Epiphanes' death a different Roman delegation sojourned in Antioch (Polybius 31.1.6–8),[15] so that Gnaeus Octavius' delegation cannot be regarded as the one despatched to inspect the situation in Antioch immediately after Epiphanes' death.

The very reason for dating the passage of Polybius under discussion to Olympic year 154.1 is not compelling: the fragment survived in the Byzantine anthology *De legationibus gentium ad Romanos*, 93. The ensuing item, no. 94, reporting Ariarathes' delegation to Rome (Polybius 31.3.1–5), says that the delegates were well received owing to Tiberius Gracchus' report (paras. 4–5). Tiberius Gracchus returned to Rome in the Olympic year 153.4 (165/164 B.C.; Polybius 30.31.19).[16] However, the Roman legate's report could have influenced the senate in favour of the Cappadocian king's envoys even more than a year later just as well, and not necessarily in the following year.[17] One of the tasks assigned to Gnaeus Octavius on his way to Syria was to inspect the kingdom of Ariarathes (31.2.13; cf. 8.1–8), which indicates that a considerable time had passed since Tiberius Gracchus' report. On the other hand, the account of Demetrius' flight from Rome (Polybius 31.11–15), which took place in November 162, shows that he left Rome shortly after the Seleucid embassy had come to apologize for the murder of the Roman delegates committed in the wake of the slaughter of the elephants (esp. 11.3–4,6, 12.2: ἐξ αὐτῆς; μετ' ὀλιγόν; εὐθέως). If we accept the dating of the passage on the despatch of Gnaeus Octavius in the Olympic year 154.1 (164/163), that would mean that Lysias sent the conciliatory delegation to Rome at least one year after the murder, which is highly unlikely. Polybius' passage on the embassy sent for the destruction of the elephants should therefore be dated to the Olympic year 154.2 rather than 154.1.

It should be added that the slaughter of the elephants was not necessarily a reaction to their utilization in Lysias' second campaign, and therefore no lengthy period of time after that expedition would be needed. The elephants were exterminated because Antiochus Epiphanes had used them in earlier battles inside his kingdom and outside it, contrary to the provisions of the Treaty of Apamea (see I Macc. 1.17, 3.34; *Ant.* 12.296; Polybius 30.25.11). In that same mission Gnaeus Octavius was charged as well with burning the Seleucid war ships (Polybius 31.2.11) which were certainly not involved in the campaign in Judaea.

---

[14] On the date of Demetrius' escape see n. 3 above, and on the dating of Demetrius' second appeal close to his flight, Polyb. 31.11.3,6,12.2,8.   [15] See Walbank 1957–79: 3.465.
[16] Ibid. 33–4,35,456.   [17] Against Walbank, ibid.

We have seen so far that the arguments made on the basis of the historical sequence and circumstances in favour of the chronology of II Maccabees do not hold water, while the references to the effects of the Sabbatical year support that of I Maccabees. What actually decides the issue are considerations related to the evaluation of these sources. It is hard to accept an error by I Maccabees precisely on this date when there are many indications that the author actually lived through the experience of the battle of Beth Zacharia, and there is no reason to question any of the other dates in that book.[18] Furthermore, since the Jewish defensive capability was greatly affected by the fallow year, and the cycle of fallow years provided a better gauge for determining that date than for any other in the history of the Revolt, is it credible that it was the author of I Maccabees who erred?

Jason of Cyrene, on the other hand, did not have personal knowledge of the events and could not verify the date on the basis of the fallow year cycles, whose observance was obligatory only in the Holy Land, and in any case his book makes no reference to any fallow year. This author could have had a verifiable reason for setting Lysias' second expedition in 149 s.e. He dates the three documents in ch. 11 (verses 21,33,38), which he relates to Lysias' first expedition, to 148 s.e., and it is possible that dating the second expedition to 149 s.e. was meant to establish some continuity between the two expeditions and yet distinguish between them. The doubts expressed by some modern scholars about the attribution of two expeditions to Lysias[19] merely illustrate the importance of such a distinction. For that reason the epitomist left the latter date in the book while eliminating all other dates from the narrative.[20]

The sequence of events in the eight months between the spring of 162 b.c. and November of the same year was thus as follows: the siege of the citadel, the delegation to Antioch, the expedition to Judaea, the siege of Beth Zur, the battle of Beth Zacharia, the siege of the Temple, Philippus' return to Syria, Lysias' conquest of Antioch, the slaughter of the elephants at Apamea, the Seleucid conciliatory delegation to Rome, and Demetrius' disembarkation at Tripolis. The battle at Beth Zacharia took place at the end of May 162 b.c. and the siege of the Temple started immediately thereafter.

The only remaining obstacle is the statement of I Maccabees that the siege of the Temple lasted 'many days' (6.51,52). The sequence and the absolute dating do not leave much time for the siege. However, this statement does not necessarily mean that the siege lasted more than a month or two: it reflects the feelings of the few remaining besieged (6.54) who suffered from famine, artillery bombardment and low morale after the defeat at Beth Zacharia, and were left on their own by their leader. The

---

[18] In stating this I refer only to dates and not to chronological sequence. On the reasons for the disruption of the correct chronological sequence in I Macc. 4.26–6.17 see pp. 281–2 above.   [19] See p. 275 above.

[20] The source of the date 'the year 149' is Jason and not the epitomist. On this and on the epitomist's intervention in the selection of material see p. 178 n. 82 and esp. p. 184 n. 98.

siege was lifted and the expedition came to an end probably some time between the end of June and the end of July 162 B.C.

This proposed dating refutes the opinion held by some scholars that the Scroll of Fasting for the 28th of Shevat ('On the 28th of it King Antiochus removed himself from Jerusalem') refers to Lysias' return to Syria, after agreement reached with the besieged in the Temple (I Macc. 6.57–63).[21] The episode in the Scroll seems to be connected with the lifting of the siege by Antiochus Sidetes in 134 B.C.[22] The description of the Sidetes siege mentions the setting of the Pleiades, rain, and the Feast of the Tabernacles (*Ant.* 13.237,241). As the siege was a lengthy one, toward the end of which tough negotiations were conducted, it can be assumed that the conclusion was not achieved before the month of Shevat. The maintenance of the siege throughout the winter is not surprising, for the expedition and the conquest of the countryside were completed before the rainy season. Only the siege of Jerusalem, at the start of which the besiegers themselves suffered from a shortage of water (ibid. 237), went on into the winter. It is also possible that it lasted longer than one year.[23]

[21] Herzfeld 1863: 1.280; Zeitlin 1922: 81; Bickerman 1935: 352.
[22] Rightly noted by Lichtenstein 1931–2: 287ff.
[23] See Schürer... 1973–9: 1.202 n. 5.

Table 7. *Chronology of Lysias' second expedition*

Date	External events	Internal events
Tishri 164–Elul 163	'The year 149' (II Macc. 3.1)	A fallow year
Kislev 164	Antiochus Epiphanes' death in Persia	End of Lysias' first expedition
		Purification of the Temple
163	Lysias' rule in Antioch, and the 'domestic purifications'	Judas Maccabaeus' expeditions to rescue Jews throughout Eretz Israel
Autumn 163		End of fallow year
Nisan 162–Nisan 161		'The year 150' (I Macc. 6.20)
April–May 162		(Continued) siege of the Akra
		Delegation to Antioch
		The expedition to Judaea
		Siege of Beth Zur
End of the spring		Surrender of Beth Zur
End of June or July		**Battle of Beth Zacharia**
Late summer 162	Elephants destroyed at Apamea	Lysias stops the siege of the Temple and returns to Antioch
Autumn 162–autumn 161	'The year 151' (I Macc. 7.1)	
November 162	Accession of Demetrius I to power	

L

The route of Bacchides' second expedition to Judaea

The route taken by Bacchides on his second expedition to Judaea which ended in the battle near Elasa is described in I Maccabees in relative detail and with more than the usual number of topographical indications. Nevertheless, the identity of the locations and the meanings of the phrases mentioned – and consequently the overall reconstruction of the expeditionary route – are in dispute. The precise determination of the route is important for an understanding not only of the particular strategy that Bacchides adopted in the expedition itself, but also of the date when extensive Jewish settlement began outside the Judaean Hills area during the period of the Second Temple.

The expedition is described as follows (I Macc. 9.2):

> καὶ ἐπορεύθησαν ὁδὸν τὴν εἰς Γαλγαλα καὶ παρενέβαλον ἐπὶ Μαισαλωθ τὴν ἐν Ἀρβήλοις καὶ προκατελάβοντο αὐτὴν καὶ ἀπώλεσαν ψυχὰς ἀνθρώπων πολλάς.
>
> (= And they went on the Gilgal[1] road and camped on (or 'at')[2] *maisalōth* in *Arbēlois* and they captured it, and they killed many human souls.)

The name Gilgal is well known in the toponymy of the Holy Land, and at least four sites bearing the same name figure in the sources and can be located. The word *maisalōth* is obviously a transcription of the Hebrew *mesīlōt*, and can be either a place-name or a noun denoting 'routes' and the like, which would mean that Bacchides camped at a crossroads. The key question for deciphering the verse is the identity of *Arbēlois*. The definition of *maisalōth* as being 'in *Arbēlois*' (and not 'by', 'near', etc.) rules out any identification of the latter as a settlement, whatever the meaning of *maisalōth* may be, and indicates that *Arbēlois* was a region or area. This discredits the identifications so far suggested for the references in the verse. In the following pages I shall raise other arguments against the various attempts at interpreting the verse.

Josephus in *Antiquitates* identifies *Arbēlois* with Arbel in Galilee (12.421),

---

[1] In the form 'Galgala' as is usual in the Septuagint. The Lucian version has γῆν Γαλααδ (= land of Gilead).　　[2] For the translation 'at' see p. 558 below.

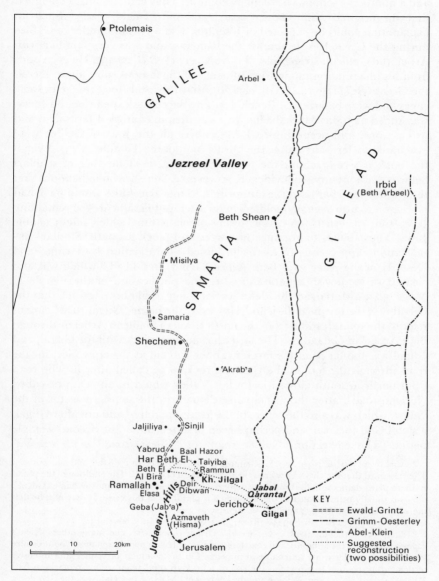

22 Proposals for the reconstruction of Bacchides' route (cf. p. 383)

and a number of scholars have followed him.[3] They consequently concluded that the original said 'Galilee road' and not 'Gilgal road'.[4] Such an explanation could be expected of Josephus who was commander of Galilee during the Great Revolt against the Romans, and was very familiar with Arbel, the Galilean stronghold (*Vit.* 188,311; cf. *Bell.* 2.573). He even adds from his imagination, under the influence of the famous story about Herod the Great (*Bell.* 1.305; *Ant.* 14.421–30), that the locals took refuge in some caves and were besieged by Bacchides. The Bacchides expedition, however, was aimed at Judas Maccabaeus who was then in control of Jerusalem and its environs, and according to I Maccabees all the Jews of Galilee were evacuated to Jerusalem after the purification of the Temple (5.23). Even if the book is wrong about the total evacuation, as a number of scholars believe (without any real evidence, however[5]), there are no indications that the Galilee Jews harassed the authorities, so that Bacchides would have had no reason to utilize 22,000 soldiers in an attempt to eradicate the remaining Jews from eastern Galilee, thus losing precious time which might enable Judas Maccabaeus to organize his forces and block his path. Similar considerations apply equally to the proposed identification by Grimm and Oesterly of the place with Beth Arbeel (Irbid) in Gilead,[6] which was also cleared of its Jewish inhabitants after the purification of the temple (I Macc. 5.45). Moreover, the identifications suggested above assume that the Gilgal was the one near Jericho.[7] However, the name 'Gilgal road' cannot refer to the roads leading from the north through Galilean Arbel or through Beth Arbeel in Galaaditis. The latter has no direct link with the Gilgal, and Gilgal was too far from the former (about 120 km as the crow flies) for the road through the foot of the Galilean rock to be called after it. The road from north to south along the Jordan Valley would in any case be called 'Jericho road', after the principal settlement in the southern sector of the valley, which was also the centre of the local toparchy,[8] and not after Gilgal, a small God-forsaken and perhaps even deserted site in the Second Temple period. The correction 'Galilee road' or 'Gilead road' is no less un-

[3] Abel 1924: 380; id. 1949: 160; S. Klein 1928a: 6–7; Avi-Yonah 1966: 66, and many others. They assumed that the Greek *Arbēlois* is the dative plural of 'Arbel'. The addition of the plural suffix to place-names is indeed rather widespread in the Septuagint. Thus the name 'Gilgal', too, was usually transliterated as *Galgala*, which is plural, as in this verse. It may also be that the plural form *arbēlōt* was prevalent in Hebrew as well.

[4] Grimm 1853: 132; Abel 1924: 381–2; id. 1949: 160; Dancy 1954: 131.

[5] Klein 1928: 1ff.; id. 1938: 1–20. See also Grintz 1969a: 164; and many others. Klein's eagerness to prove the antiquity and continuity of a large Jewish population throughout Galilee leads him to proffer quite untenable arguments. On the conquest of Galilee and intensive settlement in the area beginning at the end of John Hyrcanus' reign see my remarks in Bar-Kochva 1977a: 191–4, and see there also the analysis of I Macc. 5.15 ('Galilee of the Gentiles'), which is the decisive argument against Klein's theory. It should be noted that Nittai the Arbelite, mentioned in Tractate Aboth (1.7), lived in Hyrcanus' reign or early in Jannaeus', and consequently cannot constitute evidence of the antiquity of the Jewish settlement in eastern Galilee (against Klein 1938: 11–12).

[6] Grimm 1853: 132–3; Oesterly 1913: 96.   [7] See esp. Abel 1949: 160.

[8] On the biblical use of the term *derek* together with a place name see Aharoni 1967: 39ff.

acceptable, since the official name of such a well-known district as 'Galilee' and 'Gilead' could not have given way to 'Gilgal'.[9]

Some of the arguments mentioned above apply against Klein's interesting suggestion to connect the unknown narrow 'trails of (ševilē) Beth Gilgul', recorded in the Mishnah (Tohoroth 6.6; cf. *BT Erubin* 22b), with the 'Gilgal road, mesīlōt (routes) in Arbel', and accordingly locate Beth Gilgul somewhere in the neighbourhood of Arbel, and the 'trails' in the narrow ascent to the cliff.[10] The word *maisalōth-mesīlōt* itself can hardly refer to the steep steps climbing from the east up to the top of the Arbel cliff. Moreover, the safest way to seize control of the cliff was from the direction of the south-western plateau, and as the region was only sparsely, if at all, populated by Jews, Bacchides would have had no reason to choose another approach if he wanted to capture the cliff. However, the word *mesīlōt* is inappropriate also, if the advance was made from that direction, for movement from the south-east is unencumbered and not restricted to any particular path. The sentence 'and they camped on *mesīlōt* in Arbel' would not, in this case, make any sense. In addition, the trails which led to Arbel must obviously have been named after the latter place, and not after Beth Gilgul, wherever it may have been, which was also less well known. The 'trails of Beth Gilgul' should be looked for somewhere else, perhaps near Beth ha-Gilgal in the Judaean Hills (see below).

Ewald, who dealt first of all with *maisalōth* and 'Gilgal road', believes that *maisalōth* is the name of a place to be identified with the village of Misilya near Jenin, and 'Gilgal' with the village of Jaljilia, 28 km north of Jerusalem.[11] Grintz, who accepted the hypothesis, corrected EN ΑΡΒΗΛΟΙΣ to EN ΝΑΒΡΑΧΤΟΙΣ (= *Nabrakta*), which in his view was an early Jewish settlement district in northern Samaria.[12] Though the last correction is not impossible from the palaeographic point of view, the hypotheses of Ewald and Grintz as a whole are unacceptable. The road going from the north to Misilya (and any other destination on the road to Jerusalem) could not possibly be named after Gilgal-Jaljiliya, a remote unimportant village 50 km south of Misilya and 5 km west of the main road going south to Jerusalem. And we are not touching upon the question of the existence of a district called 'Nabrakta' in northern Samaria, or the antiquity of Jewish settlement there, which in our opinion is essentially untenable. Vilnay, who accepts Grintz's view on 'Gilgal road', believes that Arbelois is the village of Yabrud in the neighbourhood of Baal Hazor.[13] Aside from the difficulty caused by the location and unimportance of Jaljiliya, it is doubtful whether the name Arbel, which in other places became 'Irbid' for the Arabs, turned

[9] See also Klein 1938: 12. The substitution in Joshua 12.23, if indeed the verse requires correction, is understandable in view of the central position of Gilgal in the account of the conquest of Canaan.

[10] See Klein 1938; id. 1928: 6–7.

[11] Ewald 1864–8: 4.421 n. 2; cf. G. A. Smith, *Encyclopaedia Biblica*, vol. 2 (London, 1902) p. 291.   [12] Grintz 1946: 6; id. 1969a: 21–2. Cf. Schalit 1968: 130–3.

[13] Vilnay 1968: 169.

into 'Yabrud' in the Judaean Hills area. Furthermore, the word *maisalōth-mesīlōt* is not explained by this hypothesis: no place bearing a similar name can be traced in the area, and Yabrud is not located at a crossroads.

Möller and Schmitt, who also identified Gilgal with Jaljiliya, connected Arbel with the same name which appears as a Jewish foundation in the medieval Midrash *va-yisā'ū* in the legendary description of the war of the sons of Jacob against the Amorites in the Shechem area and suggested that *maisalōth* was a nearby settlement, without specifically identifying them.[14] In a recent publication, Schmitt prefers to locate Gilgal in the village of Jaljiliya, on the eastern edge of the coastal plain near modern Kefar Saba.[15] Apart from the phrasing of the verse in I Maccabees, which does not allow us to regard *Arbēlois* as a settlement, the version 'Arbel' in the Midrash is, by itself, very dubious: the earlier versions of the legend read Rôbel (Jubilee 34.8) and Iōbēl (Testaments, Judah, 6.1). All these are, as Klein rightly suggested, a garble of 'Akrab'el ('Akrab'a), which was inhabited by Jews at the time of the Hasmonaean Revolt (I Macc. 5.3).[16] The reading in the Midrash was probably affected by the Arbel Valley famous from the consolation and messianic Midrash (*PT Berakhoth* 1.1[2c]; *Ioma* 3.2[40b]; and the lamentations of Eleazar ha-Kalir for the Ninth of Ab – 'Menahem son of Amiel will suddenly appear, in the Arbel Valley...') as well as by the mediaeval identification in the Galilaean Arbel of the tomb of Dina, Jacob's daughter (see, e.g., Nachmanides' exegesis on Genesis 34.12), whose rape is described as the cause of the midrashic war with the Amorite kings near Shechem.

The discussion so far has illuminated some considerations which must guide us in the search for a proper identification of the geographic references in the verse:

(a) The military activity of Bacchides was carried out in the Judaean Hills or in their immediate vicinity.

(b) The toponymy of the area either now or in antiquity does not reveal anything similar to *maisalōth*, and the single reference to *Arbel* which appears in a mediaeval text does not stand up to criticism.

(c) In any case, *Arbēlois* must be a region and not the name of a settlement or geographical feature.

(d) The 'Gilgal road' leading to *Arbēlois* and *maisalōth* must be located in that region, and the 'Gilgal' by or very close to that road.

As we do not know of any region called Arbel in the Judaean or the south Samarian Hills, and as a whole region could hardly be neglected in the historical records of such an eventful country, there is no choice but to look for a name which bears a close phonetic resemblance and corresponds to the provisions listed above. The only name that occurs to me is *har bēt 'ēl*

[14] Möller and Schmitt 1976: 22.   [15] G. Schmitt 1983: 33–9.
[16] S. Klein 1934: 96. The verse in I Maccabees does not refer to the Ascent of 'Akrabbim in the Negev as some scholars think. Some Edomaean population is known from the Daliyah papyri as residing in the southern Samarian Hills as well (on these papyri see Cross 1963: 110–21; id. 1966: 201–11).

(= the mountain[hill country] of Beth El), the hilly region to the north-east of Ramallah, which is twice mentioned in the Bible (I Sam. 13.2; according to the Septuagint, also in Josh. 16.1). It may have been slightly garbled or shortened already in the Hebrew version to *harbē'ēl*. There were ample reasons for this: it is doubtful whether the original manuscript had spaces between the words, and in any case, they may not have been easily discernible (as for instance, in the Nash papyrus).[17] Be that as it may, the combination *har bēt'ēl*, like similar ones, could have been written without spacing.[18] The Hebrew letter *tav* could be skipped over in such a long combined word, or it may be omitted under the influence of the word *bē* (= *bēt*, 'house') current in Palestinian Aramaic.[19] The word was transliterated into Greek, with the addition of the plural suffix,[20] and one *ē* was omitted because of the haplography. It is also possible that the name was properly preserved in the original Hebrew, and the garble occurred only in the Greek version: *har bēt'ēl* was transliterated according to the transcription system used in the Septuagint as Arbethel (cf. Num. 33.23: Mount Shepher-*Arsaphar*), and the rest happened along the lines mentioned above. In any case, it should be remembered that, since he had no knowledge of the topography of Eretz Israel, the translator himself no longer understood the verse. This can also be seen from his mistake in copying the word *mesīlōt* as a place-name (see below), and the consequent construction of the word as a singular rather than a plural (προκατέλαβοντο αὐτήν = 'and they captured it').[21]

The settlements in the *har bēt'ēl* region are satisfactorily recorded in the Bible, especially in the stories about the conquest of Canaan and the Judges, as well as in the lists of the settlements and families in Joshua and Chronicles. The absence of any reference to *maisalōth* supports the suggestion, already made by some scholars, that the word is a transcription of the Hebrew *mesīlōt* (= routes).[22] This conclusion is strengthened by the fact that the

[17] Such must be the conclusion if the meaningless word *asaramēl* (I Macc. 14.27) should indeed be reconstructed through the phrase *ḥaṣar 'am 'ēl* (= court of God's people) and the like (Abel 1949: 256); the translator did not understand the phrase and thought it a place-name, so that he transcribed rather than translated it. But if we incline to Schalit's suggestion (1969: 415 n. 275) of *asara me[ga]l[ē]* (= great 'azārā, i.e. Temple courtyard), the garbling must have occurred in the copying of the Greek text.

[18] Cf. the expression *ḥerev'el* (= sword of God) in the Scroll of the War of the Sons of Light (15[22]3; 19[31]11). Rabin believes that the word *ḥerev'ēl* is a place-name (Rabin 1961: 40). But this is not necessarily so; see Flusser 1980: 445.

[19] Cf. the deletion of the *tau* (the equivalent of the Hebrew *tav*) in some of the MSS in I Macc. 7.19 (*Bēzeth* instead of *Beth Zeth* or *Bēer Zeth*?), and in the name *Bezetha*, one of Jerusalem quarters (*Bell.*2. 328,530, 5.149,151,246,504). See especially the celebrated abbreviation of Beth Shean to *bēšan* in the Palestinian Talmud (e.g. *Pea* 7.1[20a], *Abodah Zara* 1.2[39c]; *Megillah* 3.1[73d]; *Baba Meziah* 10.1 [12c]).

[20] In the Septuagint, A is used to transcribe Hebrew *hē*. For the addition of the plural suffix in I Maccabees cf. 5.23. The form *en Arbattois* is apparently a garbled version of *en Narbattois*. See Klein 1939a: 220; Grintz 1946: 12.

[21] The lack of understanding of geographical and topographical terms the translator displays is conspicuous in I Macc. 9.15 (see p. 396 above). See further p. 386 above.

[22] Robinson 1841: 2.398 n. 4; Grimm 1853: 132; Abel 1924: 380; Klein 1928: 6; Avi-Yonah 1963: 140.

word *mesīlōt*, which is not very common in the Bible, appears three times in Judges in reference to roads in the Beth El area (20.31,45, 21.19). It should be added that the preposition in the sentence 'and they camped *epi*[literally = on, toward] *maisalōth*' does not prove that *maisalōth* was a place besieged by Bacchides. The Biblical phrase 'and they camped on' ('*al*; or '*el* = toward) means also 'and they camped at'.[23]

Finally: the 'Gilgal road'. A place-name designating a road denotes the starting-point of the road, its terminus, or the route it takes.[24] Two sites called 'Gilgal' are to be found in and near *har bēt'ēl*: Gilgal near Jericho, known from the stories about the conquest of Canaan, and a settlement called Beth ha-Gilgal on the mountain itself. 'Beth ha-Gilgal' is mentioned in Nehemiah near 'the fields of Geba and Azmaveth' (12.29), present-day Jaba and Hisma. According to the north–south order in the verse, it would appear that Beth ha-Gilgal was north of Geba. And indeed, close to the village of Rammun there is a ruin known as Khirbet Jiljal, and near it, the tomb of a sheikh with the same name.[25] Some Roman-style graves are visible there, and it merits thorough archaeological investigation. It should be noted that almost all the places the Arabs call Jaljil, Jiljiliya and the like are located in a geographical context making it possible to identify them with one or another of the places called 'Gilgal' in the biblical sources. Thus, even if Khirbet Jiljal near Rammun is not identical with the biblical Beth ha-Gilgal, it does preserve the ancient Hebrew name of Gilgal.

I would suggest, therefore, that the 'Gilgal road' be identified with the ascent from the Jordan Valley, not far from Jericho, along a ridge through the village of Taiyiba to the plateau of the Judaean Hills at Beth El. It is the present-day Jericho–Beitin (Beth El) road, paved along the route of a fourth-century Roman road,[26] and running 1–1.5 km north of Rammun. A trail winding from it westward via Rammun shortens the way to the plateau, although it is less comfortable.[27] Such a local route (as distinct from a major road) could well be named after two tiny sites, one of which had many historical associations with the nation's glorious past, even in a period when that place had lost its former position; or the old name of the route could at least be preserved. We can only admire the author's great precision in choosing the specific biblical terms in his description of Bacchides' operation: 'and they went on the Gilgal Road and camped at the trails (*mesīlōt*) in *har bēt'ēl*'.

Thus, Bacchides moved through the Jordan Valley to a point north of Jericho and made his way into the Judaean Hills via a trail that climbed up to Rammun and Baal Hazor. Upon reaching Beth El, he camped at a place commanding a view of the north–south and east–west roads, apparently near Beth El.[28]

---

[23] Ex. 14.2; Num. 33.49; Jos. 11.5; Judg. 20.19; I Sam. 4.1, and cf. p. 338 above.

[24] See the reference, n. 8 above.   [25] See Conder and Kitchener 1882: 2(1). 292–3.

[26] On it see Thomsen 1917: 15.   [27] See the *PEF* maps nn. 14–15.

[28] On the military considerations for choosing that route and camping in the Beth El region see pp. 383–4 above.

It is also possible that Bacchides used the more southerly road called Tariq Abu el-Hindi by the Arabs, which goes through ancient Gilgal in the Jordan Valley and turns toward the mountain via Jabal Qarantal, going mainly along a crestline through Deir Dibwan to Beth El. That route is quite convenient, and at Beth El reaches the mountain plateau. It is shorter than the one near Rammun, and was bare and completely uninhabited.

EXCURSUS

I The chronology of
John Hyrcanus' first conquests

(see p. 163 n. 33)

It is difficult to determine the exact dates of the conquests in the first round of John Hyrcanus' campaigns of expansion (*Ant.* 254–8). One can only say that they took place during the second half of the 120s B.C. Some scholars believe that that round – which included the conquest of a number of unspecified settlements in addition to Medaba, Samaga, Shechem and Mount Gerizim, Adora and Marisa, as well as the subjection and conversion of the Idumaeans – was completed by 128 B.C. This dating is based on Josephus' statement that Hyrcanus embarked upon these campaigns 'immediately' (εὐθύς) after learning of the death of Antiochus Sidetes (129 B.C.) in order to take advantage of the cities being empty of their militia (*Ant.* 13.254), which must mean that the locals accompanied Antiochus Sidetes in his eastern adventure. As the notations there of the various conquests are short and successive, they give the impression that the operations occurred one after another without a break, as part of a single campaign. However, for various reasons it seems certain that they were spaced over the course of a number of years after 129 B.C.

The introductory sentence about the timing of Hyrcanus' campaign and its motivation does not accord with Josephus' preceding story about Hyrcanus' participation in Antiochus Sidetes' expedition against the Parthians (*Ant.* 13.251). There is no reason to doubt the information about the Jewish auxiliaries in Sidetes' camp: it appeared in Nicolaus' *Universal History* as part of the description of that expedition in the context of Seleucid history (see below), and consequently cannot be represented as Jewish propaganda (in any case, how could it serve the Jews?). As has already been pointed out by some scholars, the epithet 'Hyrcanus' may well have been acquired through that expedition, destined for the regions near the Caspian Sea. It is highly improbable that the Jewish army could embark upon a new expedition immediately after an exhausting and dangerous retreat of many hundreds of kilometres deep in hostile regions. In view of the Jewish commitment to Sidetes and of his stern character, the Jewish force does not appear to have returned early, and its remaining intact in the expedition to the east is explicable by the fact that Sidetes' army was scattered in several camps, not all of which were struck by the Parthian army and the local population (see Justin 38.10).

560

The introductory sentence to Hyrcanus' campaign against 'the cities in Syria', originates from a tradition which was not aware of his participation in Sidetes' *anabasis*. This appears from an examination of Josephus' description in *Antiquitates* of Hyrcanus' first years. The description comprises two contradictory stories: according to the first (henceforward: 'the siege story'), Antiochus Sidetes laid a heavy siege on Jerusalem, Hyrcanus was forced to surrender, and even had to rob David's tomb to compensate the king (paras. 236–49). However, later on he took advantage of Antiochus' death and the absence of the local militia to occupy 'the cities' (paras. 254ff.). According to the second story (henceforward: 'the treaty story'), Antiochus was willingly admitted into the Holy City with his army, was given a splendid reception, and signed a treaty of alliance (para. 250a). Hyrcanus accordingly took part in Antiochus' great expedition against the Parthians which ended in a great disaster (paras. 250–3).

The two stories were reported by Nicolaus of Damascus in two different places: 'the siege story' appeared in a sequence on Jewish history. It figures in *Bellum*, where Josephus, for reasons of convenience, epitomized Nicolaus alone. The same reasons probably led Josephus to avoid combining in his epitome information scattered in Nicolaus' work, but rather to content himself with abbreviating the latter's consecutive passages on Jewish history. There is no reference in *Bellum* to the story of Hyrcanus' participation in Sidetes' expedition. That 'the treaty story' was taken from Nicolaus is clear from the quotation of Nicolaus with regard to the halting of the march for two days at the request of Hyrcanus (para. 251). As indicated above, it was taken from a context on Seleucid history. This is obvious from the expression 'the Jew Hyrcanus' (ibid.; and cf. M. Stern 1974: 240), from its contents, and from its absence in *Bellum*. The question of Nicolaus' sources (the account of the siege itself was drawn from Poseidonius of Apamea), which is rather interesting, is irrelevant to the present discussion.

Be that as it may, the word 'immediately' refers to campaigns against unnamed settlements from which no real resistance was expected (para. 254). In Medaba, on the other hand, the Jewish army suffered many hardships (ταλαιπωρηθείσης) which dragged on for six months (para. 255), and presumably Hyrcanus did not immediately thereafter set out on the campaign against the Samaritans and Idumaeans which would necessarily be more complicated and difficult (cf. the later conquest of Samaria, *Ant.* 13.275–83). Furthermore, the Jewish–Roman treaty (*Ant.* 13.259–66), reconfirmed sometime between 128 and 125 B.C. (see M. Stern 1965: 150), mentions Jaffa, Pegai and Gazara as being still occupied by the Seleucids, and the Jewish demand to get them back, but does not mention (in order to approve) any new Jewish conquests and annexations, which must consequently be dated after that treaty. Finally, the danger presented by Demetrius II in 129–126 B.C., right after the death of Sidetes (*Ant.* 13.267), makes it hard to believe that Hyrcanus allowed himself so early in his reign to commit the army to successive difficult battles outside Judaea (cf. events during the siege of Samaria, *Ant.* 13.278–9). On the other hand, Josephus

(*Ant.* 13.269,273) reports that Hyrcanus signed a treaty with Alexander Zabinas after the latter's victory over Demetrius II (126 B.C.) and was expanding his realm in the time of the sole reign of Zabinas (126–123/2 B.C.). Hyrcanus' first round of conquests took place therefore after 126 or 125 B.C.

The passage in *Antiquitates* 13.254–8 compresses events that took place in the course of a number of years. It is the only passage providing any direct information on Hyrcanus' rule between 129 and 113 B.C., while for 113–105 B.C. the information is rather detailed (*Ant.* 13.275–300). In striking contrast to his report on the conquest of Samaria in the later period (*Ant.* 13.275–83), Josephus says nothing about the conquest of Shechem and Mount Gerizim, except for references to the structure of the temple there and the Sanbalat–Manasseh episode which were mentioned elsewhere in *Antiquitates* (11.310–11, 322–4). Additions of this sort are typical of Josephus in places where he felt it necessary to 'fill the vacuum' because the information available to him was inadequate. Obviously Nicolaus' book supplied only the briefest description of the first round of conquests, and the brevity of the description is no indication of the time needed to complete the activities described. See also M. Stern 1961: 8–9 for objections to the view that the conquests in the first round were all completed in 128 B.C.

II The Seleucid dates in I Maccabees

(see p. 167 n. 42)

The theory about the different systems of the Seleucid calendar used in I Maccabees for 'internal' and 'external' events, which was first suggested by Bickerman, has been questioned by various scholars who attempted to offer alternative solutions. Some claimed that there was only one chronological system in I Maccabees, differing as to what it was; others accepted the use of two systems but tried to change the base date of one or both. See a survey of the various opinions in Pfeifer 1949: 480–1; Schunck 1954: 18–19, esp. n. 1; cf. Zeitlin 1950: 257ff.; Bringmann 1983: 15–28. The arguments of the objectors deserving comment are as follows:

(a) On the basis of Bickerman's method there is no way of reconciling the chronology of Lysias' second expedition in I Maccabees with its chronology in II Maccabees, or even with the information in I Maccabees itself which seems at first sight to indicate that the expedition took place in the fallow year. However, these difficulties are only apparent: II Maccabees is mistaken and the events took place in the year after the Sabbatical (see p. 543ff. above).

(b) The use in one book of two different systems for the same count is unreasonable and unprecedented. Why would the author wish to confuse the reader? Would it not have been much easier to use a single system? However, Leviticus already uses two systems, one for holidays and another for jubilees (22.5, 25.8–10), and Josephus uses several systems simultaneously (see Schürer... 1973–9: 1.597). As to I Maccabees, the author did not do so consciously and deliberately. For domestic events that he was familiar with, he employed the system he was used to (usual in Judaea) – the Macedonian–Babylonian system – while for external events he relied directly or indirectly on a Seleucid chronicle (or a number of Seleucid sources) without realizing or taking into account that the dates were based on a slightly different chronological system. It is worth noting that the 'external' dates never have the name or number of a month, even when that seems necessary (in 10.1, e.g., because of 10.21), contrary to the practice for domestic events. This suggests that the author found it difficult to translate the Macedonian calendar into Hebrew months (just as quite a few educated orthodox Jews today find it hard to convert dates from the Julian to the Jewish calendar). Given his relatively meagre knowledge of 'foreign' matters, it is easy to understand how he erred and included in his book a set of dates based on a system different from the one prevalent in Judaea.

(c) In Judaea the year began in Tishri, and this also emerges from the Mishnah. Consequently the Jews of Eretz Israel had no reason to adopt the Babylonian variety of the Seleucid calendar that began the year in Nisan. However, the widespread use of New Year's Day in Tishri is known only from the period after the destruction of the Second Temple, it having been restricted previously to fallow years and jubilees (see Herr 1976: 843–5). Furthermore, the Mishnah itself testifies to the existence of two systems in Eretz Israel at a later period. One, 'for fallow and jubilee years', began in Tishri, and the other, 'for kings', began in Nisan (Rosh Hashanah 1.1). Even if the Mishnah ruling does not reflect the count of the Seleucid kings, the very existence of a separate count 'for kings' at a later period indicates the possibility that during the Seleucid period as well, for official matters, a chronological system that began with Nisan was adopted. Supporting Bickerman's theory are a number of 'external' dates in Maccabees that can be explained only on the assumption that they are based on the system whose count began in October 312 (e.g. 6.16 and 7.1; see Bickerman in RE s.v. 'Makkabäerbücher', col. 783; Goldstein 1976: 540) and at least two 'domestic' dates definitely based on the Macedonian–Babylonian system (4.52, 10.21). As this is still disputed, the 'domestic' dates require some elaboration.

Goldstein (1976: 540) has cogently shown that 25 Kislev 148, the date of the purification of the Temple (4.52), cannot be calculated according to the Syrian–Macedonian system; this appears from the sequence of events antedating the purification. My dating of Antiochus' departure to the eastern satrapies on the eve of the Ammaus campaign (year 147, I Macc. 3.37) at the end of the summer (see p. 472), and the conclusion that a full year elapsed between the battle of Ammaus and Lysias' first expedition (4.28; see p. 283 above), make it even more evident that 25 Kislev 148 must be counted according to the Babylonian version. Furthermore, if one takes the purification of the Temple to be dated according to the Syrian version, the event would have preceded by almost three months the famous document of 15 Xanthicus 148 (10 March 164; II Maccabees 11.27–33). The document acknowledges the wish of people to return to their homes, and guarantees safe return, amnesty and religious freedom to those who will return within fifteen days, besides permission to live according to Jewish law granted to those who remained in their homes. Menelaus' decisive role in convincing the authorities to issue the document (verses 29,32) shows that it mainly served the purposes of the Hellenized Jews. The offer is understandable in view of the circumstances prevailing before the liberation of the Temple when the rebels carried out guerrilla warfare from their hiding places. Permission to return to their homes peacefully after some rough years in mountains and deserts might have appealed to them, thus considerably weakening the rebel camp (see further pp. 525–30 and pp. 538–9 above). However, after the purification of the Temple, most of the rebels were in any case back at home: Judaea was firmly under their control, and Judas Maccabaeus even permitted himself to expand his military activity beyond the borders (I. Macc. 5; II Macc. 10.14ff.). Had the document been issued after the purification, its provisions would certainly have been defined otherwise, and there would have been a reference to the status of the Temple and the Hellenized Jews.

The second date referring to a domestic event was already pointed out by Bickerman (1936: 155). At the beginning of ch. 12, Alexander Balas' accession is dated to year 160. It was followed by a series of diplomatic communications between the two Seleucid rivals to the throne and Jonathan, at the end of which Jonathan is said to have served publicly (or been ordained) as high priest on the occasion of the Festival of Tabernacles in the seventh month of 160. As a new Macedonian year started at the beginning of the Jewish seventh month, Jonathan could not have been ordained in year 160 of the Seleucid–Syrian count. The dates can stand only if we assume that the first, which refers to an 'external' event, was counted from October 312 B.C., and the second, being a 'domestic' one, was calculated from April 311 B.C. This piece of evidence has been contested by Hanhart (1964: 61) and Bringmann (1983: 24–5), who argue that owing to the different systems of intercalation, the Jewish seventh month (Tishri) could have started one month before the first Macedonian month. The Feast of Tabernacles, which was celebrated from 15 to 22 Tishri, would thus have fallen within year 160 of the Syrian–Macedonian era. This was indeed occasionally possible (against Goldstein 1967: 541; see for December 164 B.C. p. 278 above), but still does not accommodate the two references to year 160 under the same chronological system: even those who believe that I Maccabees used the Syrian–Macedonian count for internal events must admit that it could not have been a 'pure' Syrian–Macedonian system, as is already indicated by the attachment of the number of the Jewish month. A contemporary Jew living in the Land of Israel, who was brought up and conducted his life according to the Jewish calendar, would certainly have considered the first of Tishri, the Jewish New Year 'for fallow and jubilee years', as the opening of the Syrian–Macedonian year, regardless of occasional discrepancies. Similarly Orthodox Jews in British Palestine, for instance, used to regard 1 Tabeth as the opening of the New Christian Year (and so it was taught in their schools), though it very seldom fell on that day. This applies even more to a Jewish historian who would not have bothered to consult records of the Jewish and Macedonian calendars and compare them with each other in order to date an internal event. And it has already been noted that the author of I Maccabees refrained from citing the Macedonian months he found in his source with regard to external events, and from transforming them into the equivalent Jewish months. I would not doubt likewise that the Seleucid year in its Babylonian version started in Judaea on 1 Nisan of the Jewish calendar, though it did not always run parallel to Babylonian Nisanu.

The use in Eretz Israel of the Babylonian count emerges also from the date of the letter to Egyptian Jewry in II Macc. 1.7 (see in detail Bickerman 1933: 239–41 = id. 1976–80: 2.142–4). Finally, the month count in I Maccabees, which as noted appears only in relation to domestic events, begins with Nisan. It is used also in regard to events and dates unconnected with biblical holidays (e.g. 16.14 and 13.51 compared with the Scroll of Fasting, 23 Iyyar). The use of a month count based on a different system of counting the years is not absolutely impossible, but it shows that in Eretz Israel there could have at least been a tendency to adopt the Seleucid–Babylonian system that started with Nisan and not the Seleucid–Syrian system that started with Tishri.

III Migdal Zur in the MSS of the Scroll of Fasting (s.v. 14 Sivan) and Beth Zur

(see p. 290 n. 24)

The form *ṣūr* (*ṣar*) appears in the Parma and Oxford manuscripts and the Mantua printing. Although the Babylonian Talmud generally identifies the place with Caesarea (*Megillah* 6a), the Munich manuscript (of the Babylonian Talmud) has *ṣūr* (ibid.). Furthermore, the retention of *ṣūr* in all manuscripts of the Scroll of Fasting, despite the later identification with Caesarea which appears in the mediaeval *scholion* to the Scroll (following the Babylonian Talmud), makes it necessary to accept the existing reading. The name Migdal Zur, instead of the Beth Zur known from the sources, does not impose particular difficulties. The term *migdāl* (tower), in its Greek translation *pyrgos*, denotes in I Maccabees a specific type of fortified structure (5.5,65, 16.10; cf. II Macc. 10.18,20,22,36; Jos. *Bell.* 2.513). For an attempt to define the term *migdāl* as a structure designed for the protection of farmers and their produce in the fields during the agricultural season see Applebaum et al. 1978: 91–100. This definition certainly does not apply to Beth Zur. In any case, Simeon did not occupy the settlement of Beth Zur, but the fort strengthened there by Bacchides (I Macc. 9.52), which may well have been known as Migdal Zur. The author of I Maccabees did not use that designation because he wished to stress the fact that the site conquered was the one which had previously been mentioned numerous times in his book as Beth Zur.

As to the Babylonian Talmud and the *scholion*: the forms *šūr*, *šīr* and *šar* appear in the Vatican manuscript and the Venetian printing of the Babylonian Talmud (and see the 'Aruch s.v. אחדר). Presumably *ṣūr* was garbled to *šūr* in one of the versions of the Scroll, and Rabbi Abbahu, who lived in Caesarea in the third century A.D. and strove to 'settle' with the Gentiles of his town because of their molesting of the Jewish community there during the Roman period (which is clear from the fact that his statement is a commentary on the verse in Zephaniah 2.4 ('and Ekron shall be uprooted')), exploited the linguistic similarity to the ancient name of Caesarea (Migdal Straton; Hebrew: *šaršōn*) in order to apply the text of the Scroll of Fasting to Caesarea. It may very well be that in his enthusiasm he himself, inadvertently or perhaps even deliberately, garbled the text of the Scroll. Similar forms of the name *migdal šaršōn* (*šīr*, *šar*) appear in some of the versions of the well-known Beraita on the boundaries of Eretz Israel, those in the *Tosefta* (*Shebiith* 4.11), the Palestinian Talmud (*Demai* 2.1[22c]; *Shebiith* 6.1[36c]) and in the *Sifri* (Deut. 51). Possibly that Beraita, whose distribution and influence have recently been clarified by the monumental Hebrew inscription from Rehov in the Beth Shean Valley (see Sussmann 1974: 88ff.; id. 1976: 213ff.), also contributed to the garbling of the form and the mistaken interpretation of the Scroll in the Babylonian Talmud and the *scholion*. Thus there is reason to doubt the value of Rabbi Abbahu's testimony regarding the special difficulties that Migdal Straton caused for the Jews of Eretz Israel during the Hasmonaean Revolt ('And it was a stake driven into Israel in the days of the Greeks'), for which there is no evidence in the Books of the Maccabees and which is hardly believable in light of the lack of importance and small size of Migdal Straton at the time (contrary to the opinion of Levine 1974: 63–4, and others).

IV The deployment of the armies at Magnesia

(see p. 415 n. 13)

The reconstruction of the Seleucid and Roman deployment offered by me in Bar-Kochva 1979: 168–9 (and map 14) assumes that Livy erred in describing the Seleucid deployment with light forces at the outer edges of the right and left wings (37.40.8–10,13–14), while in reality they were skirmishers positioned ahead of the two wings, as can be understood from Appian's description (*Syr.* 32(166–7)). That assumption is based on a series of considerations noted there (pp. 166–7), and is essential also for the estimation of the space occupied by the *argyraspides* in that battle and consequently of their number.

J. Briscoe (1981: 350) does not accept my arguments and gives the following reasons:

(a) Even with the deployment depicted by Livy, the Seleucid phalanx, rather than the light infantry as I claim, could have been positioned opposite the Latin *ala* (Briscoe adds: 'Even on Bar-Kochva's view, with the phalanx facing the right-hand legion and *ala*, it is the *argyraspides* who face the left *ala*', but he apparently does not realize that the *argyraspides* were heavy troops).

(b) If the forces are deployed that way, it will turn out that the edge of the left wing, which according to Livy likewise included infantry, did not extend very far beyond the Roman front line (and was therefore not superfluous, as I argue).

(c) Livy could not have erred in such an important part of the battle description.

Yet if we accept Livy's picture, we will be unable in any way to position in the Seleucid right wing opposite the Latin *ala* any heavy unit (certainly not the phalanx of the centre, nor the heavy *agēma* cavalry, nor the *argyraspides*, which were to the right of the centre). The Roman force was confined on its left wing by the river Phrygius (Livy 37.39.11). Between the Latin *ala* and the river were only four Roman *turmae*, 120 horse in all. According to Livy, at the edge of the Seleucid right wing were, from right to left, 9,500 light infantry, 1,200 Dahae cavalry, *argyraspides* whose number is not given, and 1,000 *agēma* cavalry. The 9,500 light infantry took up at least two kilometres. The Seleucid right wing was evidently not hemmed in by the river (see also the map on p. 164 of my 1979 book, and p. 165), and for that reason it may appear possible to assume that light infantry was positioned beyond the Roman front line in a way that enabled some heavy contingent to face the Latin *ala*. However, the 1,200 Dahae cavalry were already necessarily deployed beyond the Roman battle line. The deployment of 9,500 light infantry such a distance from the battle line is a definite waste of manpower and is unthinkable, certainly as the Roman wing was protected by the river from being outflanked. And if the Latin *ala* is to be positioned opposite the Seleucid phalanx in the centre, as Briscoe proposes, the 'extra' Seleucid forces beyond the Roman front line would include most of the *agēma* cavalry and all the *argyraspides* and Dahae cavalry. As that proposal falls, so does Briscoe's second argument with regard to the Seleucid left flank. If the Roman legions and *alae* are placed opposite the Seleucid heavy troops (and no one disputed that), on the basis of Livy's description the result would be an extra 12,000 Seleucid 'lights' in the left wing beyond the Roman battle line, even if we assume that the Roman columns were lengthened as much as possible. Furthermore, although Briscoe admits that Antiochus had skirmishers in that battle placed in front of the forces (as noted by both Livy and Appian and dictated by the need to place light infantry opposite the Roman *velites*), he does not explain why they are not listed by Livy (and in his view not by Appian either).

As to the argument that Livy could not have erred in such an important point, it seems superfluous to demonstrate again the lack of understanding of military matters that Livy displays, and this is not his only serious mistake in the description of the battle of Magnesia. The conception I propose emerges clearly from Livy's presentation of the sixteen elephants immediately after the listing of the light infantry which he sets at the edge of the Seleucid left wing, *et sedecim elephanti modici intervallo distantes* (= and sixteen elephants separated by moderate-sized intervals, 37.40.14). Could anyone conceivably suggest that the Seleucid elephants were deployed in battle array with the traditional intervals several kilometres beyond the battle line of the enemy?

At the same time it is not certain that Livy really intended to place the infantry 'lights' on the edges of the wings. He may simply have negligently prefaced the mentions of those units with the conjunctions *tum* and *inde* (paras. 8,13) instead of explicitly noting that the 'lights' were deployed in front of the wings. That possibility is supported by the way Livy describes the placement of the light infantry in the left wing: *Inde alia multitudo, par ei, quae in dextro cornu erat* (= Then another great crowd, corresponding to that on the right flank, para. 13). The word *multitudo* recalls Appian's *plēthos*, which precedes the latter's separate presentation of the light infantry and characterizes this group of troops. Livy's phrasing suggests that he considered the light infantry a separate group from the troops in the line on both sides of the centre. The deployment was described explicitly by Polybius, from whom the word *plēthos* (*multitudo*) was taken.

V The Seleucid 'peltasts' at Thermopylae

(see pp. 37 n. 31, 422 n. 43, 427 n. 27)

In his description of the deployment before the battle, Appian notes the participation of 'lights' and 'peltasts' in the forefront of the Seleucid phalanx which was positioned before the camp (πρὸ τοῦ στρατοπέδου, *Syr.* 18(83); the reference is undoubtedly to the *vallum*, the rampart, mentioned by Livy). Livy on the other hand does not mention 'peltasts' but only 'light' forces deployed before the rampart, backed by 'sarissa-bearers' who were likewise in front of the rampart (36.18.2). Behind them, at a certain distance, was a second line of defence (18.4), presumably inside in the rampart. According to Livy, the 'Macedonians', who were 'sarissa-bearers' and deployed before the rampart, at first succeeded in repulsing the Romans, but when the pressure increased they retreated and made a stand on the rampart itself and inside it. In the second stage, with their pikes pointed forward, they succeeded in blocking all Roman attempts at making a breach, thanks to their position on the rampart and their consequent advantage of height (36.18.5–7). The 'Macedonians' abandoned their position and fled only when they became aware of the flanking operation of Cato and his men from the direction of the ridge to the west (36.19.1– 3). According to Appian, however, at first it was the 'lights' that attacked the Romans and when repulsed retreated to a position behind the phalanx, which then successfully blocked the Romans until Cato's force appeared climbing down the Callidromus (paras. 84–7). Livy thus speaks of a retreat by 'Macedonians' and the establishment of an alternative line of defence on the *vallum*, while Appian mentions only a retreat by 'lights' and a firm stand by the phalanx.

The key to understanding the discrepancy between Appian and Livy, both of whom are based on Polybius, lies in the way that Livy presents the unit which was deployed before the rampart: *Macedonum robur, quos sarisophorus appellabant* (= the core of the Macedonians whom they call *sarisophoroi*, 36.18.2). The use of the Greek combination *sarisophoroi* shows that it is not an interpretation of Livy's but appeared in Polybius. Yet no unit called *sarisophoroi* is known in the Seleucid army, so that in Polybius the term did not designate a unit but merely described its equipment. The question is why Polybius needed to describe any unit as 'sarissa-bearers', which is not his usual practice.

The question seems more puzzling when notice is taken that the words 'Macedonians' and '*robur*' must also have been taken from Polybius; Livy, who tried to disparage the Seleucid army and describe it as 'Syrians' (see pp. 94–5 above), would not have written 'Macedonians' unless he found that term in Polybius. All the more so with regard to the word *robur* (= core, the strongest of...). The latter word indicates that Polybius described the unit as the crack force of the Macedonians. In reference to the Seleucid

army, Polybius certainly more than once used the word 'Macedonians'
alone in listing phalanx troops (e.g. 30.25.5). The designation 'the core of
the Macedonians' would have been more than required for clarifying that
they were equipped with *sarissai*, unless the tactical term attached to them
had indicated otherwise. Keeping in mind that according to Appian it was
the 'peltasts' who were positioned in front of the rampart, there is little
doubt that the unit name in Polybius was 'peltasts', which made it
necessary to specify its equipment, and that is the source of the errors in
both Livy and Appian.

As has already been stated, the term 'peltasts' was used for the heavy
Guard in the Antigonid army, and Polybius applied it to the heavy Guard
of the Ptolemies. In his report on Thermopylae he did the same to the
Seleucid Guard. However, in order not to mislead the reader who might
have thought of the 'peltasts' in their classical sense, he added that they
were *sarissa*-bearers. That definition along with their identification as Macedonians led Livy to think that there was a unit called '*sarisophoroi*'. The
latter may also have been influenced by the same name applied to a unit
in Alexander's army (reflected in Arrian, *Anab.* 1.14.1, 4.4.6; the reference
is actually to *prodromoi* = cavalry scouts).

The positioning of the crack phalanx unit in front of the rampart suggests
that the second line, within the rampart, was occupied by the ordinary
phalangites, i.e. the military settlers who were also Macedonians. As a
result, Livy disregarded the name 'peltasts' and confused their deployment
and action on the battlefield with those of the other Macedonians, for all
of them were *sarissa*-bearers. It should be noted also that Livy does not use
the term 'peltasts' in his version of the battle of Thermopylae in any
context, but only 'Macedonians'. It may perhaps be assumed that Polybius
did not use the term 'phalanx', but only 'Macedonians', in connection
with the soldiers positioned inside the rampart, which likewise contributed
to Livy's mistake.

Appian, on the other hand, with not uncharacteristic negligence, paid no
attention to the peltasts' weapons in Polybius, or perhaps believed a textual
error was involved, and thought they were 'lights' compared with the
phalanx, like the other forces deployed before the rampart and in accordance with the definition of peltasts in the Classical world and in
the writings of the Tacticians and Lexicographers.

The battle in the centre should be reconstructed as follows: the *sarissa*-
bearing 'peltasts' were positioned before the rampart together with certain
light forces in front of them and on their flanks. The phalanx itself was
positioned as a second line of defence inside the rampart. In the first stage,
with the 'lights' helping in a 'softening up' operation, the 'peltasts' tried
to breach the Roman lines. In the second, when the assault failed, they
passed over to defence. In the third stage, they retreated to beyond the lines
of the phalanx, which from the rampart succeeded in keeping the Romans
at bay until Cato's flanking force came into view.

For other attempts at harmonizing Livy and Appian see Nissen 1863:

181; Kromayer and Veith 1903–32: 2.152 n. 1 and 153, followed by Witte 1910: 394–5 n. 1; Briscoe 1981: 249. My interpretation resembles Kromayer's in some degree, but differs in a number of crucial details, notably as regards the definition of 'peltasts' and the reason for Livy's and Appian's errors.

VI The belief in resurrection and the sectarian affiliation of the authors of the two Books of the Maccabees

(see p. 484 n. 27)

Along with the apparent difference with regard to defensive war on the Sabbath, Geiger and his followers stressed in particular the absence of any reference to belief in resurrection in I Maccabees, in contrast to its being emphasized in II Maccabees, as evidence of the sectarian difference between the two books. II Maccabees expresses belief in resurrection of the flesh in the most extreme and realistic way (see the analysis in Zeitlin 1952: 55–6; Nickelsburg 1972: 93–108; Cavallin 1979: 280–2). However, the Pharisees in Eretz Israel in Josephus' time believed only in the eternity of the soul (*Bellum* 2.163–4; *Ant.* 18.14; and cf. p. 180 n. 92 above). As to the position of the author of I Maccabees, none of these ideas appears in the book. However, there is no reference to resurrection in the battle orations in II Maccabees either, though it could be expected that such a reference might have encouraged the warriors. Their unreal character and abundance of epiphanies notwithstanding, the battle descriptions in II Maccabees contain only one mention of the belief in resurrection, after the battle of Marisa in connection with idolatrous items supposedly found in the clothing of the fallen. Judas Maccabaeus is said to have offered a sacrifice to atone for their sins and prayed for them, and the author notes incidentally that he did so in the expectation that they would be resurrected (12.44). That battle is treated very briefly in I Maccabees (5.66–7) while in II Maccabees it is reported in great detail. The story of the idolatrous paraphernalia in the fallen warriors' garments is designed to excuse the defeat, and is the invention of the author, as are the offering and prayer for the souls of the dead, practices which had no roots in Jewish tradition. Belief in resurrection is expressed as well in the martyr stories of the mother and her seven sons (7.9,14,36) and the suicide of Razis (14.46). These stories and others like them do not appear in I Maccabees. The mention of belief in the resurrection of the dead is natural and comprehensible in the framework of stories of martyrdom. On the other hand, such a reference would not be congruent with the events described in I Maccabees, just as II Maccabees did not see fit to include one in the pre-battle orations or descriptions of the battles, aside from a marginal instance in connection with a fictitious event artificially attached to the aftermath of the battle of Marisa. The pathetic nature of II Maccabees also called for an unreal element like the belief in resurrection, whose absence from the realistic descriptions in I Maccabees is not surprising, even if the author of the latter book held the Pharisee, more 'refined', version of that belief.

All the above arguments still do not establish that the author of I Maccabees was a Pharisee, but they show that the claims that he was a Sadducee are unproven. As indicated above (p. 180 n. 92), Jason of Cyrene's expectation of the resurrection of the flesh does not accord with the Pharisee conception. It would certainly be completely wrong to present the author of II Maccabees as a 'Pharisee sage', as some scholars have done, for his knowledge of halakhic matters is extremely defective (see pp. 371–2 above).

For the rejection of the proposal to view Jason of Cyrene as representing 'early Phariseeism' or the Hassidism of Eretz Israel see p. 180 n. 92 above; see there also on the different versions of the belief in resurrection and their origin, especially that of II Maccabees. I Maccabees was written at a time when the points of dispute between Pharisees and Sadducees were not yet clearly formulated and defined, nor was the factional adherence of the majority of people. As is natural, the factional controversy reached Diaspora Jewry, to which the author of II Maccabees belonged, even later. It therefore seems an unjustifiable exercise to try at any cost to assign the authors to one sect or another.

Plate I. Metal parts of a sarissa (see p. 6)

No complete *sarissa* has as yet been found in archaeological excavations, un-doubtedly because it was made mainly of wood. Nor can the long infantry *sarissa* be definitely identified in illustrations and reliefs because the pike's dimensions ex-ceeded the limitations of the works of art. Still, help in reconstructing the *sarissa* is provided by metal parts found in the royal tomb at Aegae, near Vergina in Lower Macedonia, and elsewhere, and by data scattered through literary sources. All these indicate that the *sarissa* was composed in the main of a long wooden pole, sometimes in one piece, sometimes in two; a metal point was attached to the front end and a metal butt-spike to the back. To increase its stability and strength, a metal sleeve was put around the middle part of the long shaft, serving also as a coupling if the *sarissa* was in two pieces. The butt-spike was very sharp and could be used for attacking in case the front point broke, as well as to fix the *sarissa* in the ground. The shaft was made of strong wood of the cornelian cherry (*kraneia*) which provided a powerful, solid weapon even when not very thick. The diameter of the shaft was a maximum of 3.2 cm and a minimum of 2.8 cm, and its weight about 4 kg. The total, together with the metal parts, weighed about 6.7 kg.

The photograph shows the metal parts found at Aegae; from left to right: point, coupling sleeve and butt-spike.

(a) *The point.* The front end of the *sarissa* is composed of two parts, a cylindrical socket which fits on the end of the shaft, and the sharp point. The total length is 51 cm and it weighs 1,235 g. The diameter of the socket is 3.6 cm and the metal is 2–3 mm thick. The protruding central spine of the blade adds power and stability in penetration. The sides of the point, too, are well sharpened.

(b) *The butt-spike.* The back end of the *sarissa* has three parts: a cylindrical socket into which the shaft end fits, the four-sided body, and the pyramidical point. Its overall length is 44.5 cm (the point itself is 14.5 cm long), the diameter of the socket is 3.4 cm, the metal is 2–2.5 mm thick, and the total weight 1,070 g.

(c) *The central sleeve.* It is narrower toward the middle and wider toward the ends, which means that it fits a two-piece shaft. It is 17 cm long, 2.5–3.2 cm in diameter, and weighs about 500 g; the metal is 3–5 mm thick.

The material from Aegae was described by M. Andronikos (1970: 91–107). Similar *sarissa* parts found in various places in Greece and Macedonia have been discussed by Markle (1977: 323–6).

Thessaloniki, Archaeological Museum. *Photo*: Museum.

573

Plate II. Cretan phalanx officer and his armour bearer (see p. 7)

This stele was discovered in the military cemetery of Sidon, and it is to be dated to the late third century B.C. like the other funerary *stelai* of Ptolemaic mercenaries found there. The stele, published by T. Macridy, 'A travers les nécropoles sidoniennes', *Revue Biblique* N.S. 1 (1904) 547–56, was stored in the Archaeological Museum in Istanbul, but seems to have disappeared.

The stele depicts a Cretan mercenary officer in the Ptolemaic army saying farewell to his wife, as his armour bearer stands by. The officer is wearing a Macedonian helmet with crest, visor and attached cheek guards. On his shoulders is a *khlamys*, and near his right thigh is a scabbard with its loop showing. There are signs on his lower body of long leather or metal strips. The armour bearer is carrying a round shield which seems to be the size of the usual phalangite shield, and a long offensive weapon whose point is not visible. As in the Hellenistic period semi-heavy infantry were generally equipped with the long oval shield, it can be assumed that the pike in the painting is not the relatively short one used by those troops, but a *sarissa*, and the warrior was the commander of a phalanx unit.

The woman is bewailing the parting from her husband as the inscription attests: Διοδ[ότω]ι Πάτρωνος | Κρητὶ Ὑρτακίνωι | ᾿Αθαβους ἀξίως τῶι | ἑαυτῆς ἀνδρί | Διόδοτε | χρηστέ | χαῖρε. (= To Diodotus son of Patron, the Cretan from Hyrtacina, Athabus who is worthy of her man [set up the stone]; Good Diodotus, farewell!). The deceased's Cretan origin shows that natives of that island served in the Hellenistic armies not only as archers, as is often thought, but also as phalangites.

Plate III. A coat of armour and other defensive items from
Pergamum (see p. 8)

Fragment of a relief from the Athena temple at Pergamum, built (or completed) by
Eumenes II (197–160 B.C.). The collection of arms dedicated to the goddess is
meant to be a trophy, i.e. to represent booty taken from the city's foes. The variety
of advanced weapon types appearing in the reliefs suggests that the battles against
all of Pergamum's enemies, including the Seleucids, were commemorated, not just
against the Galatians, as many scholars believe. On the relief see Droysen 1885: 1.
97,105,109–10.

The relief shows personal defensive weapons: on the right is a suit of armour, with
the haft of a sword in its sheath protruding from behind it. On the left is an oblong
shield designed for semi-heavy infantry. Below it in the left-hand corner are arm
puttees and above it is a broad-brimmed Boeotian helmet with attached cheek
guards. The coat has three parts: the upper metal part (*protomē*) is shaped like a
torso with full anatomical details. The chest and back sections, somewhat overlapping, are attached by two knobs seen above the nipples and certainly also by
other knobs on the sides. This part was generally covered by the *khitōn*, the warrior's
tunic, while under the armour the warrior wore a kind of short-sleeved shirt, a
khitōniskos, to prevent the armour from rubbing. At the armholes are fasteners by
which the arm puttees were attached. From the waist down the soldier was equipped
with leather armour, a shirt composed of a belt and long leather strips (*pteryges*)
enabling him to move and bend. The arms were wrapped in puttees made of several
layers of heavy fabric. The weight of the *protomē* varied and, together with the
method and skill employed in its manufacture, determined its vulnerability to pikes,
arrows and artillery missiles. A coat of armour celebrated for its impenetrability
weighed 18 kg (Plutarch, *Demetrius* 21), but the run-of-the-mill suit was certainly
lighter. A well-preserved royal cuirass of a different design dating from just before
the Hellenistic period was discovered at Aegae; see Hatzopoulos and Loukopoulos
1980: 220,225.

Berlin (East), Staatliche Museen, Antikensammlung. *Photo*: Museum.

Plate IV. Thracian semi-heavy horseman (see pp. 10–11)

A second or first century B.C. tombstone of a Thracian horseman found in Abdera, on the southern Thracian coast, now in the National Museum at Sofia; see Avezou 1913: 118–21; Kazarow 1918: 49–51; Mikhailov 1974: 285.

The horseman's left hand is raised in order to hurl a lance at the enemy. Judging by the swing of the arm and similar reliefs of Thracian horsemen, especially of the Roman period, he is using a short thrusting spear slightly more than a metre long. In his right hand the horseman is holding an elliptical shield, seen under the horse's chin, which provided some protection for the side of the horse's head as well. At his right hip is the scabbard for a long sword. Behind the horse's head can be seen a blurred representation of a foot soldier, certainly an armour bearer, holding two lances. The cavalryman is wearing a *khitōn* and a *khlamys* over it, and trousers typical of the Thracian riders. It is impossible to tell whether he had any body armour. The horseman's equipment is principally similar to that of the famous tombstone of the Thracian horseman from the *ala Noricum* which is now in the Römisch-Germanisches Museum in Cologne.

Sofia, National Museum.

Plate V. Heavy cavalry: *xyston* and coat of mail
(see pp. 5, 11, 274)

A copy of a fresco found near Naoussa in western Macedonia, dating from the early third century B.C. The fresco, now destroyed, was published by Pfuhl 1923: 345; Couissin 1931: pls. 1–2.

The ratio of pike length to horse length suggests that the pike, known from the literary sources as a *xyston*, was about 3·6 m long, and this is confirmed by other findings (cf., e.g., the horseman from Sciatby near Alexandria, see Rostovtzeff 1940: 1.150). The coupling sleeve in the middle of the pike is likewise an indication of considerable length. The horseman's right hand holds the pike which passes through a supporting loop at the horse's neck. The end and the central sleeve are of a type different from those in Plate I. The shape of the shoulders and chest indicates that the horseman has a rigid coat of armour under his tunic. The helmet, shaped like a Phrygian turban, is a Thracian type. Facing the horseman is a foot soldier parrying the blow of the *xyston* with his concave *hoplon*, the traditional shield of the Greek heavy infantry. The warrior's clothing exemplifies the colourful appearance of the battlefield: the helmet in red; the cloak of the horseman waving in the breeze is red; the tunic has grey and dark blue on the shoulders and hips, and red in the middle; the belt in brown; and the garment of the infantry-man opposite is greenish.

577

Plate VI. Cataphract horseman (see p. 12–13)

A third-century B.C. graffito at Dura Europus shows a Sassanian cataphract-type horseman. See M. Pillet and M. Rostovtzeff, in *The Excavations at Doura Europos 1930/1* (New Haven, 1933): 13,207,216–21; Eadie 1967: 170.

Except for his eyes, legs and tail, this horse is completely covered by an armour of little scales. Judging from the straight horizontal shape of the bottom, his belly may not have been protected either, a point reported in the literary sources as a salient disadvantage. Remnants of scale armour found at Dura itself and at other places indicate that the scale armour was fashioned of individual iron or bronze plates in standard sizes, arranged side-by-side, somewhat overlapping, and sewn on a fabric or leather lining. This horseman's armour is quite varied, composed of three different types: the body down to the knees is protected by scale armour composed of rectangular metal plates, the arms and legs (up to the knees) are covered by broad parallel metal rings; the face is protected by a metallic mesh veil attached to the conical helmet, much like that of a modern fencer. The horseman is holding a long *kontos* and has a sword girded at his waist. Some items of his equipment differ from those known from literary sources. Other illustrative sources show both heavier and lighter equipment for cataphract as well as horse.

Yale University Art Gallery, Dura-Europos Collection.

Plate VII. Variations on the cataphract style: *kontos* and corselet
(see p. 14)

A silver coin from Cibyra, a city in south-western Phrygia. It dates from before
84 B.C., when the city was still ruled by the tyrants. The legend includes the names
of the magistrates, and in the exergue Κιβυράτων (= of the Cibyrans). To the left
of the horseman is a bee, the symbol of the city. On the coin see Head 1932: pl. 44,
no. 12.

The horseman is wearing a suit of armour with leather skirt and leather strips
below. On his head is a late form of the Boeotian helmet, preferred by cavalry
because it allowed better visibility (cf. Xenophon, *Eq*. 12.3). In his right hand the
horseman holds a long pike with a point different from that of the *sarissa* in Plate
I, and a sleeve and end similar to those in Plate V. The pike is clearly longer than
the *xyston*, the spear of the heavy cavalry, and seems more or less identical with the
cataphract *kontos*. The horseman is holding the pike in his right hand which is bent
back along the horse's rear thigh, thus suggesting that the pike was somehow
attached to the front part of the horse. This is reminiscent of the loop by which the
shaft of the pike was attached to the horse's neck in Heliodorus' description of
cataphract warfare (*Ethiopica* 9.15). However, despite the influence of the cataphract
type, the rider and horse are not wearing scale armour.

London, British Museum. Reproduced by Courtesy of the Trustees. *Photo*:
Museum.

579

Plate VIII. A Parthian mounted archer (see pp. 15, 77)

A Parthian terracotta of a typical Parthian mounted archer, found somewhere in Mesopotamia. The general style, being that of early Parthian art, indicates a date in the second or first century B.C. The bearded archer is wearing a heavy protective garment. The bow is of the single-arc type. In addition to the bow, the archer's right hand holds a bunch of arrows, enabling him to shoot rapidly without having to reach into the quiver at his waist or the horse's flank. Bibliography: Sarre 1923: 25,68 and pl. 54 r.; Van Buren 1930: 114; Van Ingen 1939: 35–6.

On the Seleucid side in the battle of Magnesia there were Dahaen-Scythian mounted archers (ἱπποτοξόται). Asclepiodotus, one of the Tacticians who may have drawn on Seleucid sources (such as Poseidonius of Apamea), even calls the mounted archers 'Scythians' (1.3). In addition to mounted archers drawn from Oriental peoples in the Hellenistic armies, the sources mention a unit known as the Tarentines, particularly in the Seleucid army. It has been suggested that they were mounted akontists, i.e. spear throwers (Griffith 1935: 246–50). It is difficult to determine their national origin or the connection of their name with the city of Tarentum in southern Italy.

Berlin (East), Staatliche Museen, Islamisches Museum. *Photo*: Museum.

Plate IX. Semi-heavy infantry: Pisidian mercenary in the
Ptolemaic service (see pp. 15–16, 313–16)

The colourful gravestone of a mercenary from Adada in Pisidia who served in
the Ptolemaic garrison at Sidon toward the end of the third century B.C. On the
stele see Mendel 1912: 1.264–6; Perdrizet 1904: 237–8; Robert 1935: 428–30;
Rostovtzeff 1940: 1.474; H. R. Robinson 1975: 17,164.

The soldier is equipped with the characteristic weapons of the semi-heavies: the
oval shield, a relatively short pike, and a helmet. Instead of the traditional corselet,
the soldier is equipped with a sleeveless blue-grey shirt; it is difficult to make a
definite identification of the shirt because the stone is broken in the middle of it, but
the small remaining right upper part which clearly shows winding black intersecting
lines, indicates that it is a chain armour shirt (cf. Pl. XI). This is less evident from
the lower part. Beneath the shirt there are protective brown strips (*pteryges*), made
of heavy felt and/or leather. The colourful design and the proportions may indicate
the sizes and material off the weapons: the shield, being white, is probably made of
wood, and its grey frame, bronze rib and umbo of metal. Lengthways the shield
could protect the warrior from his forehead to his waist; its width slightly surpassed
that of the warrior's body. The pike is somewhat longer than its bearer is tall, and
the bronze colour may indicate that it was of metal. The bronze-coloured helmet
is of the Boeotian type, with a visor and cheek- and nape-guards, topped by reddish
feathers. A scabbard for a short sword is presumably covered by the shield. The
inscription, which is not seen in the picture, was reconstructed by Louis Robert as
follows: Σάλμα Μολ[... ᾿Α]δαδεῦ χρησ[τέ, χαῖρε] (= Salma son of Mol... [of
A]dada the good, [farewell]).

Plate X. Pisidian signaller in a Ptolemaic semi-heavy unit (see pp. 15–16)

A Ptolemaic soldier's painted gravestone of the late third century B.C., found in Sidon. See Mendel 1912: 1.259–61; Rostovtzeff 1940: 1.150; Launey 1949–50: 1. 80–1,475–6 and passim.

The soldier is engaged in hand-to-hand combat: his left leg inclined forward and his right hand wielding a sword. He is wearing a dark red *khitōn*, a belt, and high blue-grey shoes with dark red laces. On his head is a Thracian reddish-brown helmet decorated with grey and bronze-coloured 'snails' (or, rather, enlarged ears) on the sides, and pink feathers at the top, and equipped with cheek- and nape-guards. His left hand is holding an oval Galatian-type shield, half light grey and half white. Its bracket and rib are brown and light green, and its rim red. The straight sword is grey-blue and its haft is bronze-coloured with a reddish rim. That it was used primarily for slashing and not thrusting is seen from the way it is wielded, and from its triangular profile and the absence of a protruding spine. At the soldier's left hip is the scabbard. The inscription reads: Διοσκορίδη 'Εξαβόου Πισίδη | Βα⟨λ⟩-βου⟨ρ⟩εῦ συμμάχων | σημεοφόρε χρηστέ | χαῖρε | Κεραίας ὁ ἀδελφός ἔστησε (= Dio-scorides son of Exabous, Pisidian from among the allies from Ba⟨l⟩bu⟨r⟩a, the good signaller, farewell! His brother Keraias put up [this gravestone]).

The stone was thus erected by the deceased's brother, who apparently served in the same unit. From the inscription and the other *stelai* discovered in the military cemetery in Sidon it appears that they were Pisidian mercenaries, recruited presumably according to a contract of alliance (συμμάχοι) which ensured the Ptolemies the option of hiring them, and deprived their rivals of that option. The Pisidians served as a garrison in Sidon, and were organized in a *politeuma* of their own. The deceased is described as a signalman who transmitted orders. The oblong shield indicates that his unit was semi-heavy. He is not equipped with a lance because the artist wishes to depict him in hand-to-hand combat where the sword is most effective. It is, possible, however, that for some of the Pisidians the standard equipment was a variation of the Classical Scythian peltasts or the Thracian style of the Hellenistic period consisting only of a long broad-sword and an oblong shield.

Plate XI. Chain body armour from Pergamum and other items
(see pp. 313–16)

A relief from the temple of Athena Nicephorus at Pergamum. To the left are two crossed 'Galatian' shields, and in front of them a convex round shield, smaller than the traditional *hoplon*. Such a shield appears in the sarcophagus of Alexander from Sidon, and seems to be an interim model that was used in Greece. In the lower left-hand corner is a piece of fur, or hairy leather, whose use is not clear. At bottom right is a kind of sleeveless 'shirt' or corselet made of metal mesh, used as body armour. Such shirts appear twice more in the Pergamum reliefs (see Bohn 1885: pls. 41, 44). Presumably a leather shirt was worn under the mail. Both literary sources and archaeological finds indicate that chain mail was used by the Galatians. In the upper right-hand corner is a bull's head with its tongue hanging out. The open mouth and the form of the ears suggest that it is a carnyx, a Galatian wind instrument used to raise a din on the battlefield to frighten the enemy. On archaeological evidence from Britain on the Galatian carnyx see Allen 1958: 44–6; Powell 1958: 266.

   Berlin (East), Staatliche Museen, Antikensammlung.

Plate XII. Elephant and cub, tower and archers, in the bowl
from Capena (see pp. 16–17, 317–23, 335)

A painted bowl found at Capena in Campania in south-west Italy, now at the Villa
Giulia Museum in Rome. The elephant is probably Indian, given its height, raised
head, curved back and sloping hindquarters. The trailing cub shows it to be female.
On its neck is the mahout, wielding a stick with a hook on the end to spur and guide
the animal. On the elephant's back is a red carpet and tower, tied to its body with
three straps. Two soldiers with bows are seen in the tower. The side of the tower has
a roundish object, evidently a shield, attached to it.

The Indian origin of the elephant and the place where the bowl was found make
it possible to set the scene in one of the Italian campaigns of King Pyrrhus of Epirus
(280–275 B.C.). The scene is generally considered to represent a well-known story,
derived from Roman annalists, that at the battle of Beneventum the pain of a
wounded elephant cub led its mother to stampede among Pyrrhus' warriors and
thus affect the course of battle. The later manufacture of the bowl accounts for the
errors in some secondary details of the elephant's anatomy: the Indian cow elephant
has small tusks or none at all; protruding curved tusks are more characteristic of the
African bush elephant which was never employed in battle; the end of the trunk
features two 'fingers' typical of the African elephants of both bush and forest.
Bibliography: Beazley 1928: 257; Lévêque 1957: 371–4; Scullard, 1974: 112–
13,244,271.

Rome, Villa Giulia. *Photo*: Soprintendenza Archeologia.

584

Plate XIII. War elephants (see pp. 16–17, 317–23, 334–5)

a. *Silver phalera from the Leningrad Hermitage*

Purportedly found in southern Russia, the phalera was acquired by the Hermitage in the early eighteenth century. It is of uncertain provenance, and was originally used as an ornament for a war elephant or horse. The dragon on the rug, the south Russian provenance, and especially the hat of the first soldier resembling that of King Eucratides of Bactria (toward the middle of the second century B.C.), lead to the conclusion that the elephant pictured served the Greeks in Bactria in the Hellenistic period. Bibliography: Kondakov and Tolstoi 1891: 427; Rostovtzeff 1940: 1. 433; Scullard 1974: 244. The portrait of Eucratides appears in Head 1932: pl. 41, no. 32; Tarn 1951: 563, where there are additional Bactrian hats as well.

The elephant is Indian, as shown by the curved back, the steeply sloping hind-quarters, the triangular ear, flat forehead, and shape of the trunk end. The mahout, wearing a kind of Indian fez, is seated on the elephant's neck holding a stick with a hook in the middle to spur the animal which has a relatively thin rug, with an oriental dragon design, on its back. The sides of the tower are reinforced with thin metal, and its back had an opening for the soldiers, who climbed up to it on a rope ladder. The two soldiers in it are equipped with lances. Given the proportions, they seem to be sitting on stools inside the tower.

Leningrad, Hermitage. *Photo*: Hermitage.

Plate XIII (Cont.)

b. *A terracotta from Myrina*

A painted terracotta found at Myrina in western Asia Minor with other finds of the third century B.C., now in the Louvre. The curved back, steep slope of the hind-quarters and triangular ear are typical of the Indian elephant. On its back is a heavy red carpet which provided some protection, and a kind of square tower, likewise red, on which two blue shields are fixed for both decoration and rein-forcement. The tower walls have crenellations, but it is not manned. The mahout seated on the elephant's neck is wearing a conical Macedonian helmet. The elephant has a large bell hanging around its neck. Its trunk is curled around an infantry soldier, and its tusks are goring him. The soldier has an oval shield and a sword. It is generally agreed that the terracotta commemorates the 'elephant victory' of Antiochus I against the Galatians in western Asia Minor after the First Syrian War. Bibliography: S. Reinach 1885: 485–9; id. 1888: 318–23; von Bienkowski 1928: 142ff.; Rostovtzeff 1940: 1.432; Bar-Kochva 1973a: 1–5; Scullard 1974: 122–3, and 273 n. 65.

Paris, Musée du Louvre. Photo: Chuzeville.

a

Plate XIV. War elephants (see pp. 16–17, 317–23)

a. *Terracotta from Pompei*

Now in the Naples Museum, this terracotta obviously depicts an African forest elephant, as shown by the small size of the animal, its round ear, concave back, gently sloping hindquarters, and the two 'fingers' at the end of the trunk. The mahout is an African black. The tower designed for a single soldier is fixed onto the elephant with three chains. A shield is attached to a tower wall, on which courses of large bricks are drawn. Taking into account the place where the terracotta was found, and the type of elephant, the statuette may commemorate Hannibal's campaign in Italy.

Bibliography: Scullard 1974: 244, and pl. 10. Cf. the tower for a single soldier on an African elephant in von Bienkowski 1928: fig. 222.

Naples, Museo Nazionale. *Photo*: Foglia.

b

c

d

Plate XIV (Cont.)

b. *Amulet of elephant and soldiers in an attack*

Etching on an amulet in the Cabinet de France; see Daremberg and Saglio, s.v. 'Elephas', p. 540, fig. 2624; Scullard 1974: 245.

The elephant has the small stature and slightly concave back characteristic of the African type. It thus probably originates in Ptolemaic or Punic territory, or is perhaps connected with one of the first-century B.C. European or African wars in which the Romans used elephants. The elephant's trunk is wrapped round a soldier holding an elongated shield, and the scene has certain similarities with that depicted on the Myrina terracotta (Pl. XIII b). The elephant has a mahout on its neck and a platform with low railing on its back. Two broad straps from the corners of the platform wind round the animal's belly. The two soldiers are in the throes of attacking, their right arms raised to hurl stones or spears.

c. *Coin from Campania*

A small silver coin, of unknown mintage, with no legend. The presumption is that it originated in Campania in south-western Italy, at the end of the third century B.C., and that it was issued by one of the Italian cities that rebelled against Rome after Hannibal's victory at Cannae. Most features point to an African origin of the forest type for the elephant (the head lower than the back, the two 'fingers' at the end of the trunk, and the large, round ear). The heads of three soldiers are visible above the tower. On the coin and the complicated problems involved, see F. Imhoof-Blümer, *Monnaies grecques* (Paris 1883) 459ff.; H. H. Scullard, 'Hannibal's elephants', *Numismatic Chronicle* 5[10] (1949) 158–68; H. H. Scullard and W. Gowers, 'Hannibal's elephants again', *Numismatic Chronicle* 6[10] (1950) 271–80; Scullard, 1974: 170–3, and the bibliography there in p. 277 n. 111.

d. *'Armoured' elephant* (see p. 334)

A bronze elephant head with silver eyeballs, found in Etruria in north-western Italy, now in the M. Julien Gréau collection. Reproductions appear in Daremberg and Saglio, s.v. 'Elephas', p. 540, fig. 2625; Scullard 1974: 239. The round ear and sloping forehead show it to be an African forest elephant. On the face, above the trunk (missing in the sculpture), is an armour mask with openings for the eyes. The neck, too, is covered in chain armour.

ABBREVIATIONS

AASOR	*Annual of the American Schools of Oriental Research*
AJA	*American Journal of Archaeology*
AM	*Mitteilungen des Deutschen Archäologischen Instituts, Athenische Abteilung*
ASTI	*Annual of the Swedish Theological Institute in Jerusalem*
BA	*Biblical Archeologist*
BASOR	*Bulletin of the American Schools of Oriental Research*
BCH	*Bulletin de correspondance hellénique*
BGU	*Aegyptische Urkunden aus den Königlichen Museen zu Berlin*, 1903–26. Vol. 10: W. Müller, *Papyrusurkunden aus Ptolemäischer Zeit*, 1970
BMC	*Catalogue of Greek Coins in the British Museum*
BMI	*Ancient Greek Inscriptions in the British Museum*, Oxford, 1874–1916
BPES	*Bulletin of the Jewish Palestine Exploration Society*
BT	*Babylonian Talmud*
CAH	*Cambridge Ancient History*
CP	*Classical Philology*
CPJ	V. Tcherikover, A. Fuks and M. Stern, *Corpus Papyrorum Judaicarum*, Cambridge (Mass.), 1957–64
CQ	*Classical Quarterly*
CR	*Classical Review*
Daremberg-Saglio	M. C. Daremberg and E. Saglio, *Dictionnaire des antiquités grecques et romaines*, Paris, 1877–
FGrH	F. Jacoby, *Die Fragmente der griechischen Historiker*, Berlin–Leiden, 1923–
FHG	C. and T. Müller, *Fragmenta Historicorum Graecorum*, Paris, 1841–70
GGM	C. Müller, *Geographici Graeci Minores*, Paris, 1855–61
HTR	*Harvard Theological Review*
HUCA	*Hebrew Union College Annual*
I.Cret.	M. Guarducci, *Inscriptiones Creticae Opera et Consilio Friderici Halbherr Collectae*, vol. 1, Rome, 1935
IEJ	*Israel Exploration Journal*

IG	*Inscriptiones Graecae*, Berlin 1893–
I.Lindos	C. Blinkenberg and K. F. Kinch, *Lindos, Fouilles et recherches 1902–1914*, vol. 2, Copenhagen, 1941
I.Perg.	M. Fränkel, *Die Inschriften von Pergamon*, Berlin, 1890–5
JBL	*Journal of Biblical Literature*
JEA	*Journal of Egyptian Archaeology*
JHS	*Journal of Hellenic Studies*
JJS	*Journal of Jewish Studies*
JPOS	*Journal of the Palestine Oriental Society*
JQR	*Jewish Quarterly Review*
JRS	*Journal of Roman Studies*
JSJ	*Journal of the Study of Judaism in the Persian, Hellenistic and Roman Period*
JTS	*Journal of Theological Studies*
MGWJ	*Monatschrift für Geschichte und Wissenschaft des Judentums*
Milet 3	G. Kaweran and A. Rhem, *Das Delphinion in Milet*, Berlin, 1914, in: Th. Wiegand, *Milet, Ergebnisse der Ausgrabungen und Untersuchungen seit* 1899, vol. 1.3
OGIS	W. Dittenberger, *Orientis Graeci Inscriptiones Selectae*, Leipzig, 1903–5
P.Bad.	F. Bilabel, *Veröffentlichungen aus den badischen Papyrus-Sammlungen*, vols. 2 and 4, Heidelberg, 1923–4
PCZ	C. C. Edgar, *Zenon Papyri*, Cairo, 1925–31
P.Dura	C. B. Welles, R. O. Fink and J. F. Gilliam, *The Excavations at Dura-Europos*, Final Report, v.1, *The Parchments and Papyri*, New Haven, 1959
PEF	*Palestine Exploration Fund*
P.Ent	O. Guéraud (ed.), ΕΝΤΕΥΞΙΣ. *Requêtes et plaintes adressées au roi d'Égypte au IIIᵉ siècle avant J.-C.*, Cairo, 1931–2
PEQ	*Palestine Exploration Quarterly*
PG	*Patrologia Graeca* (J. P. Migne (ed.), *Patrologiae Cursus*, series Graeca)
P.Gnomon	W. Schubart, *Der Gnomon des Idios Logos*, Berlin, 1919
P.Hamb.	P. M. Meyer, *Griechische Papyrusurkunden der Hamburger Stadtbibliotek*, Leipzig, 1911–24
PJB	*Palästinajahrbuch*
PL	*Patrologia Latina* (J. P. Migne (ed.), *Patrologiae Cursus*, series Latina)
P.Petr.	J. G. Mahaffy and J. G. Smyly, *The Flinders Petrie Papyri*, Dublin, 1891–1905
PT	*Palestinian Talmud*
RA	*Revue archéologique*
RB	*Revue biblique*
RE	A. Pauly, G. Wissowa and W. Kroll, *Real-Encyclopädie der classischen Altertumswissenschaft*, Stuttgart, 1893–
REA	*Revue des études anciennes*

REG	*Revue des études grecques*
REJ	*Revue des études juives*
RFIC	*Rivista di filologiae d'istruzione classica*
RhM	*Rheinisches Museum für Philologie*
SB	*Sammelbuch Griechischer urkunden aus Aegypten*, 1915–
SEG	*Supplementum Epigraphicum Graecum*, Leiden, 1923–
Syll.[3]	W. Dittenberger, *Sylloge Inscriptionum Graecarum*, Leipzig, 1913–24
W Chr.	U. Wilcken and L. Mitteis, *Grundzüge und Chrestomathie der Papyruskunde*, Berlin–Leipzig, 1912
VT	*Vetus Testamentum*
ZAW	*Zeitschrift für die Alttestamentliche Wissenschaft*
ZDPV	*Zeitschrift des Deutschen-Palästina-Vereins*
ZNW	*Zeitschrift für die Neutestamentliche Wissenschaft*

REFERENCES

Abel, E. L. (1968) 'The myth of Jewish slavery in Ptolemaic Egypt', *REJ* 127: 253–8

Abel, F. M. (1923) 'Topographie des campagnes Maccabéennes', *RB* 32: 495–521

   (1924) 'Topographie des campagnes Maccabéennes (cont.)', *RB* 33: 201–17, 371–87

   (1925) 'Topographie des campagnes Maccabéennes (cont.)', *RB* 34: 194–216

   (1926) 'Topographie des campagnes Maccabéennes (cont.)', *RB* 35: 206–22, 510–33

   (1927) *Grammaire du grec biblique*, Paris

   (1949) *Les Livres des Maccabées*, Paris

   (1951) *Histoire de la Palestine*, Paris

Abel, F. M. and Starcky, J. (1961) *Les Livres des Maccabées*, Paris

Adinolfi, P. M. (1964) 'Elogia di l'autore di 1 Mac. 6.43–46; il gesto di Eleazaro?', *Antonianum* 39: 177–86

Aharoni, Y. (1967) *The Land of the Bible, a Historical Geography*, Philadelphia

Akavia, A. A. (1974) *Calendar for Six Thousand Years*, Jerusalem (Hebrew)

Albeck, H. (1954) *Six Mishnah Orders*, vol. 1, *Seder Mo'ed*, Tel Aviv (Hebrew)

   (1958) *Six Mishnah Orders*, vol. 3, *Seder Nashim*, Tel Aviv (Hebrew)

   (1959) *Introduction to the Mishnah*, Tel Aviv (Hebrew)

Albright, W. F. (1923) 'The site of Mizpah in Benjamin', *JPOS* 3: 110–21

   (1924) 'Mizpah and Beeroth', *AASOR* 4: 90–111

   (1932) *The Archeology of Palestine*, New York

Allen, O. F. (1958) 'Belgic coins as illustrations of life in the Late Roman Iron Age of Britain', *Proceedings of the Prehistoric Society* N.S. 24: 43–63

   (1971) 'The Sark hoard', *Archaeologia* 103: 10–31

Alon, G. (1955) *History of the Jews in the Land of Israel in the Time of the Mishnah and Talmud*, 2 vols., Tel Aviv (Hebrew)

   (1958) *Studies in Jewish History in the Times of the Second Temple, the Mishnah and Talmud*, 2 vols., Tel Aviv (Hebrew)

   (1977) *Jews, Judaism and the Classical World*, Jerusalem

Alt, A. (1925) 'Das Institut im Jahr 1924', *PJB* 21: 5–57
  (1927) 'Das Institut im Jahr 1926', *PJB* 23: 5–51
  (1929) 'Das Institut im Jahr 1928', *PJB* 25: 5–59
  (1932) 'Das Institut im Jahr 1931', *PJB* 28: 5–47
Altheim, F. (1947–8) *Weltgeschichte Asiens im griechischen Zeitalter*, 2 vols., Halle
Altheim, F. and Stiehl, R. (1970) *Geschichte Mittelasiens im Altertum*, Berlin
Anderson, J. K. (1970) *Military Theory and Practice in the Age of Xenophon*, Berkeley
André, L. E. T. (1903) *Les Apocryphes de l'Ancien Testament*, Florence
Andronikos, M. (1970) 'Sarissa', *BCH* 94: 91–107
  (1980) 'The royal tombs at Aigai' (Vergina)', in Hatzopoulos–Loukopoulos 1980: 188–231
Applebaum, S. (1955) 'Possible Jewish military settlement in Cyrenaica', *Bulletin of the Israel Exploration Society* 19: 188–97 (Hebrew)
  (1979) *Jews and Greeks in Ancient Cyrene*, Leiden
  (1980) 'A fragment of a new Hellenistic inscription from the Old City of Jerusalem', in A. Oppenheimer et al. (eds.), *Jerusalem in the Second Temple Period* (Jerusalem): 47–60 (Hebrew)
Applebaum, S., Dar, S. and Safrai, Z. (1978) 'The towers of Samaria', *PEQ* 110: 91–100
Arenhoevel, D. (1967) *Die Theokratie nach dem 1. und 2. Makkabäerbuch*, Mainz
Artamonov, M. I. (1969) *The Splendor of Scythian Art*, New York
Arvanitopoulos, A. S. (1928) *Graptai Stelai Demetriados-Pegasae*, Athens
Atkinson, K. T. M. (1972) 'A Hellenistic land conveyance: the estate of Mnesimachus in the Plain of Sardes', *Historia* 21: 45–72
Avezou, Ch. (1913) 'Inscriptions de Macédoine et de Thrace', *BCH* 37: 84–154
Avi-Yonah, M. (1954a) *The Madaba Mosaic Map*, Jerusalem
  (1954b) 'The War of the Sons of Light and the Sons of Darkness and Maccabean warfare', *IEJ* 2: 1–5
  (1963) *Historical Geography of Palestine from the End of the Babylonian Exile up to the Arab Conquest*, 3rd edition, Jerusalem (Hebrew)
  (1964) *Essays and Studies in the Lore of the Holy Land*, Tel Aviv (Hebrew).
  (1966) *The Holy Land from the Persian to the Arab Conquest, a Historical Geography*, Grand Rapids, Michigan
  (1971a) 'Syria', in A. H. M. Jones 1971: 226–94
  (1971b) 'The newly found wall of Jerusalem and its topographical significance', *IEJ* 21: 168–9
  (1972) 'The Hasmonaean Revolt and Judah Maccabee's war against the Syrians', in A. Schalit (ed.), *The World History of the Jewish People*, vol. 6: *The Hellenistic Age*, First Series (Jerusalem), 142–82
  (1974) *Carta's Atlas for the Periods of the Second Temple, the Mishna and the Talmud*, 2nd edition, Jerusalem (Hebrew)

(1975) 'Jerusalem in the Hellenistic and Roman period', in M. Avi-Yonah (ed.), *The World History of the Jewish People*, vol. 7: *The Herodian Period* (Jerusalem): 207–49

Avi-Yonah, M. (ed.) (1978) *Encyclopedia of Archaeological Excavations in the Holy Land*, Jerusalem

Avigad, N. (1961) 'The paleography of the Dead Sea Scrolls and related documents', in C. Rabin and Y. Yadin (eds.), *Essays on the Dead Sea Scrolls in Memory of E. L. Sukenik* (Jerusalem): 107–40 (Hebrew)

(1970) 'Excavations in the Jewish Quarter of the Old City of Jerusalem', *IEJ* 20: 129–40

(1972) 'Excavations in the Jewish Quarter of the Old City of Jerusalem', *IEJ* 22: 193–200

(1980) *The Upper City of Jerusalem*, Jerusalem

Avigad, N. and Yadin, Y. (1956) *A Genesis Apocryphon*, Jerusalem

Avissar, A. (1955) *The Wars of Judas Maccabaeus*, Tel Aviv

Avnimelech, M. (1933) 'Discovery of volcanic formations between Jerusalem and Haifa', *Bulletin of the Israel Exploration Society* 3: 59–63 (Hebrew)

Aymard, A. (1953–4) 'L'auteur de l'avènement d'Antiochos IV', *Historia* 2: 49–73

(1955) 'Du nouveau sur la chronologie des Séleucides', *REA* 57: 102–12

Bächli, O. (1976) 'Zur Lage des alten Gilgal', *ZDPV* 83: 64–71

Baer, I. F. (1952) 'The historical foundation of the Halakha', *Zion* 17: 1–55, 173 (Hebrew)

(1956) *Israel among the Nations*, Jerusalem (Hebrew)

(1964) 'The Mishnah and history', *Molad* 21: 308–23 (Hebrew)

(1968) 'The persecution of monotheistic religion by Antiochus Epiphanes', *Zion* 33: 101–24 (Hebrew)

(1969) 'Pesher Habbakuk and its period', *Zion* 34: 1–42 (Hebrew)

(1971) 'Jerusalem in the times of the Great Revolt', *Zion* 36: 127–90 (Hebrew)

Bagnall, R. S. (1976) *The Administration of the Ptolemaic Possessions Outside Egypt*, Leiden

Bar-Kochva, B. (1973a) 'On the sources and chronology of Antiochus I's battle against the Galatians', *Proceedings of the Cambridge Philological Society* 119 N.S.19: 1–8

(1973b) 'The status and origin of the garrison at the Akra on the eve of the religious persecutions', *Zion* 38: 32–47 (Hebrew)

(1974a) 'Menas' inscription and Curupedion', *Scripta Classica Israelica* 1: 14–23

(1974b) 'The battle of Beth Zacharia', *Zion* 39: 157–82 (Hebrew)

(1975) 'Hellenistic warfare in Jonathan's campaign near Azotos', *Scripta Classica Israelica* 2: 83–96

(1976) 'Seron and Cestius Gallus at Beth Horon', *PEQ* 108: 13–21

(1977a) 'Manpower, economics and internal strife in the Hasmonaean state', in H. van Effenterre (ed.), *Armées et fiscalité dans le monde antique*, (Paris): 167–96

(1977b) 'The Babylonian Jews and the Galatians', in *Proceedings of the Sixth World Congress of Jewish Studies (August 1973)*, vol. 1 (Jerusalem): 55–61 (Hebrew)

(1979) *The Seleucid Army*, 2nd impression (1st impression 1976), Cambridge

(1980a) (ed.), *The Seleucid Period in Eretz Israel*, Tel Aviv (Hebrew)

(1980b) *The Battles of the Hasmonaeans, the Times of Judas Maccabaeus*, Tel Aviv (Hebrew)

(1982) 'E. Bickermann's research on the Second Temple period', *Cathedra* 23: 3–10 (Hebrew)

Barkai, G. (1977) 'On the location of the tombs of the late Davidic kings', in M. Broshi (ed.), *Between Hermon and Sinai* (Jerusalem): 75–92 (Hebrew)

Barnabei, F. (1901) *La villa pompeiana di P. Fannio sinistore*, Rome

Bartlett, J. R.(1973) *The First and Second Books of the Maccabees*, Cambridge

Beazley, J. D. (1928) 'Corpus Vasorum Antiquorum: Italia 3 = Villa Giulia 3', *JHS* 48: 257

Beek, M. A. (1943) 'Relations entre Jérusalem et la Diaspora égyptienne au 2ᵉ siècle avant J. -C.', *Old Testament Library* 2: 119–43

Begbie, C. M. (1967) 'The Epitome of Livy', *CQ* N.S. 17: 333–8

Beloch, K. J. (1886) *Die Bevölkerung der griechisch–römischen Welt*, Leipzig
(1924–27) *Griechische Geschichte*, 2nd edition, 4 (8) vols., Berlin and Leipzig.

Ben-Dov, M. (1980) 'The Seleucid Akra – south of the Temple', *Cathedra* 18: 22–35 (Hebrew)

Ben-Jehuda, E. (1908) *Thesaurus Totius Hebraitatis*, vol. 4, Jerusalem and Berlin (Hebrew)

Ben-Shalom, I. (1980) 'The Shammai School and its place in the political history of Eretz Israel in the first century A.D.', diss., Tel Aviv (Hebrew)

Bengtson, H. (1964) *Die Strategie in der hellenistischen Zeit*, 2nd edition, 3 vols., Munich

Bentzen, A. (1952) *Daniel*, Tübingen

Bequignon, P. (1934) 'Recherches archéologiques dans la vallée du Spercheios', *RA*⁶ 4: 14–33

Berve, H. (1926) *Das Alexanderreich auf prosopographischer Grundlage*, 2 vols., Munich

Best, J. G. P. (1969) *Thracian Peltasts*, Groningen

Bevan, E. R. (1902) *The House of Seleucus*, 2 vols., London
(1904) *Jerusalem under the High Priests*, London

Bévenot, H. (1931) *Die beiden Makkabäerbücher*, Bonn

Beyer, G. (1930) 'Eusebius über Gibeon und Beeroth', *ZDPV* 53: 199–211

(1931) 'Das Stadtgebiet von Eleutheropolis im 4. Jahrhundert n. Chr. und seine Grenznachbarn', *ZDPV* 54: 209–71

Bickerman, E. (1933) 'Ein jüdischer Festbrief vom Jahre 124 v. Chr.',
 ZNW 32: 233–54
  (1935) 'Some notes on Megillat Ta'anit', *Zion* 1: 351–5 (Hebrew)
  (1937) *Der Gott der Makkabäer*, Berlin
  (1938) *Institutions de Séleucides*, Paris
  (1945) 'The date of Fourth Maccabees', in S. Lieberman et al. (eds.),
 Luis Ginzberg Jubilee Volume (New York): 105–12
  (1947) 'La Coelé-Syrie: notes de géographie historique', *RB* 54: 256–
 78
  (1968) *Chronology of the Ancient World*, Ithaca
  (1976–80) *Studies in Jewish and Christian History*, 2 vols., Leiden
  (1978) *The God of the Maccabees*, Leiden
Blass, F. and Debrunner, A. (1967) *A Greek Grammar of the New Testament*
 (ed. R. W. Funk), Chicago
Blidstein, G. J. (1976) 'The first fruit in rabbinic literature', *Eshel Beer-
 Sheva, Studies in Jewish Thought*: 78–87 (Hebrew)
Bloch, H. (1879) *Die Quellen des Flavius Josephus in seiner Archäologie*, Leipzig.
Blum, H. (1969) *Die antike Mnemotechnik*, Hildesheim
Bochart, S. (1893) *Hierozoicon sive de Animalibus Sacrae Scripturae*, 2 vols.,
 Leipzig
Bohn, R. (ed.) (1885) *Das Heiligtum der Athena Polias Nikephoros*, Altertümer
 von Pergamon II.1.2, Berlin
Bornecque, H. (1977) 'Die Reden bei Livius', in E. Burck (ed.), *Wege zu
 Livius* (Darmstadt): 395–414
Bornstein, H. I. (1921) 'The count of sabbaticals and jubilees', *Ha-Tekufa*
 11: 238–60 (Hebrew)
Bosworth, A. B. (1973) 'ΑΣΘΕΤΑΙΡΟΙ', *CQ* N.S. 23: 245–54
  (1980a) *Commentary on Arrian's History of Alexander*, vol. 1, Oxford
  (1980b) 'Alexander and the Iranians', *JHS* 100: 1–21
Bouché-Leclercq, A. (1907) *Histoire des Lagides*, vol. 4, Paris
  (1913–14) *Histoire des Séleucides*, 2 vols., Paris
Bradford, A. S. (1977) *A Prosopography of Lacedaimonians from the Death of
 Alexander the Great, 323 B.C.., to the Sack of Sparta by Alaric, A.D.. 396*,
 Munich
Breccia, E. (1912) *Le necropoli di Sciatbi*, Cairo
Breitenstein, U. (1976) *Beobachtungen zu Sprache, Stil und Gedankengut des
 Vierten Makkabäerbuchs*, Basel
Briant, P. (1972) 'D'Alexandre le Grand aux Diadoques: le cas d'Eumène
 de Kardia', *REA* 74: 32–73
Bringmann, K. (1983) *Hellenistische Reform und Religionsverfolgung in Judäa*,
 Göttingen
Brink, C. O. (1960) 'Tragic history and Aristotle's School', *Proceedings of the
 Cambridge Philological Society* 186 N.S. 6: 14–19
Briscoe, J. (1969) 'Eastern policy and senatorial politics 168–146 B.C.',
 Historia 18: 49–70

(1981) *A Commentary on Livy, Books XXXIV–XXXVII*, Oxford

Broshi, M. (1979) 'The population of Western Palestine in the Roman–Byzantine period', *BASOR* 236: 1–10

(1982) 'The credibility of Josephus', in U. Rappaport (ed.), *Flavius Josephus*, Jerusalem (Hebrew)

Broshi, M. and Gophna, R. (1984) 'The settlements and population of Eretz Israel in the Early Bronze Age I–II', *Eretz Israel* 17: 147–57 (Hebrew)

Brown, T. S. (1958) *Timaeus of Tauromenium*, Berkeley

Brüne, B. (1913) *Flavius Josephus und seine Schriften*, Wiesbaden

Brunt, P. A. (1963) 'Alexander's Macedonian cavalry', *JHS* 83: 27–46

(1971) *Italian Manpower*, Oxford

(1976) *Arrian*, vol. 1, London

(1980) 'On historical fragments and epitome', *CQ* N.S. 30: 475–94

Büchler, A. (1896) 'Les sources de Flavius Josèphe', *REJ* 32: 179–99

(1897) 'Les sources de Flavius Josèphe [cont.]', *REJ* 34: 68–93

(1906) *Die Tobiaden und die Oniaden im 2. Makkabäerbuch und in der verwandten jüdisch-hellenistischen Literatur*, Vienna

(1928) *Studies in Sin and Atonement*, Oxford

Bunge, J. G. (1971) *Untersuchungen zum zweiten Makkabäerbuch*, Bonn

(1974a) '"Theos Epiphanes", zu den ersten fünf Regierungsjahren', *Historia* 23: 57–85

(1974b) 'Münzen als Mittel politischer Propaganda: Antiochus IV Epiphanes von Syrien', *Studii clasice* 16: 43–52

(1975) 'Zur Geschichte und Chronologie des Untergangs der Oniaden und des Aufstiegs der Hasmonäer', *JSJ* 6: 1–46

(1976) 'Die Feiern Antiochos' IV Epiphanes in Daphne, 166 v. Chr.', *Chiron* 6: 63–71

Burck, E. (1977) 'Einzelinterpretation von Reden', in E. Burck (ed.), *Wege zu Livius* (Darmstadt): 430–63

Burney, C. F. (1920) 'An acrostic poem in praise of Judas Maccabaeus', *JTS* 21: 319–25

Burr, D. (1934) *Terracottas from Myrina*, Vienna

Büttner-Wobst, Th. (1904) *Polybius*, Teubner edition, vol. 4, Leipzig

Cahana, A. (1957) *The Apocrypha and Pseudepigrapha*, 2nd edition, 2 vols., Tel Aviv (Hebrew)

Caley, E. R. (1964) *Orichalcum and Related Alloys*, New York

Carmon, I. and Shmueli, A. (1970) *Hebron, a Mountain City*, Tel Aviv (Hebrew)

Cary, M. (1951) *A History of the Greek World from 323 to 146 B.C.*, 2nd edition, London

Cavaignac, C. (1951) 'Launey, *Recherches sur les armées hellénistiques*' (review), *Revue de Philologie* 25: 292–4

Cavallin, H. C. (1979) 'Leben nach dem Tode im Spätjudentum und im frühen Christentum' in H. Temporini and W. Haase (eds.), *Aufstieg und Niedergang der römischen Welt*, II, *Principat*, vol. 19.1 (Berlin): 240–345

Cerfaux, L. and Tondriau, J. (1957) *Un concurrent du christianisme : le culte des souverains dans la civilisation gréco-romaine*, Tournai

Churgin, P. (1949) *Studies in the Times of the Second Temple*, New York (Hebrew)

Clermont-Ganneau, C. (1874) 'Letters from M. Clermont Ganneau', *PEF*: 137–78

(1896) *Archeological Researches in Palestine*, 2 vols., London

Clinton, H. F. (1834) *Fasti Hellenici*, vol. 3, Oxford

Cohen, G. M. (1972) 'The Hellenistic military colony: a Herodian example', *Transactions of the American Philological Association* 103: 83–95

(1978) *The Seleucid Colonies, Studies in Founding, Administration and Organization*, Wiesbaden

Cohen, N. G. (1976) 'Asinaeus and Anilaeus: additional comments to Josephus' *Antiquities of the Jews*', *ASTI* 10: 30–7

Cohen, S. J. D. (1979) *Josephus in Galilee and Rome*, Leiden

Conder, C. R. (1875) 'The hill country of Judah – first campaign', *PEF*: 66–72

(1893) *Judas Maccabaeus and the Jewish War of Independence*, London

Conder, C. R. and Kitchener, H. H. (1881–3) *The Survey of Western Palestine*, 3 vols., London

Corradi, G. (1929) *Studi Ellenistici*, Turin

Couissin, P. (1926) *Les armes romaines*, Paris

(1927) 'Les armes gauloises figurées sur les monuments grecs, étrusques et romains', *RA* 25.1: 138–76 and 25.2: 43–79

(1931) *Les institutions militaires et navales*, Paris

Crawford, D. J. (1971) *Kerkeosiris*, Cambridge

Cross, F. M. (1963) 'The discovery of the Samaria Papyri', *BA* 26: 110–21

(1966) 'Aspects of Samaritan and Jewish history in Late Persian and Hellenistic times', *HTR* 59: 201–11

Crowfoot, J. W., Kenyon, K. M and Sukenik, E. L. (1942) *The Buildings of Samaria*, London

Dancy, J. C. (1954) *A Commentary on I Maccabees*, Oxford

De Boor, C. (1903) *Excerpta de legationibus Romanorum ad gentes*, Berlin

(1906) *Excerpta de Sententiis*, Berlin

Delbrück, H. (1913) *Numbers in History*, London

Delcor, M. (1971) *Le Livre de Daniel*, Paris

Derenbourg, J. (1867) *Essai sur l'histoire et la géographie de la Palestine*, Paris

Dindorff, G. (1865) *Flavii Josephi opera*, 2nd edition, Paris

Doran, R. (1979) '2 Maccabees and "tragic history"', *HUCA* 50: 110–14

(1981) *Temple Propaganda: the Purpose and Character of 2 Maccabees*, Washington

Downey, G. (1951) 'The economic crisis at Antioch under Julian the Apostate', in P. R. Coleman-Norton (ed.), *Studies in Roman Economic and Social History in Honor of Allan Chester Johnson* (Princeton): 312–21

(1961) *A History of Antioch in Syria from Seleucus to the Arab Conquest*, Princeton

Droysen, H. (1877–8) *Geschichte des Hellenismus*, 3 vols., Gotha

(1885) 'Die Balustradenreliefs', in Bohn 1885: 93–138

(1889) *Heerwesen und Kriegführung der Griechen*, Freiburg

Drüner, H. (1896) *Untersuchungen über Josephus*, Marburg

Ducrey, P. (1968a) *Le traitement des prisonniers de guerre dans la Grèce Antique*, Paris

(1968b) 'Aspects juridiques de la victoire et du traitement des vaincus' in Vernant 1968: 231–44

Dupont-Sommer, A. (1960) *Aperçus préliminaires sur les manuscripts de la Mer-Morte*, Paris

Durrbach, F. and Roussel, P. (1935) *Inscriptions de Délos*, Paris

Eadie, J. W. (1967) 'The development of Roman mailed cavalry', *JRS* 57: 162–70

Eddy, S. K. (1961) *The King is Dead*, Lincoln, Nebraska

Edson, C. (1958) 'Imperium Macedonicum: the Seleucid empire and its literary evidence', *CP* 53: 153–70

Efron, J. (1980) *Studies in the Hasmonaean Period*, Tel Aviv (Hebrew)

Ehrenberg, V. (1960) *The Greek State*, Oxford

Eissfeldt, O. (1931) 'יהד Jos. 19.45 und ἡ 'Ιουδαῖα 1. Makk 4.15-el-jehudiye', *ZDPV* 54: 271–8

Elhorst, H. J. (1905) 'Die beiden Makkabäerbücher und die Vorgeschichte des jüdischen Freiheitskrieges', *Vierteljahrschrift für Bibelkunde*: 38–55

Epstein, J. N. (1957) *Introduction to Tannaitic Literature*, Jerusalem (Hebrew).

Errington, R. M. (1969) *Philopoemen*, Oxford

Ettelson, H. W. (1925) 'The integrity of I Maccabees', *The Connecticut Academy of Arts and Sciences* 27: 249–84

Ewald, H. (1864–8) *Geschichte des Volkes Israel*, 3rd edition, 7 vols., Göttingen

Farmer, W. R. (1956) *Maccabees, Zealots and Josephus*, New York

Farnell, L. R. (1909) *The Cults of the Greek States*, 5 vols., London

Feldman, L. H. (1984) 'Flavius Josephus revisited: the man, his writings, and his significance', in H. Temporini and W. Haase (eds.), *Aufstieg und Niedergang der römischen Welt*, II, *Principat*, vol. 21.2 (Berlin): 763–862

Feliks, J. (1963) *Agriculture in Palestine in the Period of the Mishna and Talmud*, Jerusalem (Hebrew)

Février, J. G. (1924) *La date, la composition et les sources de la lettre d'Aristée à Philocrate*, Paris

Feyel, M. (1935) 'Un nouveau fragment du règlement militaire trouvé à Amphipolis', *RA*⁶ 5: 29–68

Finkelstein, A. (1951) *Introduction to the Treatises Abot and Abot of Rabbi Nathan*, New York (Hebrew)

Fischer, M. (1979) 'Hirbat Masad (1977–1978)', *RB* 86: 461–2
(1980) 'Khirbet Mazad 1552.1360', *Archiv für Orientforschung* 28: 235–7

Fischer, Th. (1980). *Seleukiden und Makkabäer*, Bochum

Flusser, D. (1980) 'Apocalyptic elements in the War Scroll' in A. Oppenheimer (ed.), *Jerusalem in the Second Temple Period* (Jerusalem): 434–52 (Hebrew)

Forbes, R. J. (1950) *Metallurgy in Antiquity*, Leiden

Foucault, J. A. (1972) *Recherches sur la langue et le style de Polybe*, Paris

Fraser, P. M. (1972) *Ptolemaic Alexandria*, 3 vols., Oxford

Fraser, P. M. and Rönne, T. (1957) *Boeotian and West Greek Tombstones*, London

Friedländer, M. (1903) *Geschichte der jüdischen Apologetik*, Zurich.

Funk, R. W. (1958) 'The 1957 campaign at Beth Zur', *BASOR* 150: 8–20

Gafni, J. (1980) 'On the use of I Maccabees by Flavius Josephus', *Zion* 45: 81–95 (Hebrew)

Galili, E. (1954) 'The invasion of Eretz Israel by the Seleucids', *Ma'arakhot* no. 22: 57–72 (Hebrew)
(1968) 'Whom did the Hasmonaeans confront in the battlefields?', *Ma'arakhot* no. 52: 52–6 (Hebrew)
(1976–7) 'The battle of Raphia', *Scripta Classica Israelica* 3: 52–126

Galling, K. (1939) 'E. Bickermann, *Der Gott der Makkabäer*' (review), *Orientalische Literaturzeitung* 42: 225–8
(1964) *Studien zur Geschichte Israels im persischen Zeitalter*, Tübingen

Garlan, Y. (1972) *La guerre dans l'antiquité*, Paris
(1974) *Recherches de poliorcétique grecque*, Paris
(1975) *War in the Ancient World*, London
(1984) 'War and Siegecraft', in *CAH*, vol. vii.1²: 353–62

Gauger, J. D. (1976) *Beiträge zur jüdischen Apologetik*, Cologne

Gauthier, H. and Sottas, H. (1925) *Un decret trilingue en l'honneur de Ptolémée IV*, Cairo

Geiger, A. (1875) *Urschrift und Uebersetzungen der Bibel in ihrer Abhängigkeit von der inneren Entwicklung des Judentums*, Breslau

Gerleman, G. (1956) *Studies in the Septuagint*, vol. 3, *Proverbs*, Lund

Geva, H. (1983) 'Excavations in the Citadel of Jerusalem 1979–1980', *IEJ* 33: 55–71
1985 'Tryphon's sling bullet from Dor', *IEJ* 35: 153–63

Gichon, M. (1967) 'Idumea and the Herodian *limes*', *IEJ* 17: 27–42
(1980) 'Khirbet Aqed 1508.1382', *Archiv für Orientforschung* 28: 235

Giovannini, G. (1943) 'The connection between tragedy and history in ancient criticism', *Philological Quarterly* 22: 308–14

Glover, R. F. (1948) 'The tactical handling of the elephant', *Greece and Rome* 17: 1–11

Goettsberger, J. (1928) *Das Buch Daniel*, Bonn

Goldberg, R. (1979) 'The Jewish Sabbath in the Roman world up to the time of Constantine the Great', in H. Temporini and W. Haase (eds.), *Aufstieg und Niedergang der römischen Welt*, II, *Principat*, vol. 19.1 (Berlin): 414–47

Goldstein, J. A. (1976) *I Maccabees*, A New Translation with Introduction and Commentary, New York

Gomme, A. W. (1933) *The Population of Athens in the Fifth and Fourth Centuries B.C.*, Oxford

Goren, S. (1958) 'War on the Sabbath in the light of the sources', in L. L. Maimon (ed.), *'Sinai' Jubilee Book* (Jerusalem): 149–80 (Hebrew)

Graetz, H. (1888) *Geschichte der Juden*, 4th edition, vol. 3.2, Leipzig

Graham, A. J. (1960) 'The authenticity of the ΟΡΚΙΟΝ ΤΩΝ ΟΙΚΙΣ-ΤΗΡΩΝ of Cyrene', *JHS* 80: 94–113
(1964) *Colony and the Mother City in Ancient Greece*, Manchester

Griffith, G. T. (1935) *The Mercenaries of the Hellenistic World*, Cambridge
(1956–7) 'ΜΑΚΕΔΟΝΙΚΑ: notes on the Macedonians of Philip and Alexander', *Proceedings of the Cambridge Philological Society* N.S. 4: 3–10

Griffith, G. T. (with Hammond, N. G. L.) (1979) *A History of Macedonia*, vol. 2, Oxford

Grimm, K. L. W. (1835) *Das erste Buch der Maccabäer*, Kurzgefasstes exegetisches Handbuch zu den Apokryphen des Alten Testaments, Leipzig.
(1857) *Das zweite, dritte und vierte Buch der Maccabäer*, Leipzig

Grintz, J. M. (1946) 'Cities of Nabhrachta', *Zion* 12: 1–16 (Hebrew)
(1969a) *Chapters in the History of the Second Temple*, Jerusalem (Hebrew)
(1969b) *Studies in Early Biblical Ethnology and History*, Tel Aviv (Hebrew)

Grote, K. (1913) *Das griechische Söldnerwesen der hellenistischen Zeit*, Jena

Grube, G. M. A. (1965) *The Greek and Roman Critics*, London

Gruen, E. S. (1984) *The Coming of Rome*, 2 vols., Berkeley and Los Angeles

Grundy, G. B. (1901) *The Great Persian War*, London
(1948) *Thucydides and the History of his Age*, 2nd edition, 2 vols., London

Gruppe, O. (1906) *Griechische Mythologie und Religionsgeschichte*, 2 vols., Munich

Guérin, M. V. (1868–80) *Description géographique, historique et archéologique de la Palestine*, 7 vols., Paris

Gutberlet, C. (1920) *Das erste Buch der Maccabäer*, Münster
(1927) *Das zweite Buch der Maccabäer*, Münster

Guthe, H. (1882) 'Ausgrabungen bei Jerusalem', *ZDPV* 5: 271–378

Gutman, A. Y. (1949) 'The story of the Mother and her Seven Sons', in

M. Schwabe and I. Gutman (eds.), *Memorial Book to Hans J. Levy* (Jerusalem): 25–37 = Bar-Kochva 1980a: 191–204 (Hebrew)

(1958) *The Beginnings of Jewish–Hellenistic Literature*, 2 vols., Jerusalem (Hebrew)

Habicht, C. (1956) *Gottmenschentum und Griechische Städte*, Munich

(1976a) *2. Makkabäerbuch*, Jüdische Schriften aus hellenistisch–römischer Zeit, vol. 1, *Historische und legendarische Erzählungen*, Gütersloh

(1976b) 'Royal documents in II Maccabees', *Harvard Studies in Classical Philology* 80: 7–17

Hadas, M. (1951) *Aristeas to Philocrates*, New York

(1953) *The Third and Fourth Books of the Maccabees*, New York

(1954) *Ancilla to Classical Reading*, New York

(1959) *Hellenistic Culture*, New York

Halevy, I. (1901) *Dorot Harischonim, Die Geschichte und Literatur Israels*, Part 1, vol. 3, Frankfurt (Hebrew)

Hall, F. W. (1913) *A Companion to Classical Texts*, Oxford

Hammond, N. G. L. (1966) 'The opening campaigns and the battle of *Aoi Stena* in the Second Macedonian War', *JRS* 56: 39–54

(1981) *Alexander the Great, King, Commander and Statesman*, London

Hanfmann, G. M. A. and Waldbaum, J. C. (1975) *A Survey of Sardis and the Major Monuments outside the City Walls*, Cambridge, Mass

Hanhart, R. (1959) *Maccabaeorum liber II*, Göttingen

(1961) 'Zum Text des 2. und 3. Makkabäerbuches: Probleme der Ueberlieferung, der Auslegung und der Ausgabe', *Nachrichten der Akademie der Wissenschaften in Göttingen*, Phil. -hist. Kl.: 427–87

(1964) *Untersuchungen zur israelitisch–jüdischen Chronologie*, Berlin

Harkavi, Y. (1981) 'The strategy in the Jewish Wars', *Ma'arakhot* nos. 279–80: 69–71 (Hebrew)

Hartman, A. F. and Di Lella, A. D. (1978) *The Book of Daniel*, New York

Hatch, E. and Redpath, H. A. (1897) *A Concordance to the Septuagint*, 2 vols., Oxford

Hatzopoulos, M. B. and Loukopoulos, L. D. (1980) *Philip of Macedon*, Athens

Head, B. V. (1911) *Historia Numorum*, 2nd edition, Oxford

(1932) *A Guide to the Principal Coins of the Greeks*, London

Heichelheim, F. (1925) *Die auswärtige Bevölkerung im Ptolemäerreich*, Stuttgart.

Heinen, H. (1973) 'Heer und Gesellschaft im Ptolemäerreich', *Ancient Society* 4: 91–114

Helfgott, S. (1974) 'The Sabbath in the Classical writers', diss., Yeshiva University, New York

Hengel, M. (1961) *Die Zeloten*, Leiden

(1973) *Judentum und Hellenismus*, 2nd edition, Tübingen

(1976) *Juden, Griechen und Barbaren*, Stuttgart

(1981) *The Atonement*, London

(1982) 'Achilleus in Jerusalem', *Sitzungsberichte der Heidelberger Akademie der Wissenschaften*, Phil. -hist. Klasse, no. 1

Herr, M. D. (1961) 'The problem of war on the Sabbath in the Second Temple and the Talmudic periods', *Tarbiz* 30: 242–56, 341–56 (Hebrew)

(1976) 'The Calendar', in S. Safrai and M. Stern (eds.), *The Jewish People in the First Century* (Assen), vol. 2: 834–64

(1980) 'Jerusalem, the Temple and its cult-reality and concepts in Second Temple times', in A. Oppenheimer et al. (eds.), *Jerusalem in the Second Temple Period* (Jerusalem): 166–77

Herzfeld, E. (1920) *Am Tor von Asien*, Berlin

Herzfeld, L. (1863) *Geschichte des Volkes Jisrael*, 2nd edition, 2 vols., Leipzig.

Heuss, A. (1937) *Stadt und Herrscher des Hellenismus*, Berlin

(1949) 'Bengtson, *Die Strategie*' (review), *Gnomon* 21: 304–18

Hitzig, F. (1850) *Das Buch Daniel*, Leipzig

(1869) *Geschichte des Volkes Israel von Anbeginn bis zur Eroberung Masada's*, 2 vols., Leipzig

Holleaux, M. (1938–57) *Études d'épigraphie et d'histoire grecques*, 5 vols., Paris

Hölscher, G. (1904) *Die Quellen des Josephus für die Zeit vom Exil bis zum jüdischen Kriege*, Leipzig

(1940) *Die Hohenpriesterliste bei Josephus und die evangelische Chronologie*, Heidelberg

Huari, K. (1941). 'Das islamische Geschützwesen', *Studia Orientalia* (Helsinki–Leipzig) 9.3: 105–40

Hunkin, J. W. (1928) 'An emendation of the Text of I Macc. III 48', *JTS* 29: 43–6

Huss, W. (1976) *Untersuchungen zur Aussenpolitik Ptolemaios' IV*, Munich

Jacoby, F. (1923) *Fragmente der griechischen Historiker*, vol. IIB, Berlin

(1944) 'Patrios nomos', *JHS* 64: 37–66

Janke, A. (1904) *Auf Alexanders des Grossen Pfaden, eine Reise durch Kleinasien*, Berlin

Jastrow, M. (1886–1903) *A Dictionary of the Targumim, the Talmud Babli and Yerushalmi and the Midrashic Literature*, 2 vols., New York and Berlin

Jeffery, L. H. (1961) 'The pact of the first settlers at Cyrene', *Historia* 10: 139–47

Jellicoe, S. (1968) *The Septuagint and Modern Study*, Oxford

Jones, A. F. (1963) 'The military strategy of Sabbath attacks on the Jews', *VT* 13: 482–6

Jones, A. H. M. (1931) 'The urbanization of Palestine', *JRS* 21: 78–85

(1940) *The Greek City from Alexander to Justinian*, Oxford

(1971) *The Cities of the Eastern Roman Provinces*, 2nd edition, Oxford

Joüon, P. (1922) 'Quelques hébraïsmes de syntaxe dans le 1er livre des Maccabées', *Biblica* 3: 204–6

Judeich, W. (1931) 'Granikos', in Kromayer and Veith 1903–32: 4. 347–97

Kähler, H. (1965) *Der Fries vom Reiterdenkmal des Aemilius Paulus in Delphi*, Berlin

Kahrstedt, U. (1926) *Syrische Territorien in hellenistischer Zeit*, Berlin

Kallai, Z. (1954) 'An attempt to determine the location of Beeroth', *Eretz Israel* 3: 111–15 (Hebrew)
(1960) *The Northern Boundaries of Judah*, Jerusalem (Hebrew)

Kalléris, J. N. (1954) *Les Anciens Macédoniens*, Athens

Kamphausen, A. (1900) 'Das zweite Buch der Makkabäer', in E. F. Kautzch, *Die Apokryphen und Pseudepigraphen des Alten Testaments* (Tübingen), vol. 1: 81–118

Kanael, B. (1964) 'The heroic wars of Judas Maccabaeus', *Mahanayim* 77: 110–15 (Hebrew)

Kappler, W. (1967) *Maccabaeorum liber I*, 2nd edition, Göttingen

Kappler, W. and Hanhart, R. (1967) *Maccabaeorum Liber II*, Göttingen

Kasher, A. (1975) 'Some suggestions and comments concerning Alexander of Macedon's campaign in Palestine', *Beth Mikra* 20: 187–208 (Hebrew)
(1977) 'The Jewish attitude towards the Alexandrian Gymnasium', *American Journal of Ancient History* 2: 148–61
(1978) 'The first Jewish military units in Ptolemaic Egypt', *JSJ* 9: 55–67
(1980) 'Diaspora Jews in the period of the Persecution and the Revolt', in Bar-Kochva 1980a: 205–26
(1985) *The Jews in Hellenistic and Roman Egypt*, Tübingen

Katz, P. (1960) 'The text of 2 Maccabees reconsidered', *ZNW* 51: 10–30

Kaufmann, E. (1937–56) *The History of the Israelitic Religion*, 4 vols., Jerusalem (Hebrew)

Kazarow, G. (1918) 'Zur Archäologie Thrakiens (ein Reisebericht)', *Archäologischer Anzeiger* 33: 1–66

Kebric, R. B. (1977) *Duris of Samos*, Wiesbaden

Keil, C. F. (1875) *Commentar über die Bücher der Makkabäer*, Leipzig

Kellermann, U. (1978) *Auferstanden in den Himmel, 2 Makkabäer 7 und die Auferstehung der Märtyrer*, Stuttgart

Kelley, R. J. (1977) *Studies in the Speeches in the First Book of Xenophon's Anabasis*, Berkeley

Kenyon, K. (1974) *Digging up Jerusalem*, New York

Kiechle, F. (1958) 'Zur Humanität in der Kriegsführung der griechischen Staaten', *Historia* 7: 129–56

Kimming, W. (1940) 'Ein Keltenschild aus Aegypten', *Germania* 24: 106–11

Kirkpatrick, A. F. (1884–5) 'I Maccabees III.48', *Journal of Philology* 14:111–12

Kitto, H. D. F. (1966) 'Catharsis', in L. Wallach (ed.), *The Classical Tradition* (Ithaca): 133–47

Klausner, J. (1950) *History of the Second Temple*, 2nd edition, 5 vols., Jerusalem (Hebrew)

Klein, S. (1927) 'Studies in the genealogical list in the Book of Chronicles (1)', *Meassef Zion* 2: 1–16 (Hebrew)

  (1928a) *Galiläa von der Makkabäerzeit bis 67*, Vienna

  (1928b) 'Studies in the genealogical list in the Book of Chronicles (2)', *Meassef Zion* 3: 1–16 (Hebrew)

  (1930) 'Studies in the genealogical list in the Book of Chronicles', *Meassef Zion* 4: 14–30 (Hebrew)

  (1934) 'Palästinisches im Jubiläenbuch', *ZDPV* 57: 7–27

  (1938) *The Land of Galilee*, Jerusalem (Hebrew)

  (1939a) *The Land of Judaea*, Tel Aviv (Hebrew)

  (1939b) *Sefer ha-yishuv*, Jerusalem (Hebrew)

Klotz, A. (1940) *Livius und seine Vorgänger*, Stuttgart

Knabenbauer, J. (1907) *Commentarius in duos libros Machabaeorum*, Paris

Kochabi, S. (1983) 'Sources of the First Book of the Maccabees', *Beth Mikra* 28: 278–90 (Hebrew)

Kochavi, M. (ed.) (1972) *Judaea, Samaria and Golan, Archeological Survey in 1968*, Jerusalem (Hebrew)

Koerner, R. (1957) *Polybius als Kritiker früherer Historiker*, Jena

Kohut, A. (1878–92) *Aruch Completum sive lexicon vocabula et res, quae in libris Targumicis Talmudicis Midraschicis*, 7 vols., New York

Kolbe, W. (1926) *Beiträge zur syrischen und jüdischen Geschichte*, Kritische Untersuchungen zur Seleukidenliste und zu den beiden ersten Makkabäerbüchern, Berlin

  (1927) 'Die Seleukidenära des I Makkabäerbuches', *Hermes* 62: 224–42

Kondakov, N. P. and Tolstoi, I. (1891) *Antiquités de la Russie méridionale*, Paris

Koperberg, S. (1919) *Polybii historiarum liber XXX*, Amsterdam

Koster, A. (1923) *Das Antike Seewesen*, Berlin

Kosters, W. H. (1878) 'De Polemik van het tweede boek der Makkabeën', *Theologisch Tijdschrift* 12: 491–558

Kraeling, C. H. (1932) 'The Jewish community at Antioch', *JBL* 51: 130–60

Krauss, S. (1898–9) *Griechische und lateinische Lehnwörter im Talmud Midrasch und Targum*, 2 vols., Berlin

Kreissig, H. (1978) *Wirtschaft und Gesellschaft im Seleukidenreich*, Berlin

Krochmal, N. (1924) *More Neboche ha-Zeman* (= *The Writings of N. Krochmal*), ed. S. Rawidowicz, Berlin (Hebrew)

Kromayer, J. and Veith, G. (1903–32) *Antike Schlachtfelder*, 5 vols., Berlin

  (1926) *Heerwesen und Kriegführung der Griechen und Römer*, Munich

Krumbacher, K. (1897) *Geschichte der Byzantinischen Literatur*, 2nd edition, Munich

Kugler, F. X. (1907) *Sternkunde und Sterndienst in Babel*, vol. 1, Münster
(1922) *Von Moses bis Paulus*, Münster

Kutscher, E. Y. (1959) *The Language and Linguistic Background of the Isaiah Scroll*, Jerusalem (Hebrew)
(1977) *Hebrew and Aramaic Studies*, Jerusalem (Hebrew)

Laistner, M. (1947) *The Greater Roman Historians*, Berkeley

Lambert, A. (1946) *Die indirekte Rede als künstlerisches Stilmittel des Livius*, Zurich

Lammert, F. L. (1941) 'Griechisches Kriegswesen, Bericht über das Schrifttum der Jahre 1918–1938', *Jahresbericht über die Fortschritte der klassischen Altertumswissenschaft* 274: 1–114

Lane, E. W. (1863) *An Arabic-English Lexicon*, Part 2, London

Laperrousaz, E. M. (1975) 'Angle sud-est du "Temple de Salomon" ou vestiges de l'"Acra des Séleucides"? Un faux problème?', *Syria* 52: 241–59

Laqueur, R. (1904) *Kritische Untersuchungen zum zweiten Makkabäerbuch*, Strasbourg
(1911) 'Ephoros', *Hermes* 46: 347–54
(1927a) 'Griechische Urkunden in der jüdisch–hellenistischen Literatur', *Historische Zeitschrift* 136: 229–52
(1927b) 'Kahrstedt, syrische Territorien in hellenistischer Zeit' (review), *Gnomon* 3: 527–36

Latyschev, B. (1916) *Inscriptiones antiquae orae septentrionalis Ponti Euxini Graecae et Latinae*, vol. 1.2, Petrograd

Launey, M. (1949–50) *Recherches sur les armées hellénistiques*, 2 vols., Paris

Lebram, J. C. H. (1974) 'Perspektiven der gegenwärtigen Danielforschung', *JSJ* 5: 1–33

Legrain, L. (1930) *Terra-cottas from Nippur*, Philadelphia

Leo, F. (1901) *Die Griechisch–Römische Biographie nach ihrer literarischen Form*, Leipzig

Le Rider, G. (1965) *Suse sous les Séleucides et les Parthes*, Mémoires de la Mission archéologique en Iran, vol. 38, Paris

Lesquier, J. (1911) *Les institutions militaires de l'Égypte sous les Lagides*, Paris

Leuze, O. (1935) *Die Satrapieneinteilung in Syrien und im Zweistromlande von 520 zu 320*, Halle

Lévêque, P. (1957) *Pyrrhos*, Paris
(1968) 'La guerre à l'époque hellénistique', in Vernant 1968: 261–90

Lévêque, P. and Vidal-Naquet, P. (1960) 'Epaminondas Pythagoricien ou le problème tactique de la droite et de la gauche', *Historia* 9: 294–308

Levi, M. A. (1963) 'La critica di Polibio a Timeo', in *Miscellanea di Studi Alessandrini in memori di Augusto Rostagni* (Turin): 195–202

Levine, I. L. (1974) 'The Hasmonean conquest of Strato's Tower', *IEJ* 24: 62–9

Levy, H. (1960) *Studies in Jewish Hellenism*, Jerusalem (Hebrew)

Lévy, I. (1950) 'Notes d'histoire hellénistique sur le second Livre des Maccabées', *Mélanges H. Grégoire* (Brussels), vol. 2: 688–99

    (1955) 'Les deux Livres des Maccabées et le Livre Hébraïque des Hasmonéens', *Semitica* 5: 15–36

Levy, J. (1876–84) *Neuhebräisches und chaldäisches Wörterbuch über die Talmudim und Midraschim*, 4 vols., Berlin

Licht, J. (1957) *The Thanksgiving Scroll*, Jerusalem (Hebrew)

Lichtenstein, H. (1931–2) 'Megillat Taanit', *HUCA* 8–9: 257–353

Lieberman, S. (1939) *Tosefet Rishonim*, vol. 3, Jerusalem (Hebrew)

    (1962) *Tosephta Ki-Fshutah, Order Mo'ed*, New York (Hebrew)

    (1973) *Tosephta Ki-Fshutah, Order Nashim*, New York (Hebrew)

Liebeschuetz, J. H. W. G. (1972) *Antioch, City and Imperial Administration in the Later Roman Empire*, Oxford

Liebesny, H. (1936) 'Ein Erlass des Königs Ptolemaios II Philadelphos über die Deklaration von Vieh und Sklaven in Syrien und Phönikien', *Aegyptus* 16: 257–91

Liebmann-Frankfort, T. (1969a) *La frontière orientale dans la politique extérieure de la république romaine depuis le traité d'Apamée jusqu'à la fin des conquêtes asiatiques du Pompée (189–63)*, Brussels

    (1969b) 'Rome et le conflit Judéo-Syrien (146–161 avant notre ère)', *L'antiquité classique* 37: 101–20

Liedmeier, Z. C. (1935) *Plutarchus' Biographie van Aemilius Paulus, Historische Commentar*, Utrecht

Liers, H. (1895) *Das Kriegswesen der Alten*, Breslau

Lindner, H. (1972) *Die Geschichtsauffassung des Flavius Josephus im Bellum Judaicum*, Leiden

Lock, R. A. (1977) 'The origins of the Argyraspides', *Historia* 26: 373–8

Lonis, R. (1949) *Les usages de la guerre entre grecs et barbares*, Paris

Luria, B. Z. (1981) 'The location of the Akra in the north of the Temple Mount', *Cathedra* 21: 31–41 (Hebrew)

Magie, D. (1950) *Roman Rule in Asia Minor*, 2 vols., Princeton

Mahaffy, J. P. (1899) 'The army of Ptolemy IV at Raphia', *Hermathena*: 140–52

Malamat, A. (1965) 'The War of Gideon and Midian', in J. Liver (ed.), *The Military History of the Land of Israel in Biblical Times* (Tel Aviv): 110–23 (Hebrew)

Mantel, H. D. (1969) *Studies in the History of the Sanhedrin*, Tel Aviv (Hebrew)

    (1980) 'The period of the Great Synagogue', in A. Oppenheimer et al. (eds.), *Jerusalem in the Second Temple Period, Abraham Schalit Memorial Volume* (Jerusalem): 22–46 (Hebrew)

    (1983) *The Men of the Great Synagogue*, Tel Aviv (Hebrew)

Marcus, R. (1943) *Josephus*, vol. 7, The Loeb Classical Library, London
  (1966) *Law in the Apocrypha*, New York
Markle, M. M. (1977) 'The Macedonian sarissa, spear and related armor',
  AJA 81: 323–39
  (1978) 'B. Bar-Kochva, *The Seleucid Army*' (review), *The Classical World*
  71: 407–9
Marmorstein, A. (1927) *The Old Rabbinic Doctrine of God*, New York
Marsden, E. W. (1964) *The Campaign of Gaugamela*, Liverpool
  (1969–71) *Greek and Roman Artillery*, 2 vols., Oxford
Maule, A. F. and Smith, H. R. W. (1959) *Votive Religion at Caere*, Berkeley
Maxwell-Stuart, P. G. (1975) '1 Maccabees VI 34 again', *VT* 25: 230–3
Mayser, E. (1933) *Grammatik der griechischen Papyri aus der Ptolemäerzeit*,
  Leipzig
Mazar, B. (1941) 'Topographical studies II: the home of the Hasmonaeans',
  BPES: 105–7
  (1975) *The Mountain of the Lord*, New York
McCown, C. C. (1947) *Tell en-Nasbeh*, vol. 1, Berkeley
McLeod, W. (1965) 'The range of the ancient bow', *Phoenix* 19: 1–14
  (1972) 'The range of the ancient bow', *Phoenix* 26: 78–82
McNicoll, (1978) 'B. Bar-Kochva, *The Seleucid Army*' (review), *PEQ* 110:
  61–5
Meecham, H. G. (1935) *The Letter of Aristeas*, Manchester
Meisner, N. (1972) *Untersuchungen zum Aristeasbrief*, diss., Berlin
  (1973) *Aristeasbrief, jüdische Schriften aus hellenistisch–römischer Zeit*, vol. 2,
  Gütersloh
Meister, K. (1975) *Historische Kritik bei Polybios*, Wiesbaden
Melamed, E. Z. (1932) 'A. Cahana, *The First Book of the Maccabees*'
  (review), *Tarbiz* 3: 469–72 (Hebrew)
  (1951) 'Josephus and I Maccabees – a comparison', *Eretz Israel* 1: 122–
  30 (Hebrew)
  (1966) *The Onomasticon of Eusebius*, Jerusalem (Hebrew)
Melber, J. (1885) 'Ueber die Quellen und den Wert der Strategen-
  sammlung Polyäns', *Jahr. Class. Phil. Suppl.* 14: 640
Mendel, G. (1912) *Catalogue des sculptures grecques, romaines et byzantines*,
  Constantinople
Metzung, A. (1871) *De Polybii librorum* xxx–xxxIII *fragmentis ordine collocandis*,
  Marburg
Meyer, Ed. (1881) 'Die Quellen unserer Ueberlieferung über Antiochus
  des Grossen Römerkrieg', *RhM* N.F. 36: 120–6
  (1921) *Ursprung und Anfänge des Christentums*, vol. 2, Stuttgart
Meyer, P. M. (1900) *Das Heerwesen der Griechen und Römer in Aegypten*,
  Leipzig
Michaelis, J. D. (1778) *Deutsche übersetzung des ersten Buchs der Maccabäer mit
  Anmerkungen*, Göttingen
Michel, O. and Bauernfeind, O. (1962) *Flavius Josephus, Der jüdische Krieg*,
  2nd edition, 2 vols., Munich

Mikhailov, G. (1956) *Inscriptiones Graecae in Bulgaria repertae*, Sophia
   (1974) 'A propos de la stèle du Captor Decebali à Philippes', in *Mélanges helléniques offerts à George Daux* (Paris): 279–87
Milne, J. G. (1928) 'Egyptian nationalism under Greek and Roman rule', *JEA* 14: 226–34
Milns, R. D. (1971) 'The hypaspists of Alexander III', *Historia* 20: 186–96
   (1975) 'The army of Alexander the Great', in O. Reverdin (ed.), *Alexandre le Grand, image et réalité* (Geneva): 87–136
Min ha-Har, S. (1973) *The Jewish Law on Army and Warfare on the Sabbath*, Jerusalem (Hebrew)
Minns, E. H. (1913) *Scythians and Greeks*, Cambridge
Mitford, T. B. (1957) 'Ptolemy Macron', in *Studi in onore di A. Calderini e M. Paribeni* (Milan): 163–87
Mittwoch, A. (1955) 'Tribute and land-tax in Seleucid Judaea', *Biblica* 36: 352–61
Moffatt, J. (1913) 'The Third Book of Maccabees', in R. H. Charles, *The Apocrypha and Pseudepigrapha of the Old Testament* (Oxford), vol. 1: 155–73
Mölleken, W. (1953) 'Geschichtsklitterung im I Makkabäerbuch (Wann wurde Alkimos Hohenpriester?)', *ZAW* 65: 205–28
Möller, Ch. and Schmitt, G. (1976) *Siedlungen Palästinas nach Flavius Josephus*, Wiesbaden
Momigliano, A. (1929–30) 'Un' ignota irruzione dei Galati in Siria al tempo di Antiocho III?', *Bollettino di Filologia Classica* 36: 151–6
   (1930) *Prime linee di storia della tradizione Maccabaica*, Rome
   (1932) 'Per la data e la caratteristica di Aristea', *Aegyptus* 12: 161–72
   (1975) 'The Second Book of Maccabees', *CP* 50: 81–8
   (1978) 'Greek historiography', *History and Theory* 17: 1–28
   (1980) 'The date of the First Book of the Maccabees', in his *Sesto contributo alla storia degli studi classici e del mondo antico* (Rome), vol. 2: 361–6
Montgomery, J. M. (1927) *The Book of Daniel*, Edinburgh
Moore, G. F. (1932) *Judaism*, 3 vols., Cambridge, Mass.
Moore, J. M. (1965) *The Manuscript Tradition of Polybius*, Cambridge
Mooren, L. (1975) *The Aulic Titulature in Ptolemaic Egypt*, Brussels
Mørkholm, O. (1966) *Antiochus IV of Syria*, Copenhagen
Motzo, B. (1915) 'Aristea', *Atti Acad. Torino* 50: 55–78,195–225
Mugler, C. (1931) 'Remarques sur le second Livre des Macchabées', *Revue d'histoire et de philosophie religieuses* 11: 419–23
Murray, G. (1965) *Euripides and his Age*, Oxford
Murray, O. (1967) 'Aristeas and Ptolemaic kingship', *JTS* 18: 337–71
Musti, D. (1960) 'Lo stato dei Seleucidi', *Studi Classici e Orientali* 15: 61–197
Musurillo, H. A. (1954) *The Acts of the Pagan Martyrs*, Oxford
Naor, I. (1959) 'Bet Dagon and Gederoth-Kidron, Eltekeh and Ekron', *Eretz Israel* 5: 121–8 (Hebrew)

Naveh, J. (1981) 'The Aramaic ostraca from Tel Arad', in J. Aharoni, *Arad Inscriptions* (Jerusalem): 153–74 (Hebrew)

Nelis, J. T. (1983) 'La distance de Beth-Sur à Jérusalem suivant 2 Mac. 11.5', *JSJ* 14: 39–43

Neria, M. Z. (1959) *Sabbath Wars*, Jerusalem (Hebrew)

Nestle, E. (1884) 'Der Greuel der Verwüstung', *ZAW* 4: 248

Neuhaus, G. O. (1971) 'Studien zu den poetischen Stücken im I Makkabäerbuch', diss., Tübingen

   (1971/2) 'Methodische Ueberlegungen zur Retroversion des 1. Makkabäerbuches', *Institutum Judaicum der Universität Tübingen*: 100–5

   (1974a) *Studien zu den poetischen Stücken im 1. Makkabäerbuch*, Würzburg

   (1974b) 'Quellen im 1. Makkabäerbuch? Eine Entgegnung auf die Analyse um K. D. Schunck', *JSJ* 5: 162–75

Nickelsburg, G. W. E. (1971) '1 and 2 Maccabees – same story, different meaning', *Concordia Theological Monthly* 24: 515–26

   (1972) *Resurrection, Immortality, and Eternal Life in Intertestamental Judaism*, Cambridge, Mass.

Nielsen, M. P. (1961) *Geschichte der Griechischen Religion*, 2nd edition, Munich

Niese, B. (1893–1903) *Geschichte der griechischen und makedonischen Staaten*, 3 vols., Gotha

   (1900) *Kritik der beiden Makkabäerbücher*, Berlin (= *Hermes* 35: 268–307, 453–527)

   (1906) 'Eine Urkunde aus der Makkabäerzeit', in C. Bezold (ed.), *Orientalische Studien Theodor Nöldeke gewidmet* (Giessen), vol. 2: 817–29

Nissen, H. (1863) *Kritische Untersuchungen über die Quellen der vierten und fünften Dekade des Livius*, Berlin

Nock, A. R. (1952) 'The Roman army and the Roman religious year', *HTR* 45: 187–252

Norden, E. (1923) *Die antike Kunstprosa*, 4th edition, vol. 1, Berlin

North, R. (1953) 'Maccabaean Sabbath Year', *Biblica* 34: 502–15

Nussbaum, M. (1875) *Observationes in Flavii Josephi Antiquitates, Lib. XII.3–XIII.14*, Marburg

Oelgarten, T. (1914) 'Die Bethoron Strasse', *PJB* 14: 73–89

Oesterly, W. O. E. (1913) 'I Maccabees', in R. H. Charles, *The Apocrypha and Pseudepigrapha of the Old Testament* (Oxford), vol. 1: 59–124

Olmstead, O. T. (1937), 'Cuneiform texts and Hellenistic chronology', *Classical Philology* 32: 1–14

Oppenheimer, A. (1976) 'Oral law in the Books of Maccabees', *Immanuel* 6: 34–42

   (1977) *The 'Am ha-Aretz*, Leiden

Otto, W. (1908) *Priester und Tempel im hellenistischen Aegypten*, vol. 2, Leipzig

   (1928) *Beiträge zur Seleukidengeschichte des 3. Jahrhunderts v. Chr.*, Munich

(1934) *Zur Geschichte der Zeit des 6. Ptolemäers*, Munich

Pagenstecher, R. (1919) *Nekropolis, Untersuchungen über Gestalt und Entwicklung der Alexandrinischen Grabanlagen und ihre Malereien*, Leipzig

Panskin, A. G. and de Zeeuw, K. (1970) *Textbook of Wood Technology*, New York

Paret, P. (1964) *French Revolutionary Warfare from Indochina to Algeria*, New York

Parker, R. and Dubberstein, W. (1956) *Babylonian Chronology 626 B.C.–A.D. 75*, Providence

Paschokowski, I. (1966) *Die Kunst der Reden in der 4. und 5. Dekade des Livius*, Kiel

Pearson, L. (1960) *The Lost Histories of Alexander the Great*, Oxford

Pédech, P. (1951) 'Polybe et l''"Éloge de Philopoemen"', *REG* 64: 82–103

(1958) 'Deux campagnes d'Antiochus III chez Polybe', *REA* 60: 67–81

(1964) *La méthode historique de Polybe*, Paris

Perdrizet, P. (1904) 'Stèles peintes de Sidon', *RA*⁴ 3: 234–44

Peremans, W. (1951) 'Notes sur la bataille de Raphia', *Aegyptus* 36: 214–22

Peremans, W. and Van't Dack, E., (1954/5) 'A propos d'une inscription de Gortyn', *Historia* 3: 338–45

(1977) *Prosopographia Ptolemaica*, vol. 2, *L'armée de terre et la police*, Louvain

Petit, P. (1955) *Libanius et la vie municipale à Antioche au IVe siècle après J.C.*, Paris

Petzold, K. E. (1969) *Studien zur Methode des Polybios und zu ihrer historischen Auswertung*, Munich

Pfeifer, R. H. (1941) *Introduction to the Old Testament*, New York

(1949) *History of New Testament Times with an Introduction to the Apocrypha*, New York

Pfuhl, E. (1923) *Malerei und Zeichnung der Griechen*, Munich

Phillipson, C. (1911) *The International Law and Custom of Ancient Greece and Rome*, London

Plöger, O. (1958) 'Die Feldzüge der Seleukiden gegen den Makkabäer Judas', *ZDPV* 74: 158–88

(1965) *Das Buch Daniel*, Gütersloh

Poralla, P. (1913) *Prosopographie der Lakedaimonier*, Breslau

Porten, B. (1968) *Archives from Elephantine*, Berkeley

Powell, J. U. (1925) *Collectanea Alexandrina*, Oxford

Powell, T. G. E. (1958) *The Celts*, London

Préaux, C. (1936) 'Esquisse d'une histoire des révolutions égyptiennes sous les Lagides', *Chronique d'Egypte* 11: 528–52

(1978) *Le monde hellénistique*, 2 vols., Paris

Press, J. (1946–52) *Encyclopaedia of Palestine*, 4 vols., Jerusalem (Hebrew)

Pritchard, B. (1962) *Gibeon, Where the Sun Stood Still*, Princeton

Pritchett, W. K. (1965) *Studies in Ancient Greek Topography*, Part 1, Berkeley (1974–85) *The Greek State at War*, 4 vols., Berkeley

Proksch, O. (1903) 'Der Friede des Lysias vom Frühling 164 v. Chr.', *Theologisches Literaturblatt*: 457–64

Raban, N. (1962) 'On the Hebrew original version of I Maccabees', in E. Eliner, H. M. I. Gebariahu and B. Z. Luria (eds.), *Seidel Festschrift*: *Studies in the Bible* (Jerusalem): 367–96 (Hebrew)

Rabbinovicz, R. (1896) *Dikdukey sofrim, Moed Katan*, Munich (Hebrew)

Rabello, A. M. (1972) 'The "Lex de Templo Hierosolymitano" prohibiting Gentiles from entering Jerusalem's sanctuary', *Sinai* 70: 267–81 (Hebrew)

Rabin, Ch. (1961) 'The literary structure of the War Scroll', in Y. Yadin and Ch. Rabin (eds.), *Essays on the Dead Sea Scrolls in Memory of E. L. Sukenik* (Jerusalem): 31–48 (Hebrew)

Radin, M. (1915) *The Jews among the Greeks and Romans*, Philadelphia

Rahlfs, A. (1911) *Septuaginta Studien*, 3 vols., Göttingen
(1934) 'Die Kriegselefanten im 1sten Makkabäerbuche', *ZAW* 52: 78–9

Rappaport, U. (1965) 'The fourth kingdom in the Book of Daniel', *Beth Mikra* 10: 10–25 (Hebrew)
(1968a) 'The date of the Letter of Aristeas', in *Studies in the History of the Jewish People and the Land of Israel* (Haifa), vol. 1: 37–50 (Hebrew)
(1968b) 'La Judée et Rome pendant le règne d'Alexandre Jannée', *REJ* 127: 329–45
(1969) 'Les Iduméens en Égypte', *Revue de Philologie* 43: 73–82
(1980) 'The Hellenistic cities and the Judaization of Eretz Israel', in Bar-Kochva 1980a: 263–76 (Hebrew)

Rattenbury, R. M. (1942) 'An ancient armoured force', *CR* 56: 113–16

Reinach, S. (1885) 'Fouilles dans la nécropole de Myrina', *BCH* 9: 484–93
(1888) *La nécropole de Myrina*, vol. 1, Paris

Reinach, T. and Hamdy-Bey, O. (1892) *Une nécropole royale de Sidon*, Paris

Reitzenstein, R. (1906) *Hellenistische Wundererzählungen*, Leipzig

Reuter, F. (1938) *Beiträge zur Beurteilung des Königs Antiochus Epiphanes*, Münster

Reynolds, L. D. and Wilson, N. G. (1974) *Scribes and Scholars*, 2nd edition, Oxford

Richnow, W. (1968) 'Untersuchungen zu Sprache und Stil des zweiten Makkabäerbuches', diss., Göttingen

Riemer, M. (1918) 'Wo lag Emmaus?', *PJB* 14: 32–43

Risberg, G. (1918) 'Textkritische und exegetische Anmerkungen zu den Makkabäerbüchern', *Beiträge zur Religionswissenschaft* (Stockholm) 2: 6–31

Robert, L. (1935) 'Notes d'épigraphie hellénistique', *BCH* 59: 421–37
  (1949) 'Inscriptions Séleucides de Phrygie et d'Iran', *Hellenica* 7: 5–29
  (1963) '*Samothrace* 2.1: Fraser, "The Inscriptions on Stone"', (review),
    Gnomon 35: 50–79
Robinson, Ed. (1841) *Biblical Researches in Palestine*, 2 vols., London
Robinson, H. R. (1975) *The Armour of Imperial Rome*, New York
Rofé, A. (1974) 'The laws of war in Deuteronomy: their origin, intention
    and positivity', *Zion* 39: 143–56 (Hebrew)
Rösel, H. (1976) 'Studien zur Topographie der Kriege in den Büchern
    Joshua und Richter', *ZDPV* 92: 10–46
Rosenberg, G. (1927) 'Hjortspringfundet', in *Nordiske Fortiminder* (Copen-
    hagen), vol. 3: 103–14
Rostovtzeff, M. (1906) 'Angariae', *Klio* 6: 249–58
  (1910) *Studien zur Geschichte des römischen Kolonates*, Leipzig
  (1922) *Iranians and Greeks in South Russia*, Oxford
  (1933) *The Excavations at Dura Europos 1930/1*, New Haven
  (1940) *The Social and Economic History of the Hellenistic World*, 3 vols.,
    Oxford
Roussel, D. (1969) 'Remarques sur 2 batailles navales', *REG* 82: 336–41
Roveri, A. (1956) 'Tyche in Polibio', *Convivium* 24: 275–93
Rubin, B. (1955) 'Die Entstehung der Kataphraktenreiterei im Lichte der
    chorezmischen Ausgrabungen', *Historia* 4: 264–83
Rüstow, W. and Köchly, S. (1852) *Geschichte des griechischen kriegswesens von
    der ältesten Zeit bis auf Pyrrhos*, Leipzig
Sachs, A. and Wiseman, D. J. (1954) 'A Babylonian king list of the Hel-
    lenistic period', *Iraq* 16: 202–12
Safrai, S. (1965) *Pilgrimage at the Time of the Second Temple*, Jerusalem
    (Hebrew)
Samuel, A. E. (1972) *Greek and Roman Chronology*, Munich
Sarre, F. (1923) *Die Kunst des Alten Persien*, Berlin
Schachermeyer, F. (1973) *Alexander der Grosse*, Vienna
Schalit, A. (1960) 'The Letter of Antiochus III to Zeuxis regarding the
    establishment of Jewish military colonies in Phrygia and Lydia', *JQR*
    49: 289–318
  (1965) 'Evidence of an Aramaic source in Josephus' "Antiquities" of the
    Jews', *ASTI* 14: 163–88
  (1968) *Namenwörterbuch zu Flavius Josephus*, Leiden
  (1969) *König Herodes*, Berlin
  (1970/1) 'Die Denkschrift der Samaritaner an König Antiochos Epi-
    phanes', *ASTI* 8: 131–83
Schaumberger, J. (1955) 'Die neue Seleukidenliste BM 35603 und die
    makkabäische Chronologie', *Biblica* 30: 423–35
Schechter, S. Z. (1887) *Avot de Rabbi Nathan*, Vienna (Hebrew)
Scheller, P. (1911) *De hellenistica historiae conscribendae arte*, Leipzig
Schiffer, I. (1973) *Charisma, A Psychoanalytic Look at the Mass Society*, Toronto

Schlatter, D. A. (1891) *Jason von Kyrene*, Munich

Schmitt, A. (1966) *Stammt der sogenannte 'Θ' Text bei Daniel wirklich von Theodotion?* Göttingen

Schmitt, G. (1983) *Ein indirektes Zeugnis der Makkabäerkämpfe*, Wiesbaden

Schmitt, H. H. (1957) *Rom und Rhodos*, Munich
  (1964) *Untersuchungen zur Geschichte Antiochos' des Grossen und seiner Zeit*, Wiesbaden

Schneider, C. (1969) *Kulturgeschichte des Hellenismus*, 2 vols., Munich

Schober, A. (1933) *Der Fries des Hekataios von Lagina*, Baden

Schramm, E. (1918) *Die antiken Geschütze der Saalburg*, Berlin
  (1926) 'Poliorketik' in Kromayer and Veith 1926: 209–43

Schubart, W. (1900) *Quaestiones de rebus militaribus, quales fuerint in regno Lagidarum*, Breslau
  (1926) 'Bemerkungen zum Stile hellenistischer Königsbriefe', *Archiv für Papyrusforschung und verwandte Gebiete* (Leipzig) 6: 324–47

Schunck, K. D. (1954) *Die Quellen des I und II Makkabäerbuches*, Halle
  (1980) *1. Makkabäerbuch*, Jüdische Schriften aus hellenistisch–römischer Zeit, vol. 1, *Historische und legendarische Erzählungen*, Gütersloh

Schürer, E. (1901) *Geschichte des jüdischen Volkes im Zeitalter Jesu Christi*, 4th edition, 3 vols., Leipzig

Schürer, E., Vermes, G. and Millar, F. (1973–9) *The History of the Jewish People in the Age of Jesus Christ*, 2 vols., Edinburgh

Schwabe, M. (1933–5) 'The Book of the Hasmonaeans', *Kiryat Sefer* 9: 274–7 (Hebrew)

Schwabe, M. and Melamed, E. Z. (1928) 'Zum Text der Seronepisode in 1 Macc. und bei Josephus', *MGWJ* 72: 202–4

Schwartz, Ed. (1896) *Fünf Vorträge über den griechischen Roman*, Berlin
  (1897) 'Die Berichte über die Catilinarische Verschwörung', *Hermes* 32: 554–608

Schwyzer, E. (1922) *Dialectorum Graecarum exempla epigraphica potiora*, Leipzig

Scullard, H. H. (1974) *The Elephant in the Greek and Roman World*, London

Segal, M. Z. (1950) *Introduction to the Bible*, 4 vols., Jerusalem (Hebrew)
  (1951) 'Problems of the Dead Sea Scrolls', *Eretz Israel* 1: 39–44 (Hebrew)

Seibert, J. (1963) *Metropolis und Apoikie*, Würzburg
  (1967) *Historische Beiträge zu den dynastischen Verbindungen in hellenistischer Zeit*, Wiesbaden
  (1969) *Untersuchungen zur Geschichte Ptolemaios' I*, Munich
  (1981) *Alexander der Grosse*, Darmstadt

Sellers, O. R. (1933) *The Citadel of Beth Zur*, Philadelphia

Sellers, O. R. and Albright, W. F. (1931) 'The first campaign of excavations at Beth Zur', *BASOR* 43: 2–13

Sevenster, J. N. (1975) *The Roots of Pagan Anti-Semitism in the Ancient World*, Leiden

Seyrig, H. (1951) 'Antiquités syriennes', *Syria* 28: 191–228

Sherk, R. K. (1969) *Roman Documents from the Greek East*, Baltimore

Shiloh, Y. (1980) 'The population of Iron Age Palestine in the light of a sample analysis of urban plan, areas and population density', *BASOR* 239: 25–35

(1984) *The Excavations at the City of David*, Qedem 19, Jerusalem

Shotwell, W. (1964) 'The problem of the Syrian Akra', *BASOR* 176: 10–19

Sievers, J. (1981) 'The Hasmoneans and their supporters from Mattathias to John Hyrcanus', diss., Columbia University, New York

Simons, J. (1952) *Jerusalem in the Old Testament Period*, Leiden

Smith, G. A. (1894) *The Historical Geography of the Holy Land*, London

Smith, S. (1907) *Babylonian Historical Texts*, London

Snodgrass, A. M. (1964) *Early Greek Arms and Armour*, Edinburgh

(1967) *Arms and Armour of the Greeks*, London

Sokolov, G. (1974) *Antique Art on the Northern Black Sea Coast*, Leningrad

Soltau, W. (1897) *Livius' Geschichtswerk, seine Komposition und seine Quelle*, Leipzig

Spendel, A. (1915) *Untersuchungen zum Heerwesen der Diadochen*, Breslau

Spiegelberg, W. (1928) 'Beiträge zur Erklärung des neuen dreisprachigen Priesterdekretes zu Ehren des Ptolemaios Philopator', *Sitzungsberichte der Bayerischen Akademie der Wissenschaften*, Phil.-hist. Abteilung, Abh. 4: 1–24

Stählin, F. (1907) *Geschichte der Kleinasiatischen Galater*, Leipzig

Stein, M. E. (1970) *The Relationship between Jewish, Greek and Roman Cultures*, Tel Aviv (Hebrew)

Stern, E. (1973) *The Material Culture of the Land of the Bible in the Persian Period, 538–332 B.C.E.*, Jerusalem (Hebrew)

Stern, M., (1960) 'The death of Onias III', *Zion* 25: 1–16 (Hebrew)

(1961) 'The relations between Judaea and Rome during the rule of John Hyrcanus', *Zion* 26: 1–22 (Hebrew)

(1963) 'Notes on the story of Joseph the Tobiad', *Tarbiz* 32: 35–47 (Hebrew)

(1965) *The Documents on the History of the Hasmonaean Revolt*, Tel Aviv (Hebrew)

(1972) 'Nicolaus of Damascus as a source for Jewish history in the times of the Hasmonaeans and Herod', in B. Uffenheimer (ed.), *The Bible and the History of Israel*, Studies in Memory of Jacob Liever (Tel Aviv): 375–94 (Hebrew)

(1974) *Greek and Latin Authors on Jews and Judaism*, vol. 1, Jerusalem

(1976) 'The Jews in Greek and Latin literature', in S. Safrai and M. Stern (eds.), *The Jewish People in the First Century* (Assen), vol. 2: 1101–59

(1981) 'Judaea and her neighbors in the days of Alexander Jannaeus',

The Jerusalem Cathedra, Studies in the History, Archaeology, Geography and Ethnography of the Land of Israel: 1.22–47

Strassburger, H. (1952) 'W. W. Tarn, *Alexander the Great*' (review), *Bibliotheca Orientalis* 9: 210

(1966) *Die Wesensbestimmung der Geschichte durch die antike Geschichtsschreibung*, Wiesbaden

Strassmaier, J. W. (1893) 'Zur Chronologie der Seleukiden', *Zeitschrift für Assyrologie* 8: 106–13

Sukenik, E. L. (1933) 'An ancient Jewish cave on the Jerusalem–Sechem road', *Bulletin of the Israel Exploration Society* 1: 7–9

Sukenik, Y. (= Y. Yadin) (1947) 'Engines invented by cunning men', *BPES* 13: 19–24 (Hebrew)

Sussmann, Y. (1974) 'A Halakhic inscription from the Beth Shean Valley', *Tarbiz* 43: 88–148 (Hebrew)

(1976) 'The boundaries of Eretz Israel', *Tarbiz* 45: 213–57 (Hebrew)

Sweet, H. B. (1900) *Introduction to the Old Testament in Greek*, Cambridge

Syme, R. (1964) *Sallust*, Berkeley

Taeger, F. (1959) *Charisma*, vol. 1, Stuttgart

Talbert, R. J. A. (1974) *Timoleon and the Revival of Greek Sicily*, Cambridge

Tarn, W. W. (1913) *Antigonos Gonatas*, Oxford

(1926) 'The First Syrian War', *JHS* 46: 155–62

(1930) *Hellenistic Military and Naval Developments*, Cambridge

(1941) 'F. W. Walbank, *Philip V of Macedon*' (review), *JRS* 31: 172–3

(1948) *Alexander the Great*, 2 vols., Cambridge

(1951) *The Greeks in Bactria and India*, 2nd edition, Cambridge

Tarn, W. W. and Griffith, G. T. (1952) *Hellenistic Civilization*, 3rd edition, London

Taubenschlag, R. (1955) *The Law of Greco-Roman Egypt in the Light of the Papyri*, Warsaw

Tcherikover, V. (1927) *Hellenistische Städtegründungen von Alexander dem Grossen bis auf die Römerzeit*, *Philologus* Suppl. IX.1, Leipzig

(1930) 'The Documents in II Maccabees', *Tarbiz* 1: 31–45 (= Tcherikover 1961b: 181–98)

(1950) 'Antioch in Jerusalem', in *Jubilee Volume for Y. N. Epstein* (Jerusalem): 61–7 (Hebrew)

(1958) 'The ideology of the Letter of Aristeas', *HTR* 51: 59–85

(1961a) *Hellenistic Civilization and the Jews*, Philadelphia

(1961b) *The Jews in the Graeco-Roman World*, Tel Aviv

(1963) *The Jews in Egypt in the Hellenistic–Roman Age in the Light of Papyri*, 2nd edition, Jerusalem (Hebrew)

Tcherikover, V. (and Fuks, A.) (1960) *Corpus Papyrorum Judaicarum (CPJ)*, vol. 1, Cambridge, Mass.

Tchernowitz, H. (Rav Tzair) (1935–50) *Toldot Ha-Halakhah, History of the Hebrew Law*, 4 vols., New York (Hebrew)

Thackeray, H. St J. (1913) *A Grammar of the Old Testament According to the Septuagint*, Cambridge

(1929) *Josephus, the Man and Historian*, New York

Thissen, H. J. (1966) *Studien zum Raphiadekret*, Meisenheim

Thomsen, P. (1917) 'Die römischen Meilenstein der Provinzen Syria', *ZDPV* 40: 1–103

Timpe, D. (1974) 'Der römische Vertrag mit den Juden von 161 v. Chr.', *Chiron* 4: 133–52

Toki, K. (1977) 'The dates of the First and Second Books of Maccabees', *The Annual of the Japanese Biblical Institute* 3: 69–83

Tomaschek, W. (1893) *Die alten Thraker*, Vienna

Torrey, C. C. (1934) 'Three troublesome proper names in First Maccabees', *JBL* 53: 31–3

(1963) *The Apocryphal Literature*, London

Tov, E. (1978) 'Studies in the vocabulary of the Septuagint – the relation between vocabulary and translation technique', *Tarbiz* 87: 120–38 (Hebrew)

(1981) *The Text-Critical Use of the Septuagint in Biblical Research*, Jerusalem

Tramontano, R. (1931) *La Lettera di Aristea a Filocrate*, Naples

Tränkle, H. (1977) *Livius und Polybius*, Basel

Tsafrir, Y. (1972) 'The location of the Seleucid Akra in Jerusalem', *Qadmoniot* 5: 125–6 (Hebrew)

(1975) 'The location of the Seleucid Akra in Jerusalem', *RB* 82: 501–52

(1977) 'Une fois de plus! l'angle sud-est du Mont du Temple de Jerusalem et le problème de l'Acra (correspondance)', *Syria* 44: 295–7

(1980) 'The site of the Seleucid Akra in Jerusalem', *Cathedra* 14: 17–40 (Hebrew)

Uebel, F. (1968) *Die Kleruchen Aegyptens unter den ersten sechs Ptolemäern*, Berlin

Ullman, B. L. (1942) 'History and tragedy', *Transactions and Proceedings of the American Philological Society* 73: 25–53

Ullmann, R. (1927) *La technique des discours dans Sallust, Tite Live et Tacite*, Oslo

Unger, F. (1895) 'Die Seleukidenära der Makkabäerbücher', *Sitzungsberichte der Münchner Akademie*, Phil.-hist. Klasse: 236–316

Urbach, E. E. (1975) *The Sages*, Jerusalem

(1984) *The Halakha, its Origins and Development*, Jerusalem (Hebrew)

Ursinus, V. (ed.) (1582) *Ex libris Polybii Megalopolitani selecta de legationibus et alia*, Antwerp

Van Buren, E. D. (1930) *Clay Figurines of Babylonia and Assyria*, New Haven

Van Henten, J. W. (1983) 'Der Berg Asdod. Ueberlegungen zu 1. Makk. 9.15', *JSJ* 14: 43–51

Van Ingen, W. (1939) *Figurines from Seleucia on the Tigris*, Ann Arbor

Van't Dack, E. (1968) 'La date de la Lettre d'Aristée', *Studia Hellenistica* 16: 263–78

(1976) 'Epistratégie Ptolémaïque', *Ancient Society* 7: 177–84

(1977) 'Sur l'évolution des institutions militaires lagides', in H. van Effenterre (ed.), *Armées et fiscalité dans le monde antique* (Paris): 77–105

Vatin, C. (1970) *Recherches sur le mariage et la condition de la femme mariée à l'époque hellénistique*, Paris

Venini, P. (1951) 'Tragedia e storia in Polibio', *Dionisio* 14: 54–61

Vernant, J. P. (ed.) (1968) *Problèmes de la guerre en Grèce ancienne*, Paris

Vilnay, Z. (1968) *Judaea und Samaria*, Tel Aviv (Hebrew)

Vincent, H. (1913) 'Un hypogée juif à Djifneh', *RB* 10: 103–6
(1934) 'Acra', *RB* 43: 205–36

Volkmann, H. (1925) 'Demetrios und Alexander I von Syrien', *Klio* 19: 373–412
(1961) *Die Massenversklavungen der Einwohner eroberter Städte in der hellenistisch-römischen Zeit*, Wiesbaden

von Bienkowski, P. (1928) *Les Celtes dans les arts mineurs gréco-romains*, Cracow

von Destinon, J. (1882) *Die Quellen des Flavius Josephus*, Kiel

von Fritz, K. (1958) 'Die Bedeutung des Aristoteles für die Geschichtsschreibung', in *Histoire et historiens dans l'antiquité* (Geneva): 85–145

von Gutschmid, A. (1888) *Geschichte Irans und seiner Nachbarländer*, Tübingen
(1893) *Klassische Schriften*, vol. 2, Leipzig

von Wilamowitz-Moellendorff, U. (1918) 'Dichter Fragmente aus der Papyrussammlung der Kgl. Museen', *Sitzungsberichte der Akad. Berl.*: 728–51

Wacholder, B. Z. (1973) 'The calendar of sabbatical cycles during the Second Temple and the Early Rabbinic period', *HUCA* 44: 153–96
(1974) *Eupolemus, a Study of Judaeo-Greek Literature*, New York
(1976) *Essays on Jewish Chronology and Chronography*, New York

Walbank, F. W. (1938) 'ΦΙΛΙΠΠΟΣ ΤΡΑΓΩΙΔΟΥΜΕΝΟΣ, a Polybian experiment', *JHS* 58: 55–68
(1940) *Philip V of Macedon*, Cambridge
(1945) 'Polybius, Philinus and the First Punic War', *CQ* 39: 8–18
(1955) 'Tragic history: a reconsideration', *Bulletin of the Institute of Classical Studies of the University of London*: 4–14
(1957–79) *A Historical Commentary on Polybius*, 3 vols., Oxford
(1960) 'History and tragedy', *Historia* 9: 216–34
(1962) 'Polemic in Polybius', *JRS* 52: 1–12
(1965) *Speeches in Greek History*, Oxford
(1972) *Polybius*, Berkeley and Los Angeles
(1980) 'The idea of decline in Polybius', in R. Koselleck and P. Widmer (eds.), *Niedergang, Studien zu einem geschichtlichen Thema* (Stuttgart): 41–58

Wallace, J. L. (1979) 'The wars of the Maccabees', *Revue internationale d'histoire militaire* 42: 53–81

Walsh, P. G. (1963) *Livy, his Historical Aims and Methods*, Cambridge

Wardman, A. (1974) *Plutarch's Lives*, London

Watson, G. R. (1969) *The Roman Soldier*, London

Wavell, A. P. (1928) *The Palestine Campaign*, London

Wehrli, F. (1946) 'Der erhabene und der schlichte Stil in der poetisch–rhetorischen Theorie der Antike', in *Phyllobolia für Peter von der Mühll zum 60. Geburtstag* (Basel): 9–34

(1947) 'Die Geschichtsschreibung im Lichte der antiken Theorie', in *Eumasia, Festgabe für E. Howald* (Zurich): 54–71

Weierholt, K. (1932) 'Zum Ausdruck οι περι τινα in den Maccabäerbüchern', *Symbolae Osloenses* 11: 69–71

Weiss, J. H. (1904) *Dor Dor Vedorshav, Geschichte der Jüdischen Tradition*, 4th edition, Part 1, Vilna (Hebrew)

Welles, C. B. (1934) *Royal Correspondence in the Hellenistic Period*, New Haven

(1951) 'The population of Roman Dura', in P. R. Coleman-Norton (ed.), 'Studies in Roman Economic and Social History in Honor of Allan Chester Johnson' (Princeton): 251–74

Wellhausen, J. (1901) *Israelitische und jüdische Geschichte*, 6th edition, Berlin

(1905) 'Ueber den geschichtlichen Wert des zweiten Makkabäerbuchs im Verhältnis zum ersten', *Nachrichten von der Königl. Gesellschaft der Wissenschaften zu Göttingen*, Phil.-hist. Klasse: 117–63

(1924) *Die Pharisäer und die Sadducäer*, 2nd edition, Hannover

Welwei, K. W. (1963) *Könige und Königtum im Urteil des Polybius*, Cologne

(1977) *Unfreie im antiken Kriegsdienst*, 2 vols., Wiesbaden

Wernsdorff, G. (1744) *De Republica Galatarum*, Nuremberg

(1747) *Commentatio historico-critica de fide historica librorum Maccabaicorum*, Bratislava

West, W. C. (1969) 'The trophies of the Persian War', *CP* 64: 7–19

Westermann, W. L. (1938) 'Enslaved persons who are free', *American Journal of Philology* 59: 1–30

Westlake, H. D. (1938) 'The sources of Plutarch's Timoleon', *CQ* 33: 65–74

Wibbing, S. (1962) 'Zur Topographie einzelner Schlachten des Judas Makkabäus', *ZDPV* 78: 159–70

Wiegand, T. (1908) *Milet*, vol. 2 (Ergebnisse der Ausgrabungen und Untersuchungen seit dem Jahre 1899), Berlin

Wieneke, J. (1931) *Ezechielis Judaei poëtae Alexandrini fabulae quae inscribitur ΕΞΑΓΩΓΗ fragmata*, diss., Münster

Wikgren, A. P. (1932) *A Comparative Study of the Theodotionic and LXX Translations of Daniel*, Chicago

Wilhelm, A. (1937) 'Zu einigen Stellen d. Bücher der Makkabäer', *Akademie der Wissenschaft in Wien*, Phil.-hist. Klasse, Anzeiger 74: 15–30

Will, E. (1913) *Kallisthenes' Hellenika*, Königsberg

Will, Ed. (1967) *Histoire politique du monde hellénistique*, 1st edition, vol. 2, Nancy

(1979) *Histoire politique du monde hellénistique*, 2nd edition, vol. 1, Nancy

Will, Ed., Mossé, Cl. and Goukowsky, P. (1975) *Le monde grec et l'orient*, Paris

Willrich, H. (1895) *Juden und Griechen vor der makkabäischen Erhebung*, Göttingen

(1900) *Judaica*, Göttingen

(1924) *Urkundenfälschung in der hellenistisch–jüdischen Literatur*, Göttingen

Wirgin, W. (1969) 'Judah Maccabee's embassy to Rome and the Jewish Roman treaty', *PEQ* 101: 15–20

Witte, K. (1910) 'Ueber die Form der Darstellung in Livius' Geschichteswerk', *RhM* 65: 270–305, 359–419

Wolfson, H. A. (1947) *Philo, Foundations of Religious Philosophy in Judaism, Christianity and Islam*, 2 vols., Cambridge, Mass.

Yadin, Y. (1962) *The Scroll of the War of the Sons of Light against the Sons of Darkness*, Oxford

(1963) *The Art of Warfare in Biblical Lands*, Jerusalem

(1978) *The Temple Scroll*, 3 vols., Jerusalem (Hebrew)

Yalon, H. (1967) *Studies in the Dead Sea Scrolls*, Jerusalem (Hebrew)

Yeivin, S. (1941) 'Topographical notes', *BPES* 8: 83–4 (Hebrew)

Zambelli, M. (1960) 'L'ascesa al trono de Antiocho IV Epifane di Siria', *RFIC* 38: 363–89

(1965) *Miscellanea Greca e Romana*, Rome

Zegers, N. (1959) *Wesen und Ursprung der tragischen Geschichtsschreibung*, Cologne

Zeitlin, S. (1922) *Megillat Taanith as a Source for Jewish Chronology and History in the Hellenistic and Roman Period*, Philadelphia

(1950) *The First Book of Maccabees*, New York

(1952) *The Second Book of Maccabees*, New York

Zeitlin, S. and Enslin, M. S. (1972) *The Book of Judith*, Leiden

Zgusta, L. (1964) *Kleinasiatische Personennamen*, Prague

Zimmerman, (1938) 'The Aramaic origin of Daniel 8–12', *JBL* 57: 255–72

Zunz, I. L. (1832) *Die Gottesdienstlichen Vorträge der Juden*, Berlin

INDEX LOCORUM

BIBLE

BIBLE TRANSLATIONS

ARISTOTLE, PSEUDO-

De Mundo

ARRIAN

Anabasis

Tact.

ASCLEPIODOTUS

ATHENAEUS

DION HAL.

de comp. verb.

Pomp.

DURIS OF SAMOS

FGrH IIA, no.

EUSEBIUS

Chron.

Praep. Evan.

FRONTINUS

Stratēgēmata

HEGESIAS

FGrH II, no.

HELIODORUS

Ethiopica

HERO OF ALEXANDRIA

Belopoeica

HERODOTUS

HIERONYMUS

In Dan.

GENERAL INDEX*

* Compiled by Mrs Fern Seckbach

651

INDEX OF GREEK TERMS
IN TRANSCRIPTION

USING GREEK ALPHABET

IN TRANSCRIPTION